STALINISM

Stalinism is a provocative addition to the current debates related to the history of the Stalinist period of the Soviet Union. Sheila Fitzpatrick has collected together the newest and the most exciting work by young Russian, American and European scholars, as well as some of the seminal articles that have influenced them, in an attempt to reassess this contentious subject in the light of new data and new theoretical approaches.

The articles are contextualized by a thorough introduction to the totalitarian/revisionist arguments and post-revisionist developments. Eschewing an exclusively high-political focus, the book draws together work on class, identity, consumption culture, and agency. Stalinist terror and nationalities policy are reappraised in the light of new archival findings. *Stalinism* offers a nuanced navigation of an emotive and misrepresented chapter of the Russian past.

Sheila Fitzpatrick is Bernadotte E. Schmitt Distinguished Service Professor at the University of Chicago.

Rewriting Histories focuses on historical themes where standard conclusions are facing a major challenge. Each book presents papers (edited and annotated where necessary) at the forefront of current research and interpretation, offering students an accessible way to engage with contemporary debates.

Series editor **Jack R. Censer** is Professor of History at George Mason University.

REWRITING HISTORIES
Series editor: Jack R. Censer

Already published

THE INDUSTRIAL REVOLUTION AND WORK IN
NINETEENTH-CENTURY EUROPE
Edited by Lenard R. Berlanstein

SOCIETY AND CULTURE IN THE SLAVE SOUTH
Edited by J. William Harris

ATLANTIC AMERICAN SOCIETIES
From Columbus through Abolition
Edited by J.R. McNeill and Alan Karras

GENDER AND AMERICAN HISTORY SINCE 1890
Edited by Barbara Melosh

DIVERSITY AND UNITY IN EARLY
NORTH AMERICA
Edited by Philip D. Morgan

NAZISM AND GERMAN SOCIETY 1933–1945
Edited by David Crew

THE FRENCH REVOLUTION: RECENT DEBATES
AND NEW CONTROVERSIES
Edited by Gary Kates

THE ISRAEL/PALESTINE QUESTION
Edited by Ilan Pappe

REVOLUTIONS OF 1989
Edited by Vladimir Tismaneanu
Forthcoming

STALINISM

New Directions

Edited by Sheila Fitzpatrick

London and New York

First published 2000
by Routledge
11 New Fetter Lane, London EC4P 4EE

Simultaneously published in the USA and Canada
by Routledge
29 West 35th Street, New York, NY 10001

Routledge is an imprint of the Taylor & Francis Group

Typeset in Palatino by
Florence Production Ltd, Stoodleigh, Devon
Printed and bound in Great Britain by
Biddles Ltd, Guildford and King's Lynn

British Library Cataloguing in Publication Data
A catalogue record for this book is available from the British Library

Library of Congress Cataloging in Publication Data
Stalinism: a reader/edited by Sheila Fitzpatrick.
p. cm. – (Rewriting histories)
Includes bibliographical references and index.
1. Soviet Union–Politics and government—1917–1936.   2. Soviet Union—
Politics and government—1936–1953.   3. Soviet Union—Social
conditions—1917–1945.   4. Soviet Union—Social conditions—
1945–1991.   I. Fitzpatrick, Sheila.   II. Series: Re-writing histories.
DK267.S6939 1999
947.084–dc21   99–12609
                                                                                              CIP

ISBN 0–415–15233–X (hbk)
ISBN 0–415–15234–8 (pbk)

CONTENTS

SERIES EDITOR'S PREFACE

Rewriting history, or revisionism, has always followed closely in the wake of history writing. In their efforts to re-evaluate the past, professional as well as amateur scholars have followed many approaches, most commonly as empiricists, uncovering new information to challenge earlier accounts. Historians have also revised previous versions by adopting new perspectives, usually fortified by new research, which overturn received views.

Even though rewriting is constantly taking place, historians' attitudes towards using new interpretations have been anything but settled. For most, the validity of revisionism lies in providing a stronger, more convincing account that better captures the objective truth of the matter. Although such historians might agree that we never finally arrive at the "truth," they believe it exists and over time may be better approximated. At the other extreme stand scholars who believe that each generation or even each cultural group or subgroup necessarily regards the past differently, each creating for itself a more usable history. Although these latter scholars do not reject the possibility of demonstrating empirically that some contentions are better than others, they focus upon generating new views based upon different life experiences. Different truths exist for different groups. Surely such an understanding, by emphasizing subjectivity, further encourages rewriting history. Between these two groups are those historians who wish to borrow from both sides. This third group, while accepting that every congeries of individuals sees matters differently, still wishes somewhat contradictorily to fashion a broader history that incorporates both of these particular visions. Revisionists who stress empiricism fall into the first of the three camps, while others spread out across the board.

Today the rewriting of history seems to have accelerated to a blinding speed as a consequence of the evolution of revisionism. A variety of approaches has emerged. A major factor in this process has been the enormous increase in the number of researchers. This explosion has reinforced and enabled the retesting of many assertions. Significant

ideological shifts have also played a major part in the growth of revisionism. First, the crisis of Marxism, culminating in the events in Eastern
Europe in 1989, has given rise to doubts about explicitly Marxist accounts.
Such doubts have spilled over into the entire field of social history which
has been a dominant subfield of the discipline for several decades.
Focusing on society and its class divisions implied that these are the
most important elements in historical analysis. Because Marxism was
built on the same claim, the whole basis of social history has been questioned, despite the very many studies that directly had little to do with
Marxism. Disillusionment with social history, simultaneously opened the
door to cultural and linguistic approaches largely developed in anthropology and literature. Multi-culturalism and feminism further generated
revisionism. By claiming that scholars had, wittingly or not, operated
from a white European/American male point of view, newer researchers
argued that other approaches had been neglected or misunderstood. Not
surprisingly, these last historians are the most likely to envision each
subgroup rewriting its own usable history, while other scholars incline
towards revisionism as part of the search for some stable truth.

Rewriting Histories will make these new approaches available to the
student population. Often new scholarly debates take place in the scattered issues of journals which are sometimes difficult to find.
Furthermore, in these first interactions, historians tend to address one
another, leaving out the evidence that would make their arguments more
accessible to the uninitiated. This series of books will collect in one place
a strong group of the major articles in selected fields, adding notes and
introductions conducive to improved understanding. Editors will select
articles containing substantial historical data, so that students – at least
those who approach the subject as an objective phenomenon – can
advance not only their comprehension of debated points but also their
grasp of substantive aspects of the subject.

Because of the immensely controversial nature of the rule of Josef
Stalin, historians have from the beginning battled over what it all means.
The first group of scholars saw his leadership as purely totalitarian and
focused on Stalin's ideological statements. From Moscow the tentacles
of government reached out and successfully determined the texture of
life in the Soviet Union. Challenging this view were the "revisionists,"
who held the view that individuals carved out considerable autonomy.
As social historians, these revisionists were impressed by the ability of
workers and peasants to make everyday experience conform to their
own wishes. Indeed, it might be said that by acquiring positions in the
bureaucracy, the people of the Soviet Union took over the government.
Although this scholarly discussion continues, the work presented in this
volume represents a new approach, labelled here as "cultural." These
scholars seem far less interested in earlier debates which replicated a

Cold War discussion over Stalinism. They seem more concerned with assessing whether everyday practices had a traditional past or presaged modernity. This is, indeed, a more anthropological than political concern. Also, they borrow from each side in the historiographical debate, in that they examine both ideology and society. This departure, though highly original already shows a sophistication that normally takes far more time to develop. Readers will find the articles included here to be models for research and analysis in other fields.

ACKNOWLEDGEMENTS

The permission of the following publishers to reprint articles is gratefully acknowledged:

American Association for the Advancement of Slavic Studies (AAASS) for "The USSR as a Communal Apartment" by Yuri Slezkine, published *Slavic Review* 53: 2 (1994); and " 'Dear Comrade, You Ask What We Need' " by Lewis H. Siegelbaum, published *Slavic Review* 57: 1 (1998).

Blackwell Publishers for "Rituals of Stalinist Culture at Work" by Alexei Kojevnikov, published *Russian Review* 57: 1 (1998).

Cornell University Press for materials from chapter 6 of James R. Harris, *The Great Urals: Regionalism and the Evolution of the Soviet System* (1999).

Jahrbücher für Geschichte Osteuropas for "Fashioning the Stalinist Soul" by Jochen Hellbeck, published in *Jahrbücher für Geschichte Osteuropas* Bd. 44, Heft 3 (1996).

Ohio State University Press for " 'Us Against Them' " by Sarah Davies, published *Russian Review* 56: 1 (1997).

Oxford University Press (UK) for materials by Vadim Volkov from *Constructing Russian Culture in the Age of Revolution: 1881–1940*, ed. Catriona Kelly and David Shepherd (Oxford, 1998), pp. 291–313.

University of Chicago Press for "Ascribing Class" by Sheila Fitzpatrick, published *Journal of Modern History* 65: 4 (1993); and "Denunciation and its Functions in Soviet Governance" by V.A. Kozlov, published *Journal of Modern History* 68: 4 (1996).

The editor would like to thank Jack Censer, editor of the "Rewriting Histories" series, and Heather McCallum, history editor at Routledge, for their generous help and encouragement. She also thanks Joshua Sanborn and Christopher Burton for their assistance in preparing the volume.

GLOSSARY

aktiv – group of activists (for example, in Komsomol, factory)
aul – village in parts of the Caucasus and Central Asia
bedniak – poor peasant
blat – informal system of favors and connections
Bolsheviks – Communists
Bukharin, Nikolai (1888–1938) – party leader, one of "Right Opposition" at the end of the 1920s, defendant in famous show trial in 1938; executed
Cadets – liberal party of late Imperial period and 1917
Catherine II (the Great) – eighteenth-century empress of Russia
Central Committee – decision-making body of Communist Party
chistki – reviews (literally, "cleansings") of the membership of the Communist Party or the employees of state institutions
"closed distributors" – system of closed stores and cafeterias at work-places established during First Five-Year Plan; later, closed stores for elite
collectivization – movement for collectivization of peasant agriculture forcibly conducted by the Communist Party at the end of the 1920s
Comintern – Communist International, based in Moscow
Commissariat, People's Commissariat – Ministry
communal apartment – apartment with one family to a room, shared kitchen, bathroom, and hall; typical urban housing of 1930s
criticism and self-criticism: *see* **self-criticism**
Cultural Revolution – cultural upheaval of the late 1920s and early 1930s involving harassment of "bourgeois specialists" and affirmative action programs on behalf of workers
dacha – country house
dekulakization – expropriation of kulaks accompanying collectivization; many kulaks deported to Urals, Siberia
edinolichniki – non-collectivized peasants
First Five-Year Plan (1929–32) – rapid industrialization program
FZU – factory school

gigantomania – passion for the huge

Gogol, Nikolai (1809–52) – famous writer. His play *The Inspector General* is a satire on Russian bureaucracy

Gosplan – State Planning Commission

GPU – state security police, 1921–8 (see also **OGPU, NKVD**)

Great Purges – episode of state terror directed against "enemies of the people" in Communist Party and elsewhere, 1937–8

"Great Retreat" – term coined by émigré sociologist N.S. Timasheff to describe turn away from revolutionary social and cultural policies in the mid-1930s

"Great Transformation" – term for the radical policy turn of the late 1920s – collectivization, First Five-Year Plan, Cultural Revolution (1928–32) – also known as "Stalin's revolution"

Gulag – labor camp system under NKVD

intelligentsia – term used broadly for Soviet educated, white-collar classes as well as more narrowly for professionals educated before the revolution ("bourgeois specialists")

Kalinin, Mikhail (1875–1946) – President of the USSR, Politburo member

Kamenev, Lev (1883–1936) – Bolshevik leader, member of Opposition to Stalin in mid-1920s, twice tried (1935, 1936) for alleged complicity in Kirov's murder, executed 1936

Kirov, Sergei (1886–1934) – Leningrad party leader, murdered 1934

kolkhoz, kolkhoznik – collective farm, peasant working on collective farm

Komsomol – Communist youth organization for ages 14–23

krai – region

kulaks – prosperous peasants, alleged exploiters, subject to expropriation and deportation at the beginning of the 1930s

Lenin, V.I. (1870–1924) – founder and leader of Bolshevik party

lishentsy – disenfranchised persons

Lysenko, Trofim – pseudo-scientist whose agricultural panaceas were hailed by party leaders, led campaign against geneticists in late 1940s

Mensheviks – Marxist socialists, competitors to the Bolsheviks before the Revolution and in 1917

meshchanstvo – pejorative term derived from lower urban estate of *meshchane* (townsmen) in Imperial Russia; connotes philistinism, petty-bourgeois mentality

Michurin, Ivan – Russian scientist, invoked as authority by Trofim Lysenko in his fight against geneticists

militsiia – regular (not political) police

mir – traditional peasant commune (abolished 1930); *mir*-eaters – exploiters, kulaks

Molotov, Viacheslav (1890–1986) – head of Soviet Government, Stalin's closest associate in 1930s

Morozov, Pavlik – quasi-mythical adolescent murdered by relatives in early 1930s for denouncing his father as a grain hoarder

NEP – New Economic Policy (1921–8), interval of moderation seen by many Communists as a retreat

Nepmen – private entrepreneurs of the NEP period

Nicholas I – Russian emperor famed as a martinet, creator of first political police, ruled 1825–55

Nicholas II – last emperor, ruled 1894–1917

Nikolaev, Leonid – Kirov's assassin

nizy – ordinary people, people at the bottom (in contrast to *verkhi*)

NKVD – State security police (1934–46)

obkom – regional party committee

oblast – region

Obshchestvennitsa – volunteer movement of elite wives in second half of 1930s

obshchestvennitsy – activists in the *Obschestvennitsa* movement

OGPU – state security police, 1928–32 (*see also* **GPU, NKVD**)

okrug – district

oprichniki – members of Ivan the Terrible's *oprichnina*, used to suppress boyar opposition in the sixteenth century

Ordzhonikidze, "Sergo" (1886–1937) – party leader in charge of heavy industry; died, probably a suicide, in 1937

Orgburo – administrative bureau of Central Committee

People's Commissariat: *see* **Commissariat**

Piatakov, Iurii (1890–1937) – "Left Oppositionist" of 1920s, later served as Ordzhonikidze's deputy, defendant in 1937 show trial, executed

Pioneers – Communist organization for 10–14 age group

Politburo – political bureau of Central Committee, Party's highest decision-making body

Potemkin village – term for façade, built to impress (as in villages built by Prince Potemkin in the South in the late eighteenth century to impress Catherine the Great)

proletariat – Marxist term for industrial working class (proletarian = worker). The Communist Party described itself as the vanguard of the proletariat and its rule as a dictatorship of the proletariat.

Pushkin, Aleksandr (1799–1837) – beloved Russian poet, the centenary of whose death was celebrated with great fanfare in 1937

raion – district

"responsible workers" (*otvetrabotniki*) – white-collar employees in good positions, officials

RSFSR – Russian Socialist Federated Soviet Republic, largest component of USSR

shockworker (*udarnik*, f. *udarnitsa*) – worker or peasant with outstanding production achievements

sluzhashchie (sing., *sluzhashchii*) – white-collar employee

Smolny – Party and Soviet headquarters in Leningrad

soslovie, pl. *sosloviia* – social estate in Imperial Russia before the revolution

soslovnost' – *soslovie* order

soviets – organs of local self-government; national soviets – soviets of ethnically distinct districts

sovkhoz – state farm, in which peasant workers received wages rather than a share of produce and profits as in a kolkhoz.

speculation – pejorative Soviet term for trading, that is, buying and selling goods to make a profit

St. Petersburg – Imperial capital, renamed Petrograd during World War I and Leningrad in 1924

Stakhanovites – workers, employees, and peasants recognized for outstanding production achievements; movement named for record-breaking coalminer Aleksei Stakhanov in 1935

Stalin, Iosif (1879–1953) – Georgian Bolshevik, emerged as Lenin's successor in leadership struggles of the 1920s, supreme leader of Communist Party and Soviet Union 1929–53

Stolypin, Petr – prime minister of Nicholas II, responsible for agrarian reforms (1907–15) designed to foster individual small peasant farming and break up the traditional peasant commune

subbotniki – voluntary work on public projects

Torgsin – stores that sold goods for gold, silver, and hard currency in the years 1930–6

troika (pl. *troiki*) – three-person board acting outside the regular judicial system (dealing with "socially harmful elements" or, during the Great Purges, political cases)

Trotsky, Lev (1879–1940) – Bolshevik leader, headed Left Opposition in 1920s, expelled from Party 1927, subsequently deported from USSR, demonized as "Judas-Trotsky" in Great Purges

Trotskyite – political supporter of Trotsky

Tukhachevskii, Mikhail (1893–1937) – military leader, Marshal of the Soviet Union, accused of treason and executed in June 1937

verkhi (sing. *verkha*; variant, *verkhushka*) – people on top, power-holders

vozhdi – leaders

White Guards, **Whites** – officers in the so-called "White" Armies that fought the Bolsheviks (the "Reds") in the Civil War (1918–20)

wreckers – term for saboteurs, often industrial administrators and engineers, used during Cultural Revolution and Great Purges

Young Pioneers: *see* **Pioneers**

zemliaki – people from the same village or district

zemstva (sing. *zemstvo*) – organs of local self-government in late Imperial period

Zinoviev, Grigorii (1883–1936) – Bolshevik leader, headed Leningrad party organization and Comintern in 1920s, then in Opposition; tried 1935 for alleged complicity in Kirov's murder; retried and executed 1936

INTRODUCTION

Sheila Fitzpatrick

This is a reader on new directions in the study of Stalinism. Its focus is work published in the 1990s, reflecting the remarkable changes in the field that have occurred in the last ten years. The decade began dramatically with the collapse of the Soviet Union in 1991. That ended the long separation of Russian (Soviet) scholarship from Western Soviet studies and paved the way for the integration of Russian scholars, especially the younger cohort, into the international scholarly community. It also opened up Soviet archives to historians, as well as giving anthropologists, sociologists, and political scientists opportunities for fieldwork unheard of before. For historians, particularly historians of the Soviet period, this was a bonanza comparable with the opening of Nazi-period records in Germany after the collapse of the Third Reich.

In this same period, Russian historians in the United States and Europe, like their counterparts in other fields of history, were experiencing a shift away from social history, dominant in the 1960s and 1970s, towards a new cultural history.[1] This was accompanied by a growing interest in cultural and social theory that in the 1990s pulled the historical profession away from the social sciences and towards the humanities. The new wave threw up a range of theorists – Foucault, Derrida, Habermas, and Bourdieu among the most prominent – as cultural authorities, threatening to swamp the commonsense empiricism usually associated with historians. Ripples from the wave even reached the former Soviet Union, offering new possibilities to young Western-oriented scholars seeking to escape the stale clichés of late-Soviet Marxism.

The new directions in the study of Stalinism that are presented in this volume are the product of these two very different processes, whose impact on the writing of Soviet history was felt almost simultaneously. It was a fortunate coincidence. Excitement about theory was matched by an equal or even greater excitement about new archival discoveries; and as a result, "theory" in this field generally meant something vital and empirically grounded, while the absorption of vast amounts of new data was accompanied from the first by active efforts at reconceptualization. In the community of scholars that study Russia, just as in the country itself, the collapse of the Soviet Union has forced everyone to reexamine their assumptions and search for new modes of understanding. It has been a decade of breakthrough; and already the outlines of new interpretations and intellectual configurations are starting to emerge.

Within the field of Soviet studies, Stalinism has been the central problem and mystery that has preoccupied generations of scholars. It was in the Stalin period, conventionally dated from 1929 (the onset of collectivization and the First Five-Year Plan for rapid industrialization) to Stalin's death in 1953, that the shape of the new order, product of the Bolshevik revolution 1917, was established. This was the era in which the Soviet Union was at its most dynamic, engaging in social and economic experiments that some hailed as the future become manifest and others saw as a threat to civilization; claiming the status of a world power and then a superpower; and, after World War II, self-cast as the antithesis of Western capitalism and liberal-democratic values, becoming the great bogeyman of the Cold War for Western public opinion. The Soviet (Stalinist) system – a complex of political and economic institutions, values, and cultural practices – was exported wholesale to Eastern Europe and, with modifications, to China and other Asian countries that embraced Communism in the postwar era.

American Sovietology grew very rapidly in the postwar years, helped by generous US government funding, because of the overwhelming importance of "understanding the enemy." Yet at the same time, the nature of the beast remained elusive, hidden behind closed frontiers and a comprehensive system of information control that often baffled Western scholarly research (which the Soviet Union tended to construe, perhaps understandably, as spying). Similarities between the two great antagonists of the democracies, the Soviet Union and Nazi Germany, generalized in the so-called "totalitarian model," made a great impact on Western scholarship and public opinion. Hannah Arendt's *Origins of Totalitarianism* was a key text for scholars, while a wider public read Arthur Koestler's *Darkness at Noon* and George Orwell's *Animal Farm* and *1984*.

Different keys have been used to try to unlock the mystery of Stalinism. In the immediate postwar era, political scientists, sociologists, anthropologists, and even psychologists cooperated in a major study of the Soviet social system based on interviews with postwar Soviet refugees in Germany and the United States.[2] Subsequently, however, due partly to the great difficulty of obtaining social data from inside the Soviet Union, this interdisciplinary effort collapsed. Political scientists came to dominate US Sovietology,[3] and not surprisingly sought the key to Stalinism in its political system, characterized as totalitarian. In the 1970s, this was challenged by a new generation consisting mainly of social historians who wanted to bring society back in and write history "from

2

below" as well as "from above." The present move towards cultural approaches is thus the third big shift in Soviet studies.[4]

The new scholarship on Stalinism focuses on Stalinism as a culture. In some ways, this cultural emphasis is a strange choice on the part of young historians: after seventy years of Western speculation on Soviet political processes and attempts to penetrate the mysteries of Soviet statistics, one might have expected that scholars' first instincts would be to uncover the secrets of high politics and Soviet GNP. Of course there are disciplinary imperatives at work here: political and economic history are out of fashion,[5] and most of the liveliest minds of the younger generation are drawn to sociocultural issues. And there are real secrets here too, many of them in the realm of everyday life and the private sphere, considered by the Soviet regime and previous generations of Western historians alike to be inappropriate objects of historical study. Historians of the new cohort often approach Stalinism like anthropologists, analyzing practices, discourses, and rituals; sometimes, however, they seem to be reaching for yet-undeveloped methodologies to examine the Stalinist soul.

While the topics dealt with in these essays range widely from social identity to terror and from consumption to the construction of nationality, it has been necessary to exclude some good recent work that does not fit the sociocultural focus, notably studies of high politics, economics, demography, and foreign policy. Within the sociocultural field, the sub-area of gender studies is least well represented in this volume, largely because no major study dealing with the Stalin period has yet emerged.[6] This volume also and intentionally gives pride of place to young scholars – American, Russian, English, German – not long past the dissertation stage (or, in one case, just finishing his dissertation as this book goes to press). It is the young who have been the main beneficiaries of the revolution in Soviet studies of the past decade, and they are the ones from whom important new interpretations and reconfiguration of the field are most likely to come.

Something very unusual happened in Soviet historiography in the past fifteen years since the onset of Gorbachev's *perestroika*: an abrupt and radical transformation of the universe of sources and the conditions of access to information. Until the mid-1980s, Western Soviet historians had very restricted access to archives and even to many published sources. To be sure, things had improved somewhat from the 1960s, when access was still more limited, or the 1950s, when the country was essentially closed to Western scholars. But it was still the case at the beginning of *perestroika* that the central political archives (records of the Soviet Communist Party) and a large portion of the central governmental archives were inaccessible to foreign researchers; and even where foreigners were allowed into the archives, they were not allowed to see the inventories and therefore had to order their material blind. Travel to the provinces was difficult and provincial archives were largely inaccessible; systematic oral history, along with all kinds of survey research, was impossible. Russian (Soviet) historians had somewhat better access to materials; on the other hand, their work went through strict censorship processes which severely restricted what could be said in print. Contact between Western and Soviet historians was limited and slightly furtive (foreigners were segregated in a separate reading-room in the state archives until quite late in the 1980s). Western historians did not really take Soviet scholarship seriously and were repelled by its Marxist-Leninist jargon; Soviet historians still periodically denounced their Western counterparts as "bourgeois falsifiers."

Compared to this, the post-1991 situation has been a researcher's paradise, for all the financial and governmental chaos, bureaucratic problems, and archives made hazardous by falling masonry and unheated reading rooms, not to mention unpaid archivists. Huge amounts of material in the state and military archives were declassified, and the Communist Party lost control over its archives, opening them to researchers.[7] The provinces and their archives have opened up, and young American and European researchers may be found in archives and institutes from Voronezh to Vladivostok and from Baku to Samarkand. Oral history projects, along with public-opinion surveys and anthropological fieldwork, can now be done by anyone with the resourcefulness and perseverance to organize them. While oral history is a diminishing resource for the prewar Stalin period, a recent collection of life histories of elderly women published by an American scholar and a Russian collaborator shows how valuable such material can be.[8] One of the most useful initiatives of the *perestroika* period in Russia was the recording of oral histories and the gathering from the general public of unpublished memoirs and family histories, diaries, and personal correspondence – part of a popular project of recovering the hidden Soviet past, the past as experienced by ordinary people. One such diary, deposited in the newly formed "People's Archive" in the early 1990s, is the basis for Jochen Hellbeck's article in this volume.

Of the twelve authors represented in this book, three learned their trade as Soviet historians under the old dispensation (Fitzpatrick and Siegelbaum in the West, Kozlov in the Soviet Union). A fourth (Yuri Slezkine) came on the American scene as a Soviet emigré in the 1980s; his emigré status meant that when writing his dissertation he had no hope of Soviet archival access, since emigration was still regarded by the regime as an act of treachery. The remaining eight authors, barely acquainted with the old Soviet Union and what it was like to work there, belong to the post-1991 cohort whose apprenticeship as Russian historians was served in a country where archival access and working conditions, if not ideal, were closer to those of France than of North Korea. The significance of this difference can hardly be exaggerated. Instead of working, like medieval historians, with a finite and limited source base, arguing about the authenticity of key texts (for example, those smuggled abroad) because good information was so hard to come by, historians of Soviet Russia suddenly found themselves pitchforked into the twentieth century, almost buried under the avalanche of bureaucratic paper ceaselessly generated by modern governments. Just what kind of leap Russia made in 1991 is still under debate. But its historians leaped from something like a seventeenth-century source base to a twentieth-century one almost overnight.

The new cohort has other advantages. It has the enormous advantage, psychologically as well as in other ways, of arriving on the scene after the end of the Cold War and thus being free of a great amount of baggage from that era that still weighs on their elders. Young scholars of the 1990s did not go behind "the Iron Curtain" to do their graduate work; to their great benefit, they did not have to acquire the traits of political caution and self-censorship once required to work in the Soviet Union (and sometimes also in the United States). Time was when American scholars who studied Bukharin or Solzhenitsyn or even Stalin would routinely be refused visas for research in the Soviet Union because of their "dangerous" topics; and, for that matter, there were "dangerous" topics for historians and political scientists even in the United States (in the 1970s, discussion of upward mobility in a Soviet context, affirmative action, political participation, and popular support for the Soviet regime were all likely to be construed as *de facto* justification of the Soviet system[9]). I doubt that, even now, any American historian old enough to have gone through the Cold War would subtitle a book "Stalinism as a civilization," as one young historian did in 1995;[10] the old reflexes of caution would prevent it. Of course, such reflexes are very bad for scholarship. That is one reason why the arrival of a new generation of Soviet historians is so much to be welcomed.

Another important thing that happened in the 1990s was the partial bridging of the old gulf between Western and Russian (Soviet) scholarship. This process has been difficult and painful for the older generation of Russian (formerly Soviet) historians, whose professional skills included a mastery of Marxist-Leninist discourse that is now irrelevant and embarrassing, but hard to unlearn. Young Russians have had less difficulty adapting and have also been the main beneficiaries of Western training and research support from the Soros, MacArthur, and other foundations and from others active in the former Soviet Union. Some of those who have quickly made a mark in international scholarship were able to get bursaries in the early 1990s to do graduate work in the social sciences at Berkeley, Cambridge, or Paris, working with cutting-edge social and cultural theorists. The combination of theoretical sophistication and a native-speaker's feel for the language and practices is a powerful asset, especially for cultural history. It is shared, of course, by the young Russian scholars now living and working in the United States and Europe (for whom the old term "emigré" is now, happily, disappearing).

Because of the disjuncture of 1991, the new cohort of Soviet historians is to some degree detached from past debates in the field. These debates, dating from the 1970s, focused on the totalitarian model and involved a conflict between "revisionists" and (for want of a better word) traditional Sovietologists. They are still perpetuated in the literary reviews, especially *The Times Literary Supplement* and the *New York Review of Books*, where Martin Malia, Robert Conquest, and Richard Pipes continue to assail revisionists like Arch Getty and Stephen Wheatcroft for underestimating the scale of Stalin's crimes (with particular reference to the number of victims of the Great Purges and other episodes of terror) and claim that their view of the Soviet Union has been vindicated by its collapse and the archival disclosures that followed.[11] In the academic community and scholarly journals, however, the old debates no longer hold pride of place, and scholars of the younger generation have little interest in them.

There were many dimensions to the totalitarian-versus-revisionist debate that preoccupied Soviet studies in the 1970s and 1980s.[12] One was the political: revisionists thought the old-timers were full of Cold War prejudice, while traditional Sovietologists thought the revisionists were whitewashers of the Soviet Union, noting with disapproval that some were Marxists. Another was disciplinary: old-time Sovietology was dominated by model-oriented political scientists, revisionism by empirically-oriented social historians. By disposing of the Soviet Union, 1991 made the question of being "for" or "against" it irrelevant. As for the disciplines, social historians flourished and multiplied in the 1980s: as Pipes and other revisionist critics complain, former revisionists now have a dominant position in the field of twentieth-century Russian and Soviet history. Once challengers of established views in Sovietology, the revisionists themselves have become the establishment. It is now *their* conventional wisdom that is under challenge from a brash younger generation.

The main thrust of 1970s revisionism was to show that Soviet society was something more than just a passive object of the regime's manipulation and mobilization, as totalitarian theorists suggested. In one sense, this was simply an assertion that there was a social history to be written about Soviet Russia. But it also raised politically charged questions about the degree and nature of popular support for the regime, the society's capacity to generate "initiative from below," and the

6

possibility of negotiation between society, or parts of it, and the regime. One of the classic issues for revisionists was the October Revolution of 1917, represented by traditionalists as a Bolshevik coup and by revisionists as part of a genuine popular revolutionary movement.[13] Another strain of revisionism emphasized the democratic potential of Bolshevism and claimed that a viable moderate alternative to Stalinism, represented by Nikolai Bukharin, had existed in the 1920s; Stalinism, in this interpretation, was a radical departure from Leninist tradition, not a continuation of it.[14]

With regard to the Stalin period, the first debates concerned the Cultural Revolution of the late 1920s, where revisionists saw initiatives coming from below as well as from above, while traditionalists saw only "revolution from above."[15] Revisionists also pointed to upward mobility from the working class as a means of elite formation and source of legitimacy for the regime,[16] and argued that the Soviet Communist Party of the 1930s was incapable of exerting the pervasive "totalitarian" control attributed to it.[17] It would be difficult to say that a coherent overall view of Stalinism emerged in the revisionist scholarship of the 1970s and 1980s, but perhaps the most widely accepted picture, derived from Trotsky's contemporary indictment in *The Revolution Betrayed*, was that Stalinism was a form of extreme statism in which the regime "acquired a social base it did not want and did not immediately recognize: the bureaucracy."[18]

While not wholly rejecting this view of Stalinism, Stephen Kotkin, one of the aspirant leaders of the new scholarship of the 1990s, sharply disputes its underlying premise: far from being a post-revolutionary phenomenon, he claims, Stalinism *was* the revolution. What he means by this is that it was the "Stalin revolution" of the 1930s, not the Bolshevik revolution of 1917, that created radically new and durable political, economic, social, and cultural structures that were to last for half a century.[19] This proposition is probably common ground for all the authors in this volume, as indeed it was for the first generation of Western Sovietologists (and even for many revisionists). Nor is this the only commonality between the new "third generation" of Soviet scholars and the first one. Ideology, a subject of intensive study by the first generation of Sovietologists, received short shrift from the revisionists, who tended to point out impatiently that what the Bolsheviks said in their propaganda hand-outs was a completely different thing from what was happening on the ground. Two young scholars, Igal Halfin and Jochen Hellbeck, recently rebuked revisionists for their habit of "deideologiz[ing] the workings of the Soviet system, explaining its durability in terms of the 'interests' of those groups in society that were identified as its beneficiaries"; while Stephen Kotkin characterizes the Bolsheviks as "deliberately ideological," meaning not simply that they held to a particular set of ideas but "that they deemed it necessary to possess universal ideas to act at all," and warns that to dismiss ideology "is to render the behavior and thinking of contemporaries incomprehensible."[20]

But the new generation has a lot in common with the revisionists, too, notably a central interest in social practices and the local and everyday. It also has its bones to pick with the first generation of American Sovietologists: as one young commentator writes dismissively: "With its blatantly caricaturish notions of the operations of power, totalitarianism is no better than its twin, the Stalin-era short-course history,[21] at accounting for Soviet realities, change, or the interconnectedness of the USSR with the rest of the world."[22] This judgement, with its implied reference to a more sophisticated understanding of power, brings Michel Foucault to mind. Foucault has indeed been a major influence on some of the new historians,[23] particularly for his view of power, sexuality, and the construction of self. The focus on subjectivity that is one of the most novel aspects of the new scholarship on Stalinism, without precedent in either traditional or revisionist Soviet studies, has strong Foucauldian overtones.

The scholars represented in this volume, however, are not a unified group, and their sources of intellectual inspiration are diverse. Among the most obvious influences in the theoretical realm, in addition to Foucault, are Pierre Bourdieu, Michel de Certeau, Erving Goffman, Jurgen Habermas, Benedict Anderson, Edward Said, Mikhail Bakhtin, James C. Scott, and Norbert Elias. For young Russian historians of science like Alexei Kojevnikov, work on the social construction of science has had a major formative impact. For understanding Soviet-type economies and states, the economist Janos Kornai and the anthropologist Katherine Verdery (a specialist on Romania) are important. Within Soviet historiography, literary and cultural scholars like Vera Dunham, Katerina Clark, Boris Groys, Thomas Lahusen, and Vladimir Paperny are often cited. Indeed, new cultural approaches to Stalinism are coming not only from historians but also from cultural studies,[24] and at least one of our authors, Yuri Slezkine, has as close connections with the world of literary studies as with that of history.

Marxism, the dominant theoretical influence on the previous generation, has been much less important in the scholarship of the 1990s. If the revisionists often had a wistful fondness for the working class *qua* class, that attitude is rarely reproduced among the young. The workers in David Hoffman's study of Moscow are uprooted peasants who "did not constitute a class in the sense of a group united by shared experiences and common interests."[25] A deconstructionist approach to class (see Fitzpatrick's "Ascribing Class," Chapter 1 in this volume) has been gaining ground: class identities are increasingly seen as things chosen and manipulated by individuals rather than produced (as, at least of the older generation Marxists would have it) by socioeconomic circumstances.

A similar approach to nationality and ethnicity has won even more adherents. Thanks largely to the disintegration of the Soviet Union into its constituent national republics, the study of nationalities has become a booming sub-field of Soviet history, advancing by leaps and bounds from its old marginal status as a vehicle of small-nation patriotism. Ronald Suny, a Marxist revisionist of the 1970s and 1980s, has been the leading figure in the rout of notions of "primordial" nationality, which until very recently were widely if tacitly accepted by scholars in the Soviet field.[26] Following theorists like Benedict Anderson and Ernest Gellner, the new nationalities scholarship of the 1990s has taken the social constructedness of nationality as a given. In contrast to journalists and the general public, who concluded that the events of 1991 demonstrated the unappeasable strength of nationalisms that the Soviet Union had been unable to crush, scholars like Yuri Slezkine and Terry Martin have been finding almost the opposite: namely, that the Soviet regime not only fostered national identities but in many cases actually created them.

As already noted, the new Soviet scholarship draws on theory from a range of sources outside the Russian/Soviet field. That is an advantage not just for the scholarship but also for the theory. What we call "theory," after all, usually has an implicit empirical referent; and for the theories with the widest currency at the present, the referent usually comes from the historical experience of modern Western Europe, especially Britain and France, or of the United States. If the empirical referent is shifted to a completely different context, that can produce extremely interesting results, which in turn are liable to change or expand the original concept. The present volume is full of such examples: indeed, that was one of the editor's basic criteria of selection. They deserve to be carefully pondered by theorists and comparative historians as well as by Russianists.

Take the question of consumption. The birth and development of the "consumer society" is a major scholarly issue for European and American historians, the premise of which is that this is part of the history of capitalism, connected to an ever-increasing abundance of goods. In the Soviet Union, however (as Julie Hessler shows in the volume), consumerism came *without* abundance – a consumerism of scarcity in a context of state socialism, bizarrely plugged into a discourse about the civilizing process. Or take the question of nationality. Theorists of nationality emphasizing its social construction have proceeded from situations where the "imagined community" of nation was constructed by intellectuals, often in opposition to an imperial state. How much more interesting and complex the whole thing becomes when (as Slezkine and Martin demonstrate) it is the imperial state that "imagines" its own nations. Or take the self, whose emergence in modern Europe is the subject of much Foucauldian-inspired scholarship. "Modernity" looks very different if the Soviet version is included; here, paradoxically, processes of individuation take place (as Hellbeck and others suggest) in the context of *collective* practices like "purging" and "self-criticism."

The work in this volume challenges many received truths and assumptions about Soviet history. "Class" – including the "dictator class" of the revolution, the proletariat – becomes a problematic rather than a transparent category (Fitzpatrick), though we see that Russians had their own spontaneous form of "class consciousness" in the us/them dichotomy (Davies). Nationality assumes a new centrality in Soviet state-building and the myth of the Communist leaders as suppressors of ethnic/national particularism dissolves (Slezkine, Martin). Consumer goods turn out to have been vitally important because of their scarcity, and a spirit of consumerism turns out to have been actually encouraged by the Stalinist regime (Hessler). That regime has marked paternalist features (Siegelbaum) and sees itself as engaged in a "civilizing mission" *vis-à-vis* "backward" ethnic groups, peasants and women, as well as a mission to instil "culturedness" in the whole population (Volkov, Hessler, Slezkine). Soviet citizens are participants in, rather than victims of, Stalinism, devoting much energy to cultivating a Soviet mentalité and suppressing the non- or anti-Soviet elements in their souls (Hellbeck); but that participation is likely to be expressed in surprising forms, such as the "disinterested denunciation" discussed by Kozlov. Citizens learn rituals and practices from the Communist Party but then use them for private ends (Kozlov, Kojevnikov). Uncertainty about identity and fear of being unmasked as "socially alien" produce passionate commitment to the regime's values, as well as resentful alienation, on the part of "former" people (Hellbeck, Fitzpatrick) – and the reality behind that fear is demonstrated by the fate of social marginals who fell into the related, though distinct, category of "socially harmful" (Hagenloh).

The most controversial of all topics in the history of the Stalin period, terror and the Great Purges, is illuminated by two innovative contributions from young scholars included in this volume. Harris shows how the imperatives of meeting production targets of the Five-Year Plans led regional party and economic leaders into self-protective practices that involved a systematic deception of the Center that was interpreted during the Great Purges as "conspiracy." Hagenloh distinguishes a strand in the process of terror in 1937 that was essentially unknown until publication in the early 1990s of secret Politburo directives, namely the mass arrests of marginals that constituted the climax of a decade-long effort to remove from the society lower-class misfits like beggars, itinerants, prostitutes, and expropriated peasants.

This is a young scholarship, and the major interpretive lines and controversies are only starting to emerge. What is clear, however, is that some preoccupations of earlier scholarship have been discarded, at least for the time being, while new topics and problems have been proposed. In the former category come a range of questions and areas of enquiry that interested both revisionists and earlier modernization theorists, namely the Soviet analogues of structures and processes characteristic of Western development in the last two centuries (professionalization of bureaucracy, interest-group politics, political participation, upward mobility, spread of popular literacy and education, and so on).[27] In the latter category are questions of subjectivity and identity and informal networks.

In general, it is the specific characteristics of Stalinism rather than its commonalities with other cultural systems that interest the current generation. Two distinct approaches can be discerned, one stressing the "neo-traditional" aspects of Stalinism, the other its modernity. The "modernity" group, which includes Jochen Hellbeck and other young scholars who were graduate students at Columbia in the first half of the 1990s, suggests that the stereotype of modernity based exclusively on Western experience (parliamentary democracy, market economy) is inadequate, and points to the Soviet example as an important alternative form. This points up statist phenomena such as planning, scientific organizational principles, welfare-statism, and techniques of popular surveillance, on the one hand, and disciplines of the self and the collective, on the other.[28]

The neo-traditionalists (represented in this volume by Terry Martin), drawing on the work of Ken Jowitt, Andrew Walder, and Janos Kornai, do not dispute that the Soviet Union represented an "alternative type of modernity." Their interest, however, is drawn more particularly to the "archaicizing" phenomena that were also a part of Stalinism: petitioning, patron–client networks, the ubiquity of other kinds of personalistic ties like *blat*, ascribed status categories, "court" politics in the Kremlin, the mystification of power and its projection through display, and so on. Despite the invocation of tradition, this group is less interested in Russian historical precedents than in why and how Stalinism generated such "neo-traditional" phenomena: Terry Martin proposes that "extreme Soviet statism was the root cause of neo-traditional outcomes."[29]

Which one of these will become the dominant paradigm of scholarship in the 2000s is anybody's guess. Perhaps it will be something different altogether. What is already clear is that scholarship on Stalinism is in a phase of intensive development and excitement that is going to change the field. The new work published here demonstrates its variety and vitality.

Note for readers

The Glossary at the front of the book provides definitions and identifications of common terms and names used in the texts. More esoteric terms are translated in square brackets in the text.

NOTES

1 See Lynn Hunt, ed., *The New Cultural History* (Berkeley, 1989).
2 Raymond A. Bauer, Alex Inkeles, and Clyde Kluckhohn, *How the Soviet System Works: Cultural, Psychological, and Social Themes* (Cambridge, 1956); Alex Inkeles and Raymond Bauer, *The Soviet Citizen: Daily Life in a Totalitarian Society* (New York, 1968). For other scholarly works based on this Harvard Interview Project data, see list in Inkeles and Bauer, *The Soviet Citizen.*
3 Note, however, the excellent work of economists like Abram Bergson, Naum Jasny, Franklyn Holzman, Joseph Berliner, and David Granick on the Soviet economic system in the 1950s and 1960s. Apart from Merle Fainsod's *How Russia is Ruled* (1953), the political scientists produced little work of comparable quality and durability.
4 In the early post-Soviet era, history has been the discipline that has survived the upheaval most successfully. Despite a crying need for sociologists, anthropologists, political scientists, and (most egregiously) economists with area expertise to monitor developments in the former Soviet Union, the social sciences' efforts have been crippled by withdrawal of funding and poor employment prospects for new area-studies specialists. Political scientists have been demoralized by reproaches for their failure to predict the Soviet collapse, while Slavic literature departments have suffered in the 1990s from the sharp decline of Russian-language teaching in schools.
5 But note the stalwart work in newly opened political and economic archives of a handful of English and American scholars, notably R.W. Davies, Stephen Wheatcroft, and J. Arch Getty, joined on the Russian side by scholars like Oleg Khlevniuk, V.N. Zemskov, and Elena Osokina.
6 On women and gender questions in the Stalin period, see Wendy Z. Goldman, *Women, the State and Revolution: Soviet Family Policy and Social Life, 1917-1936* (Cambridge, 1993); idem., "Industrial Politics, Peasant Rebellion, and the Death of the Proletarian Women's Movement in the USSR," *Slavic Review* 55: 1 (Spring 1996); Lynne Viola, " 'Bab'i bunty' and Peasant Women's Protest during Collectivization," *Russian Review* 45: 1 (1986); Mary Buckley, "The Untold Story of *Obshchestvennitsa* in the 1930s," *Europe-Asia Studies* 48: 4 (1996); D. Healey, "The Russian Revolution and the Decriminalisation of Homosexuality," *Revolutionary Russia* 6 (1993). Note also Robert Maier, "Die Hausfrau als Kul'turtreger im Sozialismus. Zur Geschichte der Ehefrauen-Bewegung in den 30er Jahren," in Gabriele Gorzka, ed., *Kultur im Stalinismus* (Bremen, 1994), and idem., "Von Pilotinnen, Melkerinnen und Heldenmüttern. Frau und Familie unter Stalin – Vergleichsebenen zum Nationalsozialismus," in Matthias Vetter, ed., *Terroristische Diktaturen im 20. Jahrhundert* (Opladen, 1996). The chapter on "Sexuality" in C. Kelly and D. Shepherd, eds, *Russian Cultural Studies: An Introduction* (Oxford, 1998) provides a useful and up-to-date survey. For discussion of some innovative work-in-progress on gender issues, see Introduction to Part I.
7 Note however that much high-political documentation remained inaccessible in the newly formed Presidential Archive, and the foreign ministry has also been slow to open its archives to researchers. In addition, secret police archives, once the property of the Soviet KGB, now of the FSB or Federal Security service of the Russian Federation, remained closed except to a favored few – a pointed reminder that not everything has changed in Russia and that some institutions have remarkable staying power.

8 Barbara A. Engel and Anastasia Posadskaya-Vanderbeck, eds, *A Revolution of their Own: Voices of Women in Soviet History* (Boulder, Col., 1997).

9 When I wrote the first draft of this Introduction, in September 1998, I put this firmly in the past tense. As a recent spate of "anti-revisionist" journal and newspaper articles indicates (see particularly Jacob Heilbrunn, "Washington Diarist. Historical Correctness," *New Republic*, October 12, 1998, p. 54, and Robert Harris, "The West Prefers its Dictators Red," *The Sunday Times* [London], October 11, 1998), this was over-optimistic; it remains true, however, that the younger generation of Soviet scholars seems almost completely unaffected by this belated resurgence of Cold War passions.

10 Stephen Kotkin, *Magnetic Mountain: Stalinism as a Civilization* (Berkeley, 1995).

11 The arguments about the number of victims have been exceptionally bitter and long-lasting; not surprisingly, the archival disclosures since 1991 are intepreted differently by the two sides. For a non-aligned discussion, slightly dated but still valuable, see Alec Nove's "Victims of Stalinism: How Many?" in J. Arch Getty and Roberta T. Manning, eds, *Stalinist Terror: New Perspectives* (Cambridge, 1993). See also J. Arch Getty, Gabor T. Rittersporn, and V.N. Zemskov, "Victims of the Soviet Penal System in the Pre-war Years: a First Approach on the Basis of Archival Evidence," *American Historical Review* 98: 4 (1993), a "revisionists'" contribution, which presents the new quantitative data from the archives (as of that date) fully and clearly. One of the reasons the debate continues is that, while the archives show that the number of convicts in GULAG, though still substantial, was lower than Conquest and others suggested in the 1980s, they also show that the number of persons executed or sent into administrative exile during the Great Purges was higher than the revisionists (or, for that matter, their opponents) supposed. Thus, both sides can regard themselves as the victors in the old argument.

12 To declare an interest: I was one of the original 1970s revisionists, although in the mid-1980s I expressed skepticism about some revisionist approaches: see my article "New Perspectives on Stalinism" and "Afterword," *Russian Review* 45: 4 (1986), plus the comments from revisionists and others in the same issue and in *Russian Review* 46: 4 (1987).

13 For the classic statement of this position, see Ronald G. Suny, "Toward a Social History of the October Revolution," *American Historical Review* 88: 1 (1983).

14 See Stephen F. Cohen, *Bukharin and the Bolshevik Revolution: A Political Biography, 1888-1938* (New York, 1973). For a portrayal of a democratic, gradualist Lenin, not unlike Cohen's Bukharin, see Moshe Lewin, *Lenin's Last Struggle* (New York, 1968).

15 See Sheila Fitzpatrick, ed., *Cultural Revolution in Russia, 1928-1931* (Bloomington, Ind., 1978).

16 Sheila Fitzpatrick, *Education and Social Mobility in the Soviet Union, 1921-1934* (Cambridge, 1979).

17 Roberta Manning, "Government in the Soviet Countryside in the Stalinist Thirties: the Case of Belyi Raion in 1937," *Carl Beck Papers in Russian and East European Studies*, no. 301 (1984); J. Arch Getty, *The Origins of the Great Purges: The Soviet Communist Party Reconsidered* (Cambridge, 1985).

18 The quotation is from Moshe Lewin, the leading Marxist revisionist, in his *The Making of the Soviet System* (New York, 1985), p. 261.

19 Kotkin, *Magnetic Mountain*, pp. 5–6.

20 I. Halfin and J. Hellbeck, "Rethinking the Stalinist Subject: Stephen Kotkin's 'Magnetic Mountain' and the State of Soviet Historical Studies," *Jahrbücher für Geschichte Osteuropas* 44 (1996), p. 456; Kotkin, *Magnetic Mountain*, pp. 151–2.

21 The reference is to the *History of the Communist Party of the Soviet Union (Bolsheviks): Short Course* (Moscow, 1939; first published in Russian in 1938), the official history, reputedly part-authored by Stalin, which all party members were required to study.

22 Stephen Kotkin, "1991 and the Russian Revolution: Sources, Conceptual Categories, Analytical Frameworks," *Journal of Modern History* 70: 2 (1998), p. 425. This review article contains many equally trenchant comments on revisionist scholarship.

23 Notably Kotkin, whose *Magnetic Mountain* is dedicated to Foucault in memory of their conversations at Berkeley (where Kotkin was a student), but also Hellbeck, the Russian Oleg Kharkhordin, and to a lesser degree Vadim Volkov. Other young Soviet historians, however, including many authors in this volume, are either indifferent or positively antipathetic to Foucault.

24 Q.v. the important volumes edited by two literary/cultural-studies scholars, Catriona Kelly and David Shepherd: *Constructing Russian Culture in the Age of Revolution* (Oxford, 1998) and *Russian Cultural Studies: An Introduction* (Oxford, 1998), and Christina Kiaer's and Eric Naiman's forthcoming volume, *Everyday Subjects: Formations of Identity in Early Soviet Culture* (Cornell University Press), edited by an art historian (Kiaer) and Slavic literature scholar (Naiman).

25 David L. Hoffman, *Peasant Metropolis: Social Identities in Moscow, 1928-1941* (Ithaca, 1994), p. 212.

26 See Ronald G. Suny, *The Revenge of the Past: Nationalism, Revolution, and the Collapse of the Soviet Union* (Stanford, 1993). Note, however, that this is one line of current scholarship that is definitely *not* appealing to historians in the non-Russian republics of the former Soviet Union, who are all engaged in rewriting their national histories in a nationalist, deeply primordial, spirit.

27 For a clearly argued position statement on this question, see the concluding chapter of Matthew Lenoe, "Stalinist Mass Journalism and the Transformation of Soviet Newspapers, 1926–1932," PhD diss., University of Chicago, 1997.

28 On Soviet modernity, see Kotkin, "1991," p. 425, and Peter Holquist, " 'Information is the Alpha and Omega of our Work': Bolshevik Surveillance in its Pan-European Context," *Journal of Modern History* 69: 3 (September 1997). On Soviet articulation of an "illiberal modern selfhood," see Jochen Hellbeck, "Subjectivities and Policies of Subjectivization in the Stalin Period," presented at a conference on "The Stalin Period: New Ideas, New Conversations," held at Riverside, California, March 12–15, 1998. The modernity argument is the focus of a volume edited by David L. Hoffman and Yanni Kotsonis, *Russian Modernity: Politics, Practices, Knowledge* (London: Macmillan, forthcoming).

29 The "neo-traditionalists" are sometimes referred to as the Chicago group, since a number of them were graduate students at the University of Chicago in the first half of the 1990s. Terry Martin and Matthew Lenoe are the main theorists, but they draw on Golfo Alexopoulos' study of petitions of the disfranchised and Julie Hessler's study of trade practices, as well as a number of other studies of petitions and denunciations (see special issue of *Russian History*, 1997 nos. 1–2) and Sheila Fitzpatrick's recent work on petitions and denunciations, patronage and *blat*.

Part I

SOCIAL IDENTITIES

Class has been the big problem for Soviet social historians. This reflects the fact that, thanks to the Marxist ideology of the Bolshevik leaders, class was the official system of social classification in the Soviet Union; in 1926, the Bolsheviks were proud of conducting the world's first population census using class as a basic category. In the 1970s, when class categories were taken more or less at face value by Western Soviet scholars, interest in class was largely a by-product of Marxism. Marxist revisionist historians attached special importance to the working class because they saw the establishment of Soviet power in 1917 as a workers' revolution and thought that the key to understanding the Soviet system lay in the relationship of workers and the state. Soviet historians, of course, operated on similar premises. To be sure, Western Marxists, in contrast to Soviet ones, usually saw the Stalinist regime as betraying the working class and the workers' revolution[1] and enthroning a "new class" of bureaucrats in power, or at least in privilege.[2] But near-consensus reigned that the way to understand Russian (Soviet) social structure was in terms of classes.

There were two lines of discussion about class in the 1970s. One was about class differentiation of the peasantry, a subject of great concern to Soviet Marxists in the 1920s. The details of the debate need not concern us, but what is interesting for our purposes is that it prompted several Western Marxists to question the reality of the *kulak* class that was demonized as a class of rural exploiters and finally, at the end of the 1920s, expropriated.[3] The second discussion was associated with Sheila Fitzpatrick's work on upward mobility, specifically her argument that in practice the Bolshevik solution to the revolutionary promise of "power to the workers" was *not* to give workers power as a class, but rather, via "affirmative action" policies, to offer individual workers the opportunity to move upward into the administrative and professional elites.[4] In Fitzpatrick's reading, Trotsky's and Djilas's "new class" – the ruling bureaucracy whose emergence constituted a betrayal of the revolution

15

– actually consisted in large part of upwardly mobile former workers; moreover, those former workers saw their rise as a fulfilment of the promises of the revolution.

In the 1980s, the highly reified approach to class previously prevailing started to crumble under the impact of E.P. Thompson's suggestion that class consciousness is not a given but something that has to be formed.[5] But it was not until the 1990s that a distinctly new approach to class gained ground. The basis of the new approach was the perception that class is not a fixed attribute of an individual (not "primordial," to borrow a term from the nationality discussions presented in Part V) but rather an identity that can be taken up, cast off, hidden, learned, and so on. This insight was very useful in understanding types of Soviet behavior that were previously unexamined, notably those associated with class discrimination and stigmatization and Soviet "affirmative action" policies. Golfo Alexopoulos's 1996 dissertation explored the world of the disenfranchised (persons deprived of civil rights because of their "alien" class origins), showing by a close study of their petitions how they attempted to rid themselves of stigma and gain reinstatement as full Soviet citizens. Paul Hagenloh's work highlights the related category of "socially harmful elements," persons targeted for repression on grounds of their social marginality. In his study of Cossack territory during the Civil War, Peter Holquist showed how class and ethnic labels were manipulated and contested by the warring groups.[6] The Cossacks, indeed, provide a fine demonstration of the point that ethnic and class identities overlapped and – as Terry Martin argues in his essay in Part V of this volume – the same analytical approach can be applied to both categories.[7]

Sheila Fitzpatrick's article in this volume, "Ascribing Class," one of a series of essays on the subject of class dating back to the end of the 1980s, exemplifies the new approach to class and social identity. Fitzpatrick (b. 1941) was a non-Marxist revisionist in the 1970s whose earlier work on proletarian upward mobility had left her with some unanswered questions on exactly what it meant in class terms to be a proletarian *vydvizhenets* (a "promoted" or upwardly mobile worker), or, for that matter, what it meant to be a worker.[8] The argument of "Ascribing Class" is that in Soviet Russia "class" was an ascribed characteristic, not a socio-economic attribute, whose primary function, like that of social estates (*sosloviia*) under the old regime, was to define an individual's rights, privileges, and obligations *vis-à-vis* the state. Russia's class structure (in the normal Marxist sense) had never been highly developed, and in the social chaos following the revolution it came close to collapse. Yet, according to the Bolsheviks' Marxist premise, Russia *must* be a class society, otherwise how could the leaders of the proletarian revolution distinguish their allies from their enemies? Elaborate legal and administrative structures of class

discrimination put in place in the 1920s led to a variety of peculiar practices such as "masking" (assuming an advantageous social identity) and
"unmasking" (publicly revealing such deceptions). This fostered an acute
and often painful consciousness of class in Soviet citizens – but it was far
from the kind of consciousness E.P. Thompson had in mind. In fact, that
Thompsonian consciousness – hence, in a Marxist sense, the formation of
classes in Soviet society – could only be inhibited by the practices associated with ascribed or "virtual" class.

Sarah Davies (b. 1967), a young British scholar, offers another approach
to the question of social identity in her article " 'Us Against Them'," which
deals with popular opinion and the popular construction of social identities in Leningrad in the 1930s. This study is based on extensive archival
research on secret NKVD and party reports on the "mood of the population," together with unpublished letters sent by citizens to the authorities.
Davies found that the traditional "us" and "them" dichotomy by which
ordinary people distinguished themselves from those with power and
privilege was stronger than any Marxist class categories. She shows the
resentment ordinary people felt for those in power, their sense of deception and betrayal, their assertion of the superior moral worth of "toilers"
over the "parasites" at the top, and their equation of the new bosses with
the old (pre-revolutionary) ones. The popular critique often had anti-
Semitic overtones (and sometimes anti-Georgian and anti-Armenian ones
as well). Popular resentment of "the bosses" could sometimes be mobilized by the regime in its own interests, for example, during Stalin's terror against the Communist elite in the Great Purges.

Davies' work is probably best placed in the tradition of English social
history exemplified by E.P. Thompson's famous article "The Moral
Economy of the English Crowd in the Eighteenth Century."[9] It owes
something, too, to the notion of everyday resistance developed by James
C. Scott, which has had considerable influence on North American work
on collectivization and its aftermath.[10] Resistance in the more literal sense
of workers' strikes and peasant uprisings is another emerging topic made
possible by the opening of Soviet archives, notably in the work of Jeffrey
Rossman and Lynne Viola.

FURTHER READING

Social identity

Alexopoulos, Golfo, "Rights and Passage: Making Outcasts and Making Citizens
    in Soviet Russia, 1926–1936," PhD dissertation, University of Chicago, 1996.
Brooks, Jeffrey, "Revolutionary Lives: Public Identities in *Pravda* during the
    1920s," in Stephen White, ed., *New Directions in Soviet History* (New York,
    1992).

Davies, Sarah, *Popular Opinion in Stalin's Russia: Terror, Propaganda, and Dissent, 1934-1941* (Cambridge, 1997).

Fitzpatrick, Sheila, "The Bolsheviks' Dilemma: Class, Culture, and Politics in the Early Soviet Years," *Slavic Review* 47 (Winter 1988), reprinted in Fitzpatrick, *The Cultural Front* (Ithaca, 1992).

—— "The Problem of Class Identity in NEP Society," in Sheila Fitzpatrick, Alexander Rabinowitch, and Richard Stites, eds, *Russia in the Era of NEP*, (Bloomington, 1991).

Hoffman, David L., *Peasant Metropolis: Social Identities in Moscow, 1928–1941* (Ithaca, 1994).

Kimerling, Elise, "Civil Rights and Social Policy in Soviet Russia, 1918-1936," *Russian Review* 41:1 (1982).

Krylova, Anna, " 'Healers of Wounded Souls': The Crisis of Private Life in Soviet Literature and Society, 1944–46," ms.

Siegelbaum, Lewis and Ronald Suny, eds, *Making Workers Soviet: Power, Class and Identity* (Ithaca, 1994).

Weiner, Amir, "The Making of a Dominant Myth: The Second World War and the Construction of Political Identities within the Soviet Polity," *Russian Review* 55: 4 (1996).

Gender

Bernstein, Frances L., "Envisioning Health in Revolutionary Russia: The Politics of Gender in Sexual-enlightenment Posters of the 1920s," *Russian Review* 57: 2 (1998).

Fitzpatrick, Sheila, "Lives and Times," in Fitzpatrick and Yuri Slezkine, eds, *In the Shadow of Revolution: Stories of Russian Women from 1917 to the Second World War* (Princeton, forthcoming).

—— "Sex and Revolution: an Examination of Literary and Statistical Data on the Mores of Soviet Students in the 1920s," *Journal of Modern History* 50 (June 1978), reprinted in Fitzpatrick, *The Cultural Front* (Ithaca, 1992).

Gorsuch, Anne E., " 'A Woman is Not a Man': the Culture of Gender and Generation in Soviet Russia, 1921–1928," *Slavic Review* 55: 3 (Fall 1996), 636–60.

Naiman, Eric, *Sex in Public: The Incarnation of Early Soviet Ideology* (Princeton, 1997).

Reid, Susan E., "All Stalin's Women: Gender and Power in Soviet Art of the 1930s," *Slavic Review* 57: 1 (Spring, 1998).

Slezkine, Yuri, "Lives as Tales," in Fitzpatrick and Yuri Slezkine, eds, *In the Shadow of Revolution: Life Stories of Russian Women from 1917 to the Second World War* (Princeton, forthcoming).

Resistance

Fitzpatrick, Sheila, *Stalin's Peasants: Resistance and Survival in the Russian Village after Collectivization* (New York, 1994).

Rossman, Jeffrey, "The Teikovo Cotton Workers' Strike of April 1932: Class, Gender and Identity Politics in Stalin's Russia," *Russian Review* 56: 1 (1997).

—— "Weaver of Rebellion and Poet of Resistance: Kapiton Klepikov (1880–1933) and Shop-floor Opposition to Bolshevik Rule," *Jahrbücher für Geschichte Osteuropas* 44: 3 (1996).

Viola, Lynne, *Peasant Rebels under Stalin: Collectivization and the Culture of Peasant Resistance* (New York, 1996).

Zubkova, Elena, *Russia After the War: Hopes, Illusions, and Disappointments, 1945–1957*, ed. and trans. by Hugh Ragsdale (Armonk, NY, 1998).

NOTES

1 See, for example, Solomon Schwartz, *Labor in the Soviet Union* (New York, 1952); Donald Filtzer, *Soviet Workers and Stalinist Industrialization: The Formation of Modern Soviet Production Relations, 1928–1941* (Armonk, NY, 1986).

2 See Leon Trotsky, *The Revolution Betrayed* (London, 1937); Milovan Djilas, *The New Class: An Analysis of the Communist System* (London, 1957).

3 See Moshe Lewin, *Russian Peasants and Soviet Power: A Study of Collectivization* (London, 1968); and Teodor Shanin, *The Awkward Class: Political Sociology of Peasantry in a Developing Society, Russia, 1910–1925* (Oxford, 1972).

4 See Sheila Fitzpatrick, *Education and Social Mobility in the Soviet Union, 1921–1934* (Cambridge, 1979); "Stalin and the Making of the New Elite" (first published 1979), in Fitzpatrick, *The Cultural Front* (Ithaca, 1992); "The Russian Revolution and Social Mobility: a Reexamination of the Question of Social Support for the Soviet Regime in the 1920s and 1930s," *Politics and Society*, Fall, 1984.

5 E.P. Thompson, *The Making of the English Working Class* (London, 1980; first published 1963). For a discussion of the impact of this destabilization on Soviet labor history, see Lewis H. Siegelbaum and Ronald Grigor Suny, "Class Backwards? In Search of the Soviet Working Class," in Siegelbaum and Suny, eds, *Making Workers Soviet: Power, Class, and Identity* (Ithaca, 1994).

6 Peter Holquist, "Conduct Merciless Mass Terror: Decossackization on the Don, 1919," *Cahiers du Monde russe* 38: 1–2 (1997).

7 Gender identity has been less explored for the Stalin period than social and national identity; so far, no major paradigm challenge or original hypothesis comparable to that of Eric Naiman's on the NEP period, *Sex in Public* (1997). Anna Krylova's current work on the role of women as healers of male war-inflicted trauma in the literature of the late Stalin period may be a precursor of new themes in Stalinist gender studies.

8 Fitzpatrick is often described as an atheoretical historian. Some theoretical works that did influence her thinking to some extent were Erving Goffman's *Presentation of Self in Everyday Life* (New York, 1959), Benedict Anderson's *Imagined Communities: Reflections on the Origins and Spread of Nationalism* (London, 1983), and Ian Hacking, *The Taming of Chance* (Cambridge, 1990).

9 *Past and Present* 50 (1971).

10 For example, Sheila Fitzpatrick, *Stalin's Peasants* (New York, 1994); Lynne Viola, *Peasant Rebels under Stalin* (New York, 1996); Gabor Rittersporn, "Enjoying Carnival, Breaking Step: Soviet Unorthodox Folklore in the 1930s," paper presented at conference on "The Stalin Period: New Ideas, New Conversations," held at Riverside, California, March 12–15, 1998. The works of James C. Scott most often cited in this scholarship are *Weapons of the Weak: Everyday Forms of Peasant Resistance* (New Haven, 1985) and *Domination and the Arts of Resistance* (New Haven, 1990).

1

ASCRIBING CLASS

The construction of social identity in Soviet Russia*

Sheila Fitzpatrick

To ascribe, according to one of the definitions offered by the OED, means "to enroll, register, reckon in a class." But there is no known process of enrollment in Marxist classes. A class in the Marxist sense is something to which a person belongs by virtue of his socioeconomic position and relationship to the means of production (or, in some formulations, the class consciousness engendered by socioeconomic position). In this it differs fundamentally from the kind of class to which one might be ascribed: for example, a social estate (soslovie, Russian; état, French; Stand, German), which is first and foremost a legal category that defines an individual's rights and obligations to the state.

This article is about the peculiar conjunction of two incompatible concepts, ascription and Marxist class, that existed in Soviet Russia in the 1920s and 1930s. This conjunction was the product of a Marxist revolution that occurred in a country where class structure was weak and social identity in crisis. While the Marxist framing of the revolution required that society be properly "classed" in Marxist terms, the society's own disarray prevented it. The outcome was a reinvention of class that involved the ascription of class identities to citizens so that the revolutionary regime (a self-defined "dictatorship of the proletariat") could know its allies from its enemies.

The marriage of ascription and Marxist class produced an offspring: stigma. There were "untouchable" classes in revolutionary Russia, notably the much-vilified kulaks and Nepmen (private entrepreneurs), whose fate it was to be "liquidated as a class" at the end of the 1920s. At the other end of the spectrum, to be sure, were the proletarians, whose favored class status was a guarantee of advancement, at least for all those who were young and ambitious (and preferably male) in the first fifteen years after the revolution. But this aspect of the

20

matter, which is by now relatively familiar, will be less emphasized in this article.[1]

The main thesis of this article is that the process of revolutionary ascription produced social entities that looked like classes in the Marxist sense, and were so described by contemporaries, but might more accurately be described as Soviet *sosloviia*. Whether, in addition to these "*sosloviia*-classes," postrevolutionary Russian society was also in the process of making real Marxist classes is a question that lies outside my scope here. But I would tentatively suggest that processes of class formation in the Marxist sense were much inhibited in Soviet Russia in the 1920s and early 1930s, partly as a result of the ascriptive use of Marxist class categories that is the subject of this article.[2]

* * *

Social identity in early twentieth-century Russia

Russian society was in flux at the turn of the century. The crisis of identity that had long preoccupied educated Russians extended to the basic categories of social structure. At the time of the country's first modern population census in 1897, citizens of the Russian Empire were still officially identified by *soslovie* rather than occupation.[3] *Soslovie* categories (noble, clergy, merchant, townsman, peasant) were ascriptive and usually hereditary; historically, their main function had been to define the rights and obligations of different social groups toward the state. To all educated Russians, the survival of *sosloviia* was an embarrassing anachronism, pointing up the contrast between backward Russia and the progressive West. Liberals asserted that *soslovie* had "lost its practical significance as a social indicator" and even claimed (unconvincingly) that many Russians had forgotten which *soslovie* they belonged to.[4]

Judging by the entries in the St Petersburg and Moscow city directories,[5] however, urban citizens of substance remembered their *soslovie* but did not always choose to identify themselves by it. Many directory entries gave a *soslovie* description such as "noble," "merchant of the first guild," and "honored citizen" (or, even more frequently, "widow of," "daughter of"). But those who had a service rank ("privy counsellor," "retired general") or profession ("engineer," "physician") tended to list it, in rare instances adding *soslovie* if that lent weight to the persona ("noble, dentist").

The *soslovie* structure offended educated Russians because it was incompatible with the modern, democratic, meritocratic principles they saw emerging and admired in Western Europe and North America. They assumed – not entirely accurately, as historians have recently pointed

21

out – that the Russian *sosloviia* had no vitality or raison d'être other than tradition and state inertia.[6] Following Kliuchevskii and other liberal historians, it was fashionable in the early years of the twentieth century to condemn the Russian *soslovie* system, past as well as present, as an artificial creation that the tsarist state had foisted on society.[7] (The estates of early modem Europe, by contrast, were seen as "real" social groups whose existence and corporate life were independent of the state's imprimatur.) Dissatisfaction with the *soslovie* system focused particularly on its failure to incorporate the two "modern" social entities that were of particular interest to educated Russians: the intelligentsia and the industrial working class.[8] This was regarded, not without reason, as a reflection of the regime's suspicion and fear of these groups.

It was taken for granted in educated circles at the turn of the century that the *soslovie* system would soon wither entirely, even in backward Russia, and that a modern class society on the Western pattern would emerge. While this reflected the popularity of Marxism among Russia's intellectuals, it was by no means only Marxists who thought that a capitalist bourgeoisie and industrial proletariat were necessary attributes of modernity. The belief was widespread; even Russia's conservative statesmen and publicists shared it, though they had a different value judgment of modernity. Even though Russia was still lacking one of the two great classes of modern society, the notoriously "missing" bourgeoisie, this did not disturb the general assumption of educated Russians that when (as must inevitably happen) classes finally superseded *sosloviia* as the structural underpinning, Russian society would have made the transition from the "artificial" to the "real."[9]

The definitive transition to a class society came – or seemed to come – in 1917. First, the February Revolution created a "dual power" structure that looked like a textbook illustration of Marxist principles: a bourgeois, liberal Provisional Government dependent for its survival upon the goodwill of the proletarian, socialist Petrograd Soviet. Class polarization of urban society and politics proceeded apace in the months that followed: even the Cadet party, traditionally committed to a liberalism that was "above class," found itself inexorably drawn to the defense of property rights and an image of politics as class struggle.[10] In the summer, the landowning nobility fled the countryside as peasants began to seize their estates. In October, the Bolsheviks, self-described "vanguard of the proletariat," drove out the Provisional Government and proclaimed the creation of a revolutionary workers' state. The centrality of class and the reality of class conflict in Russia could scarcely have been more spectacularly demonstrated.

Yet the moment of clarity about class was fleeting. No sooner had word reached the outside world that Russia had experienced a

Marxist class revolution than its newly revealed class structure started to disintegrate. In the first place, the revolution deconstructed its own class premises by expropriating capitalists and landowners and turning factory workers into revolutionary cadres. In the second place, the turmoil attendant upon revolution and civil war led to a breakdown of industry and flight from the cities that, in one of the great ironies of revolutionary history, temporarily wiped out the Russian industrial working class as a coherent social group.[11] The proletarian revolution had indeed been premature, the Mensheviks crowed; and within the Bolshevik party harsh words were exchanged about the vanishing of the proletariat. ("Permit me to congratulate you on being the vanguard of a non-existent class," an opponent taunted the Bolshevik leaders in 1922.)[12] But in a sense the debacle was even worse: in addition to leading a premature revolution, the Bolsheviks apparently had achieved a prematurely "classless" society in which the absence of classes had nothing to do with socialism.

Class principles

For the Bolsheviks, it was imperative that Russian society be "reclassed" forthwith. If the class identity of individuals was not known, how was it possible for the revolution to recognize its friends and enemies? Equality and fraternity were not among the immediate goals of the Marxist revolutionaries, for in their view members of the former ruling and privileged classes were exploiters who (in the transitional period of "dictatorship of the proletariat") could not be granted full citizenship. Thus, the immediate political thrust of the new rulers' interest in class was to find out who should be stigmatized as a bourgeois class enemy, on the one hand, and who should be trusted and rewarded as a proletarian ally, on the other.

Class rule and the dialectics of class conflict were the key concepts about class that the Bolsheviks derived from Marx and their own revolutionary experience. Every society had a ruling class (they believed), and every ruling class had a potential challenger; as a result of the October Revolution, the proletariat was Russia's new ruling class and its potential challenger was the old ruling class that had been overthrown in October, the counterrevolutionary bourgeoisie. In fact, according to strict Marxist-Leninist analysis, this "bourgeoisie" was actually a composite of capitalist bourgeoisie and feudal aristocracy. But the distinction was really irrelevant, since by the early 1920s neither capitalists nor feudal lords remained in Russia as a result of the expropriations of the revolution and the large-scale emigration from the old upper classes at the end of the Civil War. In their absence, the symbolic mantle of the bourgeoisie fell on the intelligentsia, the most visible survivor from Russia's prerevolutionary elites and the Bolsheviks' only serious competitor for moral authority in postrevolutionary society. For this reason, as well as for baser purposes of insult and polemic, the group was commonly referred to by Bolsheviks of the 1920s as "the bourgeois intelligentsia."[13]

The term *bourgeois* was also applied in the 1920s to members of a variety of other social and occupational groups that had little in common with each other or, in most cases, with capitalism. One set of "bourgeois" groups, whose members were collectively known as "former people" (the Russian term, *byvshii*, is comparable with the French Revolution's *ci-devant*), derived its class identity from social or service status under the old regime. It included nobles (both former landowners and former tsarist bureaucrats), former industrialists, members of the old merchant estate, officers of the Imperial and White Armies, former gendarmes, and, somewhat anomalously, priests. A second set, the emerging "new bourgeoisie" of the 1920s, consisted of persons whose class identity was derived from their current social position and occupation under the New Economic Policy (NEP), introduced in 1921, which gave a qualified license to private trading and manufacturing. The urban private entrepreneurs of the 1920s were known as "Nepmen."

On the other side of the equation was the proletariat, defined as the new ruling class in Soviet society. As a socioeconomic class, its main constituent groups were the urban industrial workers and landless agricultural laborers (*batraks*). As a sociopolitical entity, however, it necessarily included the Bolshevik party, "vanguard of the proletariat." Bolsheviks who were not of proletarian origin considered themselves to be "proletarians by conviction."[14]

The peasantry – four-fifths of the total population, poor, still farming by the primitive strip system, and maintaining the traditional communal organization in much of Russia – was difficult to categorize in class terms, but the Bolsheviks did their best, using a tripartite classification according to which peasants were either "poor peasants" (*bedniaki*), "middle peasants" (*seredniaki*), or "kulaks," the last being regarded as exploiters and proto-capitalists. Lenin's 1899 monograph *The Development of Capitalism in Russia* had pointed out early signs of class differentiation in the Russian countryside. The Stolypin agrarian reforms in the years immediately before the First World War furthered the process, but then rural revolution of 1917–18 reversed it. During the Civil War, the Bolsheviks' attempts to stimulate class conflict in the villages and ally themselves with the poor peasants against the kulaks were largely unsuccessful. Nevertheless, the Bolsheviks continued to fear a resurgence of kulak power, and Soviet statisticians and sociologists diligently monitored the "balance of class forces" in the countryside throughout the 1920s.

Large segments of the society that were neither clearly proletarian nor clearly bourgeois were supposed to be drifting between the two poles, capable of responding to the attraction of either. Such groups included urban white-collar workers (usually called "employees" (*sluzhashchie*) in the 1920s and 1930s), middle peasants, and artisans. While one might logically argue that the Bolsheviks should have done their utmost to draw them to the proletarian cause, the opposite was true in practice. The Bolsheviks were much too anxious about the class purity of the proletariat and the validity of their own proletarian credentials to do any such thing. "A distrustful, ironic, and sometimes hostile attitude" toward white-collar workers prevailed in party circles and Soviet public discourse for many years after the revolution.[15] A similar distrust, mingled with patronizing contempt, was often directed toward peasants and artisans, who were perceived as nonmodern (*otstalye*) as well as petit bourgeois.

The revolutionary "classing" of Soviet society required a definitive rejection of the old *soslovie* system of social classification. Thus, *sosloviia* were officially abolished, along with titles and service ranks, within a month of the October Revolution.[16] Yet from the very beginning there was a hint of *soslovie* in the Soviet approach to class, as indeed was natural in terms of the society's heritage. The white-collar "employee" class, for example, was anomalous in strict Marxist terms. White-collar workers should by rights have been put in the same "proletarian" category as blue-collar workers (and sometimes were, for purposes of academic Soviet-Marxist analysis);[17] yet popular usage persisted in giving them a separate class status, distinctly nonproletarian in political flavor. The pejorative term *meshchanstvo*, derived from the lower urban *soslovie* of *meshchane* and denoting a petit bourgeois, philistine mentality, was so regularly used by Bolsheviks to describe white-collar office workers as to suggest that the new class of *sluzhashchie* was in effect a Soviet version of the old estate of *meshchane*.

Priests and members of clerical families constituted another anomalous "class" in Soviet popular usage that was clearly a direct descendant of the old clerical *soslovie*.[18] In contrast to the "employee" class, which was merely an object of suspicion and disapproval, priests belonged to a stigmatized class deemed unworthy of full Soviet citizenship. They figured prominently in Soviet thinking about potentially counter-revolutionary "class enemies" in the 1920s, and efforts were made to prevent their children, who were also stigmatized, from getting higher education or "penetrating" (in the terminology of the time) the teaching profession. The assumption that priests were *ipso facto* class enemies was so strong that large numbers of village priests were "dekulakized"– that is, stripped of their property, evicted from their homes, and arrested or deported along with the kulaks – at the end of the decade.

Structures of class discrimination

Class was built into the very constitutional foundations of the new Soviet state. The 1918 Constitution of the Russian Republic extended full citizenship and the right to vote only to "toilers." Those who lived parasitically off unearned income or the exploitation of hired labor, including private entrepreneurs and kulaks, were deprived of the right to vote in elections to the soviets, along with priests, former gendarmes and officers of the White Army, and other "socially alien" groups.[19] Although these class-based restrictions on voting rights merely formalized the established (pre-October) practice of the soviets and cannot be regarded as a Bolshevik innovation or even a conscious policy decision, the effect of their incorporation in the constitution of the new Soviet state was to make class a legal category, a situation never envisaged by Marx but nevertheless quite familiar to any Russian brought up under the *soslovie* system.

Virtually all Soviet institutions practiced some kind of class discrimination in the 1920s, giving highest preference to proletarians and lowest to disenfranchised persons and members of various "bourgeois" groups.[20] High schools and universities had class-discriminatory admissions procedures, as did the Communist party and the Komsomol (the Communist youth organization). Purges of "class aliens" from government employment, party membership, and student status in universities occurred from time to time, often as a result of local initiative rather than central instructions. The judicial system operated according to the principles of "class justice," treating proletarian defendants leniently and favoring their claims in civil cases over those of bourgeois plaintiffs. Municipal housing bodies and rationing boards discriminated on the basis of class, and there were special punitive tax rates for social undesirables like kulaks and Nepmen.

In order for this system of class discrimination to work really efficiently, it would have been necessary to have citizens carry internal passports showing their social class (just as they had shown *soslovie* under the old regime), but this was going too far for the Bolsheviks in the 1920s. Internal passports had been abolished with the revolution as a symbol of autocratic repression, and they were not reintroduced until 1932. In the interim, there was no truly effective means of class identification, and discrimination was usually conducted on an *ad hoc* basis with unpredictable results. Among the types of documentation that could be used were birth and marriage certificates, which recorded class ("social position") in the place where tsarist authorities had registered *soslovie*, and letters of attestation from the workplace or rural soviet.[21] Personal testimony about an individual's class origins could also be cited, as could the lists of disenfranchised persons (*lishentsy*) maintained in each soviet electoral district maintained by local electoral commissions.

Since the procedures of class discrimination tended to be haphazard and informal, they were also to some degree negotiable. In judicial practice, for example, one form of appeal by a defendant identified as "bourgeois" or "kulak" (and thus liable to a heavy sentence) was a petition to change the class label: "Relatives, and sometimes the accused themselves, obtain documents after the trial to *change their economic and social position*, and the supervisory committees permit them [to raise] the question of transferring from one [class] category to another."[22]

In the higher educational system, too, class identities were often contested by persons refused admission on class grounds or expelled in the course of social purges. The whole issue of class discrimination in education was a painful one to Bolsheviks old enough to remember the time when, in a policy shift universally condemned by Russian radicals, the tsarist government had sought to restrict the educational access of members of lower *sosloviia* ("children of cooks and washerwomen"). Nobody went so far as to raise the issue of a new Soviet *soslovnost'* (*soslovie* order) explicitly in public debates. But the "quota politics" that developed in education in the 1920s had disconcerting overtones. When, for example, teachers pressed a government spokesman on the issue of "parity of rights with workers" in regard to university admissions, it was almost as if a time warp had plunged Russia back to 1767 and Catherine the Great's Legislative Commission was arguing about *soslovie* privileges.[23]

If Soviet class-discriminatory laws were creating new "*sosloviia*-classes," however, this was an involuntary process that went unnoticed by the Bolsheviks. Russian Marxist intellectuals were deeply committed to the belief that classes and class relations were objective socioeconomic phenomena and that gathering information on them was the only way to gain a scientific understanding of society. It was in this spirit, undoubtedly, that even before the Civil War was over Lenin was pressing for a population census that would provide data on occupations and class relations.[24]

A national population census, designed and analyzed according to impeccable Marxist principles, was conducted in 1926 and published in fifty-six volumes. Its basic socioeconomic categories were wage and salary earners (proletariat), on the one hand, and "proprietors" (*khoziaeva*), urban and rural, on the other. In the latter group, which included the entire peasantry[25] as well as urban artisans and businessmen, those employing hired labor (capitalists!) were rigorously differentiated from those working alone or with the assistance of family members.[26] The census, which was exhaustively analyzed and studied by contemporary demographers, sociologists, journalists, and politicians, constituted a major step in the "classing" of Russian society.[27] Of course it did not and could not create classes in the real world. But it created something that might be called *virtual classes*: a statistical representation that enabled Soviet Marxists (and future generations of historians) to operate on the premise that Russia was a class society.

Class stigma

There were stigmatized, "untouchable" groups in Soviet society in the 1920s: kulaks, Nepmen, priests, and *byvshie*. People in all these stigmatized groups were *lishentsy* – that is, they shared the common legal status of disenfranchisement and the civil disadvantages that flowed from it. The "untouchables," however, were not members of a traditionally separate caste, and they could not be distinguished by visible physical characteristics such as skin color or gender. If the kulak left the village or the priest stopped wearing his vestments and became a teacher, who but their old acquaintances would know that they bore the stigmata of class?

Like Russian society as a whole in the first third of the twentieth century, but to an even greater degree, the stigmatized population of the 1920s was unstable and in constant flux. People of all sorts frequently changed occupations, statuses, familial arrangements, and places of residence as part of the general turmoil of war, revolution, civil war, and postwar readjustment. But people who found themselves with class stigmas were even more prone to change, because they hoped that change would rid them of the stigma. For example, a former high-ranking civil servant of noble birth might work as a humble Soviet bookkeeper not only because he needed a job but also as a way of shedding the old identity.

The class identity of a very large number of Soviet citizens was both contestable and contested in the 1920s.[28] This was not only because of high geographical, social, and occupational mobility in the previous decade and the evasive strategies of the stigmatized but also because there were no hard-and-fast criteria for class identification or rules about how to resolve ambiguous cases. The three basic indicators of class were generally considered to be current social position, former (prewar or prerevolutionary) social position, and parents' social status. But there was disagreement on the relative importance of these indicators. The most popular method of identification, inside and outside the Bolshevik party, was "genealogical" or *soslovie*-based, especially in the case of stigmatized identities: a priest's son was always "from the clergy," regardless of occupation; a noble was always a noble.[29] But party intellectuals were unhappy about this approach on Marxist theoretical grounds; and the Communist Party itself used a much more complicated procedure to determine the class identity of its members, using the two indicators of "social position" (usually defined in this context as an individual's basic occupation in 1917) and current occupation, and disdaining "genealogy."[30]

Avoiding ascription to a stigmatized class was among the basic concerns of many Soviet citizens in the 1920s, as was achieving ascription to the proletariat or the poor peasantry in order (for example) to get into university or secure a paid job in the rural soviet. There were numerous behavioral strategies for avoiding class stigma, and outright fraud, such as the purchase of documents attesting to a false class identity, was not uncommon. But these practices generated their own "dialectical antithesis": the more prevalent became evasion and manipulation of class ascription, the more energetically Communist militants strove to "unmask" the evaders and reveal their true class identity.

The unmasking of class enemies rose to a pitch of hysteria and became a real witch-hunt at the end of the 1920s and beginning of the 1930s. The most remarkable episode of "class war" in this period was the dekulakization campaign whose purpose was to "liquidate kulaks as a class." This involved not only the expropriation of all those ascribed to the kulak class and their "hirelings" (*podkulachniki*) but also the deportation of a substantial part of the group to distant regions of the country.[31] Urban Nepmen were being forced out of business and in many cases arrested at the same period, as the entire urban economy was nationalized. In the Cultural Revolution, "bourgeois specialists" came collectively under attack, and a number of those who had held senior posts in the state bureaucracy were accused of counterrevolutionary wrecking and sabotage.[32]

The "heightened class vigilance" of the Cultural Revolution meant that the situation of *lishentsy* became ever more precarious even as the lists of officially disenfranchised persons grew longer. *Lishentsy* were liable to be fired from their jobs, evicted from housing, and declared ineligible for rations, while their children were unable to enter university and join the Komsomol or even the Young Pioneers (for ages ten to fourteen). A wave of social purging (*chistki*) swept through government offices, schools, universities, Komsomol and party organizations, and even factories in 1929–30. Rural schoolteachers lost their jobs because they were sons of priests; kulaks who had fled the village and found work in industry were denounced; elderly widows of tsarist generals were "unmasked" and subjected to various indignities. Neighbors and professional colleagues accused each other of hiding class stigmas. Persons from stigmatized classes sometimes publicly repudiated their parents in a vain effort to wipe out the stain.[33]

Then, as was inevitable, the witch-hunt for class enemies died down. In reaction to its excesses, the institutional structures of class discrimination were largely dismantled in the period 1931–36. Kulaks and their children recovered some (though not all) civil rights; class discrimination in university admissions was abolished; first the Komsomol and then the Communist Party changed recruitment rules to make it easier for nonproletarians to join.[34]

It was time to move toward full equality of citizens and abolition of all class restrictions, Molotov said in 1935, since those had merely been "temporary measures" to counteract the "exploiters' attempts to assert or reestablish their privileges."[35] The government had decided that it was important to lift class stigmas, reported a member of the Soviet Control Commission, "in order that a person can forget his social origins. . . . The offspring of a kulak is not to blame for that, since he did not choose his parents. Therefore they are saying now: don't persecute people for their [class] origins."[36] Stalin made the same point with his famous interjection: "A son does not answer for his father." The remark was made at a conference of peasant Stakhanovites in response to the complaint of one delegate about the discrimination he had suffered because his father had been dekulakized.[37]

The move away from class discrimination and class stigma was completed with the adoption of the new "Stalin" Constitution of the USSR of 1936. The new constitution stated that all citizens of the country had equal rights and that all could vote and hold elective office "regardless of race and nationality, religious creed, . . . social origin, property status, and past activity."[38] This restored voting rights to kulaks, priests, *byvshie*, and others formerly stigmatized and disenfranchised.

"A son does not answer for his father"– or does he?

Stalin's interjection quickly became part of Soviet folklore.[39] Untypically, however, it was not followed up by approving commentary and elaboration in the press, and it was never republished after the initial press report.[40] This suggests that the conciliatory policy it implied remained controversial – not least, perhaps, in Stalin's own mind. It was a question on which Stalin must surely have had mixed feelings. The kulaks' sons who had become honest toilers might be "innocent" in class terms, but did that mean they were harmless as far as the state was concerned?

Stalin himself was not a man to forget an injury done to him or his, and the Soviet regime had undoubtedly injured the kulaks' sons. Might they not be cherishing bitter resentment behind an outward show of loyalty and obedience?

In 1929, on the eve of the great onslaught against class enemies in the countryside that was described as "liquidation of the kulaks as a class," Stalin had predicted that, as the defeat of the class enemy became more certain, his resistance would become all the more vicious and desperate.[41] This introduced a psychological twist to Marxist doctrine on class conflict that discomforted some theoretically minded Communists. All the same, if what Stalin was saying was that "class enemies" become real enemies once you liquidate them as a class, it is hard to disagree with him. As he reflected somberly a few years later, destroying a class did not eliminate its (anti-Soviet) consciousness, for the former members of the class remained, "with all their class sympathies, antipathies, traditions, habits, opinions, [and] world views. ... The class enemy survives ... in the person of living representatives of those former classes."[42]

It is clear that fear of the (former) class enemy remained very strong in the Communist Party through the 1930s and that, even more than the similar fears of the 1920s, it was directly related to the perception that people whose lives had been shattered, either by the original revolution or Stalin's "revolution from above," were likely to remain irredeemably hostile to the Soviet regime. This was particularly frightening because – as a result of Soviet policies liquidating the rural and urban bourgeoisie and discriminating against persons who had once belonged to these classes – many of the enemies were now dispersed and hidden. For every kulak or kulak family member who had been deported or sent to labor camp in the early 1930s, for example, there were several who had fled from the village during collectivization and made new lives elsewhere, usually as urban wage earners. For obvious reasons, such people tried to hide their past from workmates and the authorities because their former identities carried a stigma.

In principle, there was nothing illegal about this, any more than it was illegal for a former noble to work quietly as an accountant without advertising his lineage: after all, it was not only the right but also the obligation of all Soviet citizens to work. In practice, however, the discovery that former kulaks or former Nepmen were employed in the workforce always produced alarm, and the most sinister interpretation was put on their attempts to "pass" as normal citizens. Melodrama hinging on the "hand of the hidden class enemy" theme was one of the standard genres of Soviet mass culture in the 1930s. In the film *Party Card* (1936), for example, an unknown youth turns up in a factory town and meets a woman worker, Anna, who falls in love with him.

Through her, he gets a job at the plant and is even able to join the party. But he is really a kulak who fled from his native village during collectivization. Anna gets some inkling of this but decides not to tell the party. It turns out that this is a terrible mistake. Not only is he a kulak and a murderer but he is also a spy in the pay of foreign intelligence.[43]

Class stigma proved very resilient in Soviet society, despite the sporadic attempts of the party leadership to move away from policies of stigmatization. Both in the leadership and the party's rank and file, there was a basic ambivalence on the class issue throughout the 1930s, interludes of comparative relaxation alternating with fresh outbursts of paranoia right up to the bacchanalia of the Great Purges and its hungover aftermath in the last prewar years. Policies of destigmatization were neither wholeheartedly recommended by party leaders nor systematically implemented by officials at the local level.

In addition, there are indications of considerable grassroots suspicion of destigmatization policies, especially in the now-collectivized villages. At a national conference of kolkhoz activists in 1935, the Central Committee secretary for agriculture floated the idea of allowing deported kulaks to return home, but the proposal received an extremely tepid response and was not pursued further.[44] (Any "return of the dekulakized" obviously would have led to monumental conflicts between peasant households about the houses, cows, and samovars that once had belonged to kulaks but were now in other hands.) In the Smolensk region the next year, two Communist district officials took the new constitution's guarantee of equality of all citizens seriously, ordering that the old stigmatizing lists of kulaks and *lishentsy* be destroyed and that competent former kulaks and traders be employed in places where their skills could be useful – for example, in Soviet trading institutions. These actions were subsequently interpreted as counterrevolutionary sabotage during the Great Purges, in a context that strongly suggests that they offended the local population.[45]

For *Homo sovieticus*, the left and right brain were often at odds on questions involving class and the class enemy: the rational man might accept that class-discriminatory policies had outlived their day and the class enemy was no longer a real threat, but the intuitive man remained dubious and fearful. In each successive political crisis of the 1930s, Communists hastened to round up "the usual suspects," knowing instinctively that the class enemy must be somehow to blame.

This happened during the crisis of the winter of 1932–33, when the introduction of passports was accompanied by a purge of the urban population in which large numbers of disenfranchised persons and other class aliens were refused urban registration cards, summarily evicted from their homes, and expelled from the city.[46] It happened again in Leningrad in 1935 after the murder of Kirov, then the number 2 man in the party. In response to the murder (which had no apparent connection with any "class enemies"), the NKVD rounded up many *byvshie*, including forty-two former princes, thirty-five former capitalists, and more than a hundred former gendarmes and members of the tsarist police.[47]

The Great Purges of 1937–38 marked an apparent change in the pattern. In the first place, the witches in this witch-hunt were called "enemies of the people," not "class enemies." In the second place, as was clearly signaled by Stalin and Molotov in their speeches and reiterated day after day in the press, the prime candidates for the "enemies of the people" title were not the old class enemies but highly placed Communist officials – regional party secretaries, heads of government agencies, industrial managers, Red Army leaders, and the like.

But old habits die hard, and "the usual suspects" often found themselves caught up once again. In Leningrad in the autumn of 1937, Zakovskii, head of the local NKVD, identified university students who were sons of kulaks and Nepmen as a particular category of "enemies of the people" who should be exposed and rooted out.[48] The Komsomol organization in Smolensk province expelled dozens and probably hundreds of its members on grounds of alien social origin, connection by marriage with class aliens, concealment of such origins and connections, and so on.[49] In Cheliabinsk (and surely also elsewhere), former class enemies were among those executed as counterrevolutionaries in 1937–38.[50]

Hidden former kulaks who had "wormed their way" into the factories and government institutions were frequent targets of exposure during the Great Purges. In the villages, denunciations of "kulaks" (or "kulak, Trotskyite enemies of the people" – usually kolkhoz chairmen) by other peasants were even more frequent in 1937 than in previous years; and it was not uncommon for the NKVD to arrest as a counterrevolutionary in 1937 someone whose brother or father had been arrested or deported as a kulak earlier in the decade.[51] The newspaper *Krest'ianskaia gazeta*, recipient of many peasant complaints and denunciations, had to rebuke one correspondent for sending in a denunciation that confused the old stigmatized categories and the new: "In giving information about the kolkhoz veterinarian, A.P. Timofeev, you write: 'His brother was arrested by organs of the NKVD as a former Junker.' Obviously you meant to say 'arrested for counter-revolutionary work.' "[52]

Data recently released from NKVD archives indicate that the gulag labor camps took in almost 200,000 prisoners classified as "socially harmful and socially dangerous elements" in the Great Purge years (1937–38) – not a negligible quantity even in comparison with the half-million-odd "counterrevolutionaries" flooding into the gulag at the same period, and particularly striking in light of the fact that class enemies were not officially a target in this witch-hunt.[53]

Passports and Stalinist *soslovnost'*

At the end of 1932, the Soviet government introduced internal passports for the first time since the fall of the old regime. This was a reaction to the immediate threat of a flood of peasant refugees from the famine-stricken countryside overwhelming the towns, which were already drastically overcrowded as a result of the large-scale out-migration associated with collectivization and the rapid expansion of industry under the First Five-Year Plan. But it also turned out to be something of a milestone in the evolution of the new Soviet *soslovie* order (*soslovnost'*), just as tsarist passports had identified the bearers by *soslovie*, so the new Soviet passports identified them by "social position" – in effect, by class.[54]

Notable features of the new passport system were that the passports were issued to urban inhabitants by the OGPU (forerunner of the NKVD and KGB), along with city residence permits (*propiski*), and that passports were not automatically issued to peasants. As in tsarist times, peasants had to apply to the local authorities for a passport before departing for temporary or permanent work outside the district, and their requests were not always granted. Kolkhoz members also needed permission from the kolkhoz to depart, just as in the old days of *krugovaia poruka*[55] they had needed permission from the mir. It was hard to ignore the *soslovie* overtones, once the peasantry was placed in such a juridically distinct (and, of course, inferior) position. The rules on passports were not significantly changed in the course of the 1930s, despite the equality-of-rights principle that was declared to be a foundation of Soviet law and government by the constitution of 1936.

The normal passport entries under the "social position" heading in the 1930s were worker, employee, kolkhoznik, and, for members of the intelligentsia, a designation of profession, such as doctor, engineer, teacher, or factory director.[56] With the exception of "kolkhoznik," these passport listings seem usually to have been an accurate representation of the individual's basic occupation.[57] No doubt the fact that passports came under NKVD jurisdiction improved their accuracy; but in addition it should be noted that, with the decline of class-discriminatory laws and procedures, there was a corresponding decline in contestation of social identity. No stigma in the old sense attached to any of the class identities given in passports. "Kolkhoznik" and "*edinolichnik*" (noncollectivized peasant) – the two juridical categories of peasant in the 1930s, which replaced the three quasi-legal, quasi-economic categories of the 1920s – were certainly inferior statuses in Soviet society. But neither can be regarded as having the pariah status of the old "kulak."

When the Communist party and Soviet society emerged from the maelstrom of collectivization and cultural revolution in the second quarter of the 1930s, the depth and sincerity of the leaders' commitment to Marxist principles on class had noticeably waned. As has already been noted, the regime started moving away from practices of class stigmatization and class discrimination. If this meant little in the case of the new constitution, real changes in Soviet practice occurred in other areas; for example, educational opportunity and elite recruitment via Komsomol and party membership. The decline of genuine concern about class was also manifest in the abrupt collapse of social statistics, a major research industry in the 1920s – particularly the disappearance of the formerly ubiquitous tables showing the class breakdown of every imaginable population and institution.

All the same, it would be misleading to leave the impression that the Soviet authorities no longer bothered to collect data on social origin and class background. The concerns about hidden enemies discussed in the previous section were reflected in Soviet recordkeeping practices, but this was mainly in the context of personal dossiers. As Malenkov told a national party conference as late as 1941, "When an official is appointed in many party and economic organs, despite the Party's instructions, people spend more time establishing his genealogy, finding out who his grandfather and grandmother were, than studying his personal managerial and political qualities [and] his abilities."[58] The standard questionnaire filled out by all state employees and party members in the 1930s pursued every possible circumstance bearing on social identity, including class origins (former *soslovie* and rank, parents' basic occupation), occupation before entering state employment (or, for party members, occupation before joining the Communist Party), year of first job in state employment, and current social status.[59]

One question about class that remained very relevant in the 1930s was that of an individual's social trajectory. It remained extremely important to differentiate between, say, a worker whose father had also been a worker and a worker who had left the village, perhaps fearing dekulakization, in 1930, or between an official who had started off life as a priest's or noble's son and one who had struggled up from village to factory and then in 1929 become a beneficiary of "proletarian promotion." In the comparatively few large-scale social surveys conducted and published in the 1930s, such questions were also central.[60]

The population censuses of the 1930s, in contrast to the 1926 census, dealt briskly and briefly with social position. In a sense, this simply reflected changing external circumstances, notably the "liquidation as a class" of kulaks and other private employers of hired labor. But it was also clear that, in an unarticulated reversion to the spirit of the 1897 census, the question about class (identical in the 1937 and 1939 censuses) had suddenly ceased to be complicated and had become almost as straightforward as the old question about *soslovie*. Class position no longer had to be deduced on the basis of painstakingly assembled and analyzed economic data; for a large part of the population, it was conveniently written in the passport and just had to be reported. In the 1937 and 1939 question on social position, respondents were simply required to say which of the following groups they belonged to: "workers, employees, kolkhozniks, *edinolichniki*, craftsmen, free professionals or servants of a religious cult, and non-toiling elements." In addition, in an evocative turn of phrase that would not have displeased Peter the Great, they were asked to identify their present "service" (*sluzhba*) – that is, their branch of employment if they worked for the state.[61]

The term *class* was not used in the census forms, suggesting some uncertainty about its continuing relevance as a category.[62] In the mid-1930s, after all, the Soviet Union had officially reached the stage of socialist construction (*sotsialisticheskoe stroitel'stvo*): it was possible, despite the lack of theoretical clarity about the relationship of socialist construction to socialism, that this implied that the achievement of a classless society was imminent. Stalin, however, confirmed that classes did indeed remain in Soviet society, although they were classes of a special, non-antagonistic kind due to the ending of exploitation and class conflict.[63] He did not bother to justify this assertion with elaborate theorizing. "Can we, as Marxists, evade the question of the class composition of our society in the Constitution?" he asked rhetorically. The laconic answer was, "No, we cannot."[64]

In the spirit of Catherine the Great clarifying the principles of *soslovnost'* in the eighteenth century, Stalin laid out the three major groupings of Soviet society: workers, collectivized peasants (*kolkhoznoe krest'ianstvo*), and intelligentsia.[65] This was a reasonable adaptation of Catherine's four basic *soslovija* divisions to contemporary Soviet circumstances, except for one peculiarity.[66] This was the merging of the old "employees" category with both the intelligentsia and the Communist administrative elite to form a single white-collar conglomerate called "the Soviet intelligentsia."

It would, of course, be an exaggeration to claim that a full "blown *soslovie* system emerged in the Soviet Union in the 1930s. Nevertheless, there were many signs of a tendency toward *soslovnost'* in Soviet social organization at this time, starting with the entry of social position in internal passports discussed above. The peasantry had the most clearly defined *soslovie* characteristics. Unlike the other basic *sosloviia* classes, workers and intelligentsia, peasants did not have the automatic right to passports and thus had special restrictions on mobility. They bore a corvée obligation to the state to provide labor and horses for roadwork and logging from which the other *sosloviia* classes were exempt. On the positive side of the ledger, peasants were alone in having the collective right to use land,[67] and they also had the right, which was strictly denied to all other Soviet citizens, to engage in individual trade.[68]

More subtle distinctions in the rights and privileges of different social groups also existed in Soviet society in the 1930s. Some of them were enshrined in law: for example, the right of noncollectivized peasant households – in contrast to kolkhoz households and members of urban *sosloviia* – to own a horse and the right of "worker" and "employee" households to the use of village plots or urban allotments of a designated size.[69] Cossacks, one of the traditional minor *sosloviia* under the old regime, recovered quasi-*soslovie* status with regard to military service privileges in 1936, after twenty years in disgrace because of their opposition to Soviet power during the Civil War and collectivization.[70] Kulaks deported at the beginning of the 1930s and other "special settlers" (*spetsposelentsy*) in Siberia and elsewhere must also be regarded as a separate estate, since their rights and restrictions as agriculturalists and industrial workers were carefully spelled out in laws as well as secret instructions.[71]

We can also distinguish at least one "proto-*soslovie*" whose existence was recognized by custom and official statistical classification, if not by law. This was the new Soviet upper class, the administrative and professional elite that constituted the top layer of the general white-collar group that Stalin called "intelligentsia." The formal designation of this elite, used in statistical analyses of the 1930s that were usually unpublished, was "leading cadres and specialists."[72] Members of the group enjoyed a range of special privileges, including access to closed stores, chauffeured cars, and government dachas.[73]

In this connection, it should be noted that the whole economy of scarcity and "closed distribution" networks[74] that developed in the 1930s tended to encourage the trend toward *soslovnost'*. This applied not only to the new upper class of "leading cadres and specialists" but also to groups lower in the social hierarchy that also enjoyed access to privileges of various kinds. At the beginning of the 1930s, for example, the closed distribution and public dining room system in factories often distinguished three categories: managers and engineers (known as ITR), privileged workers,[75] and ordinary workers.[76] Later, with the development of the Stakhanovite movement in the latter part of the decade,

Stakhanovites and *udarniki* [shockworkers] came to constitute a distinct stratum of workers who received special privileges and rewards for their achievements.[77] In theory, Stakhanovite status was not permanent but was dependent on performance. But it is clear that many workers perceived it as a new "honored worker" status – comparable perhaps with the "honored citizens" *soslovie* of tsarist times? – that, once earned, was bestowed for a lifetime.[78]

Conclusion

I have argued in this article that class became an ascribed category in Russia after the revolution. The main proximate causes were the legal and institutional structures that discriminated on the basis of class and the societal flux and disintegration that made an individual's "real" socioeconomic class elusive and indeterminate. More generally, one can say that the Soviet practice of ascribing class arose out of a combination of Marxist theory and the underdeveloped nature of Russian society.

In a sense, class (in its Soviet form) can be seen as a Bolshevik invention. The Bolsheviks, after all, were the rulers of the new Soviet state and the framers of class-discriminatory legislation, and Marxism was their professed ideology. All the same, it is too simple to give the Bolsheviks all the credit for the Soviet invention of class. This invention also had Russian popular roots: after all, it was the popularly created workers' soviets of 1905 and 1917 whose class-based franchise set the pattern for the restriction of voting rights in the 1918 constitution and thus indirectly for the whole corpus of class-discriminatory legislation of the early Soviet period. Moreover, the *soslovie* overtones of class in the 1920s – particularly evident with regard to the "class" status of the clergy and the *meshchane*-like category of "employees" – also suggests popular rather than Bolshevik imagination.

Where a specifically Bolshevik (or Marxist intellectual) construction of class was most evident was in the realm of social statistics. Convinced that a scientific analysis of society required class categories, Soviet statisticians of the 1920s painstakingly built such categories into their data, including the volumes of the 1927 population census dealing with occupation. In this chapter, I have suggested that the great corpus of social statistics of the 1920s was part of the creation of a "virtual class society" – that is, a representation whose purpose was to sustain the illusion of classes. One inference to be drawn is, of course, that historians should be extremely wary of taking these statistics at face value.

In the 1920s, the ascription of stigma was a very important – if not crucial – aspect of the general process of ascribing class. Here we are obviously in the realm of popular revolutionary passion as much as that of Marxist theory or even Bolshevik ideology. Bolshevik intellectuals (including Lenin and other party leaders) were uncomfortable with the stigmatizing and scapegoating implications of their class policies; in particular, they resisted the popular notion that a person's class origins should be the basis of stigma. But these objections went largely unheeded. Class stigmatization reached its height in the outburst of state-incited witch-hunting of the Cultural Revolution.

In the 1930s, after the orgy of collectivization, dekulakization, and Cultural Revolution at the beginning of the decade, many things changed. Revolutionary passions waned; Marxism became routinized and lost its charisma for Communists; and, in 1937–38, Soviet witch-hunting was at least partly diverted away from class channels. Nevertheless, class was still a basic category of identity for Soviet citizens, and this was institutionalized in a new way when internal passports including a "social position" entry were introduced at the end of 1932. This "social position" entry was an almost exact counterpart of the old *soslovie* notation in tsarist identification documents. No longer a matter of contestation or (with the dismantling of legal and institutional structures of class discrimination) of stigma, Soviet "class" increasingly assumed the meaning of Imperial *soslovie*.

The implications of a "Stalinist *soslovnost'* " model of Soviet society obviously cannot be adequately explored here, but it may be useful to suggest a few possible lines of enquiry. In the first place, *soslovnost'* provides a framework within which it becomes immediately comprehensible that the "classes" of Stalinist society should have been defined, like *sosloviia*, in terms of their relationship to the state rather than, like Marxist classes, in terms of their relationship to each other. This gives us a new perspective on the much-remarked "primacy of the state" in the Soviet state-and-society relationship.

In the second place, the *soslovnost'* model helps us deal with the issue of social hierarchy. While it has often been pointed out that an unmistakable social hierarchy emerged in the Stalin period, its nature has remained conceptually blurred. It is easy to agree with Trotsky and Djilas that a new upper class, strongly associated with office holding, emerged in the Stalin period, but it is much more difficult to accept the Marxist proposition that this was a new *ruling* class rather than simply a new privileged one. Within the framework of "Stalinist *soslovnost'*," this class becomes a latterday "service nobility"[79] whose status and functions are as transparent to historians as they were to contemporaries, and other *sosloviia*-classes fall into place in the social hierarchy with equal ease.

Finally, it is worth asking whether the same framework might be applied to the study of Soviet nationalities. In Imperial Russia, there

39

were ethnic/national *sosloviia* (e.g., Bashkirs or German colonists) as well as social ones. Nationality, like class, was a category that achieved full legal recognition only with the revolution. Its Soviet construction at first seemed to proceed on very different lines from the Soviet construction of class. In the Stalin period, however, things changed, especially in connection with the deportations of nationalities in the 1940s. There is an intriguing possibility that the shadow of *soslovnost'* hung over the construction of national as well as social identity in the Stalin period.

NOTES

This chapter is reprinted from *Journal of Modern History*, 65: 4 (December 1993), 745–770.

* Previous versions of this article were presented at the University of Chicago, Johns Hopkins University, and the first Midwestern Workshop of Russian Historians in Ann Arbor. Thanks are due to all those who contributed to the discussion on these occasions, especially Jeffrey Brooks and Ronald G. Suny. I am also grateful to Pierre Bourdieu for his comments and encouragement at an earlier stage of the project and to Laura Engelstein, Jean Comaroff, and Steven L. Kaplan, whose careful readings of the manuscript were extremely helpful.

1 See Sheila Fitzpatrick, *Education and Social Mobility in the Soviet Union, 1921–1934* (Cambridge, 1979), and "Stalin and the Making of a New Elite, 1928–1939," *Slavic Review* 38 (1979): 377–402, and reprinted in Fitzpatrick *The Cultural Front* (Ithaca, N.Y., 1992), pp. 149–82.

2 This applies particularly to those Marxist concepts of class formation (e.g., E.P. Thompson's) that emphasize consciousness. Consider, e.g., the problems of (re)formation of the Russian working class in the early Soviet period, given the Bolsheviks' appropriation for their party of a version of "proletarian consciousness" that actual industrial workers neither wholly accepted nor wholly disowned.

3 Form A of the 1897 population census is reproduced in Vl. Plandovskii, *Narodnaia perepis'* (St Petersburg, 1898), app. 1. Respondents were required to give their "Social estate, status, or title" (*soslovie, sostoianie, ili zvanie*), as well as the branch of the economy in which they worked (agriculture, industry, mining, trade, and so on).

4 Ibid., p. 339. The only example cited is that of peasant respondents to the 1897 census who were unable to identify their families' pre-1861 status (*razriad,* not *soslovie*) under serfdom, i.e., whether they were manorial serfs, state peasants, and so on.

5 *Vsia Moskva* and *Ves' Peterburg*, published annually or biannually from the turn of the century.

6 For discussion of the general problems of *soslovie*, see Gregory L. Freeze, "The Soslovie (Estate) Paradigm and Russian Social History," *American Historical Review* 91 (1986): 11–36; Leopold H. Haimson, "The Problem of Social Identities in Early Twentieth Century Russia," *Slavic Review* 47 (1988): 1–20; Alfred J. Rieber, *Merchants and Entrepreneurs in Imperial Russia* (Chapel Hill, N.C., 1982), pp. xix–xvi, and "The Sedimentary Society" in *Between Tsar and People: Educated Society and the Quest for Public Identity in Late Imperial Russia*, ed. Edith W. Clowes, Samuel D. Kassow, and James L. West (Princeton,

N.J., 1991); and Abbott Gleason, "The Terms of Russian Social History," in Clowes, Kassow, and West, eds, pp. 23–27.

7 See V.O. Kliuchevskii, *Istoriia soslovii v Rossii; Kurs, chitannyi v Moskovskom Universitete v 1886 g.* (St Petersburg, 1913).

8 The intelligentsia emerged out of the nobility in the mid-nineteenth century as a distinct group of educated Russians not in (or not committed to) government service. Its non-noble members, many of whom were sons of clergy, were sometimes given the estate classification of *raznochintsy* (various ranks). As separate professions such as law and medicine became more important in the society in the late nineteenth century, the state showed some inclination to treat them as new *sosloviia* – a development to which Russian intellectuals, already focused on Marxist classes as the necessary "modern" unit of social aggregation, paid little attention. The rapid growth of the urban industrial working class was a result of Russia's pell-mell industrialization under the leadership of Count Witte from the 1890s. Most industrial workers, recent or not-so-recent migrants from the villages, were legally peasants by *soslovie*.

9 On this perception, see Freeze, p. 13. Yet, as Leopold Haimson has pointed out ("The Problem of Social Identities in Early Twentieth Century Russia," pp. 3–4), if *sosloviia* were the state's representation of society, so Marxist classes were essentially an "alternative representation" offered by a quasi-dissident intelligentsia on the basis of observation of Western rather than Russian society.

10 See William G. Rosenberg's comment that "for a brief historical moment, at least, dominant identities allowed the lines of social conflict to be very clearly drawn" ("Identities, Power, and Social Interactions in Revolutionary Russia," *Slavic Review* 47 (1988): 27) and the data on liberal perceptions of class polarization in his *Liberals in the Russian Revolution* (Princeton, N.J., 1974), esp. pp. 209–12.

11 On the demographic process, see Diane P. Koenker, "Urbanization and Deurbanization in the Russian Revolution and Civil War," *Journal of Modern History* 57 (1985): 424–50; on its political significance, see Sheila Fitzpatrick, "The Bolsheviks' Dilemma: Class, Culture and Politics in the Early Soviet Years," *Slavic Review* 47 (1988): 599–613, and reprinted in *The Cultural Front* (n. 1 above), pp. 16–36.

12 *XI syezd RKP(b). Mart-aprel' 1922 g. Stenograficheskii otchet* (Moscow, 1961), pp. 103–4.

13 The insult was particularly effective because *bourgeois* was as much a term of opprobrium in the lexicon of the Russian intelligentsia as it was in Bolshevik discourse.

14 Workers made up about 60 percent of the party's membership in October 1917, but this dropped to around 40 percent in the course of the Civil War (partly as a result of peasant recruitment via the Red Army); moreover, most of the party's leaders came from the intelligentsia. Energetic efforts were made to increase the party's working-class membership in the 1920s. But the process of worker recruitment was matched by an equally intensive process of worker "promotion" to cadre status and administrative jobs. The associated practical and conceptual problems are discussed in Fitzpatrick, "The Bolsheviks' Dilemma."

15 *Pravda* (April 20, 1936), p. 1.

16 Decree of TsIK and Sovnarkom (November 11 [24], 1917) signed by Sverdlov and Lenin, "Ob unichtozhenii soslovii i grazhdanskikh chinov," in *Dekrety sovetskoi vlasti* (Moscow, 1957), 1: 72.

17 See, e.g., the detailed class breakdown of Soviet society, based on census returns, in *Statisticheskii spravochnik SSSR za 1928 g.* (Moscow, 1929), p. 42.

18 In a context of serious social-statistical analysis, however, priests and other religious servitors (*sluzhiteli kul'ta*) were subsumed under the category of "free professionals" (*litsa svobodnykh professii*).

19 "Konstitutsiia (osnovnoi zakon) RSFSR, priniataia Piatym Vserossiiskim syezdom Sovetov" (July 10, 1918), in *Sobranie uzakonenii i rasporiazhenii rabochego i krest'ianskogo pravitel'stva*, no. 51 (1918), art. 582. Section 4 (pt 13) of the constitution deals with voting rights.

20 For a detailed discussion of this question, see Elise Kimerling, "Civil Rights and Social Policy in Soviet Russia, 1918–1936," *Russian Review* 41 (1982): 24–46.

21 The 1926–27 registration forms for marriage, birth, divorce, and death are reproduced in V.Z. Drobizhev, *U istokov sovetskoi demografii* (Moscow, 1987), pp. 208–15. The options listed under the heading of "social position" (*sotsial'noe polozhenie*) were worker, employee, proprietor. assisting family member (in a family enterprise such as a peasant farm), free professional, and other.

22 *Sovetskaia iustitsiia*, no. 1 (1932), p. 20; my emphasis.

23 The government spokesman was Lunacharsky, People's Commissar of Education, who was being questioned at a teachers' conference in 1929. (He advised the teachers to rely on the goodwill of the admissions boards rather than pushing their luck by trying to get this enacted into law.) Gosudarstvennyi Arkhiv Rossiiskoi Federatsii (GARF), f. 5462, op. 11, d. 12, l. 37.

24 The failure of the 1897 census to provide such data had been a source of great frustration to Lenin when he was writing *The Development of Capitalism in Russia*. A census was duly taken in 1920, during the last stages of the Civil War, but because of the social turmoil and dislocation of the period its occupational data turned out to be of little value. *Massovye istochniki po sotsial'no-ekonomicheskoi istorii sovetskogo obshchestva* (Moscow, 1979), p. 24; Drobizhev, pp. 47–48, 53.

25 With the exception of agricultural laborers.

26 See *Vsesoiuznaia perepis' naseleniia 17 dekabria 1926 g. Kratkie svodki*, vyp. 10 (Moscow, 1929): *Naselenie Soiuza SSR po polozheniiu v zaniatii i otrasliam narodnogo khoziaistva*.

27 On the general question of the uses of statistics for purposes of social construction and control, see Ian Hacking, *The Taming of Chance* (Cambridge, 1990); and Joan Scott, "Statistical Representation of Work: the Politics of the Chamber of Commerce's *Statistique del' Industrie à Paris, 1847–48*," in her *Gender and the Politics of History* (New York, 1988).

28 For a more extended discussion, see Sheila Fitzpatrick, "The Problem of Class Identity in NEP Society," in *Russia in the Era of NEP: Explorations in Soviet Society and Culture*, ed. Sheila Fitzpatrick, Alexander Rabinowitch, and Richard Stites (Bloomington, Ind., 1991), pp. 12–33.

29 Communists did not usually apply the "genealogical" approach to the working class. Those workers (a high proportion of the whole) who had been born peasants were still regarded as "proletarian."

30 The two headings were "*po sotsial'nomu polozheniiu*" and "*po zaniatiiu*." See questionnaire for the 1927 party census, reproduced in *Vsesoiuznaia partiinaia perepis' 1927 g.*, vyp. 3 (Moscow: Statisticheskii otdel TsK VKP[b], 1927), pp. 179–80. On the "genealogical" issue, the Central Committee's statisticians

believed that parents' class status was "less characteristic of a party man" and "lays a less bright imprint on his whole spiritual profile" than his own immediate class experience and occupational history: *Sotsial'nyi i natsional'nyi sostav VKP(b). Itogi vsesoiuznoi perepisi 1927 goda* (Moscow, 1928), p. 26.

31 On dekulakization, see R.W. Davies, *The Socialist Offensive: The Collectivisation of Soviet Agriculture, 1929–1930* (Cambridge, Mass., 1980), chaps 4–5.

32 See Kendall E. Bailes, *Technology and Society under Lenin and Stalin* (Princeton, N.J., 1978), chaps 3–5.

33 See Sheila Fitzpatrick, "Cultural Revolution as Class War," in *Cultural Revolution in Russia, 1928–1931*, ed. Sheila Fitzpatrick (Bloomington, Ind., 1978), pp. 8–40.

34 On restoration of rights to kulaks and their children, see "O poriadke vosstanovleniia v izbiratel'nykh pravakh detei kulakov," *Sobranie zakonov i rasporiazhenii raboche-krest'ianskogo pravitel'stva S.S.S.R.*, no. 21 (1933), art. 117; and "O poriadke vosstanovleniia v grazhdanskikh pravakh byvshikh kulakov," *Sobranie zakonov*, no. 33 (1934), art. 257. On college admissions, see Fitzpatrick, *Education and Social Mobility in the Soviet Union, 1921–1934* (n. 1 above). On party admissions rules, see T.H. Rigby, *Communist Party Membership in the U.S.S.R., 1917–1967* (Princeton, N.J., 1968), pp. 221–26. On changes in the basis of Komsomol enrollment, see speech by Central Committee secretary Andreev at the Tenth Komsomol Congress, *Pravda* (April 21, 1936), p. 2.

35 Molotov, speech to Seventh Congress of Soviets on forthcoming changes in the Soviet Constitution (February 6, 1935), *Komsomol'skaia pravda* (February 8, 1935), p. 2.

36 A.A. Solts, in *Sovetskaia iustitsiia*, no. 22 (1936), p. 15.

37 *Komsomol'skaia pravda* (December 2, 1935), p. 2. The delegate, A.G. Tilba, a combine driver from Bashkiriia, claimed that local party officials had tried to prevent him from attending the conference, despite his merits as a Stakhanovite, and he had been able to attend only after intervention by the head of the party Central Committee's agriculture department.

38 "Konstitutsiia (Osnovnoi Zakon) Soiuza Sovetskikh Sotsialisticheskikh Respublik" (1936), in *Istoriia sovetskoi konstitutsii (v dokumentakh) 1917–1956* (Moscow, 1957), p. 726.

39 Note, e.g., its use in Aleksandr Tvardovskii's poem, "Po pravu pamiati," which began to circulate in Soviet samizdat in the 1960s. Tvardovskii's parents and brothers were deported as kulaks at the time he was embarking on a successful career as a people's poet in Smolensk.

40 While most newspapers simply failed to react, the Komsomol paper ran an editorial a few weeks later calling for more revolutionary vigilance against class enemies that sounded like an oblique rebuttal: *Komsomol'skaia pravda* (December 28, 1935), p. 1.

41 "O pravom uklone v VKP(b)," in I.V. Stalin, *Sochineniia* (Moscow, 1952), 12: 34–39.

42 Speech by State Prosecutor Nikolai Krylenko, allegedly paraphrasing unpublished remarks by Stalin, delivered to judicial officers in Ufa, March 1934: *Sovetskaia iustitsiia*, no. 9 (1934), p. 2.

43 The plot summary, which may not be strictly accurate, is taken from the film's very favorable review in a local newspaper, *Magnitogorskii rabochii* (Magnitogorsk) (May 5, 1936), p. 3.

44 See *Vtoroi vsesoiuznyi syezd kolkhoznikov-udarnikov. 11–17 fevralia 1935 g. Stenograficheskii otchet* (Moscow, 1935), pp. 60, 81, 130.

45 See the report of the Sychevka trial – one of many provincial show trials of 1937 in which rural Communist officials were accused of abusive, arbitrary, and repressive behavior toward the local peasant population – in *Rabochii put'* (Smolensk) (October 16, 1937), p. 2.

46 See Sheila Fitzpatrick, "The Great Departure: Rural–Urban Migration, 1929–33" in *Social Dimensions of Soviet Industrialization*, ed. William G. Rosenberg and Lewis Siegelbaum (Bloomington, Ind., 1993), pp. 15–40.

47 *Za industrializatsiiu* (March 20, 1935), p. 2.

48 Reported in *Komsomol'skaia pravda* (October 5, 1937).

49 A large number of these victims were formally reinstated in the Komsomol in 1938 after appealing their expulsions. Their rehabilitation hearings are in Smolensk Archive, WKP 416.

50 See data from local NKVD files cited in G. lzhbuldin, "Nazvat' vse imena," *Ogonek*, no. 7 (February 1989), p. 30.

51 These observations are based on reading archival files of peasant letters of complaint in 1938. The files, which come from the Soviet archive Rossiiski gosudarstvennyi arkhiv ekonomiki (RGAE), f. 396, op. 10, are discussed in Sheila Fitzpatrick, *Stalin's Peasants: Resistance and Survival in the Russian Village after Collectivization* (New York and Oxford, 1994), see esp. app. "On Bibliography and Sources."

52 RGAE, f. 396, op. 10, d. 121, 1. 6.

53 Figures from N. Dugin, "Otkryvaia arkhivy," *Na boevom postu* (December 27, 1989), p. 3, based on NKVD archival data classifying prisoners on the basis of the articles of the Criminal Code on which they had been convicted.

54 The basic coordinates of personal identity given in the passports of the 1930s were age, sex, social position (*sotsial'noe polozhenie*), and nationality: see resolution of TsIK and Sovnarkom USSR of December 27, 1932, "Ob ustanovlenii edinoi pasportnoi sistemy v SSSR," published in *Pravda* (December 28, 1932), p. 1. "Social position" remained as an entry in Soviet passports until 1974.

55 Collective responsibility for redemption and tax payments of households in the peasant commune in the post-Emancipation era.

56 *McGraw Hill Encyclopedia of Russia and the Soviet Union*, ed. Michael T. Florinsky (New York, 1961), s.v. "passports," p. 412; information from Harvard Refugee Interview Project cited in Alex Inkeles and Raymond A. Bauer, *The Soviet Citizen: Daily Life in a Totalitarian Society* (New York, 1968), pp. 73–74.

57 "Kolkhoznik" falls into a special category because the passport-holding kolkhoznik was almost by definition not occupied full-time in kolkhoz agriculture. As in the tsarist period, this was often the designation of a former peasant who had in practice become an urban worker but had not yet succeeded in changing his legal status.

58 Reported in *Pravda* (February 16, 1941), p. 3.

59 GARF, f. 5457, op. 22, d. 48, ll. 80–81 (personal dossier [*lichnyi listok po uchetu kadrov*] of P.M. Grigorev, member of knitting workers' trade union, 1935).

60 See, e.g., the trade union census of 1932–33, which paid special attention to union members from the village and their former class status there (*Profsoiuznaia perepis' 1932–1933 g.* [Moscow, 1934]); the 1935 census of personnel in state and cooperative trade, which focused on the employment of former Nepmen and employees from the private sector (*Itogi torgovoi perepisi 1935 g.*, pt. 2: *Kadry sovetskoi torgovli* [Moscow, 1936]); and the 1933 survey of the Soviet administrative and professional elite (published in

1936), which distinguished not only those cadres who were of working-class background but also those who had still been "workers at the bench" in 1928 (*Sostav rukovodiashchikh rabotnikov i spetsialistov Soiuza SSSR* [Moscow, 1936]).

61 See census forms for 1937 and 1939 censuses, published in TsUNKhU pri Gosplane SSSR, Vsesoiuznaia perepis' naseleniia 1939 g., *Perepisi naseleniia. Al'bom nagliadnykh posobii* (Moscow, 1938), pp. 25–26. The 1937 census was suppressed and never published because the population total was unacceptably low.

62 Instead, a completely new term was introduced: *social group* (*obshchestvennaia gruppa*).

63 "O proekte konstitutsii Soiuza SSR" (November 25, 1936), in I.V. Stalin, *Sochineniia* I (XIV), ed. Robert H. McNeal (Stanford, Calif., 1967), pp. 142–46.

64 Ibid., p. 169.

65 Ibid., p. 142. For reasons of doctrinal orthodoxy, Stalin called the first two groups "classes" and the third (which was not defined by relation to the means of production) a "stratum"(*prosloika*). This was sometimes referred to irreverently as the "two-and-a-half" formula.

66 The four divisions were nobility, clergy, urban estates, and peasantry.

67 Noncollectivized peasants had an individual (household) right in their native village, though not elsewhere.

68 This right was limited to certain designated spaces, the "kolkhoz markets" in towns to which individual peasants and kolkhozy brought surplus produce.

69 Note that for most practical purposes, "employees" (*sluzhashchie*) were still treated as a separate estate in the 1930s, despite Stalin's "two-and-a-half" formula.

70 See the letter from Cossacks of the Don, Kuban, and Terek pledging loyalty to the Soviet regime in *Pravda* (March 18, 1936), p. 1, and the statute on their new status passed by the Central Executive Committee of the Congress of Soviets of the USSR on April 20, 1936, cited in *Bol'shaia sovetskaia entsiklopediia*, 2nd edn. (Moscow, 1953), 19: 363 (s.v. *Kazachestvo*). It is possible that the new Cossack *soslovie* also received the right to own horses, a much-coveted privilege in the 1930s, but I have so far been unable to determine this.

71 See V.N. Zemskov, "Spetsposelentsy (po dokumentatsii NKVD–MVD SSSR)," *Sotsiologicheskie issledovaniia*, no. 11 (1990), pp. 3–17, and (on the removal of legal restrictions from this group in the 1950s) "Massovoe osvobozhdenie spetsposelentsev i ssyl'nykh (1954–1960 gg.)," *Sotsiologicheskie issledovaniia*, no. 1 (1991), pp. 10–12.

72 *Rukovodiashchie kadry (rabotniki) i spetsialisty.* See *Sostav rukovodiashchikh rabotnikov i spetsialistov Soiuza SSR* (Moscow, 1936); "Iz dokladnoi zapiski TsSU SSSR v Prezidium Gosplana SSSR ob itogakh ucheta rukovodiashchikh kadrov i spetsialistov na 1 ianvaria 1941 g.," in *Industrializatsiia SSSR 1938–1941 gg. Dokumenty i materialy* (Moscow, 1973), pp. 269–76; and other surveys cited in Nicholas de Witt, *Education and Professional Employment in the USSR* (Washington, D.C., 1961), pp. 638–39. In industrial statistics of the 1930s, the category of "ITR" (engineering-technical personnel) was used in the same way: it included administrators as well as professionals, but excluded lower-status office workers, who were put in a separate "employees" category.

73 See Mervyn Matthews, *Privilege in the Soviet Union: A Study of Elite Life-styles under Communism* (London, 1978), chap. 4.

74 That is, distribution of rationed and scarce consumer goods via workplaces and professional organizations.

75 That is, "shockworkers" (*udarniki*), so designated in recognition of their high productivity as workers.

76 See Leonard E. Hubbard, *Soviet Trade and Distribution* (London, 1938), pp. 38–39, 238–40.

77 On Stakhanovism, see Lewis H. Siegelbaum, *Stakhanovism and the Politics of Productivity in the USSR, 1935–1941* (Cambridge, 1988).

78 See, e.g., the heartfelt complaint from an illiterate woman worker in the flax industry who wrote (via her literate daughter) to Maria Kaganovich, the national head of her trade union, to complain of the gross injustice committed when she was deprived of Stakhanovite status (and forbidden, therefore, to sit in the front row at the factory club) just because her health declined and she could no longer work as well as she used to. GARF, f. 5457, op. 22, d. 48 (letter of November 1935).

79 For a similar suggestion, see Robert C. Tucker, "Stalinism as Revolution from Above," in *Stalinism: Essays in Historical Interpretation*, ed. Robert C. Tucker (New York, 1977), pp. 99–100.

2

"US AGAINST THEM"

Social identity in Soviet Russia, 1934–41[*]

Sarah Davies

According to Stalin, by the mid-1930s the Soviet Union had evolved into a socialist society without private property or antagonistic classes, in which workers, peasants and intelligentsia shared common interests. Since then, much energy has been expended on debates over whether the USSR could be considered a class society in the Marxist sense.[1] This theoretical question will not be addressed directly here. Instead, the focus will be upon the subjective perceptions of ordinary workers and peasants from 1934 until World War Two, and, in particular, on the *language* they employed to construct representations of their social identity.[2]

As this is a vast subject, the article will consider only identities articulated as "us against them" in the sense of the "people" (in various guises) against those perceived as power-holders. This image coexisted and competed with many others. David Hoffmann's work on Moscow in this period reveals the existence of identities based on cleavages between new and cadre workers, men and women workers, and workers of different nationalities. Stephen Kotkin suggests that workers sometimes articulated their identity through the use of the official "Bolshevik" language. Sheila Fitzpatrick shows how some peasants continued to define themselves as *bedniaki* [poor peasants], in implicit opposition to kulaks.[3] Divisions also existed between peasants and workers, Stakhanovite and ordinary workers, and so on. People were rarely consistent in their self-identification. Cleavages among workers or between workers and peasants were not incompatible with broader solidarities based on identification with "the people" against "them," the power-holders. Simply, different identities were articulated on different occasions and for different purposes.

The "us/them" (*nizy/verkhi*) identification was typical of language that was "popular," in the sense of nonofficial. While the official language of the Soviet regime under Stalin stressed the harmony of social interests, popular language emphasized conflict. Although the categories of "official" and "popular" cannot be absolutized, since both emerged from a common culture, shared a frame of reference, and appropriated each other's terms, it is also clear that the conflictual image was characteristic of unauthorized, or what the regime termed "anti-Soviet" and "negative" expressions, and the following analysis is based entirely on comments and letters highlighted by the regime for their unorthodoxy.

Party and NKVD informants recorded the comments in highly classified reports on the popular mood. These reports, and the letters written by ordinary citizens, are problematic sources, partly because their representativeness and authenticity are difficult to ascertain,[4] and partly because there is little indication of the context of the views enunciated in them, apart from a few sparse details contained in the opinion reports about the originators of pronouncements (their name, place of work, party affiliation, occasionally their job). The lack of contextual information makes it hard to attribute meaning to particular statements. Therefore, the article will try to focus as much as possible on the language itself, and to identify recurring themes and images. In particular, it will reveal the way in which the sense of cleavage between "us and them" drew on a variety of repertoires – traditional, nationalist, populist, and Marxist – as well as from the official propaganda.

This dichotomous image of society is common to many cultures, as Ralf Dahrendorf shows. It is articulated as "them" and "us," "die da oben" and "wir hier unten," "ceux qui sont en haut" and "en bas."[5] Stanislaw Ossowski maintains that the spatial metaphor of vertical stratification of people into two main groups – those above and those below – has an ancient lineage stretching back to biblical times.[6] In Russia this perception of social polarization was acute in the prerevolutionary period, partly because of the sharp division between state and society, "official Russia" and the people, which gave rise to an image of "dual Russia."[7] During the revolutionary period, Leopold Haimson has shown, workers felt this sense of polarization very keenly. Ronald Suny suggests that the 1917 Revolution was a "struggle between classes in the inclusive sense of the *verkhi* [the people on top] . . . versus the *nizy* [the people down below]."[8] According to Lenin, "the whole world [of the workers] is divided into two camps: " 'us', the working people, and 'them' the exploiters."[9] This sense of polarization did not vanish with 1917: it continued in a modified form throughout NEP, found a partial outlet during the Cultural Revolution, and reemerged in the 1930s, when the social divide became pronounced and egalitarianism was officially denounced.

In the period 1934–41 the "us/them" conflict was signified by a variety of means. Ordinary people defined themselves with such categories as "we," "the workers," "the people," "the *nizy*," "the peasants," "the Russians," and "the masses." These categories tended to overlap and be used rather indiscriminately to identify the whole stratum of people

48

excluded from power. They reveal the influence of SR, nationalist, populist, as well as Bolshevik language. Likewise, the categorization of the "other," the "enemy," drew on a number of sources in both pre- and postrevolutionary discourse.[10] The "other" was defined most commonly as "they," "the *verkhi*," "responsible workers," "party members," "the state," "the rulers," "the new bourgeoisie," "the new capitalists," "engineers and technical workers" (ITR), "Jews"; and, less, commonly, "rotten intelligentsia," "academics," and "*tsar'ki* [little tsars]." Popular self-identification had a rather negative quality in that it often appeared to rely on identification *against* more than identification *with*. The role played by the "them" in defining "us" therefore assumed a disproportionate weight.

The fundamental dichotomy between elite and people, us and them, was represented and explained in different ways, but rarely involved Marxist criteria. One common interpretation of the conflict was that it lay in an unequal distribution of political power. This was articulated through the use of analogies such as slaves and masters. Another means of representing the divide was in terms of ethical criteria, of good versus evil. A final representation was of a division based on economic power, the cleavage between rich and poor. Often representations of the social dichotomy relied on more than one explanatory factor: however, in the following analysis, each type of explanation will be examined separately.

It seems likely that this sense of dichotomy did much to legitimize certain aspects of the terror in the eyes of the ordinary people, and that the regime may have to a certain extent deliberately manipulated and promoted the us/them thinking, particularly in 1936–37.[11] In official discourse, the terror was portrayed as a battle between the "people" and the "enemies of the people." This opposition, people/enemy of the people, shared many similarities with the us/them dichotomy. Both were directed against those in positions of responsibility (although of course the terror targeted other groups as well, including ordinary workers and peasants), and both highlighted the political, economic and moral corruption of those in power. However, it is also clear that popular understandings of the official representation of "people" versus "enemies of the people" could differ from those intended by the regime. As Fredric Jameson points out, "the dialogue of class struggle is one in which two opposing discourses fight it out within the general unity of a shared code."[12] The same code could be used for divergent purposes. While the regime intended this language to mobilize support, subordinate groups could use it to indicate disaffection: to highlight inequality, the powerlessness of ordinary people, and distrust of *all* those in power, not simply the officially designated enemies.

The political dichotomy

According to the propaganda, power in the USSR belonged to the people, namely, the workers and peasants. This power was vested in the people's representatives: the *vozhdi naroda* [leaders of the people]. In practice, and in the perceptions of many of the supposed powerholders, it actually rested in an elite of officials, Jews, and so on. Ordinary people felt that they were excluded from power, that those in power did not consult with the masses and ignored their opinions. The repercussion of this was indifference to politics among some people, although others adopted a more positive stance, considering it necessary to take action to put "their own people" in power. The predominance of "higher-ups" implicated in the show trials encouraged the perception that all power-holders must be "enemies" and "wreckers" and that this would only be remedied when the government contained a higher proportion of workers and peasants.

The imagery employed to represent the distribution of political power derived from the traditional language of power relationships: "We nonparty workers are slaves"; "Workers were slaves and remain slaves"; "The Communists have white bones, and the nonparty people, black. If you look at it in the old way: the Communists are the nobility and the nonparty people, the workers"; "The masses are the manure of history"; "The people are pawns, they understand nothing, you can do what you want with them"; "The workers are lumps, drop them where you like"; "Workers are treated like dogs." Those in power were bosses (*khoziaeva*), "Soviet directors," "our gentlemen Bolsheviks."[13]

A concerted propaganda campaign tried to portray the country's leaders in a populist guise as *vozhdi naroda*, an image that clearly had the potential to resonate with the people's own representations of the "ideal" leader. Although this propaganda undoubtedly worked to an extent, as the popularity of the leader cult demonstrates, others questioned the veracity of the image. Leaders were perceived as being nonproletarian: "Our leaders are not from the workers, Stalin is from an artisanal family. How could Kirov [the Leningrad party leader] get an education if he was a *bedniak*?" Kalinin, who had been a worker at Krasnyi Putilovets (later, the Kirov Works) before his rise to power, was distrusted for having lost his proletarian roots: "Kalinin has broken away from the masses and does not want to know the working class." It was felt that most of the *vozhdi* were afraid of the people. Stalin and his *soratniki* [comrades-in-arms] "are afraid of us, and do not trust us workers." Zhdanov (Kirov's successor as Leningrad party leader) too was a "leader without the people."

The people did draw distinctions between the behavior of leaders. Kirov was sometimes represented as the ideal leader, perceived as being on the side of Leningrad workers: "Kirov was close, simple, completely one of us (*tselikom nash*)."[14] He set the standard against which others, particularly his successor, Zhdanov, were compared. Thus at a *kruzhok* [study group] of Krasnyi Treugol'nik at the end of 1935, workers complained that while Kirov often used to visit the factory, Zhdanov had not been there once, and they asked that he rectify this.[15] A cadre worker expressed a similar comparison between Kirov and Zhdanov in a letter of 1938, maintaining that Zhdanov knew about events at the grassroots only from reports:

> You do not hear stories about [workers'] lives, or ask questions of thousands of ordinary Communists, Komsomols and nonparty people which they could answer directly in their own words, and that is very bad. It's bad that you are never at factories and in the districts. In this you are not like the late Sergei Mironovich Kirov. He was close to the people. It was impossible for all the workers not to love him; it was impossible for his enemies to hate him. The party always relied and relies on the working class. Therefore it was and is victorious. There is no other way. Therefore there's no need to fear the workers, but you must come to us at the factories. The tsar was afraid to come to the people – and they killed him. . . . You must come to the factories, that will be more useful than your presence at the academic theater in Moscow.[16]

It was indeed the case that, unlike Kirov, Zhdanov was heavily involved with work in Moscow and had little time for ordinary factory workers in Leningrad.

This feeling that those in power ignored grassroots opinions was quite widespread. Thus, a smith, speaking at a soviet election meeting in December 1934, denied that popular suggestions and amendments to the soviet had any influence, because "the bourgeoisie and landowners (*pomeshchiki*) are in power . . . poor peasants have been exiled, kulaks remain, and there are only Jews in power."[17] This feeling emerged especially when decisions were taken which seemed quite contrary to popular wishes, and it was accompanied by demands for ordinary people to be given a consultative role. For example, at the end of 1934, when the decision to abolish bread rations was announced, a worker asked why they could not have a plebiscite in order to find out about popular opinion, as had been done in Germany. Another said that the party was a "handful of people ruling not in 'our' interests. They ought to first of all ask the workers' opinion, have a meeting, and only if we agreed, only then sign a government decree." Similarly, after the publication of the labor decree of June 1940, supposedly at the workers' behest, there were complaints at several factories that in the USSR, in contrast to Britain and America, the government never *asked* the people for help in improving the national economy, it simply issued a decree.[18]

Despite the considerable social mobility of this period, the power elite was often represented as inaccessible to workers and peasants, no doubt because when any of the latter did move up the hierarchy, their lifestyle changed radically.[19] Elections were regarded as a formality, for it was believed that ordinary people were never elected. The 1937 elections to the Supreme Soviet provoked remarks that the existing power-holders had already arranged matters so that they would be elected – "Who was in power, will be again, we won't get in" – and that once they had grown accustomed to the good life they were unlikely to give it up.[20] This system was effective because it relied on fear, as one worker explained:

> It's just talk that the people will take part in the Supreme Soviet elections. It's nothing like that. Some person suggests the candidacy of Stalin or Kalinin and everyone begins to vote for them. They are afraid not to vote for them, because those who don't want to get arrested. After the elections to the Supreme Soviet, the situation will not change because the same people will remain.[21]

In practice, few workers and peasants were elected in party or soviet elections. Of the deputies elected to the Supreme Soviet of the USSR in 1937, only 11.5 percent were workers and 8.5 percent kolkhozniks.[22] Likewise, in the elections to primary party organizations in Leningrad in 1938, only 20 percent of those elected were workers, prompting one old worker to ask, "Why do they not elect us, but only engineers?"[23]

While for this worker "engineers" epitomized "them," for others the target was the Jews. Jews more than any other ethnic group were singled out, not only because of the tenacity of Russian anti-Semitism but also because the largest ethnic minority in Leningrad was Jewish. According to the 1939 census Jews comprised 6.3 percent of the city's population (compared with 1.7 percent Ukrainians, the next largest nationality), and Leningrad had the highest proportion of Jews in the RSFSR.[24] Persistent stereotypes connecting Jews with positions of power were partly based on the fact that few Jews worked in factories, and even fewer in agriculture. For example, in Leningrad in 1924, at nineteen industrial enterprises whose ethnic composition is known, out of six hundred non-Russian workers, only sixteen were Jews. In the 1930s the proportion of Jewish workers remained small.[25] A disproportionately large number of Jews had always been leading members of the party, although this number declined a little in the 1930s. They also came to be identified with state power, since state service was one of the few outlets for Jews after NEP, when many had been engaged in trade and commerce. They dominated the Leningrad intelligentsia, comprising, in 1939, 18 percent of scientists and teachers in higher education, 20 percent of engineers, one-third of writers, journalists and editors, 31 percent of store managers, 38 percent of physicians, 45 percent of lawyers and 70 percent of dentists.[26]

As a result, Jews were naturally identified with the (non-Russian, nonworker) "other." Leningrad Party Secretary Irklis received a letter shortly after the murder of Kirov which implicated Jews in the murder and declared that "the sacred revolutionary Smolny is full of the Jewish nation." According to the letter, this fact was well known to all workers and was causing unrest among them:

> All the traders' sons have set themselves up well with you in Smolny and behave brutally toward the old party members and toward the masses in general. . . . They shelve valuable applications and arrange responsible jobs for Jews and Jewesses at a fast pace, and now you can meet people of all nations among the unemployed with the exception of Jews, as they are all sitting in the leading jobs.

The letter went on to report conversations indicative of a desire to get rid of the Jews, warning Irklis, "a valuable worker and old party member," so that he should not suffer like Kirov. The masses were apparently planning a St Bartholomew's Night Massacre to eliminate Jews, or preparing for a new revolution.[27]

Another letter expressed similar feelings that Jews had taken over all the positions of power. The letter, signed by "A Russian," referred to the party organization of the Leningrad Industrial Institute, whose leader, Zakhar Zabludovskii, was apparently "not indifferent to people of Jewish extraction." The writer claimed that Jews "with dark pasts" occupied 80 percent of the apparat, and that Jews were given priority in housing, stipends and other privileges, and never excluded from the party. Zabludovskii allegedly had once drunkenly shouted, "For one Jew, we'll expel a thousand Russians from the institute."[28]

The Jewish dream of world domination was the subject of another anonymous letter, sent to Zhdanov. The letter argued that the Jews advocated world revolution because Russia was too small for them. Reflecting on the fall in the real standard of living since the Revolution, the writer concluded that socialism and communism were not viable, and simply a mask for the Jews to gain equal rights. The Jews organized 1917; Russians and other nationalities were simply pawns. Stalin, Kirov and other leaders had been bought up by the Jews and forced to subscribe to the doctrines of Comintern, the "international Yiddish cabal." Zhdanov was warned that he too would be sucked in, bought products from Torgsin, given cars, flattered, and have his speeches and portraits printed, all so that the Jews could realize their dream of world power.[29]

Although these three letters to party secretaries referred specifically to Jews, the sentiments they professed reveal a more general hostility toward the existing power structure, an anxiety that power was in the hands of a self-seeking alien group with its own interests and rules. Similar sentiments were expressed about other power-holders, although without the particular language associated with anti-Semitism. Jews were often associated with Bolsheviks, as in the assertion that "the Bolsheviks and Yids will destroy us."[30] The term "Jew" was sometimes applied indiscriminately, simply as a general term of abuse; for example, "Better had they killed Stalin than Kirov – Stalin is a Jew, but Kirov was Russian."[31] The letters were therefore part of a wider phenomenon of hostility to and resentment of power and privilege by impotent groups, rather than purely a manifestation of ethnic hostility.[32]

The sense of impotence, of being superfluous to the workings of power, generated some apathy and alienation from politics on the part of workers. The show trials were designed to mobilize the population, but when asked about their reactions to the trial of Piatakov and others, cleaners at Proletarskaia Pobeda [factory] replied. "We sweep the floor, that does not concern us."[33] Even the more politically literate expressed their alienation:

> The working class never fought for political rights. Only unconscious workers took part in the October Revolution. For the worker it is all the same who is in power, as long as he lives well. Each lives only for himself, and is not bothered about the rest. Workers were slaves and remain slaves. For us it makes no difference what kind of power there is, Soviet or fascist.[34]

The traditionally indifferent peasant also took the line of least resistance: "It's all the same to us, who's for Stalin, who's for Trotsky; better if they demanded fewer deliveries after the trials, but as it is they hurt each other, and the muzhik takes the rap."[35]

While these people ignored the machinations at the top, others appear to have considered the show trials and purges an opportunity to express their disaffection with the "other." The officially sanctioned punishment of authority figures in 1936–38 merely accentuated preexisting popular hostility toward power-holders. The scapegoating intention and/or effect of the terror against officialdom is clear and has often been highlighted.[36] Like the Cultural Revolution of 1928–31, the terror served as an outlet for popular hostility and hitherto thwarted social mobility. However, rather than deflecting criticism from Stalin and the evils of the system itself, it seems, in some cases, to have stimulated the already existing hostility toward all those in power, including Stalin.[37]

That the terror against those in power met with popular enthusiasm from some quarters is beyond doubt. Complaints that Kamenev and Zinoviev had been treated too leniently in 1934–35 were legion. It was felt that workers in such a situation would have been treated far worse, and that Zinoviev and Kamenev had been spared only because they were famous leaders.[38] One soldier described the situation in a letter to his parents in February 1935:

> The old counterrevolutionaries – Zinoviev, Kamenev and Evdokimov – have been sentenced as follows: Zinoviev ten years, Evdokimov eight years, Kamenev five years and the rest they don't describe who, where and how long, previously they wrote – shooting for this one and that one, and there is no sense in it at all, and a simple worker gets ten years for nothing.[39]

After the trial, a worker asked a question that would, as the terror developed, become ever more common: "Why is it only the educated (*uchenye*) who are involved in all these affairs, and not workers?" The fall of Enukidze (Secretary of the Central Executive Committee of the Soviets) in mid-1935 led to demands that all the *verkhi* be checked, including those in the Central Committee, since the real root of the country's problems lay with them and not with the *nizy*.[40] These sentiments grew more pronounced as the regime itself encouraged vigilance toward those in positions of power and Stalin recommended listening to the voices of the "little people."[41]

During the August 1936 trial of Zinoviev and Kamenev, fears were expressed that once again they would be let off: "If a worker does something, then he is sent to court for trifles, but if the *verkha* does something, he is treated less strictly":[42]

> More likely they'll shoot us fools. Nikolaev killed Kirov, and do you think he was shot, no, they sentenced him but only on paper. They have covered the eyes of us dark people. If they are shot, the Communists will get it from the capitalists.[43]

The news of the death sentences handed down to Zinoviev and Kamenev was therefore greeted with some jubilation and regarded as yet another blow against authority. One peasant commented: "All the leaders in power and Stalin should be shot," while a worker said in a similar vein, "Let them sentence the Zinovievites to shooting, and anyway the *vozhdi* will be stifled one by one, especially Stalin and Ordzhonikidze."[44] Another noted the number of Jews featuring in the trial. This became quite a common observation at the successive trials. At the trial of the "Anti-Soviet Trotskyite Center" at the beginning of 1937, there were many questions and observations of this type, including one by a Komsomol: "There are many Jews in this trial, because the Jewish nation loves power, and so they struggled for power so strongly."[45] Not only Jews but also "big people" and *sluzhashchie* [white-collar workers] stood out: "Look at the people sitting there. They are *sluzhashchie*, and *sluzhashchie* create these things. Now if only they would send old workers from the Karl Marx Factory and a couple of young ones to tell Stalin to rebuild and change things."[46] The reputation of party members continued to decline, particularly in the wake of the turnover in party personnel of 1937–38 and the Bukharin–Rykov trial, when workers observed that only Communists were involved, and one even asked if all members of the party had been accused.[47]

By the time of elections in 1937–38 the cumulative effect of the official and unofficial attacks on authority was often popular distrust of anyone in a position of power. The fall from grace even of the "hero" (Marshal) Tukhachevskii caused particular shock. Everywhere people asked, "Whom do we trust now?" for the old regime and its servants had been discredited in the eyes of many at the grassroots. Stalin, Molotov or any member of the Central Committee might turn out to be a "Trotskyist" or a "wrecker." As one engineer put it, "Now being in power means to wreck."[48] It was felt that those in power had been corrupted "because among the *verkhi* there is not one worker."[49] The us/them feelings were thus exacerbated, and there was a tendency to blame the authorities for every misfortune. A kolkhoznik explained: "That's why life is bad in the kolkhoz; wreckers destroy and we have to try to pay for it. We achieve nothing, they wreck and we restore with our backs."[50]

The popular representation of society as split between the people on one side and the "powers" on the other legitimized the terror against the *verkhushka* since it already predisposed them to regard power-holders as *ipso facto* guilty. To a certain extent the popular hostility toward "them," and the regime's image of the "enemy" coincided. However, it is clear that this popular hostility was directed not simply toward officially sanctioned enemies, but sometimes also toward Stalin, his colleagues and the whole party leadership. Likewise, some of those officially denounced as enemies, such as kolkhozniks and workers, clearly did not fall within the category of power-holders despised by the ordinary people. Nevertheless, the construction of the image of the enemy was not simply a one-way process.

The moral dichotomy

In their characterization of the social divide, people often had recourse to moral metaphors. The importance of the moral and religious dimension as a source of legitimacy in popular struggles against authority has been widely noted.[51] Mark Steinberg has shown how workers in the Russian printing industry rarely used Marxist language, preferring to define their opponents using ethical criteria:

> Although workers often accepted the notion of irreconcilable conflict between labor and capital, they viewed it less as a structural conflict of interest between classes than as a moral battle between, to use their own vocabulary, good and evil, light and darkness, honour and insult.[52]

This practice, Steinberg shows, continued after 1917. Ideas of suffering, redemption and salvation enabled the worker to make sense of his own experience in a more comprehensible way than the unfamiliar language of Marxism – capital, accumulation, labor value – would allow.[53]

The moral dimension was always a part of the idealist populist language. This, and the influence of the church, left its impact on the language of ordinary workers and peasants in the 1930s. It appealed both to the more literate and also to those who only had elementary ideas about good and evil. It emerged in the practice of attributing positive moral characteristics to the "people," and negative ones to their oppressors. The people were represented as naturally honest, defenseless and childlike. They were the innocents. Those in power were by contrast dishonest, sinful, drinkers of blood (*krovopiitsy*), hangmen, and murderers. They were unequivocally guilty. Their relationship to the people was based on deception and mockery or insult (*izdevatel'stvo*). An important distinction between the two groups was that the people worked, while "they" lived off them in a morally reprehensible way.

The moral superiority of the toiler was contrasted with the immorality of those who had made it into the ruling elite using dishonest means, or who had become corrupted as a result of being in power. In its most idealist form, this notion emerged in the populist belief that truth resides only in the people. An anonymous letter sent to the head of the Leningrad NKVD, Zakovskii, after the death of Kirov illustrates this view. The letter criticized the government for being unaware of the people's real feelings behind the façade of peace:

> It does not see that every destroyed church resounds with the most terrible echo throughout the whole country. It does not hear the curses of millions of people every day. It does not hear what the tortured people say in the queues created by Soviet power. It does not hear that *people's truth*. . . . Soviet power is " blat" [connections] plus bureaucratism, boorishness and vandalism. No Soviet "truths" can wipe out this genuine *people's truth*. . . . Soviet

power is racing toward its destruction. The more and the quicker it does so, the faster does the cup of the people's patience fill up.[54]

Because of this stereotype of the innate honesty of the people, and the corresponding dishonesty of those in power, the official discourse on wreckers and sabotage within the leadership found a resonance in the minds of ordinary people, who already assumed that they must be guilty. The words of a worker, Kuznetsov, seem representative:

> I do not trust your VKP(b) [initials of Communist Party] – they are all wreckers. I believe only in the worker, who works in production. None of the Communists are honest. You get together on your own at your meetings, and what you are sorting out is a mystery. You don't tell the workers about it.[55]

Those in power were constantly represented as deceiving the people, as breaking their promises, pulling the wool over people's eyes, saying one thing and doing another. This feeling was particularly profound in a period when the media was saturated with stories of happiness and prosperity which contradicted sharply with the reality of everyday life. An "honest worker" from the Samoilov Factory expressed this feeling:

> What is there to say about the successes of Soviet power. They're lies. The newspapers cover up the real state of things. I am a worker, wear torn clothes, my four children go to school half-starving, in rags. I, an honest worker, am a visible example of what Soviet power has given the workers in the last twenty years.[56]

"Deception" and "betrayal" were some of the most commonly employed words in this period. The Constitution was a deception, the elections were a deception, the government's economic policies were a deception. The people's enemies had deceived them and betrayed their trust.

In 1935 workers from the Kirov Works wrote a lengthy letter to Zhdanov, full of strong words against the regime and the "soap-bubble comedy" it was enacting: "The time of respect for the Bolsheviks has passed, for they are traitors and oppressors of everyone except their *oprichniki*." The end of rationing was "Molotov's vile deception," especially as the leadership was well aware of the conditions in which workers lived, particularly those with a family: "Oh, how criminal, how base to deceive the toilers (*truzheniki*), especially his family. And the children, about whom you shout a lot in the press, constant deceivers and scoundrels." With reference to the party's attention to youth in mid-1935, they wrote:

And you Bolsheviks – fighters for the people (*narodnoe delo*), for liberty, equality and fraternity, you still shout at the present time, speak about the education of contemporary youth, and in the spirit of communism as well. Are you not embarrassed to deceive the young so shamefully, surely you Bolsheviks can see, and how can it be educated and be a genuine reserve and helper of your treacherous party.[57]

The feeling that "you are deceiving us" recurs time and time again.[58] The deception of the people was represented as a constant attribute of power: "The tsarist government deceived the people and Soviet power deceives them." The people were easy to deceive because of their naive and trusting nature: "We have been deceived for nineteen years, and, fools, we understand nothing, like sheep." "We are deceived like fools."[59]

The moral distinction between the honest people and the dishonest rulers was often based on the perception that the people, unlike their rulers, actually worked. The assumption behind this was that toil in itself is redemptive, and suffering is good. Since those in power did not actually work, they became morally corrupt. The characteristics applied by the people to their rulers suggest moral degeneration – they were lazy, fat, drinkers of blood, cowardly, thieving. Sloth is a sin, and those in power did no real work, but just sat in offices and issued decrees: "Party members lead and nonparty members work."[60] Sometimes this representation was given a nationalist coloring. Georgians and Jews were portrayed as loafers (*lodyri*) living at the expense of the Russians.[61]

The much-vaunted moral precept in the new Constitution, "He who does not work shall not eat," was treated with irony by many ordinary people, who argued that, on the contrary, "he who works does not eat, and he who does no work [those in power] eats."[62] The greed of those in power was constantly emphasized: "Look at the military, responsible workers, the GPU, they live well, just get fatter"; and, on Kirov's corpse, "Kirov is so fat lying there. No doubt he didn't get the pay a worker does."[63] Attributing the sin of greed to "them" was one way ordinary people coped with the fact that they themselves were hungry, for hunger was associated with moral virtue. This sense of moral righteousness can be discerned in a letter from a group of domestic workers to the Leningrad Soviet in 1936. Among their demands was one that cafés selling vodka should be reduced by 80 percent, and serve tea and coffee instead, for "we see how responsible workers with briefcases wait at eight o'clock for the opening of the cafe with vodka and beer; having drunk a couple of pints of beer, the *sluzhashchii* goes to work. Is that normal?"[64]

Since those in power did no work themselves, they lived off the labor of others. This idea of exploitation was often expressed through the use of the concept of theft: "They" robbed the workers with loans and deprived them of what was theirs by right, the fruits of their labor: "Soviet power robs the peasants, takes everything, while people are left to go hungry. You won't build socialism that way." Other nationalities were innately predisposed to theft: "There is not one sensible person in power, they are all Yids, Armenians and other *zhuliki* [thieves, swindlers]".[65]

In contrast to those in power, the laboring people were by definition good and free from sin. The idea of redemptive suffering was an essential aspect of the moral superiority of the worker. He suffered because his work was so hard and life so difficult. In contrast to the official doctrine of work in the USSR as creative, joyful and liberating, people continued to see labor as a curse to be endured. The writer of a letter to Zhdanov in 1935 signed off as "Stradalist pravdist" (roughly, sufferer for truth), and described his life as a poor worker in Leningrad, his miserable, exhausting day at the factory with little to eat but bread and water:

> That, dear comrade Zhdanov, is how we Leningrad workers work and suffer and torture ourselves in our lives. Our life is very tortured and suffering, what else can one say, when living people begin to envy the dead, that they sleep without any torture, while we live and suffer terribly.[66]

The idea of suffering was often expressed in terms of torture and blood – those in power "drink the blood" of the worker and "have become carried away with exaggerated successes at the expense of the blood and sweat of the Russian people." There was a tendency to equate this suffering and patience with Russianness. Only "workers in the USSR can bear such difficult torture, for the Russian can be patient for long," but not forever: "The Russian people have waited for a long time, but even Russian patience has an end." This view of the Russian people was often, but not exclusively, the product of the more literate and it was associated with a certain amount of idealization: The Russian had "a large and broad soul," according to one party member writing to Zhdanov.[67]

The final aspect of the moral dichotomy that should be considered is that of the authorities' insulting attitude to the people. As Steinberg points out, some workers firmly believed in the idea of the dignity and equality of all men, partly because of the influence of Christian teaching.[68] This belief provided a vocabulary with which to protest against the behavior of the *verkhi*. The millions of petitions sent to the highest party leaders were full of complaints about the rude, boorish and insulting behavior of individual bureaucrats. The comments and letters also indicate that *izdevatel'stvo* [insulting behaviour] was considered morally unacceptable. One letter sent to the Leningrad Executive Committee shortly after the end of bread rationing stressed this idea several times:

> Better first to bury all our rulers of Soviet power, so that they do not insult the working class. . . . That's enough watching the mockery of the working class. So here's a task for you, the bosses, if prices on food are not lowered and on bread by 40 percent, it will be bad for you. . . . No, that's enough slavery and mockery of the working class.[69]

Another anonymous letter to Zhdanov from the end of 1935 echoed this theme: "That's enough laughing at the workers, enough starving, enough teasing them like dogs, who suffers like the poor worker, our enemies are our aristocrats who harm the working people."[70] This objection to the people being treated like dogs also emerges in a comment in 1940 that, under Catherine II, landowners exchanged their peasants for dogs, while now Soviet directors sell workers to each other over drinks in restaurants.[71]

Underlying many of these representations of a moral dichotomy were often questions of political and economic difference. Nevertheless, the moral dimension should not be underestimated. The moral difference between "us" and "them," between good and evil, was for many ordinary people as valid as the more obvious political and material inequality. Official representations of the "enemies of the people" in 1937–38 also played up the moral degeneracy of those concerned, portraying them as the embodiment of evil. Gábor Rittersporn, echoing Moshe Lewin, argues that the "conspiracies" of the 1930s relied on the "allegorization of an ineffable evil that came to possess the world of every social category, the projection of the regime's elusively hostile universe in identifiable deeds and agents," and that this corresponded with traditional popular beliefs.[72] In the official discourse, moral turpitude was criticized, not only that of Trotsky (the "Judas") but also of ordinary Communists. Thus, in September 1937, *Pravda* in its leader, "The Moral Aspect of a Bolshevik," attacked the "bourgeois" morality of some Communists and Komsomols and their excessive drinking.[73] Once again, the official and popular languages echoed each other.

The economic dichotomy

While inequalities of power were frequently articulated using political and moral language, the reality of economic difference was the most immediately perceptible and intelligible facet of everyday life. As one peasant put it succinctly, "They say that everyone is equal, but in fact not everyone is equal – some are well dressed, and others badly."[74] The fact that one family had 150 rubles a month, while another had 3000, that leaders were chauffeured around in cars and shopped in Torgsin, that the state bought grain from peasants for one price and sold it for twenty times more – all these basic inequalities were the most visible signs of the existence of two groups in society. Popular interpretations of economic difference were not usually related to questions concerning the relationship to the means of production; they did, however, use Marxist concepts such as exploitation and capitalism. More often, though, they focused on inequality in income and lifestyle, and in particular on access to privileges. The main observation was that those in power seemed to get a lot more money or privileges than the people, and hence that the people were being exploited in order to keep the privileged in power.

This theme was replayed hundreds of times. A sophisticated version emerges in the words of a worker at the Lenin Works in the middle of 1934:

> How can we liquidate classes, if new classes have developed here, with the only difference being that they are not called classes. Now there are the same parasites who live at the expense of others. The worker produces and at the same time works for many people who live off him. From the example of our factory it is clear that there is a huge apparat of factory administrators, where idlers sit. There are many administrative workers who travel about in cars and get three to four times more than the worker. These people live in the best conditions and live at the expense of the labor of the working class.[75]

This refrain was powerful after 1934, a period that witnessed the turn toward the market and greater income differentials. Despite Stalin's denunciation of egalitarianism at the Seventeenth Party Congress, demands for leveling persisted. Referring to the congress, one cleaner commented that:

> the speeches are good, but there's no bread, at the factory there are three bones: pure white, they have a canteen of a closed type; whitebone, they have their own one; and black [workers], they have a general one where there is nothing. We are all workers and we should be fed equally.[76]

Likewise, a request to the Leningrad Soviet in 1934 highlighted the need to improve children's food "and not open various better canteens for ITR [technical specialists]. They should have achieved equality of food for all."[77] The end of rationing in 1935 seemed to signal the end of the preferential treatment of workers, and it provoked many comments that prices would be only accessible to "craftsmen and businessmen" (*kustari i chastniki*), *sluzhashchie*, "white guards," "Stalin's shockworkers and Red Partisans," "scientists," "kulaks and bourgeois," and "alien elements."[78] Many women feared that the more highly paid and the technical specialists would buy up everything, leaving nothing for the rest. Interestingly, certain academics regarded the end of rationing in a similar light. The orientalist Krachkovskii, for example, interpreted the decree abolishing rations on meat, fish and other food as a regression to a new class system:

> This decree, like all recent measures is aimed mainly at high-paid groups. For those who get 1000–1500 a month the reduction is very important. For the average Soviet citizen, in particular for a young academic, the decree is useless. It does not even provide a meager minimum, that ration which used to be given. In a word, however much we shout about socialism, in fact we're moving to new classes.[79]

A common perception existed that the elite made policies that promoted their own economic interests rather than those of the workers and peasants. Many workers interpreted the end of rationing in this way: "Power sees that the people have begun to live only on rations, and no one buys bread at the expensive price, and it gets little profit, so they have to sell unrationed bread, as it will be more profitable. Power only worries about its own profit, and does not want to bother about the people." A similar reaction greeted all price rises during this period – it must be good for the "new capitalists," responsible workers [officials], Communists, and so on. One worker even thought that price reductions were "a fiction carried out for the benefit of the higher class." Likewise, such labor policies as the Stakhanovite movement and the laws of 1938–40 were regarded as a way of extracting more profit from the worker in order to benefit the elite. Typical of comments was, "The Stakhanovite movement has been thought up by our rulers in order to squeeze the last juice from the toilers."[80]

The Stakhanovite movement was accompanied by the public promotion of consumer values and a status revolution.[81] This made the growing economic inequality glaringly obvious to the *nizy*. A question addressed to propagandists in a region of Western Siberia in 1936 summed up the economic disparity between elite and people: "Isn't what is prevailing in practice in the USSR the principle of socialism for the masses and the principle of communism for the *vozhdi*?"[82]

The privileged lifestyle of the elite, symbolized by holidays, cars, servants, special closed shops, flats, and clothes, was one of the most visible signs of social injustice, of a two-tier system. Ordinary people tended to associate this visible wealth with enemies; that is, with those in power. At an election meeting in 1934 at Krasnyi Putilovets, someone complained that "trips to resorts and rest homes are given to alien (*chuzhdye*) people, lawyers, *sluzhashchie* travel with their wives, and there is no room for the worker." At another meeting at the Munzenberg Factory, the complaint was similar: "Our children never get to go to rest homes, it costs 112 rubles, a female worker cannot afford it, and only the children of responsible workers go."[83]

There were constant complaints about those with cars, the ultimate status symbol.[84] The insinuation – again – was that those with cars were enemies. Remarking on the fall of Enukidze, a chauffeur said, "How many are there of his kind in Leningrad. They go out to the dacha at the weekend in cars, bought with the people's money, wasting petrol, which we lack." Some people interpreted the new phenomenon as symptomatic of the development of middle-class values: "A new bourgeoisie has appeared in our country, they travel around in cars, go around the workshops, grow paunches"; "Soviet power is bad because it has created many Soviet bourgeois, for example . . . the secretary of the RK [district committee] VKP(b) Osip. He travels round in cars, while the kolkhoznik doesn't have that chance."[85]

The Torgsin stores, which during 1930–36 sold goods for gold and hard currency, were particularly reviled. Although Torgsin stores were not in fact as luxurious and opulent as they have sometimes been portrayed, they nevertheless had great symbolic significance, epitomizing the inequities of the system.[86] In jokes and leaflets, which relied on transmitting ideas in a symbolic and concentrated form, the symbol of the Torgsin stores frequently appeared. One leaflet of 1934 read, "Comrades! Unite. Russia is perishing. Stalin is wearing the people out. Torgsin caters for Russian gentlemen, who served the emperor Nicholas."[87] A joke was made by deciphering Torgsin as "Tovarishchi opomnites', Rossiia gibnet, Stalin istrebliaet narod" (Comrades remember, Russia is perishing, Stalin is exterminating the people).[88] At the time of the end of rationing, another joke ran, "There are four categories: (1) *Torgsiane*, (2) *Krasnozvezdiane*, (3) *Zaerkane*, (4) *Koe-kane* [this translates roughly 'the Torgsiners, the Red Stars, the Closed Workers' Cooperative people, the Somehow or Others']."[89] There was some popular pressure for the shops to be closed. An anonymous letter with just such a demand landed on Zhdanov's desk in 1935 from a group of workers at the Kirov Works. The letter clearly reveals how workers tended to associate class with privilege:

> Comrade Zhdanov. At all the meetings they speak of a classless society, but in fact it turns out not like that, we have a handful of people, who live and forget about communism. It's time to stop the fattening-up of responsible workers. It is time to close the

Soviet Torgsins . . . for they are a disgrace, the worker must buy expensive products with his pennies, while the responsible worker, who receives 600–750 rubles a month, gets butter in this shop for 7 rubles per kg, and they give him 4 kilos a month, while the worker for his pennies gets butter for 27 rubles, in general it's a disgrace to have such shops now, it's simply squandering the people's resources, if they get everything there virtually gratis. It's clear that responsible workers cost the state a lot, they get dachas, even those without children, they go to resorts, and get benefits, take our factory director, he doesn't come to our shop, why should he, it's expensive there. No, we've still got a long way to go before a classless society if this carries on.[90]

There are numerous examples of such attitudes berating those in power for their economic privileges, but one that stands out is the letter already mentioned, written by a group of low-paid domestics. These workers were barely mentioned in the official press or statistics, but they were most exposed to the glaring differences in lifestyle between rich and poor in this period. In the letter they described how they earned about 125 rubles for fourteen hours' work for employers who were receiving anything from four to twenty times as much. Their bosses (doctors, engineers, directors) also had access to free cars, holidays and luxury flats. They particularly resented the wives of these people who engaged in "light work for amusement," such as being school directors, and whom they considered worse than the "former ladies," since they demanded so much work (up to eighteen hours a day) from their servants. They directly stated that they felt themselves to be the *nizy*, and they resented the fact that the press ignored them, that, according to responsible workers, there were no longer any *nizy*, only "low-paid groups."[91]

Although the writers of this letter were more directly exposed to the privileged lifestyle of the new elite, many others shared their views and were keen to accord enemy status to those enjoying a life so conspicuous in its opulence. The terror clearly had popular support because it was perceived as hitting those with economic privileges. The expulsion of "former people" and other undesirables from Leningrad in early 1935 was greeted with satisfaction by those who hoped that workers would be the beneficiaries: "Finally all the parasites will be expelled from Leningrad and the working class will have at least a little improvement in housing at their expense."[92]

It is revealing to compare the type of criticism made by workers in 1937 with official accusations against "enemies," since both highlighted the material excesses of the elite. Popular complaints tended to be more vehement and to articulate more general grievances about, for example, the low standard of living and the state loans. Workers said to agitators,

"What are you saying that life has become better; in our hostel the stoves have not been lit for three days, there's no food and linen. In the administration of the artel they say there's no money, while fifteen–twenty thousand are being spent on the chairman's office alone." Likewise, old cadre workers and Communists at the Kirov Works complained during the loan campaign that "the people who demand loans are those who decorate their flat for twenty thousand, like the head of the factory committee, Podrezov."[93] Fitzpatrick cites some of the official accusations leveled against the accused, such as the director of Molodaia Gvardiia, who "ripped off the state shamelessly. In the rest houses that the publishing firm is building, a luxurious apartment has been equipped for Leshchintser. Furniture of Karelian birch has been bought for that apartment. He is a bourgeois degenerate."[94] These words echo the unofficial language of workers and peasants, with the difference that the latter tended to blame all those in power, or the entire system, as well as concrete individuals. As one party worker explained in a letter to Stalin of 1937:

> The logic of the peasant is very simple. For him, all leaders are plenipotentiaries of the regime, and correspondingly, he considers that the regime is responsible for all his woes. . . . And the situation of the kolkhozniks is such that mentally they have sent us all to the devil.[95]

Despite the official representation of a socialist society without antagonistic classes, some people continued to view their world as polarized between two groups, those with power, and those without. For these, the dream of socialism seemed far away. As one person wrote in a note to a speaker at an election meeting at the end of 1934, "Comrades, how can you say this, we are enserfed, hungry and cold. This is called a classless socialist society. It's all lies."[96] People felt divided from the elite on political, economic and moral grounds. The way these divisions found expression owed as much to traditional conceptions of social justice as it did to the ideas of Marx and Lenin. The terror of 1937 was one way in which the people could satiate their appetite for revenge against at least some of those in power.

For a while, the officially sanctioned image of the enemy and that constructed by the people partially coincided. However, by early 1938 the "quasi-populist" aspect of the terror was already receding, with the stress henceforth on stability of cadres.[97] In its wake came a new policy of appeasing and extolling the intelligentsia, one symbol of which was the award of Stalin Prizes worth thousands of rubles. Those disbursed in March 1941 for science, technology, art, and literature provoked such comments from workers as: "We agree that they should get prizes, but why do they need such big sums when they are well off? We ourselves are creating capitalists living off interest, and then those millions will be squeezed out of us workers as loans."[98] Such feting of the intelligentsia in the difficult years 1938–41, when harsh laws were being applied to workers and peasants, probably ensured that the latter groups' sense of social polarization, if anything, increased in this period. Possibly, only the appearance in 1941 of an external enemy provided the necessary stimulus for at least some of the disaffected *nizy* to feel part of a "united people."

NOTES

This article is reprinted from the *Russian Review*, 56 (1) (January 1997), 70–89, with minor changes requested by the author.

* The author is grateful to those who commented on earlier versions of this article presented at the conference "Rossiiskaia povsednevnost', 1921–1941 gg.," St Petersburg, 1994, and at the panel "Popular Opinion in Soviet Russia in the 1920s and 1930s" (ICCEES World Congress, Warsaw, 1995). She also thanks Sheila Fitzpatrick, David Hoffmann, Mary McAuley, David Priestland, Chris Ward, and two referees for their criticisms and suggestions. The British Academy and the Leverhulme Trust provided the financial support that made this research possible.

1 For example, Alec Nove, "Is There a Ruling Class in the USSR?" *Soviet Studies*, vol. 27, no. 4 (1975): 615–38; idem, "The Class Nature of the Soviet Union Revisited," *Soviet Studies*, vol. 35, no. 3 (1983): 298–312; and David Lane, *Soviet Economy and Society* (Oxford, 1985), 163.

2 On language and social identity see Gareth Stedman-Jones, *Languages of Class: Studies in English Working-class History* (Cambridge, 1983), 22, 101; Lewis Siegelbaum and Ronald Suny, eds, *Making Workers Soviet: Power, Class and Identity* (London, 1994); and Sheila Fitzpatrick, "Ascribing Class: the Construction of Social Identity in Soviet Russia," Chapter 1 in this volume.

3 David Hoffmann, *Peasant Metropolis: Social Identities in Moscow, 1929–1941* (London, 1994); Stephen Kotkin, *Magnetic Mountain: Stalinism as a Civilization* (London, 1995); Sheila Fitzpatrick, *Stalin's Peasants: Resistance and Survival in the Russian Village after Collectivization* (Oxford, 1994).

4 This is a question that I have dealt with at greater length elsewhere. See S.R. Davies, "Propaganda and Popular Opinion in Soviet Russia, 1934–1941" (PhD diss., Oxford University, 1994). Most of my sources are from the former Leningrad Party Archive (now TsGAIPD). Equivalent material in other archives suggests that Leningrad was not a particularly special case: workers and peasants in different regions used similar language, although perhaps less frequently and less articulately.

5 Ralf Dahrendorf, *Class and Class Conflict in Industrial Society* (Cambridge, 1959), 285.

6 Stanislaw Ossowski, *Class Structure in the Social Consciousness* (London, 1963), 19–37.

7 Robert Tucker, *The Soviet Political Mind: Stalinism and Post-Stalin Change* (London, 1972), 122.

8 Ronald Grigor Suny, "Toward a Social History of the October Revolution," *American Historical Review* 88 (February 1983): 51. See also Leopold Haimson,

"The Problem of Social Stability in Urban Russia 1905–17," *Slavic Review* 23 (Autumn 1964): 619–42, and 24 (Winter 1965): 1–22; and idem, "The Problem of Social Identities in Early Twentieth-century Russia," *Slavic Review* 47 (Winter 1988): 1–20.

9 Cited in Timothy McDaniel, *Autocracy, Capitalism and Revolution in Russia* (London, 1988), 389.

10 On representations of enemies in the Soviet period, see William Chase, *Workers, Society and the Soviet State: Labor and Life in Moscow, 1918–1929* (Urbana, 1987); Diane Koenker, "Class and Class Consciousness in a Socialist Society: Workers in the Printing Trades during NEP," in *Russia in the Era of NEP: Explorations in Soviet Society and Culture*, ed. Sheila Fitzpatrick, Alexander Rabinowitch, and Richard Stites (Bloomington, IN, 1991); and Hiroaki Kuromiya, *Stalin's Industrial Revolution: Politics and Workers, 1928–1932* (Cambridge, 1988).

11 See Sheila Fitzpatrick, "Workers against Bosses: the Impact of the Great Purges on Labor–Management Relations," in *Making Workers Soviet*, 312.

12 Fredric Jameson, *The Political Unconscious: Narrative as a Socially Symbolic Act* (London, 1981), esp. 83–89. For more on the idea of "dialogue" and in general on Bakhtin's philosophy of language and culture see Mikhail Bakhtin, *The Dialogic Imagination* (Austin, 1981); idem, *Tvorchestvo Franzua Rable i narodnaia kul'tura srednovekov'ia i renessansa* (Moscow, 1965); and V.N. Voloshinov, *Marksizm i filosofiia iazyka* (Leningrad, 1930).

13 Tsentral'nyi gosudarstvennyi arkhiv istoriko-politicheskikh dokumentov Sankt Peterburga (TsGAIPD), f. 25, op. 5, d. 46, l. 109 (p/34), f. 24, op. 2v, d. 1914, l. 58 (p/36), d. 2286, l. 12 (p/37), d. 1914, l. 3 (p/36), d, 4306, l. 176 (n/40), d. 3563, l. 32 (n/39), and d. 4313, l. 279 (n/40), op. 5, d. 2696, l. 90 (p/35), and op. 2v, d. 4306, l. 213 (n/40), and d. 4300, l. 275 (n/40). The information in parentheses that follow archival citations indicates the type of source and the year it was produced; for example, (p/34) denotes a party report, (n/34) an NKVD report, (l/34) a letter and (k/34) a Komsomol report, all from 1934.

14 Ibid., f. 24, op. 5, d. 2288, l. 100 (p/34), f. 25, op. 5, d. 53, l. 59 (p/34), and d. 2288, l. 61 (p/34), and op. 2v, d. 2286, ll. 97, 78 (p/37).

15 Ibid., f. 25, op. 10, d. 17, l. 80 (p/35).

16 Ibid., f. 24, op. 2g, d. 149, 1. 129 (l/38).

17 Ibid., f. 25, op. 5, d. 49, l. 117 (p/34).

18 Ibid., f. 24, op. 5, d. 2286, ll. 67, 93 (p/34), and op. 2v, d. 4306, l. 128 (n/40).

19 When workers did move up the ladder, there was some resentment, as in the case of some leading Stakhanovites. For example, in 1936 one worker asked, "Why did Stakhanov develop the Stakhanovite movement, and does not work himself, but is a boss (*nachal'nik*)?" (ibid., f. 25, op. 10, d. 36, l. 68 [p/36]).

20 Ibid., f. 24, op. 10, d. 303, l. 162 (p/37), and op. 2v, d. 1855, l. 210 (n/36), and d. 2499, ll. 24, 26 (n/37).

21 Ibid., f. 24, op. 2v, d. 2499, l. 27 (n/37). See also ibid., ll. 48, 79, 105 (n/37).

22 *Rossiiskaia Federatsiia*, 1993, no. 2: 55.

23 TsGAIPD, f. 24, op. 2v, d. 3179, ll. 110–13 (p/38).

24 Iu.A. Poliakov *et al.*, eds, *Vsesoiuznaia perepis' naseleniia 1939 goda: Osnovnye itogi* (Moscow, 1992), 62–63.

25 Michael Beizer, "The Jewish Minority in Leningrad, 1917–1939" (paper presented to BASEES conference, Cambridge, England, March 1995), 8–10.

26 Ibid., 10.

27 TsGAIPD, f. 24, op. 2v, d. 727, 1. 367 (l/34).

28 Ibid., d. 1543, l. 10 (l/35).
29 Ibid., d. 1518, ll. 9–10 (l/35).
30 Ibid., op. 5, d. 3202, l. 109 (p/36).
31 Ibid., f. K598, op. 1, d. 5343, l. 17 (k/34).
32 The tendency for class and nationalist languages to overlap in Russia has been noted by Ronald Suny, "Nationalism and Class in the Russian Revolution: a Comparative Discussion," in *Revolution in Russia: Reassessments of 1917*, ed. E. Frankel, J. Frankel and B. Knei-Paz (Cambridge, 1992).
33 TsGAIPD, f. 24, op. 2v, d. 2267, l. 27 (p/37).
34 Ibid., d. 1914, ll. 56, 58 (p/36).
35 Ibid., op. 10, d. 163, l. 141 (p/37).
36 For example, by Rittersporn and Fitzpatrick in much of their work.
37 Fitzpatrick also argues this in *Stalin's Peasants*, 312.
38 For example, TsGAIPD, f. 25, op. 5, d. 48, ll. 1, 3 (p/34).
39 Ibid., f. 24, op. 2b, d. 33, l. 43 (l/35). I have opted to retain the original grammar and punctuation in this and subsequent quotes.
40 Ibid., f. 25, op. 5, d. 48, l. 12 (p/34), f. 24, op. 2v, d. 1367, ll. 71–72 (p/35).
41 I. Stalin, *Sochineniia* (Stanford, 1967), 1: 253–55.
42 TsGAIPD, f. 24, op. 2v, d. 2061, l. 115 (p/36).
43 Ibid., d. 1851, l. 74 (n/36).
44 Ibid., l. 72 (n/36).
45 Ibid., d. 2061, l. 141 (p/36), and d. 2267, ll. 14, 25ob (p/37), and f. K598, op. 1, d. 5423, l. 11 (k/37).
46 Ibid., f. 24, op. 10, d. 291, l. 77 (p/37), and f. K598, op. 1, d. 5423, l. 65 (k/37).
47 Ibid., f. 24, op. 2v, d. 3178, ll. 19, 23, 29 (p/38).
48 Ibid., d. 2664, ll. 1–8 (p/34), d. 2498, ll. 1–2, 150 (n/37), d. 2286, l. 13 (p/37), d. 2665, ll. 2–4 (p/37), d. 3178, ll. 23, 28–29 (p/38), and d. 2499, l. 24 (n/37), and op. 10, d. 291, l. 78 (p/37).
49 Ibid., op. 2v, d. 2499, l. 24 (n/37).
50 Ibid., op. 10, d. 163, l. 68 (p/37).
51 For example, by N. Cohn in *The Pursuit of the Millennium: Revolutionary Millenarians and Mystical Anarchists of the Middle Ages* (London, 1970).
52 Mark Steinberg, *Moral Communities: The Culture and Class Relations in the Russian Printing Industry, 1867–1907* (Berkeley, 1992), 234.
53 Mark D. Steinberg, "Workers on the Cross: Religious Imagination in the Writings of Russian Workers, 1910–1924," *Russian Review* 53 (April 1994): 213–39.
54 TsGAIPD, f. 24, op, 2v, d. 1518, l. 1 (l/37).
55 Ibid., d. 2664, l. 265 (p/37).
56 Ibid., d. 2282, l. 109 (p/37).
57 Ibid., d. 1518, ll. 184–88 (l/35).
58 For example, ibid., op. 5, d. 2696, l. 90 (p/35), and d. 3202, l. 92 (p/36), and op. 2v, d. 1833, l. 185 (n/36).
59 Ibid., op. 2v, d. 2499, ll. 77, 104 (n/37), and op. 5, d. 3202, l. 109 (p/36).
60 Ibid., op. 2v, d. 3720, l. 339 (p/39). See also ibid., d. 3563, l. 32 (p/39).
61 Ibid., op. 2v, d. 2286, l. 137 (p/37), and f. 25, op. 10, d, 17, l. 80 (p/36).
62 Also, "There are many intelligentsia, and they live off us, they say that he who does not work does not eat, but we work and there is nothing to eat" (ibid., f. 24, op. 2v, d. 1914, l. 92 [p/36]), and d. 1846, l. 123 [n/36], and op. 5, d. 3732, l. 88 [p/36]).
63 Ibid., op 2v, d. 1049, l. 20 (p/35), and op. 5, d. 47, l. 31 (p/34).
64 Ibid., op. 2v, d. 1748, l. 171 (l/36).

65 Ibid., d. 3563, l. 61 (n/39), d. 1049, l. 23 (p/35), and d. 4306, l. 198 (n/40).
66 Ibid., d. 1518, l. 183 (l/35).
67 Ibid., l. 184 (l/35), d. 2500, l. 62 (n/37), and d. 2499, l. 29 (n/37), and op. 2g, d. 47, l. 197 (l/37).
68 Steinberg, *Moral Communities*, 112–22.
69 TsGAIPD, f. 24, op. 2v, d. 1518, l. 14 (l/35).
70 Tsentral'nyi gosudarstvennyi arkhiv Sankt Peterburga, f. 7384, op. 2, d. 49, l. 432 (n/35).
71 TsGAIPD, f. 24, op. 2v, d. 4306, l. 213 (n/40).
72 Gábor Rittersporn, "The Omnipresent Conspiracy: On Soviet Imagery of Politics and Social Relations in the 1930s," in *Stalinist Terror: New Perspectives*, ed. J. Arch Getty and Roberta Manning (Cambridge, 1993), 115.
73 *Pravda*, 20 September 1937.
74 TsGAIPD, f. 24, op. 2v, d. 1914, l. 92 (p/36).
75 Ibid., f. 25, op. 5, d. 38, l. 46 (p/34).
76 Ibid., d. 38, l. 44 (p/34).
77 Ibid., f. 24, op. 5, d. 2286, l. 6 (p/34).
78 Ibid., f. 25, op. 5, d. 48, l. 52 (p/34), d. 46, l. 141 (p/34), d. 54, l. 27 (p/34), and d. 49, l. 116 (p/34), and f. 24, op. 2v, d. 1200, l. 70 (n/35), and op. 5, d. 2286, l. 80 (p/34), and d. 2691, l. 35 (p/35).
79 Ibid., f. 24, op. 2v, d. 1200, l. 71 (n/35).
80 Ibid., d. 1049, l. 22 (p/35), f. 25, op. 10, d. 74, l. 11 (p/37), and f. 24, op. 2v, d. 1829, l. 63 (n/36).
81 See Sheila Fitzpatrick, *The Cultural Front: Power and Culture in Revolutionary Russia* (London, 1992), 216–37.
82 Gosudarstvennyi arkhiv Novosibirskoi oblasti, Novosibirsk, f. 3, op. 10, d. 926, l. 52 (p/36).
83 TsGAIPD, f. 25, op. 5, d. 46, l. 180 (p/34), and d. 49, l. 11 (p/34).
84 Fitzpatrick, *Cultural Front*, 230.
85 TsGAIPD, f. 24, op. 2v, d, 1367, l. 71 (p/35), f. 25, op. 5, d. 83, l. 24 (p/36), and f. 24, op. 2v, d. 1851, l. 124 (n/36).
86 E.A. Osokina, "Za zerkal'noi dver'iu Torgsina," *Otechestvennaia istoriia*, 1995, no. 2: 97–98.
87 TsGAIPD, f. 24, op. 2v, d. 772, l. 15 (n/34).
88 Tsentr khraneniia dokumentov molodezhnykh organizatsii, Moscow, f. 1, op. 23, d. 1128, l. 64 (k/35).
89 TsGAIPD, f. 25, op. 5, d. 46, l. 73 (p/34).
90 Ibid., f. 24, op. 2v, d. 1518, l. 32 (l/35).
91 Ibid., d. 1748, ll. 166–68 (l/36).
92 Ibid., op. 5, d. 2714, l. 106 (p/35).
93 Ibid., op. 2v, d. 2665, ll. 61–2 (p/37).
94 Fitzpatrick, *Cultural Front*, 230.
95 TsGAIPD, f. 24, op. 2g, d. 49, l. 114 (l/37).
96 Ibid., f. 25, op. 5, d. 48, l. 53 (p/34).
97 Sheila Fitzpatrick, "Stalin and the Making of a New Elite, 1928–1939," *Slavic Review* 38 (Summer 1979): 396.
98 TsGAIPD, f. 24, op. 2v, d. 4814, ll. 116–17 (n/41), and d. 5134, ll. 30–36 (p/41).

Part II

PRIVATE AND PUBLIC PRACTICES

The practices of Stalinism have become a major focus of investigation in recent studies. One of the questions historians have to grapple with is the relationship between private and public practices, and by implication between private and public spheres of life, in Stalin's Russia. Because of the strong pressure for conformity and orthodoxy in Stalinist society, it is clear that a Soviet citizen's public face was often at odds with his or her private one (this presumption, indeed, lay at the root of the regime's zeal in "unmasking"). Yet there was no impermeable barrier between the two spheres: even the hero of Orwell's *1984*, with his strong private feelings of alienation from the official values and rituals he has to follow in public, ended up "loving Big Brother." In an influential work, Stephen Kotkin argued that not only did Soviet citizens need to learn to "speak Bolshevik," that is, to master the language and practices associated with the post-revolutionary order, they also inevitably internalized its values.[1] How far this internalization went is, of course, a matter of dispute.

Of the contributors in this section, Jochen Hellbeck, examining the diary-writing of Stepan Podlubnyi, goes furthest and is most explicit in arguing for thorough-going internalization of Soviet values. Dealing with denunciation, a practice connecting the private and the public spheres, Vladimir Kozlov also suggests that Soviet citizens often "thought Bolshevik" as well as speaking it, though he demonstrates the manipulative uses of denunciation. In Alexei Kojevnikov's reading of the public rituals of the Soviet scientific community, by contrast, the scientists' use of officially endorsed practices such as "disputation" (*diskussiia*) and "self-criticism" appears more a matter of rational manipulation of the regime than embrace of its values.

Stalinism was rich in practices involving self-scrutiny, confession, and the telling of one's life in public, among them purges (*chistki*), self-criticism sessions, application for party or Komsomol membership, and Stakhanovite conferences. Workers were encouraged to record their life stories; schoolchildren were encouraged to keep diaries. As Vadim Volkov describes in his essay in Part III, "working on oneself" (*rabota nad soboi*) was an essential discipline of a civilized Soviet person. All this has led a number of scholars to the paradoxical conclusion that individuation – the "making of selves" characteristic of modernity – was one of the basic processes of Stalinism.[2]

Jochen Hellbeck (b. 1966) is a young German historian trained both in Germany and the United States who draws on the theories of Michel Foucault as well as work by scholars such as Stephen Greenblatt and Stephen Kotkin[3] in his analysis of a Soviet diary of the 1930s.[4] The diarist, Stepan Podlubnyi, was a young man with a tainted past: his father had been expropriated as a kulak, a fact that Podlubnyi was obliged to conceal. Accepting the premise that he was a flawed person because of his background, Podlubnyi used his diary-writing as a way of over-coming this spiritual deficiency and re-creating himself as a true Soviet citizen. Even when he became disenchanted after his mother's arrest during the Great Purges, he criticized the actions of the Soviet regime in terms of its professed values and "continued to regard himself as an active participant in the Soviet project of civilization." Hellbeck rejects the commonly held notion that under Stalinism individuals said things they regarded as lies in public and told "the truth" in private. In his view, the public and private spheres were interconnected: individual subjectivity was a constitutive element of the Stalinist system.

While Podlubnyi's diary-writing, despite its quasi-public purpose, was a private practice, the denunciations studied by Vladimir Kozlov addressed an external audience. Denunciations are one of a variety of types of individual communication with the authorities, ranging from appeals and petitions to anonymous letters abusing Soviet leaders and criticizing the regime, that have received a lot of attention from Western and Russian scholars since the opening of the Soviet archives.[5] (Lewis Siegelbaum's article in Part III uses another kind of citizen's letter from the archives as its source base.) Writing to the authorities with a complaint, denunciation, or appeal was part of the everyday repertoire of Soviet citizens in coping with the world – all the more important because so many other ways of coping with problems (for example, through political organization, collective bargaining, collective protests, or individual law-suits) were outlawed or ineffective in the Stalin period.

Vladimir Kozlov (b. 1950) is a Russian historian who is currently deputy director of the State Archive of the Russian Federation. His article, origi-nally written for a conference on comparative denunciation held in Chicago in 1994,[6] draws on materials of the Ministry of State Security of the 1940s held at his archive, GARF, that are still not freely available to scholars. Kozlov classifies denunciations as "disinterested" and "interested," showing that the first – a flourishing category, akin to American whistle-blowing – served an important function as a check on the abuses of local bureaucracy and a channel for the expression of popular grievances. Kozlov sees denunciation as a manifestation of "paternalistic statism in an 'underdeveloped' country." In addition to its utility to the regime, he argues, denunciation was an important resource in a society where law and other mechanisms of settling conflicts and redressing grievances were poorly developed.

Alexei Kojevnikov (b. 1966) is one of a talented group of young Russian historians of science whose work has commanded considerable attention in the 1990s. In touch with Western scholarship and theory but also possessing direct practical knowledge of the functioning of Soviet science (many were originally trained in science or came from families of scientists), their common interest is in the mentalités and practices of Soviet scientific communities and their interaction with power.

In his "Games of Soviet Democracy," Kojevnikov rejects a notion that the familiar formula "the party dictated" provides an adequate explanation of the development of Soviet science. Taking an anthropological approach to ritual and drawing on Wittgenstein's notion of language games, Kojevnikov investigates some key rituals of scientific life, notably disputations (*diskussii*) and "criticism and self-criticism" sessions. These were rituals borrowed from the sphere of party politics, Kojevnikov notes, but that does not mean that they were purely ceremonial, fully scripted occasions when the party leadership made its will known to the scientists. Outcomes were not always predetermined (Kojevnikov calls the Stalinist decision-making system "chaotic," in the scientific sense of the term) and different groups of scientists pursued their own agendas, sometimes successfully. Substantive professional issues could be contested in such forums; what was obligatory was to play the game in the approved manner and end up with a resolution. As in Stalinist politics, there was no middle ground, no theoretical tolerance of plurality: in cases of scientific disputation, one side had to be judged right and the other wrong.

FURTHER READING

Self-fashioning

Alexopoulos, Golfo, "Portrait of a Con Artist as a Soviet Man," *Slavic Review*, 57: 4 (1998).

Fitzpatrick, Sheila, "Lives under Fire: Autobiographical Narratives and Their Challenges in Stalin's Russia," in *De Russie et d'ailleurs: Mélanges Marc Ferro* (Paris, 1995).

—— "The Two Faces of Anastasia: Narratives and Counter-narratives of Identity in Stalinist Everyday Life," in Christina Kiaer and Eric Naiman, eds, *Everyday Subjects: Formations of Identity in Early Soviet Culture* (Cornell University Press, forthcoming).

Halfin, Igal, "From Darkness to Light: Student Communist Autobiography during NEP," *Jahrbücher für Geschichte Osteuropas* Bd. 45, Heft 2 (1997) .

Hellbeck, Jochen, "Self-Realization in the Stalinist System: Two Soviet Diaries of the 1930s," in Manfred Hildermeier, ed., *Stalinismus vor dem Zweiten Weltkrieg. Neue Wege der Forschung/Stalinism before the Second World War: New Avenues of Research* (Munich, 1998).

Kharkhordin, Oleg V., *The Collective and the Individual in Russia. A Study of Practices* (Berkeley, 1999).

Krylova, Anna, "In Their Own Words? Autobiographies of Women Writers, 1930–1946," in Adele Barker and Jehanne Gheith, eds, *Russian Women Writers* (Cambridge University Press, forthcoming).

Oral histories, autobiographies, and diaries

Engel, Barbara A. and Anastasia Posadskaya-Vanderbeck, eds, *A Revolution of Their Own: Voices of Women in Soviet History* (Boulder, Col., 1997).

Fitzpatrick, Sheila and Yuri Slezkine, eds, *In the Shadow of Revolution: Life stories of Russian Women from 1917 to the Second World War*, (Princeton, forthcoming).

Garros, Véronique, Natalia Korenevskaia, and Thomas Lahusen, eds, *Intimacy and Terror: Soviet Diaries of the 1930s* (New York, 1995).

Holmes, Larry E., "Part of History: the Oral Record and Moscow's Model School No. 25, 1931–1937," *Slavic Review* 56: 2 (1997).

Rituals, myths, mentalités

Brooks, Jeffrey, "Socialist Realism in *Pravda*: Read All About It!", *Slavic Review* 53 (Winter 1994).

Lahusen, Thomas, *Life Writes the Book: Real Socialism and Socialist Realism in Stalin's Russia* (Ithaca, 1997).

Lenoe, Matthew, "Agitation, Propaganda, and the 'Stalinization' of the Soviet Press, 1925–1933," *Carl Beck Papers*, no. 1305 (1998).

McCannon, John, *Red Arctic: Polar Exploration and the Myth of the North in the Soviet Union, 1932–1939* (New York, 1998).

Petrone, Karen, " 'Life has Become More Joyous, Comrades': Politics and Culture in Soviet Celebrations, 1934–1939," PhD dissertation, University of Michigan, 1994.

Sartorti, Rosalinde, "Stalinism and Carnival: Organisation and Aesthetics of Political Holidays," in Hans Günther, ed., *The Culture of the Stalin Period* (New York, 1990).

von Geldern, James, "Cultural and Social Geography in the Mass Culture of the 1930s," in Stephen White, ed., *New Directions in Soviet History* (New York, 1992).

Petitions and denunciations

Alexopoulos, Golfo, "Exposing Illegality and Oneself: Complaint and Risk in Stalin's Russia," in Peter H. Solomon, ed., *Reforming Justice in Russia, 1864–1996* (Armonk, N.Y., 1997).

—— "The Ritual Lament: a Narrative of Appeal in the 1920s and 1930s," *Russian History/Histoire russe*, 24: 1–2 (1997).

Fitzpatrick, Sheila, "Supplicants and Citizens: Public Letter-writing in Soviet Russia in the 1930s," *Slavic Review* 55: 1 (1996).

—— "Signals from Below: Soviet Letters of Denunciation of the 1930s," in Sheila Fitzpatrick and Robert Gellately, eds, *Accusatory Practices: Denunciation in Modern European History, 1789–1989* (Chicago, 1997).

Science culture

Aleksandrov, D.A., "The Historical Anthropology of Science in Russia," *Russian Studies in History*, Fall (1995), 62–91.

Joravsky, David, *The Lysenko Affair* (Cambridge, Mass., 1970).

—— *Russian Psychology: A Critical History* (Oxford, 1989).

Krementsov, Nikolai, *Stalinist Science* (Princeton, 1997).

Rossiianov, Kirill, "Editing Nature: Stalin and the 'New Soviet Biology,' " *Isis* 84 (1993).

NOTES

1 Stephen Kotkin, *Magnetic Mountain: Stalinism as a Civilization* (Berkeley, 1995), ch. 5. The editor regrets that she was unable to include a chapter from this book in the present volume because the author denied permission.

2 See, for example, Oleg Kharkhordin, "By Deeds Alone: Origins of Individualization in Soviet Russia," in Christina Kiaer and Eric Naiman, eds, *Everyday Subjects: Formations of Identity in Early Soviet Culture*, (Cornell University Press, forthcoming); Yanni Kotsonis, "A Modern Paradox: Subject and Citizen in Nineteenth and Twentieth Century Russia," Introduction to David L. Hoffman and Yanni Kotsonis, *Russian Modernity: Politics, Practice, Knowledge*, forthcoming; and the essays by Hellbeck (Chapter 3) and Volkov (Chapter 7) in this volume.

3 Stephen Greenblatt, *Renaissance Self-fashioning: From More to Shakespeare* (Chicago, 1980); Kotkin, *Magnetic Mountain*.

4 The diary comes from the People's Archive (*Tsentr Dokumentatsii "Narodnyi arkhiv"* or TsDNA), a collection of personal and family documents created in Moscow since the collapse of the Soviet Union, as part of a civic effort to recover lost aspects of the Russian past. The complete diary has appeared in German in Jochen Hellbeck, ed., *Tagebuch aus Moskau, 1931–1939* (Munich, 1996). A portion of the diary was published in English in Véronique Garros, Natalia Korenevskaia, and Thomas Lahusen, eds, *Intimacy and Terror: Soviet Diaries of the 1930s* (New York, 1995).

5 See, for example, the special issue of the journal *Russian History/Histoire russe* 24: 1–2 (1997) on "Petitions and Denunciations in Russia from Muscovy to the Stalin Era" with contributions on the Stalin period by Lewis Siegelbaum, Matthew Lenoe, Golfo Alexopoulos, Sarah Davies, Chris Chulos, Vladlen Izmozik, and Sheila Fitzpatrick; the joint US–Russian publication edited by Lewis Siegelbaum and Andrei Sokolov, *Stalinism as a Way of Life: A Documentary Narrative* (Yale University Press, forthcoming), which is based on unpublished letters to the authorities from the 1930s; and an interesting collection of letters from the 1920s, available only in Russian, *Pis'ma vo vlast'*,

1917–1927. Zaiavleniia, zhaloby, donosy, pis'ma v gosudarstvennye struktury i bol'-shevistskim vozhdiam, compiled by A. Ia. Livshin and I. B. Orlov (Moscow: ROSSPEN, 1998).

6 Articles from this conference, edited by Sheila Fitzpatrick and Robert Gellately, were published in a special issue of the *Journal of Modern History* 68: 4 (1996) and later in book form as *Accusatory Practices: Denunciation in Modern European History, 1789–1989* (Chicago, 1997).

3

FASHIONING THE STALINIST SOUL

The diary of Stepan Podlubnyi, 1931–9[1]

Jochen Hellbeck

How members of Soviet society subjectively experienced the Stalinist system has traditionally received insufficient attention from historians. Until recent years, the Soviet government's restrictive archival policy provided a convenient justification for this research lacuna. Investigations of popular attitudes toward the Stalinist regime had to limit themselves largely to published documents, which were generally considered to have been manufactured or manipulated by the Soviet state and to reflect little, if any, authentic beliefs. Whether the recent opening of secret archival files will enable scholars to gain fundamentally new insights into the subjective dimension of Stalinism remains to be seen. What kind of source material can be expected to make visible individuals' "real" beliefs, if the repressive political environment continuously forced them to censor themselves?[2]

What at first sight seemed to be a question of finding the right source is really a conceptual problem. At issue is whether individuals living in Stalinist Russia were able to articulate a private identity distinct from the political system and, more fundamentally, if such an identity can be presupposed to have existed. The present study takes up this question by exploring an extraordinary source recently discovered in a Moscow archive – the diary of Stepan Podlubnyi, a young worker and student of peasant origins, who recorded his life experience throughout the 1930s. On the basis of Podlubnyi's diary it investigates how an individual perceived and understood himself outside of the public realm. Throughout the focus is on Podlubnyi's evolving self-portrayal and the ways in which it was shaped by his environment. In this connection, the study treats Podlubnyi's diary not as a mirror of an external social reality; rather, it analyzes the journal as a means of self-construction and self-fashioning – as a tool that he applied onto himself in order to express himself. The goal of the study is to comprehend individual subjectivity as a constitutive element of the Soviet system.[3] Studying the notions of the self that individuals embraced reveals the active nature of their involvement in the formation of the political system of Stalinism.

* * *

In assessing the impact of the Stalinist system on Soviet society, historians have developed three different explanations. Scholars adhering to the totalitarian theory understood the Bolshevik regime as a terror state that effectively subjugated society, to the extent that individuals were "atomized" – deprived of the means to organize themselves independently and forced into silence. Only within the shelter of the precarious private sphere – the family or a few trusted friends – and even then only at great risk, could individuals articulate their "real" selves and expose the false premises of the ruling system.[4] This viewpoint has rightly been questioned for its inability to account for the striking stability of the Soviet system except through a policy of coercion and terror. One scholar modified the totalitarian paradigm to suggest that the propagandistic efforts of the Bolshevik regime succeeded in programming large segments of Soviet society. According to this view, "homo Sovieticus" had the properties of a *homunculus* – a soulless creature of the Stalinist system.[5] Compelling as this concept might appear, it falls to explain how the regime succeeded in manipulating the thoughts and attitudes of an entire society.

Criticizing the prevailing concept of Soviet society as solely victimized by the Bolshevik regime, a number of social historians pointed to large population groups, which they identified as active agents in the establishment of the Stalinist system. Specifically, they focused their attention on the processes of education and social advancement in which a great number of young people, mostly of worker or peasant background, were engaged during the Stalin years. This "revisionist" interpretation emphasized what it perceived to be individual self-interest, namely the pursuit of material concerns and status benefits, as the principal source of stability of the Stalinist system.[6] Yet the question remains, how in the context of the political system did individuals define their interests?

Both the "revisionist" and totalitarian concepts rest on problematic notions of the self. Implicit in the term "self-interest" or in the question of what people "really" thought is an assumption of a transcendental self, lacking historical specificity, which is then opposed to the Stalinist system. It is this specificity that the present study seeks to regain by exploring an individual's subjective understanding of himself during the Stalin era. Methodologically, this approach is indebted to Stephen Kotkin's recent study of a Soviet city during Stalinism. Kotkin effectively refutes the simplistic notion that Soviet society was either victim or agent of the political system. According to him, the Stalinist system functioned as a set of rules, including the rule of social identification, which were enforced by the state but by the same token appropriated and actively used by members of society. Soviet identities were "unavoidable," Kotkin states, but "playing the identity game" granted individuals meaning, purpose, and power.[7] This study seeks to take Kotkin's approach one step further, by inquiring how an individual thought about himself outside of the official realm of publicly enforced norms. Its goal is to investigate the potential of the Soviet regime to define Podlubnyi's social identity and the effects this power had on his conceptualization of self and the Stalinist political order.

Questions to be raised in the course of the investigation include Podlubnyi's view of his diary; the purpose in writing and, connected to this, what he considered proper or improper to write about; which role in society he hoped to play; how he defined his own place in society and how he viewed other social groups. A separate section is devoted to the relationship between the public and private spheres, as illustrated in the diary. Another section deals with Podlubnyi's understanding and usage of ideology, called "personal Bolshevism." The goal is to show the potential for reshaping and redirecting Bolshevik ideological tenets in the process of their reception. While this section points to the latitude as well as the inherent vulnerability of a ruling culture, the emphasis of the study overall is on the cultural logic residing within an individual. It seeks to reveal how Podlubnyi's notion of himself as an agent was informed by the program of the Bolshevik state. As the final section devoted to the issue of unbelief makes clear, the degree of Podlubnyi's implication severely affected the way in which he experienced his growing disenchantment with the Stalinist state in the course of the 1930s.

A typical case?

Stepan Podlubnyi was born in 1914 into a family of wealthy peasants living in the Vinnitsa district of Ukraine. After the Revolution of 1917 his father was stripped of all but a modest portion of his previous landholdings. However, as his son recounted, in the Soviet village of the 1920s he was considered a *kulak*, a member of the exploiting classes, on the basis of the living memory among fellow villagers of his wealthy past. In 1929 the family was dekulakized: household, land, and cattle were confiscated, and Stepan's father was deported to Arkhangel'sk for a three-year term of administrative exile. Stepan and his mother also had to leave the village. They obtained forged documents showing them to be of worker origin and settled in Moscow. Podlubnyi found employment as an apprentice in the factory school (FZU) of the *Pravda* printing plant. He immediately joined the Komsomol in which he assumed a variety of functions. After attending a middle school, Podlubnyi was accepted into the Moscow Medical Institute in 1935. In the following year, the Komsomol learned about Podlubnyi's concealed *kulak* origins. Although he was publicly expelled from the Komsomol, this incident did not damage his standing at the institute where he continued to study.

Any study focusing on an individual biography has to confront the question of representativeness. How typical was this young man's experience? This essay argues that Podlubnyi's autobiographical account has general value in terms of the ways in which it is phrased, the emphases it makes, and the broader arguments it contains. Podlubnyi's attempt to structure his own life can be read as an effort to endow it with cultural meaning, and it follows a recognizable pattern dictated by that culture's logic. Podlubnyi's story would not substantially differ from that of a young Kalmyk coming to urban Soviet Russia on general issues, such as his experience of the self *vis-à-vis* the state order. Nor did Podlubnyi's account stand out due to his non-Soviet class status. To be sure, because of the stigma he carried with him, Podlubnyi was certainly more preoccupied with the question of social identity than a young worker with proletarian ancestors would have been. But this only meant that he articulated sharply what others may have felt intuitively. Furthermore, no one in Stalinist Russia, not even a proletarian with impeccable ancestry, could individually determine his class status and therefore evade being relegated into the camp of the class enemy. Two points should be kept in mind, however: Podlubnyi's rural background and young age combined to make his embrace of the Stalinist system compelling and uncompromising. Because of the degree of his commitment and the lack of alternative sources of identity, both in terms of memory and intellectual capacity, Podlubnyi's attempts to detach himself from the ruling culture proceeded painfully and eventually proved to be unsuccessful.

Source basis

The central source used in this study is Podlubnyi's diary which he began to write in 1931 after settling in Moscow and kept up to 1939.[8] In addition, interviews with Podlubnyi have helped elucidate biographical details and events mentioned only in passing in the diary.

Podlubnyi's recollections often conflict with what he wrote in the diary, illustrating the risk of reconstructing a past subjective life experience on the basis of memoirs.

How authentic are the diary entries? Can they be regarded as sincere and spontaneous enunciations? Was the diary strictly secret, or was it addressed to an outside audience? From the outset Podlubnyi considered his diary both a tool and a record. As a tool, it was to help him master two distinct languages: the Russian language, which was not his primary language until he arrived in Moscow, and the Soviet political language which he had not previously faced as the carrier of an all-embracing cultural system. The diary's early entries were phrased in awkward Russian and contained numerous orthographic errors. They were devoted exclusively to events at the workplace and in the Komsomol, complete with painstakingly drawn sketches of the printing equipment in the *Pravda* plant.

Podlubnyi's mastery of the Russian language improved quickly, as his entries after 1932 show. His dream was to become a writer. This goal was one reason why Podlubnyi kept exhorting himself to write regularly, but in addition he was convinced that "more easily" than other people, writers could "perceive and better understand the whole depth of a text" (entry of 10.10.1932). Writing could thus help him raise his consciousness and foster his maturation into a legitimate Soviet citizen. Podlubnyi also wrote because he saw himself as participating in an transformational process of epic dimensions. One day he wanted to tell his children about the "1930s," when the whole country had been built (2.9.1932; 18.9.1935).

The longer he wrote, the more Podlubnyi came to regard the diary as his "sole friend." Only to his diary could he confide the secret of his past as well as his doubts and torments, attempting to fit into the new society. He hoped to overcome these doubts through writing. He regarded the diary as a "rubbish heap" onto which he could discard all the "dirt" that had accumulated in his "soul." Eventually, however, he also used the diary as a training ground for a project that he hoped to be able to undertake one day – an autobiographical novel devoted to "the life of an outdated class and its spiritual rebirth and adaptation to new conditions" (25.9.1934). Podlubnyi not only hoped to remake himself through writing, but his projected novel – and, by extension, also the diary – were to serve as evidence for the process of learning and reconstruction that he had undergone. By means of his literary work he would be able to substantiate his claim for full citizenship in Soviet society. To what extent the private and public dimensions of his diary overlapped in Podlubnyi's own understanding is apparent in the role of "chronicler" that he chose for himself. In this context, his chronicle described a two-fold project: the project of his own reconstruction in the wider frame of the history of the Soviet Union as a whole (2.9.1932; 10.10.1932).

In spite of the seemingly cacophonic voice in which this document speaks – "rubbish heap" and training ground for developing consciousness on the one hand, source of relief and best friend on the other – its evolution followed a discernible pattern. Judging from both its format and the title selected by Podlubnyi,[9] the diary probably started as a Komsomol or school assignment. Podlubnyi himself mentioned that several of his colleagues also kept diaries at the time. It thus appears that diaries were assigned in school as both instruments and records of individuals' work performance and consciousness. Over the years, Podlubnyi's diary documents how he took on a "technical" task assigned by the regime, gradually infusing it with his own agenda of self-improvement and self-perfection. In the process, the diary became a laboratory of Podlubnyi's self. This development renders the diary unique as a source, for it sheds much light on Podlubnyi's subjectivity, his own evolution as a subject of the Soviet order. In this connection, Podlubnyi's growing doubts over the success of his project and, concomitantly, his increasingly critical view of the Stalinist order as a whole provide valuable insights into the extent of critical thought in a repressive political system. They also illustrate the barriers that an individual faced in his attempts at constructing a self that would transcend the official norms of the Stalinist order.[10]

Toward becoming a new Soviet man

In 1931, when Stepan Podlubnyi came to Moscow, a campaign of unprecedented scale to transform the socio-economic landscape of the Soviet Union had been underway for several years. This campaign for the collectivization of agriculture and industrialization was acted out as a crusade: a battle for socialist construction, war against class enemies, and eradication of backwardness. The social policies employed in this campaign were two-fold. They entailed, on the one hand, the technical and political education of millions of young workers, mostly of peasant background, who had come to the cities and industrial sites to join the socialist battle. On the other hand, encapsulated in the formula of class war, incessant attempts were undertaken to identify and expunge from the ranks of workers and laboring peasants all supposed opponents of socialism. For the most part, this signified a war against peasants. Beginning in 1929 peasant households deemed *kulak* were systematically expropriated and several million *kulaks* deported into administrative exile. But the language of class war pervaded the country's cities and industrial centers as well. There the Party and Komsomol staged campaigns for vigilance and the unmasking of the class enemies who had infiltrated the working class.[11]

The class identity of an individual in the Soviet Union was purportedly defined by "scientific" sociological criteria. Scores of statisticians tracked the class divisions among the peasantry during the 1920s. In question-naires that had to be filled out for employment or admission to educational institutions, applicants had to specify their "class origins" and current "class position." Ultimately, however, class identity was determined politically. The Bolsheviks regarded a proletarian conscious-ness as the chief criterion in an individual's claim to membership in Soviet society. As a rule, an individual had to prove his consciousness on the strength of a corresponding class background. But consciousness could also transcend sociological origins. Thus descendants of the exploiting classes could be ascribed to the working class when they denounced their origins and displayed proletarian consciousness. In turn, even "hereditary proletarians" risked being relegated into the camp of the class enemy if they manifested a class-alien consciousness.

As his diary strikingly demonstrates, Podlubnyi fully accepted the stigma that he carried as a son of a *kulak*, believing it to be legitimate. He harbored no doubts that class aliens such as himself were imbued with a "sick psychology" and were unfit even to live unless they under-went massive reeducation (9.7., 28.7., 14.8.1933). But this meant that any attempt on his part to lead a double life and conceal his "real identity" – be it peasant or anti-Soviet – simply by assuming the appearance of a conformist would not succeed. The only way to overcome his nega-tive identity was to reconstruct it through his own efforts.

The question that he faced – in fact his entire diary can be read as both an expression and function of this question – was how to become a New Man. Podlubnyi realized that achieving success in his work and public activities would not only provide for acceptance into Soviet society, but also for self-respect. Upon entering the *Pravda* plant as an appren-tice, he immediately joined the Komsomol, where he was appointed leader of a brigade of shockworkers. Both in school and at work he soon stood out as one of the best apprentices. In spite of his successes, which were reflected in good grades at the factory school (FZU), a budding career in the Komsomol administration, and Podlubnyi's own satisfac-tion at having acquired "authority" among his peers, he often expressed the fear that his performance did not rise to the demands imposed upon him. Anxious that "the entire reservoir of my knowledge, my entire progressive development is beginning to evaporate" (1.10.1932), Podlubnyi repeatedly chided himself to work harder to speed up his "reconstruction." But he also knew that work was supposed to come about effortlessly when performed in the right spirit. What worried him was the fact that, due to his background as a class alien, his work performance and its relevance for his social standing seemed an imposition rather than a natural and painless expression of his consciousness. Did this detachment between labor and consciousness not indicate that he was inherently different from others?

> *13.9.1932* [. . .] Several times already I have thought about my production work. Why can't I cope with it painlessly? And in general, why is it so hard for me? My successes in production work don't make me happy. A thought that I can never seem to shake off, that sucks my blood from me like sap from a birch tree – is the question of my psychology. Can it really be that I will be different from the others? This question makes my hair stand on end, and I break out in shivers. Right now, I am a person in the middle, not belonging to one side nor to the other, but who could easily slide to either. But the chances are already greater for the positive side to take over – but still with a touch of the negative left. How devilishly this touch torments me.

Adding to Podlubnyi's problems was his responsibility as leader of the Komsomol brigade for the performance of his co-workers. He frequently complained about his futile attempts to instill in them a revolutionary passion for work. In turn, the Komsomol repeatedly took him to task for the low labor discipline among the group as a whole. Moreover, probably due in large measure to Podlubnyi's profile as an ardent and outspoken Komsomol activist, he was singled out for harsh treatment by his technical instructor. In his diary Podlubnyi characterized the workplace as a "snake pit" filled with "enemies" attempting to exploit his moments of weakness in order to denounce him as a wrecker and class enemy. As he reflected on an incident in which he had been held responsible for damaging a machine and received a reprimand from the Komsomol, Podlubnyi discovered a fundamental rule:

> *18.8.1932* [. . .] Now I don't regret that I was in such a position. This struggle, this experience – they taught me a lot. I have worked out a new approach to life. . . . I've learned something that one cannot learn in school. . . . From my observations I have noticed that when you approach a task recklessly, without any thought, in a hot-tempered way, the results are very bad. You have to gradually get used to the work, "without partisanship in the bad sense of the word." Now I'm gradually getting used to the work, am a member of the board, an activist, etc. I don't know what my path will be paved with. But the fact from

the past suggests that you always have to reach out to the interests of the state, and particularly those of production. You must
not consider the moods of the other guys and let yourself be
contaminated by them. Well, fate, don't let me down. Head in
the clouds, feet on the ground, and off to work.

Podlubnyi understood that it was for the state that he worked, whether
in the production process, as a Komsomol activist, or in school, and that
it was solely on the basis of performance that his social identity would
be determined – again by the state. Persistent work for the "interests of
the state, and of production in particular" would save him from falling
victim to the intrigues at the workplace and assure him good standing
in Soviet society.

Podlubnyi became acutely aware of the role of the state in determining
social identity in early 1933, when a passport system was introduced in
the Soviet Union. By issuing passports to the urban population and
making mandatory individual registration with the city administration,
the government attempted to curtail in-migration to the cities. With the
agricultural crisis produced by collectivization, and with the first indications of a famine spreading over the countryside, peasants were leaving
the villages in unprecedented numbers, threatening to exceed the
resources of the rationing system in the cities. At the same time the passport law was introduced to purge the cities of class aliens and to bind
the peasantry, who did not receive passports, to the newly established
kolkhozes.

For several months while the purge went on among the population
of Moscow, Podlubnyi remained uncertain about his fate. He asked
himself what the decisive criterion in the purge would be: his social
origins, or his current work performance? As he interpreted it, the passport campaign was a purge enacted by the state – a process of "sifting"
– in order to sort out the useful from the useless elements in society.
The latter, who faced expulsion from the city, included not only "speculators," "alcoholics," and "thieves," but also *"lishentsy"* [disfranchised
persons] and in general, people "with a wealthy past." What distinguished these people was their tainted psychology, precluding them from
performing socially useful work. To members of this group he opposed
the exemplary image of the "honest citizen": someone like himself, who
was reconstructing his psychology and showing readiness to work for
the state. Podlubnyi hoped that the new passports would come to constitute a contract between state and citizen, a contract requiring each
individual to work harder but in turn granting distinct benefits: not only
a ration card and an assured salary, but also – and more importantly –
a clearly defined and unquestioned social identity.

Podlubnyi did receive his passport in April 1933, but remained inse-
cure about his social standing. In reply to the questions, "How am I
supposed to live?! How am I to be?!! Where is the mirror for me to look
into?" (15.1.1933), he received mixed signals. By receipt of the passport
he was publicly confirmed as a member of the working class and received
all the benefits that this privilege entailed, but with the continuing hunt
for class enemies in the Komsomol and the press, the risk of being uncovered remained high; validation given by the state could just as easily be
taken away.

In Podlubnyi's view the unresolved question of his social status was
his "psychology," as he put it, his inadequate consciousness. This issue
preoccupied him more than anything else in the diary. One obvious way
to develop consciousness seemed to be to read and internalize the fundamental texts of Soviet culture, which were prescribed at school and in
study circles:

> *2.8.1932*   Asked the leader of the political circle: what should I
> read first, Marx or Lenin? He said that I should read both at the
> same time. That is very significant. He advised me to work with
> a pencil. In Marx, in his philosophy, he says so many obscure
> things, so much in it is difficult to understand, there are such
> depths, that you read it for the third time and still discover the
> significance of something new. You don't grasp everything at
> once. I noticed that too. Given my present development, today
> I understand one part, the easiest and most understandable part,
> and the next time I'll understand something new, the part that
> I couldn't understand at the first time. The work with the pencil,
> I mean reading with the pencil, is really a good thing! For news-
> papers as well as for books. I need to get used to this by writing
> down interesting quotations in a special note-book.

A few weeks later, however, expressing a sense of futility, Podlubnyi
dropped Marx again from his agenda. He showed greater perseverance
in reading novels and going to museums and to the theatre – expecting
there to find guidelines for thought and behavior. A particularly disap-
pointing experience for him was reading the three volumes of [Maxim]
Gor'kii's novel, *The Life of Klim Samgin*. Podlubnyi worshipped Gor'kii
as the leading Soviet writer, and also as a role model who had assisted
"thousands of young writers" in their work and who would perhaps
help him too (6.10.1932). Part of his fascination with Gor'kii lay in the
fact that he supported as possible the reeducation of class aliens through
labor – an idea Podlubnyi endorsed for obvious reasons. As to *Klim
Samgin*, Podlubnyi found the novel "boring, monotonous and foggy."

Specifically, he deplored that Samgin remained an "undefined" person throughout the book (6.2.1933). Podlubnyi expected to find in Soviet culture models of determination and a clear way to think, and not merely replicas of the "indeterminable" and "unsystematic" life he was still leading (1.1.1934, 18.2.1934, 15.10.1934).

In his program of acquiring consciousness Podlubnyi was operating under two-fold pressure. He viewed his life in Moscow as part of a larger race against time, in which the whole country was engaged. The rapid development of industry had to be matched by an equally "stormy growth" of the culture and consciousness of each individual. This especially applied to someone with an educational background as "backward" as his. Podlubnyi felt that he had to accelerate the process of his "growth" to eradicate the remnants of his secret past before they were uncovered by state officials.

Podlubnyi was made even more aware of this when he became involved with the GPU. In the fall of 1932 the secret police turned to him – presumably on the strength of his performance in the Komsomol – to collaborate as a secret informer. He was to report on counterrevolutionary behavior among his colleagues in school and at work. Podlubnyi experienced enormous anxiety whenever a scheduled appointment was approaching, as he expected his *kulak* past or innermost thoughts to be uncovered at any moment by the all-powerful GPU. Continuously reminded of his concealed origins, Podlubnyi could not help view his new life as a pretense:

> *8.12.1932* My daily secretiveness, the secret of my inside – they don't allow me to become a person with an independent character. I can't come out openly or sharply, with any free thoughts. Instead I have to say only what everyone [else] says. I have to walk on a bent surface, along the path of least resistance. This is very bad. Unwittingly I'm acquiring the character of a lickspittle, of a cunning dog: soft, cowardly, and always giving in. How trite and how disgusting! It makes me sick to mention this, but that's the way it is. I'm afraid that this is exactly the character that I'm developing.

In his longing for "independence" and the ability to articulate "free thoughts," Podlubnyi essentially expressed the desire to reach a state of natural conformity with the Soviet system. What he condemned was not the coercive nature of the system but his own behavior in it, and he saw no way out of his dilemma as long as he concealed his secret. As a result Podlubnyi felt increasingly exasperated, to the point that he longed for the moment when the GPU would uncover him (18.6.1934).

While the passport campaign went on, Podlubnyi groped for a notion of "freedom" that stood in marked contrast to his previous views:

> *12.3.1933* Often when you sit down to think your position over [...], and you don't find a way out, a thought appears: I can't stay in Moscow and I don't have to! I want to be free! I'll live at the end of the world! In Arkhangel'sk! In the tundra!! I don't care, I just want to be free, so that nobody can reproach me any longer: ah, so you are one of *those*? We know who you are, etc ... – and whatever else they say in these cases.

Freedom thus came to mean for him freedom from the social identity inflicted upon him by his surrounding culture, and could only be achieved in exile, outside the boundaries of Soviet culture.

Yet in spite of his ability, at various moments, to discern the outer contours of the system he lived in and thereby to gain a degree of detachment from it, Podlubnyi continued to view the state as both the source and the model for his social identity. This is particularly lucidly expressed in the "balance-sheets" that he drew up at the end of each year in his diary to record his achievements. Explaining why he needed to create such records, Podlubnyi pointed to an established practice among state institutions:

> *30.12.1933* Everywhere in the Union and in all countries the balance of the yearly work is being drawn. Everywhere in the Union, in many cities, and also in Moscow, conferences, congresses etc. are convoked in order to review the work of the year.

On his own balance-sheets Podlubnyi reviewed his performance at work, in school, and in the field of "cultural growth." Repeatedly he chided himself for his lack of determination and his "uselessness" to anyone, reverting to his earlier model of a "socially useful" person (30.12.1933, 1.1.1934, 27.12.1934).

In his program of reconstruction, Podlubnyi expected support from the state. Specifically, he turned to the GPU and the Komsomol as moral institutions, whose *raison d'être* was to correct the consciousness of an erring individual. Referring to the "counterrevolutionary" sentiment rampant among youth at the *Pravda* plant, Podlubnyi called on the GPU to intensify radically their "educational work" (27.11.1932). In his own case, Podlubnyi hoped to receive "indications from above" (26.5.1934) on how to think correctly and what place to occupy in society. He thought that such a moment of truth had finally arrived in October 1934, when the GPU unexpectedly confronted him with his real social origins during one of their regular meetings. In his entry of that day, Podlubnyi hailed the incident as a "historical moment," because it signalled the end of his "illegal" life (5.10.1934). But contrary to his expectations, he continued to remain uncertain about where he stood and what would happen to him. His GPU contacts told him only that no action would be undertaken as long as he continued to do good work for them. In the months following the uncovering of his secret, Podlubnyi became increasingly critical of state policies and institutions. At the same time, however, he criticized himself for developing such "reactionary" thoughts. In his eyes the responsibility for his personal degeneration lay with the GPU: Instead of curing him of his sick "psychology," they made matters only worse by constantly reminding him of his past:

> 5.1.1935 [. . .] Previously I did not think about my past: I was an ordinary rank-and-file member of society, I was even progressive. But now they, they themselves, have forced me to think differently. They will beat me for that. No doubt, when they find out, they'll beat me. It is so horrible, what is happening. Instead of curing me, they are making a cripple of me.

In spring 1935 Podlubnyi witnessed the exposure of a colleague at work as the son of a *kulak*. Surprisingly, though, nothing happened to him, he was not even expelled from work. To Podlubnyi this clearly indicated that the Soviet state was changing its policy toward class aliens. What mattered now was not one's past but one's current work performance. His reaction was exuberant:

> 2.3.1935 [. . .] This is a historical moment. Perhaps, from here on my new worldview will begin to emerge. The thought that I've been made a citizen of the common family of the USSR like everybody else obliges me to respond with love to those who have done this. I am no longer with the enemy, whom I fear all the time, every moment, wherever I am. I no longer fear my environment. I am just like everybody else, and therefore I have to be interested in various things, just like a master is interested in his farm, and not like a hireling toward his master.

This entry reveals to what extent Podlubnyi was dependent on the state in defining himself. The state had made him a citizen "like everybody else" and thus relieved him of his false consciousness. To work for the state now was not just his individual obligation but also his declared will. Only the state could imbue him with the notion of being a free agent. It was through the Soviet state that Podlubnyi acquired a sense of purpose, indeed the norms to define and guide his personal life. As his case makes clear, Soviet man could realize himself only by working for the state.

In fall 1935, Podlubnyi was accepted into Moscow's Second Medical Institute. For years he had dreamed of becoming a student, but his social origins seemed to prevent this dream from becoming true. Prior to admission to higher education, the biography of each student candidate was thoroughly scrutinized, and Podlubnyi had to fear that the authorities would discover his *kulak* past. Yet, equipped with recommendations from the Komsomol and the *Pravda* plant, he was able to secure admission to the institute. On the face of it, he now fully conformed to the ideal of the New Man. A career in the Soviet state apparatus seemed to be within his reach. But Podlubnyi also thought that now the time had come when his inner transformation would complete itself. By being accepted into the institute, he entered "a new stage ... of my being and consciousness" (18.9.1935).

Alternative social identities

One important aspect of his personal history seems to have compounded Podlubnyi's dependence on the state as the source of his identification. This was his conflictual relationship with his father which dated back to his childhood. As he described it in his diary, he experienced a euphoric moment when he was separated from his abusive father, who was sentenced to administrative exile during the dekulakization campaign. It was a moment of liberation and a turning point in his life. Only with the removal of the "tyrant" could he start to gain consciousness and "grow" (13.8.1932). This description suggests that Podlubnyi's conflict with his father greatly contributed to his need for identification with the Stalinist system, since this system – by stamping his father a *kulak* and enemy – provided a powerful catalyst in the articulation of Stepan's defiance of parental authority.

Podlubnyi's father, Filipp Evdokimovich, was reunited with his family in Moscow upon completion of his three-year term of exile in 1933. Stepan expressed his revulsion at how "old," "backward," and "useless" his father remained, despite the opportunity to remake himself in exile. By the same token this characterization of his father in the pejorative terms of the Soviet language served to underscore the positive Soviet identity of the son:

> *9.7.1933* [...] Now about F.E. himself. A halfway old man, of no use to anybody and completely superfluous. He has left the

old behind in many ways, but not altogether. But in the material sense definitely. Yet he hasn't been able to join the new. And if he doesn't succeed, it will be bitter for him and for us. This old man's weak will can destroy us as well as him. We have to help him with many things. We must force him to work on himself. Well, this will become clearer in the process. I look at him as at an acquaintance. Coldly. I can see in him only qualities negative for me. [...] His character is one of a wretched old man. Actually he's not really an old man.

Throughout the diary, Stepan addressed his father not with name and patronymic; instead, he frequently referred to him simply as "F.," or "F.E.," to demonstrate his lack of respect for him. Furthermore he felt compelled to emphasize his emotional and intellectual detachment from his father. Calling him a "father by conception but a stranger by education" (24.1.1934) or simply his "former father" (9.5.1934), he made a point of contrasting relationships based on blood to those forged by consciousness. Bonds of consciousness superseded those of kinship and thus justified his claim to be recognized as a member of the new order, in spite of his blood ties to the old.

Stepan greatly admired his mother. Specifically he praised her for the "proletarian views" that she had gradually come to exhibit, implying that, like him, she had accepted the necessity to rework herself. His mother attended evening school and performed outstanding social work, for which she even received awards. At one point he received a letter from her after she had been sent to a summer work camp to cut peat:

2.9.1932 [...] Received a letter from Mama. Am very happy that she has reeducated herself a little in the course of her "emigration." She writes that, notwithstanding the great difficulty of the work, "I'll stay for the entire month until the victorious end." This is very good. This is the proletarian way.

One way to view these relationships and how they informed Podlubnyi's social and political identity would be to explain them in psychological terms: as a struggle for identity fought against an oppressive father. This approach, however, is problematic because it accepts the concepts and emphases selected by Podlubnyi as psychological truth. Instead, these concepts can be situated historically as parts of a larger cultural text. The epithets used by Podlubnyi to establish the opposition between himself and his father strikingly resemble the epithets with which the battle for Soviet industrialization was fought: a struggle between "old" and "new" elements in society, "backward" and "progressive," darkness and light. But the similarity between Podlubnyi's rebellion against his father and the war gripping the country at large was not confined to the way in which they were phrased; it extended to content as well. The Party appealed to youth, and especially to those with tainted backgrounds, to dissociate themselves from their fathers and denounce them. Ritualistic declarations made by sons and daughters of supposedly anti-Soviet class origin filled the local and national press, repudiating their parents and stating that they had severed all ties to them. Among these sons was the famous Pavlik Morozov, who allegedly denounced his *kulak* father to the authorities and was then slain by an uncle. Pavlik was declared a martyr and a model to be emulated by Soviet youth.[12]

If Podlubnyi's relation toward his *kulak* father replicated a cultural pattern, we may conclude that he articulated this conflict because he felt encouraged by his environment to do so. He knew this articulation to be legitimate and, moreover, meaningful. The fundamental reason why his rebellion against his father occupied such a prominent place in Podlubnyi's diary was that he could situate it on the cultural axis – the struggle between old and new – which ultimately provided meaning in his life in the early 1930s.

Podlubnyi's descriptions of his social environment similarly appear to be organized around the binary terms of "backwardness" and "culture." During the early 1930s, Stepan and his mother lived in a humid cellar room in central Moscow which was occasionally flooded. In 1934 they moved to the first floor of the same building where they managed to claim some free space: half a room in a communal apartment shared by thirteen families. Of all their neighbors, the Podlubnyis appear to have been on good terms only with the Rodin family, in-migrants from Kaluga province, who occupied another apartment in the building. Stepan referred to that apartment as the "Rodin village," because it served as a temporary shelter for all the relatives and acquaintances of the Rodins who came to Moscow in search of work.[13] The apartment was also a meeting point of the local youth. Podlubnyi went there on occasion, to chat and have a good time. Notwithstanding the pleasure that he received from these encounters, his descriptions of the "Rodin village" were consistently rendered as a bulwark of peasant backwardness and barbarism:

> *12.2.1933* [. . .] The young people who come together to dance and sing in the kitchen of the Rodins: These young people are all from the village – girls and fellows from a backward, extremely low milieu. You stand there and look at them, a pleasant picture at first sight. But when you think about it more

deeply, you draw back, because you remember that these are living people. People! Not animals. But their relation toward each other, their thoughts and manners are just animal-like . . . Let's just take this evening. One of many. A dance, a "virtuoso" dance accompanied by an accordion. The fellows with drunken mugs and even sober guys with insolent expression paw the girls, shoving, and being rowdy. Vas'ka Godunov, a lad who has lived in Moscow since 1928. He is only 20, in the prime of his life. He is dead drunk; on clumsy, drunken legs he taps out the Russian dance. He has forgotten that it's time to go to work, that his comrades there are waiting for him, that the driver is waiting with the car (he is a loader). . . . He has emptied a whole bottle, he couldn't care less. But tomorrow? Tomorrow he'll get up with a heavy, aching head – without work, without his bite of bread, torn and sick. And then? Well, they won't give him work, where can he go? Perhaps do some trading on the market. A number of these fellows will come together, and they'll begin to steal. If it works, fine, but if not, they will literally die of hunger. Without a home, they'll freeze to death. There you see a thief, a bandit and what have you, someone who it is very difficult, if not impossible, to put on their feet, and lead to the path of truth, the path of a cultured person.

Fascinating in this entry is what it reveals about Podlubnyi's understanding of the opposite terms of culture and backwardness. Culture in his understanding subsumed work, the right to live in Moscow, consciousness, and virtue (the conduct of an honest, sober, and law-abiding life). By contrast, he associated backwardness with indifference toward work, unconsciousness (drunkenness), banditry, and even death. Again, as in the conflict with his father, Podlubnyi wrote so extensively about the "Rodin village" because it illustrated the fundamental problem of culture versus backwardness, which had been defined by the culture in which he lived. He wrote about what he recognized as meaningful.

Podlubnyi applied these concepts also to his attempts to build an environment for himself. He was proud of having a number of "cultured" friends, which referred to their level of education, cleanliness, and material resources. He was equally unhappy when he realized that he seemed to have particular success among uncultured friends, especially girlfriends, "from the lowest class" (18.6.1933; 1.1.1936). For a while he frequented a girl called Tania, whom he liked for her looks and the sincere love that she felt for him. But a letter from her confirmed his previous suspicion that she was virtually illiterate and could not possibly be a suitable girlfriend. An entry captures well the contrast between the two "milieus," to use one of Podlubnyi's favourite terms, of Tania and Polina, a university student. Especially striking is his use of the attributes of darkness and depth, expressed in the image of the "black cellar," to underscore Tania's backwardness:

> *30.1.1936* [...] On the 23rd in the evening I was at Tania's birthday party. . . . A black, dreadful cellar apartment consisting of a small room and a kitchen. After reading the leaflets from the calendar and the old newspapers, which are glued to the wall, or more precisely: after a boring hour the table was set. There were few drinks, little food, and no music. Hellishly boring. All in all, Galankin made the right conclusion: what can you expect from these people? [...]
>
> On the 22nd Polina Lakernik called. She invited me and Nikolai [Galankin] to a dance at her apartment. We danced magnificently. I got to know a different society, more cultured and totally different from the one with which I have mingled so far. Apart from Polina's sister, there were her acquaintance Vit'ka and his sister Lida, and also Shura Smorodinova. On the 27th I went ice-skating with Polina on the skating-rink of the TsDK[A].[14]

Podlubnyi's views of his social environment reveal the extent to which his social identity was prescribed by a certain cultural logic. He viewed his life as a struggle to overcome backwardness and attain culture, to eliminate remnants of the old in his social environment as well as his personal life.

This struggle, even if it clashed with other loyalties, was visible in his attitude toward his former home in Ukraine and his old friends. Feeling increasingly homesick and longing for the warmth and a sense of protection that he missed in his Moscow life as an imposter, Podlubnyi began to write to old friends from Ukraine in 1932, notwithstanding the threat to the preservation of his false identity. But how insignificant this partly Ukrainian, partly peasant identity remained for him and how little suited it seemed to him to define his role in society became particularly evident during his two visits to Ukraine in 1934 and 1936. He felt appalled by the villagers' lack of education, the pervasive patriarchal culture, and the misery of kolkhoz life. In contrast he made a point to appear as an educated and well-dressed Muscovite, in order to gain respect in the village. The overwhelming response was envy and resentment.[15]

Confronted with his old home, Podlubnyi resorted to the attributes of the urban, "cultured," New Soviet man. This posturing reveals Podlubnyi to be a beneficiary of the Soviet system, which gave him authority, culture, and the assurance that he had emancipated himself from the idiocy of rural life. This identity also obliged him to retain his loyalty to the state, in spite of the increasing pains that his illegal position inflicted upon him.

The private and the public

Podlubnyi's commitment to public values was all-embracing and unconditional because he possessed no positive notion of a private sphere in which to anchor a sense of self and personal values divergent from public norms. To be sure, he did develop a distinct notion of the private, as is evidenced by his diary. The diary represented his "only friend," the only partner to whom he confided those thoughts that he knew would be dangerous to voice to anyone else, even close friends. But by the same token Podlubnyi conceived of these thoughts as illegitimate. This attitude was rooted in Marxist ideology, which denounced the private sphere as a constituent element of the capitalist system. The function of the private world was to deceive the oppressed worker, to give him respite and make him oblivious to his fundamental state of alienation. Under socialism, by contrast, any notion of the private had to be anachronistic. Freed from capitalist oppression, man regained his nature as a social being. His inner being and outer function became one.

Faithful to the Marxist concept of man, Podlubnyi could not conceive of his diary as a record of a private sphere to be remembered. Rather, it served him as a "rubbish heap" onto which he could discard all the "garbage" and "dirt" accumulating in his mind (23.1.1933). Podlubnyi envisioned writing as a struggle from which he would ultimately emerge cleansed, in full conformity with the public values and thereby ridden of any alternative private sphere. This notion of the private radically differs from the concept offered by totalitarian theorists. Their view of society as being "atomized" by the totalitarian regime comes tantalizingly close to Podlubnyi's experience. But this argument is based on a problematic understanding of the private as a preserve of subjective truth conflicting with, and embattled by, a system of propaganda and lies.[16]

Podlubnyi conceptualized the relation between the private and the public realm in terms of an inner and an outer self. In his diary he often mentioned the feelings of his "inside" (*vnutrennost'*), using this expression synonymously with his "soul" (*dusha*). As he understood it, the soul of a Soviet citizen was to be filled with a distinctly political spirit and should form a realm of enthusiasm. He was dissatisfied when noticing that "all the inside [was] asleep" or when he found himself in an "idiotic and nonpolitical mood" (7.6.1932). In turn, when a sense of elevation toward the political sphere pervaded him, Podlubnyi experienced great relief:

1.6.1933 [...] Lately I've come to view my social work not as careerism, but as a system, as an intrinsic part of my body and existence, as the bread that is indispensable in order to exist, meaning not a struggle for existence, but a system that I willingly embrace. And with every day this continuity, this system, which is necessary for my organism, becomes stronger. I have noticeably reeducated myself from a careerism to a system that is as necessary as food, to which I devote my time without any effort. That is good. I'm happy about it.

Podlubnyi understood the importance of belief as a central distinguishing feature of the New Man. He considered it illegitimate to be "careerist" in the Stalinist system. An individual's outward achievements did not count as much as his inner disposition. Podlubnyi was describing the experience of belief when he wrote about a social spirit entering his body, becoming a part of his organism, and thereby merging with his inner self. In this connection it is of little importance to ask whether Podlubnyi truly believed. More important is to recognize that the Soviet regime required members of society to believe. This is why Podlubnyi felt impelled to describe himself in his diary as a believer. He understood that without demonstrating belief one would not be accepted into the Soviet system.[17]

This perceived necessity to believe also explains the troubles Podlubnyi experienced when he realized that, under the pressures of his concealed social origins, his soul was increasingly turning into a realm of critical thought, preventing the sensation of natural, uncoerced belief. Podlubnyi longed for a close friend, a "soul mate" as he put it, with whom he would be able to engage in "conversations of the heart," and to whom he could confide his difficulties and doubts. In spite of his fear of informants who would denounce him to the authorities, he did find such a friend, Mitia. Interestingly, in Podlubnyi's description this friendship turned into an extension of his illegitimate private sphere. Reacting to a poem that Mitia once read to him in which he deplored the "unhappiness" of his life, Podlubnyi noted that Mitia was a "pessimistically disposed subject, with petty-bourgeois views" (23.12.1933). However, he tried to situate Mitia's views in the broader picture of the political attitudes of Soviet youth:

23.12.1933 Youth, in other words the way in which youth views the world, can be divided into two groups. One group that enjoys great respect in the current order is a group of state parrots. Some of them don't understand anything at all, but the majority simply does what is being dictated to them. They never have their own opinion. They do everything the way they are ordered to, without any thought. These people have a shallow understanding of science and they resemble each other like a herd of sheep.

There is another category of people, which I would call more or less liberal. Liberal in the sense that they occupy a different place and have evolved differently, perhaps due to their upbringing. Well, these are unconventional people with progressive views or so. It is very noticeable that the category of these people is deeper, more developed and more gifted than the first one. They do everything silently and have a critical opinion on everything. Having said something, they don't turn around when they feel that they have said it right. They would never say anything for no reason. In terms of their knowledge one can feel that they don't know things in general, like the first category, but they know the depths. These are profound people. Profound, because they look at life with clear, not dull, eyes, and aren't afraid to face the truth. Often they are among the lists of the people who, as it is said, don't belong to "us." ... So, Mitia belongs to the second category of people, although he doesn't express their views very clearly.

Podlubnyi's conceptualization of these groups seemed to turn his initial judgement about Mitia on its head. A "pessimist," "petty-bourgeois," and by extension "reactionary" at the beginning, he now appeared to represent the truly "progressive" youth: critical, liberal, reflective – in a word a conscious young man. But the frailty of Podlubnyi's private thoughts in the face of the overwhelming body of public norms can also be seen in his reasoning. His most intuitive response condemned the conversation with Mitia in the official language of the time, underscoring his reflexive and unreflecting usage of such labels. Podlubnyi then attempted to categorize his friend on the basis of his own experience, which led him to invert the polar categories of "progressive" and "reactionary," as defined by the regime. In concluding his entry, Podlubnyi shifted again to the perspective of a citizen commited to the goals of the state, viewing his encounter as "illegal" and inauspicious for his own future:

23.12.1933   All in all, the whole business[18] is a reflection of the youth's "illegal" views. Soon it will be New Year, time to establish a balance sheet. There will be little to brag about. In the year before I did more than in this one. But let's look and compare.

It was probably no accident that Podlubnyi reminded himself at exactly this moment to draw up the "balance sheet" of his yearly achievements. This reminder suggests how uneasy he felt about his private criticism of the regime and how threatening he considered it to be.

Through his conversations with Mitia, Podlubnyi came to realize that there were "two people" inside of him. One of them was a "bureau-crat": "Daily he reminds me to be on my guard, to observe the rules and be careful ... This person is present in me for most of the time." The other person was one "who collects all sort of dirt in my soul, all the remaining garbage, and he waits for the right moment to splash out this refuse over someone else's head in order to relieve himself from the burden of the dirt. This person lives more rarely in me, but he exists. This old wound of my origins and memories occasionally makes itself felt" (25.9.1934).

Speaking of the two people inside of him, Podlubnyi was referring to a duality of mind and soul. He saw his mind as the state agent inside of him, an agent reminding him continuously to follow the rules of public conduct. It was present most of the time. The anti-realm to the state and its values resided in his soul. It was nourished by the "old wound of my origins and memories." From this open wound dirt flowed into the soul, so heavily that it had to be discharged from time to time, in order not to smother the soul. Podlubnyi's conversations with Mitia were moments when he silenced his mind by articulating his soul.

As his diary shows, Podlubnyi experienced his private life as an inces-sant act of purging his soul. This task became exceedingly difficult for him after his involvement with the GPU, as his soul became the shelter for his illegitimate, dirty inner secret (*sekret vnutrennosti*). Podlubnyi hoped that the moment of his unmasking would send him through a purgatory. But although the NKVD eventually discovered his secret, no action was taken, and he continued to be fraught with his "illegal" life. Ironically the only place where he felt now freed from the weight of his "garbage" and experienced a unity of private and public was with the NKVD: "Somehow you purge your soul from some kind of garbage. Because you can speak sincerely and truthfully, while everywhere else your whole life is a lie" (26.10.1934).

Podlubnyi's personal Bolshevism

During his program of personal reconstruction, Podlubnyi sought to embrace Bolshevik values and behavioral norms. He tried to attain such a model behavioral type by following what he conceived of as binding guidelines or laws, the validity of which he did not question. But in Podlubnyi's reception of elements of the ruling ideology one can also discern a redirection and refashioning of some of these values. His individual appropriation of public norms can be called Podlubnyi's personal Bolshevism.

In March 1933 Podlubnyi "fulfilled an age-old dream." He went to a graphologist to have his handwriting analyzed, in order to find out about his "flaws, qualities, and talents." He put all of his savings, seven rubles, into that analysis, but did not regret the expenditure because he knew the graphologist to be the greatest authority in the field: "Zuev-Insarov himself" (16.3.1933).

The written analysis is quoted in full because it reads like a catalogue of publicly proclaimed values of the time, against which Podlubnyi's personal qualities are assessed:

Graphological examination
A personality full of initiative, who easily grasps the essence of a matter. Materialistic worldview. Politically oriented. At an early stage escaped the ideological influence of his family. Has a gift for observation. Can distinguish lies from sincerity in the voice of another. Sociable and pleasant; soft, even good-natured, in the company of others; but when decisive action is called for, or when an obligation or a strong desire has to be fulfilled, neither the pleas of close friends nor any other temptations can distract him from the goal he has set himself. Does not let himself be coerced in any fashion. Persistent in the realization of intentions, although perseverance is occasionally unsystematic and lacks precision; more concentration of will is indispensable. Able to do many things at once, but has a tendency to defer things already started. Lazy. Shows little trust and is suspicious, has developed professional caution. Leans toward formal and logical reasoning, shows talent for treating issues with a scientific methodology, suited for activities in law and administration, is also mechanically talented. Can command respect, has a literary vein. A character suited for various social work. Gravitates toward self-education. Should in this regard strive for a deepening, rather than broadening, of his knowledge. A great experimentator in terms of passions, occasionally displays more curiosity than passion. Unsteady in his passions. Able to control his emotions, but not after releasing them. Uneconomical in his relation toward money and cannot economize it. Does not lose his head in moments of danger, is fearless, of course not because he stands above universal human weaknesses, but simply because he believes in his strength and maintains a presence of mind.

Implicitly underlying this characterization of Podlubnyi is a set of exemplary behavioral norms, which taken together defined the New Man. This was a politically inclined individual with a materialistic world-view, who in his character displayed firmness and determination – as evidenced in his "concentration of will" – expressed interest in science and in furthering his education, but by the same token a good manual worker. For the most part, Podlubnyi lived up to this model type, according to Zuev-Insarov's analysis. When he received the document, Podlubnyi was impressed how accurately he had been characterized, but also surprised that Zuev-Insarov had assigned to him many positive qualities. Specifically with respect to his willpower, "I didn't even expect to have strong willpower. But he says that I'm persistent." He concluded: "The letter was useful for me. I've begun to know myself, to trust myself, to trust my behavior and strength" (1.4.1933).

In his diary Podlubnyi was obsessively concerned with his willpower. In his understanding, will and consciousness were interdependent; one could not be attained without the other. Thus willpower was the key to becoming a New Man. This link becomes evident in many entries in which Podlubnyi blamed his "weak will" for setbacks in his work and for his "idiotic and nonpolitical mood" (7.6.1932):

> *30.12.1933* [...] With full confidence I can say that this year I have received nothing. Studied at the FZU – with bad results. Began to study in middle school – also with bad results. I am neglecting my classes horribly, lagging behind in all subjects. I don't have enough willpower to control myself. Right now I have a big, huge, horrible weakness of will. This is the cause of all my troubles, this is my biggest deficiency. Of all the dangers in my life, this deficiency is the most horrible and dangerous. Because everything depends on it.

But willpower was not only to raise his consciousness, it was also to help him preserve the double secret of his social origins and noncon-formist political viewpoints. Only through "will," "determination" and "cold-bloodedness," all of which Podlubnyi regarded as "proletarian" virtues, could he seal his private thoughts from his public behavior (6.12.1933). Podlubnyi thus tried to adopt proletarian values in order to protect himself against the proletarian state.

This paradoxical understanding of "proletarian" is especially well captured in an entry in which Podlubnyi described a trip that his parents took to Ukraine in 1933, hoping to resettle there. Due to Filipp's "foolish" behavior, which raised the suspicion of the local GPU, they were forced to leave shortly after arriving in their home village. In striking contrast to Filipp, Stepan's mother was described by her son as consistently "bold," "resolute" and "energetic." She warned Filipp not to get involved with the GPU, as this would cause trouble, but he went ahead anyway in order to seek their legal registration. The GPU threatened him with arrest and ordered him to disappear within 48 hours. The mother then managed to procure falsified documents enabling them to buy train tickets back to Moscow. In the meantime the ultimatum set by the GPU had elapsed, and Filipp ran away in panic, stranding her without money. Nevertheless she found a way to return to Moscow. Summing up the story, Stepan lauded his mother for her "purely proletarian views" (14.8.1933). As suggested by the context, "proletarian" subsumed in Stepan's understanding the ability to cope with one's political environment, including the necessity to shield oneself against its adversities. Stepan called his father "weak-willed" because he proved unable to defend himself against the encroachments of the Soviet political order.

Podlubnyi conceived of life as a constant struggle. To corroborate his view, he cited a Soviet authority: "I don't know who, but I think it was Gor'kii who said that 'life is a struggle.' A very pointed observation. If life is without struggle, it is not human; it is an animal's life" (2.5.1933). In Podlubnyi's life, the struggle took place on several "fronts," to use his terminology: in the first place, he struggled with himself to "overcome" the "reactionary" part within, but he also struggled against "enemies" at work bent on denouncing him as a wrecker. Finally, there was his struggle against Soviet authorities to preserve his secret life. Podlubnyi once likened himself to a lonely sailor at sea, facing the sudden outbreak of a terrible storm (23.3.1934). The only way to survive in an environment, the overwhelming forces of which could destroy him at any moment, was to listen to one's "instincts" and develop a "plan of self-preservation." Having these abilities was a sign of great willpower. Repeatedly Podlubnyi reminded himself in his diary to stay prepared to accept imminent challenges from any direction. He was especially suspicious about calm periods, when nothing seemed to threaten him, neither at work nor from the GPU. They reminded him of the "calm before the storm" (10.10.1933; 8.12.1935).

Podlubnyi's metaphoric use of nature to describe his own life as well as his concept of willpower replicated popular imagery of the time. The Soviet literary canon of the early 1930s represented the program of socialist construction and the social conflict erupting in the course of this process as man's conquest of an unwieldy nature. The chief force available to master the anarchic and "elemental" forces of nature was human willpower.[19] Podlubnyi faithfully adopted the imagery of this conflict with nature, but he redirected it in such a way that it helped him abide by his peculiar standing in society and the problems which stemmed from it. In Podlubnyi's interpretation, the state order itself had assumed the role of the elemental forces of nature against which he, as an individual, had to protect himself in a lifelong struggle. Socialism in this particular imagery came to mean the survival of man in savage nature.

If "willpower" constituted for Podlubnyi the key element necessary for his survival in socialist society, it was also what he thought differentiated classes in Soviet society. As already mentioned, he considered "proletarian" to be someone who possessed great willpower and therefore could cope with the conditions of Soviet life. In an unnerving extension of this logic, Podlubnyi defined those groups in society who could not cope with the Soviet environment as "weak-willed" and unfit for life. When Podlubnyi's mother returned from a visit to Ukraine in summer 1933, she brought him the horrible news of the famine ravaging their home village. Stepan wrote:

> *14.8.1933* [. . .] By the way, about the news that Mama reported: an incredible famine is going on over there. Half of the people have died of hunger. Now they are eating cooked beet tops. There are plenty of cases of cannibalism. . . . All in all it's a terrifying thing. I don't know why, but I don't have any pity for this. It has to be this way, because then it will be easier to remake the peasants' smallholder psychology into the proletarian psychology that we need. And those who die of hunger, let them die. If they can't defend themselves against death from starvation, it means that they are weak-willed, and what can they give to society?

Podlubnyi's notion of will was not simply tied to the purpose of individual self-preservation. In his eyes, an individual's will had to first serve the interests of society. In this aspect, Podlubnyi's life philosophy differed from both Darwinism and Nietzscheanism, with which it had many elements in common.[20] Socialist man's struggle for existence was not decided by his physical strength, nor by his will for life. The decisive factor was his social usefulness. On the basis of an uninterrupted process of selection, the Soviet state divided the population into the strong-willed and weak-willed, the useful and useless, good and evil people. It welcomed the former and discarded the latter.

Podlubnyi's interpretation turned the official view of Soviet man as a selfless, collective builder of socialism on its head. In his eyes, socialism came to denote individual self-preservation through collective labor. Podlubnyi built his idiosyncratic life philosophy by using certain building blocks of Bolshevik ideology, but by rearranging their positions. Particularly striking was his understanding of "willpower" and other virtues of the model "proletarian." These qualities were not to be mobilized primarily to build socialism as official ideology demanded, but to protect oneself from the encroachments of the socialist state. This potential for reinterpretation of official dogma points to the vulnerability of the Soviet conception of truth and to its susceptibility to erosion, as Bolshevik ideology turned in part against Soviet state power.

Yet in spite of his freedom in appropriating and manipulating the ruling ideology, Podlubnyi remained committed to two fundamental assumptions of Bolshevism: 1. An individual counted only as long as he demonstrated his social usefulness; 2. His service to society was a function of his will. These convictions would have fateful implications for Podlubnyi. What if his quest for integration into Soviet society remained unsuccessful? Wouldn't this indicate that he himself was weak-willed and – like the dying peasants in Ukraine – had no right to live? Podlubnyi's capacity to escape this destructive logic hinged on his ability to transcend the official self-representation of Bolshevik ideology as an exclusionary, all-encompassing truth.

Unbelief in the Stalinist system

Podlubnyi's diary provides particularly valuable insights into the character and significance of dissent in the Stalinist system. Especially in the latter part of the 1930s he increasingly articulated opinions critical of the Soviet political system. His diary seems to endorse the widespread notion that the Soviet regime could survive only on the strength of a systematic policy of manipulation and intimidation. Through a reign of terror, the Stalinist leadership enforced the submissiveness of a society which had lost its belief in the goals of the revolution. Even though this study places its emphasis on other areas of governance, it by no means seeks to deny the repressive character of the Stalinist order. The purpose is rather to demonstrate how deeply an individual internalized elements of a system of rule – to the extent that his attempts to detach himself from the system could not but have destructive implications for himself as well. Podlubnyi experienced his rebellion against the Stalinist regime in part as a rebellion against himself.

Following a methodology introduced by Lucien Febvre, intellectual resistance to a political system can be analyzed in terms of unbelief. In his study of the Renaissance poet François Rabelais, Febvre examines the popular notion that Rabelais was an atheist. He demonstrates that the sixteenth century lacked the conceptual vocabulary to formulate, let alone articulate, "unbelief." Notwithstanding Rabelais' heretical appearance, Febvre concludes, the poet remained entirely bound within the Christian cosmos.[21]

This study defines unbelief in opposition to the regime of truth of the Stalin era. The questions to be addressed in Podlubnyi's particular case are whether he was able – and if so, by what means – to broaden his critical opinion to question the goals to which the Stalinist regime had publicly committed itself. On which issues did Podlubnyi's criticism center, and how did he justify it? What was the frame of reference underlying his criticism? This approach requires a particular sensitivity to what could be said or thought in Soviet culture and what remained unthinkable.

Podlubnyi experienced his gradual detachment from the state order as an exceedingly difficult and painful process, largely for two reasons. First, this order functioned on the basis of tight censorship, massive agitation, and a formidable apparatus of investigative and punitive agencies, the purpose of which was to insure the regime's monopoly over interpretation of the ruling ideology. Therefore any attempt at formulating an intellectual framework divergent from the values of the regime had to be confined to the private and, moreover, had to be undertaken with great caution. Compounding the difficulty of articulating dissent was the fact that the Soviet order of the 1930s resembled a closed society with sealed borders and virtually no information flow from abroad except for the fables of life abroad presented by the Soviet press. Thus most people lacked even the most basic precondition for the articulation of dissent: an outside frame of reference against which to evaluate the performance of the Stalinist system.

Second, and more importantly, Podlubnyi experienced his condemnation of the state order as an act of self-destruction. All the sources and elements of his positive self-definition as a subject were grounded in the Soviet regime. Bound as he was to the conceptual language of the regime in defining his identity, Podlubnyi's attempts at detaching himself from the values of the state invariably entailed a rejection of his positive self and forced him to condemn himself as a "useless," "pessimistic," and "reactionary" person.

In December 1934, the Leningrad Party secretary Sergei Kirov was murdered. The Soviet leadership reacted with outrage, demanding the relentless prosecution of the murderers who were suspected to come from the political opposition. Podlubnyi, however, suspected that the government itself had fabricated the murder in order to rid itself of a bothersome member.[22] He distrusted the official version of the murder, "just the way that one distrusts a thief who had stolen before." Along with his criticism, Podlubnyi also leveled serious accusations against himself, chiding himself for his "too realistic" perspective on things. No longer was he a member of the "progressive" Soviet youth; his "ideology" had become "rotten" (5.1., 26.1.1935). In the long run, two possibilities were available to him to accommodate his "reactionary" unbelief. One was to rearrange the categories of self-definition, so that his illegitimate thoughts would appear legitimate. If he proved unable to remake the world for himself, he was bound to marginalize himself: to accept his individual thoughts as an exception to the norm and to seek the reasons for such a deviation in himself.

Podlubnyi became implicated in both of these processes. His diary provides a graphic illustration of the ways in which he managed to rearrange his political vocabulary. The following entry was written only a few weeks after the excerpts quoted above:

> *12.2.1935* [. . .] This is the onset of a time of such reaction and persecution . . . – I can't describe this in a few words. It only reminds me of studying the history of the Party in 1907: a raging black reaction, going on right now. A raging reaction, and the persecution of free thought. You have to fear not only your comrades, you must also be afraid of yourself. They don't just persecute you for conversations, but they even persecute you for hinting at unfavorable speech.

These sentences reveal a pattern of literal inversion which enabled Podlubnyi to rid himself of his "reactionary" thoughts by defining the regime as "reactionary" and, by implication, portraying himself as "progressive." More striking even is Podlubnyi's reference to the source which inspired this new conceptualization, and which brought him to denounce the party state: a Bolshevik Party history textbook. To use an analogy, Podlubnyi used the Holy Scripture against the Church in legitimizing his unbelief. This example illustrates the extent to which Podlubnyi's critical thought was rooted in the Soviet regime of truth. The only way in which he could articulate oppositional views was by pointing to discrepancies between the regime's policies and its proclaimed goals. But by invoking these goals as a higher truth, he remained bound to the fundamental principles and values of the regime.

At one point, Podlubnyi described his disposition as an incurable "illness,"[23] thereby implying that he believed his environment to be "healthy" (17.2.1936). Specifically he thought that he was suffering from an illness of will. Previously he had attempted to acquire consciousness through the mobilization of will, but now he realized this goal to be unattainable due to a lack of willpower. He wrote that he felt "paralyzed," a condition that he attributed to the complete erosion of his willpower (28.10.1935, 17.2.1936, 5.3.1936). As this instance reveals, Podlubnyi remained fully bound to the conceptual language of the Stalinist regime and was unable to sustain a self-representation divergent from its norms. Therefore he felt compelled to individualize his experience of unbelief and turn it against himself. Since it was the Soviet state that formed Podlubnyi's positive identity as an individual and defined his ability to act, it was only logical that Podlubnyi experienced his detachment from the state order as his personal paralysis.

In early 1936 Podlubnyi's social origins were publicly uncovered at a Komsomol meeting and he was expelled from the youth organization. His diary brings to light how much this incident affected his sense of self-worth: as he described it, he felt physically and psychologically "broken" on the days following his unmasking (17.2.1936). He had a conversation with Egor Kozhemiakin, another son of a kulak:

> *21.2.1936*   The whole evening I sat together with Kozhemiakin, my friend in misery. Only he has already gone through everything. It boiled over and then it was business as usual. So many offspring from the other class are being uncovered, in every corner, it's amazing. . . . And they all are wonderful people, they are the best – celebrated heroes of labor. One could draw a very interesting conclusion.

With particular lucidity this entry shows both the perceptiveness and the structural limits of Podlubnyi's unbelief. Challenging the social identity imposed on him by the regime, he argued that those stamped as "offspring from the other class" were in fact "best" people. Yet in justifying such a reversion of the official categories, he resorted to the regime's concepts. Podlubnyi pointed to the fact that all of these offspring were "celebrated heroes of labor," implying that they had successfully reconstructed themselves and were entitled to full membership in Soviet society. Following this reasoning, Podlubnyi's final enigmatic remark "one could draw a very interesting conclusion," meant that he considered the policy of the regime toward these specific individuals unjustified and erroneous. Still faithful to the belief that class aliens had to redeem themselves through labor, he did not criticize the general nature of class policies in the Soviet state.

Podlubnyi also gradually came to reevaluate his former views of the private and public spheres. Referring to his encounters with Kozhemiakin, he wrote that they gave him "consolation." In particular they restored some of his self-worth, which had been lost in the public sphere. Podlubnyi now viewed the private sphere, in which he could voice his grievances, as a "morally" positive realm – a striking departure from his previous condemnation of it as morally polluted. He recounted an evening he spent together with another close friend, Vladimir Vorontsov. Vorontsov confided to him that his biography was also tainted: his father was a Trotskyite and had been sentenced to administrative exile in 1928. Concluding his description of the evening, Podlubnyi wrote:

> *5.3.1936* [. . .] Somehow this made both of us happy. Morally we became even closer on that evening. "I told that only to you," he said. "I just thought that I had to tell this to Stepa, as my best friend."

Whereas Podlubnyi previously had felt weighed down by the burden of his "dirty" origins, he now appeared to derive strength from sharing the secret of his friend's origins. Clearly the private sphere had turned into a notion that he now endowed with positive value. Yet, as his friend Vorontsov emphasized, this sphere was limited, as it could include only a few trustworthy individuals. Moreover it was permanently contested by a public sphere, which decreed a social reality standing in marked contrast to the private anti-realm.

In December 1937, Podlubnyi's mother was arrested. This incident became a turning point in his life. During the following months he concentrated all his energy on trying to help her, sending her packages, and writing petitions to the Moscow Procuracy. Compelled to earn money to support himself and his mother, he quit the institute. Looking back on the year 1937, he acknowledged the failure of his new life:

> *1.1.1938* There it is, the beginning of 1938. What awaits me in this year? Won't fate finally smile on me? I don't regret that 1937 is over. There was nothing good in it for me, only lots of bad. My life has fallen apart before it could settle. If before 1938 there was a perspective for something positive, namely to study at the institute, this singular dream, this bright spot in the midst of my dark life, has vanished. I'm robbed of perhaps the most valuable of all valuables that I possessed. The beacon toward which I oriented myself, in making my way through life, is extinguished. It was a difficult way, curvy and blocked by obstacles, but the bright spot of the beacon drew me toward it, showing the goal, for which I was striving. What is my goal in life now?! I don't see a goal. Life without a goal is like an animal's life. What sort of life is that? There is nothing, absolutely nothing, that could give me moral support. Ah, you people, how incredibly difficult is it to live. If I didn't have the desire to see how people live and what will happen further on, it would probably not be worth living. Ah, how disgusting! This gives me the creeps, and shivers just ran up my spine. What am I to do

tomorrow and the following days? Look for work!? Sell my labor power for 200 rubles per month. Where will that leave me? And also, what kind of work can I do? Who needs my head that knows things in general but has no specialized knowledge? Who needs my hands, which have learned no skill? Yet I still need to look for work. Much will depend on whether I find a suitable job. I must look for a good job.

"Robbed" of his only goal of higher education, Podlubnyi felt left without a purpose in life. A life without a purpose was an "animal's life," it was devoid of consciousness. Podlubnyi continued to measure himself according to the state's categories of knowledge, labor, consciousness, and usefulness. His ultimate sense of failure was underscored in thoughts of suicide. Suicide could be understood as a logical final step undertaken by an individual who realized his "uselessness" in a system that defined him solely on the basis of his "social usefulness."[24]

However, paralleling his self-image as "paralyzed," "broken," and "useless," Podlubnyi continued to solidify the body of his critical thought after 1937. His denunciation of the regime's policies now became unequivocal – he no longer embedded it in qualifications and self-accusations. The diary exhibits a veritable explosion of intellectual development by 1938. He denounced the celebration of the return of the Papanin polar expedition as an "unprecedented hullabaloo," the principal purpose of which was to deflect popular attention from the Bukharin trial (18.3.1938). After reading *Quo Vadis?* by Henryk Sienkiewicz, situated in Imperial Rome during the first century AD, Podlubnyi characterized Stalin as "our Russian Nero," specifically addressing his personal cult: "It appears that the unjustified lavishing of praise and attribution of good deeds, and also deification, are possible in our times too, if only in a more subtle form" (15.4.1938). Podlubnyi now appeared to be reading in order to corroborate his critical political views: a striking departure from his earlier program of reading to provide himself with a "correct" outlook. Nevertheless, his continued voracious reading habits and, moreover, the very fact that he deemed necessary to record it in his diary shows how much Podlubnyi remained committed to the Bolsheviks' understanding of a *conscious* citizen.

Podlubnyi's denunciation of life in Soviet Russia did not center on political issues, however. The focus of his criticism lay on the material standard of living and the state of cultural development. A trip to Iaroslavl' to visit his father, who had resettled there, was an eye-opening experience. Although he now lived an urban life, his father shared a room not only with other workers but also with a piglet and swarms of bugs and lice. On a tour through the outskirts of Iaroslavl' Podlubnyi discovered with amazement and shock that such living conditions appeared to be the rule (3.4.1938, 5.4.1938). Yet all the people whom he questioned replied that they were doing well. Only his "fresh perspective" as a visiting outsider, Podlubnyi wrote, allowed him to understand the "inhuman" nature of these living conditions. "We must not live like this," he exclaimed (9.4.1938).[25] He implicitly accused the regime of failing to live up to its commitment as a socialist welfare state and to bring about cultural progress and material enrichment.[26] In place of progress, Podlubnyi saw only persistent backwardness and barbarism:

> *17.4.1938* When will the Russians finally begin to lead a human life? The older generation says that 20 years ago there was a time when a person could calmly enter a store and buy whatever he wanted within 15 minutes, provided he had the money. I and my generation have not seen such times. ... When will we finally begin to live the life that our leaders promise us?

Podlubnyi's damning criticism of the Stalinist regime notwithstanding, the Russian Revolution remained the focal point of his reasoning. He compared the present to the first year of the Revolution, not to the prerevolutionary period. It was inconceivable to him to claim that living conditions in Tsarist Russia had been better than at present. Podlubnyi was also convinced that a brighter future awaited Soviet society. This orientation allowed him to rationalize the present as a temporary aberration, as a period in which "swine" had come to replace the "good people." Ultimately, however, present injustices would be corrected, and justice be restored (11.1.1938).

Even while discrediting the policies of the Soviet government, Podlubnyi continued to adhere to the fundamental assumption of Stalinist culture, that the evolution of the country proceeded on a path preordained by history. Characteristically, even his mother's arrest did not lead Podlubnyi to question the legitimacy of the regime's policies. Commenting on the charge of her being a Trotskyite, he reacted incredulously:

> *18.12.1937* [...] Of course I know a lot of rumors about the arrests of various people. This doesn't come as a surprise to anybody these days. But to number Mama, a half-illiterate woman, among the Trotskyites, that would have never occurred to me. Not even in my dreams would I be able to imagine this, as I know her very well.

But his very reasoning showed that he believed the accusation against her, as well as the mass arrests in the country at large, to be grounded in more than a random policy of terror. Accordingly, he looked for means to "persuade" the "dumb bureaucratic blockheads" of the Procuracy of the "actual (*istinnaia*) injustice" of her punishment (30.11.1938). That such a conviction was widespread in society at the time, is confirmed by the memoir literature on Stalinism.[27] Since terror presented a threat to virtually anybody, the only way to live with that threat was to understand the terror as rational.[28] This need for rationalization was compounded by the fact that the very thought of irrationality – of a departure from the laws of history – was difficult, if not impossible, to conceptualize in postrevolutionary Russia.

Podlubnyi could not challenge the legitimacy of the revolutionary process, because he was personally implicated in it, even if his own life was a "failure." His life in Moscow evolved on the axis of his personal transformation and self-perfection toward the ideal of the New Soviet Man. Notwithstanding his growing criticism toward the Bolshevik regime, he remained faithful to the program of enlightenment as proclaimed by the Soviet state. Even though he had failed in his new life, Podlubnyi continued to regard himself as an active participant in the Soviet project of civilization.

Conclusion

Podlubnyi's case strikingly reveals how deeply the self-consciousness of an individual living in the Soviet system was informed by Bolshevik notions of what man should be. Podlubnyi not only internalized the Bolshevik system of class and the role that it allocated to him personally, but using his diary, he actively wrote himself into the Soviet order, attempting to acquire a sense of personal meaning and purpose. By means of the diary, Podlubnyi engineered his own soul, to paraphrase Stalin's famous phrase. In search for a positive identity, he invariably oriented himself toward the program of the Soviet state as the source of his individual existence. His self-definition as a subject was inextricably linked to the cause of the state as a whole. In keeping with the Bolshevik concept of man, Podlubnyi did not accept the notion of a positive, legitimate private identity divergent from public norms. He envisioned writing as a purgatory from which he would ultimately emerge clean, fully identical with the public values and thereby rid of any alternative, "selfish" sphere. Through confession and self-improvement, he sought to constitute himself as a good Soviet citizen. To be sure, over the years the diary did turn into a distinctly "private" document, of whose dangerous content the author became painfully aware. However, Podlubnyi could not help but perceive this process as his estrangement from the collective and evaluate it as a token of his personal degeneration.

The effacement of the boundaries between the public and the private in defining the individual sets this diary apart from a long tradition of diary writing in Russia and the West. To be sure, as a record and instrument of self-perfection, Podlubnyi's diary seems to replicate a familiar genre. But unlike diary writers in the Western liberal tradition, Podlubnyi did not strive for autonomy. Quite to the contrary, his notion of individual emancipation was wholly contained within the larger political project defined by the Soviet state.[29]

Podlubnyi's account of his life testifies to the power of the Stalinist regime over the self-definition of its subjects. By illustrating how the Soviet system of social identification pervaded even the individual's personal domain, this diary sheds light on an arena of power that has been overlooked in most existing studies on the social history of Stalinism. Focusing on methods of censorship and administrative surveillance, these studies have tended to view Soviet state power largely in negative terms, as a distorting and repressive force. This view is based on a problematic distinction between the Soviet order and the individual. It posits state power – conceptualized in only two ways, as the exercise of physical violence or ideological influence – in opposition to the individual self, which is understood as an essentially pure and power-free domain.

By contrast, the approach taken in this study is founded on the belief that power and meaning are interdependent and therefore inseparable. As Podlubnyi's case makes eminently clear, an individual living in the Stalinist system could not conceivably formulate a notion of himself independently of the program promulgated by the Bolshevik state. Our analysis conducted on the micro level has shown how Soviet state power instilled an individual with subjecthood – how it shaped Podlubnyi's self. In striving for culture and consciousness, Podlubnyi sought to realize his notion of individual subjectivity, but by the same token he himself acted as a carrier of the Stalinist system. As Podlubnyi's account shows, an individual and the political system in which he lived cannot be viewed as two separate entities. For this reason, the present study did not set itself the goal of measuring the effects of the Stalinist system on Podlubnyi's individual existence. Rather it sought to locate this system within the individual, and read the diary as a laboratory of his Soviet self. Thus, while not seeking to downplay the repressive qualities of the Stalinist regime (which, incidentally, figure prominently in Podlubnyi's diary), it reveals a productive side of Bolshevik government, namely how it induced an individual to appropriate the Soviet program of civilization for himself and become engaged in a process of self-transformation and self-perfection.

How deeply did Podlubnyi believe in the principles and goals of the Soviet system? As his diary shows, the principal source of individual loyalty toward the political order was not belief, but rather an inability to articulate unbelief consistently. Podlubnyi was not a true believer. One might even go so far as to insinuate that he wrote his diary out of a manipulative intent, without any inner conviction – in order solely to play the role of a good Soviet citizen. However, as the diary makes eminently clear, Podlubnyi staged this role not only, and not primarily, for his social environment, but in the first instance for himself, trying to convince himself of the authenticity of his Soviet identity.

More important even is to recognize that Podlubnyi, while trying to instrumentalize the Soviet political language for his own purposes, kept being shaped by it. His thought and behavior could not escape the logic inherent in the Bolshevik concept of class. Nowhere is the operation of this logic more visible than in Podlubnyi's criticism of the Stalinist state. Characteristically, his condemnation of the regime's inability to live up to its promises did not extend into an indictment of the Soviet project as a whole. Podlubnyi stopped short of such criticism, because it threatened to destroy his positive sense of self and marginalize him in Soviet society. He exercised a considerable degree of self-censorship, aware that by articulating anti-Soviet statements he risked not only being publicly relegated into the camp of the class enemy, but would also be forced to condemn *himself* as bourgeois or, even worse, as a hereditary *kulak*. To the extent that he did assume a critical voice, his criticism reproduced the Bolshevik regime of truth. Podlubnyi could denounce Stalin or even the entire Bolshevik leadership as inhuman and cruel, but he could not question the overall configuration of the world in which he was living, nor the purposes to which the Soviet state had committed itself.

NOTES

This article is reprinted from *Jahrbücher für Geschichte Osteuropas*, Bd 44, Heft 3 (1996), pp. 344–373.

1 Of all the people who supported me in this project, I would like to thank in particular Leopold Haimson, Igal Halfin, and Peter Holquist for their comments and suggestions, and Nadieszda Kizenko and Daniel Brandenberger for their editorial help. I am indebted to Bernd Bonwetsch for his relentless support, and to the Deutsche Forschungsgemeinschaft for funding the research and writing of this study.
2 In this connection, researchers pin high hopes on the recently declassified surveys (*svodki*) conducted by the Soviet secret police on the "moods of the population." It would be misleading, however, to treat this source body as an unmediated window to popular belief. First, if we assume that Soviet citizens in the 1930s lived in fear of being surrounded by GPU informants, they tended to present themselves – even to friends – in a way conforming to Soviet values. It is therefore difficult to imagine how GPU informers could penetrate beyond what were once more public appearances and attitudes.

Second, and more important, while writing their reports, informants subjected their observations to a process of selection, organization, and translation, so as to make them fit with the GPU's peculiar agenda and preconceptions. Consequently, these reports are more telling about the security police and its interests (the political stability of the Soviet regime in the first place) than about "real" popular beliefs.

3 This approach is inspired by Michel Foucault whose studies seek to make visible the operation of microscopic networks of power relations within the modern individual. Whereas the early Foucault viewed the individual solely as an object dominated by a variety of heteronomous agents – language and the modern state, in particular – he later came to reconsider the self as agent and ethical subject. These seemingly contradictory views are bracketed by Foucault's conceptualization of the self as a construct and site of domination. In his final works, Foucault drew particular attention to a range of self-practices – such as confessing and record-keeping – as catalysts of individual subjectivity (*Technologies of the Self. A Seminar with Michel Foucault*, ed. Luther Martin *et al.*, Amherst, 1988; see also Michel Foucault, The Subject and Power. Afterword, in: Michel Foucault, *Beyond Structuralism and Hermeneutics*, eds. Hubert Dreyfus, Paul Rabinow Chicago 1982).

4 Carl Friedrich, Zbigniew Brzezinski, *Totalitarian Dictatorship and Autocracy*, 2nd rev. edn. Cambridge, MA, 1965, especially pp. 295–298. This viewpoint has also found support in memoirs of the Stalin era written by members of the intelligentsia; cf. Nadezhda Mandelshtam, *Hope Against Hope*, New York, 1970; Eugenia Ginzburg, *Journey into the Whirlwind*, New York, 1967.

5 Aleksandr Zinov'ev, *Gomo Sovetikus*, Lausanne, 1982.

6 See in particular Sheila Fitzpatrick, *Education and Social Mobility in the Soviet Union, 1921–1934*; Cambridge, 1979; by the same author: *The Russian Revolution 1917–1932*, Oxford, New York, 1982; J. Arch Getty, *The Origins of the Great Purges: The Soviet Communist Party Reconsidered, 1933–1937*, Cambridge, 1985; Gabor Rittersporn, *Simplifications Stalinistes et Complications Sovietiques*, Paris, 1987; Hiroaki Kuromiya, *Stalin's Industrial Revolution. Politics and Workers, 1928–32*, Cambridge, 1988.

7 Stephen Kotkin, *Magnetic Mountain: Stalinism as a Civilization*, Berkeley, 1995, pp. 151–152, 223–225.

8 In late 1939 Podlubnyi was arrested on charges of speculation and sentenced to 18 months of labor camp. He was freed in May 1941. At that point Podlubnyi resumed writing his diary, and he has been writing to the present day. The diary for the period 1931–1939 is deposited in the Moscow based *Tsentr Dokumentatsii "Narodnyi Arkhiv"* (TsDNA), fond 30, opis' 1, dela 11–18. It consists of 980 hand-written pages. The frequency of the entries in general is high; breaks of over a month or so are rare, except for the period of January to November 1937, during which he did not write at all. An abridged version of the diary has been published in German: *Tagebuch aus Moskau 1931–1939*, ed. Jochen Hellbeck (München, 1996). Russian and English editions are in preparation.

9 The title read: "Work diary of the '9th Komsomol Congress' brigade and daily notes of the brigadier and FZU student St[epan] Fil[ippovich] Podlubnyi."

10 Although a great number of diaries from the Stalin period have become accessible to researchers in recent years, few of them match Podlubnyi's diary in scope and the level of introspection. Most known diaries of the period were produced by high-ranking Soviet officials, writers, or artists who felt

especially exposed to the threat of the Great Terror and therefore exercised a considerable degree of self-censorship; to cite just a few: A.G. Solov'ev, "Tetradi krasnogo professora (1912–1941 gg.)," in: *Neizvestnaia Rossiia. XX vek.* T. 4. Moskva, 1993, pp. 140–228; A. Afinogenov, *Pis'ma, dnevniki*, Moskva, 1977 = *Izbrannoe v dvukh tomakh.* T. 2; A. Afinogenov, "Dnevnik 1937 goda," in: *Sovremennaia dramaturgiia* (1993) no. 1, pp. 219–233, no. 2, pp. 223–241, no. 3, pp. 217–239; K.I. Chukovskii, *Dnevnik 1930–1969*, Moskva, 1994. Two especially noteworthy diaries from the younger generation, roughly Podlubnyi's age, should be mentioned: Iu. Baranov, *Goluboi razliv: dnevniki, pis'ma, stikhotvoreniia, 1936–1942*, Iaroslavl', 1988; A.G. Man'kov, "Iz dnevnika riadovogo cheloveka (1933–1934 gg.)," in: *Zvezda* (1994) no. 5, pp. 134–183. A compilation of fascinating diary selections, for the most part not published before, has just appeared: *Intimacy and Terror: Soviet Diaries of the 1930s*, eds, Veronique Garros, Natalia Korenevskaya and Thomas Lahusen, New York, 1995.

11 The best treatments of collectivization and industrialization and their social repercussions include Merle Fainsod, *Smolensk under Soviet Rule*, New York, 1958; Moshe Lewin, *The Making of the Soviet System: Essays in the Social History of Interwar Russia*, London, 1985; Sheila Fitzpatrick, in "Ascribing Class: The Construction of Social Identity in Soviet Russia," Chapter 1 in this volume; Kuromiya, *Stalin's Industrial Revolution*; David Hoffmann, *Peasant Metropolis: Social Identities in Moscow, 1929–1941*. Ithaca, London, 1994.

12 Iurii Druzhnikov, a Soviet writer who later emigrated, discovered in the 1970s that Morozov's story had been fabricated at least in part. Among other things his father was not a *kulak* but the chairman of a rural soviet (Sheila Fitzpatrick, *Stalin's Peasants: Resistance and Survival in the Russian Village After Collectivization*, New York, Oxford, 1994, pp. 255–256).

13 This instance strikingly illustrates the patterns of peasant in-migration to the cities, in particular the use of village networks (*zemliachestvo*), investigated by Hoffman, *Peasant Metropolis*, pp. 54–72.

14 TsDKA: The Central House of the Red Army.

15 In an interview I conducted with Podlubnyi, he remembered that during his second trip to the Ukraine in 1936, when he was already a student, he feigned the appearance of an *intelligent* and wore fake glasses, in order to impress people in his old village. The same pattern of self-identification is visible in Podlubnyi's correspondence. Throughout the 1930s he actively sought to sustain a connection with his childhood friends from the village. Most of them had left the Ukraine; some had been dekulakized like him, others had left on their own for the cities and industrial sites; In these letters Podlubnyi portrayed himself as a committed and "cultured" student, mentioning how much money he earned and emphasizing the difference in the quality of life between Moscow and the "periphery," where the recipients of his letters lived; see for example his letter of April 7, 1935, to a cousin, Kornei Krivoruka (TsDNA, f. 30, op. 1, ed. khr. 46).

16 Friedrich and Brzezinski, *Totalitarian Dictatorship and Autocracy*, pp. 295–298. For a popular textbook replicating the dichotomy of private versus public beliefs, see Geoffrey Hosking, *The First Socialist Society: A History of the Soviet Union from Within*, Cambridge, MA, 1985, pp. 218–219.

17 The Bolsheviks were less concerned with man's outward attitude than with the state of his soul. Their goal was to persuade the population that the revolutionary process was a manifestation of historical necessity. Man was to engage himself in the program of building socialism out of his own will.

This urge to appropriate the soul also explains the Bolsheviks' obsession with transparency in public life, as evidenced in the frequent practice of purges and show trials. The goal of a show trial was to bare the soul of the defendant, in order to reveal his "real" attitude toward socialism. Accordingly, party members facing trial attempted to persuade the public that their "conscience" was "clean." (A case in point is Bukharin's letter "To a Future Generation of Party Leaders" which he dictated to his wife shortly before his arrest. See Roy Medvedev, *Let History Judge: The Origins and Consequences of Stalinism*, New York, 1989, pp. 366–367; see also Boris Groys, *The Total Art of Stalinism*, Princeton, 1992, pp. 58–62.)

18 Read: Mitia's poem.

19 Katerina Clark, *The Soviet Novel: History as Ritual*, Chicago, London, 1981.

20 Bolshevism and Nietzschean thought both viewed the will as the central moving force of human development. In distinction to Darwin, who discarded any psychic influence on evolution, Nietzsche proclaimed the birth of superman through an act of will. To be sure, official Stalinist culture never acknowledged its indebtedness to Nietzsche, as the philosopher was regarded as an exponent of "nihilism" and "individualism" (Michael Agursky, "Nietzschean Roots of Stalinist Culture" in *Nietzsche and Soviet Culture*, ed. Bernice Glatzer Rosenthal, Cambridge, 1994, pp. 261–262).

21 Lucien Febvre, *The Problem of Unbelief in the Sixteenth Century: The Religion of Rabelais*, Cambridge, MA, 1982. I am indebted to Stephen Kotkin for his suggestion to apply this method to the study of Stalinism.

22 Western historians are largely in agreement that Stalin masterminded the Kirov murder; cf. Robert Conquest, *Stalin and the Kirov Murder*, New York, 1989; Robert Tucker, *Stalin in Power: The Revolution from Above, 1928–1941*, pp. 288–302. One of the first to indict Stalin for the murder was Nikita Khrushchev in his secret speech to the Twentieth Congress of the CPSU in 1956. A well-researched recent publication on the subject concludes, however, that Stalin's responsibility for the murder cannot be established. Pointing to the close relationship between Stalin and Kirov – the Leningrad secretary was the only comrade with whom Stalin would go to the bathhouse – the author is convinced that Kirov was not murdered on Stalin's orders: A.A. Kirilina, *Rikoshet, ili, skol'ko chelovek bylo ubito vystrelom v Smol'nom*, St. Petersburg, 1993; a similar position has been maintained by J. Arch Getty, "The Politics of Repression Revisited," in *Stalinist Terror: New Perspectives*, ed. J. Arch Getty, Roberta Manning, Cambridge, 1993, pp. 40–64. There is no doubt, however, that Stalin used the murder as a pretext to launch a terror campaign against his foes.

23 In her diary, Iuliia Piatnitskaia, the wife of a high-ranking Komintern official, reached the same conclusion that her unbelief was the manifestation of an "illness," isolating her from society (entries of 21.3.1938 and 28.5.1938). Piatnitskaia began to keep her diary when her husband was arrested in 1937 (Iuliia Piatnitskaia, *Dnevnik zheny bol'shevika*, Benson, VT, 1987).

24 The antithetical nature of Podlubnyi's thought of suicide in relationship to the norms of the Stalinist system is further confirmed by the way in which he phrased it: "One can always stop living, but one can do that only once" (6.12.37). This phrase stands in implicit dialogue with Ostrovskii's novel *How the Steel Was Tempered*, whose main argument is that one lives only once (Nikolai Ostrovskii, *Kak zakalialas' stal'*, in: *Sochineniia v trekh tomakh*, T. 1. Moskva, 1969, especially pp. 374–375). I am grateful to Al'bert Nenarokov for this insight.

25 This is a famous quote from Gor'kii's *Lower Depths*. Podlubnyi's usage of this phrase illustrates both the boundaries and logic informing his critical thought.

26 As Stephen Kotkin has compellingly demonstrated, a core component of the Stalinist system's self-definition resided in its claim as a socialist welfare state. Kotkin further argues that this claim was most effective in neutralizing all conceivable sources of opposition toward the regime, because any attempt to challenge it would have been tantamount to endorsing the capitalist system, which was unthinkable in the Soviet 1930s (Kotkin, *Magnetic Mountain*, pp. 18–21, 227–228). Podlubnyi's case suggests, however, that Kotkin underrates the resources available to members of Soviet society to undermine the system's claims "from within."

27 Robert Thurston, "Fear and Belief in the USSR's 'Great Terror': Response to Arrest, 1935–1939," *Slavic Review*, 45 (1986), 213–244, esp. 224.

28 Bernd Bonwetsch, "Der Stalinismus in der Sowjetunion der dreißiger Jahre. Zur Deformation einer Gesellschaft", in: *Jahrbuch für Historische Kommunismusforschung* 1 (1993) pp. 11–36, here pp. 33–34.

29 In her essay on the evolution of Russian legal culture, Laura Engelstein overlooks the potential for subjectivity in an illiberal society. Defining subjectivity strictly in the liberal sense as the body of rights that assure the inviolability of an individual, she argues that after 1917, with the law becoming a tool in the hands of the Soviet state, subjectivity could no longer exist – it turned into "submission." In effect, her judgment seems to be based on a misunderstanding of the Foucauldian term of "subjectivity." Engelstein understands it as synonymous with the liberal notion of individualism, whereas Foucault had in view the general phenomenon of the modern self, as it is shaped by mechanisms of introspection and self-perfection; Laura Engelstein, "Combined Underdevelopment: Discipline and the Law in Imperial and Soviet Russia," *American Historical Review*, 98 (1993), no. 2, pp. 338–353.

4

DENUNCIATION AND ITS FUNCTIONS IN SOVIET GOVERNANCE

From the Archive of the Soviet Ministry of Internal Affairs, 1944–53

Vladimir A. Kozlov

According to Vladimir Dahl, author of the *Interpretive Dictionary of the Living Great-Russian Language* published in the second half of the nineteenth century, a denunciation is "not a petition or complaint on one's own behalf, but the revelation of the illegal acts of another."[1] In the nineteenth century the word "denunciation" did not convey a clear pejorative meaning. Alexander Pushkin considered "Kochubei's denunciation of the evil hetman to Tsar Peter" a completely positive act [the reference is to the treason of the Ukrainian hetman Mazeppa during a war between the Swedes and the Russians in the early eighteenth century]. Most probably it was only in the Soviet period, especially after the wave of bloody political denunciations in the 1930s, that the word "denunciation" took on a negative, even repugnant, connotation. S.I. Ozhegov, compiler of the *Dictionary of the Russian Language*, noted this development along with his definition: "a secret revelation to government representatives of some kind of illegal activity."[2]

The negative connotation of the word "denunciation" in the modern Russian language not only reflects essential shifts in the traditional culture of Russian society, but also sets up psychological obstacles to understanding the actual social phenomenon signified by the word. The fact is that archaic survivals within the political culture of the USSR – the almost complete absence of a tradition of legal resolution of conflicts between political institutions and the individual, between the rulers and the ruled; the extremely limited legal rights of the population to organize autonomously; the anxiety generated in the individual by the feeling of a direct psychological connection to the central power

– made denunciation more than anything else an essential element in Russia's traditional system of bureaucratic governance, and only secondarily a moral problem, understood within the context of conceptions of good and evil.

While the denunciation of those close to one – of a relative, a neighbor or a co-worker – was always considered an act deserving of moral censure (thus "everyday ethics" did mark out and protect the boundaries of the autonomous personality against the state), matters stood otherwise when it came to the denunciation of the malfeasance of "the bosses" – local officials and bureacrats. Making such a move often demanded courage and a readiness to suffer "for the people." It is simply impossible to imagine how the central government could have maintained any control over its local agents without many such acts, carried out every day, year in and year out. For long periods of time bureaucrats scattered throughout the vast spaces of Russia were able to act independently and arbitrarily, following the dictates of their own self-interest rather than the greater good of the state. Within the complex of interrelations among the populace, the bureaucracy, and the central power (and in this instance it is not important who the central power was, whether the monarch, the Party chiefs, or even the Central Committee of the Communist Party), the institution of the denunciation functioned as a communicative back channel in the cumbersome, ineffective, but nonetheless stable governing apparatus. Denunciation was an important element of the culture of governance for many centuries.

The denunciation, along with petitions of complaint to the "big bosses" over the heads of the bureaucrats and officials who oppressed and abused the people, substituted for courts and other institutions of civil society. The denunciation gave the population a final hope that justice would be done, preserved for the central power an aura of infallibility and righteousness, and redirected the population's dissatisfaction down the channel of "local criticism." For these reasons, I would argue that the evolution of the institution of denunciation in Russia must be viewed within the framework of overall research into the history of Russian government, as a specific case of paternalistic statism in an "underdeveloped" country. [. . .]

I should note right away that in my opinion the denunciations sent in to the NKVD[3] from 1944 to 1953 differ little from denunciations of earlier or later periods in motivations for composition, the denouncers' psychology, or the rhetoric employed (which usually either was borrowed from official propaganda or used the traditional Russian schema of the "Good Tsar," protector of the people, versus his evil servants). This latter case illustrates the stability and persistence of denunciation as a back channel in the system of bureaucratic governance of Russia and the USSR. [. . .]

There are very few instances of political denunciation among those I have studied. This is due to the fact that after the division of the NKVD into two independent People's Commissariats, political denunciations were investigated (and stored) by the People's Commissariat of State Security of the USSR (NKGB), which had the functions of a secret political police. The NKVD principally retained regular police functions, such as battling crime, management of places of incarceration, utilizing and controlling forced labor, organizing the passport system, and so on. In addition, some of the denunciations that served as the basis for juridical or extrajuridical repression ultimately ended up in the files of courts and investigative agencies, which were stored in other archives.

Most denunciations in the NKVD/MVD archive are devoted to the ordinary themes of Russian denunciation: abuse of power; bureaucratic neglect of duties or financial misdemeanors; and so-called "moral breakdown," ranging from alcoholism to marital infidelity, corruption, bribe taking, and theft of state funds. In this sense they have a routine, "timeless" character, and they give us the opportunity to look into the ordinary, traditional forms of denunciatory activity in Russia and the USSR. These forms differ somewhat from the hysterical denunciations made during the "Great Terror" in the 1930s, but the differences lie more in their numbers than in their motivations, techniques of composition and rhetoric. At the same time it is obvious that precisely this persistent tradition of denunciation, existing at all times as an instrument of back channel communication in the Russian administrative system and as a part of the political culture of the people, could in certain situations be dry kindling for a bonfire of massive political repression. The leader's exhortation and the eagerness of subordinates and deputies to get their bosses' jobs no matter what the cost were enough to get the machinery of denunciation working at full speed. This machinery always had an opportunity to use experienced, clever "cadres," a numerous "reserve army" of "amateurs," and it enjoyed great legitimacy in the eyes of the people, who hungered for order and for the punishment of the bureaucrats who constantly abused and insulted them. [...]

The structure of this chapter mirrors the social history of the denunciation, addressing in turn the types of authors, their motivations for writing, the peculiarities of their style and rhetoric, the means of registering their complaints, the procedural controls and investigative routines, the bureaucracy's self-defense mechanisms, the efficacy of denunciation, and the subsequent fates of both denouncers and denounced.

Clearly, it is impossible to present the results of such a broad investigation in one chapter. I shall focus only on a few of the more important points, attempting to formulate a series of working hypotheses without making any claim to comprehensive research coverage or to totalizing conclusions. Nor have I set myself the task of presenting a complete classification of denunciations and denouncers: there are too many facets to the subject. One could do an entire study of the characteristics of lower-level denunciation of managers or of co-workers within the bureaucracy, or of the distinction between rural/provincial denunciations and those written by city residents. For the latter, the local government was too abstract and distant an entity to justify a general denunciation of corruption within the entire urban apparatus. Such broad denunciations were more typical of rural localities or small towns where bureaucrats' activity and personal relationships were constantly in public view, where administrative connections had a deeply personalized character, and where the circle of collective accountability among bureaucrats (*krugovaia poruka chinovnikov*) was more developed. Another entirely separate topic might be the comparison of anonymous denunciations, written over pseudonyms or made-up names, with those whose authors did not hide their identity.

This chapter touches on all these questions, but I have chosen to base my typology on the identity of the denouncer and on his or her motivation – in particular, on the presence or absence of motives of personal gain in his or her turning "to those above."

"Disinterested" denunciations

Among the documents of the NKVD denunciations are often found which are written without any obvious personal motives and which are imbued with an abstract striving toward justice, a desire to expose "the enemies of the party and the people." In such denunciations the authors do not achieve anything for themselves – at least not directly. One denunciation from the Zaporozh'e district reads:

> Prosecutor Ostrokon' of the Mikhailovskii district is a criminal. He destroys Red Army families, misappropriates kolkhoz produce, undermines the kolkhoz finances, and is rude to those who register complaints. Such plaintiffs get bad treatment. Often the prosecutor refuses to receive a plaintiff who has traveled many kilometers. During working hours he goes about his personal business. It is time to investigate this person!
>
> He is repeating the year 1933. This fellow has traveled down the wrong path. Although he cheers, "Long Live Soviet Power!" he quails before Soviet power. There are many signs of trouble here, and the people are concerned.
>
> Red Army soldier K. Sokolov
> Let's finish the war and clean things up!
> 2 December, 1944.4

Such attempts to unmask others are often so angry and convoluted that they seem nonsensical. They were authored by people who sincerely believed in the fairness of the central government and in the possibility of restoring justice. Often such a complaint was simply a cry from the soul of a person from the lower levels of society, directed to the higher arbiter and not referring to any real facts. The role of selfless defenders of justice was also often filled by members of the local intelligentsia, and in taking it on, they condemned themselves to long and fierce battles with corrupt bureaucrats.

Such "disinterested" denunciations were directed against specific individuals (immediate supervisors and co-workers). One example is the official report of the Deputy Chief of Police of the Estonian Soviet Socialist Republic, Golubkov, to a Deputy Commissar of the Estonian NKVD, Kiselev.[5]

> I consider it essential to inform you of the following:
>
> On Saturday, 8 August of this year I had a discussion with the Director of the NKVD Police Command, Comrade Logusov. In the discussion he told me that one of the Deputy Commissars of the NKVD, Comrade Kal'vo, is a nationalist and has a very bad attitude toward Russians.[6] According to Comrade Logusov, Comrade Kal'vo once asked him during conversation (they always speak in Estonian) if he were concealing something from him (Kal'vo), since it seemed to him that Logusov was not passing on to him necessary information.
>
> On receiving Logusov's answer that he (Logusov) was concealing nothing from him (comrade Kal'vo), comrade Kal'vo then said to Logusov: "All right, don't worry. When we go to Estonia, we'll show them our teeth."
>
> This "We'll show them our teeth," Logusov explained to me, "refers to Russians."[7]

The above "report" demonstrates, or in any case allows us to assume, the existence of a specific personality type especially inclined to write denunciations. It is characteristic that the main source of compromising information in the "report" – Logusov – did not write the denunciation. This dirty job was taken on by another person, who himself had no compromising information on Kal'vo.

The author of the denunciation of Kal'vo does not put forward any personal requests: this is a classic example of the selfless "announcement of the illegal actions of another person." Devoid of any special rhetorical strategies, it contains only information touching upon a single fact known to the denouncer. The only thing of which the author can be suspected is a concealed careerism, and the documents we have reviewed neither refute nor confirm this suspicion. However, there is a more important point here. The report quoted above was swiftly used in a complicated judicial intrigue. Logusov's oral communication went into the written report of Lieutenant Colonel Golubkov, which in turn became an extremely important part of the denunciation that followed – presented this time not as a "report" (*raport*) but as "reference materials" (*spravka*) on Deputy Commissar of Internal Affairs of the Estonian Soviet Socialist Republic, Police Colonel A.Ia. Kal'vo, signed by Deputy Commissar Kiselev. This document is a typical denunciation, but its author is obviously attempting to make the details it includes more believable by labelling it "reference materials," like an ordinary bureaucratic document.

[. . .] In using this term [*spravka*] for his denunciation Kiselev was attempting to follow the canons of composition for such a document. In trying to prove the devotion of Kal'vo to the ideas of Estonian nationalism, he was creating the impression of objective research into Kal'vo's life. The author of the *spravka* quoted "several verbal signals about the 'strange' position and line of conduct which Kal'vo maintained in relation to colleagues of Russian nationality." "They [Kal'vo's Russian colleagues] report," he wrote, "that Kal'vo carries out any requests made by Estonian colleagues and refuses all those made by Russians. Recently he has begun to surround himself with Estonian police workers who are under investigation by the counterintelligence department SMERSH."[8]

In his *spravka*, Colonel Kiselev utilized Lieutenant Colonel Golubkov's written "report" as the only real evidence of Kal'vo's guilt. The *spravka* initiated a whole series of political accusations and graphically demonstrates how denunciation could serve not only as an effective instrument of official intrigue but also as an important means of forcing government bureaucrats to adhere to state policies. In this case the attack on Kal'vo fizzled out: in the upper margin of the *spravka* there was noted the bureaucratic resolution typical of such cases: "To be filed." The central authorities probably did not consider the accusation serious enough. However, the resolution of this particular case does not change my overall interpretation of the social function of such communications to the upper-level "bosses."

An officer of the NKVD was always threatened with denunciation, and this constant fear guaranteed his political and bureaucratic loyalty. In fact, most Soviet bureaucrats lived under the weight of the illusion of total oversight (*kontrol'*) over their political reliability and behavior. (I speak of an "illusion" because it was not the oversight that was total but, rather, the fear generated by the potential for continuous oversight, the unrelenting sense of looming danger.) The fear of the "stool-pigeon" (*stukach*) so characteristic of Soviet life was founded not on a myth of mass denunciation but on the perpetual risk of being "misunderstood" and becoming the victim of a routine "disinterested" denunciation.

While the denunciation of colleagues and immediate supervisors leads one to suspect concealed bureaucratic intrigue and secret personal motives, the "disinterested" denunciations of local authorities' malfeasance appear to be the offspring of a peculiar denunciatory "graphomania." Some such denunciations may indeed have been born of the play of demented imagination and paranoia. The deputy director of the Moscow district NKVD office, one Polukarov, described in this way the author of more than 300 denunciations, addressed to every imaginable (and unimaginable) destination: "He systematically wrote letters of a troublemaking and slanderous character . . . to central and regional organizations, both Party and Soviet,"[9] adding that "as a rule, investigation did not confirm the allegations made in the letters."[10] In contrast, the author of another denunciation, Ivanov, confessed: "I have also given you information in the past. While I have never been charged with deceiving you, I have suffered unpleasantness at the hands of several individuals."[11] Ivanov represented an unusual type, the professional fighter for justice (*borets za spravedlivost'*) – though it is true that he did strongly resemble a traditional "troublemaker" (*sklochnik*). It was not coincidental that while serving with troops of the Moscow anti-aircraft defense force (MPVO) he was deputy chairman of the People's Court and a member of the cafeteria "control commission": in short he was constantly watching the people around him and "educating" them. Ivanov carried a reputation with him from one workplace to the next. Co-workers feared him and told potential victims of Ivanov's "vigilance": "he is a very dangerous man; when he was serving in the battalion, he informed on us . . . "[12] Word that someone was capable of a "disinterested" denunciation of co-workers or acquaintances spread widely, surrounding the denouncer with a wall of estrangement and fear. (Ivanov complained about this to Beria, head of the NKVD, incidentally.) "Writers" afflicted with the mania of suspecting and exposing others were not loved even within the NKVD system, especially if their "artistic compositions" were directed against co-workers. They "got the squeeze," "got nailed," or were denied promotion.[13]

Another fighter against malfeasance and disorders, Kovalev, a prisoner at the NKVD labor camp in Noril'sk, was, judging by the texts of his denunciations, as sincere and disinterested as Ivanov. He was in the habit of numbering his statements at the top, and his persistence may be judged by a document I came across bearing the number 318. Naturally, this flood of complaints aroused the ire of the camp's administrators, who accused him of making "provocative declarations." (These same administrators had originally proposed Kovalev for early release from camp; it was only later that his accusations began to escalate.) The Deputy Commissar of the All-Union NKVD was relatively tolerant of this behavior, but he also instructed the administrators to give the truth-seeker "a really serious warning" about "the inappropriateness of submitting one statement after another, to a total of over 300," and to rebuke him on that account.[14]

Such denunciations frightened those in the vicinity precisely because they were written, as it were, "from love of the art," and so it was not possible to use standard defenses against them – discrediting the denouncer or exposing his personal interest in the matter. Nonetheless, most of the authors of the denunciations I studied did not suffer from this kind of denunciation mania. I have encountered many "pure" denunciations – "pure," that is, from the point of view of the authors' motives – that were written by completely normal people who despaired of getting justice on the local scene.

(When I had nearly finished this chapter, I was surprised to discover that I had been unconsciously using a certain "code" to reflect the difference between "interested" and "disinterested" denunciations. The authors of "interested" denunciations I unhesitatingly called "informers" [donoshchiki], using a word that has clear pejorative connotations in contemporary Russian. But to refer to those who did not have obviously self-serving motives, who did not engage in slander but fought for justice however they understood it, I used the term "denouncer" [donositel'], which has a more neutral meaning and simply signifies a type of activity without conveying a negative attitude to that activity.)

As a rule, the authors of "disinterested" denunciations give the impression of being fearless and ready to fight stoically for justice. Some of them appear to be driven by forces beyond normal dedication or even denunciation mania; we might think of such individuals as being afflicted by a particularly severe and incurable sort of "denunciation virus," whose symptoms include the use of highly politicized rhetoric and a set of images and metaphors standard for Soviet political culture.

"Disinterested" denunciations based not on concrete facts but on a general moral indictment of "the bosses' " corruption were often anonymous or had in place of a signature a pseudonym or label – "One of your own" (Svoi), "Partisan," "Red Army soldier," "Party member" and so forth – designed to present the author to the higher authorities as "one of their own." A pseudonym might also be used to forestall the unfortunate psychological impression created by anonymity: the absence of a signature would automatically provoke doubts about the "pure motives" of the denouncer, leading to suspicions that he was personally interested in the results of his denunciation.

Local authorities often criticized "disinterested" denunciations as an "anti-Soviet activity" growing out of an alternative political culture that transgressed the limits of permissible Communist rhetoric. In denunciations of this kind, criticism and exposure of "unjust state servitors"[15] went beyond the conventional dichotomy between a "good" central authority and "bad" local bureaucrats, and turned into criticism of the political system itself. During Khrushchev's time this type of denunciation evolved into a specific form of "anti-Soviet propaganda": anonymous letters, addressed to the highest Soviet leaders, criticizing the regime. Copies of these letters were mailed to many people and usually dealt with problems in the country at large rather than focussing on any particular district.

I offer as an example one of these "proclamation denunciations," which was written in 1944:

> I want to scream!
>
> When I look around at what is happening, I cannot keep silent. Once upon a time there was the autocracy of the Tsar. Things were clear: there was the lord and his workers. One had rights and the other responsibilities. But in the so-called socialist republic where there is supposed to be socialist rule of law (*zakonnost'*), the purity of which is supposed to be maintained by the Soviet government, something unbelievable is going on.
>
> This government, the only of its kind in the world, was born with such difficulty, so much priceless workers' blood was spilled, so many strong young lives were given with total faith in the shining future. Happy are they who died in that faith, the faith in a shining future for their oppressed, forgotten, but nonetheless beautiful motherland. They did not live to see the scandalous injustice of today.
>
> For three long years, the Soviet land has been drinking human blood, even as it still soaked in the blood of previous wars. For three long years the Soviet people has carried on its back the heavy burden of war. The weight presses upon people, crushing them into the earth. And this burden has been distributed very unevenly. For some the war is immeasurable physical sufferings and spiritual torture; for others it is not so much war as pleasure. Beside those who have emaciated faces, who are wracked by scurvy, who are barefoot and unclothed, you see others who are sated, who have more than they need, who are dressed smartly, lack nothing and live in spacious apartments which are light, warm, dry and well-furnished. What is the war to them? ... [*sic*] And right next to them ... [*sic*] naked degradation. People huddle together in dugouts, crushed in until no more can fit. It's humid, the air is unbearably heavy. The so-called "healthy" are here and also the sick. Dressed in rags, people die from hunger although there is food, die in cold, damp shelters although there is firewood. Nobody helps them. And this is inside Soviet territory, thousands of kilometers from the front.

Where is this sad corner? It is the Turukhansk district of the Krasnoiarsk region . . . [sic] The town of Turukhansk – a regional center with a district Party Committee, a Party Executive Committee, a Prosecutor's office, a People's Court, and so on and so forth, where there sit (and I do mean sit – on their behinds) leaders who do not care for the condition of the district, but only for their personal well-being. They don't care that people are dying of hunger, are dying in the dugouts; it doesn't matter to them that hundreds, indeed thousands of tons of foodstuffs are rotting . . .

Money does not make it easier to buy things. And there's no money anyway. There is only one exit: death by starvation. We've got the right to "employment" (as forced labor!) and the right to eternal rest. The greatest number of deaths occur in transport contingents (Volga Germans and Greeks). But among the regional authorities the opinion about these people is: "It's all the same if they croak." And so people die . . .

Can one protest? Say a word, and you'll disappear! Lawless arbitrariness . . . [sic] It can be compared only with serfdom. That was a hundred years ago. . . . Wartime is used to cover up all kinds of incompetence, indifference and even crime, like a "fig-leaf." And this is happening thousands of miles from the front. If only this leaf were torn away as if should be, that would be a lesson to others!

I just don't have the time or energy to describe all the dirt. No energy, when I see the uselessness of it all. For I am not cheering "Hurrah!" but shouting "Danger!" And that, only as long as I still have my voice. And for that I could lose my voice, too. What I lose once, I won't have to lose again, but the best I can hope to get is prison. You new gentry bastards! It's hard to acquire new habits, forget old ones . . . [sic]

These are all trifles. But when will trifles be treated as great, important matters, and the great matters as trifles? Surely great matters boil down to trifles.

"A Partisan".[16]

The author of this denunciation makes no personal requests or demands. Against the background of a typical denunciation of the local authorities and the usual wartime charges that "the rats in the rear" are "provisioning themselves" (*samosnabzhenie* – the Stalinist equivalent of "corruption"), the author trumpets much louder political motifs: the bureaucratic degeneration of the socialist system ("You new gentry bastards!"), the leaders' betrayal of their avowed principles, and an indictment of the government for demagogy and deception.

"Interested" denunciations

"Interested" denunciations are those written to protect the personal interests of their authors. They occupy an intermediate position between the ordinary petition and the denunciation in the narrow sense of the word, as it was understood by Vladimir Dahl. It is not surprising that documents like these are addressed against immediate supervisors, co-workers, and neighbors. They are almost never found to have in them an abstract desire to achieve justice.

I know of one curious case in which a denunciation that was apparently a "disinterested" exposure of local corruption and "counterrevolutionary statements" among NKVD agents turned out upon investigation to be an "interested" document. Sakhnenko, the regional fire inspector of the Buriat-Mongolian Autonomous Soviet Socialist Republic (the fire command was a part of the NKVD system) accused some collective farm directors of engaging in sabotage during the 1943 harvest. He also accused some local NKVD officials of Buriat nationality (names were not provided) "of rubbing their hands in satisfaction at the prospect of Japan's arrival, saying that when the Japanese come, we Buriats will show you Russians."[17]

The higher leadership of the NKVD naturally became interested in this denunciation, but an investigation proved it to be totally false. It turned out that Sakhnenko wanted only to be transferred back from Buriat-Mongolia to Ukraine. According to the author's own naive confession, the denunciation was written "as a supplement to my official request to be sent on a mission to Ukraine," with the sole "aim of making an 'argument' for a positive decision."[18] The only thing the author achieved with his denunciation was a transfer to another district within the same Buriat-Mongol Republic he disliked so much.

The "interested" denunciation was sometimes used as a means of self-defense. People who were themselves accused of abuses and indicted took to writing denunciations against their persecutors, hoping to carry off a preemptive strike that would make them appear to be victims of "suppression of criticism." In materials related to the investigation of such cases there appeared supplements of the following type: "I must also note that the authors of this statement, Ermakov and Sharapov, were themselves involved in embezzlement of government property and are violators of labor discipline, for which they were removed from their responsibilities by the director of Enterprise Group No. 100. Materials related to their case have been handed over to the proper organs for indictment."[19]

A typical example of such a denunciation is the accusation of one Fediainov, a former employee in the prosecutor's office, against the Chief Military Prosecutor, Afanasiev. In August 1941 Fediainov was caught in a surrounded pocket and lived for two years in German-occupied territory. By the standards of that time this was in itself a serious transgression. Nor was Fediainov able to produce any proof that he had taken part in the resistance against the Germans. In short, he had been "sitting things out" in the German rear. After an investigation, Fediainov was expelled from the Party and thus automatically lost the right to work in the prosecutor's office.

In the opinion of officials at the Communist Party's Central Control Commission (TsKK pri TsK VKP), Fediainov had written a denunciation against his long-time acquaintance, the Chief Military Prosecutor, "only because he himself was in a bad position, as he had lived in occupied territory, and Comrade Afanasiev, as the Chief Military Prosecutor, was obligated (for there was nothing else he could do) to hold off on the decision whether to restore Fediainov to his former job as a military prosecutor until a clarification of the question about his party standing."[20]

Fediainov had chosen not to wait for that decision, but instead had answered with a preemptive strike against Afanasiev, charging that he had ties with an "enemy of the people," former Chief Military Prosecutor Rogovskii, who had been arrested six years earlier. Afanasiev was fortunate. The Control Commission concluded: "Everything that Fediainov writes about Afanasiev has been collected or thought up by him only now, six to seven years after the fact."[21]

One motive for an "interested" denunciation could be the desire to take secret revenge on someone who had offended the writer. One example of this was an anonymous denunciation against the commander of the First Detached Division of the NKVD Special Service troops, Engineer-Major Iadroshnikov. Iadroshnikov had had longtime relations with a former commander of the division, Colonel Khrychikov. Khrychikov used a tried-and-true tactic: he created a commission composed of people loyal to him that was to collect compromising material against his deputy and "drown" him. Even this commission, which the Leningrad District (*okrug*) NKVD counterespionage department (SMERSH) concluded had "tendentious origins," was not able to find any evidence of corruption on Iadroshnikov's part. A repeat attempt to use the same tendentiously selected commission against Iadroshnikov was undertaken, in the opinion of a newly created commission of inquiry, "with clearly slanderous intent by persons Engineer-Major Iadroshnikov had 'offended.' "[22]

A special type of "interested" denunciation is the "petition-denunciation." The authors of such documents are clearly pursuing personal goals as they struggle against some sort of injustice done against them, but the pathos of appealing to central authorities goes beyond the limits of a single episode (for example, "Help a family that was robbed get back their stolen goods") and reaches the level of generalization ("No one is fighting against crime in our region; the people's complaints are ignored"). In this manner a petition on the writer's behalf is given a higher status – one of a denunciation or complaint which is "not for oneself" but "a declaration of the unlawful acts of another." This is meant not only to make a personal petition more convincing but also to wash away any taint of suspicion that the author had self-interested motives in turning to the highest authorities.

Once a personal request was turned into a denunciation, it was cast as part of a fight for higher justice in the name of the "common good," of "the people," of "the state." Authors of such declarations to the authorities tended to be more educated and consciously or unconsciously exploited Russian statist traditions in order to achieve their personal goals. Not only did they place their request within the symbolic system of the dominant political culture but also they used the most effective rhetorical tactics for that system.

For example, Captain N.A. Beliaev wrote to the Deputy Commissar of the NKVD, Kruglov:

> This is why, Comrade Kruglov, I am turning to you concerning this small matter and asking you to demand from the authorities of the city of Serpukhov that effective measures be taken to protect the families of soldiers, especially at such a difficult time. One understood the situation when it was the fascists who pillaged and burned, but something must be done now about the Russian bandits. Send help from Moscow to Serpukhov and protect our families and workers. This situation is a major political issue in Serpukhov.[23]

Having opened with a request for the return of his family's stolen property (for they had lost everything), Beliaev veiled his main motive behind a concern for the common good, presenting his own problem as one brushstroke in the terrifying total picture of a city submerged in a crime wave. This folding of a personal problem into a "big political question" through constant references to the heavy lot of the families of the military servicemen defending the fatherland was a typical rhetorical approach. It was not coincidental that this passage of the petition-denunciation was underlined in blue pencil by an upper-level NKVD official.

Beliaev's request was the product of high-quality creative work by an experienced petitioner. Ordinary petitioners would often, without giving it any deep thought, simply reinforce their very specific petition with more general accusations against the people they were complaining about.[24] Thus they composed supplementary accusations, often of a political nature, in transparent attempts to fortify their personal requests with "higher" motives, to present the petition as "selfless," to obscure their private motives with concern for the general welfare. The existence of various methods for making ordinary petitions mimic denunciations both demonstrates the latter form's higher status and confirms the proposition that denunciations had a special social function in post-revolutionary Russian society.

The rhetoric of denunciations

In almost any denunciation one can find a kind of compulsory minimum of ideological beliefs and moral judgments. The widespread logic was: Soviet power is the best and most just in the world, so how can it bear the illegal and amoral actions of its bureaucrats? Or: A war is on, millions of people are dying at the front, and these traitors who have dug in at the rear are committing offenses against the wives and children of the fighting troops. Or: The authorities are disgracing the title of Communist. Sometimes denunciations against the malfeasance of local authorities concluded with symbolic threats ("Just let us finish the war and we'll clean things up"[25]).

As noted above, such pronouncements – intended to signify that the author of the denunciation was "one of ours," to key into the ideological codes that would open the door to mutual understanding with the higher authorities – often concealed quite different motives. Some authors used standard ideological "frames" sincerely, almost subconsciously; others quite cynically exploited the Communist regime's "favorite" themes. All strove to establish their right of petition to the higher authorities by presenting positive facts about themselves; often this presentation resembled that used in "the lives of the saints."

The motif of "a few words about myself" (*nemnogo o sebe*) was one of the most popular rhetorical ploys. When the author of one denunciation wrote that he was a participant in the October Revolution, a Red Guard in 1917, twice wounded, with permanent war injuries and so on, he was actually trying to "activate" in the consciousness of the reader a whole system of symbols that reflected the basic ideological and political preferences of the government – in this case including the revolutionary past, the author's worker origins and social status, and Soviet patriotism.

The use of applicable ideological codes was supposed to set up a special, almost intimate connection between the informer or denouncer and the regime and to indicate also that the author was deserving of special trust. An ably (professionally?) written denunciation invariably utilized at least one of the rhetorical strategies described above. In the majority of the denunciations I examined, however, the authors also strove not to overuse political rhetoric. Only in a few, relatively rare cases did the denunciators deviate from the principle of the "quick prayer" – that minimal expression of moral and political sentiments that was almost as routine as saying grace before meals in a religious family, which would be enough to activate in the mind of the bureaucrat the system for "recognizing one's own." In the unusual cases where more than a "quick prayer" was offered, the denunciation came to resemble a front-page article from *Pravda*, with a quotation from the latest "great" speeches of Comrade Stalin serving as the central support for the argument (for example, "People must be evaluated and judged according to the results of their activities, according to their abilities").[26] The abuses detailed in the denunciation would then be presented to the reader as contravening the Great Chief's Great Precepts; that is, they would be turned into a political crime.

In addition, some "writers" clearly misused references to their "revolutionary services." As a result the effective approach of "a few words about myself" turned into its opposite: "a lot of words about myself." And this was bound to provoke a negative reaction from the bureaucrats who were required to read and verify the long confessions and autobiographies.

The techniques employed in the writing of denunciations depended primarily upon the author's motives – disinterested pursuit of the truth or personal gain – as well as upon his or her level of education. In spite of superficial similarities, such as the use of rumors or fabrications, there were also fundamental differences.

The phraseology of "disinterested" denunciations against local authorities was directly determined by the educational level of the denouncer. Semi-literate people usually just detailed concrete facts, making no claim to generalization. As a rule they did not employ the devices of political demagogy. "Disinterested" denunciations of this type were founded on a deep conviction that it was possible to get the "real truth" and justice "up there" (*naverkhu*). Their authors not only lacked the ability (because of their educational deficiencies) to provide proof of things that were self-evident to them but, to all appearances, also lacked the desire to do so. They simply appropriated the traditional Russian myth (which could still be applied in a Soviet context) about "the good tsar" and his "bad servants" who deprived the people of truth and justice. In such a system of social concepts, the central authority was supposed to act as an agent "of the people"; it was through this authority that the people were supposed to achieve justice. Without a doubt, the morality of this authority was accepted as a kind of given. In the traditional view, the higher authorities had but one problem: that the immoral and self-serving bureaucrats who represented authority in the regions were not telling them "the whole truth." And since this was so, there was no need for further verbal "stimulation" of the "chiefs" (*vozhdi*): once they knew the truth, they themselves would restore justice.

The naive traditional faith in the limitless fairness of the highest authorities normally accompanied another traditional motif: "The lord (*barin*) will come, and then the lord will sort it out (*nas rassudit*)." Authors of many denunciations wrote insistently to Stalin or Beria: "I beg you to come here yourself." Many denunciations repeated this request in various forms and contexts, but one can always discern the paternalistic traditions of the authoritarian Russian state and the last hope of the "oppressed and debased" for the personal intervention of the leader who was almost as powerful as the Lord God Himself.

It was not only in such petitions to higher authority that traditional consciousness found its expression. Archaic rhetoric, including the expression of values at least officially condemned by Communist ideology, such as anti-Semitism, was generally characteristic of many types of denunciation. It was as if traditional consciousness slipped up here, introducing forbidden motifs. Yet at the same time there was an essential difference between the truly archaic everyday anti-Semitism of the uneducated, with their complaints that Jews dominated trade, and the appeals of educated and semi-educated denouncers who called upon Beria to save "Georgian sports" from Jewish sabotage.[27] This latter denunciation was written a few years before the beginning of the anti-Semitic political campaign officially dubbed "the battle against cosmopolitanism." The author of the denunciation apparently was attempting to make use not only of the official system of political symbols but also of the chauvinistic prejudices deeply rooted (and carefully concealed) in the consciousness of the regime leaders. And quite probably (as the text of the denunciation allows us to suppose) the author knew that these prejudices existed.

Denunciations were often rigged with a system of supplementary arguments that were supposed to strengthen their emotional and logical power. "Social origins as a factory owner," kulak, Nepman, landowner and so on were often cited as incriminating circumstances. In the political culture of Stalinist Russia, belonging to one of these categories was in itself no small sin. And again, some of the authors sincerely believed that simply belonging to such social categories was practically a crime, while others obviously were using the class preferences of the authorities to further their personal interests.

In many cases "disinterested" accusations were clearly written by people who were mentally ill or (as one bureaucrat who had to check out denunciations observed) were inclined to interpret facts incorrectly, giving them a wider meaning than necessary. In other words, "disinterested" informers of this type saw "enemies of the people" everywhere, and their brains built up logical frameworks of "betrayal" from completely innocuous facts.

Such pathological cases would not merit even passing mention here except that I have discovered an analogous logic in "self-serving" denunciations written by completely normal people. For example, the only more or less real fact mentioned in a denunciation against the chairman of the All-Union Arts Committee, Khrapchenko, was the nationality of his wife's relatives (German). Everything else was conjecture and innuendo. On these grounds Khrapchenko was portrayed as the next thing to a German spy, since he had the opportunity to meet with Stalin and might then tell what he heard to his German relatives (who, by the way, lived in another town).[28]

Most slanderous denunciations, in fact, were constructed according to this ingenuous schema. For example, the denunciation written by one Dombrovskii against the director of a Moscow institution of higher education was based on the following real fact: he had recently dismissed eight persons from the institute. On this basis the denouncer concluded that the director was "poisoning and smashing cadres [meaning here 'personnel' or 'human resources']." Investigation revealed that some of the workers had been fired before the tenure of the present director and that others had simply been transferred to new posts upon their graduation from the institution. Only one relevant case was found: "The management of the Institute intends to relieve Comrade Chernaia ... from her post for neglect of her clerical duties."[29]

Other accusations made use of a similar method. In actuality Dombrovskii's slander of the director was constructed like a myth: it contained one real fact and a completely fantastical interpretation. Some "disinterested" denunciations following this rule were written by people who were clearly mentally ill – but the difference between these letters and Dombrovskii's slander is obvious. What was for them a genuine "model of the world" was for Dombrovskii a consciously applied stratagem, a pretense.

A comparison of the rhetorical devices and techniques of "disinterested" and "interested" denunciations suggests that we are dealing with two completely different cultural systems: one that is traditional, sincere, and naive and one that is its cynical imitation. On the one hand, we have the genuine sacralization of leaders; on the other, hypocritical paeans to them. On the one side, there is an almost mystical belief in the traditional paternalism of the higher authorities; on the other, a sanctimonious appeal to that paternalism that relies on the "concern for the common good" sanctioned by official ideology. We have the sincere faith in socialism as heaven on earth, which for many replaced religious faith, contrasting starkly with the calculated use of the symbols and substance of that faith for personal gain.

In truth the legitimacy of the Communist regime rested on a system of traditional Russian values only lightly swathed in the clothing of socialist ideology. This legitimacy was destroyed not by Gorbachev or the democratic movement but by an egotistical individualism which had begun to develop at the core of Stalinist society, which understood the value of socialist demagogy and was able to use it for its own goals. This individualism touched not only "the people," but also the party elite itself.

Those who destroyed the traditional system of values and concepts, among them the authors of many "interested" denunciations, seem unappealing as historical actors. However, the "knights of the era of primitive capitalist accumulation" – representatives of the young and greedy bourgeois class – looked equally unappealing, especially in comparison with the "noble lords" of the waning feudal era.

Fortunately, cynicism was not the only refuge for people torn out of their traditional culture. Oppositional defiance and the beginning of a new ideology of protest existed in embryo within the shell of the traditional "disinterested" denunciation. It is enough to recall, for example, the letter from "A Partisan" quoted above, with its criticism of the system, as opposed to the system's own devious servants, in order to understand that the base compromise and hypocritical egotism were not the only product of the decomposition of the old value system. From it also sprouted sincere and noble protest. [. . .]

Methods of bureaucratic obstruction of denunciations: the circle of collective accountability (*krugovaia poruka*)

The existence of denunciation as a specific form of political culture in traditional society and as a means of social control over the behavior of local authorities in the vast spaces of the USSR was a sword of Damocles hanging constantly over the heads of the bureaucrats. The population, which had no means of democratic control over officials' actions, used denunciation as a means to bring in the central power to resolve this or that conflict, and to defend itself against the malfeasance of local bureaucrats, and to restore justice.

It would have been strange indeed had the bureaucracy not found ways to counteract denouncers and to defend itself against the intervention of the central power. In a situation where even potential centers of opposition were totally suppressed, especially following the "Great Terror" of the 1930s, the chances that low- and middle-level bureaucrats would be able to block the denunciatory activity of the population were substantially higher. The key was to not to "get into anything political," for the authorities could hope to avoid responsibility for economic crimes and malfeasance.

The most farsighted bureaucrats understood this, and strove to make sure that things did not get so bad that the oppressed population would send the most dangerous form of denunciation (the "disinterested" variety) to the highest leaders of the country. Others took a riskier path.

They "broke the rules of the game" by which the "people's government" was supposed to be concerned solely with the people's needs, and created in their jurisdiction, their small city or district, an atmosphere of "suppression of criticism" that made any attempt at denunciation extremely dangerous. Consider, for example, the following description: "The party committee secretaries are completely under the influence of Iosif'ian. Surrounding himself with his own people, Iosif'ian feels himself total master of the situation, he suppresses criticism without fear of reprisal, he does whatever he wants."[30] Such was the picture that many denouncers painted as they embarked on the gamble of joining battle with "the bosses."

At times the local authorities of distant regions and remote places felt that they could act with impunity. A.S. Semenova, a party member from Kursk oblast, wrote to Beria as follows:

> In response to my letter and public statement at the district party meeting about the defects of the work of the district and the kolkhoz in which I live, the district leaders, comrade Shamanin and comrade Abrosimov, organized unprecedented harassment against me. District party representative I.A. Per'kov, together with rural soviet chairman P.A. Kostin and kolkhoz chairman A.P. Golovin, told the kolkhozniks that "Anna Semenovna sent in a denunciation because we lost interest in her" and similar insinuations.
>
> They didn't give me the work assignment I requested. They took away my bread ration. They told Golovin: "Do everything you can to make her leave." He did it with a will.
>
> They tried to get my landlady to evict me from my hut . . . Life became really impossible. Anyway, the hut needed repairs and there was nothing to heat it with. The kolkhoz chairman had the nerve to say: "You're not a fine lady, you can bring some wood from the forest." He knows perfectly well that I can't walk half a kilometer without getting out of breath . . .
>
> One could die from this kind of life.
>
> But I will not die in the hope that Moscow Bolsheviks will investigate the questions that I have raised and protect me from all these horrors.[31]

In many such cases, "the Moscow Bolsheviks" really did intervene and take measures. The central authorities, of course, had to worry about their popularity and their legitimacy in the eyes of the population: this was in the interest of the entire ruling class of Communist Russia. There is nothing more dangerous for rulers than allowing the population to lose all hope of protection and support from the government. So those who "broke the rules of the game" were actually opposing their own estate, and they could expect severe retribution.

For Russian bureaucrats the biggest risk lay not in breaking the laws themselves but in losing their "sense of proportion," their "feeling for their turf," their knowledge of what they could and could not get away with. It was precisely this simple truth that denunciation authors and the regime leaders had in mind when they referred to "out-of-control bureaucrats."

Among the permissible methods of suppressing criticism were various softer forms of pressure on subordinates and the population. Preventing the "critic's" (the denunciation author's) promotion at work, denying him or her use of a collective farm horse, seizing upon minor violations of formal rules and instructions, so as to put the squeeze on the actual or potential denouncer – none of these went beyond the bounds of bureaucratic propriety or put the bureaucrat in a compromising position.

It was another matter to go beyond the accepted bounds, not of the law, but of community ethics. This occurred, for example, when officials were not content simply to "put the squeeze on" authors of complaints and petitions sent to central organs, but went further and actually seized their letters. Yet it was quite widely known that such things happened. People who took the road of confrontation with "the bosses" constantly feared that the local authorities were simply seizing their letters at the post office, acting just as they had in the time of Nicholas the First. (The postmaster in Gogol's play, *The Inspector General*, acted in this way.)

A kolkhoznik named Khoron'ko, author of a denunciation of the malfeasance of officials in Osokarovskii district (Karaganda oblast, Kazakhstan), demonstrated that at least two of his letters had been intercepted by local authorities using the services of the military censor, who had the legal right to seize correspondence or to blank out any information of military significance. According to Khoron'ko, his enemies "were in bed with" the local NKVD and the military censor and "under the pretext of state security protect themselves from Moscow and Soviet justice . . . I have written two letters to Comrade Stalin about the above-mentioned facts. But obviously they did not reach him, but fell into Loshman's hands." (Loshman was a local official persecuting Khoron'ko.) Complaints of this sort were normal in letters reaching the NKVD. It is not surprising that denouncers preferred to avoid using the regular post if they could, sending their letters instead by more exotic routes: they would, for instance, drop them in the boxes set up at the entrances of the NKVD or NKGB buildings or at other offices and organizations, sometimes without an envelope.

In general the conviction of informers and denouncers that local bureaucrats were seizing their letters, and that the country's leaders simply did not know the truth, fed the legend of the "good tsar" and his "evil servants." And indeed the "good tsar" in the person of one Party hierarch or another would, in the name of the central power, severely punish the violators of bureaucratic propriety, those who deviated from the generally accepted rules of the bureaucratic game. They would be removed from their positions and expelled from the party; some were arrested and tried. To judge by the material I have seen, sometimes there were full-scale purges of local bureaucracies or the officials of this or that department, not only for suppression of criticism but also for serious financial malfeasance, abuse of power, corruption, and so on. In the early period such purges were referred to in bureaucratic parlance as "lancing the boil."

In short, there were both legal and illegal methods of suppressing criticism. The corporate morals of the bureaucrats censured gross and obvious violations of law that would discredit the entire bureaucracy in the eyes of the population, but they accepted, or at any rate took a neutral stance toward, more refined traditional methods of self-defense. Intercepting correspondence, using the military censor and postal workers for one's own purposes, was obviously a "shady practice." But other methods yielding analogous results did not provoke distaste even in the central authorities, much less in the lower levels of the bureaucratic estate.

The common practice of returning a denunciation to local authorities was in essence little different from the interception of correspondence. In this case the denunciation most often fell into the hands of those against whom it was written, or of one of their friends and associates, none of whom had any interest in "airing dirty laundry." Such an "investigation" resulted in much unpleasantness for the denouncer. This in turn strengthened the conviction of the populace that the only place to seek justice was at the very top of the pyramid of power – from the just and sinless "chiefs" (*vozhdi*).

Those bureaucrats who avoided gross violations of the rules of the game and did not overstep the bounds of bureaucratic morals were often saved from accountability by patrons at higher levels. Every "big boss" had his own people in local positions, upon whom he depended, whom he trusted, and who were personally devoted to him. If they had good relations with higher-ups the local "bosses" could avoid accountability for serious misbehavior and even crimes.

"Loshmanov knew of these disorders, yet he was merely transferred to another jurisdiction, without punishment." Such phrases appear often in denunciations sent to the NKVD. One usual method of saving "one's own man" from accountability was to punish him for internal disciplinary infractions, even in cases of criminal misconduct. In one of the denunciations I found an egregious example: a man implicated in the rape of one of his female subordinates received as punishment twenty days in jail and a demotion. Cases that developed according to a similar scenario appear frequently in the NKVD Secretariat files: formal measures were taken and the case was filed. In one case, for example, Beria removed an acquaintance from his post as NKVD commander of rear security forces on the Second Belorussian Front for misappropriation of captured materiel, compelling female subordinates to sleep with him, and other crimes and misdemeanors. Without bringing the case to trial, Beria prevented his acquaintance from sinning further – by removing him to another post on another front.

In the bureaucrats' system of defense against denunciation, discrediting the character of the denouncer had an important place. If the denouncer frequently relied on "a few words about myself" to strengthen his case, refutation of the denunciation offered a mirror image of the same ploy. The denouncer, pointing to his services to the regime, tried to show that he was right because he was "one of our own" (*svoi*), while the bureaucrats tried to show that he was wrong because he was "an outsider" (*chuzhoi*). One distorted logic confronted another: it was the denouncer who was discredited rather than his or her information. In general the accused's defense was based on the same rhetorical tactics as the slanderous denunciation: the clear facts were not disputed but simply given another interpretation, more favorable to the denunciation's target. The Soviet bureaucrats' system of corporate self-presentation included one very important postulate: that any "personal motive" of a denouncer who appealed to the central authorities devalued his information, bringing it into question morally and in many cases entirely obviating the necessity of seeking counterarguments or offering a defense. This was especially the case with anonymous denunciations. Refusal to sign almost automatically evoked doubt about whether the denouncer's motives were "pure," leading to suspicion that there was an element of personal interest in the results of the investigation. When an investigation concluded that an anonymous denunciation was slanderous, the revelation of the author's identity, together with some evidence of his or her personal interest in the results of the investigation, were the final stroke proving the complete innocence of the denunciation's victim. (And the search for an anonymous author under the pretext of seeking further information was an important part of any investigation.)

As noted earlier, bureaucrats who observed the rules of the game and knew the limits of the permissible could feel that they were relatively safe and did not need to fear denunciations: they were protected by the network of "collective accountability" based on personal ties. Only the "transgressors," those who grossly violated the written and unwritten rules of behavior and bureaucratic ethics, could seriously suffer from denunciations.

However, under certain circumstances the system of bureaucratic defense against denunciations could malfunction. In the first place, this could occur if the rules of the game were broken by those same higher authorities who had set them up. In unstable or crisis situations, or in the course of major reforms ("revolution from above"), the "chiefs" would appeal directly to the masses, calling on them to expose "enemies" and "saboteurs" and smashing the bureaucracy's congenital conservatism. In this way the stable relationships and the predetermined behavior of the bureaucratic layer of society were broken up. The political symbiosis of "the chiefs," the masses, and the bureaucrats would cease to exist, one part of the bureaucracy would attack another, the denunciatory activity of the masses and of the bureaucrats themselves would reach an apogee, and the investigation of denunciations would become a mere formality. The denunciation as a "normal" instrument of administrative oversight and control, allowing the exposure and punishment of "transgressors," would be converted into a means of political struggle. The system of bureaucratic self-defense against denunciations would cease to work. The destructive potential of denunciation would be fully realized. "The people" would take their revenge upon the bureaucracy, but having smashed the complex, self-regulating equilibrium of the social system at the chiefs' call, they themselves would then become victims of yet greater lawlessness.

In the second place, in certain rare cases the denunciatory activity of the population of one or another region, in combination with an influx of complaints, letters to newspapers, and so on, would reach such magnitude that it became a political rather than an administrative problem. This would force the central power to intervene to reestablish "law and order," breaking up the circle of collective accountability (*krugovaia poruka*) and the whole system of personal ties. In this situation it was no longer safe to save "one's own" people.

In the third place, local "hitches" in the bureaucrats' system of collective accountability in the localities did sometimes occur. One or another institution within the local government structure might begin a struggle for power or attempt to widen its sphere of influence. A wave of mutual denunciations and exposures would begin. The "disinterested denunciations" written "from below" would become a dangerous weapon in the internecine struggle, whether they were truth or slander. This sharply raised any given denunciator's chances of success and stimulated the composition of more and more denunciations. Intervention of the central authorities, undesirable under normal circumstances, would become the only exit from the local crisis of authority.

To use Marx's apt expression, bureaucrats treat the state as their private property. However, the paternalistic statism of the communist regime imbued "the people," at least its more active representatives, with the same feeling. In the resulting conflict between these two positions, neither side could gain the upper hand without smashing the system as a whole. The regime chiefs were the arbiters of the inevitable compromise: indeed, their own power depended upon this conflict between the "masses" and the "apparatus." The denunciation in its turn was one of the instruments of control that maintained the equilibrium of the entire system of relationships which constituted Soviet society. Under certain conditions, it could become one specific factor in dynamic changes in that system, facilitating turnover in the bureaucratic elite and political transformations of the regime. The "ignition key" for these functions was always in the hands of the ruling Communist oligarchy.[32]

NOTES

This is an abridged version of an article published in the *Journal of Modern History*, 68: 4 (December 1996), 867–898. The translation from the original Russian is by Christopher Burton, Matthew Lenoe, and Steven Richmond, edited by Sheila Fitzpatrick.

1 V. Dal', *Tolkovyi slovar' v chetyrekh tomakh. Tolkovyi slovar' zhivogo velikorusskogo iazyka*, vol. 1, A–Z (Moscow, 1989).

2 S.I. Ozhegov, *Slovar' russkoqo iazyka*, 3rd edn (Moscow, 1953), p. 149.

3 Translators' note: The NKVD (= USSR People's Commissariat of Internal Affairs) was renamed as the USSR Ministry of Internal Affairs, or MVD, in 1946. This change was part of a general shift in nomenclature from People's Commissariats to Ministries. But the NKVD also suffered other organizational changes during the war and postwar periods. From 1943 to 1953, the political security administration (Glavnoe Upravlenie Gosudarstvennoi Bezopasnosti) was separated from Internal Affairs as a distinct People's Commissariat–Ministry of State Security, the NKGB/MGB. Other police functions, including issuing passports and administering the labor camp system (gulag), remained with NKVD/MVD.

4 Gosudarstvennyi arkhiv Rossiiskoi Federatsii (GARF), f. 9401, op. 1, d. 2184, l. 1413.

5 Estonia had recently been incorporated into the USSR as the Estonian Soviet Socialist Republic. Its republican NKVD was subordinate to the "All-Union" NKVD in Moscow (editor's note).

6 There were two deputy commissars, Kal'vo and Kiselev (translators' note).

7 GARF, f. 9401, op. 1, d. 4935. l. 273.

8 Ibid., l. 272 ob.

9 Ibid., d. 4933, ll. 119 ob.-20.

10 Ibid., l. 120.

11 Ibid., d. 4934, l. 273.

12 Ibid., d. 4934, l. 277.

13 See, for example, ibid., d. 4930, ll. 363–68.

14 Ibid., d. 4933, l. 57.

15 The Russian phrase ("*nepravednykh gosudarevykh slug*") is archaic, recalling the language of traditional Russian petitions to the Tsar (translators' note).

16 GARF, f. 9401, op. 1, d. 2184, ll. 836–39.

17 Ibid., d. 2141, l. 1441.

18 Ibid., l. 1440.
19 Ibid., d. 4935, l. 60.
20 Ibid., d. 4930, ll. 542–43.
21 Ibid., d. 4930, l. 538.
22 Ibid. , d. 4936, l. 60–64.
23 Ibid., d. 4933, l. 123.
24 See, for example, ibid., d. 4934, ll. 291–92.
25 Ibid., f. 9401, op. 1, d. 2184, l. 1413.
26 Ibid., d. 4934, l. 400.
27 Ibid., d. 4932, ll. 420–23.
28 GARF, f. 9401, op. 1, d. 4930, l. 372
29 Ibid., l. 388.
30 Ibid., l.298
31 Ibid., d. 4931, l. 239.
32 A brief concluding section on the post-Communist era is omitted (editor's note).

5

GAMES OF STALINIST DEMOCRACY

Ideological discussions in Soviet sciences, 1947–52[1]

Alexei Kojevnikov

The Lysenko case has become a symbol of the ideological dictate in science and its damaging consequences. It is often explained that in the years following World War II, the Stalinist leadership launched an ideological and nationalistic campaign aimed at the creation of a Marxist-Leninist and/or distinctively Russian, non-Western science. Concepts and theories which were found idealistic or bourgeois were banned, their supporters silenced. In no other science was this process completed to the same degree as in biology after the infamous August 1948 Session of the Soviet Academy of Agricultural Sciences, at which Trofim Lysenko declared the victory of his "Michurinist biology" over presumably idealistic "formal" genetics. The August Session, in turn, served as the model for a number of other ideological discussions in various scholarly disciplines.

This widely accepted interpretation, however, encounters two serious difficulties. The first arises from a selective focus on one particular debate which best fits the stereotype. It was critics of the Stalinist system who singled out the Lysenko case as the most important example of the application of Soviet ideology to science. The Soviet Communist party viewed it differently. It did regard the event as a major achievement of party ideological work and a great contribution to the progress of science (until 1964, when the mistake was quietly acknowledged). But what is more interesting, and less expected, is that Communists claimed five, not one, major ideological successes in the sciences: philosophy (1947), biology (1948), linguistics (1950), physiology (1950), and political economy (1951).[2] The additional four cases did not become as widely known outside the USSR as the biological one, apparently because they did not fit as well the standard picture of the campaign as an ideological purge.

Their effect on scholarship was not obviously damaging, patterns and outcomes were much more confusing than that of the "clear" Lysenko case, and they did not present the critics of communism with such a perfect example of scandalous failure that could be used in Cold War propaganda.

The second difficulty concerns the apparent incoherence of events. Any straightforward generalization based on the single case of Lysenko could hardly be sustained against a wider factual background. Those who assume that the goal of the campaign was to subordinate science to ideology disagree considerably on what constituted the ideology which had to be applied in the sciences. Indeed, many different ideological principles were pronounced, they often contradicted each other, and none was consistently carried through the entire campaign. Dialectical materialist and Cold War slogans suffused the rhetoric, calling for unity in struggle against idealism, cosmopolitanism, and obsequiousness before the West. At the same time, however, one also frequently encounters attacks on monopolism in science and encouragement of creativity and free criticism. David Joravsky has characterized this ideological mess as a "bizarre mixture of elements," "obvious self-contradiction" for "the outsider," and the "most astonishing incongruity in the Stalinist drive for monolithic unity." At the same time, he noted that, for Stalin, there was no self-contradiction here.[3]

These particular five ideological cases acquired the importance of a general political event and had to be publicized far beyond the circle of directly concerned scholars because Stalin participated in them either openly or behind the scenes. But even having been approved by the same authority, they still form a rather chaotic set, in light of their conflicts, contents, and outcomes. Philosophers met in June 1947 to criticize a book by Georgii Aleksandrov, a high party official who, although demoted, was later appointed to direct the work of his critics.[4] The August 1948 Session, as mentioned above, led to the banning of international genetics in favor of an idiosyncratic and specifically Soviet version.[5] The linguistics controversy presents quite a contrast. In June 1950, after a series of polemical publications in *Pravda*, the candidate for Lysenkoism in linguistics – revolutionary and anti-Western Nikolai Marr's "new doctrine on language" – was silenced in favor of a very traditional and internationally accepted comparative approach.[6] Conceptual disagreements in physiology were not so pronounced when, in July 1950, representatives of this field gathered at the joint session of the Academies of Sciences and of Medical Sciences. Nevertheless, the disciples of Ivan Pavlov fought a serious battle over which of them followed the orthodoxy of their deceased teacher more closely and should therefore direct his physiological institutes.[7] Finally, in November 1951 a closed panel of economists and politicians at the party's Central

Committee discussed the project of a new textbook on political economy. This meeting apparently did not end up with any resolution, but it provided the pretext and inspiration for Stalin to write his last major theoretical opus, *Economic Problems of Socialism in the USSR*.[8]

The variety already displayed in these most-controlled cases increases considerably when one takes into account dozens of other critical discussions reported in the press in 1947–52. They could be as large as an all-Union conference and as small as an institute's meeting devoted to the review of a book or a textbook. Political authorities at some level were occasionally involved, but most of the meetings were organized solely by academics. Ideological argumentation and accusations sometimes were used very heavily, in other cases the discourse was almost scholarly in style and paid only lip service to political rhetoric. In the majority of episodes it is difficult or even impossible to classify the participants according to two categories, such as "Lysenkos" and "true scientists." Disputes could reflect serious conceptual disagreements, but also institutional conflicts or merely personal animosities. Some critical discussions led to serious changes in the academic hierarchy, others only confirmed existing power relations. Their general effect on scholarship can be described as confusing: sometimes negative, sometimes, as in linguistics, more positive, and in many other cases largely irrelevant.[9]

Diverse patterns and results notwithstanding, these discussions taken together constituted a political campaign in the Soviet sense: several highly publicized model events and a number of local reactions and imitations. The very fact of holding a discussion already had a political meaning prior to what its particular outcome would be. My goal is to understand what in this campaign made it look coherent to insiders, Communist practitioners, although it appears irregular and chaotic to us, cultural outsiders.

Understanding the logic of a different culture – Stalinist culture, in this case – asks for anthropological approaches. Elsewhere I have already suggested that regularity can indeed be found, but on the level of formal rules and rites of public behavior rather than in the contents and results of disputes. This idea has helped to explain events in physics and why they ended up differently than in biology.[10] The argument I sketched in earlier papers will be developed here further and applied to three other crucial cases. The Philosophical Dispute of 1947 was not only chronologically the first but also the purest performance staged by politicians themselves. Its analysis will reveal the rules of the Communist games of *diskussiia* (disputation) and *kritika i samokritika* (criticism and self-criticism). An inquiry into the rituals of Stalinist political culture and its special domain called "intra-party democracy" will then be needed to understand both the ascribed functions of these games and the possible motivations of politicians who proffered them to scholars as methods for handling scientific disputes.

Provoked from above, scholars engaged in a variety of academic conflicts while pursuing their own agendas and inventively using available cultural resources in dialogues with politicians. An important thing about these games was that, in theory and often also in practice, their outcomes were not predetermined, but depended upon the play. How scholars interpreted and exploited this particular feature will be shown by analyzing two further contrasting cases – in biology and linguistics.

The campaign of ideological discussions will thus be reinterpreted as the transfer of the rites of intraparty democracy from Communist political culture to academic life. In this process, the rules of public behavior and, to some degree, rhetorical vocabulary, were relatively stable, but they left sufficient room for the unpredictability and diversity that actual events displayed. This model allows me in the end to draw some general conclusions about the relationship between science and ideology, and between scholars and politicians, in Stalinist Russia.

Exercises on the philosophical front

> In Marxism perfectly, / he could express himself and write,
> / admitted mistakes easily, / and repented elegantly.
> Soviet folkloric play on line from Pushkin's *Eugene Onegin*[11]

Even in dictatorial and hierarchical Stalinist Russia, authorities were not entirely exempt from grass-roots criticism. On special occasions such criticism was not only possible but also welcomed, and even required. Soviet philosophers knew this when the Central Committee summoned a representative gathering of them to a meeting on 16 June 1947. Andrei Zhdanov, the Politburo member responsible for ideology and Stalin's current favorite, presided over the meeting and, in a few introductory words, informed the participants that their task was to discuss Georgii Aleksandrov's *The History of West European Philosophy*. Having expressed the hope "that the comrades invited to the discussion will take an active part in it and will freely voice all critical remarks and suggestions," but stopping short of providing any more detailed instructions, Zhdanov opened the meeting and let the panel go.[12]

To understand the humor of the situation, one has to imagine oneself in the shoes of a rank-and-file philosopher who also had to be a party member and for whom Aleksandrov was the official authority, within both the profession and the party. Having not yet turned forty, Aleksandrov had accomplished an extraordinary career within the party apparatus. Zhdanov's protégé, he was appointed in 1940 as director of the Department of Propaganda and Agitation (Agitprop), which together with the Department of Cadres was the most important office in the Central Committee. The following year he was elected candidate member of the Central Committee and member of its Orgburo. Aleksandrov's philosophical publications were devoted to topics more original than one would have expected from a party bureaucrat: Aristotle and pre-Marxist philosophy. In the fall of 1946 he reached the apex of his political career and added to it signs of academic recognition by receiving a Stalin prize for his textbook, *The History of West European Philosophy*, and by becoming a full member of the Academy of Sciences. Zhdanov's rise to favor in 1946 and renewed stress on ideological work placed Agitprop, and Aleksandrov as its head, into the center of the party's political activity. Under normal circumstances, he would be the one who would call in philosophers, scold them for mistakes, and deliver instructions on their job, while they would have considered it a great honor to be invited to publish a laudatory review of his book.[13]

At the Philosophical Dispute, however, the roles were reversed, and philosophers were encouraged to develop a principled critique of the book and its highly placed author. The sort of criticism expected was not an obvious guess: the first attempt to engage in a serious discussion had already been made in January 1947 at the Academy's Institute of Philosophy. It had been prepared by Aleksandrov's colleague from Agitprop, Petr Fedoseev, but the level of criticism failed to satisfy the Central Committee. In Zhdanov's words, discussion was "pale (*blednaia*), skimpy (*kutsaia*), and ineffective." For the second try, Zhdanov himself presided over the meeting, and more participants, in particular from outside Moscow, were invited and encouraged to freely express their disagreements.[14]

The audience fulfilled Zhdanov's hopes and demonstrated a great deal of activity. For more than a week, almost fifty speakers presented their critical comments on the book, and twenty more who had not received time to speak insisted on including their texts as an addendum to the published minutes. Several remarks made it clear that the event was taking place because Stalin had expressed his dissatisfaction with the book.[15] Historian Vladimir Esakov has suggested that the entire chain of events was started by a letter of criticism, or denunciation, by one of Aleksandrov's foes, Moscow University philosopher Zinovii Beletskii. The letter, dated November 1946 and addressed to Stalin, was discussed at the Central Committee Secretariat and prompted the decision to organize a critical discussion.[16]

The philosophers did not know the particularities of Stalin's and the Central Committee's criticisms, if indeed there were any, so they had to develop critiques of their own, guessing about the essence and seriousness of Aleksandrov's mistakes. Within certain limits, the gathering produced a variety of conflicting views on the book's scholarly and political shortcomings. Mark Mitin and Pavel Yudin, the "old guard" of Communist philosophy and Aleksandrov's personal foes, apparently hoped that the event would shake up the young Turk's career and restore their own importance in the field. Supported by Beletskii and Aleksandr Maksimov, they spoke against "conciliatory attitudes" displayed during the previous discussion of the book and called for a "principled criticism" and for "militant struggle" with bourgeois ideology.[17] More moderate critics included a group of up-and-coming young philosophers like Bonifatii Kedrov and Mikhail Iovchuk, who proposed such slogans as "creative criticism" and "further creative elaboration of Marxist philosophy." Many who did not belong to either "militant" or "creative" camps and had no personal reason to be for or against Aleksandrov used the opportunity to speak before Zhdanov, demonstrate their talents, loyalty, and activity, while not forgetting to mention various personal agendas.[18]

Only after having listened to the others did Zhdanov deliver his talk, in which he summarized the results of the discussion and drew further conclusions. According to him, although deserving encouragement as the first attempt to write a Marxist textbook on the history of philosophy, the book had in general failed to meet its goals. Zhdanov criticized several examples of bad style and unclear definitions and accused Aleksandrov of committing not only factual mistakes but also such political ones as "objectivism" – insufficient criticism of pre-Marxist bourgeois philosophy. According to Zhdanov, the textbook's deficiencies reflected the generally unsatisfactory situation "on the philosophical front." The uncritical reception and laudatory reviews of the book, until Stalin intervened, had demonstrated "the absence of Bolshevik criticism and self-criticism among Soviet philosophers." Combining the slogans of rival philosophical parties, Zhdanov said that Soviet philosophical publications were often scholastic and conciliatory rather than creative and militant, that they stopped short of developing Marxist doctrine further and of fighting against idealistic perversions. Aleksandrov failed to ensure good leadership in the field; "moreover, he relied in his work too much on a narrow circle of his closest collaborators and admirers" – at this point Zhdanov was interrupted by the applause and shouts of "Right!" – and "philosophical work had thus been monopolized by a small group of philosophers."[19]

At the end of the Session, Aleksandrov was given an opportunity to engage in self-criticism. His role was technically the most difficult one: on the one hand, the ritual strictly forbade the use of a defensive tone; on the other, his career would not benefit were he to accept the most serious accusations. For the game to be performed and resolved successfully, and to convince the spectators that his repentance was sincere, Aleksandrov had to estimate correctly the mood of the audience and higher referees and find the right tone of self-accusation. Having done this in the first part of his speech, having thanked everybody for exposing his mistakes, and having summarized them once again, Aleksandrov then shifted his tone to that of a philosophers' instructor and urged everybody to learn from his case and to improve work on the philosophical front.[20]

The Stalinist system preferred distinct black and white colors over shaded tones and had difficulty drawing an intermediate line between unequivocal political praise and complete political denigration. In Aleksandrov's case, however, the discussion did not destroy him either as a politician or as a person, but did constitute a turning point in what had been an extraordinarily rapid and successful career. Although Aleksandrov survived for another three months as director of Agitprop, and even submitted a proposal for further work, his career was in danger.[21] In September 1947 the Central Committee Secretariat reviewed the results of the philosophical discussion and decided to remove Aleksandrov from his influential party post.[22] Demoted, he was appointed as director of the Institute of Philosophy, in which position, presumably, he had to supervise in person how his critics were learning from his mistakes. Stigmatized by the event, Aleksandrov was repeatedly criticized within the party apparatus, especially after the death of his patron Zhdanov in August 1948. In July 1949, Aleksandrov was accused of political mistakes, fired from the editorial board of the party's main theoretical journal, *Bol'shevik*, and disappeared for a while from the public political arena. He managed to return to it in 1950 and even to come back into favor during the political changes which followed Stalin's death. In 1954, Aleksandrov was appointed minister of culture, only to be removed the following year in a sex scandal. He was transferred to Minsk and died there in 1961 as a rank-and-file member of the Belorussian Institute of Philosophy. Such was the end of this turbulent and unusual career for a Soviet bureaucrat.[23]

Games of intraparty democracy

We cannot do without self-criticism, Aleksei Maksimovich. Without it, stagnation, corruption of the *apparat*, and an increase of bureaucratization would be inevitable. Of course, self-criticism provides arguments for our enemies, you are completely right here. But it also gives arguments (and a push) for our own progressive movement.
Joseph Stalin to Maxim Gorky, 1930[24]

The ritualistic performance described in the preceding section may seem weird to a modern reader, but for Soviet audiences it was an example of the familiar cultural games of *diskussiia* (disputation) and *kritika i samokritika* (criticism and self-criticism). These games originated and were usually played within party structures and belonged to the repertoire called "intraparty democracy."

Soviet, and more narrowly, intraparty democracy is a controversial topic. Merle Fainsod described it as mere propaganda and a "verbal masquerade." Roy Medvedev took it seriously as an element of true democracy and argued against violations of its principles in party life. More recently, Arch Getty called attention to its function of controlling local party bosses with the help of rank-and-file members, and argued that under certain conditions the process could get out of control and produce a massive purge.[25] Communists themselves, in public and in private, viewed intraparty democracy as a mechanism for making officials accountable to the party masses and as the main tool in the struggle against bureaucratism and corruption in the party apparatus. Although openly preferring administrative centralization and hierarchical discipline as the organizing principles of social life, they were also aware that local bosses were in a position to abuse their power and to prevent higher authorities from receiving objective reports about local conditions. The Stalinist leadership tried to establish a system of counterbalances designed to provide feedback as well as to define situations and limits within which grass-roots control of the apparatus was possible. In combination with the principle of administrative hierarchy, this system was called by the idiosyncratic term "democratic centralism"; and, as we shall see later, it could lead to idiosyncratic results.

Intraparty democracy could perform all of the above-mentioned functions – propagandistic, democratic or populistic, controlling, and purging – but it would be a simplification to reduce it to any particular one of them and to define it by its function. The phenomenon is more complex and might be better understood as a system of cultural rituals specific to, and of central importance to, Stalinist society. For members of that culture it had a high ideal value in its own right, not only because of its presumed practical goals. It also had sufficient power to ensure the public compliance of even the highest officials, such as Zhdanov. In modern anthropological studies, rituals are no longer described as rigid, strictly repetitive, and noncreative activities, but as forms of life: they are formalized collective performances, a unity of spatial movement and verbal discourse, which constitute the core of social identity in all communities and have both sacred and practical meanings. Although being rule-governed, the activity is not a petrified or simply symbolic one: rituals "are not just expressive or abstract ideas but do things, have effects on the world, and are work that is carried out." "[Ritual] is an arena of contradictory and contestable perspectives – participants having their own reasons, viewpoints, and motives and in fact is made up as it goes along."[26]

Social life under Stalinism was ritualized to a very high degree. In its political sphere, the most typical space of formalized collective action and discourse was a local meeting of a party organization or some institution. The repertoire of distinctive types of meetings, with their specific genres of discourse, was quite rich, and there were also many words for "meeting with discussion" in the political language: *sobranie, soveshchanie, zasedanie, vstrecha, obsuzhdenie, priem, sessiia,* and others. Some correspondence, although not one-to-one, between genres and names can be established. The English word "discussion" is too general and too neutral to account for that diversity. In the following I will use "discussion" as a generic term, and more specific words to stress when necessary the differences in genres. For instance, a local meeting (*sobranie*) which invited participants to discuss and draw conclusions from an authoritative decision or decree would be typically called an *obsuzhdenie* (consideration). When a meeting was announced as a *diskussiia* (disputation), this was a sign that participants were invited to demonstrate polemical skills in a theoretical matter which had not yet been decided by authorities. A *diskussiia* allowed for temporary, public disagreement over important political questions. It was often used for, or followed by, resolving the controversy and formulating a decision, after which further expressions of disagreements were ruled out. The decision was sometimes taken by participants' voting, sometimes by authorities who either observed the meeting in person or reviewed its minutes later. In the most serious *diskussii* that threatened to split the party several times during the 1920s, it was the party congress, or *s"ezd*, that resolved the controversy. Officially, a *s"ezd* was the highest party authority. By voting, it settled the disputes once and forever, and the opposition, or the losing party, had to stop any further polemics with the majority.[27]

Besides *diskussiia, kritika i samokritika* (criticism and self-criticism) also belonged to the repertoire of intraparty democracy, but it usually dealt with personal rather than theoretical matters. Berthold Unfried has already described it as a ritual central to the culture of the party and as a dialectical combination of two functions: initiation (educating and enculturating party cadres) and terror (exposing and destroying enemies). Standing the trial of *kritika i samokritika* was a necessary part of the training of new party members and officials. Subordinating one's personal views to those of the collective, accepting criticism and delivering self-criticism in the proper way, were the proof of successfully internalized cultural values and of one's status as an insider. The same ritual could also be used as a mechanism for purging, for revealing and accusing internal (but not external) enemies. Its cultural force was so strong that even Communist oppositionists who faced the death penalty were still proving their insider status by admitting imaginary crimes and accusing themselves in the *public* performance of Moscow trials, while denying their guilt in last *private* letters to Stalin or to the party.[28]

Another role of *kritika i samokritika*, identified by Arch Getty, allowed and provided an institutional framework for grass-roots criticism of local bosses.[29] Party secretaries normally would rule in an authoritarian way, exempt from criticism from below, but within ritualistic space-time constraints, the usual hierarchy could be temporarily reversed and horizontal or upward critique welcomed. The requirement of self-criticism forbade the local authority under fire from using his power to suppress criticism. In Communist self-descriptions, this democratic institution supplemented the hierarchical structure of the party and was steadily at work revealing and repairing shortcomings and local abuses of power, "however unpleasant it might be for the leaders." In practice, *kritika i samokritika* was performed mainly on special occasions and usually required permission or initiative from above. It could be applied when higher authorities wanted popular justification for their desire to remove a local functionary, when they were not sure about denunciations against him and wanted to test him publicly, during elections to party posts, or simply as a substitute for the Christian ritual of "penance" for the regular cleansing of the system.

Analyzing the Philosophical Dispute of 1947 as a combination of two rituals, *diskussiia* and *kritika i samokritika*, reveals some of their rules. Rule-governing in the ritual does not necessarily imply the existence of an explicit code, but the shared perception that there are some rules: "Even when neither observers nor participants can agree on, understand, or even perceive ritual regulations, they are united by a sense of the occasion as being in some way rule-governed and as necessarily so in order [for a public ritual] to be complete, efficacious, and proper."[30] Party members learned most of their cultural rituals not from such texts as party statutes, but from watching and participating in actual performances; their behavior and discourse at a meeting depended in the most crucial way on the announced type of ritual. The feeling of definite rules permeated the entire procedure of the Philosophical Dispute: participants watched each other's behavior and often criticized perceived violations. They protested when, in their opinion, speakers were expressing personal animosities instead of principled criticism, and especially strongly when self-defense was being offered in place of self-criticism. The ritual could not be considered completed without a solo performance of "sincere self-criticism." Aleksandrov displayed a good example of playing according to the rules, and thus proved his loyalty and his status as an insider. But at the 1950 physiological discussion, when Leon Orbeli protested against the accusatory style of criticism, the audience got more infuriated at this "violation of rules" than at his other alleged mistakes, and at the end of the meeting Orbeli had to deliver another, much more humble talk.[31]

Both *discussiia* and *kritika i samokritika* were rule-governed public performances, the results of which did not have to be fixed in advance. Although the structure of the discourse was quite rigid, the critical content and the outcome of the discussion depended very much upon the activity of players. On the theoretical side, Aleksandrov's mistakes were not exactly known to participants, but had to be found out during *diskussiia*. On the career side, the ritual of *kritika i samokritika*, like the ritual of confession, could be constructive as well as destructive. In the regular training and elections of party cadres, self-criticism could often be followed by a promotion. At a trial of an official, such as in Aleksandrov's case, the procedure was certainly a purgatory for him, but it could still end up anywhere between purge and practical acquittal. Public contestations which, like *diskussiia* and *kritika i samokritika*, had more or less fixed rules but open results, would be more appropriately termed "ritual games."[32]

The Philosophical Dispute can also illustrate the characteristic role structure of both games. Since both constituted a temporary challenge to the normal order – conceptual or hierarchical – the play often required a permission or encouragement from a higher authority, either in a concrete form or as an announcement of a general campaign of, say, *samokritika*. A representative from an agency further up the administrative hierarchy typically moderated the meeting: he was not directly associated with actively contesting parties – he played above them – but was not completely impartial, either.[33] Thus Zhdanov's presence in this role at the Philosophical Dispute was needed to announce the type of ritual to be played and the topic, to suppress by his aura of power the usual hierarchy between Aleksandrov and his subordinates, and to enforce procedures and rules. Various agencies could fulfill the role of referee. Many participants at the Philosophical Dispute included indirect appeals to the Central Committee in their speeches. As it turned out, the Central Committee Secretariat played referee with regard to *kritika i samokritika* by deciding about Aleksandrov's career, whereby minutes of the dispute were certainly taken into account. Zhdanov himself refereed the *diskussiia*, when at the end of the meeting he summarized its theoretical results and fixed the consensus.

The roots of these rituals are not to be found in Marxist doctrine, either in its original form or as it was developed by Lenin. Apparently, they were first established in Communist practice and only later in theory. *Diskussiia*, as a way of sorting out and resolving factional disagreements within the party, existed in some form before the Revolution, and in a fully developed version certainly by 1920. Within its space-time constraints, the opposition was arguing for and partially achieving the *freedom to criticize* party authorities. *Samokritika* as a political slogan and campaign first appeared in 1928 and meant "the purge of the party from below," which allowed young radicals to criticize authorities and do away with NEP.[34] By 1935 the ritual had changed its name to *kritika i samokritika* and was playing an important role in the party purges. Among Soviet leaders, Zhdanov always appeared as its chief promoter and propagandist. It was familiar to all members, applied on various occasions within party and Soviet structures, and considered one of the main principles of party life. But by the time of the 1947 Philosophical Dispute, it had not yet received a higher justification from Marxist theory.

In his talk at the dispute, Zhdanov presented the first outline of such a theory:

> The party long ago found and put into the service of socialism this particular form of exposing and overcoming contradictions in socialist society (these contradictions exist, although philosophers are reluctant to write about them), this particular form of the struggle between old and new, between withering away and emerging in our Soviet society, which is called *kritika i samokritika* . . . Development in our society occurs in the form of *kritika i samokritika*, which is the true moving force of our progressive development, a powerful tool in the party's hands.[35]

In what was further developed as the theoretical rationalization for existing practice, *kritika i samokritika* was supposedly doing for socialist society what "bourgeois democracy" did for capitalism – providing mechanisms for change. In the one-party system, so the argument ran, when no competing political party was providing external criticism, the Communist party had to carry the burden of self-criticism to reveal and repair its own defects if it were to cleanse and improve itself. Such was the Communist interpretation of the democratic idea as applied to the party itself.[36]

Opening Pandora's box

> The great and serious tasks arising before Soviet science can be solved successfully only through the wider development of *kritika i samokritika* – "one of the most serious forces that pushes forward our development."
>
> *Vestnik Akademii nauk*, 1948, quoting Stalin

According to the official point of view, the Philosophical Dispute "enlivened work on the philosophical front and stimulated further progress in it." The immediate consequence was the establishment of the professional journal *Voprosy filosofii*. Bonifatii Kedrov, who during the meeting argued in favor of such a journal and managed to pass a note to Zhdanov asking for a personal appointment, became editor-in-chief.[37] The entire first issue of the journal was devoted to the minutes of the discussion. The theory of *kritika i samokritika*, developed by Zhdanov and sanctioned by Stalin, was thus introduced to wider audiences as an important new contribution to Marxism-Leninism. It offered a basis and inspiration for mid-level politicians to develop derivatives and applications. A demonstration of zeal by initiating and carrying out a successful interpretation of the general slogan could certainly bring rewards and push one's career ahead. At the same time, risks could never be eliminated entirely. We shall see later that, no matter how correct the official might try to be in his actions, the chance always remained that he might come under fire for real or assumed mistakes.

Although the minutes of the Philosophical Dispute did not suggest yet that the method ought to be applied within other academic disciplines, the slogan *"kritika i samokritika* in science" soon became one of the policies of Agitprop under its new leadership, the official director and Central Committee secretary, Mikhail Suslov, and the acting director Dmitrii Shepilov. However, it was mainly lower-level politicians whose names became directly associated with the initiative. Kedrov was apparently the first to publish, in February 1948, a theoretical paper on the topic. Later the entire campaign was reviewed and praised by former Agitprop officer Mikhail Iovchuk and by Iurii Zhdanov, a young Moscow University graduate and the son of Andrei Zhdanov, who came to Agitprop in late 1947 to head the Sector of Science.[38] Extending *kritika i samokritika* to the sciences could well have seemed a safe bet. The word "sciences" in Russian, *nauki*, embraces not only the natural and social sciences but also the humanities and ideological scholarship. The Dispute of 1947 was performed by party members who just happened to be philosophers. But since philosophy was also one of the *nauki*, it was just as natural to apply the same, presumably so effective method to other fields as well. The double status of philosophy as both a party business and an academic field made it easier for the games of *diskussiia* and *kritika i samokritika* to be transferred from party culture to academia.

When Kedrov published his theoretical essay in February 1948 in *Vestnik Akademii Nauk*, the official monthly of the Soviet Academy of Sciences, readers could still regard the work as the author's personal opinion. The appearance of the editorial, "The First Results of Creative Disputations," in the subsequent issue, however, signified to readers the existence of an ongoing political campaign. Unsigned editorials in newspapers were the usual means for delivering messages from authorities regarding sanctioned opinions and policies. The March 1948 editorial reviewed several early examples of "creative disputations": the Philosophical Dispute, the disputes on E.S. Varga's book on world economics, on textbooks in linguistics, law, and on the history of the USSR, discussions at Moscow University and the Academy of Sciences on intraspecies competition, and a few others. The editors mentioned that the initiative had come from the party press and appealed to scientists from other fields to follow these examples. Methods of creative *diskussii* and of *kritika i samokritika* had to be applied in the work of scientists in order to "reveal our own mistakes and to overcome them."[39]

This new Agitprop initiative differed markedly from Andrei Zhdanov's earlier crusade of 1946, which hit mainly literary journals, films, theater, and music, but also some academic institutes in law and economics. In his talk in August 1946, Zhdanov had called for an increased level of criticism in various cultural fields: "Where there is no criticism, there solidifies stagnation and rot; there is no room there for progressive movement."[40] However, the initiative was expected then to come from the party. When first plans for such an extension of ideological work were discussed at a closed meeting of Agitprop on 18 April 1946, Zhdanov was particularly concerned about the weakness of internal criticism in such hierarchically governed organizations as the Writer's Union and the State Committee for Cultural Affairs: "Who can correct these departments' attitude which spoils the work and contradicts the interests of people? Of course, only the involvement of the party ... through the organization of party criticism in order to counterbalance the department's own criticism."[41] Open party involvement in cultural affairs followed. Politicians apparently considered themselves competent enough in literature and film to make expert judgments and to issue them publicly in the name of party bodies. Writers and film directors convened afterwards and held *obsuzhdeniia* (considerations) of authoritative decisions.[42]

In contrast, when it came to scholarly disputes in the fall of 1947, politicians preferred to act behind the scenes, left most public performances to scholars, and let decisions be issued in the name of a representative academic meeting. This choice was not a random one, but very characteristic of the place of *nauka* in Stalinist society. In their theoretical views about science, Soviet Marxists tried to combine adherence to objective scientific truth with the idea of an inseparable relationship between knowledge and social values. A typical solution drew a line between specific problems in science, where scholars were recognised experts, and philosophical interpretations, where politicians had the right and duty to intervene and interact with professionals. Politicians alone did not possess the knowledge and authority to define agendas in sciences, but required the active participation of, and dialogue with, experts. They therefore recommended games – *diskussiia* (with a special adjective, *tvorcheskaia* – "creative") and *kritika i samokritika* – from their repertoire of intraparty democracy which implied grass-roots initiative and criticism.[43]

Scholars were thus invited to play, within their own ranks, party games, and they could respond in a number of different ways. A sufficient demonstration of loyalty would be to hold an *obsuzhdenie* of the Philosophical Dispute at a local meeting and adopt a resolution with assurances that disputes and criticism had always been, and continued to be, crucial for their work. Some interpreted the invitation as permission for more freedom in academic discourse.[44] Many reacted with discussions imitating the Philosophical Dispute. Since the model event was a dispute over a textbook, most of the early imitations also took the form of a discussion of a certain book or textbook.[45] Being the best informed about the rules of the game, philosophers staged one more smooth performance. In January 1948 a *diskussiia* was organized in the Institute of Philosophy, and it became a miniature replica of the 1947 Dispute. The cast of characters included Aleksandrov, who had become director of the institute, presiding over the meeting as mini-Zhdanov; and Kedrov, with his book *Engels and the Natural Sciences*, playing mini-Aleksandrov. Both were apparently in control of the situation, and the meeting only confirmed the existing hierarchy. While presenting a mixture of moderate praise and criticism of the book, the audience turned largely against Kedrov's main opponent, Aleksandr Maksimov, blaming him for unfair and dogmatic use of criticism.[46]

While agendas and outcomes were not predetermined, the rhetorical and cultural resources, in a certain sense, were. Rival groups of scholars were already used to including political argumentation in academic discourse, and to sending political authorities letters of denunciation and complaints against colleagues. Agitprop files are filled with such letters, only a relatively few of which could receive any serious attention. With the new agenda of critical discussions, a tempting possibility emerged for scholars to proceed with existing academic conflicts in more open and politically sanctioned forms. The campaign stimulated public as well as unofficial dialogue between scholars and politicians, wherein the common language was mainly that of current politics and ideology; by appealing to politicians as referees and striving for their support, scholars competed in translating scientific concepts and agendas into that language. Conflicting academic parties were developing ideological pictures of their fields in ways that would support their positions in controversies.

In these scenarios, politicians could fulfill different roles. That "*kritika i samokritika* is the law of the development in science" quickly became a commonplace for them.[47] In fields like philosophy, political economy, and law, Agitprop initiated and set the direction of some discussions. More often, it did not have its own agenda but welcomed scholars' critical initiatives and was more interested in the very fact that a discussion came about than in its particular result. In these cases, disputes were performed within the academic hierarchy and depended largely upon internal conflicts and power relations. In some situations, politicians listened to appeals for support by rival groups of scientists and, if convinced by the rhetoric, could accept the role of referee. The following section applies this interpretation to an analysis of the events in the field of biology leading to the August Session. This case has served as the core model for most previous interpretations and therefore requires special treatment.

Resolving the controversy and achieving consensus

> In science as in politics, contradictions are resolved not through reconciliation, but through an open struggle.
> Andrei Zhdanov and Georgii Malenkov, July 1948

The conflict in biology had ripened long before 1948. Geneticists had suffered serious losses in the late 1930s, with Nikolai Vavilov and several other prominent figures perishing in the great purges and Lysenko rising to head the Academy of Agricultural Sciences and the Institute of Genetics in the Academy of Sciences. After World War II geneticists tried to regain some ground and to undermine Lysenko's position. Anton Zhebrak, a geneticist, and in 1945–46 an Agitprop officer, wrote letters to the Central Committee arguing that Lysenko's monopoly was damaging the reputation of Soviet science among the Western Allies, and lobbied for opening another institute of genetics in the Academy, with himself as its future director.[48] Perhaps as a result of a denunciation that too many Agitprop workers were seeking membership in the Academy of Sciences in major elections during the fall of 1946, it was not Zhebrak but another geneticist, Nikolai Dubinin, who was elected corresponding member despite Lysenko's opposition, and the Academy proceeded with the plan to organize an institute for him. Soon after Iurii Zhdanov became the head of the Science Sector in Agitprop on 1 December 1947, he was visited by several of Lysenko's opponents, who complained about the unsatisfactory situation in biology.[49]

Once the campaign of *tvorcheskie diskussii* (creative disputation) started, a new dispute about Darwinism and the problem of intraspecies competition erupted between Lysenko and his opponents on the pages of *Literaturnaia gazeta*. With silent permission from Agitprop, and in line with the new policies, biologists organized conferences at Moscow State University (November 1947 and February 1948), and at the Biology Division of the Academy of Sciences (December 1947), where they criticized some of Lysenko's views.[50] On 10 April 1948, Zhdanov, Jr, entered the discussion with a lecture at a meeting of party propagandists on "Controversial Questions of Contemporary Darwinism," in which he partly sided with Lysenko's critics. According to him, the struggle was between two schools of Soviet biology, rather than between the Soviet and bourgeois sciences. Both Neo-Darwinians (geneticists) and Neo-Lamarckists (Lysenkoists) had accomplishments, and both had succumbed to an undesirable radicalism during the struggle. Lysenko, in particular, should not claim to be the only follower of the great Russian selectionist, Michurin. Having started as a pathbreaker, Lysenko later lost his self-critical attitude and, by suppressing other approaches, he had brought about direct damage. Monopolies in every field of scientific research should be liquidated: creative disputations, developing *kritika i samokritika* in science, and cultivating a variety of research methods would help achieve this.[51]

A young and inexperienced *apparatchik*, Iurii Zhdanov prematurely tried to referee the biological controversy. Although he had consulted with his boss, Shepilov, he spoke up too early and secured neither definite approval from higher authorities nor the means to drive Lysenko toward *samokritika*. Zhdanov made it clear to the audience that he was delivering his personal rather than the official opinion. Although Lysenko was not invited to the lecture, he managed to hear it secretly and became intimidated, for he had apparently almost lost this round of *kritika*. Cleverly enough, he started a new one. Since Lysenko was a major authority in the field of biology, he would have committed a rhetorical mistake had he decided to complain about the criticism from below. Instead, he built a new triangle of *kritika i samokritika* by presenting his school as the minority constantly attacked by biological authorities, complaining against the actions of Iurii Zhdanov, who was the party authority for scientists, and appealing to Stalin as referee. In his letter of 17 April to Stalin and Andrei Zhdanov, Lysenko appears as a nonparty but loyal scientist who was upset by Iurii's lecture and did not know whether the party had lost trust in him, or whether the critique was just the result of a young official's incompetence. Were the former true, Lysenko offered in another letter his resignation as president of the Agricultural Academy.[52]

Lysenko's complaint impressed Stalin. At a Politburo meeting in June, Stalin expressed his dissatisfaction with Zhdanov's talk. In later interviews with Valery Soyfer, Iurii Zhdanov and Shepilov made contradictory and obscure remarks about who in the ideological hierarchy, and in what form, admitted responsibility for the mistake. A committee was established to investigate the case. Following the unwritten rules of the bureaucratic *modus operandi*, Shepilov advised the younger Zhdanov to write a letter of self-criticism. According to Iurii, rivals of Zhdanov, Sr among the upper level of the Soviet leadership used the occasion to criticize the youngster for "insufficient disarmament" and the father for protecting the son.[53] Whether Iurii's precipitate action may have thus contributed to his father's fall, or whether it was Andrei Zhdanov's loss of power that helped the agricultural bureaucracy to prevail over the ideological one, is still difficult to tell with certainty.[54] But some connection apparently existed, for Politburo decisions on the Lysenko case and on the Central Committee apparatus coincided. Andrei Zhdanov became the main victim of these changes, while most other concerned party officials managed to improve their positions. Malenkov, his chief rival, was added to the Secretariat on 1 July and took over the chairmanship there one week later when Zhdanov took two months' vacation (during which he would die under suspicious circumstances). On 10 July the Politburo effected a major reorganization of the Central Committee apparatus, shifting its emphasis in work from propaganda to cadres. Suslov took charge of international relations, Shepilov was promoted to the official directorship of Agitprop, and Malenkov, besides cadres, oversaw the reestablished Agricultural Department. The younger Zhdanov received a severe moral reprimand, but Stalin spared him from any more serious punishment. He remained in his position at Agitprop, but only for so long as Stalin was alive. Learning the rules of apparatus intrigue required years of experience; a hasty and amateur involvement in high politics could be very dangerous.[55]

On 15 July the Politburo met to discuss questions presented by the agricultural establishment – the Academy, ministries, and the new Central Committee Agricultural Department – and to repair the damage caused by "the incorrect report of Iu. Zhdanov on matters of Soviet biology, which did not reflect the position of the Central Committee." Stalin's expression of sympathy for Lysenko could possibly suffice to ruin the career of a Politburo member, but not to close the scientific dispute. On behalf of the committee investigating the case, Andrei Zhdanov had written, and Malenkov cosigned, a draft resolution on the situation in biological science and the mistakes of Iurii Zhdanov, but the party again stopped short of issuing the decision in its name. Instead, the Politburo approved the agricultural lobby's proposal to appoint a number of Michurinists as new members of the Academy, and decided to reimburse Lysenko for moral damage by allowing him to present to the Academy, and publish, a report "On the Situation in Soviet Biology."[56]

The session of the Lenin Academy of Agricultural Sciences of the USSR opened on 31 July with a major presentation by Lysenko. Stalin had edited the manuscript and corrected its ideological profile, but party support was not announced at first. Lysenko's task was to prove that he could control the field, mobilize enough grass-roots support, and stage a smooth performance. Only after he had passed this test, on the last day of the meeting, was Iurii Zhdanov's repentant letter published in *Pravda*, and Lysenko allowed to say that the Central Committee had approved his talk.[57] Having been sanctioned both by the voting at the representative scholarly meeting and by Stalin's support, the victory of Michurinist biology became final.

One can recognize behind this pattern the model provided by another game of intraparty democracy: the party congress, or *s"ezd*. The first important feature is that, officially, the decision adopted by the representative collective body had more strength than the decision of any individual leader. Even Stalin could later be declared fallible by Khrushchev, but none of the decisions of party congresses could be. Second, everyone knew from the party *Short Course* history that congresses had served several times in the 1920s as the method for final resolution of the most important party disputes. Factions and propaganda on behalf of opposing views were allowed before the *s"ezd*, but after the ballot further polemics were forbidden. The opposition had to "disarm itself" and to cancel all organizational activity. For the Central Committee, preparing such a *s"ezd* was a challenge: the election of deputies on the local level had to be manipulated to ensure the necessary majority.

Lysenko proceeded in a similar way. His difficulty was that the Agricultural Academy, where he had many supporters, was not the only natural authority to adjudicate theoretical problems in biology. Early interference from the Academy of Sciences could have spoiled the smooth scenario. Hence preparations were made very quickly, and most of Lysenko's opponents from the outside did not know of them and did not attend the session. Iosif Rapoport learned about the meeting only by chance and at the last moment. With some difficulty he managed to get into the building and to become one of the very few who raised a dissident voice.[58] These few were just enough to create the impression of a militant, but numerically insignificant, opposition. One cannot say that almost everybody in the hall was a convinced Lysenko follower, but many who in a different setting would have preferred to remain aloof from the polemics or even take the opposite side joined the common chorus at the August Session.

This behavior was for all intents and purposes enforced by the genre of discourse set by Lysenko's main talk and the subsequent initial speeches. Opponents tried unsuccessfully to change the game being played, and therefore the style of polemics. They argued that the dispute had not been organized properly and that the other side had not been informed and given time to prepare and explain its views. "We have to hold another free *diskussiia* in a different place," demanded P.M. Zhukovskii – but many other speakers made it clear that the game was different and that time was up.[59] "*Diskussiia* had been finished after the meeting at the editorial office of the journal *Under the Banner of Marxism*. Since then ... on the part of formal genetics ... there is not a scientific creative *diskussiia*, but factionalism and struggle, which took most unnatural and useless forms," proclaimed the Lysenkoist Nuzhdin. The intended meaning was that geneticists had failed to meet the basic rule of a loyal party opposition: to "disarm" after being defeated during the *diskussiia*. Their status therefore changed, from tolerable partners for dispute to disloyal saboteurs who needed to be suppressed administratively, rather than verbally.[60]

According to the rules of the game of *s"ezd*, the voting at the session resolved the dispute forever. Further *diskussiia* was off the agenda. The only possible games to play were *obsuzhdenie* and *kritika i samokritika*, which had already started on 7 August, the last day of the session, and which continued on 24–26 August, at the Presidium of the Academy of Sciences. The local authority subjected to criticism was the secretary of the Biology Division, Leon Orbeli. President of the Academy Sergei Vavilov played the role of moderator and opened the meeting with a dose of *samokritika*, reproaching the Presidium for "neutrality" and its attempts to preserve parity between two directions in biology. In the discussion that followed, Orbeli failed to convince the audience of the sincerity of his repentance. Vavilov then suggested that Aleksandr Oparin be elected as the new secretary of the division.[61] While the Academy was allowed the privilege of purging itself, a dozen directors of large agricultural institutes and biological departments were replaced after the August Session by direct decision of the Central Committee Secretariat, and over one hundred professors by an order of the Ministry of Higher Education. The minister's proposal to remove a number of biology books from public libraries gathered support from Agitprop but was finally rejected by the Secretariat. In most biological institutions, non-Michurinists had to "disarm themselves" through *samokritika*; teaching and research plans were changed according to the results of the controversy.[62]

Paradigm shift, Soviet style

It is generally recognized that no science can develop and flourish without a battle of opinions, without freedom of criticism.

Joseph Stalin (1950)[63]

161

Nineteen forty-nine passed without a major *diskussiia*, although there were plans for the All-Union Council of Physicists. The conflict behind these plans was institutional rather than conceptual: physicists of Moscow University proved to be more active and better equipped for political discussion in the Organizing Committee, and they were determined to push some of their more privileged colleagues from the Academy of Sciences toward *samokritika*, thus challenging the existing hierarchy in the field. The meeting, scheduled for March 1949, was indefinitely postponed by the Central Committee Secretariat, and the rehearsed performance was never played publicly. The credit for preventing the discussion has been usually given to nuclear physicists and their political boss Lavrenty Beria. However, archival documents suggest that it was not the atomic bomb, but a quiet bureaucratic intrigue by Dmitrii Shepilov and possibly Sergei Vavilov, which directed the Secretariat to corroborate the opinion that the council had not been properly prepared.[64]

The Lysenko Session therefore was not eclipsed by another important political event in the sciences until 1950, when two discussions occurred almost simultaneously. The July meeting on physiology, the Pavlov Session, had been under preparation for about a year. The main moving force behind it was Iurii Zhdanov, who later claimed that he wanted to stage something more reasonable than the August Session. It is clear from the archival documents, however, that he wanted to end the monopoly of Leon Orbeli, who had inherited from Ivan Pavlov the main physiological institutions. Other pupils of Pavlov were quite willing to criticize Orbeli and to get their share of the institutes. Every politically important event in those days needed an ideological rationalization: the high principle applied in this case was strict faithfulness to Pavlovian doctrine, despite the fact that it did not belong to the body of Marxism-Leninism. This also brought under fire several other unorthodox physiologists and psychologists, and resulted in another monopoly in the field. Zhdanov had learned the lessons of the Lysenko case and rehabilitated himself: he prepared the Pavlov Session without haste, in a professional bureaucratic way, and secured Stalin's approval for it.[65] In contrast, even Agitprop was unprepared for the sudden outbreak of the "Free Discussion on linguistics in *Pravda*" in May 1950. The controversy shattered the emerging order and reversed the consensus that nearly had been achieved in the field, which already had passed through several consecutive rounds of *kritika i samokritika*.

A figure in Soviet linguistics who was in some aspects similar to Lysenko, Nikolai Marr was a mixture of genius and insanity, with a tendency to develop from the former toward the latter. He spoke an enormous number of languages, in particular those of the Caucasus and other linguistically complicated parts of the world. The Caucasus remains

162

a problem for standard systems of linguistic classification even now. Marr's pathbreaking studies of this area challenged the accepted Indo-European theory. In 1923 he announced a complete break with that theory and started developing what would become known as the "new doctrine on language." In place of the existing picture of multiple languages developing from few common ancestors, Marr substituted a reverse evolution from initial variety, through mixture, toward the future unification of languages. In Marr's scheme, independent languages passed through common stages which corresponded to the level of the development of the society. This offered him later an opportunity to connect his theory with Marxism, declare it materialistic, and oppose it to bourgeois Western linguistics.[66]

In the battles of the Cultural Revolution, around 1930, Marr and his school defeated their non-Marxist and Marxist opponents and achieved a monopoly in the field. Upon his death in 1934, Marr was beatified as one of the "founding fathers" of Soviet science along with Michurin, Pavlov, and Williams. "The new doctrine on language" became the official Soviet linguistics. Its keeper, and the heir to Marr's position in the Academy, Ivan Meshchaninov, adopted a conciliatory approach: heresies and pluralism in actual research were tolerated, so long as ritualistic loyalty was expressed and the political status of Marrism as the Marxism of linguistics was not challenged.[67] Alas, this compromise did not survive the test of the discussion campaign.

The genres of discussion in linguistics in 1947–50 were dictated by the need to respond to and hold *obsuzhdeniia* on the model events: Zhdanov's 1946 critique of the literary journals *Zvezda* and *Leningrad*, the 1947 Philosophical Dispute, and the 1948 August Session. Correspondingly, linguists reviewed the work of their journals, discussed the quality of their textbooks, and criticized idealism. But, driven largely by the aspirations of two deputy directors (of the Moscow Institute of Language and Thought, Georgii Serdiuchenko, and of the Institute of Russian Language, Fedot Filin), these ritualistic performances were suffused with exposing and criticizing those who deviated from Marr.[68]

The titles of the two main talks at a joint meeting of the Leningrad branches of these institutes in October 1948, "On the Situation in Linguistic Science," and "On the Two Trends in the Study of Language," were borrowed from Lysenko's address to the August Session. In fact, there were three trends, for Marrists attacked modern structuralism as well as classical Indo-European linguistics, but the ritual of imitation proved to be stronger than logical considerations. Meshchaninov, who spoke first, took a softer theoretical approach, which showed his reluctance to fight. He could not avoid, after all, some self-criticism for having tolerated idealists too long, Trying to draw parallels between linguistics and biology, he equated Wilhelm Humboldt's "spirit of the nation" with "hereditary substance," and both Indo-European theory and genetics with racism. The second speaker, Filin, provided a more militant and practical criticism, calling for the "total scientific and political exposure" of open and hidden non-Marrists, and arguing that peace in Soviet linguistics was only illusory and that the struggle between materialism and idealism had to break out.[69]

Besides conceptual considerations, institutional ones were obviously in play, since the main target of criticism was Viktor Vinogradov, who was not the most open non-Marrist but definitely the most highly placed one. He directed the Philological Department of Moscow University and had recently become a full member of the Academy. At the 1947 discussion Vinogradov's textbook, *Russian Language*, had been criticized.[70] Now Filin accused him of sticking to his views even *after* that dispute. "Undisarmed Indo-Europeanists among us have to think carefully! They must abandon incorrect methodological principles not only in words but also in deeds," he concluded.[71]

Several similar local battles took place during 1949, in which Marrists gradually suppressed heretics one by one, institute by institute.[72] The main administrative success occurred in the summer of 1949, when the Ministry of Higher Education ordered changes in the curriculum and the Academy corrected research plans of its institutes. Vinogradov was driven to engage in *samokritika* a couple of times, repented in words, and resigned as the department's dean, but survived as chair of the university's *kafedra* of Russian language. A few were fired, but many more were forced to denounce former views and at least formally subscribe to the prevailing orthodoxy. Only on the periphery, in particular in Georgia and Armenia, had a few open dissidents not yet been disciplined.[73] The community was straightening itself out and approaching a consensus. In order to fix it, one would have needed a real political event. Starting in July 1949 the Academy of Sciences sent reports to the Central Committee about its decisions against anti-Marrists and about the continuing struggle. Agitprop supported its position and was quite willing to host a meeting with linguists (all Marrists) "in order to finish the work of discussing the situation in Soviet linguistics and to submit to the Central Committee a proposal on the improvement of work." The Secretariat answered in January 1950 that the discussion should be organized by the Academy itself.[74]

Meanwhile, disagreements were developing among Marrists. Meshchaninov was still trying to keep to the middle ground, accepting that there were mistakes in Marr's doctrine, too, and that it needed *creative* development. But his position as the institutional leader was becoming shaky as radicals criticized him ever more often and openly. On the other hand, on 13 April 1950, Suslov received a report that referred to information received from the Academy of Pedagogical Sciences and accused Serdiuchenko of intolerance, lack of professionalism, denying any mistakes in Marr's works, and opposing *samokritika*. Suslov showed a willingness to distinguish between what was ideologically wrong and right in Marrism: in a draft of his remarks he wrote that "scientific problems cannot be solved administratively" and mentioned the need to organize a *diskussiia*.[75] But the crucial moment had already occurred three days before, when leaders of the Republic of Georgia presented Stalin with a new *Encyclopedic Dictionary of the Georgian Language*. They also introduced him to the dictionary's editor, Arnold Chikobava. Probably the most open fighter against the "new doctrine on language," Chikobava had called it anti-Marxist and racist because it placed Indo-European languages higher than Georgian on the developmental scale. Supported by republican party leaders and enjoying a stronghold in the Georgian Academy of Sciences and the University of Tbilisi, Chikobava remained one of the few who had not yet been subdued.[76]

As a result of his meeting with Stalin, Chikobava got the commission to write down his views as a discussion note: "You will write, we will consider," said Stalin. They met two more times to discuss the text, and on 9 May 1950 the linguistic order was broken again: "In connection with the unsatisfactory state of Soviet linguistics, the editors consider it essential to organize an open *diskussiia* in *Pravda* in order to overcome, through *kritika i samokritika*, stagnation in the development of Soviet linguistics and to give the right direction to further scientific work in this field. ... Chikobava's article 'On Certain Problems of Soviet Linguistics,' is printed as a matter of dispute."[77] In this essay Chikobava accepted Marr's early works on the theory of Caucasian languages, but not the general linguistic theory, and praised his desire to become a Marxist, but denied the thesis on the class nature of language, thus accusing Marr of being "unable to master the method of dialectical materialism and to apply it to linguistics."[78]

Reportedly, *Pravda* received over two hundred letters in response to the article.[79] In numbers, Marrists should have prevailed, but the papers selected for publication constitute a very symmetrical set. In articles as long as Chikobava's, Meshchaninov praised Marr, and Vinogradov was inconclusive. The same structure of one positive, one negative, and one opportunistic letter was preserved in three other issues. Every Tuesday, workers and peasants, intellectuals and policemen, received a sophisticated scholarly-ideological reading in linguistics, knowing neither why it had suddenly become a matter of general political importance, nor what the truth was. Then, on the seventh week, came the following message: "We continue to print articles sent to *Pravda* in connection with the dispute in Soviet linguistics. Today, we publish articles by I. Stalin, 'Concerning Marxism in Linguistics,' and Prof. Chernykh, 'Toward a Critique of Some Theses of the "New Doctrine on Language." '[80]

It may be that Stalin originally planned to participate and gave himself some time to develop an opinion, or that his contribution was triggered by one of the articles of the previous week, which was devoted almost entirely to the question of class and language. Having admitted in the beginning that he was "not a linguistic expert and, of course, cannot fully satisfy the request of the comrades," Stalin continued: "As to Marxism in linguistics, as in other social sciences, this is directly in my field." From the linguistic point of view, the paper consisted of trivial but surprisingly competent statements; from the point of view of orthodox Marxism, it certainly would have been considered heretical, had the author been anybody else. Stalin denied not only that language was a class phenomenon but also that it had a place in the superstructure, which none of Marr's harshest critics dared to do. The stress on the class issue, once a very powerful ideological resource, proved to be a misfortune for Marrism. By the 1940s internationalist class rhetoric had lost its central role in Soviet ideology to nationalist themes, although it received lip service. In the end, Stalin approved *Pravda*'s (in fact, his own) decision to open the dispute, and accused Marr's school of suppressing critics and a free discussion, which could have revealed the mistakes and the non-Marxist nature of the theory. "Elimination of the Arakcheev [police] regime in linguistics, rejection of N.Ia. Marr's errors, and the introduction of Marxism into linguistics – that, in my opinion, is the way in which Soviet linguistics could be put on a sound basis."[81]

The "Free Discussion in *Pravda*" lasted another few weeks, but the discourse changed from *diskussiia* to *obsuzhdenie* (commentary, praise, and further applications), *kritika*, and *samokritika*. Then came the time for more practical meetings in ministries and institutes, and for administrative changes. Meshchaninov, Filin, and Serdiuchenko lost their administrative jobs and became ordinary scholars. Their institutes were merged into the Institute for the Study of Language, with Vinogradov as its director and the new leader of the field.[82] "Stalin's doctrine on language" was the hottest ideological topic until 1952, when the "Corypheus of science" wrote another theoretical piece on political economy. Dozen of volumes and hundreds of articles commented on Stalin's paper and were "introducing Marxism into linguistics." The result of this party involvement in science and of the suppression of a scientific theory by Stalin's heavy hand was, in the case of linguistics, the rehabilitation of the classical and international, comparative Indo-European approach. One older academic even spoke of Stalin's piece as of a "sobering voice of reason."[83] Structuralism would have to wait a few more years, until Khrushchev's liberalization.

Conclusion

Following the end of World War II, science in the Soviet Union became a top state priority. This was not limited to physics and other military-related disciplines, but embraced all fields of scholarship, or *nauki*, in the Russian sense. *Uchenye* (scholars in this wider sense) came to form an elite social group next to party *apparatchiki*, industrial administrators, and the military, and became more privileged than engineers. In material terms, this change of status was decreed by the Council of Ministers on 6 March 1946.[84] Not only resources for research, but individual salaries as well, were raised higher than at any other time in Soviet history. As in the case of other elites in Stalinist society, with increased privileges came increased dangers, and with attentive care, tighter control. As an elite group, scientists came into a closer dialogue with politicians and accepted some of their values, language, and games.[85]

Increased concern with science prompted politicians to undertake a conscious effort to stimulate progress by available cultural means. In particular, several rituals of party life which were thought to provide mechanisms for change and repair of local defects were applied in academic fields. The choice of these rituals reveals a characteristic distribution of authority between politicians and experts in Stalinist society. The politics prescribed certain operative procedures with open agendas and outcomes, which provoked initiatives, criticism, and conflicts. Scholars were invited to fill them with more substantive matters and policies. Although politicians rarely had their own agendas in sciences, they reserved the right to intervene if and when, some important political, philosophical, or ideological issue was at stake. This possibility had the effect of stimulating appeals to them to serve as referees. In order to make politicians understand and intervene, scholars competed in translating conceptual, institutional, group, and personal agendas and conflicts into the language of current politics and ideology. Such behavior was not an unknown phenomenon – at least since the 1920s – but in the 1940s it reached an unprecedented scale.

Soviet ideology, as any rich ideology, was inconsistent enough to allow the presentation of a great many academically meaningful positions in ideological terms. Still, the ideological language was not sufficient to ensure adequate translation. Scholars and politicians thus participated in Wittgensteinian language games, communicating by means of a language with severely limited resources.[86] Some of the confused results of the ideological discussions campaign in the sciences can be ascribed to the indeterminacy of translation.

An important feature of the party games was that they closed with a single definite resolution, even though at the initial stages pluralism and freedom had been encouraged. This offers an explanation of why policies announced as, in Mao's later words, "let a hundred flowers bloom," usually ended up with the opposite result. Actually, this is characteristic of many political games in general, in contrast to many regular academic ones. Stalinist culture, however, was particularly strong in its belief in the single truth, as well as in the desire to reach a conclusion without delay, often to its own self-defeat.[87] No matter how strongly the struggling parties diverged in their specific views, they usually agreed in their denial of an even temporary pluralism of truth, and in their intolerance to the opposing opinion.

The main discussion – which saw higher politicians acting as referees and which brought about an effective resolution and official conformity – were, although the most publicized, still exceptional cases. Many scholars tried to gain the support of the political leadership, but only very few succeeded. The chances of organizing a scholarly meeting that would be representative enough to definitely settle a serious academic controversy, and even more, of getting Stalin to intervene and adjudicate, were very small. In the majority of fields, discussions were held but their impact was either indecisive or limited. This vast majority of events still has to be studied.

In communists' own theories, the party and the state had the obligation and power to decide on all politically important issues. This idea of omnipresence and total control was, of course, utopian and impossible to realize in practice, and it often resulted in sporadic interventions in arbitrarily selected cases.[88] In the events discussed above, rarer instances when the leadership did actually interfere were determined by peculiar constellations of circumstances rather than any consistent logical criterion. It was impossible to predict, for instance, which of the thousands of letters addressed to Stalin would manage to reach his desk, attract his attention, and stir his emotions. But once this had happened, the case would immediately be declared supremely important. The Stalinist system thus reacted on a random basis but with excessive power, producing outputs which were quite inadequate to the level of the incoming "signal from below." In modern physics, systems with similar behavior are called "chaotic": they can be deterministic on the microscopic local level, but produce unpredictable global results.

Each of the important political decisions, however, including those caused by internal chaos, had to be publicly presented as the logical outcome of high principles. Portraying itself as an ideologically governed and effectively controlled society, Stalinism developed ideological rationalizations for all its major actions. The notion of ideology determining the master plan, and of the totalitarian regime as capable of directing society toward its implementation, has been a very powerful explanatory model. Insiders were often deceived by it, therefore miscalculating the consequences of their moves. Even some critics who opposed the ideology and politics of the regime still depended upon the very same rationalizations in their constructions of the enemy as "Manichean" – logical and powerful – evil. Such interpretations of Stalinism were inspired by a political or moral desire to expose and defeat the dangers of totalitarianism, either in its original form, or its direct legacy. Presently, as those conditions have ceased to exist, it becomes possible to examine Stalinism as "Augustinian" – controversial and chaotic – evil.[89] Reconsidering simple pictures of the dead version of totalitarianism provides better tools for recognizing its new forms and species.

NOTES

This article appeared in the *Russian Review*, 57: 1 (January 1998), 23–52, under the title "Rituals of Stalinist Culture at Work: Science and the Games of Intraparty Democracy circa 1948." It is reprinted with slight revisions by the author.

1 Earlier versions of this chapter were presented at the Russian/Soviet History Colloquium at the University of Chicago, the 1995 Midwest Russian History Workshop, the Max-Planck-Institut für Wissenschaftsgeschichte, and at several other meetings and colloquia. My thanks to all participants for their comments, and to the US Information Agency for granting me a 1994–95 Junior Faculty Development Fellowship at Indiana University. I am very grateful to Dietrich Beyrau, Eve Greenfield, David Joravsky, Edward Jurkowitz, Dorinda Outram, Judy Johns Schloegel, Ethan Pollock, Kirill Rossiianov, Skuli Sigurdsson, and Susan Solomon for comments and suggestions on the manuscript. The chapter also benefited from criticism by Mark Adams and Nikolai Krementsov.

2 *Istoriia Kommunisticheskoi Partii Sovetskogo Soiuza* (Moscow, 1959), 606. Later editions dropped the biological discussion as damaging to the party's reputation. For the same list of major discussions see "Bol'shevistskaia kritika i samokritika," *Bol'shaia sovetskaia entsiklopediia*, 2nd edn, 51 vols (Moscow, 1949–58), 5: 515–18; Iu.A. Zhdanov, "O kritike i samokritike v nauchnoi rabote," *Bol'shevik*, 1951, no. 21: 28–43; and M.T. Iovchuk, "Bor'ba mnenii i svoboda kritiki – vazhneishee uslovie razvitiia peredovoi nauki," *Voprosy filosofii*, 1952, no. 2: 14–31.

3 David Joravsky, *Russian Psychology: A Critical History* (Oxford, 1989), 405–6.

4 "Diskussiia po knige G.F. Aleksandrova 'Istoriia zapadnoevropeiskoi filosofii,' 16–25 iiunia 1947 g.: Stenograficheskii otchet," *Voprosy filosofii*, 1947, no. 1; V.D. Esakov, "K istorii filosofskoi diskussii 1947 g.," ibid., 1993, no. 2: 83–106.

5 *The Situation in Biological Science: Proceedings of the Lenin Academy of Agricultural Sciences of the USSR, Verbatim Report* (Moscow, 1949); David Joravsky, *The Lysenko Affair* (Cambridge, MA, 1970).

6 I.V. Stalin, *Marksizm i voprosy iazykoznaniia* (Moscow, 1950); V.M. Alpatov, *Istoriia odnogo mifa: Marr i marrizm* (Moscow, 1991).

7 *Nauchnaia sessiia posviashchennaia problemam fiziologicheskogo ucheniia akademika I.P. Pavlova, 28 iiunia–4 iiulia 1950 g.: Stenograficheskii otchet* (Moscow, 1950). For a history see Joravsky, *Russian Psychology*, and " 'Pavlovskaia sessiia' 1950 g. i sud'by sovetskoi fiziologii," *Voprosy istorii estestvoznaniia i tekhniki*, 1988, no. 3: 129–41, no. 4: 147–57, and 1989, no. 1: 94–108.

8 I.V. Stalin, *Ekonomicheskie problemy sotsializma v SSSR* (Moscow, 1952); L.A. Openkin, "I.V. Stalin: Poslednii prognoz budushchego (Iz istorii napisaniia raboty 'Ekonomicheskie problemy sotsializma v SSSR')," *Voprosy istorii KPSS*, 1991, no. 7: 113–28.

9 The discussion in cosmogony was almost academic in style and did not involve politicians. See A.E. Levin, "Bitva bez izbieniia: Soveshchanie po planetnoi kosmogonii 1951 g.," *Priroda*, 1991, no. 9: 99–107. Changing the institute's director was apparently the main goal of a discussion in literary criticism ("Protiv idealizatsii ucheniia A. Veselovskogo," *Izvestiia Akademii nauk SSSR; Otdelenie literatury i iazyka*, 1948, no. 4: 362–64. A major discussion, which did not allow a revolt against the existing academic hierarchy, took place in chemistry. See Loren Graham, *Science, Philosophy, and Human Behavior in the Soviet Union* (New York, 1987); and A.A. Pechenkin, "Antirezonansnaia kampaniia 1949–1951 gg.," in *Metafizika i ideologiia v istorii estestvoznaniia* (Moscow, 1994), 184–219. The institutional conflict between Moscow University and the Academy of Sciences was the driving force behind the discussion in physics (G.E. Gorelik, "Fizika univeritetskaia i akademicheskaia," *Voprosy istorii estestvoznaniia i tekhniki*, 1991, no. 1: 15–32).

10 A.B. Kozhevnikov, "O nauke proletarskoi, partiinoi, marksistskoi," in *Metafizika*, 219–38; Alexei Kojevnikov, "President of Stalin's Academy: the Mask and Responsibility of Sergei Vavilov," *Isis* 87 (March 1996), 18–50.

11 Pushkin's original: "On po-frantsuzski sovershenno/Mog iz"iasniat'sia, i pisal/Legko mazurku tantseval/I klanialsia neprinuzhdenno"; its Soviet variation: "On po-marksistski sovershenno/Mog iz"iasniat'sia, i pisal/Legko oshibki priznaval/I kaialsia neprinuzhdenno."

12 "Diskussia," 6. On Zhdanov's episode in Soviet politics, see Werner Hahn, *The Fall of Zhdanov and the Defeat of Moderation, 1946–1953* (Ithaca, NY, 1982).

13 On Aleksandrov, see *Bol'shaia sovetskaia entsiklopediia*, 3rd edn (Moscow, 1970), 1: 413; Hahn, *Fall of Zhdanov*, 58–68; *Pravda*, 27 June 1946; and *Filosofskaia entsiklopediia* (Moscow, 1960), 1: 43.

14 For the report on the first discussion, see Rossiiskii Tsentr Khraneniia i Izucheniia Dokumentatsii Noveishei Istorii (RTsKhIDNI), Moscow, f. 17, op. 125, d. 477.

15 "Diskussiia," 267, 289; RTsKhIDNI, f. 17, op. 125, d. 477, l. 4.

16 Esakov, "K istorii," 87. A few others also claimed to have signaled to the Central Committee about mistakes in the book (RTsKhIDNI, f. 17, op. 125, d. 477, l. 111; ibid., d. 527, ll. 9–37.

17 On the feud between Mitin and Aleksandrov and groupings among philosophers, see D. Chesnokov's and Agitprop's reports to Georgii Malenkov and Mikhail Suslov in 1949, RTsKhIDNI, f. 17, op. 132, d. 155, ll. 20–26; and ibid., d. 161, ll. 8–36.

18 For a comparison of the slogans of the "creative" and "militant" parties, see the editorials, "Za tvorcheskuiu razrabotku marksistskoi filosofii," and "Za boevoi filosofskii zhurnal," in *Voprosy filosofii*, 1948, no. 1, and 1949, no. 1, respectively.

19 "Diskussiia, " 269.

20 Ibid., 188–99.

21 Esakov, "K istorii," 96–97; RTsKhIDNI, f. 17, op. 125, d. 543, ll. 154–58.

22 "Stenogramma soveshchaniia Upravleniia propagandy i agitatsii TsK VKP(b) ot 19 sentiabria 1947 g. 'O sostoianii raboty v oblasti propagandy i agitatsii'," RTsKhIDNI, f. 17, op. 125, d. 493. Petr Fedoseev, who had organized the discussion of January 1947, was criticized for a lack of principles.

23 RTsKhIDNI, f. 17, op. 132, d. 160, ll. 91–98; ibid., d. 155, ll. 1–51; [Roy Medvedev], *Politicheskii dnevnik, 1964–1970* (Amsterdam, 1972), 215, 221; *Belaruskaia savetskaia entsyklapedia*, vol. 1 (Minsk, 1969); B. Kedrov and G. Gurgenidze, "Za glubokoi razrabotku leninskogo filosofskogo nasledstva," *Kommunist* 32 (September 1955): 45–46.

24 The letter was published only in 1949, in I.V. Stalin, *Sochineniia*, vol. 12 (Moscow, 1949), 173.

25 M. Fainsod, *How Russia is Ruled* (Cambridge, MA, 1953), 180–86; Roy Medvedev, *Kniga o sotsialisticheskoi demokratii* (Amsterdam, 1972), 124–56; J. Arch Getty, *Origins of the Great Purges: The Soviet Communist Party Reconsidered* (New York, 1985), 97–98, 141–42.

26 Daniel de Coppert, ed., *Understanding Rituals* (London 1992), 1–4, 13–18.

27 Of course, theoretical openness did not exclude manipulations and intrigues, in which the Central Committee had to engage in order to secure the necessary majority. Another attempt to flirt with the idea of democracy in Stalinist times is discussed in J. Arch Getty, "State and Society under Stalin: Constitution and Elections in the 1930s," *Slavic Review* 50 (Spring 1991): 18–35.

28 Berthold Unfried, "Rituale von Konfession und Selbstkritik: Bilder vom stalinistischen Kader," *Jahrbuch für historische Kommunismusforschung* (1994): 148–64. See also Klaus-Georg Riegel, *Konfessionsrituale im Marxismus-Leninismus* (Graz, 1985).

29 Getty, *Origins*, 50, 67, 134–35, 145, 224.

30 Coppert, *Understanding Rituals*, 15.

31 *Nauchnaia sessiia*, 94, 187, 501.

32 The metaphor is used here not in the narrow sense of game theory, but in the wider Wittgensteinian sense. See examples of games in L. Wittgenstein, *Philosophical Investigations* (London, 1958), 66–71. A comparison with a game like amateur soccer, where players follow certain models, but can also argue and improvise about rules, suffices for the purposes of this essay.

33 Although Getty does not assign a special role to the moderator as the third party (besides the mob and the local boss) in the performance of *kritika i samokritika*, this figure appears in his narratives whenever he describes a meeting in detail (*Origins*, 72, 151–53). The moderator did have his own agenda and usually tried to direct the meeting, but he had to avoid being explicitly partisan. Sometimes the discussion could get out of his control: Getty describes a *kritika i samokritika* meeting during which angry communist insurgents ousted the district party secretary, despite the protective attempts of the higher representative.

34 On the 1928 campaign of *samokritika*, see *Spravochnik partiinogo rabotnika*, 7th edn (Moscow-Leningrad, 1930); G. Alikhanov, *Samokritika i vnutripartiinaia demokratiia* (Leningrad, 1928); and *O samokritike* (n. p., 1928). For a description of *samokritika* in the Moscow party structure, see Catherine Merridale, *Moscow Politics and the Rise of Stalin* (Basingstoke, 1990), 198–215.

35 "Diskussiia," 270. Originally, Zhdanov tried to ascribe authorship of the concept to Stalin, but Stalin crossed this out from the manuscript (Esakov, "K istorii," 92).

36 "Bol'shevistskaia kritika i samokritika." For more on the theory of *kritika i samokritika*, see "Samokritika – ispytannoe oruzhie bol'shevizma," Stepanian, "O protivorechiiakh pri sotsializme," and "Pod znamenem bol'shevistskoi kritiki i samokritiki," all in *Pravda*, 24 August 1946, 20 August 1947, and 15 March 1948, respectively.

37 Esakov, "K istorii," 93–102. See also B.M. Kedrov, "Kak sozdavalsia nash zhurnal," *Voprosy filosofii*, 1988, no. 4: 92–104.

38 Kedrov, "Znachenie kritiki i samokritiki v razvitii nauki (K voprosu o role otritsaniia v dialektike i metafizike)," *Vestnik Akademii nauk*, 1948, no. 2: 68–100; Zhdanov, "O kritike"; Iovchuk, "Bor'ba mnenii." See also "Za svobodnuiu, tvorcheskuiu nauchnuiu kritiku," *Vestnik Akademii nauk*, 1950, no. 8: 10–20.

39 "Pervye itogi tvorcheskikh diskussii," *Vestnik Akademii nauk*, 1948, no. 3: 15.

40 "Doklad t. Zhdanova o zhurnalakh 'Zvezda' i 'Leningrad'," *Pravda*, 21 September 1946.

41 "Stenogramma soveshchaniia v TsK po voprosam propagandy, o rabote tsentral'nykh gazet i izdatel'stv, 18 aprelia 1946 g. pod predsedatel'stvom A.A. Zhdanova," RTsKhIDNI, f. 77, op. 1, d. 976, l. 40.

42 The campaign for *tvorcheskie diskussii* in science also has to be distinguished from the 1947 campaign for teaching patriotism to scientists as well as from the 1949 anti-cosmopolitan witchhunt. On the former, see V.D. Esakov and E.S. Levina, "Delo 'KR' (Iz istorii gonenii na sovetskuiu intelligentsiiu)," *Kentavr*, 1994, no. 2: 54–69; and Nikolai Krementsov, "The 'KR Affair': Soviet Science on the Threshold of the Cold War," *History and Philosophy of the Life Sciences*, 1995, no. 3: 3–30. On the latter, see G. Kostyrchenko, *V plenu u krasnogo faraona: Politicheskie presledovaniia evreev v SSSR v poslednee stalinskoe desiatiletie: Dokumental'noe issledovanie* (Moscow, 1994). Although they shared many common rhetorical themes, the formal rules of public games differed and these campaigns needed separate treatment.

43 On the border between the spheres of cognitive authority of politicians and experts, see Kojevnikov, "President of Stalin's Academy," 38–39. For a contrasting view on *kritika i samokritika* as a method of subordinating science, suppressing all signs of independent thinking, and creating a specifically Marxist science, see N.L. Krementsov, "Ravnenie na VASKhNIL," in *Repressirovannaia nauka* (St Petersburg, 1994), 2: 94–95. This view is based on the standard interpretation of the campaign as "the intention of party agencies to establish complete control over the scientific community and to affirm the status of the Central Committee . . . as the supreme authority in scientific questions," and on unjustified generalizing upon the single case of biology. See Nikolai Krementsov, *Stalinist Science* (Princeton, NJ, 1997), 193.

44 This led to the publication of a paper on the philosophy of physics and to a subsequent *diskussiia*. See M.A. Markus, "O prirode fizicheskogo znaniia," "Diskussiia o prirode fizicheskogo znaniia: Obsuzhdenie stat'i M.A. Markusa," *Voprosy filosofii*, 1947, 2: 140–76, and 1948, 3: 212–35.

45 See, for example, "Obsuzhdenie uchebnika prof. A.I. Denisova 'Sovetskoe gosudarstvo i pravo'," and "Rasshirennoe zasedanie Redaktsionno-Izdatel'skogo soveta AN SSSR," *Vestnik Akademii nauk*, 1948, no. 4: 103–5, and no. 6: 73–80, respectively.

46 "Obsuzhdenie knigi prof. B.M. Kedrova 'Engel's i estestvoznanie," *Vestnik Akademii nauk*, 1948, no. 3: 100–5.

47 See, for instance, G.F. Aleksandrov, "Ob oshibochnykh vzgliadakh B.M. Kedrova v oblasti filosofii i estestvoznaniia," 23 February 1949, RTsKhIDNI, f. 17, op. 132, d. 180, ll. 48–97.

48 On this and other attacks on Lysenko, see Esakov and Levina, "Iz istorii bor'by s lysenkovshchinoi," *Izvestiia TsK KPSS*, 1991, no. 4: 125–41, no. 6: 157–73, and no. 7: 109–21; E.S Levina, *Vavilov, Lysenko, Timofeev-Resovskii – Biologiia v SSSR: Istoriia i istoriografiia* (Moscow, 1995); RTsKhIDNI, f. 17. op. 125, d. 359, ll. 5–8; ibid., d. 449, ll. 48–49, 108–11; and S.I. Alikhanov to Stalin, 6 May 1948, ibid., d. 71, ll. 4–41.

49 Iu.A. Zhdanov, "Vo mgle protivorechii," *Voprosy filosofii*, 1993, no. 7: 74.

50 "Nauchnye diskussii," *Literaturnaia gazeta*, 29 November, and 10 and 27 December 1947; "O vnutrividovoi bor'be za sushchestvovanie sredi orga-nizmov (Reshenie Biuro Otdeleniia biologicheskikh nauk AN SSSR)," *Vestnik Akademii nauk*, 1948, no. 3; "Moskovskaia konferentsiia po problemam darvinizma," *Priroda*, 1948, no. 6: 85–87.

51 Zhdanov, "Vo mgle," 74, 81, 85–86.

52 Lysenko to Stalin and Andrei Zhdanov, 17 April 1948, and Lysenko to I.A. Benediktov, minister of agriculture, 11 May 1948, published in Valery Soyfer, *Lysenko and the Tragedy of Soviet Science* (New Brunswick, NJ, 1994), 172–77.

53 Zhdanov, "Vo mgle," 87. On D.T. Shepilov, see "Problemy istorii i sovre-mennosti," *Voprosy istorii* KPSS, 1989, no. 2: 48–55.

54 Shepilov's recently published memoirs support the former option. See: D.T. Shepilov, "Vospominaniia," *Voprosy istorii*, 1998, no. 6: 4.

55 On the conflicting principles of the TsK organization and the Zhdanov–Malenkov rivalry, see Fainsod, *How Russia is Ruled*, 172–77. Kedrov also lost his job as the editor of *Voprosy filosofii* in November 1948 as an indirect conse-quence of the August Session (RTsKhIDNI, f. 17, op. 132, d. 34).

56 A. Zhdanov and G. Malenkov, "O polozhenii v sovetskoi biologicheskoi nauke," RTsKhIDNI, f. 17, op. 77, d. 991; and the protocols of Politbiuro meet-ings on 10 and 15 July 1948 in ibid., f. 17, op. 3, d. 1071.

57 Kirill Rossianov, "Editing Nature: Joseph Stalin and the 'New Soviet Biology'," *Isis* 84 (1993): 728–45. See also *The Situation in Biological Sciences*. On 6 August the Agricultural Department sent a long report to Malenkov, proving that the majority at the ongoing session was supporting Lysenko (RTsKhIDNI, f. 17, op. 138, d. 30, ll. 1–39).

58 E.D. Manevich, "Takie byli vremena," *Voprosy istorii estestvoznaniia i tekhniki*, 1993, no. 2: 124–5.

59 *The Situation in Biological Sciences*, 391. Another attempt to change the genre of discourse by proposing a different political model was made by B.M. Zavadovskii, who reminded the audience that the party had fought "an ideo-logical struggle on two fronts," "against right- and left-wing deviations" and "against mechanistic vulgarization of Marxism, on the one hand, and against Menshevistic idealism, formalism, and metaphysics, on the other." Zavadovskii called for defending the middle line of "correct Darwinism" against both Neo-Lamarckism and Neo-Darwinism (ibid., 338, 345).

60 Ibid., 101 (see also 165, 233, 254, and 510). The *diskussiia* at the editorial office of *Pod znamenem marksizma* occurred in 1939 and ended rather unfavorably for geneticists (Krementsov, *Stalinist Science*).

61 "Rasshirennoe zasedanie Prezidiuma Akademii nauk SSSR, 24–26 avgusta 1948 g.," *Vestnik Akademii nauk*, 1948, no. 9: 26. On Orbeli, see RTsKhIDNI, f. 17, op. 132, d. 40, ll. 65–68. The academy's report to the Central Committee is in ibid., ll. 176–82.

62 See the protocols of the Central Committee Secretariat from 6, 9, 11, 16, and 20 August in RTsKhIDNI, f. 17, op. 116, dd. 364–69. On the Ministry of Higher Education, see ibid., op. 132, d. 66. On library books, see ibid., ll. 7–21. For other administrative consequences of the August Session, see Krementsov, *Stalinist Science*.

63 J.V. Stalin, "Concerning Marxism in Linguistics (1950)," in Stalin, *Marxism and Problems of Linguistics* (Peking, 1972), 29.

64 See Kojevnikov, "President of Stalin's Academy," 43–47.

65 Zhdanov, "Vo mgle," 88. On the preparations for the Pavlov Session and the role of Zhdanov, see RTsKhIDNI, f. 17 op. 132, d. 161, ll. 43–73, 180–86; ibid., d. 177, ll. 144–62; and ibid., d. 347, ll. 1–10.

66 Alpatov, *Istoriia*, chs 1–2; R. l'Hermite, *Marr, Marrism, Marristes: Une page de l'histoire de la linguistique soviétique* (Paris, 1987). Linguistic theories had very important political meanings, as they were related to issues of nationality policies, Soviet views on nations and ethnicities, and to the big practical work on constructing languages and nationalities in the USSR. For penetrating analysis which pays attention to these themes, see Yuri Slezkine, "N.Ia. Marr and the National Origins of Soviet Ethnogenetics," *Slavic Review* 55 (Winter 1996).

67 Alpatov, *Istoriia*, chs 3–4; Slezkine, "N.Ia. Marr."

68 "Obsuzhdenie rabot po iazykoznaniiu," *Vestnik Akademii nauk*, 1948, no. 2: 113–18; "Obsuzhdenie raboty zhurnala 'Izvestiia AN SSSR: Otdelenie literatury i iazyka',," and "Ocherednye zadachi sovetskogo iazykoznaniia," *Izvestiia Akademii nauk SSSR: Otdelenie literatury i iazyka*, 1948, no. 5: 463–66, and 466–68, respectively.

69 I.I. Meshchaninov, "O polozhenii v lingvisticheskoi nauke," F.P. Filin, "O dvukh napravleniiakh v iazykovedenii," and "Rezoliutsiia," *Izvestiia Akademii nauk SSSR: Otdelenie literatury i iazyka*, 1948, no. 6: 473–85, 486–96, and 497–99, respectively.

70 "Obsuzhdenie rabot po iazykoznaniiu."

71 Filin, "O dvukh napravleniiakh," 496.

72 Aplatov, *Istoriia*, 149–67.

73 A.V. Topchiev, "I.V. Stalin o problemakh iazykoznaniia i zadachi Akademii nauk SSSR," *Vestnik Akademii nauk*, 1950, no. 7: 8–19; A.M. Samarin, "O sostoianii uchebnoi i nauchnoi raboty po iazykoznaniiu v vuzakh i mery po ee uluchsheniiu," *Vestnik vysshei shkoly*, 1950, no. 9; Alpatov, *Istoriia*, 150–51, 158, 167.

74 I.P. Bardin (Academy of Sciences) to Malenkov, 30 July 1949 and November 1949, and Kruzhkov and Zhdanov (Agitprop) to Suslov, 19 August 1949, November 1949, and 10 January 1950, in RTsKhIDNI, f. 17, op. 132, d. 164, ll. 16–114.

75 Suslov's remarks are in RTsKhIDNI, f. 17, op. 132, d. 336, ll. 4–9. See also Meshchaninov "Dokladnaia zapiska," 12 April 1950, Academy of Sciences to Malenkov, 17 April 1950, ibid., ll. 10–76, and P. Klimov and P. Tret'iakov to Suslov, 13 April 1950, ibid., ll. 4–9.

76 A. Chikobava, "Kogda i kak eto bylo," in *Ezhegodnik iberiisko-kavkazskogo iazykoznaniia* (Tbilisi, 1985), 9–52.

77 A.S. Chikobava, "O nekotorykh voprosakh sovetskogo iazykoznaniia," *Pravda* 9 May 1950. "As a matter of dispute" (*v diskussionnom poriadke*) – a necessary remark to let readers know that, despite publication in *Pravda*, the text should not be considered authoritative.

78 *The Soviet Linguistics Controversy*, trans. John V. Murra, Robert M. Hankin, and Fred Holling (Morningside Heights, 1951), 10.

79 Alpatov, *Istoriia*, 169.

80 *Pravda*, 20 June 1950.

81 J.V. Stalin, "Concerning Marxism in Linguistics," 29, 32.

82 "Prezidium Akademii Nauk, Postanovlenie," and "V institute iazykoznaniia," *Izvestiia Akademii nauk SSSR: Otdelenie literatury i iazyka*, 1950, no. 1: 80–85, and 86–88, respectively.

83 I.I. Tolstoi, "Otrezvliaiushchii golos razuma," ibid., 62–63.

84 "O povyshenii okladov rabotnikov nauki i ob uluchshenii ikh material'no-bytovykh uslovii," Decree No. 514 of the USSR Council of Ministers. This document was marked "secret," and only a short note on it appeared in *Pravda* on 7 March 1946.

85 On the notion of the elite group being extended to include the intelligentsia, see "Introduction: On Power and Culture," in Sheila Fitzpatrick, *The Cultural Front: Power and Culture in Revolutionary Russia* (Ithaca, NY, 1992), 1–15.

86 Wittgenstein, *Philosophical Investigations*, 7.

87 Compare this to Joravsky, *Lysenko Affair*, 97–98.

88 When describing this pattern, Joravsky used the words "authoritarian caprice," "zigzag party line," and "fluctuations." See his "The Stalinist Mentality and Higher Learning," *Slavic Review* 42 (Winter 1983): 575–600.

89 On images of the enemy, Manichean and Augustinian, see P. Galison, "The Ontology of the Enemy: Norbert Wiener and the Cybernetic Vision," *Critical Inquiry* 21 (Autumn 1994): 228–66.

Part III

CONSUMPTION AND CIVILIZATION

Consumption is a very different topic in a Soviet historiographical context than in a Western European or American one. With reference to the United States and modern Europe, the topic involves an exploration of abundance, advertising and marketing, "conspicuous consumption," and consumer lobby groups. In the Soviet case, by contrast, the society was socialist, not capitalist; there was no private sector and little advertising; the regime's Marxist ideology would scarcely seem encouraging to acquisitiveness (a "petty-bourgeois" attribute) or luxurious life-styles (associated with the upper classes under the old regime); and shortages, not abundance, were the norm. This makes it all the more remarkable that discerning consumerism and the cultivation of good taste received official valorization in the 1930s.

The current discussion has several roots. The first comes from Vera Dunham's observation that, contrary to Marxist principles and Bolshevik practice in the revolutionary years, the acquisition of goods and a "cultured" life-style was highly recommended in the popular literature of the postwar period.[1] She called these values "middle class" and associated their emergence with embourgeoisement and the emergence of what Milovan Djilas labelled "the new class." Trotsky's *The Revolution Betrayed* and Timasheff's *The Great Retreat* were important influences for Dunham. She argued that, in a "big deal" with this new privileged class, the regime implicitly agreed to endorse its bourgeois values, including consumerism, in return for political loyalty. The topic was further developed in Fitzpatrick, "Becoming Cultured,"[2] which put the consumerism of the 1930s in a context of the discourses of "culturedness" (*kul'turnost'* – the subject of Volkov's chapter in this volume) and socialist realism.

The second set of roots comes from the Hungarian economist Janos Kornai's analysis of the functioning of socialist-type economies, in particular his emphasis on shortages and hoarding as core characteristics and his ideas about state paternalism and societal dependency as products of the state's preeminent position as a distributor of goods. This notion of the centrality of the state's *allocative* function is developed by Katherine Verdery.[3] Associated with it, however, was always a "second economy" of informal, non-state distribution of goods, which attracted the attention of economic historians such as Gregory Grossman and James Millar in the Brezhnev period.[4]

The third major contribution to this discussion came from a young Russian scholar, Elena Osokina, who in the early 1990s began publishing (in Russian) her work on the Soviet distribution system. The title of Osokina's work was *Hierarchies of Consumption*, and what she did in the book was to provide a detailed analysis of the rationing systems practised for a large part of the Stalin period, emphasizing the special privileges of elites.[5] Implicit in Osokina's argument is the idea that *access* is the key to privilege in Soviet-type systems. Those who have preferential access to goods are the equivalent of our moneyed and propertied classes; and the state is the main distributor of access preferences. Another conclusion that could be drawn from Osokina's work is that it was consumption (that is, degrees of access to goods), not production (as Marxist class analysis implies), that was the basis of Soviet social stratification.

Goods and their distribution are still a comparatively new subject in American scholarship. The most extensive treatment is in Julie Hessler's 1996 dissertation, "Culture of Shortages," dealing with the practices and discourses of Soviet trade, as well as its policies and economic structures, over the period 1917 to 1953. In the dissertation from which her chapter in this volume is drawn, Hessler (b. 1966) analyses in detail the processes of formal and informal distribution of goods in the Stalin period. But this chapter focusses specifically on the discourse of consumerism associated with Stalin's slogan "Life has become better, comrades."

While Vera Dunham provides a starting point, Hessler goes beyond Dunham's interpretive frame of embourgeoisement, in addition to predating the turn from the postwar years to the mid-1930s. Modernity is a key value in the discourse she presents. She describes a process whereby consumer goods, and particularly the process of their sale in new large department stores, came to be valorized as modern and civilizing. Salespeople were exhorted to become exemplars of civilized modernity by providing polite service in hygienic and tasteful surroundings. They were also encouraged to assume an instructional role *vis-à-vis* the customer, with the result that "the campaign for cultured trade aimed at transforming shopping into an exercise in modernity, in which the store would become a site of education parallel to the school, the workplace, and the political meeting." America was the model, particularly department stores like Macy's (bathed in an almost paradisal light in the contemporary Soviet descriptions Hessler quotes). In the new consumerist discourse, Stakhanovite workers and peasants – high achievers who received awards of "cultured" goods like radios and sewing machines from the state – played an important role. There was also a gendered aspect: housewives were encouraged to create well-appointed, tasteful home environments in which they would exert a civilizing influence on their husbands and children. All this existed, remarkably, in a real-life context where goods of all kinds were in chronically short supply and Soviet citizens were in the habit of joining any queue they saw, regardless of what goods were on offer.

Vadim Volkov (b. 1965) is a Russian historical sociologist who received his PhD in 1995 at Cambridge under Anthony Giddens with a dissertation on "Forms of Public Life: the Public Sphere and the Concept of Society in Imperial Russia," and is now Dean of Social Sciences at the European University in St Petersburg. He belongs to a Russian cohort that is schooled in Western social and cultural theory and has a foot in both worlds. His chapter in this volume, which takes off from Vera Dunham's study of kul'turnost' and Norbert Elias's concept of the civilizing process, explores the notion of "culturedness" which is also to be found in Hessler's study of "cultured trade."

The Soviet disciplines of civilization – hygiene, manners, ways of comporting oneself in public, modes of consumption – were specifically related to certain sociological developments: the mass migration of workers to towns and large-scale upward mobility into the new elite, both requiring large numbers of individuals to become socialized in new environments. In content these disciplines resembled those of Western Europe at an earlier period; but the Soviet version was distinguished by the fact that the civilizing disciplines coexisted with more familiar forms of Stalinist discipline, violence and terror. Kul'turnost', however, was not simply something imposed from without. While the society collectively worked to produce cultured individuals (with women playing an important role), "working on oneself" was also a key part of the project.[6]

Lewis Siegelbaum (b. 1949) comes to the subject from his earlier study of Stakhanovism. The chapter in this volume is one of a number of recent works dealing with letters and petitions (see Introduction to Part II), and it draws inspiration from the writings of Kornai, Verdery, and Ferenc Feher on the function of state allocation of goods in an economy of shortages. The data on which Siegelbaum's essay are based are unpublished letters from award-winning peasant workers on state farms – forerunners of Stakhanovites, though technically distinct – who were asked by their trade union to identify their needs with regard to housing, furniture, clothing, food, cultural amenities (newspapers, books), and health care. The awardwinners' requests for winter clothes, shoes, beds, passes to sanatoria, opportunities to go away and study, and the like tell us a great deal both about how they constructed their "needs," as well as their actual living conditions; it turns out that even these peasant writers, close to the bottom of the social scale, often drew on the discourse of *kul'turnost'*. As Siegelbaum observes, citizens' requests for needed goods to a paternalist state are likely to have a tone of supplication. But sometimes a note of entitlement to "decent (*normal'nye*) cultural and living conditions" comes in too, although it appears that among these rural folk, many of them women, the sense of entitlement was much less developed than among Sarah Davies's Leningraders (see Part I).

One of the phenomena Siegelbaum notes in passing is that of client–patron relations. This is not a new topic in Soviet studies – the organizers of the Harvard Project of the 1950s were very much aware of its importance – but it has recently taken new directions in studies of the informal distribution channels of patronage and *blat* by scholars such as the anthropologist Alena Ledeneva, Julie Hessler, and Sheila Fitzpatrick. The current scholarship tends to focus as much on networks of sociability as on economic structures; and the subject is of particular interest to those who see personalistic ties as a crucial aspect of the culture and cast the Stalinist system in a "neo-traditional" light.

FURTHER READING

Dunham, Vera S., *In Stalin's Time: Middleclass Values in Soviet Fiction* (Cambridge, Mass., 1976).

Fitzpatrick, Sheila, "Becoming Cultured: Socialist Realism and the Representation of Privilege and Taste," in Fitzpatrick, *The Cultural Front: Power and Culture in Revolutionary Russia* (Ithaca, 1992).

Kornai, Janos, *The Socialist System: The Political Economy of Communism* (Oxford, 1992).

Verdery, Katherine, *What Was Socialism, and What Comes Next?* (Princeton, 1996).

Consumption

Barnes-Cox, Randi, "Soviet Commercial Advertising and the Creation of the Socialist Consumer, 1917-1941," in Christina Kiaer and Eric Naiman, eds, *Everyday Subjects: Formations of Identity in Early Soviet Culture*, (Cornell University Press, forthcoming).

Fitzpatrick, Sheila, *Everyday Stalinism: Ordinary Life in Extraordinary Times. Soviet Russia in the 1930s* (New York, 1999), chs. 2 and 4.

Hessler, Julie, "Culture of Shortages: A Social History of Soviet Trade, 1917–1953," PhD dissertation, University of Chicago, 1996.

Kotkin, Stephen, *Magnetic Mountain: Stalinism as a Civilization* (Berkeley, 1995), ch. 6.

Osokina, Elena, *Za fasadom "stalinskogo izobiliia". Raspredelenie i rynok v snabzhenii naseleniia v gody industrializatsii, 1927–1941* (Moscow: 1998); forthcoming as *Our Daily Bread: Socialist Distribution and the Art of Survival in Stalin's Russia, 1927–1941*, ed. and trans. Kate S. Transchel and Greta Bucher (Armonk, NY: M.E. Sharpe, 1999).

Rimmel, Lesley, "Another Kind of Fear: the Kirov Murder and the End of Bread Rationing in Leningrad," *Slavic Review* 56: 3 (1997).

Patronage and *blat*

Berliner, Joseph, "Blat is Higher than Stalin," *Problems of Communism* 3: 1 (1954).

Fitzpatrick, Sheila, "*Blat* in Stalin's Time," in Alena Ledeneva, Stephen Lovell, and Andrei Rogachevskii, eds, *Bribery and Blat in Russia: The Rights and Wrongs of Reciprocity*, (London: Macmillan, forthcoming 1999).

—— "Intelligentsia and Power: Client–Patron Relations in Stalin's Russia," in Manfred Hildermeier, ed., *Stalinismus vor dem Zweiten Weltkrieg. Neue Wege der Forschung /Stalinism Before the Second World War: New Avenues of Research* (Munich, 1998).

Ledeneva, Alena, "The Origins of Blat," in Christina Kiaer and Eric Naiman, eds, *Everyday Subjects: Formations of Identity in Early Soviet Culture* (Cornell University Press, forthcoming).

—— *Russia's Economy of Favours: Blat, Networking and Informal Exchange* (Cambridge, 1998).

NOTES

1 Vera S. Dunham, *In Stalin's Time: Middleclass Values in Soviet Fiction* (Cambridge, Mass., 1976).

2 "Becoming Cultured: Socialist Realism and the Representation of Privilege and Taste," in Sheila Fitzpatrick, *The Cultural Front: Power and Culture in Revolutionary Russia* (Ithaca, 1992). This article was originally published in a Festschrift for Vera Dunham: see Terry L. Thompson and Robert Sheldon, eds, *Soviet Society and Culture: Essays in Honor of Vera S. Dunham* (Boulder, Col., 1988).

3 See Katherine Verdery, *National Ideology under Socialism: Identity and Cultural Politics in Ceaucescu's Romania* (Berkeley, 1991), 74–83.

4 See Gregory Grossman, "The 'Second Economy' of the USSR," *Problems of Communism* 26: 5 (1977), and James R. Millar, "The Little Deal: Brezhnev's Contribution to Acquisitive Socialism," *Slavic Review* 44: 4 (1985).

5 E.A. Osokina, *Ierarkhiia potrebleniia. O zhizni liudei v usloviiakh stalinskogo snabzheniia, 1928–1935 gg.* (Moscow, 1993) is not available in English, but an English translation of her second book, *Za fasadom "stalinskogo izobiliia"*, will shortly be published in the US. For a different approach, comparing the Soviet system of "closed distributors" for the Soviet elite in the seventeenth-century Muscovite practice of *kormlenie*, see Tamara Kondratiéva, "Stalinizm: novizna fenomena i reaktualizacija proshlogo," presented at conference on "The Stalin Period: New Ideas, New Conversations," held at Riverside, California, March 12–15, 1998.

6 For development of these ideas, see Vadim Volkov, "Limits to Propaganda: Peasant Readers and the Soviet Power in the 1920s," in James Raven, ed., *Non-commercial Uses of Print in Comparative Perspective* (Amherst: University of Massachusetts Press, forthcoming), and the work of Kharkhordin cited in the "Further Reading" section of the Introduction to Part II.

6

CULTURED TRADE

The Stalinist turn towards consumerism

Julie Hessler

In 1927, the newspaper *Economic Life* published a *Commodity Encyclopedia*, the first major reference book on goods under the Soviet regime. Intended for use by "anyone needing information about one or another commodity," the *Encyclopedia* purported to provide a comprehensive survey of "all the goods that have trading significance" in modern society, and especially in Soviet Russia. According to its editors, the volume attempted to address the following questions: "What does the given commodity represent in essence, which of its qualities merit attention, what does it derive from, how can it be falsified?"[1] A perusal of the encyclopedia confirms these basic concerns. Its tone is technical and dry. Its alphabetical entries catalogue the basic physical and chemical properties of each commodity; describe the process of production and the requirements for storage or preservation; enumerate the uses of the commodity; and indicate its geographical sources and wholesale price range. In their selections as well as the amount of space devoted to each entry, the editors exhibited a marked preference for producers' over consumer commodities, for bulk commodities and raw materials over finished goods.

Thirty years later, a second major reference work on the subject of goods appeared. Published by the Ministry of Trade in nine volumes over the course of 1956–61, with contributions from a long list of "major specialists in trade and industry, Ph.D.s, professors, and lecturers," the new *Commodity Dictionary* was intended more narrowly for store managers and other trade personnel. Again, its stated aim was to provide the critical information about all of the goods on the Soviet market. This time, however, the "growing material demands of the working population" and the "rapid expansion of industries producing goods for popular consumption" justified an overwhelming focus on consumer goods. According to the editor:

More and more goods are appearing for sale. The role of trade personnel has become elevated; new demands have materialized in the culture of customer service. So as to help the customer correctly select the goods that he needs, and so as to place orders from industry intelligently, salesclerks, trade specialists, and store managers require a close familiarity with the goods subject to trade.[2]

Like the new dictionary's individual entries, this statement registers a subtle transformation of official views on trade and goods in the three decades since the publication of the original handbook. If the *Commodity Encyclopedia* at the outset of the industrialization drive oriented businessmen of all stripes toward production processes and "the essence of goods," the 1950s' handbook urged commercial people to turn and face the consumer, and to distinguish between goods on the basis of style as well as substance. Lavish color illustrations and numerous engravings of, for example, different fashions in women's hats, or various styles of crystal wineglasses, reinforced the point that the retailer's expertise rested as much on aesthetics and a sensitivity to customer demand as on a technical knowledge of production and supplies. In this sense, the *Commodity Dictionary* can be seen as a belated answer to NEP-era criticisms that socialist trade functionaries did not know how to sell.

At the same time, the reorientation of trade entailed a reconceptualization of commodities and their meaning to Soviet society. The dictionary's focus on consumer goods provides one index of this change. In the 1920s, an interest in material possessions was portrayed in official publications as a sign of bourgeois decadence, a deviation from the ascetic values of the socialist revolution.[3] By the mid-1950s, by contrast, the "growing material demands" of Soviet citizens were cited with pride, while the author of the dictionary's opening article on lampshades could assert in all seriousness that "A lampshade is an integral part of the light fixture; it serves to adorn the lamp and plays an important role in the architectural and aesthetic arrangement of the living space."[4] The unstated backdrop to such formulations was a valorization of materialist values. Far from repudiating material possessions, Soviet consumers were now expected to care about their stylistic statements. With its beautiful illustrations of the luxury goods produced in "ever-greater numbers" by Soviet industry, the *Commodity Dictionary* imbued its technical discussions of goods with an advertisement's appeal and a celebratory tone.

I have argued elsewhere that in most respects, it was the rationing periods (1917–24, 1928–35, 1939–47) which served as the crucible of consumer culture in Stalin's Russia.[5] Specifically, the rationing years taught Soviet citizens to expect subsidized goods from the state, but to mistrust the state's execution of its responsibilities for provisionment –

which in turn led them to queue up at the first sign of shortages, to manipulate the system through unofficial exchanges of a semi-legal or illegal nature, and to hoard. Soviet officials tolerated such behaviors to a point, but attempted to contain them through limits on the quantity of goods that customers could purchase and the threat of punishment if they overstepped the legal bounds. In addition, the rationing periods instituted a system of hierarchical entitlements, which structured consumer access for their duration. The geographical hierarchy of supplies and the social hierarchy of access that came into being under rationing shaped both the functional economy of the Stalin era and the practices, attitudes, and social relations of what I have termed the Soviet Union's culture of shortages.

It was the post-rationing periods, however, and in particular the hiatus of 1935–8, which would provide the institutional and intellectual skeleton of official distribution and consumption from the end of the Second World War to the fall of the regime. During these years, asceticism gave way to cultured consumerism as the recognized relation of the individual to material possessions. Individuals' interests became identified with their aspirations for consumption, while these aspirations became consecrated as a new kind of public value. At the same time, Soviet trade was decentralized, reorganized, and brought more into line with practices in the capitalist West. In short, if the years 1935–8 brought the renewed ferocity of Stalinist terror, they were also the harbinger of a characteristic brand of economic normalization and the dawn of an officially sanctioned Soviet consumerism.

Focussing on the non-rationing periods of the mid-1930s, this chapter examines the official turn to consumerism in relation to the campaign for "cultured trade." In a manner typical of Soviet propaganda efforts, this campaign combined media hype over "improving conditions" with the selective implementation of what it described. It brought real advances in high-end marketing, and a real enhancement of high-end wares. Its prime beneficiaries were thus high-end consumers, such as worker celebrities and Kremlin wives. For Stalin and his associates, however, this elitism connoted not the "betrayal" of the revolution, but the visible demonstration of what it could achieve.[6]

As official spokesmen would have it, the end of rationing and the establishment of "cultured" stores represented milestones on the road to prosperity. During the first years of the industrialization drive, Soviet leaders had interpreted scarcity as the price of modernization: the "heroic abstinence" of Soviet consumers was to make possible the "heroic achievements" of Soviet metallurgy, the multiplication of the means of production, and the rapid attainment of the industrial levels of the capitalist world. A condition of industrial development, scarcity was never imagined as its outcome; rather, policy-makers assumed that their temporary subjection of Soviet citizens to scarcity would lead to unprecedented affluence for individuals and society. Seven years after the start of the Stalinist revolution, however, collectivization and industrialization had resulted only in unprecedented deprivation in village and city; prosperity seemed as distant as ever before. Anxious to make progress toward that ever-receding goal, Soviet leaders attempted to bridge the gap between scarcity and abundance through culture, and to use symbolic advances in material life as a vehicle for replacing the regressive, unruly, and ultraindividualist culture of shortages with a consumer culture of socialist modernity.

From rationing to "free trade"

The identification of consumption as a public good came from no less a spokesman of Soviet power than I.V. Stalin. From 1931 on, every major speech of Stalin's contained some mendacious reference to the increasing well-being of Soviet citizens, as well as rosy projections into the prosperous socialist future.[7] Around the time of the end of rationing, however, the tenor of these pronouncements changed. From vague assertions of material progress, Stalin's remarks on consumption became pointed and present-minded. They increasingly took the form of policy statements as to the necessary measures for achieving societal affluence, and at the same time stressed individual opportunities for material advancement through work. This reconfiguration of consumption culminated in a speech to the First All-Union Congress of Stakhanovites in November 1935, when Stalin suggested that the fulfilment of the socialist Revolution required "material benefits" (*material'nye blaga*) to complement its hard-won political benefits for the Soviet citizen. His announcement that "Life has become better, comrades. Life has become happier" was widely cited at the time to legitimize popular aspirations for a higher standard of living.[8] Its import was no less than the conversion of public values; for the first time since the Revolution, the Soviet leadership conceded that the satisfaction of individuals' private material interests could further the public good.

The decision to end rationing in the mid-1930s reflected this rethinking of consumption at the upper echelons of state power. From the time of the economics reforms of 1932 on, central executives increasingly viewed rationing as an embarrassing retrogression in the country's evolution, incommensurate with a modern, socialist state. Stalin himself stressed the necessity of improving trade and increasing production of consumer goods in his public speeches of 1933–4.[9] More strikingly, Andrei Zhdanov, soon to replace Kirov as secretary of the Leningrad obkom, expressed his unease with the rationing system during a closed Politburo commission meeting in November, 1934: "We are in favor of changing the system of food distribution precisely for the sake of liquidating the vestiges of a war era in that sector."[10] The only war whose vestiges affected food distribution in 1934, however, was the war waged by the Soviet state against peasants during collectivization.[11] Tacitly acknowledging the hardships that Soviet policies had engendered, Zhdanov's remark drew into question the continuing validity of the rationing-era policy of deprivation once the apogee of the crisis had passed.

That the highest Soviet leaders now considered non-rationed trade an essential article of progress and normalization could be seen in the choice of the new Commissar of Domestic Trade. I.Ia. Veitser had served as the Soviet trade representative in Berlin in 1931 and seems to have had a genuine appreciation of the effectiveness of a market system. Consciously invoking the language of capitalism, Veitser waxed eloquent on the advantages of "free trade," the new shorthand for non-rationed distribution and consumer choice. In meetings with trade administrators from around the country, he rebuked any trade personnel who "thought that the rationing system would last for a long time yet, with a minimum of commercial trade," and insisted that the historical meaning of rationing lay in its position in a trajectory of progress – in the fact that it "laid the foundations and created a basis for the future development of free trade."[12] The Central Committee resolution on the end of bread rationing confirmed this proposition, announcing that under the present circumstances, "the rationing system for bread and certain other foods can only act as a brake on the improvement of provisionment and therefore must be repealed."[13]

The rationing system was repealed in two stages: bread rationing was abolished as of January 1, 1935, while rations for other goods were eliminated in October. Policy-makers simultaneously reorganized the trade sector and increased prices for those consumers with access to rationed foods.[14] The majority of the institutional changes were directed at the quantitative goals of profit and efficiency. Indeed, whether or not "free trade" would bring about an improved standard of living in the long run, the termination of the working-class food subsidy threatened to alienate the regime's primary constituency in the short run.[15] To defuse discontent over the price hikes, Soviet leaders mounted a highly publicized campaign to enhance the quality and atmosphere of Soviet stores. Not only did 13,500 new bread shops open across the country between September 1934 and January 1935, model shops were equipped with new weights and sharp knives; their salesclerks outfitted in new white smocks and caps; and samples of the bread displayed in new glass counters, with clearly marked prices.[16] From a rationing-era assortment of white bread or black bread, stores now boasted up to 35 varieties of bread and related baked goods.[17] New regulations expanded the hours of trade and required bread shops to remain open seven days a week.[18] Planned deliveries were increased; in

Gorky, bread shops now received six deliveries a day from the local bread factories, beginning at 4:00 a.m.[19] Stricter sanitary regulations banned sales of warm bread; required salespeople to wash their hands frequently with soap and to handle the bread as little as possible; and stipulated that floors and shelves be cleaned daily.[20] In addition, the trade administration called upon store managers to use their own initiative to make their stores and wares attractive to consumers, whether by ordering white curtains for the display cases, piping in music, decorating the store with plants, or adding benches where tired customers could sit down and rest.[21]

Politicians and publicists portrayed such innovations as concrete evidence of the country's material progress. From the backward sector of the national economy, as Stalin had labelled it just one year earlier, Soviet trade was becoming "cultured."[22] "Culturedness" had become the catchword of a newly enshrined ethic of civilized modernity. According to Vera Dunham, it made a public virtue of personal propriety, above all in relation to material goods: it "encode[d] the proper relationship between people through their possessions and labels" and "channel[ed] the direction of sanctioned aspirations" along lines determined both by petit-bourgeois tastes and a heightened sense of social hierarchy.[23] In January 1935, every newspaper offered paeans to "cultured" bread stores, whose cleanliness, inviting decor, polite service, packaging for the items purchased, and lack of cursing not only compensated for the higher prices now charged, but served as catalysts for the cultural elevation of the customer. A feuilleton in the leading industrial newspaper, written by an incognito observer in a newly opened bread store, recorded this civilizing process:

> Inexperienced in this art, we clumsily wrapped the bread in paper. These grey sheets of rough wrapping paper provoked an uninterrupted stream of delighted commentary. Many were confused by the packaging. A housewife announced: "You don't need to wrap it ... I always just carry bread in my purse."
>
> "Take it, take it," said another. "That purse probably hasn't been cleaned in three years ... We've become accustomed to dirt!"
>
> An hour later, a young worker refused the wrapping paper. "I don't need it ... It's unnecessary waste ... I'm going to eat it right away anyhow."
>
> "Take a look at your hands!" an older worker interrupted him. "Your hands are covered with kerosene, they're filthy, and you want to handle bread with them ..."
>
> And he himself asked me to wrap the bread as carefully as possible.[24]

In such depictions, publicists diverted attention from the high prices and continuing shortages in Soviet stores by identifying the problems in distribution with the learned behaviors of Soviet citizens. Unable to satisfy their material wants, Stalinist leaders invited citizens to become more hygienic and more discriminating, or more "cultured," through exposure to "modernity" embodied in consumer commodities and the cultured milieu of the store.

The campaign for "culturedness" thus had two thrusts: to cultivate consumers and to civilize trade. As the crux of both projects, the store became both a measure of cultural progress and the agent of further progress. In the broadest sense, the campaign for cultured trade aimed at transforming shopping into an exercise in modernity, in which the store would become a site of education parallel to the school, the workplace, and the political meeting. In the later 1930s, Soviet stores experimented with customer service and manipulated images of culture, appropriateness, and style to peddle goods, while the Soviet leadership used coveted consumer goods and cultured stores to promote a new image of the proper citizen.

Models of civilization, or the Americanization of Soviet trade

The campaign for culturedness was supposed to affect every store, down to the humblest bread shop or small-town cooperative. Accordingly, the trade census of 1935 included such information as the number and percentage of clothing stores with separate men's and women's departments, fitting rooms, and mirrors, and the number of food stores with accurate control weights.[25] At the same time, Trade Commissariat spokesmen admitted that store managers even in the largest cities did not always know the regulations on these questions, and that without enforcement the chances of improvement were slim.[26] Rather than devote the necessary resources to turn every store into a paragon of culturedness, the trade administration followed a policy of selective implementation. The campaign for cultured trade in fact devolved onto an embedded series of "models": stores were supposed to provide citizens with a model of cultured interaction and behavior, but certain stores – any stores in Moscow, as well as the "Bakaleia" and "Gastronom" groceries, and the so-called "model" department stores of the USSR's largest cities – were to serve as models for all the rest. Finally, these stores were patterned on their own model of civilization: the department stores and groceries of the capitalist West.

Refurbished in connection with the campaign for cultured trade, the premier stores of the mid-1930s were in most cases either "commercial" stores during the rationing era or "closed distributors" for Soviet elites.

"Bakaleia" was the name given to the commercial bread shops opened in medium to large cities as of 1933–4, for non-rationed sales of bread, cereals, pastries, and in some places, flour, while "Gastronom" designated groceries opened in 1931–4 with such delicacies as smoked fish, caviare, fruits, confectionery, and liquor. Though far better supplied than ordinary stores during the rationing era, these "commercial" stores sold their stocks at extremely high prices, and at least in the case of the Gastronoms, catered primarily to Soviet elites. After the end of rationing in 1935, all stores became "commercial" in that they sold their wares to anyone who could pay for them, but the elite orientation of the former commercial stores and closed distributors dictated that they enjoyed connections to the best suppliers, occupied the best premises, had the highest turnover, and received the most resources, as well as autonomy, from the state.[27] In Leningrad, trade experts reported that "Gastronom and Bakaleia command the best stores as to external appearance, internal equipment, quality and assortment of goods, and as to their methods of cultured customer service."[28] One grocery in particular was said to "represent a truly extraordinary phenomenon in the development of Soviet trade"; occupying the palatial premises of the prerevolutionary Eliseev supermarket, this "food department store" boasted chandeliers, frescoes, and a rich assortment of luxury foods.[29]

"Model" department stores followed essentially the same path as the premier groceries: they too were opened as commercial stores under the auspices of the Commissariat of Provisionment, satisfied high-class demands, and served as paradigms of cultured trade.[30] From Leningrad to Tashkent, local officials celebrated the inauguration of a model store as a milestone in the cultural development of their city. Gala openings provided the occasion for a media blitz, replete with speeches by city authorities, festive banners, and in the case of one model store in Leningrad, a performance by a local chamber orchestra in the central hall.[31] Like the restored Eliseev grocery, many of the Soviet Union's twenty or so model department stores were installed in the sumptuous buildings of prerevolutionary stores, where administrators consciously recreated an atmosphere of luxury to match the high-end goods that they purveyed.[32] A 1936 newsreel on Moscow's Central Department Store, converted from the prerevolutionary emporium Muir and Merilees, portrayed the results: an "abundance of high-quality goods," in the form of gleaming electric teakettles, enameled pans, silk neckties, and women's pumps; and an "attentive approach to the customer," with saleswomen, often young and pretty, hovering at every elbow. Unlike earlier newsreels, this film unabashedly exalted the elite orientation of the store. Nearly every woman shopper appears in a full-length fur coat, sheer stockings, and high heels, while every child sports a sheepskin cap. Snob appeal was perhaps most prominent in a scene in the "women's room" (*zhenskaia komnata*), where lady customers could peruse pattern books and place individual orders with the store's tailor from the comfort of an armchair, surrounded by gilt side-tables, brocade drapery, and mannequins dressed in evening gowns. Each frame of the newsreel reinforced the general image of an opulent and civilized store, where bourgeois housewives could satisfy their every desire.[33]

The campaign for cultured trade was especially prevalent in Moscow, which was currently the focus of its own drive for culturedness as the Soviet Union's model city. The mid-1930s saw the construction of the first metro line, with stations described as palaces of daily life. Similarly, trade was to "play a significant role in the transformation of the Red Capital into the most cultured and the most beautiful city in the world."[34] Although remnants of "old, merchant Moscow" still survived in the form of the dirty, disorganized stores periodically lambasted in metropolitan trade publications,[35] Moscow officials informed store managers that the era of the backward trading-row shop had come to an end. Now, managers had a duty not merely to keep their stores clean, but also to make them "pretty, according to the artistic requirements of socialist urban construction, for the external (and internal) layout of a store is at the same time one of the most visible aspects of the city."[36] In Moscow as elsewhere, however, trade department efforts were mainly directed at the "model" stores, and though these indeed became palaces of consumption, their focus on high-class demand – costly luxuries and the top end of everyday wares – prevented ordinary workers and peasants from experiencing their civilizing effects in daily life.[37]

Soviet administrators evaluated a store's culturedness in relation to four indices: the civilizing interaction of salesperson and customer, the physical appearance and organization of the store, the selection of goods, and the store's efforts at customer service. In all of these areas, but perhaps above all with respect to the last, commentators agreed that the premier stores "can and must take upon themselves higher obligations than those expected of a small or medium-sized store."[38] Bakaleia, Gastronom, and the model department stores initiated a wide variety of customer services, followed to greater or lesser degrees by other urban stores. These included, among others, packaging goods with a special store label; taking advance orders for out-of-stock wares; delivering goods to the customer's home; accepting returns of defective goods; and providing furniture where customers could sit down.[39] Home delivery, in particular, received an enormous amount of publicity during this period and was seen as the *sine qua non* of a model store.[40] This fixation seems to have had its source in Soviet bureaucrats' sense of inferiority to, and competition with, the West: at a conference at the Commissariat of Domestic Trade, the decisive argument as to the importance of home delivery was that in America, 95 per cent of all milk was delivered to the home.[41]

In fact, many of the mid-1930s innovations in customer service were inspired by examples in the West. In keeping with the new rhetoric of "free trade," the Soviet trade establishment turned to the capitalist world for instruction in commercial techniques. During 1935–7, the Trade Commissariat sponsored several study trips to the United States, Great Britain, and Germany. While British trade was quickly dismissed as a "realm of small shopkeepers" – petty trade by the petite bourgeoisie[42] – the scale of American department stores evidently appealed to the *gigantomania* so prevalent in Soviet industrialization and collectivization a few years earlier. The Soviet delegations dispatched wildly enthusiastic articles on American methods to the official Soviet trade journal, with only the briefest of caveats to the effect that, since America was a capitalist country, Soviet trade should not adopt its stores' methods "mechanically."[43]

The image of the West that resulted from these investigations bore as much relation to reality as a socialist realist hero to the typical Soviet industrial manager. Selecting to study only the largest and most innovative American stores, then exaggerating their main features, the Soviet delegations painted a mythical, futuristic portrait of shopping in America. This image obviously fascinated the trade administration, whose leaders added their own preconceptions of what was modern to the developing ideal. Nearly every stenographic report of a mid-1930s conference at the Commissariat of Domestic Trade contains some reference to America. When a feisty provincial trade representative suggested that current efforts to improve selection by offering different grades of the same item were misplaced, as fifteen grades of butter would only confuse the customer, he was quelled by a comparison with America: "Fifteen grades are still too few ... look how many kinds there are in America, there every food comes in forty varieties."[44] To objections from the floor that the extreme division of labor currently advocated by the Commissariat was not practical for the small stores that constituted the vast majority of Russia's trade network, Commissar Veitser again invoked competition with the West:

> Don't laugh! In major stores in other countries there is exactly this kind of arrangement, exactly this kind of division of labor. There is the person who shows you the commodity – say, an overcoat. You select this item. Then you are passed on to another person, who looks to see whether that style of overcoat suits you, how that overcoat hangs on you and so forth. In a word, he advises you. You select a fashion, but you are helped in selecting the fashion, given advice about color and so on. Then you go to a tailor, who measures you and takes notes, makes up your order. After all that, when you have passed through all

these stages, the so-called "senior shop assistant" comes over and finally makes arrangements with you about everything further.[45]

In these and similar comments, the trade establishment clearly identified its goals for "cultured Soviet trade" with a conception of modernization derived from the West.

At the same time, Veitser's comments illustrate the contradictory sources of the Soviet conception of modern trade: on the one hand, the rationalization of a factory assembly line, and on the other hand, the personalized service of a high-class boutique. The capitalist stores that most perfectly combined these two attributes were the largest emporia of the West, or, in Soviet terminology, the "model" department stores of cities such as New York, London, and Berlin. With their fixation on the achievements of the vanguard, Soviet trade officials were more interested in techniques for enhancing their flagship stores than in the humbler technologies relevant to ordinary shops. Chain stores and major department stores formed their basis for comparison, not rural general stores or five-and-dimes. Characteristically, the single store that enthralled them most was the world's largest, New York's Macy's. In two long feature articles about Macy's published in the official trade journal, the head of a 1936 delegation identified Macy's customer service with "culturedness," which – the Great Depression notwithstanding – transformed shopping into an educational experience for the American customer.[46]

Macy's culturedness, in the published analysis, derived from several sources: its almost infinite stock and variety of goods, its technical innovations in organization and marketing, and its orientation toward customer service, among others. However, in this period when "cadres decide everything," most commentators specified the interaction between salesperson and customers as the linchpin of the cultured store. The campaign for cultured Soviet trade was accompanied both by "professional" education in the form of courses on trading techniques and by education in "culturedness" of a more basic kind. Possibly connected to a devaluation of manual labor after the early-1930s' industrialization drive, salesclerks were urged to make a practice of washing their hands and to assimilate such rudiments of cultured trade as politeness, attractive dress and appearance, and the appealing display of wares.[47] Above all, salespeople were instructed to address their customers with the polite form *vy* instead of the familiar *ty*, the usual form of address among workers and peasants.[48] Yet by most indices, salespeople remained near the bottom of the Soviet social hierarchy, and their "cultural" attainments left administrators with a great deal to desire.[49] Macy's sales staff, by contrast, personified "culturedness" to the Soviet visitors' eyes:

In a word, the demands Macy places on its salesclerks are exceed-ingly high. Only a sufficiently cultured person can quickly accom-modate himself to these demands and quickly become familiar with all the complex conditions of this work. For that reason, Macy does not hire any salespeople who lack an education.[50]

Salesclerks at Macy's proved consistently helpful, tasteful, and friendly toward customers as well as knowledgeable about the operation of the store and its contents.

The Soviet delegates in New York were particularly interested in how stores could establish a pedagogical relationship between salesclerks and customers. Macy's resolved this dilemma for American customers in sev-eral ways, all appealing to the Soviet delegates, and some surely imaginary. The first such method was simple consultation; Macy's had apparently established a consultation desk in every department, so that customers could learn how best to dress their children and how to decorate a dining room.[51] In departments with special equipment, consultation went beyond mere description. Salespeople in the sewing department, for example, would act first as taste consultants in helping their female customers select fabric and a pattern, then as instructors, teaching them how to sew on in-store machines.[52] The educational component of selling appears more exag-gerated in this description of Macy's sporting goods department:

> Take, for example, the sporting goods department. There you see the necessary equipment for playing golf, but you do not know how to play. Macy's will send you a golfing instructor, who will take you off into a special room and teach you all the rules of the game. You want to learn to play tennis or croquet? Macy's will take you into a different room and teach you how to play tennis or croquet.[53]

Exaggerated or no, high-class Soviet stores tried to emulate these edifying techniques; at one point, Leningrad's Passazh (department store) brought in a music professor every afternoon for consultation and music lessons, while another model store installed a listening room for phonograph records.[54]

The focus on the interaction between a cultured salesperson and a pliable, ignorant customer mirrors other didactic relationships idealized in the public discourse of the mid-1930s. With Stalin increasingly portrayed as the Great Leader, the image of the authoritarian educator gained new currency as the decade progressed. "*Prosveshchenie*," enlight-enment, a buzzword of the 1920s and early 1930s, gave way to "*vospitanie*," upbringing in conventional morals and mores – cultured-ness – in a broad range of situations as the goal of education. In the schools, experimental teaching methods were abandoned in favor of a traditional pedagogy emphasizing good behavior, teacher authority, and rote memorization. The authority of parents over their children was similarly buttressed, and their educational role idealized.[55] In literature, young heroes constantly had to swallow the advice of their older Party comrades.[56] Acquiring culture, in short, most often meant listening to the wise counsel of an older mentor figure.

In this context of didacticism, it was not surprising that salespeople should be constituted discursively as instructors. In the best of worlds, salesclerks would both teach their customers and respond to them. Trade archives are full of discussions about the dual role of the salesperson: on the one hand, as the representative of cultured goods to the customer; on the other hand, as the advocate of consumer demands to industry.[57] In this latter capacity, salespeople were encouraged to study the tastes and demands of their clientele, and to fight to bring the commodities consumers needed to the market (*borot'sia za ego prodvizhenie na rynok*).[58] The advocacy aspect of a salesclerk's work, however, was never to supersede the counseling aspect, as Commissar Veitser reminded "outstanding workers" in Soviet trade:

> How can we serve the customer well? . . . You think that your task is simply to know what the consumer wants and to satisfy his demand. That is necessary; you have to know the consumer's demand . . . But your task is not merely this. You must educate the taste of the consumer [*vospityvat' vkus u potrebitelia*]. You trade workers must create new tastes in the consumer, a new Soviet taste and new wares for the consumer. You must educate him: that is what good consumer service means. Good service does not mean that if a consumer has bad taste, I will drag myself after his demands to the end [*chto ia pletus' v kontse za ego sprosom*].[59]

An express implication of this injunction was that taste deserved to be the object of education. With greater prosperity, Soviet consumers were expected to be faced with a bewildering multiplicity of goods.[60] Only some demands, however, were deemed appropriate to a cultured population, and the untrained consumer could not be expected to tell one from the other. As a result, Soviet citizens had to learn what and how to consume; they had to be educated in taste as well as in the practices involving new commodities and implements.

The cultivated consumer

During the rationing era, Soviet citizens had come under public criticism for the behaviors associated with the culture of shortages: hoarding, speculating, skipping work to buy food, getting into fights while standing in line. In 1935, however, publicists and trade administrators revealed the real problem with the rationing-era consumer, oddly overlooked in previous years. Like the stores that had relied on "mechanical distribution," the consumer of the rationing era had succumbed to "mechanical" acquisition. Publicity surrounding the end of bread rationing offered this paradigmatic representation:

> There he is, yesterday's client. I know him well. Only recently he would hurriedly stop in here out of necessity, sullenly receive his portion of standard bread, and just as quickly leave.[61]

While this description abbreviated the process of buying bread during the rationing era, publicists used it as a foil for a new model of consumption, more in keeping with the principle of free trade. If the "mechanical," rationing-era consumer had gone to his assigned store, waited in line, and passively accepted the bread being issued there, customers were now portrayed as thinking about their purchases and comparison-shopping for the freshest bread.[62] The end of rationing gave rise to parables of transformation, in which "yesterday's client" became an active and conscious consumer:

> How he has changed! Today he is spending a *long time* CHOOSING. With visible enjoyment he wavers between buying a Warsaw loaf and a Minsk loaf. Already he is *no longer an indifferent customer; he wants to know when the bread was baked, how it tastes, who made it* . . . [63]

In a wide variety of official contexts, this image of a new consumer became the human counterpart to cultured trade. Disinclined to emphasize the role of central policies in the scarcity of the previous years, the trade establishment reacted to the turn towards consumer-goods production and the end of rationing by hailing the "cultural" transformation of Soviet consumers and their "tempestuously growing demands."[64] Even Commissar Veitser, who urged salespeople to educate their customers, maintained that the transition to free trade reflected the spontaneous cultural elevation of Soviet consumers:

> The second way in which the situation has changed consists in the fact that the consumer has grown more cultured. He demands more culture in the way he is addressed and he demands that we offer him entirely different goods . . . This is an altered

consumer – a new consumer, who has grown more cultured; a literate consumer, who lives well, for whom life has become happier and easier; a consumer who has already ceased to think, as he thought before, that all he needs in life are his rations for bread or meat. Now he is already thinking about how to buy a piano, a musical instrument, attractive furniture for his home, a good lamp.[65]

As the decade progressed, peasants were said to have suddenly conceived a desire for books and musical instruments, and even children, one mother proclaimed at a [trade] conference, were becoming "more demanding."[66] The Stalinist state went out of its way to create reality in the image of this representation by encouraging citizens to develop the hitherto unknown demands of a cultured, modern population. In addition to the educational efforts of high-class stores, Soviet citizens were incited to desire goods by public displays of desirable objects and by publicized images of citizens as consumers.

Soviet citizens encountered publicity for consumer commodities in many places in the mid-1930s, from articles in women's magazines to newsreels to the display windows of "model" stores. In major cities, trade departments dedicated entire shops to novel fashions and wares in an attempt to stimulate new demands for "entirely different" goods.[67] Similarly, commodity exhibitions presented a vivid display of the goods promoted for popular consumption. Borrowing from such capitalist sensations as the 1851 Crystal Palace in London, the Commissariats of Light Industry and Domestic Trade mounted exhibitions of consumer goods in major cities from Khar'kov to Vladivostok. In the capital, residents could visit as many as four in a single day, from the shoe show at the All-Union Institute of Leather Technology to the blockbuster "Parade of the Best," which exhibited everything from sewing machines to suitcases, underwear, cameras, guitars, barometers, and teapots.[68] Expositions in Moscow and Leningrad garnered considerable attention from the press, especially if they featured "modern" goods signifying technological and cultural progress. Soviet-produced motor cycles, automobiles, radios, and washing machines received especially extensive coverage as the object of innumerable adulatory articles and photographs,[69] but even more mundane wares could dazzle consumers with the material possibilities of modern life. Overtly didactic, commodity expositions both celebrated Soviet industrial achievements and trumpeted the improved standard of living that its products would bring about.[70]

The Soviet trade establishment favored commodity exhibitions as a vehicle for stimulating consumer demand largely because of their adaptability to didactic ends. In contradistinction to other forms of publicity about goods, expositions provided proof of material progress in the tangible objects placed on display. Though Soviet officials were not absolutely averse to print advertisement, they had reservations about it on precisely the grounds that under capitalism, at least, it unleashed irrational desires by the deceptive manipulation of images.[71] Hoping to stimulate "rational" demand by transmitting information about actual products, trade administrators focussed their advertising energies on brand labels and store window displays. An exhibition of Soviet advertising in 1938 was almost entirely devoted to exemplars of these two forms of "advertisement," though half of the display cases featured political themes such as the twentieth anniversary of the Red Army instead of commodities.[72] Importantly, consumers encountered labels and display windows in the context of the store, where their desires were mediated by salespeople and the selection of goods available.

Surely the most popular method of eliciting demand in the capitalist West, print advertising was relatively scarce in the mid-1930s.[73] Major newspapers ran rather dry ads for only a few industries, notably cosmetics, and even women's magazines included very few ads. In the prewar period, the working-class women's journal *Rabotnitsa* carried one full-page color ad on cosmetics or food products on the back page of about two of every three issues, while the upper-class women's journal *Obshchestvennitsa* ran virtually none. Though few in number, such advertisements offered an image of appropriate needs for the targeted population. The food advertisements in *Rabotnitsa* appealed to readers as working mothers, who needed such products as canned pork and beans to prepare a tasty, nutritional, and economical meal for their children in just five minutes, while advertisements for cosmetics endorsed readers' aspirations for feminine beauty.[74] Portraying the advertised products in a context of "cultured" consumption – a world of snow-white tablecloths and napkins, china teacups, flowers, pretty women's and children's dresses, and cut-glass bowls of jam – the advertisements purveyed a bourgeois and civilized lifestyle along with the goods that formed their nominal subject.[75]

From the point of view of most citizens, advertisements, commodity expositions, and "model" department stores stimulated demands that were essentially unsatisfiable, either because the goods were unavailable or because their prices were out of reach. This was demonstrated vividly at a 1936 conference accompanying an exhibition of children's wares, sponsored by the Commissariat of Domestic Trade. Speaking to an audience of interested consumers, the Commissariat representative dutifully recited the Stalinist litany on "culturedness" and the "new consumer":

> We mustn't forget that our life has become better, that "life has become happier," and if just a short time ago our customers accepted everything that they were given, today they don't want to be limited to that. The consumer says, "It's not enough that

an item fits, it's not enough that it suits my price range; I want it to be attractive, I want it to be pretty in its external appearance." The same object can be made attractive and festive or crude and ugly ... It should be the kind of thing, as one Stakhanovite said, to make the soul rejoice when one buys it or wears it.[76]

Though citizens at the conference expressed their eagerness to supply their children with "cultured," attractive goods, Deputy Commissar Levenson sparked anger and derision for this outrageous assertion of material satisfaction. "Now we've seen that at the exhibition there are all imaginable things, and that's all very well, but they aren't in the stores and you won't find them," one listener jeered, while another added, "You may talk about the soul rejoicing at pretty goods, but the only reason the 'soul rejoices' when we buy things now is that goods are so hard to get."[77] These sentiments correspond closely to dozens of anonymous letters to the Leningrad Communist Party headquarters in the late 1930s, in which Stalin's slogan, "life has become happier," appeared exclusively as a taunt.[78]

The Stalinist leadership dealt with this objection through the same logic of "models" that informed its administration of cultured trade. While publicists and bureaucrats promoted the ethic of cultured consumerism to the entire Soviet citizenry, they contented themselves with its achievement in practice by a relatively privileged few. In his oft-cited "life has become happier" speech, Stalin himself sanctioned disparities in consumption between "manual" and "mental" laborers until shortages were vanquished and cultural inequalities between workers and managers overcome. Stakhanovites, Stalin's audience for this speech, were to constitute the one exception to this rule; though manual workers, their amazing feats of productivity entitled them to participate immediately in managerial-class privileges, avatars of a day when all workers could enjoy the benefits of cultural and material advance.[79] Alongside the "model" stores of the late 1930s, Soviet leaders thus promoted a specific group of "model" consumers – industrial managers, engineers, and award-winning workers – whose enjoyment of material perquisites was supposed to inform the behavior and redeem the privations of everyone else.[80]

This group was not quite coterminous with the wealthiest stratum of Soviet consumers. According to Wallace Carroll, the highest income group in the Soviet Union in 1941 comprised members of the cultural elite – authors, playwrights, musicians, actors, orchestra conductors, and ballet dancers – and the generous level of Soviet royalties would tend to substantiate this claim.[81] As Mervyn Matthews has pointed out, successful creative and performing artists also had a chance of winning one of the recently inaugurated "Stalin prizes," which conferred a one-time cash award of 25, 50, or 100,000 rubles on its recipients, or up to twenty-five times the average annual wage.[82] Another, equally prominent and unpublicized, group of privileged consumers included the "responsible workers" (that is, senior officials) of the party and state apparatus. Topping off at 500 rubles a month, their published salaries were considerably lower than the highest level of artists' and specialists' salaries, but they purportedly received periodic supplements in the form of packets of money delivered to their door. "Responsible workers" also enjoyed a variety of services and benefits in kind, such as the automobiles that were made available for their personal use, free travel, large and in some cases rent-free apartments, vacations, and the like.[83] As during the rationing period, however, the lifestyles of the nation's highest elites were shrouded in a silence pierced only by obstreperous emigrés like Leon Trotsky and by the publicized denunciations of particular executives during the Great Purges.[84]

The newsreel on Moscow's Central Department Store highlighted upper-class shoppers, but it was above all Stakhanovites who came to represent the "citizen-consumer" in Stalinist depictions of the prosperous life.[85] From the early 1930s on, Soviet leaders had attempted to link productivity to well-being by offering preferential provisionment to award-winning workers. Rationing-era privileges included supplementary rations, access to closed stores and cafeterias, and the right to circumvent lines. After the transition to free trade, elite workers lost these perquisites, but their large incomes nonetheless supported a more affluent lifestyle than they had enjoyed in the past. Newspaper biographies of Stakhanovites always underscored their high wages, and individual Stakhanovites' budgets were periodically offered as evidence of the increasing well-being of the working class.[86] But Stakhanovites received still more in the form of publicly presented and highly publicized rewards: apartments or automobiles for the lucky few, silk dresses, record players, the collected works of Marx or Lenin for the rest. Stakhanovites themselves were encouraged to view their achievements in light of the prizes they received; conferences of Stakhanovites turned into forums for open boasting about prizes.[87] The biographies of Stakhanovites, newspaper summaries of their conferences, and newsreels like "Stakhanovite Busygin gets a new apartment" appealed to workers' material interests, suggesting that a richer, more comfortable life would result from higher labor productivity. At the same time, this publicity suggested an array of objects that a prosperous and cultured person could now, and should now, buy.[88] Conspicuous consumption by Stakhanovites in this sense functioned as advertisement to cultivate consumer demand.

Soviet spokesmen used Stakhanovites as role models for cultured consumption, but as in the case of the "model" stores, the ideal that they represented originated outside the proletarian milieu. As Stalin framed it, Stakhanovites occupied a position midway between the "manual" and "mental" classes. Like managers, they were encouraged to enjoy material perquisites, but the educated stratum adopted a patronizing stance toward them on the premise that their cultural outlook was more developing than developed. Like other workers, Stakhanovites were now portrayed as inexperienced in the matter of consumption. They purportedly needed guidance in consumption from the gifts of a patriarchal state, as well as from salespeople, now obliged not simply to sell their wares, but to "educate the tastes of the population." Above all, they purportedly needed guidance from the women of the upper class.

The post-rationing years of the late 1930s saw the emergence of an intriguing alliance between bourgeois housewives and the Soviet state. Along with Stalin and the trade administration, managerial-class housewives became the country's leading exponents of consumerism and cultured trade. Like Stakhanovism, the housewives' movement was launched in 1935 by Ordzhonikidze and his Commissariat of Heavy Industry as an innovative mobilization strategy. Distinguished by the elevated moral tone of its rhetoric, the movement brought housewives into the public sphere as volunteer "*Kulturträger*," a time-honored role for the women of the upper class. Between 1935 and the outbreak of the Second World War, Soviet executives' wives declared a "war for cosiness, for culture in daily life" among the workers in their husbands' employ.[89] They decorated dormitories for workers and Stakhanovites; sponsored competitions for the best homemakers among Stakhanovites' wives; ran sewing, foreign-language, and political circles for working-class men and women; tendered advice about consumption; and even bought clothes for Stakhanovites, since, in the words of one housewife activist, "bachelor workers often don't know what to buy, they don't know how to select the right things," but "with our help, they will be dressed in the best of taste."[90]

The Soviet leadership took these "lady activists" (*aktivistki*) very seriously; not only Ordzhonikidze, but Kalinin, Kaganovich, Molotov, Voroshilov, and even Stalin himself attended the opening ceremonies of the first All-Union Meeting of the Wives of Managers and Engineering-Technical Personnel in Heavy Industry at the Kremlin Palace in May, 1936.[91] The movement quickly spread to other sectors of the economy, as witnessed by a conference of wives of Red Army officers just seven months later.[92] From the perspective of Soviet policy-makers, the housewives' movement mobilized an otherwise unemployed population to perform "socially useful work,"[93] and it harnessed their arts of procurement to the needs of the public at large. Put differently, these women kept factories in the business of supplying goods to their workers after the dismantling of the rationing system, and they did so with low over-heads and no official personnel.

Housewife activism was partly about social mobilization, but equally importantly, it projected a traditional social order *vis-à-vis* gender and class, and associated cultural progress with material goods. In this latter respect, the underlying premise of the managerial wives' movement was identical to that of the campaign for cultured trade: "cultured" surround-ings and consumer commodities would exert a civilizing influence on the laboring population. In the pages of their journal and in speeches at their national conferences, activists over and over described the trans-formations wrought by a civilized environment and the tutelage of a cultured woman:

> One dormitory for bachelor workers stood out for its lack of culture. Drunken parties and brawls often took place there. But we took over the management of this dormitory, and you wouldn't recognize it any more. A radio was introduced and a recreation room organized, where workers now hold readings of newspapers and literary works.[94]

Or in another example:

> Go to our oil industry dormitory today. Cleanliness, comfort, light, greenery, warmth. Viennese chairs, pretty curtains at the windows, portraits of our leaders, flowers, carpets on the freshly painted floor, with no spit and no cigarette butts anywhere to be seen.[95]

Invariably, they claimed that the refurbished dormitories and newly planted flowerbeds had inspired workers to pay greater attention to personal hygiene and to keep their rooms tidy, while at one factory, the housewives' influence was putatively sufficient to persuade bachelor workers to quit drinking and to devote their free time to chess, billiards, and playing in the newly organized jazz orchestra.[96]

In their own self-understanding and in public discussions of consump-tion, wives of engineers and executives were considered a natural repository of "good taste." The styles and goods that they endorsed had a lasting impact on Soviet culture, as the approved objects of consump-tion for the next twenty years. Nearly every illustration in the 1950s' *Commodity Dictionary* would have been at home in the housewife-activists' journal of the late 1930s, and one has to imagine that these women exercised considerable sway over the offerings of "cultured trade." Trotsky attributed their influence to the "laws of the market," which the end of rationing had putatively restored to Soviet life:

> When the people's commissar of food industries, Mikoian, boasts
> that the lowest kind of confections are rapidly being crowded
> out by the highest, and that "our women" are demanding fine
> perfumes, this only means that industry, with the transfer to
> money circulation, is accommodating itself to the better quali-
> fied consumer. Such are the laws of the market, in which by no
> means the last place is occupied by highly placed wives.[97]

The "laws of the market," however, could equally foster manufacturing for the masses as "fine perfumes" for executives' wives. Popular demands might have been less expensive than those of "our women," but they offered still greater opportunities for profit, given the potential size of the mass market. Prices, after all, bear no necessary relationship to profits, which depend on the marginal profit per unit times the number of units sold. The reorientation of consumer-goods industries towards the elite consumer reflected not the revival of capitalism, as Trotsky alleged, but the inherent partiality of the Stalinist command economy. It was policy-makers' priorities, not the market, which were so peculiarly susceptible to the influence of "highly-placed wives."

Conclusion

Official consumerism from the mid-1930s through the early 1950s reflected three characteristic elements of Stalinist political culture: *socialist realism* (the tendency to equate the real or symbolic achievements of a "vanguard" with general societal advance); *mobilization* (the attempt to achieve state objectives by marshalling citizens' individual efforts towards those ends); and *social traditionalism* (a revival of traditional attitudes towards gender and class). Official discourse and policies on trade and consumption inscribed present deprivations in an evolving future of prosperity and culture for individual and society. The state provided the blueprints for this happy outcome in the form of commodity exhibitions, high-end department stores, newsreels depicting consumer goods, and publicized consumption by Stakhanovite workers. By positing the good life as a reward for exceptional productivity, Soviet leaders averred that the road to prosperity could be paved only through the concerted efforts of the citizens themselves. At the same time, however, by focussing on the model department stores of the capitals over provincial general stores, and by catering primarily to the "tempestuously growing demands" of "our women" and the "better-qualified" Soviet consumers, the Stalinist leadership demonstrated that its conception of the "vanguard" bore a striking resemblance to what the jaundiced observer might call the ruling class.

Soviet citizens proved only partly susceptible to official efforts to cultivate consumerism. They did become "active consumers," as publicists

evidently wanted, but their habits remained mired in the culture of shortages that had evolved over the years. By the early 1950s, the Stalinist
economy had succeeded only in proving that deprivation was permanent: deprivation had been the one constant in citizens' experience for
the past twenty-five years. Still more debilitating to the Stalinist project
of cultured consumerism, the wartime exposure to conditions in central
Europe seemed to prove that deprivation was uniquely a product of the
Soviet regime. When, in this context, Soviet newspapers continued to
trumpet the regime's "achievements" in the consumer economy, it could
hardly be surprising that individuals rejected the legitimacy of official
values, and looked after their interests by unofficial means.

NOTES

This is an abridged version of chapter 6 of Julie Hessler's PhD dissertation,
"Culture of Shortages: A Social History of Soviet Trade, 1917–1953," University of Chicago, 1996. The abridgement is by the author.

1 *Tovarnaia entsiklopediia*, ed. Vl.Rob. Vil'iams and F.V. Tserevitinov (Moscow:
Ekonomicheskaia zhizn', 1927), iii–iv.
2 *Tovarnyi slovar'*, ed. I.A. Pugachev, 9 vols (Moscow: Gos. izdat. torgovoi literatury, 1956–-61), vol. 1, unnumbered preface.
3 This contrast has been made before: Vera Dunham, *In Stalin's Time: Middle-class
Values in Soviet Fiction*, rev. edn (Durham, NC: Duke University Press), 3–23, 43–5.
4 *Tovarnyi slovar'*, vol. 1, 1.
5 Julie Hessler, "Culture of Shortages: A Social History of Soviet Trade", PhD
dissertation, University of Chicago, 1996, ch. 3.
6 Trotsky took the former line in *The Revolution Betrayed: What Is the Soviet
Union and Where Is It Going?* (New York: Doubleday, Doran, 1937).
7 See, for example, I.V. Stalin, "Novye obstanovka – novye zadachi khozi-
aistvennogo stroitel'stva," June 23, 1931, speech to a conference of
industrialists, *Sochineniia, XIII*, 51–80, esp. 59–60; "Itogi pervoi piatiletki,"
January 7, 1933, speech at the joint plenum of the Central Committee and
Central Control Commission, ibid., 161–215, esp. 196–202; untitled February
19, 1933 speech at the first All-Union Congress of Udarnik Kolkhozniks, ibid.,
236–56, esp. 245–50; January 26, 1934, report at the Seventeenth Party
Congress, ibid., 282–379, esp. 333–9.
8 Stalin, *Sochineniia*, I [XIV] (Stanford, California: Hoover Institution, 1967),
79–101, esp. 81–2, 89–90.
9 See the speeches listed above. The sections on consumption were invariably
followed by discussions of trade.
10 Rossiiskii tsentr khraneniia i izucheniia dokumentov noveishei istorii (henceforth, RTsKhIDNI), f. 77, op. 1, d. 418, l. 9 (stenogram of a meeting of the
commission on decentralized agricultural procurements), reprinted in
Stalinskoe Politbiuro v 30-e gody, ed. O.V. Khlevniuk, A.V. Kvashonkin, L.P.
Kosheleva, L.A. Rogovaia (Moscow: AIRO – XX, 1995), 55.
11 This interpretation has been elaborated by Moshe Lewin in "Taking Grain,"
in his *The Making of the Soviet System* (New York: Pantheon, 1985), and more
recently by Andrea Graziosi, in "The Great Soviet Peasant War: Bolsheviks

and Peasants, 1917–33," paper presented to the Russian Research Center, Harvard University, March 1995.

12 Rossiiskii gosudarstvennyi arkhiv ekonomiki (henceforth, RGAE), f. 7971, op. 1, d. 105, ll. 54–5.

13 *Pravda*, November 29, 1934 (Central Committee plenum resolution of November 26, 1934).

14 For information on the restructuring of the trade system, see Hessler, "Culture of Shortages".

15 Secret police agents confirmed this premise with their reports of continual grumbling in the food lines of blue-collar districts. Tsentral'nyi gosu-darstvennyi arkhiv istoriko-politicheskoi dokumentatsii Sankt-Peterburga (henceforth, TsGAIPD), f. 24, op. 2v, d. 1373, ll. 1–5. In contradistinction to the 1937 bread crisis (qv. Hessler, "Culture of Shortages" ch. 3) these agents appear to have restricted their activities to information gathering. In any case, their secret reports make no mention of arrests.

16 RGAE f. 7971, op. 1, d. 105, l. 16; *Izvestiia*, January 1, 1935.

17 *Izvestiia*, January 2, 1935.

18 *Biulleten' finansovogo i khoziaistvennogo zakonodatel'stva* 1935, no. 7 (March 10) (Narkomvnutorg regulations on bread trade).

19 RGAE f. 7971, op. 1, d. 105, l. 16. On the first few days of rationing, trans-portation problems prevented bread factories from fulfilling all their planned deliveries in many cities. See, for example, *Izvestiia*, January 2 and 6, 1935; *Za industrializatsiiu*, January 2 and 4, 1935.

20 *Za industrializatsiiu*, January 2 and 3; *Sovetskaia torgovlia* (newspaper), January 4, 1935. The publicized firing of several Moscow bread shop managers for sanitary violations less than three weeks later put teeth into the new regu-lations. *Za industrializatsiiu*, January 21, 1935.

21 Ibid., January 2, 1935; *Izvestiia*, January 2, 1935. The reader should view claims to "radiofication" with skepticism.

22 Stalin, *Sochiineniia*, XIII, 340–6.

23 Dunham, *In Stalin's Time*, 22.

24 *Za industrializatsiiu*, January 2, 1935. This article was entitled "Prazdnik rabochego potrebitelia" [Holiday for the working consumer]. I should note that packaging never became widespread in Soviet bread shops; this must have been a shortlived experiment, indeed.

25 *Roznichnaia torgovaia set' SSSR. Itogi torgovoi perepisi 1935 g.* (Moscow: TsUNKhU, 1936), vol. III, 292. Out of 26,892 clothing and shoe stores in the Soviet Union, 1,970 had separate male and female sections; 3,176 had fitting rooms; and 5,910 had mirrors. Only 5,544 of 53,415 food stores had control weights.

26 G. Aronshtein, "Bor'ba za sovetskuiu politiku tsen," *Sovetskaia torgovlia* (journal), 1935 no. 2–3 (Feb.–March): 22.

27 The decree establishing rights and obligations of stores under free trade specifically placed Bakaleia and Gastronom stores in the class of stores with the greatest control over their own supplies. *Biulleten' finansovogo i khozi-aistvennogo zakonodatel'stva* 1935 no. 34–5 (Dec. 20): 45–6. Another indicator both of the fact that these stores were unusually well-supplied and of the higher quality of their personnel is the high percentage of udarniks among their managers and salespeople. As against a national average of 21.1 per cent of managers and 19.6 per cent of salesclerks, 31.5 per cent of Bakaleia managers and 37.8 per cent of Gastronom managers were udarniks, and 23.6 per cent and 30.2 per cent of salesclerks respectively. These figures were exceeded only by the staff of department stores, of whom 46.2 per cent of

managers and 44.0 per cent of salesclerks were udarniks. *Kadry sovetskoi torgovli. Itogi torgovoi perepisi 1935 g.*, vol. II, 129. On the class divisions of Soviet model stores, see also Leonard E. Hubbard, *Soviet Trade and Distribution* (London, 1938), 214, 240–1.

28 *Sovetskaia torgovlia Leningrada i Leningradskoi oblasti, 1931–1934 gg.*, ed. A.A. Ivanchenko and V.N. Ge (Leningrad, 1935), 31–2.

29 Ibid., 32. The interiors of the Eliseev grocery stores in Moscow and St Petersburg even now retain the incongruous splendor of Russia's turn-of-the-century art nouveau.

30 Narkomsnab issued instructions to open "model" [*pokazatel'nyi*, or *obraztsovo-pokazatel'nyi*] department stores in major cities on June 3, 1933. Tsentral'nyi gosudarstvennyi arkhiv Oktiabr'skoi revoliutsii i sotsialisticheskogo stroitel'stva goroda Moskvy (henceforth, TsGAOR g. Moskvy), f. 2458, op. 1, d. 227 (NKSnab instructions of June 3, 1933, and related materials).

31 Rossiiskii Gosudarstvennyi Arkhiv Kino-Foto Dokumentov (henceforth, RGAKFD), reel 1650a and 2524 (newsreels of gala openings in Leningrad and Tashkent).

32 The first three model stores were supposed to be Moscow's TsUM and Leningrad's Dom Kooperatsii (both reequipped and redecorated prerevolutionary stores), and a new store to be built in Khar'kov. TsGAOR g. Moskvy, f. 2458, op. 1, d. 227. The number twenty was an estimate by Hubbard, *Soviet Trade and Distribution*, 241.

33 RGAKFD, reel 2455.

34 TsGAOR g. Moskvy, f. R–346, op. 1, d. 57, l. 1 (city general plan for 1936–7 and related materials).

35 See, for example, *Stakhanovets torgovli*, November 18 and December 26, 1936, and the article on the "dirtiest bread shop in Moscow" in *Za kul'turnuiu torgovliu*, April 20, 1937.

36 TsGAOR g. Moskvy, f. R–346, op. 1, d. 57, l. 1.

37 Interestingly, this was also the case with the subway, which at least initially was too expensive for ordinary people to afford.

38 M.S. Epshtein, "Kak sdelat' magazin stakhanovskim?," *Stakhanovets torgovli*, November 7, 1936.

39 According to the 1935 trade census, out of 53,415 food stores, 4,351 sold prepackaged goods; 1,492 delivered food to the home; and 1,689 took advance orders. The trade census did not provide information on the number of stores that accepted returns, but it did identify 4,656 (out of a total of 26,892 clothing and shoe stores) which offered customers a place to sit. Statistics were also given on whether the clothing stores took individual tailoring orders (only 511 did). *Roznichnaia torgovaia set'*, III, 292.

40 For example, Epshtein, "Kak sdelat' magazin stakhanovskim?"; A. Shtukel, "Kak magazin zavoeval zvanie peredovogo," *Sovetskaia torgovlia* (journal), 1937, no. 2 (March–April): 59; Ivanchenko and Ge, *Sovetskaia torgovlia Leningrada*, 32.

41 RGAE, f. 7971, op. 1, d. 246, l. 56.

42 *Sovetskaia torgovlia* (newspaper), February 20, 1935.

43 For example, M. Smirnov, "Iz opyta amerikanskoi prodovol'stvennoi torgovli," *Sovetskaia torgovlia* (journal), 1935 no. 5 (May): 53–5. Enthusiasm for American stores also resonated at the Narkomvnutorg conference on American trading techniques: RGAE f. 7971, op. 1, d. 246 (November 21, 1936).

44 RGAE f. 7971, op. 1, d. 100, l. 28 (Veitser speaking at 1935 conference). I should note that this observation was true, at least as regards America's

largest stores: Macy's grocery department, for example, sold 186 different kinds of cheese in 1939. Cf. Ralph M. Hower, *History of Macy's of New York, 1858–1919: Chapters in the Evolution of the Department Store* (Cambridge, Mass., Harvard University Press, 1943), 403.

45 Ibid., l. 37.
46 T. Gumnitskii, "Kak zavoevyvaiut pokupatelia," *Sovetskaia torgovlia* (journal), 1937, no. 1 (January): 62–72; idem, "Priemka, khranenie i kontrol' v magazine firmy Meisy," ibid., 1937, no. 2 (February): 64–70.
47 *Sovetskaia torgovlia* (newspaper), January 2 and February 20, 1935; *Stakhanovets torgovli*, December 14, 1936. The number of salespeople attending "technical minimum" and similar courses reached nearly 76,000 in 1938. RGAE, f. 7971, op. 2, d. 116, l. 79 (archival trade statistics based on a one-time check on November 1, 1938).
48 This theme appears in a number of articles on cultured trade: for example, *Sovetskaia torgovlia* (newspaper), February 2, 1935; *Za industrializatsiiu*, Jan. 1, 1935.
49 As of November 1938, out of 121,749 salesclerks in the Narkomvnutorg system from whom educational data were available, around 3 per cent had completed secondary schooling, and even among Gastronom and department-store salesclerks, that figure only rose to 5 per cent and 10 per cent respectively, well below the average for the working-age population, especially in the cities. In 1939, 14.7 per cent of the total working-age population and 26 per cent of the urban working-age population had completed at least secondary school. RGAE, f. 7971, op. 2, d. 116, ll. 83, 86; Russia (1923 – U.S.S.R.) Tsentral'noe statisticheskoe upravlenie, *Itogi vsesoiuznoi perepisi naseleniia 1959 goda*, vol. 1: USSR (Moscow: Gosstatizdat, 1962), 81 (table of educational statistics for 1939 and 1959).
50 T. Gumnitskii, "Kak zavoevyvaiut pokupatelia," 65–6. Unfortunately, I have been unable to find figures on the actual educational attainments of Macy's salesclerks. According to a sympathetic but reliable historian from the 1940s, Ralph Hower, Macy's made a concerted effort to increase the educational levels of its employees after 1914, first by mandating elementary schooling (and providing it, where necessary, through continuing education), then by shifting its personnel policy to favor formal education over work experience. Hower suggests that a college degree became the norm for all levels of managers, but he provided no information on salesclerks after the First World War. Hower, *History of Macy's*, 378–9, 401–2.
51 Gumnitskii, "Kak zavoevyvaiut pokupatelia," 62.
52 Ibid., 62.
53 Ibid., 62. Although farfetched, this is not altogether out of the question, given that Macy's floor area exceeded 45 acres at this time. Hower, *History of Macy's*, 400.
54 *Sovetskaia torgovlia* (newspaper), January 10, 1935; RGAE, f. 7971, op. 1, d. 100, l. 26 (1935 conference).
55 Essential reading on this subject is Nicholas S. Timasheff, *The Great Retreat: The Growth and Decline of Communism in Russia* (New York: E.P. Dutton 1946).
56 On these themes in socialist realist fiction, see Dunham, *In Stalin's Time*, 143–9, and Katerina Clark, *The Soviet Novel: History as Ritual* (Chicago: University of Chicago Press, 1981), 119–20.
57 RGAE, f. 7971, op. 1, d. 105, ll. 64–5.
58 *Sovetskaia torgovlia* (newspaper), February 4, 1935; A. Petrunin and M. Evzovich, "Izuchenie potrebitel'skogo sprosa v Tsentral'nom Univermage NKVnutorga SSSR," *Sovetskaia torgovlia* (journal), 1937 no. 3 (March): 51–7; V. Kuibyshev, Speech at the 17th Party conference, *Stat'i i rechi* (Moscow:

Partizdat, 1935), 113. This last phrase was always used in discussions of the trade networks' relationship to industry; it did not have to do with selling.

59 RGAE, f. 7971, op. 1, d. 105, ll. 59–60.

60 Some commentators even claimed that the age of plenty had already arrived, for example, Epstein, "Kak sdelat' magazin stakhanovskim?" *Stakhanovets torgovli*, November 7, 1936.

61 A. Gudinov, "Prazdnik rabochego potrebitelia," *Za industrializatsiiu*, January 2, 1935.

62 *Sovetskaia torgovlia* (newspaper), January 2, 1935 ("Pokupatel' vybiraet"); *Za industrializatsiiu*, January 2, 1935 ("Eshche luchshe, eshche kul'turnee obsluzhit' potrebitelia").

63 Gudinov, "Prazdnik rabochego potrebitelia," *Za industrializatsiiu*, January 2, 1935 (stress in original). On newspaper images of the "new consumer," see also Sheila Fitzpatrick, "Becoming Cultured," 224–5.

64 The phrase "burno rastushchie zaprosy" or "sprosy" appears frequently in the speeches and writings of the trade establishment in 1935. See, for example, *Sovetskaia torgovlia* (journal) 1935, no. 1 (January): 5–14.

65 RGAE, f. 7971, op. 1, d. 105, l. 55.

66 On peasants' desires for musical instruments, see the daily newspaper *Sovetskaia torgovlia*, Jan. 30, 1939. Publicity about rising consumption in the villages began a little later than the urban consumption campaign, in 1937 rather than 1935. On demanding children, see RGAE f. 7971, op. 1, d. 250, l. 31 (1936).

67 *Sovetskaia torgovlia* (newspaper), January 1, 1941.

68 The official trade daily, *Sovetskaia torgovlia*, recorded such conferences continually in the mid-1930s. See, for example, January 12 and 20, and February 6, 1935.

69 Cf. *Za industrializatsiiu*, January 30 and March 5, 1935.

70 A particularly graphic example of this didacticism was the "Victory Exhibition" in January 1935, which made its points about Soviet industrial progress through carefully edited graphs and statistics about consumer-goods production since 1913. *Sovetskaia torgovlia* (newspaper), January 12, 1935 ("Vystavka pobedy").

71 RGAE, f. 7971, op. 1, d. 105, ll. 57–8 (1935 Narkomvnutorg conference); Gumnitskii, "Kak zavoevyvaiut pokupatelia," 64; *Snabzhenie, kooperatsiia, torgovlia*, December 3, 1932.

72 V. Vinogradov and T. Gunina, "Organizatsiia vitrinnoi reklamy," *Sovetskaia torgovlia*, 1937 no. 5 (May): 45–8; Gumnitskii, "Kak zavoevyvaiut pokupatelia," 64, and "Primeka, khranenie i kontrol' v magazine firmy Meisy," 68–70; *Sovetskaia torgovlia*, (newspaper) February 27, 1938.

73 Radio advertisement was still less common, according to an advocate of the former in the trade bureaucracy (RGAE, f. 7971, op. 1, d. 100, l. 29).

74 For example, *Rabotnitsa*, back cover, 1936 no. 22 and 23 (July); no. 26 (September); no. 28 (October). The message of the cosmetics ads was reinforced in the text of the magazine in such articles as "Culture and Beauty," which advised every woman to use facial creams every day. Ibid., 1936, no. 22 (July).

75 Randi Barnes-Cox's dissertation on Soviet advertisement "Heroic Commodities and Sentimental Households: Soviet Commercial Advertising and the Economic Self, 1921–1941," in progress at Indiana University, promises to provide a thorough content-analysis of print advertisement for this period. On the ubiquity of these particular images, see also Vadim Volkov, "The Concept of Kul'turnost'," Chapter 7 in this volume.

76 RGAE, f. 7971, op. 1, d. 250, l. 2.

77 Ibid., ll. 16, 18.

78 In one letter, for example, a group of maids complained about their living conditions as against the comfort enjoyed by their employers, Soviet executives: "For them life has become better, life has become happier, comrades." Another anonymous letter-writer declared, "Those who are well-paid shout that life has become better, life has become happier. [Otherwise] this slogan of comrade Stalin's is pronounced ironically and is used whenever people experience some kind of hardship or difficulty." TsGAIPD, f. 24, op. 2v, d. 1748, ll. 166–71 (1936); op. 2g, d. 149, ll. 129–32 (1938).

79 Stalin, *Sochineniia* I [XIV] (Stanford: Hoover Institution, 1967), 81–2, 89–90.

80 Note that these were the same people whose consumption received public attention during the rationing era.

81 Wallace Carroll, *We're in This with Russia* (Boston, 1942), 72, cited in Mervyn Matthews, *Privilege in the Soviet Union* (London: George Allen & Unwin, 1978), 107. Matthews cites information published in *Pravda* to the effect that fourteen Soviet authors received over 10,000 rubles a month in royalties in 1936 (less 20–40 per cent in taxes) – a year when the average monthly wage was around 200 rubles, and rents were fixed at 1 ruble 32 kopecks per square meter for the highest income bracket.

82 Matthews, *Privilege*, 98. Stalin prizes were instituted in 1937, a little over a year after the cessation of the more modest Lenin prizes. In addition to their monetary award, winners of state prizes were released from progressive rates of rent payment.

83 Ibid., 99–101; interviews with Galina Petrovna, Liliana Isaevna (March–April 1993).

84 Trotsky directed his best polemics against elite perquisites. *Revolution Betrayed*, 99–122. On the anti-privilege thrust of the Great Purges, see Fitzpatrick, "Becoming Cultured," 230.

85 The following discussion draws heavily on Lewis Siegelbaum, *Stakhanovism and the Politics of Productivity in the USSR, 1935–1941* (Cambridge: Cambridge University Press, 1988), ch. 6 "Stakhanovism in the cultural mythology of the 1930s," and Fitzpatrick, "Becoming Cultured," 226–7.

86 Stakhanovite Khairulin of the Stalin automobile factory, for example, earned three times as much in 1938 as in 1933; spent eight times more on clothing, linens, and shoes; more than nine times as much on furniture, household supplies, and interior decorating; and more than twelve times as much on "cultural" needs. At the same time, his family was eating better than ever before. *Sovetskaia torgovlia* (newspaper), January 1, 1939.

87 Again, see Fitzpatrick, "Becoming Cultured," 226–7, and Siegelbaum, *Stakhanovism*, 226–31.

88 In the 1936 newsreel, "Stakhanovite Busygin gets a new apartment," these items included lace curtains for the window, lace runners, and a lace coverlet on the metal bed; an immense, fringed, hanging lampshade; perfume bottles and mirrors for Busygin's well-dressed wife; a bookshelf with the "classics of Marxism-Leninism"; a record player and gaily painted furniture for the children; houseplants; and comfortable, soft chairs. RGAKFD, reel 1414.

89 *Soveshchanie zhen khoziaistvennikov i inzhenerno-tekhnicheskikh rabotnikov tiazheloi promyshlennosti. Stenograficheskii otchet mai 10–12, 1936* (Moscow: Partizdat, 1936), 41; "Culture and daily life" was also the slogan of their journal *Obshchestvennitsa*. Sheila Fitzpatrick first drew attention to the *obshchestvennitsa* movement among civic-minded executives' wives in her excellent article,

"Becoming Cultured," 232–3. See also Volkov, "The Concept of Kul'turnost'," Chapter 7 in this volume.

90 Ibid., 32, 81, 106–7 and *passim*. Not surprisingly, the efforts of the housewife "activists" were not universally appreciated by their working-class beneficiaries. In 1937, a group of women workers complained to the Leningrad obkom about these officious bosses' wives, who had persuaded the factory director to release women workers from their regular employment for a couple of weeks for the purpose of embroidering a banner of Stalin. The women workers complained that their bonuses were at stake, since the factory was not fulfilling its plan, although the director had already received a bonus for "overfulfilment." TsGAIPD, f. 24, op. 2g, d. 89, l. 74.

91 A glossy fold-out photograph of these statesmen alongside the activists' presidium serves as the frontispiece to the meeting's stenographic report. Ibid., unnumbered page.

92 *Vsesoiuznoe soveshchanie zhen komandirov i nachal'stvuiushchego sostava RKKA, 20–23 dekabria, 1936. Stenograficheskii otchet* (Moscow: Gos. voen. izdat., 1937).

93 This aspect of the movement became more striking after 1938, when the movement's journal, *Obshchestvennitsa*, was increasingly dominated by defense themes. Although the decoration of dormitories was hardly abandoned as a worthy pursuit of a civic-minded factory manager's wife, activists were exhorted to learn to perform their husbands' jobs, so that they could take over production in the event of a war.

94 *Soveshchanie zhen ITR*, 80–1.

95 *Obshchestvennitsa*, 1936, no. 2 (August): 8.

96 Ibid., 8–9; *Soveshchanie zhen ITR*, 45–6, 64, 80–1, 92, 106–7, 132.

97 Trotsky, *Revolution Betrayed*, 101.

7

THE CONCEPT OF
KUL'TURNOST'

Notes on the Stalinist civilizing process

Vadim Volkov

In *The Civilising Process*, Norbert Elias has examined historical changes
of people's social standards of dealing with each other in everyday life,
corresponding to general patterns of public behaviour and interaction
in different epochs – from early-modern Europe to the times of creation
of modern nation-states.[1] The unifying trend of the evolution of even
the subtlest features of human intercourse was, according to Elias, the
change of human affective moulding through a transformation of
constraint by others into the apparatus of self-restraint. The study of the
civilising process, therefore, included an inquiry into the origins of the
disciplined shaping of behaviour typical to a modern society.

Elias conceived of the development of the apparatus of self-restraint
as a corollary of the process whereby spontaneity of bodily expression
and freedom of immediate realisation of natural affects gave way to a
tight frame of normative behavioural regulations. These included the
code of manners, the rules of hygiene, dress-codes, forms of conversation, and the like. The macrostructural conditions in which these changes
were situated were those of centralisation of authority over an increasing
number of territories and the creation of monopoly of force – the rise
of absolutist states. The concept of the civilising process provided a relatively coherent framework which connected the rise of centralised states
with the transformation of everyday behaviour. The inculcation of civil-
isational self-controls, the changes of emotional standards of human
interaction, the alteration of the thresholds of shame and tolerance, the
growing divide between the public and the private, and other elements
of the civilising process led to the emergence of a less violent and more
complex type of society.

Admittedly, the concept of the civilising process, as it was developed
by Elias, originated from the study of specific historical conditions of

210

West European societies and cannot be applied to other cultures and epochs without substantial modification. It seems possible, however, to dissociate some elements of the theoretical model from its historical application. Or, at least, his approach can justify scholarly attention to the seemingly unimportant and subtle changes in social organisation of everyday life, such as manners, public comportment, standards of hygiene, speech, food consumption, things of everyday use, dwelling space, and so on, because they carry significant structural effects in the long term. Using some interpretative techniques invented by Elias, I shall examine the process of inculcation of disciplines that proceeded without recourse to open violence and terror.

Although the main protagonists of the following story are not former knights turned into courtiers, as in the now classic study by Elias, but mainly former peasants becoming urban dwellers becoming Soviet citizens, the subject of this chapter can still be referred to as the "Stalinist civilising process". However contradictory, this term can refer to a range of policies, which the Bolsheviks did not invent (despite the heavy rhetoric of the "new socialist culture"), but which they were led to employ in response to the pressing problems accompanying the building of the new state in the 1930s. In order to highlight these policies, I shall account for the pragmatic contents of the concept of *kul'turnost'* ("culturedness"), especially prominent in everyday discourse from 1935. It should be noted from the start that the practices and policies in question did not derive from any unified explicitly formulated political project. Their unity can be better seen with reference to their social and individual effects, their long-term consequences, rather than from the point of view of intentional projects of political authorities.

Kul'tura and *kul'turnost'*

Until the 1880s the term "culture" (*kul'tura*) was not popular in Russian society. It is not encountered in the language of Pushkin. Dobroliubov, Chernyshevsky, and Pisarev, the prominent literary critics of the 1860s, did not use this word in writing either. Belinsky mentioned it occasionally in 1845, speaking of a "literary culture" (*literaturnaia kul'tura*); otherwise, the term was used in its original etymological meaning, that is with regard to agriculture.[2] The very first mention of *kul'tura*, however, is registered in the lexicon by Zimmerman in 1807; and Tatishchev's dictionary of 1826 translates it from French as *obrazovannost'* (educatedness).[3] In Western Europe, a range of terms such as *courtoisie, civilité, Bildung, cortezia* and others were used to denote different cultural phenomena, and later, in the eighteenth century, they evolved into either "culture" or "civilization". In the absence of *kul'tura* in the language of Russian society, the general meaning of this term was conveyed by the words "enlightenment" (*prosveshchenie*), "education", "civilisation", "literature", "spirituality" (*dukhovnost'*). With regard to a person, such words as "educated" (*obrazovannyi*), "well-bred" (*vospitannyi*) and the like were used in the same way as "cultured" (*kul'turnyi*) came to be used later.

The emergence of *kul'tura* in the discourse of the Russian intelligentsia is usually connected with German influence. The German *Kultur* referred to the original national spirit as opposed to the alien French influence expressed by the concept of *Zivilisation*. *Kultur* was also central to the self-identity of German middle-class intellectuals, as they sought to distinguish themselves from the superficially refined aristocracy, whom they associated with *Zivilisation*.[4] The Russian Slavophiles, who constructed a similar opposition between the true national spirit of pre-Petrine Russia and the Westernized elite, employed "enlightenment" and "educatedness", respectively. According to Pavel Miliukov, the author of *Essays on the History of Russian Culture*, first published in 1892–5, culture (*kul'tura*) and civilization (*tsivilizatsiia*) emerged as oppositional terms in the discourse of the Slavophiles of the 1880s, most prominently in the writings of Konstantin Leontiev, who associated the authentic and rich *kul'tura* with the earlier period of exuberant growth and complexity, and *tsivilizatsiia* with the age of secondary simplification and decline of a national culture.[5] In his *Essays* Miliukov tried to avoid the opposition set by Leontiev, suggesting a broad definition of *kul'tura* as a specific relationship between the material culture and the spiritual culture of the nation. He argued that the cleavage between traditional culture and the culture of the educated elite in Russia was not a sign of crisis or decline, but the result of the historical transition from spontaneous cultural development to the reflexive stage typical of any mature nation. Sharing the hopes of contemporary liberals, Miliukov predicted that the cleavage between the two cultures would be gradually eliminated through the "transmission of cultural achievements from the intelligentsia to the masses".[6]

It is in connection with the missionary idea of the transmission of education and culture to the backward masses and in the context of the first attempts (in the late 1870s) to put it into practice that the term *kul'-tura* and its derivatives *kul'turnyi* and *kul'turnost'* started to gain prominence. Liberals working at *zemstvo* schools for peasant education (see Glossary), teachers at Sunday schools for workers and peasants, and intellectuals (liberals as well as populists) studying popular reading habits, as well as other groups involved in similar activities, saw themselves as doing "cultural work" (*kul'turnaia rabota*) and, accordingly, were sometimes referred to as *kul'turniki*.[7] Through their activity *kul'tura* came to be understood as a kind of value that could be accumulated, purposefully transferred to and acquired by wider groups of the population. So we can assume that originally the term *kul'tura* became widely adopted in Russia in connection with the idea of cultural policy. It is probably this genetic relationship with the nascent practices of mass policy that constitutes a subtle difference between *kul'tura* and the earlier cultural phenomena denoted by other terms.

Kul'turnost', then, referred to the effects of this policy. Formally, the term can only be used in relation to a person or a group, and points to a relative level of personal culture and education.[8] It is unclear whether the term was of any significance in Imperial Russia and whether it was used by groups other than Marxists, for the only pattern of contextual usage given by all dictionaries comes from Plekhanov's *The Russian Worker in the Revolutionary Movement*, first published in the 1890s: "The more I got acquainted with Petersburg workers, the more I was impressed by their *kul'turnost'*."[9] Beyond doubt is the centrality of *kul'tura* and *kul'-turnost'* for the post-1917 period, and there is no need to reproduce lengthy passages by Gorky, Lenin, Stalin, and other authorities to illustrate this. *Kul'tura* was one of the main value-charged ideological terms; *kul'turnost'* was of semi-official order and referred to the background everyday practice. If *kul'tura* gradually came to constitute one of the central spiritual values of Soviet civilization, if it became firmly rooted in official discourse and in the consciousness of the intelligentsia, it is because its specific use-value was, under certain historical circumstances, rediscovered and deployed by the Soviet power. Then in order to understand why *kul'tura* was so important ideologically, we should consider its pragmatic aspects, that is the specific rationalities, expressed in *kul'-turnost'*, and the corresponding effects of power. Vera Dunham, the first scholar to underscore the importance of the concept of *kul'turnost'* for Soviet society, defined it as "a fetish notion of how to be individually civilized".[10] Her definition can be taken as a starting point but only to raise further questions: why did this concept emerge in the Soviet 1930s? What had one to do to become civilised? What did "being civilised" mean with reference to the Soviet individual and society?

Kul'turnost' in context

In 1946 the sociologist Nicholas Timasheff suggested in his pioneering study of the pre-war USSR that there was a major historical discontinuity in the development of the Soviet system under Stalin. Timasheff studied what he called a "Great Retreat" in all major spheres of life, which began in 1934, and which represented an all-out, albeit surreptitious, reversal of the communist revolutionary experiment. Once the early Bolshevik values were abandoned, the main pattern of the Great Retreat became "the amalgamation of traits of the historical and national culture of Russia with traits belonging to the Communist cycle of ideas and behaviour patterns".[11] Yet the Great Retreat was also a "return to normalcy" in politics and society: it meant a series of concessions in the spheres of distribution of wealth, education, consumption, family, religion, and leisure. Alongside the massive influx of "raw" rural population into the cities, the era of the Great Retreat saw extensive changes in everyday behaviour, manners, and tastes – a conspicuous emergence of patterns of cultural life which tended to emulate some features of educated urban society under the Old Regime.

A transformation similar to Timasheff's "Great Retreat", or rather a continuation of it in the late 1940s, was studied by Dunham in relation to "middleclass values" as reflected in Soviet fiction. She conducted her study on the assumption that "in Stalin's time – and even in Stalin's worst times – the regime was supported by more than simple terror, a truism", as she ironically put it, "still overlooked from time to time".[12] The Soviet system owed its regenerative power and stability to what Dunham called "The Big Deal" – the officially undeclared but firmly observed contract between the Stalinist regime and "its own indigenous middle class", whose values were accommodated by the regime in exchange for loyalty and efficiency. The Big Deal also included a conversion of public values: a transition from militant revolutionary asceticism and selfless devotion to public deeds to individual consumption, a prosperous private life, and civilised conduct. "Private values were converted into public values".[13]

The changes described by Timasheff and Dunham occurred in the aftermath of the all-out drive for industrialisation which started in 1928. It brought millions of uprooted peasants into the cities and new construction sites. "Ruralization of the cities", as Moshe Lewin called it, dramatically changed the composition of the urban population. During 1926–39 the cities grew by some thirty million people; during the First Five-Year Plan alone the cities grew by 44 per cent, absorbing up to three million people each year, mainly former peasants.[14] Consequently, housing conditions became appalling, and much of the new workforce had to be housed in barracks and dormitories. The body social was profoundly shaken: as the traditional rural mechanisms of control and customary laws were loosing their grip on the former peasants, an epidemic of violent crimes, hooliganism, rape, alcoholism, and other forms of deviance overwhelmed the urban environment.[15] Industrial production also suffered from the breakdown of labour discipline and massive labour turnover. The barracks, as the worried press reports described, were turned into sites of social filth and anomie: rumours, hooliganism, wife beating, foul language, the absence of elementary hygiene.[16] The new urban masses were peasants by origin and workers by occupation. Theoretically, they were the stronghold of the new regime. But uprooted by the regime's policies, they were marginal by culture and behaviour, and therefore dangerous to the regime's very existence. According to recent archival research into Soviet penal institutions under Stalin, the majority of "socially harmful and dangerous elements" and "counterrevolutionaries" detained and executed throughout the 1930s were in fact arrested for violent crimes, robbery, crimes against property, theft, swindling, hooliganism, and similar violations of legal and public order. The politicisation of these forms of delinquency was fostered by the tendency to regard them as a political threat to the regime.[17] The resulting confusion by the regime of the problems of political order and public order and the absence of a clear conceptual differentiation between the two led to a one-sided vision of the predominantly political nature of the Stalinist terror. But even the recognition that severe punitive sanctions were frequently used as measures of social defence does not imply that violence was the main reaction of the regime to the growing social anomie.

In the conditions in which the crisis of public order was turning into a systemic crisis, one could envisage a strategy which served to counter the ruralisation of the cities: the urbanisation of the new workforce. The new masses had to be introduced to urban forms of life. This presupposed an inculcation of norms and types of discipline dictated by the industrial organisation of labour as well as by the kind of public order characteristic of the urban setting. As the authorities, for obvious ideological and pragmatic reasons, were unable to apply full-scale punitive and violent measures to workers, the logical alternative was more subtle and "positive" (that is, non-violent) policies to restore and maintain public order. In order to discipline the new urban population the regime had to civilise it. Thus the former peasants had to be turned into members of modern society. This chapter considers the productive rather than the repressive effects of power as they were expressed in everyday cultural policies under Stalin. From 1935, and especially during 1936–7, these policies revolved around the concept of *kul'turnost'*.

The other side of industrialisation was the rapid growth of the administrative and managerial hierarchies – of the new ruling stratum of the state. They were recruited from "below", educated in colleges and high schools, promoted to command positions in the economy, and, accordingly, received vast material benefits and privileges. The 1930s were characterized by sudden reshufflings in the top leadership, purges of the "old" cadres, and consequent spectacular promotions of the new proletarian-peasant intelligentsia.[18] Many members of the new elite were workers or peasants by origin but upper-middle class by their newly acquired place in hierarchy and material benefits. The conflict between these two formal attributes had to be resolved in practice without questioning the basic ideological tenets of the "worker-peasant's socialist state".

When in 1935 the right to a prosperous (*zazhitochanaia*) life was officially sanctioned, the notion of *kul'turnost'* was linked to new higher standards of individual consumption.[19] While in reality, material well-being and a civilised life were mainly accessible to the new administrative elite, the possibility of a prosperous and cultured life was promised to everyone in exchange for efficient work. As Sheila Fitzpatrick put it: "One of the great advantages of the concept of *kul'turnost'* in a post-revolutionary society burdened by the hangovers of revolutionary puritanism was that it offered a way of legitimizing what had once been thought of as 'bourgeois' concerns about possessions and status: one treated them as an aspect of *kul'tura*."[20] On the whole, the policies of *kul'turnost'* met at least two complementary objectives, pragmatic and ideological: to discipline the new masses by means of shaping everyday behaviour in accordance with uniform social ("cultured") norms and to justify inequalities by integrating the lower strata into a system of quasi-elitist consumption values. Since the consumerist ideology has received scholarly attention in the aforementioned studies, I will concentrate more on the pragmatic dimension.

The structural dynamic of *kul'turnost'*

Kul'turnost' was never a clearly defined concept, and no party authority gave coherent instructions on how to become cultured. Concrete applications of the term, scattered across the pages of official and popular texts and periodicals between 1935 and 1938, do not display any single pattern. Rather, they point to a complex of practices aimed at transforming a number of external and internal features of the individual. If we put them together we can easily arrive at the model of the cultured man (*kul'turnyi chelovek*) which is, disappointingly, nothing new and nothing more than a Stalinist variation on the theme of the individual in a modern society externally civilised and internally committed to its values. What is unique, though, is that this model functioned in the years of the Great Terror. In relation to terror, which exemplified arbitrary and repressive, negative power, the inculcation of the disciplines of *kul'turnost'* by way of leading people to transform themselves into cultured individuals can be associated, following the insights of Foucault, with creative and productive modality of power.[21] Foucault's well-known argument holds that power is not necessarily negative, that its effects are not limited to posing constraints.[22] Power should be equally seen as carrying positive effects, creating possibilities for individual and group actions. On the level of the state, the exercise of power takes the form of a "combination of the political structures of individualization techniques, and of totalization procedures".[23]

The functioning of power as violence, confinement, terror was no doubt vital for the survival of the Stalinist regime. No one would question the repressive nature of this regime. But perhaps not all of the regime's policies fit the purely repressive model; otherwise it would be difficult to envisage how the regime managed to increase the productive potential of the predominantly peasant country within the framework of the new urban-industrial organization. As Stephen Kotkin has argued in his recent study of the politics of daily life in the USSR, an inquiry into the actual functioning of Stalin's system "should include not only what was repressed or prohibited but what was made possible or produced".[24]

In the practical sense, what should one do to become cultured? This question, I believe, haunted many contemporaries, and the periodical press offered a range of answers. The recipes, sometimes quite contradictory, changed over time between 1935 and 1938. With the same question in mind, we shall now look at the structural dynamic of *kul'- turnost'* – at the changing practices associated with this concept and the logic of their relationship.

Appearance and fashion

The simplest and least demanding aspect of *kul'turnost'* referred to one's clothes. The sphere of dress was the first to be associated with this concept, in 1933–4. The formerly popular military uniforms and their derivatives, the style which originated in a combination of scarcity and early-Bolshevik values, were giving way to a more civil type of clothes.[25] The ascetic ideal was dropped as the official propaganda endorsed smart clothes, clean shaving for men and the use of perfumes and make-up for women.[26] As an inquiry into youth patterns of *kul'turnost'* between 1934 and 1936 indicates, already by 1934 a young male worker dreamt of a "Boston" suit, yellow shoes and nice shirts; and a young *udarnitsa* (female shockworker: see Glossary) from the Kirov plant in Leningrad planned to spend her salary on a crêpe de Chine dress, beige shoes, an "Oxford" suit, and a nice winter coat.[27] In January 1936 the new trend was supported by the opening of the first Soviet House of Fashions in Moscow and the publication of a number of French fashion magazines, *Saison Parisienne*, *Grand Revue des Modes*, and *Votre Gout* as well as their Soviet equivalents, the *Journal of the House of Fashions*, the *Fashions of Autumn and Spring of 1936*.[28]

Care for one's appearance came to include other aspects of the public self. In the beginning of 1936 the press claimed that the Soviet Union surpassed France in the gross production of perfumes and moved up to third place in the world after the US and Britain.[29] At the end of 1936 the Institute of Cosmetics and Hygiene opened in Moscow in order to satisfy the "great interest of the population in the hygiene of facial and bodily skin".[30] The promotion of perfumes and regular facial massage did not correspond to working-class patterns and official socialist culture. Yet there was no problem with the public advertising of these and other "cultural skills" of the new assertive elite as long as they remained part of the ideologically positive notion of *kul'turnost'*.

Personal hygiene

Concern with mere appearance was joined by the demand to keep the body clean and to wear fresh underwear. "Cleanliness and tidiness are justly considered the attributes of *kul'turnost'*. A person cannot be referred to as cultured if he does not keep his body clean."[31] Thus one of the primary forms of *kul'turnost'* was associated with personal hygiene. As attention to bodily hygiene heightened, practices related to this kind of self-care were also changing in a certain direction. The traditional public bathhouse with big common washing rooms gradually evolved into a more complex and partitioned washing space, equipped with individual showers. In official language this tendency was referred to as "the substitution of individual bath-shower washing for the (common) bath".[32] This also included new "individual bath-shower complexes" in the newly built apartment blocks.

The cleanliness of the body was part of a wider practical framework of personal care. The latter also included such "equipment" as bedlinen, underwear and handkerchiefs. The study cited earlier of young Leningrad workers took the use of bedsheets and underwear as the main indicator of *kul'turnost'*. The researcher found that all the workers included in his sample had, in 1936, at least one set of bedlinen; 5 per cent of the respondents had two, 38 per cent had three or four, and 57 per cent used five or more sets of bedlinen. This, the study claimed, indicated a steady growth of *kul'turnost'* in comparison with 1934, when 2 per cent of the workers used no bedlinen, 17 per cent had only one set, 34 per cent had two sets and 47 per cent had three to four or more sets of bedlinen. A similar tendency was registered with regard to the use of underwear.[33]

It was not by chance that the growing attention to personal hygiene coincided with the campaign for labour efficiency (the Stakhanovite movement: see Glossary) which became fully fledged in 1936. Cleanliness testified to self-discipline and efficient organisation of one's activity. So *kul'turnost'* in private life (*v bytu*) corresponded to efficiency and discipline at the workplace. "Strict discipline, elimination of carelessness (*raspushchennost'*)" was that which characterized a true Stakhanovite, who "must be the model of cleanliness, tidiness, and culturedness at work and in private life".[34] A connection between personal hygiene and the culture of production (*kul'tura proizvodstva*) was articulated in the discussion of *kul'turnost'* in a series of articles in the press in April 1936.

Kul'turnost' was persistently associated with individual achievement, the source of personal dignity and pride. Demands that workers should "look after themselves" (*sledit' za soboi*) and "hold themselves in a cultured way" (*kul'turno sebia derzhat'*) were invoked. At the same time, culturedness as self-discipline and self-monitoring was integrated into the industrial system: the cultured individual was identified with the efficient worker. Cleanliness was also conceived instrumentally: "The white collar and the clean shirt are the necessary working instruments providing for the fulfilment of production plans and the quality of products."[35] Grigorii Ordzhonikidze, the minister of heavy industry, especially accentuated the need to look tidy and to shave regularly. Thereafter, a number of enterprises issued orders compelling all engineers and managers to make sure that they were clean-shaven and that their hair was appropriately styled. Some factories were specially provided with mirrors, so that the personnel could monitor their proper appearance. In the concluding article *Pravda* stressed that the discussion of *kul'turnost'* was not a passing campaign, but the beginning of "a long systematic effort in the sphere of cultural self-training to inculcate cultural skills in the widest layers of the working population. The struggle for culture and cleanliness must embrace all spheres of our life."[36] The following months saw the creation of a social movement which focused on a systematic reform of the everyday life of workers, peasants, and Red Army personnel along the lines of *kul'turnost'*.

The wives' movement ("Obshchestvennitsa")

The idea of mobilising the wives of top managers and engineers in order to introduce workers to the basic skills of *kul'turnost'* was born, so legend says, in the head of Ordzhonikidze in 1934 when he visited a Ural factory and saw, in the yard, a flower-bed cultivated by a manager's wife (Surovtseva, later one of the leaders of the movement). It then resulted in an All-Union Meeting of Wives of Industrialists and Engineering-Technical Personnel of Heavy Industry in May 1936 and a number of similar meetings in other branches of industry, the Red Army, and communal services. This started a movement for the all-out civilisation of everyday life. The journal *Obshchestvennitsa* became the printed organ of the movement, and the women involved were further referred to as *obshchestvennitsy*. No straightforward translation of the word is possible; it derives from the term *obshchestvennost'* (literally, "socialness"), a term that came to signify the public as an active social force. In this particular case, *obshchestvennitsy* were the wives of administrative-professional stratum, engaged in voluntary social or public activity.[37]

They were to reform the everyday life of workers along the lines of *kul'turnost'*. Initially, the main principle of their activity had nothing to do with propaganda of "high" ideas and ideals. It was plain and simple: "cultured environment raises the culturedness of those who live in it", or "environment compels and edifies".[38] "Environment" here means the things proximate to one's existence: the arrangement of space, the structure of things at hand (*obikhod*, which can also be captured by the word "equipment"), and elementary habits of self-care, like hygiene and diet. It was these aspects of daily life that *obshchestvennitsy* attempted to reform.

The worker's barracks, which accommodated up to several hundred workers with their families all in one space, were no longer tolerated: they were seen as repositories of deviance, violence, filth, offensive smells, and coarse speech – the problems to which the state had become more sensitive. "Unculturedness" emanated from there. Where it was impossible to build new workers' hostels, changes in the living space were achieved through elementary partitioning. The practice was reminiscent of what Foucault has referred to as the principle of creation of disciplinary space: "Each individual has its own place; and each place is individual."[39] On the pages of the journal, *obshchestvennitsy* shared their experience in erecting partitions and dividing the space of a barrack into smaller living areas. One could read numerous reports of how the bosses' wives planned and directed the rebuilding of barracks, "those big dirty halls".[40] New standards were implemented:

> Each room must accommodate not more than four people. One bed must not touch another, even with its head; common bunks are unacceptable . . . A free passage between the beds must be not less than 0.35 meter wide, there must be a common passage of no less than 1.5 meter wide along the beds . . . From which it follows that the norm for each bed must be not less than 4 square meters.[41]

Such norms were introduced under a twofold motivation: they led to improvements in physical hygiene as well as in public order. As a result, they also made the living space more individual. Social activities were separated from natural ones. Special rooms were reserved for common leisure and cultural activities, removing them from the place where one slept; tenants were prohibited from sitting or eating on their beds. Special isolated "rooms of hygiene" were constructed. Their purpose was to improve hygiene, but at the same time they served to remove the natural functions of the body from public view.

Things and symbols of private life

In the context of the activities of *obshchestvennitsy*, things that surrounded people – their material environment – became instrumental in changing people's habits and attitudes. A recurrent set of things was supposed to instil *kul'turnost'*. Among the items of everyday "equipment" associated with the norms of civilised life three became fetishised: curtains, lampshades, and tablecloths. Curtains, lampshades, and tablecloths are mentioned in one journal after another. Sometimes the set included flowers and carpets. The achievements in introducing *kul'turnost'* often sounded like this: "There are snow-white curtains on the windows, tablecloths and flowers on the tables. Things appear that were never known before: bookshelves, wardrobes, and silk lampshades."[42] Wives of Red Army officers reported how barracks and canteens were equipped with portieres, curtains, and tablecloths made by the caring women's hands. Concern with the objects of *kul'turnost'* was obsessive. Curtains, lampshades, and tablecloths provided by *obshchestvennitsy* reached the North Pole. In 1938 the ship *Taimyr* went to rescue the members of the heroic Papanin Arctic expedition. *Obshchestvennitsy* turned their attention to the ship's interior: "It was decided to make two beautiful lampshades and a tablecloth for a gramophone ... Many nice things were made by our women: portieres, tablecloths, serviettes, carpets, and lampshades."[43] Curtains, lampshades, and tablecloths served to transform the uncultured people; they also figured as little symbols of culturedness. What was their social significance? What social effects did these things generate?

Curtains turned into a universal symbol of *kul'turnost'*. They served symbolically to constitute a home, a cultured dwelling. The "effect of curtains" consisted in the creation – both real and symbolic – of a private space through a limitation of its observability. Curtains organically accompanied the partitioning of big communal spaces; they functioned, as it were, as a diaphragm that controlled the degree of seclusion of a private space from the outside world. (A person opening or shutting the curtains is a widespread symbolic image in painting, a cliché in the cinema.) It was often emphasised that curtains were "snow-white", which implied cleanliness and proper hygiene.

A lampshade combines the function of regulating the tonality of lighting and the aesthetics of the interior. Lighting, however, is also part of the social microstructure. To a certain extent, it defines the genre of an event or activity. Techniques of lighting are also social techniques. They create and maintain certain social dispositions, but are themselves barely discernible in everyday life, because their function is to render other things discernible and present them in "this or that light". The introduction of lampshades – the journal *Obshchestvennitsa* offered instructions on how to make lampshades from various fabrics – was part of such techniques. Delimiting and condensing living-space, soft lighting helped to make one's dwelling more comfortable, private, and self-contained.

Finally, the tablecloth was the third normative element of a cultured setting. An article giving instructions on "rational diet" concluded: "If the table is draped with a white tablecloth, the dinner tastes good and is digested perfectly. To live in a cultured way also means to eat in a cultured way."[44] The white tablecloth figured as a symbol of *kul'turnost'*, and also tied together diet, hygiene, and manners. The introduction of tablecloths in workers' canteens implied further changes. Long wooden tables and common benches were removed, and were replaced with tables for four or six and separate chairs. No doubt at a small table, covered with a white tablecloth, one could no longer eat in the same way as at a crude wooden table shared with a dozen other people. The "snow-white" tablecloth would immediately testify to the person's table manners. "Now I cannot sit down at such a table with my hands dirty", wrote a worker.[45]

Kul'turnost' implied systemic changes in material environment. The things associated with *kul'turnost'* were not just single random objects that people encountered in the course of their daily lives. Rather, such things tended to form a specific "object-system" or an "equipmental matrix", in which all the elements presupposed one another and together constituted the material infrastructure of *kul'-turnost'*. On the one hand, this material infrastructure contained an implicit concept of its user, including the user's practical skills, rhythms of activity, levels of self-discipline, elementary habits. On the other hand, people used the elements of this infrastructure not only for practical purposes, but also to constitute themselves as cultured individuals. And in so doing they were bound to develop new habits which derived from the patterns of usage carried by the objects of *kul'turnost'*. In the long term, such an equipmental matrix, once introduced, would require neither permanent persuasion nor external coercion in order to mould individuals.

Brought to life by the policies of *kul'turnost'* in 1936, the movement of *obshchestvennitsy* had changed its objectives by 1939. As Europe witnessed the outbreak of the Second World War, a different set of policies aimed at military build-up and mass mobilisation was launched in the Soviet Union. Everyday life, including the cultural sphere, was reorganised to meet the needs of defence. The original civilising pursuit of *obshchestvennitsy* was also redirected. The inculcation of cultural skills was supplanted by military training. But even though the movement did not revive after the war, the processes that it had helped to set in motion continued, and what in the 1930s was still largely the projects of power to be realised – norms of hygiene, manners, elements of private life – became more habitual in the 1950s.

Speech

The framework of *kul'turnost'* was not limited to appearance or material possessions. It also included social activity: speech, for example. In March 1936 the Komsomol press started a campaign against "dirty talk", arguing that it was incompatible with the norms of *kul'turnost'*. Denouncing the impoverished, bureaucratic, criminal jargon of the Komsomol leaders, an article in a popular youth magazine proceeded to ask: "Is it possible that culture only means that Stakhanovites wear cheviot suits and 'attend theatre and cinema not less that three times a month'?"[46] Proper appearance was no longer sufficient for being cultured. This idea was stressed by Kosarev, the secretary of the Komsomol Central Committee, at the tenth congress in April 1936: "We have now a breed of people, who mistake different petit-bourgeois (*meshchanskie*) attributes for a prosperous, cultured life. Their thoughts (*pomysly*) do not go further than a suit of foreign make, a gramophone, and books published by 'Academia' [translations of light foreign novels]."[47]

The external attributes and the formal criteria expressed in attending the theatre and cinema were no longer sufficient for being a cultured person. One should not only appear but actually be cultured. Thus, culturedness would be increasingly sought in and in fact projected on to the individual's inner world. Unlike material attributes, the "culture of speech" (*kul'tura rechi*) was naturally perceived as inalienable from the personality, related more to the internal rather than the external qualities. The mastery of a correct, literary speech-manner required greater self-monitoring and a more continuous effort than buying smart clothes and gramophones. The linguistic aspect of *kul'turnost'* was further articulated during the celebration of the centenary of Pushkin's death at the beginning of 1937. The celebration, planned and prepared long in advance – the decision of the Central Executive Committee to form the special Pushkin Committee (which included the members of the government and the cultural elite) dates back to December 1935 – marked a specific fusion of two grand cultural traditions, the old Russian and the new Soviet. Pushkin, it was declared, truthfully expressed the Russian national spirit. On the individual level, however, the significance of Pushkin was more pragmatic. It was associated with correct patterns of speech: "Beyond any doubt is the positive effect of Pushkin's speech on the struggle for a cultured, correct, precise language."[48]

Reading and the common cultural horizon

The culture of speech derived from good literature; and reading was also directly connected with the acquisition of culturedness. Initially, the word "literate" was a synonym of "cultured", but as more people read more books, "educatedness" (*obrazovannost'*, the word from Pushkin's vocabulary) superseded literacy in designating the main feature of the cultured individual. Literacy was more of a technical skill; educatedness referred to knowledge and, significantly, to the common cultural horizon. *Kul'turnost'* as educatedness (a personified modality of "education") implied knowledge acquired through reading. In a speech in 1936 the secretary of the Moscow Komsomol organisation presented a model of the cultured and educated person – a female fitter from Leningrad, Nina Elkina, age 20: "in the course of the year she had read 78 books including such authors as Balzac, Hamsun, Goncharov, Hoffmann, Hugo, Rostand, Flaubert, France, Chekhov, Shakespeare, Veresaev, Novikov-Priboi, Serebriakova, A. Tolstoy, Tynianov, Chapygin, B. Iasenskii."[49]

Retaining its earlier "superficial" elements, *kul'turnost'* gradually turned into a standard stock of cultural knowledge which shaped the common cultural horizon. The cultural life-world of *sovetskii chelovek* (Soviet man), or at least its normative aspects, was formalised and presented as a specific self-test entitled "Are you a cultured person?", published in every single issue of the ever-popular weekly magazine *Ogonek* in 1936. Every self-test contained ten questions, accompanied by the following instruction: "Remember, if you are not able to answer any one of the ten suggested questions, you, apparently, know very little about a whole sphere of science or arts. Let this compel you to WORK ON YOURSELF (*porabotat' nad soboi*)."[50] The instruction also suggested testing one's friends and colleagues. Here is the questionnaire of the first week of 1936:

1 Recite by heart at least one poem by Pushkin.
2 Name and characterise five plays by Shakespeare.
3 Name at least four rivers in Africa.
4 Name your favourite composer and his three major works.
5 Name five Soviet automobiles.
6 Convert 3/8 into a decimal.
7 Name the three most significant sport tournaments of the last year and their results.
8 Describe the three paintings which you liked most at last year's exhibitions.
9 Have you read *Red and Black* by Stendahl and *Fathers and Sons* by Turgenev?
10 Explain why the Stakhanovite movement became possible in our country.

Let the educated reader answer. There are reasons to assume that by the end of 1936 many contemporary Soviet readers could. The *Ogonek* questionnaires were mentioned in other periodicals. Cultural clubs were advised to copy and hang them up as posters; so they may indeed have been a popular conversational theme and a form of self-training in 1936–7. They are remarkable documents, representing the width and limits of the original matrix of cultural and ideological knowledge required of the contemporary Soviet citizen. The first question of the first questionnaire implies the reading of Pushkin; the last, knowledge of the four points from Stalin's speech of 1935 on the Stakhanovite movement. Other issues of the journal presupposed, for example, knowledge of the gods of war, love, and trade in Ancient Greece and Rome, three types of warplanes, and the names of seven Stakhanovites (no. 2); or of two British newspapers and two representatives of Utopian socialist thought (no. 3). In one and the same questionnaire the reader could have been asked to name two poems by Heine and two Soviet icebreakers (no. 23).

It would be tempting to classify and analyse the several hundred *Ogonek* questions to the cultured person, but suffice it to say that the questionnaire can be taken as evidence of a further evolution of the concept of *kul'turnost'*. To become a cultured person one must read classical literature, contemporary Soviet fiction, poetry, newspapers, works by Marx–Engels–Lenin–Stalin, as well as attend the cinema and exhibitions with the purpose of self-education. A cultured person must have a broad cultural horizon (broad within the frame set up at a given historical moment) and a cultured inner world.

There were two important features of the process of becoming cultured. First, personal *kul'turnost'* was acquired through a combined effort by the public (*zabota obshchestvennosti*) and the individual (*rabota nad soboi*, the work on oneself), where the public concern would normally result in the individual ability to live in accordance with the norms of *kul'turnost'* without explicit external compulsion. Second, all aspects of *kul'turnost'* were related to one another systemically, as organic units constitutive of the public order. It is through the individual habituation of *kul'turnost'* that many aspects of urban public order were formed and reproduced.

Kul'turnost' *and Bolshevik consciousness*

There was yet another aspect of *kul'turnost'*. The logic of becoming cultured implied a movement from the concern with mere appearance and manners to matters of the individual's inner world, as if discovering this inner world of knowledge and spiritual commitments.

In 1938 a new doctrine was put forward by the authorities: "mastering Bolshevism" (*ovladenie bol'shevizmom*). It called for an extensive theoretical education in dialectical materialism and implied the cultivation of Bolshevik consciousness. The "acquisition of culturedness" was overshadowed by the concept of political self-education. Between them, however, was a certain connection. The tendency that preceded and, to some extent, legitimated the demand to master Bolshevism can be called the problematisation of the external aspects of *kul'turnost'*. Smart clothes, elegant behaviour, and even refined speech were associated with the image of the enemy. The sphere of leisure and private life came under constant attacks in the summer of 1937, and the criticism reached its culmination at the Fourth Plenary Meeting of the Komsomol Central Committee at the end of August 1937. The Komsomol press launched vigorous attacks on the sphere of leisure. The enemies, it was declared, operated in youth hostels and on dance floors; dressed in smart clothes in the "Harbin" style (*kharbinskii stil'*), they introduced young Komsomolers to their "beautiful and joyous lifestyle", and eventually recruited them into the ranks of spies.[51] At the Komsomol congress in 1936 young men were still urged to acquire *kul'turnost'* and to treat each other, and especially women, gallantly. Later, the external aspects of *kul'-turnost'*, including refined speech, were condemned, and what was demanded was internal convictions and healthy consciousness. In 1938 the Komsomol periodical summed up the new vision of the enemy:

> The image of the hooligan has changed! The enemy is dressed according to the latest fashion. He is gallant. He dances nicely, speaks beautifully. He knows how to enchant women. But if you delve into such a person, you will uncover his beastly, alien interior [*zverinoe, vrazhdebnoe nutro*].[52]

The transformation of the image of the enemy is indicative of the dynamic of *kul'turnost'*. In 1934–6, the first phase of *kul'turnost'*, the "hostile elements" were dirty, badly dressed, ill-mannered, and illiterate people; while the model heroes of the popular press were neatly dressed, clean, well-bred, and lived a joyous cultured life. In 1936–7, as culturedness became increasingly associated with inner culture, with broad knowledge and education, those obsessed with superficial attributes and consumerism could be labelled "petit-bourgeois". Finally, in 1937–8 the earlier aspects of culturedness came under suspicion, and, although no one officially rejected personal hygiene and educatedness, the true virtues of Soviet Man were relegated to the sphere of consciousness and private ideological commitments. Even though according to the logic of the individual acquisition of culturedness the external comes first and the internal, the inner self as the corollary of self-discipline, appears last, in the emerging official hierarchy of values it is the inner commitments that are to be regarded as the true identity of the individual. One should now take care of one's soul, the name for which became the Bolshevik consciousness. The semi-official beginning of the age of *kul'turnost'* was marked by

Stalin's motto of November 1935: "Life has become better, life has become more joyous"; its official decline coincided with the new motto "To master Bolshevism!", put forward in September 1938 in connection with the publication of the *Short Course of the Communist Party*.

The decree of the Central Committee of 14 November 1938 prescribed the correct method of mastering Marxism-Leninism: individual reading (*samostoiatel'noe chtenie*). Dialectical materialism, the decree assured, was now accessible to all rank-and-file communists and intelligentsia, if they would undertake a continuous individual (the term was repeatedly invoked) effort of self-education through the reading of the *Short Course*, in classes and at home. A month earlier A. Zhdanov, addressing the Komsomol activists in the Bolshoi theatre, emphasised that Komsomol "must make a very serious turn in the sphere of propaganda, concentrating on the quality, on the individual work of the Komsomol members with the book".[53]

In 1935–6 Stakhanovites were presented as models of *kul'turnost'*. They were involved in a kind of "conspicuous consumption", purchasing expensive suits, overcoats, gramophones, furniture, and other items of cultured life.[54] Later, another vital ingredient was added to this image. We find it in the biography of the Stakhanovite A. Busygin, published in 1939. Having described his comfortable private apartment and his involvement in cultural life, he tells the reader about his new engagement:

> Now I am working on the history of VKP(b) [implying *The Short Course*]. Slowly, in nocturnal silence I read it line by line, paragraph by paragraph. Dozens of questions, of new ideas emerge – I write them down. It is only recently that I started practising this way of working with the book. When you work with the book yourself, when you think over every line, you feel that you are learning the Bolshevik way of thinking.[55]

This sketch creates an image of extreme privacy, of a quiet dark room with the curtains shut and a table lamp casting light on the book – an ideal setting for careful reading and reflection.

Busygin's "new experience" hints at two features of private life: private living-space and silent reading intensifying individual reflection. Many aspects of *kul'turnost'* point in a similar direction. As was suggested in this article, "soft" forms of discipline, higher standards of consumption, and individual self-consciousness were indispensable tools for the consolidation of the Soviet system. Their effects, however, went beyond the narrow functional purposes for which they were re-invented by the Soviet authorities.

One way to describe their longer-term effects is by using the term "privatisation of life" suggested by the French social historians.[56] In the

West European context, the concept of privatisation of life highlights interconnections between gradual changes in material culture, manners and practices of everyday life, arrangements and divisions of the living space over more than five hundred years and gives them a sense of common direction. They all helped to establish the sphere of private and family life as distinct from public or collective life. Western self-identity thus became increasingly dependent upon the sense of privacy and individualism.

In the pre-war Soviet Union it was not just privacy as such, or *kul'-turnost'* for the sake of *kul'turnost'*, that the party authorities endorsed. The privacy that Busygin cultivated, for example, was connected with political self-education and the cultivation of Bolshevik consciousness, and an official ideological text, the *Short Course*, served as its major instrument. Nevertheless, whatever the initial purposes of regime-approved privacy, its further development was more and more likely to escape direct control. If, in the postwar period, private life and *kul'turnost'* tended to be less fetishised than before the war, that only signified that they had become less problematic.

NOTES

This is a revised version of a chapter that will appear in *Everyday Subjects: Formations of Identity in Early Soviet Culture*, ed. Christina Kiaer and Eric Naiman, Cornell University Press, forthcoming. Some of the materials contained in the chapter have been published in *Constructing Russian Culture in the Age of Revolution: 1881–1940*, ed. Catriona Kelly and David Shepherd (Oxford: Oxford University Press, 1998).

1 Norbert Elias, *The Civilizing Process*, vol. I: *The History of Manners*, trans. E. Jephcott (Oxford: Basil Blackwell, 1978).
2 R. Budagov, *Istoriia slov v istorii obshchestv* (Moscow: Nauka, 1971), 128.
3 Nikolai Shanskii, *Etimologicheskii slovar' russkogo iazyka*, vol. 2 (Moscow: Nauka, 1982).
4 Elias, *The Civilizing Process*, 4.
5 Pavel Miliukov, *Ocherki po istorii russkoi kul'tury*, vol. 2 (Paris, 1937).
6 Ibid., 980.
7 Boris Bank, *Izuchenie chitatelei v Rossii (XIX v.)* (Moscow: Nauka, 1969).
8 Dmitrii Ushakov, *Tolkovyi slovar' russkogo iazyka*, vol. 1 (Moscow: Nauka, 1935).
9 *Slovar' russkogo iazyka*, vol. 5 (Moscow: Akademiya nauk, 1956).
10 Vera Dunham, *In Stalin's Time: Middleclass Values in Soviet Fiction* (Cambridge: Cambridge University Press, 1979), 22.
11 Nicholas Timasheff, *The Great Retreat: The Growth and Decline of Communism in Russia* (New York: Dutton, 1946), 354.
12 Dunham, *In Stalin's Time*, 13.
13 Ibid., 18.
14 Moshe Lewin, "Society, State, and Ideology during the First Five-Year Plan", in S. Fitzpatrick (ed.), *Cultural Revolution in Russia, 1928–1931* (Bloomington: Indiana University Press, 1979), 52.

15 See Nataliia Lebina, "Tenevye storony zhizni sovetskogo goroda 20–30 kh godov", *Voprosy istorii* 2 (1994): 30–32.
16 See *Revoliutsiia i kul'tura* 11 (1930): 24–28; *Kul'tura i byt* 25 (1932): 11.
17 Arch Getty, Gabor Rittersporn, Vladimir Zemskov, "Victims of the Soviet Penal System in the Pre-war Years: a First Approach", *American Historical Review* October (1993): 1032–1033.
18 Sheila Fitzpatrick, *The Cultural Front: Power and Culture in Revolutionary Russia* (Ithaca: Cornell University Press, 1992), 149–182.
19 See Iosif Stalin, "Rech' na pervom Vsesoiuznom soveshchanii stakhanovtsev, 17 noiabria, 1935", in *Voprosy leninizma*, 11th edition (Moscow: Partizdat, 1939), 499.
20 Fitzpatrick, *Cultural Front*, 218.
21 Michel Foucault, "The Ethic of Care for the Self as a Practice of Freedom", in *The Final Foucault*, ed. J. Bernauer and D. Rasmussen (Cambridge, Mass.: MIT Press, 1988), 1–20.
22 Michel Foucault, "Subject and Power", in *Michel Foucault: Beyond Structuralism and Hermeneutics*, ed. H. Dreyfus and P. Rabinow (Chicago: University of Chicago Press, 1983), 129.
23 Ibid., 213.
24 Stephen Kotkin, *Magnetic Mountain: Stalinism as a Civilization* (Berkeley: University of California Press, 1995), 22.
25 See Nataliia Lebina, "Oksfor sirenevyi i zheltye botinki", *Rodina* (1994): 112–117.
26 Timasheff, *Great Retreat*, 317.
27 *Gigiena i zdorov'e*, 21 (1936): 7.
28 *Obshchestvennitsa*, 1 (1937): 63.
29 *Ogonek*, 5 (1936): 19.
30 *Gigiena i zdorov'e*, 8 (1937): 9.
31 *Stakhanovets*, 2 (1937): 53.
32 *Sotsialisticheskii gorod*, 1 (1936): 35.
33 *Gigiena i zdorov'e*, 20 (1936): 12–13.
34 *Pravda*, 28 October 1935.
35 Ibid., 24 April 1936.
36 Ibid., 6 May 1936.
37 On the gender dimension of this movement, see Mary Buckley, "The Untold Story of *Obshchestvennitsa* in the 1930s", *Europe-Asia Studies* 4 (1996): 569–586.
38 *Obshchestvennitsa* 3 (1937): 12.
39 Michel Foucault, *Discipline and Punish: The Birth of Prison* (London: Peregrine Books, 1979), 143.
40 *Obshchestvennitsa* 2 (1936): 9.
41 Ibid. 3 (1937): 30–31.
42 Ibid. 2 (1936): 9.
43 Ibid. 4 (1938): 13.
44 Ibid. 5 (1936): 12.
45 Ibid. 3 (1937): 12.
46 *Smena* 3 (1936): 26.
47 *X s"ezd VLKSM. Sbornik materialov* (Moscow: Partizdat, 1938), 41.
48 *Klub* 1 (1937): 4.
49 Ibid. 6 (1936): 1.
50 *Ogonek* 1 (1936): 22, original emphasis.
51 *Smena* 8 (1937): 25–26.
52 Ibid. 12 (1938): 20.
53 Ibid. 10 (1938): 5.

54 See Lewis Siegelbaum, *Stakhanovism and the Politics of Productivity in the USSR, 1935–1941* (Cambridge: Cambridge University Press, 1988), 225–233.
55 Aleksei Busygin, *Zhizn' moia i moikh druzei* (Moscow: Profizdat, 1939), 70.
56 See *A History of Private Life*, ed. R. Chartier *et al.*, vols. II–IV (London: Belknap Press, 1989).

8

"DEAR COMRADE, YOU ASK WHAT WE NEED"

Socialist paternalism and Soviet rural "notables" in the mid-1930s

Lewis H. Siegelbaum

In their *Dictatorship over Needs*, Ferenc Fehér, Agnes Heller, and Gyorgy Markus sought to analyze the nature of domination and subordination in Soviet-type societies in terms of the direct administration of production and distribution by a self-selecting corporate ruling group. This dictatorship, initially justified by the interests of the proletariat and the party's self-assigned role as its vanguard, was perpetuated not merely by coercion but also by various mechanisms of legitimation. Among these was the construction of a self-image of the state as a wise, stern, but also beneficent father. Thus, "everything that a subject may get (consumer goods, a flat, heating, clothes, theatre tickets, etc.) is 'due to the state'; it is not granted as a right or given in exchange for something else, but provided as an amenity that can be revoked." It follows that "Soviet subjects ask for favours, their right proper is *ius supplicationis*."[1]

The authors implicitly restrict this form of legitimation to the post-Stalin era in the Soviet Union and eastern Europe. Other scholars, however, have interpreted paternalism as endemic to state socialism and rooted in its political economy of shortage. For example, Janos Kornai argues that "the classical system has a paternalistic nature. ... The bureaucracy stands *in loco parentis*: all other strata, groups or individuals in society are children."[2] And for Katherine Verdery, who follows Kornai's "single analytical model," "socialist paternalism" was "at the center of both the Party's official ideology and its efforts to secure popular support." It "justified Party rule with the claim that the Party would take care of everyone's needs by collecting the total social product and then making available whatever people needed – cheap food, jobs, medical care, affordable housing, education, and so on."[3]

This model is useful in pointing to a pattern of expectations and behaviors that transcended both national and temporal boundaries among state socialist countries. But socialist paternalism did not emerge all at once and was not without disruptions, circumventions, and modifications. Within the Soviet Union, periods of rationing, the vagaries of the harvest, and the cult of Stalin were among the forces that powerfully affected the paternalistic posture of the party, in a sense, overdetermining it. But even in the "Soviet normal" situation of shortage, the definition of needs and the degree of their fulfillment were in near constant flux. They depended inter alia on what the regime was willing and able to distribute and to whom, on rival bureaucratic claims on goods and services to distribute, and on the degree to which individuals conformed to their expected roles of supplicants and grateful recipients.[4] These factors shaped what might be thought of as the politics of distribution in Soviet-type societies.

The aim of this essay is to examine these politics by focusing on a particular moment or episode in the determination of needs by the Stalinist state. The episode involves a discrete group of Soviet "subjects," namely workers from cattle and dairy state farms (*miaso-molochnye sovkhozy*) who had received prizes in a contest to provide the best winter quarters for livestock in their care during 1934–35. Individuals had been honored for their labor achievements with medals, monetary awards, and a variety of consumer goods ever since the early 1920s, and both contests (*konkursy*) and bouts of socialist competition (*sotssorevnovanie*) assumed systematic dimensions during the first Five-Year Plan.[5] Rather more unusual, indeed quite extraordinary, was the invitation to the prizewinners from one of the trade unions administering the contest to articulate their needs and a great deal else about themselves. The resulting correspondence, extending into 1936 and in some cases beyond, constitutes the main body of material on which this essay is based.[6]

This correspondence affords a window onto the living conditions and material culture among a segment of Soviet rural society much neglected by scholars, as well as on authority relations among the party, trade union, and sovkhoz [state farm] apparatuses.[7] The window, however, is not transparent. In describing their lives, the prizewinners were responding to a series of questions put to them by trade union functionaries and reporting what they deemed appropriate under the circumstances. But, as with other epistolary forms, the ways these letter-writers represented themselves is an important dimension of the culture of which they were a part. Thus, in addition to the politics of distribution, I am also interested in using the correspondence as well as stenographic records of meetings of rural notables (shockworkers and Stakhanovites) and newspaper accounts to explore the cultural practices constitutive of these identities.

The contest

Contests can serve many purposes, not the least of which is to enable their organizers to identify, reward, and thereby evoke gratitude among the winners. The distribution of prizes (or at least the announcement that prizes are forthcoming) is an integral part of such events. In the Soviet Union, contests were occasions when the state demonstrated its munificence and indicated the appropriate monetary value of the extra effort expended or, if the awards were in-kind, which material goods it prized. The itemization of prizes – as, for example, the bicycles, sewing machines, coats, calves, pigs, and cows distributed to the "best shock-workers" of Dnepropetrovsk's sovkhozes – was thus no less revealing of officially endorsed values than the idealized description of the interiors of a North Caucasus grain sovkhoz's dwellings ("brighter than on the street, clean, orderly, painted in vivid colors"). Both appeared in *Sovkhoznaia gazeta* within the two-week period prior to the announcement of "the first all-Union contest for the best fulfillment of plans of livestock state farms for the wintering of cattle in 1934–35."[8] [. . .]

The contest, which ran from 1 November 1934 to 1 April 1935, was organized by the Department of Cattle and Dairy Sovkhozes of the People's Commissariat [Ministry] of State Farms (Narkomsovkhoz) and the three corresponding trade unions – those of the Center and South, the Urals and Siberia, and Central Asia.[9] [. . .] The selection of prizewinners was a three-stage process: contest commissions at the sovkhoz level [. . .] chose winners and forwarded their *kharakteristiki* [references] to regional (oblast or *krai*) trade union committees. The latter nominated candidates for additional prizes to be awarded by the corresponding contest commissions at their level. Finally, the same process was repeated at the central level. Only those who had received two awards were eligible to receive prizes from the Central Contest Commission.[10] In submitting lists of candidates to the regional commissions, the regional committees of the Union of Cattle and Dairy Sovkhoz Workers of the Center and South were advised by the union's central committee to select "really the best, socially appropriate [*proverennye*] workers, enthusiasts of socialist animal husbandry, who have achieved positive results not only this winter but in the past."[11] The achievement of outstanding results during the period of the contest thus did not guarantee a prize.

Sovkhoz commissions awarded prizes to upwards of ten thousand workers. These were in the range of 30 to 100 rubles or their equivalent in material goods (tea sets, bolts of cloth, piglets, and so on). Regional commissions selected 1,319 workers from cattle and dairy sovkhozes of the Center and South. Each received 200 rubles, with an occasional pig, calf, or heifer thrown into the bargain.[12] The entire selection process culminated in August 1935 with the announcement by the Central

Contest Commission that 200 livestock sovkhoz workers had been awarded prizes ranging from 300 to 600 rubles.[13] An additional 36 of the "most active participants in the contest" received in-kind awards. These included a house valued at 4,000 rubles (the lucky recipient of which was Gari Nasunov, a 53-year-old Kalmyk head drover from Stalingrad krai), complete or partial furnishings for apartments, outer garments, accordions, sewing machines, and additional monetary bonuses.[14] Of the 236 prizewinners, 193 belonged to the Union of Cattle and Dairy Sovkhoz Workers of the Center and South.

The contestants

Livestock workers formed the largest category of agricultural wage earners, that is, workers on state farms. As of October 1934 they numbered 597,900, of whom 306,900 were permanently employed. Over half (56 percent) worked on farms in the Center and South, that is, European Russia, Ukraine, Belorussia, and Transcaucasia; the remainder were divided between the Urals and Siberia (27 percent) and Kazakstan and Central Asia (17 percent).[15] Until 1934, workers on state farms could not legally own domestic livestock or private plots, concessions that collective farmers had extracted from the regime several years earlier. But within two years, more than half of permanent workers reportedly possessed a cow, and over 70 percent had gardens.[16]

As far as monetary wages were concerned, the 118 rubles per month paid on average to the more than two million sovkhoz workers and employees in March 1935 put them at the very bottom of 37 categories of wage earners.[17] When administrative personnel and clerical-technical staff are excluded from the category of sovkhoz workers, the figures are even lower – 112 rubles for permanent workers, and 78 rubles for seasonal workers.[18] Differentiated according to the type of sovkhoz, workers engaged in animal husbandry earned considerably less than those on farms devoted to grain cultivation, but more than sugar-beet cultivators.

The three "leading" occupational groups on cattle and dairy farms for which we have aggregate data – cattlehands, milkers, and calfherds – respectively earned on average 108, 117, and 122 rubles in 1934.[19] In Russian, "cattlehands" is typically given in the masculine form (*skotniki*), while "calfherds" (*teliatnitsy*) and "milkers" (*doiarki*) are rendered in the feminine. This did not necessarily mean – and probably was not intended to convey the impression – that all cattlehands were male. Like "workers" (*rabochie, rabotniki*) and other plural nouns, the masculine form conventionally stood in for the universal. Indeed, a survey of 573 machine-tractor stations and 7,030 collective farms from January 1936, found that half (50.7 percent) of the 24,462 skotniki were actually women.[20] In the case of calfherding and milking – both of which were overwhelmingly female occupations – using the masculine form would have made no sense. [. . .]

The gender composition of the prizewinners contacted by their union generally conformed to the linguistic constructions of their occupations. Their self-reported wages also did not deviate markedly from the above-cited national figures, although the 135 rubles earned on average by the 33 milkers who provided such information was 18 rubles per month more than the national average.[21] Wages did vary a good deal within each occupational group. At 150 rubles per month, Lidiia Alfantyr's wage was considerably above the 80 rubles reported by Mariia Kubanova, even though both worked as calfherds in the same oblast (lvanovo). A similar spread can be observed between the wages of the two stable-hands, A. Morozov of the Northern krai and Ignat Adamovich of Belorussia, although in this case, and many others, the difference might be explained by the fact that Morozov was a brigade leader.[22]

The wages cited by prizewinners referred to the summer or autumn of 1935, that is, several months after the conclusion of the contest that brought these workers to the attention of the trade union authorities. But this is getting ahead of the story.

Caring about people

Even before the Central Contest Commission issued its final list, the union's central committee began sending congratulatory letters. These were addressed, not to the prizewinners themselves, but to the respective workers' committees. The letters, identical except for the addressee, the name and occupation of the prizewinner, and the amount of the award, read as follows:

> To the Workers' Committee of
> the Armavir Cattle/Dairy Sovkhoz
> By resolution of the All-Union Contest Commission with respect to the contest for the best wintering of livestock, the milkmaid, A.P. BESEDINA is awarded 300 rubles. The central committee of the union congratulates comrade Besedina on her achievement. We hope that the decision of the TsKK [Central Contest Commission] inspires a new wave of socialist competition and shockwork and transforms the sovkhoz into a profitable and exemplary socialist enterprise.
> Vice-Chair of TsK (Kryzhov)[23]

There was nothing extraordinary in this. Some time before September 1935, however, the central committee resolved to contact the prizewinners themselves. What precipitated this decision is not clear.[24] It may have been in response to one of those signals that periodically came down from above, in this case Stalin's 4 May 1935 speech to Red Army cadets, which contained the subsequently much advertised slogan "cadres decide everything." The message of the speech – that leaders were to "devote the most solicitous attention to our workers, to the 'small' and the 'great' wherever they work ... help them when they need support, encourage them when they achieve their first successes, advance them forward" – had general applicability, as the press soon made clear. But the story the Genial Leader told to elaborate on this point was particularly relevant to functionaries of a union of livestock workers and may have set in motion the process that resulted in their action.

"I recall an incident in Siberia when I was in exile," Stalin began. A group of thirty peasants had gone to the river, then at high water, to retrieve logs, but only twenty-nine had returned. The peasants, explaining why they had abandoned their fellow villager, said they had to water the horses. "To my reproach that they cared more about cattle than people, one answered, to the general approval of the others, 'What do we care about people? We can always make more people, but try to make a mare.' " The published version of the speech indicates that this little tale provoked "general animation" in the hall.[25]

Stalin's speech was not, however, a bolt from the blue. His earlier (December 1934) statement that "people must be cultivated as tenderly and carefully as a gardener cultivates a favorite fruit tree," the solicitude he and other party leaders showed kolkhoz shockworkers at their second congress in February 1935, the Kolkhoz Charter issued shortly thereafter, the unprecedented and never-to-be-repeated audiences he granted to visiting delegations of awestruck peasants from the provinces and non-Russian republics, and the massive publicity given to these occasions bespoke a new, more elaborately paternalistic relationship between the regime and the rural population – or rather, that segment of the rural population that had earned the right to a more prosperous life.[26] Translated into practical activity, the new line called for distinguishing the "best shockworkers and notables from the general working masses and ... satisfy[ing] their material and cultural requirements." In the words of K. Soms (in charge of political departments in the People's Commissariat), "Books, newspapers and journals, pictures, a radio, and flowers must become as much a part of the daily life [*byt*] of the notable as quality furniture, a good suit, tasty food, and clean sheets."[27]

Like the North Caucasus ("Potemkin") village referred to above, this cultural repertoire reflected the regime's definition of socialist modernity in the Soviet countryside. All rural residents would ultimately enjoy the benefits of a cultured existence (*kul'turnost'*), at which point the contradiction between town and country would be eliminated. Distributing such benefits among the best rural workers was a crucial stage in this process.[28] If, in the cultural geography of the mid-1930s, "social legitimacy was concentrated in the centre," it was "not as a monopoly, but as a point of distribution."[29] But who were these fortunate workers and in what conditions did they live?

Letters to prizewinners were sent on 1 September 1935. Although signed by at least eight different instructors from the union's central committee, the letters were identical in content and form. After brief salutary congratulations, they asked about achievements and deficiencies in work since the end of the contest. The thrust of the letters concerned not production but rather consumption, not what prizewinners were doing for the sovkhoz, but what the sovkhoz was doing for them. These concerns were grouped in five basic questions:

1   Family situation. Number, ages, and educational level of children; income during the last three months.
2   Material conditions. What do you need in terms of housing, furniture, clothing?
3   Food. Do you eat in the cafeteria? Does the cafeteria provide special services for shockworkers? Do you have a garden and storage facilities for preserving fruit and vegetables? Do you possess domestic animals, and if so, does the sovkhoz provide shelter and feed for them?
4   Degree of literacy. What newspapers and books do you read? Do you want to study further?
5   State of health. Do you need to go to a health resort or rest home?

If the higher authorities required evidence that their subordinates were "caring about people" who had achieved their first successes and needed further encouragement, this was surely it.

We have many needs

The 145 prizewinners who responded to the questionnaire seemed uncertain about, or at least differed in their interpretation of, what form their responses should take. The difference may be attributed to the unprecedented nature of the questionnaire as well as, perhaps, different degrees of prior experience in communicating with official bodies. A few crafted – or had crafted for them – their responses as official documents (*otnosheniia; zaiavleniia*); most, however, took a more personal approach, addressing their letters to the individual instructors who had contacted them, and employing "Dear" or "Respected" as a salutation. While some wrote discursively, combining or skipping answers to some of the questions, others listed them in point-by-point fashion. Only one prizewinner seized the opportunity to tell the story of her life, explaining by way of apology that she "wanted to acquaint you with my autobiography and my work."[30]

Several prefaced their answers with expressions of gratitude. The calfherd L.A. Romashova thanked "respected Comrade Odintsov" for "not forgetting about us." "Dear comrades," wrote G. Arshak from Armenia, "I am very glad that 5,000 kilometers from our district they are thinking of me, and for this I am very thanks from you [*ia ochen' spasibo ot vas*]." In addition to giving thanks, some demonstrated their political awareness. S.A. Arkacheev, a Tatar drover, thanked not only the union's instructor but "mainly the party and government," adding that "not in one capitalist country would I be surrounded by such attention." "Earlier I worked for *mir*-eaters and kulaks," wrote the milk-maid P.I. Aleksandrova in her opening paragraph. "But now, under Soviet power where the proletarian Communist Party, led by Stalin, rules, I occupy an honored place. Long live the Communist Party and our glorious Red Army and its leaders, comrades Voroshilov and Stalin. Long live the central committee of our [trade] union." Still others, such as the senior drover Vladimir Sychev, seemed to be responding to the union's earlier communication by promising to work better "for the fulfillment of all state plans and to raise all backward workers of the drove to the advanced."[31]

Since no promise of assistance was made in the instructors' letters, it is not clear whether respondents expected any. Having already received – or at least been promised – rewards from the contest commissions, they may have concluded that the purpose of the questions was simply what we would call sociological, a matter of the union's gathering of data. Whatever the case, the questions contained in the letters did structure the responses. The questions referred to four subjects – the individual prizewinner, the prizewinner's family, shockworkers, and the entire sovkhoz – but needs were addressed most explicitly in connection with the first two, only tangentially with respect to the third, and not at all in relation to the fourth. Thus, while a few respondents invoked their shockworker status (as in Romashova's complaint that "we shockworkers work from morning to night") or membership in the Komsomol ("With Komsomol greetings!" is how Klavdiia Maksimovskaia concluded her letter), they limited their articulation of needs almost exclusively to themselves and their families.[32]

Perhaps because there was no local community of "notables," respondents initially shunned the term. A few, though, learned to adapt. In his letter of 13 September to "his" instructor, Sychev identified himself as "senior drover of Armavir dairy and cattle sovkhoz no. 32, Sychev, Vladimir Afanasievich." But writing two months later to Trubacheev, the chair of the union's central committee, he inserted "noted" (*znatnyi*) in place of "senior." Others, however, seemed to resist the label. Having received a letter informing him that he had "achieved the title [*zvanie*] of noted fighter in the struggle for a socialist way of life," G. Shmakov, a senior drover from Stalingrad oblast replied, "This is true." But, he added, "I am not abandoning [*nesnizhaiu*] the title of shockworker and will not abandon my achievement as a first-rank shockworker until the end of socialism [*tsotsialis'm*]."[33]

Short of not responding at all, the only alternative to this assertion of a Soviet self was supplication. In this case, the very absence of an occupational or political identity underscored the impression of indigence and utter helplessness, as in the following letter from the Karavaevo sovkhoz, Ivanovo oblast:

> From Volkova, A.M.
> You wrote [*soobchali*] about an apartment. Our apartment is 3 meters wide and 5 meters long. We have lived for two years without windows, in winter wearing coats. I have two children, both in school, one in the fourth grade and the other in the second. They have no shoes or coat and go barefoot and only in a shirt. You wrote about the cafeteria. We don't go to the cafeteria [*u nas stolovat'sia ne na chto*]. I earn 108 to 116 and no more. You wrote about health. My health is very bad and all this depends on food, and you wrote about vouchers to the health resort, but with whom [can] I leave the children[?] I am completely illiterate. I am 48 years old and it is [too] late to learn. You wrote about animals. We don't have any. We were given a piglet on 3/IX.35 but it was undernourished and diseased. I have been forgotten in this respect. Nowhere is there a work corner where my children can write or read. There are no tools or materials for a labor corner. They don't give milk to schoolchildren [who] must go with crusts of bread. We have a garden [but] I don't know where to put the produce. We live badly. Give help![34]

The letter was signed by "Volkov, V.K.," probably the older of the two children.

Although – or perhaps because – Volkova was so obviously needy, she did not specifically request anything. Other respondents were not so reticent. Living space, consisting of either a single-story dormitory or barrack accommodation or separate earthen huts sometimes located several kilometers from the farms, was tight, "very tight," wrote M.N. Kubanova, a calfherd on the Communard sovkhoz (Ivanovo oblast) who lived with her husband and two daughters in a room that measured six square meters. "We have a very small and crowded apartment," reported V.A. Voronova whose family consisted of eight members, "but they don't give anything larger." Nastia Lemeshchenko, a calfherd on the Victory of Socialism sovkhoz in Belorussia, also complained about the size of her apartment as well as the lack of heating, but added hopefully that a building for workers (*rabotniki*) was under construction.[35]

Furnishings and clothing were in short supply as well. The drover Arkacheev wrote to Petrov that his apartment consisted of "a bad wooden bed, a small table, a chest, samovar, sewing machine, and nothing else." He continued, "of course, I would like to obtain an iron bed, bureau, mirror, bed linens, portraits of leaders, veterinary literature, clothes for myself, my wife, and three children [and] shoes." The items in this wish list appear, not necessarily in their entirety, in other letters with depressing frequency. What the milkmaid, Agaf'ia Maksimova, found most "unsatisfactory" was that her room contained neither a sink nor a mirror ("so that coming from work, I can wash and look at myself"). Irina Malashnikova, an unmarried milkmaid, shared a room with seven other people that contained eight cots and one table. "Now, I would like my own room with furniture: a cot, a table with two or three chairs, a small cupboard for plates and books." As for clothes, a warm jacket and felt boots would do.[36]

Indeed, the shortage of clothing and footwear evoked the most complaints and requests. Having wished a long life to Stalin and Voroshilov, P.I. Aleksandrova noted that "there are no clothes and also we are poorly supplied with shoes in this out-of-the-way place." Sychev wrote that "the whole brigade goes barefoot because we have nowhere to buy shoes"; "All drovers wear bast shoes," wrote A.K. Karpov from Bashkiria, because "nowhere can one buy leather shoes." "I have clothes, but no shoes . . . or felt boots and the workers' committee does not help," wrote Voronova. After describing her living conditions, Kubanova wrote: "Dear Comrade, you ask what we need. We have many needs. For example, winter clothes and shoes for the children."[37]

The institution that was supposed to supply state farm workers with consumer goods was the network of workers' cooperative (*rabkoop*) stores. Respondents were unanimous, however, in asserting that the stores contained very little – "not even matches," according to Sychev. "I have been a member for five years," related Alzhan Ishambaev of Orenburg oblast, "and have paid my share punctually, but . . . not one meter of cloth have I received from the coop." The cooperative "does not care about us" was the common refrain.[38]

Complaints about the dearth of manufactured goods in the country-side were hardly new. "There has been no soap for over a month," a grain procurement agent wrote to Stalin from the Central Black Earth region in August 1929, "and there are no soles, a necessary item for the peasant. Only three handkerchiefs, ten pairs of gray felt boots, and, oh yes, half a shelf of vodka. There you have the rural cooperative."[39] Sovkhoz workers, we are informed in a recent study of the "hierarchy of consumption" under rationing, were assigned to the second of three categories of industrial workers. Their norms of supply, which were rarely filled in any case, fell from year to year.[40] By 1935 when rationing was terminated, the network of 35,000 rural cooperative stores reportedly contained only one pair of shoes for every eight workers.[41]

Still, when considering the neediness of the respondents, the cultural component in their determination of needs should not be ignored. Aside from their material qualities, leather (as opposed to bast) shoes, iron or nickel-plated beds (instead of those with wooden frames), chairs (instead of benches or stools), mirrors, and other manufactured items were valued as symbols of the more cultured life to which sovkhoz workers aspired. It is even possible that these articles were the material markers of rural "notability," the indigenous adaptation, as it were, of the "good suit, tasty food, and clean sheets" cited by political department officer Soms. That the prizewinners were capable of fashioning their own sense of *kul'turnost'* is further suggested by the fact that although many indicated the absence of sheds, none explicitly cited them as needed. For their part, union officials considered the practice of keeping animals "under the bed" indicative of a "shameful lack of culture" and "Russian backwardness."[42]

Turning to nonmaterial needs, the two that appear most frequently in respondents' letters were the opportunity to study and rest. Nearly three-quarters of the respondents provided information about their degree of literacy.[43] Many of those who declared themselves illiterate or semiliterate were enrolled in "liquidation of illiteracy" (*likbez*) courses, though some were doubtful about their capacity to learn ("I am too old").[44] For those who had completed the four years of instruction available in the local primary schools, further education was sought as a means of upward mobility. But this required outside intervention, for, as Sychev put it, "technical education courses are not offered, have not been offered, and probably will not be offered ... I know nothing aside from what I have learned by practice because nobody is concerned with us."[45] Romashova, who expressed her desire to be educated in mathematics, Russian, physics, and social sciences, as well as to raise her qualifications in animal husbandry, indicated that she had been promised time off to study. But "to study one needs to be healthy, strong, and in this respect all is not well."[46]

Indeed. Of the 106 who commented on their health, only 23 did not report ailments and most of these were in their twenties. The most common complaint, reported by 29 respondents, was rheumatism, sometimes expressed as pains in the hands, arms, and legs. This appeared to be something of an occupational disease among milkers. Nearly half of the 35 milkers who reported on their health cited it, while an additional three merely indicated that their health was "not good."

Respondents also claimed to be suffering from malaria, anemia, stomach problems, tuberculosis, brucellosis (contracted from personal contact with or consumption of unpasteurized milk from infected cattle), general exhaustion, and a variety of other ailments.[47]

It is probably unfair to doubt them. Working with animals out of doors, often in subzero weather, or in poorly heated enclosures and lacking adequate nourishment, they were bound to contract illnesses of one sort or another. Still, the fifth question almost invited requests for a medical leave that under ordinary circumstances would have required certification from a doctor attached to the sovkhoz for the very purpose of distinguishing between shammers and the genuinely ill. This, at least, is how the Stalingrad drover, Shmakov, interpreted the question. "Our health so far is not bad [*nechevo*]," he wrote. "But if you are distributing passes to the health resort, then I won't object."[48]

"Life has become better"

On 31 August 1935, the day before the trade union's instructors initiated this correspondence, Aleksei Stakhanov performed his record-breaking feat of hewing 102 tons of coal. Anxious to celebrate and reward achievements in production that could serve as stimuli to other workers, the party launched the Stakhanovite movement, which spread throughout industry and to other branches of the economy. The title of Stakhanovite, conferred on workers and peasants who set production records or otherwise demonstrated mastery of their assigned tasks, quickly superseded that of shockworker. Day by day throughout the autumn of 1935, the campaign intensified, culminating in an All-Union Conference of Stakhanovites which met in the Kremlin in late November."[49]

Stalin captured the upbeat mood of the conference when, by way of explaining how such records were only possible in the "land of socialism," he uttered the phrase, "Life has become better, and happier too." Widely disseminated, and even set to song, Stalin's words served as the motto of the movement.[50] As we shall see, both the phrase and the movement would intrude on the correspondence. But even before they did so, life did take a turn for the better for many of the prizewinners.

Letters collectively signed by the chairs of the trade union's central committee, the Department of Cattle and Dairy Sovkhozes of the People's Commissariat, and the corresponding party committee began arriving in the sovkhozes in October. The "directive" sent to the director of the Natal'evsk sovkhoz and the chair of the workers' committee was typical: "We have information that you have not provided decent [*normal'nye*] cultural and living conditions for comrade Adamovich, awarded a prize by the Central Contest Commission," it began. There followed a list of measures (the provision of milk and fats to Adamovich, shoes and clothing to his children, and furniture for his apartment; the assignment of a tutor to further his education; and the dispatch of his medical report – he had complained of a weak heart – to the union's regional committee), about which the director and the union official were to report no later than 1 November. Adamovich himself received a letter from the trade union instructor, Koleskov, informing him of the action taken on his behalf and asking him to report on what the leadership of the sovkhoz had done to carry out its obligations. It also requested that Adamovich provide information on the workers' club or red corner, the union organizer and committee, and his own civic activism (*obshchestvennaia nagruzka*) but not to limit himself to these questions.[51]

These instructions to Adamovich and analogous letters to other prizewinners represented the other side of paternalism, namely surveillance.[52] As prizewinners' visibility increased, so did the demands placed on them. They were expected to comport themselves in a manner befitting their new status as notables and to serve as the eyes and ears of the regime. Such demands were, in effect, the price extracted by the union's instructors for their patronage of prizewinners. The responses, however, suggest that not all prizewinners were willing to betray their local patrons, the sovkhoz triumvirate (*treugol'nik*) that had nominated them in the first place and provided favorable kharakteristiki. Adamovich, for instance, restricted himself to thanking the union for the parcel he had received and conveying news about the number and types of animals assigned to him and the 50-ruble prize he won at a regional exhibition. This earned him a rebuke from Cherniak, another instructor, who wanted to know "by what does the sovkhoz live and breathe, what is good and what is bad," and "most importantly" (and in conformity with the rapidly spreading Stakhanovite movement) "how you yourself work."[53]

Other prizewinners, enmeshed in these crosscutting patron–client relations, were anything but shy about denouncing sovkhoz officials. Several complained that they and their fellow workers had not been paid at all for several months.[54] In his second letter, Vladimir Sychev related that the sovkhoz triumvirate had assigned him a teacher and furnished his apartment with a table, four chairs, a wardrobe, and a gramophone. But, he added, he still needed shoes, and the director had refused to sell him a cow. As for general conditions, the winter cowshed lacked glass for windows and kerosene for heating, and there were no wash basins, soap, or towels for the workers. This information was turned over to the central committee whose chair wrote to the sovkhoz's triumvirate demanding rectification. In the meantime, the union's instructor, Nesterenko, wrote back to Sychev asking for further details about the chair of the trade union committee ("how often does he visit your brigade and converse with you?") and promising to reply.[55]

A.A. Zhukova, a thirty-one-year-old milkmaid from Moscow oblast, also made it clear where her loyalties lay. Her letter to Nesterenko bubbled over with joy as she related how with her bonus of 350 rubles from the contest she had purchased a suit, which she wore to the oblast conference of the Komsomol, a pair of slippers, and a dress for her mother, adding that "Life has become better, and happier too!" In a second letter, she repeated the slogan ("Now, it is clear to us that 'life had become better ... ' ", "and yet," she went on, "except for having received a cow, nothing has been provided. Furniture has been 'promised'; no teacher has appeared ... everyone is silent about the health resort."[56]

Sovkhoz officials reacted in various ways to the directives they received from the union and the Department of Cattle and Dairy Sovkhozes. In some instances, they simply ignored them and, judging by the absence of letters in the files, even follow-up inquiries that were laced with comments about negligence and bureaucratic indifference.[57] According to Ivan Mikhailenko, a drover from the Azov–Black Sea krai, "All your [the union's] instructions and directives are inoperative for our triumvirate because they do nothing, and I consider this some kind of mockery because they receive all the directives but don't consider it necessary to carry them out."[58] But in other cases administrators at least gave the impression of carrying out what they had been told to do. Indeed, in the case of V.D. Vorob'eva, "the best shockworker-milkmaid" on the Khom'kovo sovkhoz (Western oblast), they went further. Vorob'eva had complained to the union's instructor about her small, poorly furnished apartment, the lack of clothes and shoes for her children, and no cellar space to store vegetables. She also reported that she had had no opportunity to further her education, which amounted to two years in the local school, because there was nobody to look after her two children. Within a matter of weeks, the triumvirate could announce that not only had it rectified these problems, but it had provided her with a heifer valued at 500 rubles, three kilograms of potatoes, and, "despite the fact that she claimed to be in good health," a medical examination. The letter also indicated that she was attending study circles for party candidates.[59]

Relations between prizewinning notables and their fellow sovkhoz workers also reflected the double-sidedness of their status. Some prizewinners, particularly if they were brigade leaders or had achieved a certain seniority, could serve as patrons. Thus, having received a letter from the union's instructor expressing disappointment with his work ("You can understand what a disgrace this is for a noted person ... "), Stepan Velikosel'tsev, a drover from the North Caucasus, replied that he and his brigade had overcome earlier difficulties. Indeed, he claimed, several members of his brigade deserved to be recognized as Stakhanovites. A testimonial on his behalf, collectively signed by the entire brigade, accompanied his letter.[60] Another senior drover, Abukhamir Adilov of Saratov oblast, scandalized the union investigator who reported that he gave away furniture provided by the sovkhoz (in effect, undermining the dictatorship over needs), sold off dung briquettes, organized card games, and engaged in drinking bouts. But these actions probably enhanced his local standing.[61] Then again, notoriety could also provoke resentment. That notables added water to the milk produced by cows under their care, were from kulak families, or had engaged in thievery were among the rumors reported by prizewinners or cited at meetings of shockworkers and Stakhanovites.[62] In one case, workers from the Korolevo sovkhoz (Belorussian republic) sent a collectively signed letter to the union's central committee claiming that their prizewinning brigade leader, Mariia Iuzhkevich, had "done nothing to fulfill the tasks assigned during the contest."[63]

Notables abandoned

By offering praise for so many liters of milk produced or calves raised, by commiserating with those who were experiencing difficulties, and by chastising those who had ceased to reply to letters or had failed to provide information on what made the sovkhoz "live and breathe," the trade union's instructors went beyond the merely perfunctory. Their instruction of prizewinners in how to live up to the image of a notable, which meant justifying the attention being devoted to them, was a case of power and identity constituting themselves and each other. The power exercised by instructors was not raw, coercive power. It came cooked in the rhetoric of "caring about" the people.[64] "Write and we will reply, helping each other in work," was how they frequently concluded their follow-up letters. And help they did, at least for a while.

Yet, even as they inserted themselves into the lives of these people, instructors were careful to stress their link with higher authority, typically employing the first-person plural. Nesterenko, the most prolific of instructor correspondents, pointed out to a number of prizewinners that she was not the source of their good fortune. "To thank us for the parcel is unnecessary," she wrote to the calfherd, Mariia Kubanova. "We are obliged to assist, by creating the best material and cultural conditions for our shockworkers and their children." To the milkmaid Matrena Dziuba, she noted that "the party and government now set as a basic task the provision of the best conditions for the best people, in production and in life [byt]."[65]

Sovkhoz notables were supposed to understand that their benefactors were institutional, in contrast to the traditional practices of relying on familial and familiar connections (for example, bol'shaki [heads of families], *zemliaki* [fellow countrymen]) or their local patrons. This was a hard lesson to absorb – in part, because it was so frequently contradicted by local practice, not to mention the cult of the big *batiushka* [father], Stalin – but another, more flattering lesson may have sunk in. This was that one really should consider oneself among the "best people" of the sovkhoz, the district, or even the USSR as a whole.

Inquiring whether the sovkhoz cafeteria provided special food and facilities for shockworkers, soliciting their needs, and exerting pressure on local administrators to fulfill them encouraged a sense of self-worth but also of dependency. The problem was that the dependency was not mutual, or at least was revocable. Even while the correspondence with prizewinners continued, the trade union had become ever more deeply involved in promoting the Stakhanovite movement. Evidently, it was one thing to rename rural notables as Stakhanovites (as the instructors initially did), but another for the prizewinners to justify the new, exalted title. As Gol'din, one of the instructors, wrote to the calfherd, M.M. Chernobab:

> Your letter did not entirely satisfy us. You write that you under-
> stand the substance of the Stakhanovite movement, and that
> by its application you reduced your brigade from twelve to
> nine people, but you say nothing about the method itself. . . .
> How is the work organized among milkmaids and herders? Are
> the milkmaids freed from auxiliary tasks? After all, this is the
> whole point.[66]

To speak of the union's disenchantment with the prizewinners would be an exaggeration. But by early December 1935, Trubacheev was criti-cizing union activists for not distinguishing between notables and Stakhanovites, and, by implication, failing to privilege the latter. Notables, he pointed out, were conscientious workers who fulfilled assigned tasks in the course of the all-Union contest; Stakhanovites were "*new people*, who smash old technical norms, accomplish a revolution in production and squeeze everything out of technology."[67]

Such people were soon found. Assembled in regional conferences, they impressed each other and union officials with accounts of their records. The milkmaid, Anna Naumenko, from the Azov sovkhoz (Azov–Black Sea krai), reported how, by applying a new method of milking and treating each cow differently ("they are not machines"), she increased output. From one of her cows, Valia, she obtained an astonishing 46 liters during a "short period" in October 1935. But Anna did not want to slacken her tempo. "I want to work like Stakhanov and increase Valia to 50 liters," she stated in typical Stakhanovite fashion.[68] Another milk-maid, Tat'iana Guzenko, from the Victory of October sovkhoz (Stalingrad krai), was so proficient and keen to compete with other milkmaids ("If Evdokiia Vinogradova can work on 100 weaving machines, we can handle 25 cows") that those taking up her challenge were referred to as "Guzenkoites."[69]

In February 1936, over one thousand Stakhanovite livestock workers from throughout the USSR came to Moscow to receive medals and hear each other describe their experiences – in half a dozen languages.[70] Among them were Naumenko and Guzenko. Indeed, of the 487 "delegates" from cattle and dairy farms (both kolkhozes and sovkhozes) 304 (62 percent) were milkmaids. Unlike the introduction of female tractor brigades, the prominence of women among outstanding cattle and dairy sovkhoz workers did not disrupt the gendered division of labor. But it did underscore the regime's "strong and consistent support for the promotion of women to positions of authority in the countryside" and the fact that "in its dealings with the village in the 1930s . . . the positive stereotypes . . . tended to be female."[71] The message of female emancipation from (local) patriarchal authority was vividly conveyed by the milkmaid, Natalia Tereshkova, one of the few prizewinners who also figured among the "new people." In an article entitled "Great Joy" that appeared under her name in *Sovkhoznaia gazeta*, she asked:

What dream have I fulfilled? . . . I am a widow. My husband passed away three years ago after working in a kolkhoz and then as an electrician in Smolensk. What I have experienced since his death, I cannot describe . . .

Now I am a noted milkmaid, a Stakhanovite from Pridneprov'e sovkhoz. I have become a human being. I stand on my own feet, raising my children and keeping house. I am twice as happy as any man. Earlier I sat in my room, but now almost every evening I go see friends: we dance, go to the cinema, and sometimes watch actors perform [in the theater].[72]

Unfortunately, we lose track of Tereshkova after 1935. But it is possible to follow the trajectory of Naumenko, awarded a Badge of Honor in February 1936. At that time, she was living with her father and younger sister. Responding to her list of needs, the sovkhoz administration provided her with a new apartment, a table and chairs, curtains, a bed, clothes, shoes, and a "library." But, as she wrote to the union's instructor, she still needed rubber boots and a coat, items which she claimed the cooperative reserved only for those who were "close to the bosses." She also requested a cow.[73]

Two letters from the instructor Nesterenko, sent in September 1936 and June 1937, went unanswered. But more than a year later, in September 1938, Naumenko wrote to another instructor "with Komsomol greetings." Claiming that she needed an operation for an unspecified condition, she poured out her frustrations:

> My husband [a tractor driver] works while I cook, look after the children [a two-year-old and an eight-month-old], and procure foodstuffs. There is neither daycare nor a cafeteria, so I must prepare the food, which, because there is nothing in the shops, I have to search for somewhere. The children need milk but I have no cow. The party *raikom* [district committee] ordered the director to give me a cow, but he apparently does not consider such directives obligatory. When I reminded him, he and the head of the politotdel [political department] became upset with me that I would dare to ask.
>
> They have forgotten about raising my general and cultural standard. Not only is there no teacher, but no literate person comes to me. Neither the party nor the Komsomol wants to bother. Books for me are difficult; movies are a rarity. . . . And, so, like before I remain dark and illiterate, not knowing what goes on around me. . . . From a Stakhanovite of production, I have become a slave of the kitchen. . . . Help me, help me escape from the kitchen and return to production and once again [to] the ranks of the honored people of our Great country.

The union sent a copy of this plea for help from the "order-bearing former milkmaid of the Azov sovklioz, comrade Naumenko" to the sovkhoz's director, but no further action is indicated.[74]

Conclusion

The establishment of a centralized distributional system in the late 1920s and early 1930s gave the Soviet state enormous potential to dictate needs. As Fehér, Heller, and Markus noted in reference to the generic qualities of such a system, "The paternal authority metes out punishments to its naughty, disobedient and rebellious offspring; it approves or disapproves of its children's behaviour: those who behave well will be rewarded, even decorated."[75] The state under Stalin, however, was not a unitary entity, nor did "it" exhibit much consistency about the criteria of behavior according to which punishments and rewards were distributed. The provision of goods and services could be determined *a priori* via the Five-Year and shorter-term plans, but only in the most approximate way. Unanticipated imbalances and ruptures were endemic to the shortage economy. In any case, the ability of commissars, managers, and trade union officials to garner resources for "their" workers was always highly circumscribed and contested.[76] Other than by being promoted or migrating to where resources were less scarce, workers themselves had few opportunities to improve their position within the hierarchy of distribution.

Nevertheless, a politics of distribution did exist during the Stalin era. This was never more evident than during the mid-1930s when the individuation of rewards and their significance as symbols of the acquisition of culture assumed unprecedented proportions. The primary sites of cultural acquisition were the cities, but demonstrating that "Moscow's" beneficial reach could extend into the countryside was an important task for party and trade union activists.

The contest sponsored by the Union of Cattle and Dairy Sovkhoz Workers of the Center and South in the winter of 1934–35 was a modest example of these politics. Like other forms of competition that were crowded into the Soviet calendar, it enabled authorities to identify and reward deserving workers, thereby reinforcing the importance of work as self-validation and their own authority as arbiters of who deserved what. The contest also exemplified what recently has been referred to as "Potemkinism," public rituals that were "the real-life counterpart of the discourse of socialist realism in literature and the arts."[77] Inquiring into such mundane practices as contests and their consequences for participants is to pursue at once the exercise of paternalistic power and the formation of subjectivities. It is to engage in a kind of rural ethnography not at the point of production, but rather at a point where materials and values were being distributed and discussed.

The union's request that prizewinners report on themselves and their bosses added a new wrinkle to the politics of distribution. Not only did it make these individuals more visible – as "notables" – but it also enlisted them as agents of surveillance. In return for information about what worked and what did not work on their farms and, most intriguingly, about their needs, prizewinners could anticipate the union's assistance. This was not Potemkinism: although frequently expressing themselves in the ritualistic language of Soviet public discourse, they also wrote from the heart and sometimes in desperation. Moreover, many *were* helped, although they were soon abandoned in favor of a new crop of notables, the Stakhanovites.

The case of Naumenko, aside from demonstrating that Stakhanovite status could also be provisional, illustrates how power produced effects at the level of desire. Her "slavery" was no different from that of millions of other rural women who performed labor that by Soviet – and not only Soviet – standards was considered nonproductive. What set her apart was that she had had the experience of being celebrated as a noted, highly productive worker, and evidently enjoyed her status. Her previous contact with the trade union gave her the wherewithal to complain about having returned to her previous "dark" condition.

Naumenko's fate was no more typical of rural notables than Stakhanov's was with respect to Stakhanovites in industry. The union's extraordinarily rich files contain letters from other "order-bearers" (*ordenonostsy*) who were pursuing their studies (or seeking the means to do so) at regional centers; who expressed gratitude for the attention they received; who complained that they had not received goods promised to them; and who, even if not asked, continued to articulate their needs in other respects.[78] All were touched in one way or another by a regime that knew what was in their best interests, but had more than a little difficulty fulfilling their needs.

NOTES

Reprinted in slightly abridged form from *Slavic Review*, 57: 1 (Spring 1998): 107–132.

Research for this paper was funded by the International Research and Exchanges Board and an All-University Research Grant from Michigan State University. I wish to express my thanks to these institutions as well as to Leslie Moch, the anonymous readers for *Slavic Review*, and its editor. The views expressed herein are exclusively those of the author.

1 Ferenc Fehér, Agnes Heller, and Gyorgy Markus, *Dictatorship over Needs: An Analysis of Soviet Societies* (New York, 1983), 180. Elsewhere, Fehér has argued that "charismatic legitimation" and the frequent resort to repression under Stalin precludes "the guarantees without which paternalism is meaningless." See Ferenc Fehér, "Paternalism as a Mode of Legitimation in Soviet-type Societies," in T.H. Rigby and Ferenc Fehér, eds, *Political Legitimation in Communist States* (London, 1982), 66–67.

2 Janos Kornai, *The Socialist System: The Political Economy of Communism* (Princeton, 1992), 56. Kornai characterizes the soft budget constraint as a "manifestation" of paternalism (144).

3 Katherine Verdery, *What Was Socialism and What Comes Next?* (Princeton, 1996), 19, 24. Verdery defines socialist paternalism as a "cultural relation between state and subject" that "emphasized a quasi-familial dependency" and "posited a moral tie linking subjects with the state through their rights to a share in the redistributed social product" (63).

4 As Stephen Kotkin argues, "Scarcity, far from being the Soviet system's Achilles heel, was one of the keys to its strength. The tighter the overall balance of services or supplies, the more leverage the authorities could exercise." At the same time, however, tightness of supplies engendered the "little tactics of the habitat," viz., informal distribution networks, theft, "bazaaring," and so forth, all of which can be subsumed under the category of the "second economy." See his *Magnetic Mountain: Stalinism as a Civilization* (Berkeley, 1995), 246, 253.

5 L.S. Rogachevskaia, *Sotsialisticheskoe sorevnovanie v SSSR: Istoricheskie ocherki 1917–1970 gg.* (Moscow, 1977), 59–64. The distinction between contests and competitions was that whereas the former were initiated from above, the latter depended on challenges ostensibly issued by one group of workers to others. Such challenges could coincide with or be sparked by the announcement of a contest.

6 The correspondence is in Gosudarstvennyi arkhiv Rossiiskoi Federatsii (GA RF), f. 7689, op. 11, dd.50, 51, 125, 127, 128, 129 (correspondence of the union's central committee with Stakhanovites of sovkhozes awarded prizes in the contest).

7 Western historians of the Soviet countryside have overwhelmingly concentrated on the collective farm sector, treating sovkhoz workers almost as an afterthought. To take one recent example, the peasants in Sheila Fitzpatrick's *Stalin's Peasants* (Oxford, 1994) consist almost exclusively of *kolkhozniki*.

8 *Sovkhoznaia gazeta*, 12 October 1934, 1; 4 October 1934, 1; 17 October 1934, 3.

9 Both the department and the unions had been in existence for a short while: the former emerged from the reorganization of Narkomsovkhoz, in April 1934; the latter consisted of three of the seven new unions created after the dissolution of the Union of Workers of Animal-breeding Sovkhozes in September 1934. For details see Peter J. Potichnyj, *Soviet Agricultural Trade Unions, 1917–70* (Toronto, 1972), 63–66.

10 The chair of the Central Contest Commission was Erikh Kviring, head of the Cattle and Dairy Department of Narkomsovkhoz and younger brother of the Ukrainian party *apparatchik* and Communist Academy administrator, Emmanuel.

11 GA RF, f. 7689, op. 11, d. 52, l. 34. The process of selection in the Western oblast seems typical: of the 505 names submitted by sovkhoz commissions to the *obkom* of the union, 25 were forwarded to the oblast commission. As of 25 May 1935, the latter had awarded prizes to 13, 10 of whom were nominated for consideration by the Central Contest Commission. GA RF, f. 7689, op. 11, d. 49 (protocols of sessions of contest commissions), ll. 112–116ob. For the North Caucasus krai, see the report in d. 55, l. 48–48ob.

12 The list of recipients of regional commission prizes is in GA RF, f. 7689, op. 11, d. 46, ll. 23–55. For data on their gender, age, occupations, social backgrounds, and party status, see Zaidner, *Partiinoe rukovodstvo*, 91–92.

13 *Sovkhoznaia gazeta*, 8 August 1935, 3. The range of monetary awards, which were pegged to occupational categories, is somewhat at variance with the resolution of the Central Contest Commission in GA RF, f. 7689, op.11, d. 47, ll. 24–28. Although undated, the resolution must have been earlier, for only 113 recipients are listed.

14 *Sovkhoznaia gazeta*, 8 August 1935, 3. Between 1932 and the spring of 1935, Nasunov had received awards on eight occasions. For details, see GA RF, f. 7689, op. 11, d. 50, l. 202.

15 *Trud v SSSR: Statisticheskii sbornik* (Moscow, 1935), 62. The next largest category was grain workers (517,900). Workers on pig, sheep, and horse farms totaled 568,700. Altogether, 2.83 million people worked on state farms.

16 I.E. Zelenin, *Sovkhozy SSSR v gody dovoennykh piatiletok, 1928–1941* (Moscow, 1982), 210–11. Limits on the number of animals and the size of plots prescribed in the legislation for both collective and state farms were frequently transgressed, leading to further restrictions – and violations.

17 *Trud v SSSR*, 32. The next two lowest categories were public cafeteria workers (122 rubles) and forestry workers (130 rubles).

18 Ibid., 27–28.

19 Zelenin, *Sovkhozy SSSR v gody dovoennykh piatiletok*, 130–31.

20 *Trud v SSSR*, 325.

21 Calfherds averaged 116 rubles and cattlehands 108. Among the main occupational groups, the best paid were the drovers. The 24 who reported their wages averaged 185 rubles per month. Wage data were calculated on the basis of what

was reported for the three-month period immediately preceding the date of the letters sent by prizewinners.

22 GA RF, f. 7689, op. 11, d. 50, l. 158; d. 128, l. 166; d. 51, l. 202; d. 127, l. 67.

23 GA RF, f. 7689, op. 11, d. 52, l. 24.

24 On 11 December 1934, the presidium of the central committee resolved to produce for mass circulation a "red book of notables of sovkhozes" consisting of "the best, most advanced, shockworkers" awarded by the regional commissions and the Central Contest Commission. Although names began to be collected in February, no such book ever appeared. GA RF, f. 7689, op. 11, d. 1, l. 8; d. 52, l. 1.

25 *Pravda*, 6 May 1935, 2–3. In December 1935, Trubacheev, the chair of the union's central committee, invoked Stalin's speech after denouncing a sovkhoz director who allegedly said, "I will work for the calves, but will do nothing for people." GA RF, f. 7689, op. 11, d. 42 (stenogram of meeting of chairs of oblast and krai committees with union activists and Stakhanovites), l. 47.

26 And not merely the rural population. For the now classic analysis of "The Stalinist Myth of the 'Great Family' " within "High Stalinist Culture" of the mid-1930s, see Katerina Clark, *The Soviet Novel: History as Ritual* (Chicago, 1981), 114–35. For Stalin's statement that adumbrated the slogan "cadres decide everything," see *Izvestiia*, 29 December 1934, 1. On the kolkhoz shockworker congress and the charter, see Fitzpatrick, *Stalin's Peasants*, 117–27. Fitzpatrick refers to the "conspicuous consultation between the regime and representatives of the peasantry" over the size and use of private plots (103).

27 *Sovkhoznaia gazeta*, 26 August 1935, 1. This was an editorial that cited a letter Soms had sent to politotdely on 3 August.

28 Of course, to remain faithful to the canons of socialist realism, it was important to demonstrate that this contradiction was already being overcome. See, for example, *Sovkhoznaia gazeta*, 29 October 1934, 2, which criticized the author of a book on the subject for failing to notice that "in our sovkhozes former *bedniaki*, *batraki*, and *seredniaki*, having become tractor-drivers, combiners, machinists, etc., have transformed themselves literally before our eyes into industrial workers."

29 James von Geldern, "The Centre and the Periphery: Cultural and Social Geography in the Mass Culture of the 1930s," in Stephen White, ed., *New Directions in Soviet History* (Cambridge, 1992), 62–80 (quotation on 68).

30 This was Klavdiia Maksimovskaia. GA RF, f. 7689, op. 11, d. 129, l. 137.

31 GA RF, f. 7689, op. 11, d. 50, l. 163 (Romashova); d. 50, l. 1 (Arshak); d. 51, l. 295 (Arkacheev); d. 51, l. 50 (Aleksandrova); d. 50, l. 34 (Sychev).

32 GA RF, f. 7689, op. 11, d. 51, l. 163–163ob. (Romashova); d. 129, l. 137 (Maksimovskaia). For exceptions, see GA RF, f. 7689, op. 11, d. 125, ll. 46; 69, 88–88ob.

33 GA RF, f. 7689, op. 11, d. 50, ll. 34, 42 (Sychev); d. 125, l. 23 (Shmakov).

34 GA RF, f. 7689, op. 11, d, 50, l. 151. Volkova's situation is all the more remarkable in that the Karavaevo sovkhoz was something of a showpiece.

35 GA RF, f. 7689, op. 11, d. 128, l. 166 (Kubanova); d. 129, l. 124 (Voronova); d. 50, l. 57 (Lemeshchenko).

36 GA RF, f. 7689, op. 11, d. 51, l. 295ob. (Arkacheev); d. 128, l. 125ob. (Maksimova); d. 51, l. 78ob. (Malashnikova).

37 GA RF, f. 7689, op. 1, d. 51, l. 50 (Aleksandrova); d. 50, l. 35 (Sychev); d. 50, l. 84 (Karpov); d. 129, l. 124 (Voronova); d. 128, l. 166 (Kubanova).

38 GA RF, f. 7689, op. 11, d. 50, l. 35ob. (Sychev); d. 51, l. 88ob. (Ishambaev).

See also d. 51, l. 78 (Malashnikova); d. 51, ll. 100 (Shenkliuev), 116 (Koriakina), 163 (Romashova); and d. 128, l. 9ob. (Gorusova).

39 E.A. Osokina, *Ierarkhiia potrebleniia: O zhizni liudei v usloviiakh stalinskogo snabzheniia, 1928–1935, gg.* (Moscow, 1993), 51. See also the letter sent to *Pravda* in September 1930 from Mordovia in RGAE, f. 7486, op. 1, d. 102, l. 239: "To buy, but where? In the rabkoop? It would be better not to mention it."

40 Osokina, *Ierarkhiia potrebleniia*, 54.

41 GA RF, f. 7689, op. 11, d. 42, l. 192 ob. The official from the Central Union of Cooperative Societies (*Tsentrosoiuz*) who reported on the dearth of shoes and other consumer goods pleaded a lack of funds and suggested that the cattle and dairy sovkhoz union "go to VTsSPS [the Central Council of Trade Unions] and raise a ruckus" (ll. 194ob.–195).

42 GA RF, f. 7689, op. 11. d. 44 (stenogram of discussions with sovkhoz notables), l. 21 ob.; d. 125, ll. 35, 58.

43 Of the prizewinners, 15 percent of males and 10 percent of females declared themselves literate; 27 percent and 32 percent of each group declared themselves semiliterate. One might assume that in other cases respondents were at least semiliterate, but it is not always clear that they – as opposed to relatives, friends, or sovkhoz officials – actually wrote the letters.

44 These reported rates of illiteracy and semiliteracy were significantly *higher* than official figures that put the proportion of union members who were illiterate at 9.9 percent and semiliterate at 17.5 percent, as of November 1934. GA RF, f. 7689, op. 11, d. 1, l. 7. Even these figures were characterized as among the highest of any of the 163 trade unions in the USSR (*Sovkhoznaia gazeta*, 6 March 1936, 3). Whatever the case, the expressed aim of liquidating illiteracy by 1 May 1935 was a pipe dream.

45 GA RF, f. 7689, op. 11, d. 50, l. 35. See also d. 50, l. 110 (Vorob'eva).

46 GA RF, f. 7689, op. 11, d. 51, l. 163ob.

47 For more on the occupational diseases of milkmaids and other livestock workers, see Roberta Manning, "Women in the Soviet Countryside on the Eve of World War II," in Beatrice Farnsworth and Lynne Viola, eds, *Russian Peasant Women* (New York, 1992), 217–18.

48 GA RF, f. 7689, op.11, d. 125, l. 26.

49 See Lewis H. Siegelbaum, *Stakhanovism and the Politics of Productivity in the USSR, 1935–1941* (Cambridge, Eng., 1988), 66–98.

50 For Stalin's speech, see I.V. Stalin, *Sochineniia*, 3 vols (Stanford, 1967), 1: 86–99. For an English translation of the proceedings of the conference, see *Labour in the Land of Socialism: Stakhanovites in Conference* (Moscow, 1936). The song, by Aleksandr Aleksandrov with lyrics by Vasilii Lebedev-Kumach, can be found in James von Geldern and Richard Stites, eds, *Mass Culture in Soviet Russia: Tales, Poems, Songs, Movies, Plays, and Folklore, 1917–1953* (Bloomington, 1995), 237–38.

51 GA RF, f. 7689, op. 11, d. 127, ll. 68–69ob.

52 Katherine Verdery (*What Was Socialism*, 24) considers surveillance "the negative face" of socialist regimes' problematic legitimation as opposed to "promises of social redistribution and welfare," that is, socialist paternalism. My argument is that these two "faces" were genetically part of the same body. For interesting reflections on surveillance in the twentieth century, see Peter Holquist, " 'Information Is the Alpha and Omega of Our Work': Bolshevik Surveillance in Its Pan-European Context," *Journal of Modern History* 69 (September 1997): 415–50.

53 GA RF, f. 7689, op. 11. d. 127, ll. 70–71ob.

54 GA RF, f. 7689, op. 11, d. 51, ll. 128, 130 (Koriakina); d. 125, ll. 27ob. (Shmakov) and 134 (Arsenteva).
55 GA RF, f. 7689, op. 11, d. 50, ll. 41–43ob. For another case of denunciation involving the alleged refusal of the Gorniak (Azov–Black Sea krai) farm administration to allow Tat'iana Gubkina to take her sick daughter – who later died – to the hospital, see GA RF, f. 7689, op. 11, d. 239 (correspondence of central committee with oblast committees and order-bearing workers about their work and improving living and cultural conditions), l. 28. This case went to the RSFSR Procurator's office.
56 GA RF, f. 7689, op. 11, d. 129, ll. 59ob., 63.
57 See, for example, GA RF, f. 7689, op. 11, d. 125, ll. 35, 58.
58 GA RF, f. 7689, op. 11, d. 127, l. 25. Mikhailenko's letter concluded: "I await with impatience your reply and send regards to our best leaders, strong and mighty."
59 GA RF, f. 7689, op. 11, d 50, ll. 112, 117, 118.
60 GA RF, f. 7689, op. 11, d. 125, ll. 79, 88–88ob.
61 Ibid., ll. 38, 46, 49. Adilov included raincoats and boots for young drovers in his initial letter. For another case of a prizewinner hosting a "drunken party" among "doubtful" types, see ibid., l. 134.
62 GA RF, f. 7689, op. 11, d. 41 (stenogram of meeting of Stakhanovites of Stalingrad krai sovkhozes, 1–2 December 1935), ll. 6–7, 30, 56; d. 43 (stenogram of meeting of Stakhanovite livestock workers with specialists and workers' committee chairs, 7–9 December 1935), l. 71; d. 45 (memoranda and information from oblast and krai committees to union central committee on socialist competition and development of Stakhanovite movement), l. 7. Klavdiia Maksimovskaia, a twenty-three-year-old milking brigade leader in the Northern krai, contemplated suicide after learning of the rumor that she "was fulfilling her plan with water" and had been "shunned" by the sovkhoz administration. GA RF, f. 7689, op. 11, d. 129, l. 134–134ob.
63 GA RF, f. 7689, op. 11. d. 127, l. 101.
64 As Michel Foucault noted in a Gramscian vein, "power would be a fragile thing if its only function were to repress, if it worked only through the mode of censorship, exclusion, blockage and repression. . . . If, on the contrary, power is strong this is because . . . it produces effects at the level of desire." Michel Foucault, *Power/Knowledge: Selected Interviews and Other Writings, 1972–1977* (New York, 1980), 59.
65 GA RF, f. 7689, op. 11, d. 128, l. 181; d. 127, l. 5. Nesterenko had earlier carried on a correspondence with Kubanova's daughter (initiated by the latter), urging the ten-year-old Niura to study better "so that there will not be a single mistake in your letters," inquiring about whether her sister, Raia, was also a Pioneer, and informing her that "we" had sent a pair of combed *valenki* [felt boots]. GA RF, f. 7689, op. 11, d. 128, ll. 170–80.
66 GA RF, f. 7689, op. 11, d. 129, l. 110ob. The letter was dated 26 January 1936.
67 GA RF, f. 7689, op. 11, d. 42. l. 79 (emphasis mine). Cf. the earlier statement by Soms (*Sovkhoznaia gazeta*, 26 August 1935, 1), which criticized politotdely for failing to distinguish "the best shockworkers and notables from the general mass of workers."
68 GA RF, f. 7689, op. 11, d. 42, l. 84; d. 45, l. 7.
69 GA RF, f. 7689, op. 11, d. 41, ll. 16, 19; d. 45, l. 111. Evdokiia was one of the two Vinogradova "sisters" (they were unrelated) who pioneered the Stakhanovite movement in the textile industry.
70 *Sovkhoznaia gazeta*, 14 February 1936, 1–2; 16 February 1936, 1, 3; 17 February 1936, 2; 18 February 1936, 2; 24 February 1936, 1–4. In 1935, medals were

awarded to milkers for so many thousands of liters of milk produced, to calfherds for so many calves reared, and so on.

71 Fitzpatrick, *Stalin's Peasants*, 182. The same point is made in Matt F. Oja, "From *Krestianka* to *Udarnitsa*: Rural Women and the *Vydvizhenie* Campaign, 1933–1941," *The Carl Beck Papers in Russian and East European Studies*, no. 1203 (1996): 5–16; Jennifer Fleming, " 'Private' Gardens and 'Public' Farms: Cultivating Soviet Rural Womanhood in the 1930s" (MA thesis, Michigan State University, 1997), drawing on mainly literary sources; and on the "semantic system of visual propaganda," Victoria E. Bonnell, "The Peasant Woman in Stalinist Political Art of the 1930s," *American Historical Review* 98, no. 1 (February 1993): esp. 72–82. One also thinks especially of Vera Mukhina's monumental sculpture from 1937, *Worker and Collective Farm Woman*.

72 *Sovkhoznaia gazeta*, 26 November 1935, 3.

73 GA RF, f. 7689, op. 11, d. 239, ll. 39–40.

74 GA RF, f. 7689, op. 11, d. 328 (correspondence of the union central committee with order-bearers [1938]), l. 58–58ob.

75 Fehér, Heller, and Markus, *Dictatorship over Needs*, 180.

76 Besides, as Katherine Verdery has noted, "the whole point was *not* to sell things: the center wanted to keep as much as possible under its control, because that was how it had redistributive power; and it wanted to give away the rest, because that was how it confirmed its legitimacy with the public" (*What Was Socialism*, 26).

77 Fitzpatrick, *Stalin's Peasants*, 16.

78 See GA RF, f. 7689, op. 11, d. 239, 328, 422 (correspondence of union central committee with oblast and workers' committees and individual order bearers [1939]).

Part IV

VARIETIES OF TERROR

The Great Purges of 1937–8, also known as the Great Terror, is one of the central mysteries of Stalinism. The natural question, "What caused the Great Purges?," has yet to receive a satisfactory answer, either in Russian or Western scholarship. Post-Soviet Russians tend to cast this (like most other historical questions) in terms of "Who is to blame?," offering answers like "Stalin" or "the administrative-command system" that only invite more questions. Western scholars and journalists have also been preoccupied with questions of blame and guilt (including blaming colleagues for "wrong" interpretations). There have been attempts at structural explanations, for example that as a totalitarian system Stalin's regime needed to maintain its citizens in a state of fear and uncertainty, and recurrent random purging provided the mechanism.[1] More recently, Arch Getty has argued that it was the leaders' own obsessive fears that generated the terror.[2] Consensus has not been achieved on the objects of terror in 1937–8, some seeing the elites as the prime target, others the whole population. There are also differences of opinion as to the status of the Great Purges *vis-à-vis* other episodes of state terror such as collectivization. Most Western scholars have treated the Purges as a unique event, different in kind from anything that preceded or followed it, but in his *Gulag Archipelago* Solzhenitsyn makes an eloquent case against this view.

The angry debates of the 1970s and '80s between "traditional" and "revisionist" scholars over the number of Great Purge casualties focussed attention on an aspect of the topic that was peculiarly vulnerable to political passion and, given the almost total inaccessibility of data at that time, unamenable to solution.[3] Analogies with the Holocaust – and Holocaust denial – were drawn, creating a discouraging climate for serious study. Revisionists who persevered with the subject, such as Arch Getty, Roberta Manning, and Gabor Rittersporn,[4] were in the double bind of being denied research access in the Soviet Union while being pilloried as "white-washers of Stalinism" in the West.

Since the collapse of the Soviet Union, archives have opened sufficiently to provide some answers on the numbers question, as well as an abundance of fascinating documents on the process of terror in 1937–8, many of them translated in a new volume by Getty.[5] A young Russian historian, Oleg Khlevniuk, has addressed the topic as part of his major study of the high politics of the 1930s,[6] as have other Russian historians such as Volkogonov, albeit at a more popular and less analytical level.[7] A few other Western historians have tackled the subject from various angles.[8] It would be misleading, however, to suggest that this work, admirable though much of it is, has provided an answer to that big question.

One of the reasons for this may be that the question as posed is simply too general and abstract for the specific, data-based explanations that come naturally to historians. As with cognate questions about man's inhumanity to man (for example, "Why war?"), there are dimensions of the "Why terror?" question that belong more properly to the realm of moral philosophy than history. In addition, however, it may be that the events that we label "The Great Purges" may best be understood not as a single phenomenon but as a number of related but discrete phenomena, each susceptible of specific historical explanation in a way that the universal phenomenon is not. In this sense, the question "Why the Great Purges?" may be an inept historical question in the same sense that "Why the Renaissance?" is inept: that is, the category is too large and the term too loaded with preconceptions to allow a coherent answer. To advance the process of explanation, the historian must break down the big composite phenomenon into separate, analyzable parts.

The great importance of the work of James Harris and Paul Hagenloh[9] published in this volume (Chapters 9 and 10) is that it shows, for the first time, how this can be done. Working with specific, discrete bodies of recently available archival material from the 1930s, each of them discerns a coherent process that, in 1937, produced *one kind of terror*. The emphasis on "one kind" is crucial, since neither author claims that the process he has uncovered was universal. To the degree that these specific explanations are convincing, however, they implicitly call into question our usual assumption that "the Great Purges" was a unitary process – a standard-model vacuum cleaner, as it were, systematically applied first to one area, then another.

The aspect of the Great Purges examined by James Harris is terror against regional leadership cliques. Harris (b. 1964) defended his PhD on center–periphery relations, based on the case study of Sverdlovsk, at the University of Chicago in 1996. Sverdlovsk was one of the beneficiaries of large-scale state industrial investment under the First Five-Year Plan (1929–32). Its successful industrial development was the main preoccupation of regional party leaders in the 1930s (a situation duplicated in many other regions), and they had lobbied intensively to receive major capital investment from the state. As Harris's study demonstrates, the Sverdlovsk leaders ran into big trouble during the Second Five-Year Plan (1933–7), when Moscow started insisting on exact fulfilment of targets and the exaggerated nature of some of their earlier claims started to become visible. Like other regional leaderships,[10] the Sverdlovsk leadership constituted a clique that regularly engaged in self-protective practices to conceal production shortfalls and other problems from Moscow. As the self-protective efforts started to unravel in 1936, the central party leaders came to believe (not wholly without reason) that the Sverdlovsk clique was engaged in large-scale "conspiracy" to deceive Moscow – and the usual consequences of mass arrests of "enemies" in the regional leadership followed. Much of Harris's data come from a unique source: NKVD interrogations of the regional leaders, in which they described the self-protective practices of the clique (or "conspiracy" in NKVD terminology) in detail.

Paul Hagenloh (b. 1968) is still in the process of completing his PhD at the University of Texas at the time of writing. He takes a quite different aspect of the Great Purges: the mass arrests of social marginals following a secret instruction of the Politburo in July 1937. This instruction was unknown until a few years ago. Indeed, the whole phenomenon of rounding-up marginals like prostitutes, beggars, wanderers, horse thieves, and (a typically Stalinist touch) religious sectarians is a new subject in the literature, though its relevance to the problems of social classification and ascription presented elsewhere in this volume is clear. The relationship of Soviet purging of marginals and Nazi "eugenic" approaches to population cleansing in Germany will undoubtedly be explored in the future. Hagenloh, however, focusses primarily on the dynamics of internal policing, showing how in the wake of collectivization the state's efforts to systematize and rationalize social control, particularly via the passport system, led to an ever more acute problem of what to do with social misfits and deviants. Hagenloh's topic is particularly important in the context of general discussion of the Great Purges because the process he describes is so strikingly different in genesis and kind from the more familiar processes of elite purging that it virtually forces us to think of terror in 1937–8 as a non-unitary phenomenon.

How many different strands of terror can be discerned? So far, in addition to the purging of regional leadership cliques dealt with by Harris and others, we have the emerging shape of a nationalities purge with its own historical dynamics and context,[11] as well as glimpses of the dynamics of the Red Army purge.[12] Even the show trials of the Great Purge period, whose Moscow manifestation is so memorably described by Conquest, turn out to have come in different varieties, the provincial variant differing significantly in its origins, procedures and purposes from those of the capital.[13] No doubt there are more individual strands still waiting to be identified. When that work of identification and analysis is done, we will be immeasurably better equipped to tackle the task of synthesis.

FURTHER READING

Conquest, Robert, *The Great Terror* (Harmondsworth, Mx, 1971).

Fitzpatrick, Sheila, "How the Mice Buried the Cat: Scenes from the Great Purges of 1937 in the Russian Provinces," *Russian Review* 52: 3 (1993).

Getty, J. Arch, *The Road to Terror. Stalin and the Self-Destruction of the Bolsheviks, 1932-9* (New Haven, 1999).

Getty, J. Arch, Gabor T. Rittersporn, and V.N. Zemskov, "Victims of the Soviet Penal System in the Pre-war Years: a First Approach on the Basis of Archival Evidence," *American Historical Review* 98: 4 (1993).

Getty, J. Arch and Roberta T. Manning, eds, *Stalinist Terror: New Perspectives* (Cambridge, 1993).

Khlevnyuk, Oleg, "The Objectives of the Great Terror, 1937–1938," in Julian Cooper *et al.*, eds, *Soviet History, 1017–1953: Essays in Honour of R.W. Davies* (London, 1995).

Medvedev, Roy A., *Let History Judge: The Origins and Consequences of Stalinism*, ed. and trans. George Shriver (revised edn, New York, 1989).

Solzhenitsyn, Aleksandr I., *The Gulag Archipelago* I–II, trans. Thomas P. Whitney (New York, 1974).

Tucker, Robert C. and Stephen F. Cohen, eds, *The Great Purge Trial* (New York, 1965).

Memoirs, diaries, and novels

Chukovskaia, Lydia, *Sofia Petrovna*, trans. Aline Worth (Evanston, 1988) (novella).

Ginzburg, Eugenia, *Journey into the Whirlwind*, trans. Paul Stevenson and Max Hayward (New York, 1967) (memoir).

—— *Within the Whirlwind*, trans. Ian Boland (New York, 1981) (memoir).

Kosterina, Nina, *The Diary of Nina Kosterina*, trans. Mirra Ginsburg (New York, 1968) (diary).

Rybakov, Anatoli, *Fear*, trans. Antonina W. Bouis (Boston, Mass., 1992) (novel).

Trifonov, Yuri, *Disappearance*, trans. David Lowe (Ann Arbor, 1992) (novella).

—— "House on the Embankment," in *Another Life and House on the Embankment*, trans. Michael Glenny (New York, 1983) (novella).

Weissberg, Alex, *Conspiracy of Silence* (London, 1952) (memoir).

NOTES

1 Zbigniew Brzezinski's *The Permanent Purge* (Cambridge, Mass., 1958) is the clearest statement of this hypothesis.

2 J. Arch Getty, "Afraid of Their Shadows: the Bolshevik Recourse to Terror, 1932–1938," in *Stalinismus vor dem Zweiten Weltkrieg. Neue Wege der Forschung / Stalinism before the Second World War: New Avenues of Research*, ed. Manfred Hildermeier with Elisabeth Müller-Luckner (Munich, 1998).

3 For scholarship on this question since the opening of the archives, see Introduction, note 11.

4 J. Arch Getty, *The Origins of the Great Purges: The Soviet Communist Party Reconsidered, 1933–1938* (Cambridge, 1985); Roberta T. Manning, "The Great Purges in a Rural District: Belyi Raion Revisited," *Russian History* 16: 2–4 (1989); Gabor Rittersporn, *Stalinist Simplifications and Soviet Complications* (Philadelphia, 1991); Robert W. Thurston, "Fear and Belief in the USSR's 'Great Terror': Response to Arrest, 1935–1939," *Slavic Review* 45: 2 (1986).

5 J. Arch Getty, *The Road to Terror: Stalinism and the Self-Destruction of the Bolsheviks* (New Haven, 1999).

6 O.V. Khlevniuk, *1937 g. Stalin, NKVD i sovetskoe obshchestvo* (Moscow, 1992), and idem., *Politbiuro. Mekhanizmy politicheskoi vlasti v 1930–e gody* (Moscow, 1996); and Oleg Khlevnyuk, "The Objectives of the Great Terror, 1937–1938," in Julian Cooper *et al.*, eds, *Soviet History, 1917–1953: Essays in Honour of R.W. Davies* (London, 1995).

7 Dmitry Volkogonov, *Stalin: Triumph and Tragedy*, trans. Harold Shukman, (Rocklin, CA, 1992).

8 J. Arch Getty and Roberta T. Manning, eds, *Stalinist Terror: New Perspectives* (Cambridge, 1993); Robert W. Thurston, *Life and Terror in Stalin's Russia 1934–1941* (New Haven, 1996); Sheila Fitzpatrick, *Everyday Stalinism* (New York, 1999), ch. 8; idem., "Workers against Bosses: the Impact of the Great Purges on Labor–Management Relations," in Lewis H. Siegelbaum and Ronald Grigor Suny, eds, *Making Workers Soviet: Power, Class, and Identity* (Ithaca, 1994); Robert A. McCutcheon, "The 1936–1937 Purge of Soviet Astronomers," *Slavic Review* 50: 1 (1991).

9 To these two names should be added that of David R. Shearer, whose paper "Policing the Soviet Frontier: Social Disorder and Repression in Western Siberia during the 1930s" – dealing, like Hagenloh's, with the round-up of marginals that was part of the Great Purges – was presented at the same panel of the annual meeting of AAASS in Seattle in November 1997.

10 For other regional studies of the Great Purges, see Jörg Baberowski, "Stalinismus an der Peripherie: Das Beispiel Azerbaidjan 1920–1941," in *Stalinismus vor dem Zweiten Weltkrieg. Neue Wege der Forschung*, ed. Manfred Hildermeier with Elisabeth Müller-Luckner (Munich, 1998); Manning, "The Great Purges in a Rural District" (see note 4, above); Stephen Kotkin, *Magnetic Mountain* (Berkeley, 1995), ch. 7; Robert Weinberg, "Purge and Politics in the Periphery: Birobidzhan in 1937," *Slavic Review* 52: 1 (1993); Hiroaki Kuromiya, *Freedom and Terror in the Donbas: A Ukrainian–Russian Borderland, 1870s-1990s* (Cambridge, 1998), ch. 6.

11 See N.V. Petrov and A.V. Roginskii, "Pol'skaia operatsii NKVD 1937–1938 gg.," in *Repressii protiv poliakov i pol'skikh grazhdan*, comp. A. E. Gurianov (Moscow, 1997); Terry Martin, "The Origins of Soviet Ethnic Cleansing," *Journal of Modern History* 70: 4 (December, 1998).

12 See Roger R. Reese, "The Red Army and the Great Purges," in Getty and Manning, *Stalinist Terror*, and idem., *Stalin's Reluctant Soldiers: A Social History of the Red Army, 1925–1941* (Lawrence, Kansas, 1996).

13 See Sheila Fitzpatrick, "How the Mice Buried the Cat: Scenes from the Great Purges of 1937 in the Russian Provinces," *Russian Review* 52: 3 (July, 1993); and Elena Osokina, *Za fasadom "stalinskogo izobiliia". Raspredelenie i rynok v snabzhenii naseleniia v gody industrializatsii, 1927–1941* (Moscow, 1997), p. 203, n. 2.

9

THE PURGING OF LOCAL CLIQUES IN THE URALS REGION, 1936–7

James R. Harris

At the time of the Seventeenth Party Congress in early 1934, the center–region relationship was at a dangerous crossroads. Four years earlier, the center and the regions had been united in their enthusiasm for high-tempo industrialization. In the late 1920s, regional leaders had anticipated that high levels of state investment and new construction would bring enormous wealth to the local economy.[1] What had followed was a series of economic crises, brutally violent upheavals and year after year of underfulfilled plans. Central leaders had begun to blame the regions for the problems of the planned economy: overspending, poor organization of labor, poor use of new equipment, accidents and under-fulfillment. They had developed the impression that central legislation was being ignored in the regions. This sudden turn of events and attitudes profoundly upset the regions. The regions were angered that Moscow had radically reduced the flow of investment and the tempos of construction, and were disturbed by Moscow's categorical demands for prompt and complete fulfillment. By 1934, the center and the regions were testing the boundaries of a new relationship: the regions were trying to defend a modicum of autonomy, while the center was testing the regions' responsiveness to its leadership.

The relationship was not initially conflictual; 1934 marked the beginning of two years of promising economic growth. There was no shortage of evidence of administrative incompetence and inertia, but central leaders were not inclined to take radical action against this ill which they labeled "bureaucratism" as long as the indicators of overall plan fulfillment appeared to be good. When things did go wrong, central leaders tended to accept that the fault lay at the factory or district (*raion*) level. They were not inclined to doubt the loyalty of the apparatus at the regional level. Likewise, regional leaders resented Moscow for unilaterally increasing their responsibilities and reducing the benefits of construction and investment, but they could point to a long list of concrete accomplishments of so-called "socialist construction." In the course of the first five-year plan (1929–32), the Urals region (*oblast'*) had overcome a cycle of industrial backwardness that had troubled it since the middle of the nineteenth century. Particularly in the context of the world economic crisis, the future probably seemed quite promising. It seemed likely that the tensions of the center–region relationship would relax once the plants under construction during the first five-year plan were brought to capacity.

The process of starting up first five-year plan projects may have seemed straightforward, but it proved to be exceedingly difficult. Incomplete and incompetent planning, rushed and low-quality construction and the shortage of skilled workers made the efficient use of new enterprises a herculean task. In the face of Moscow's unwillingness to accept excuses or delays, it had become politically impossible to raise and discuss economic problems with central officials. As the second five-year plan (1933–7) progressed, an ever higher percentage of production was to come from new plants, thereby compounding the difficulty of plan fulfillment. In response to these pressures, regional leaders employed a series of adaptive strategies. They tried to control Moscow's access to information. Economic "successes" were exaggerated, or invented. Underfulfillment was hidden. Production and construction costs were exaggerated, production capacity was hidden. Central policies and campaigns perceived to complicate plan fulfillment – such as the Stakhanovite movement – were pursued in such a way as to limit their effects while promoting an image of vigorous action.

In this period, a close-knit, regional leadership "clique" developed. In order to protect their positions and mask their adaptive strategies, top leaders of the regional party committee (*obkom*) formed a group which could present a united front in the face of central pressures. The Party purges (*chistki*) of 1933–6,[2] as well as the periodic and connected campaigns to uncover vestiges of the former oppositions, were controlled and limited in order to protect the "clique" and eliminate those on whom it could not rely. The cynical use of purges and the labelling of "enemies" was common at all levels of the regional apparatus. When shortcomings of any kind, from industrial accidents to resistance to central campaigns, were uncovered, scapegoats were found and fired – or arrested and tried. Local show trials were a convenient alternative to explaining the systemic causes of underfulfillment. If plan targets could not be met or policies not implemented, it was easier to find a culprit or culprits, and by shifting blame evade the consequences of non-fulfillment. The tendency was so strong as to provoke Moscow to restrain the use of trials in the regions.

The quickness to scapegoat was the Achilles heel of the regional leadership. As long as plan fulfillment was sufficient to satisfy the central leadership, the group remained relatively cohesive and the task of masking failures manageable. But when plan fulfillment suddenly declined, as it did in the first half of 1936, tensions within the regional apparatus flared dramatically. Because of the interconnectedness of the regional economy, any attempt to mask failures in one branch of the economy heightened the impression of failure in another. And the systematic misrepresentation of regional activities to Moscow made each member of the "clique" cruelly aware of his vulnerability. Blameshifting flourished among factory managers and local Party organizations as well. Rather than risk being fired for underfulfillment or other production problems, they tried to deflect blame onto subordinates or other organizations. Tensions were further aggravated by the resentment of workers against high work norms, low pay rates and poor living conditions.

Under different circumstances, the regional leadership would have been able to deal with the flare-up of Moscow's hunt for oppositionists in the summer of 1936. They had succeeded in the past. But the poor economic results of the time found the whole regional apparatus on a hair-trigger of mutual denunciation. Moscow's demands to unmask members of the "Trotskyist–Zinovievist band" – which the press declared had been "routed, reduced to ash," "crushed to bits"[3] – accelerated the use of denunciation at the factory and district level. The attempts of regional leaders to stem the flow of denunciations were hampered by tensions within the clique. They were unable to prevent the progress of denunciations up the bureaucratic hierarchy into the oblast administration itself. With each arrest, Moscow learned more about the systematic resistance to central policy that had been sponsored in the regions. Central leaders came to believe that they had uncovered a regional conspiracy against the regime.[4] The Terror was not solely an NKVD action. It was also fueled by the combustion of tensions within the bureaucracy – tensions created by central plans which were unfulfillable.

The second five-year plan: the problems of fulfillment

In successive versions of the second five-year plan, the fifth-year targets were substantially reduced. The production of pig iron, which had been projected at 50–60 million tons in 1931, was reduced to 16 million tons in the 1934 plan. The target for coal extraction was reduced from over 390 million tons to 152.5 million tons. The final target for the production of refined copper was less than one-sixth of the figure projected in 1931.[5] In part, the moderation of the plan was necessitated by the underfulfillment of current production targets in each of the three years that separated the first and the final versions. But the moderation of the plan was also driven by a rough consensus among central leaders that over-ambitious plans created disorder.

Central "moderation" meant lower overall targets, but also higher expectations for the realization of returns on every ruble invested. What had replaced the "gigantomania" of construction of the first five-year plan was a sort of "gigantomania" of efficiency. Great hopes were placed on the economic impact of the introduction of the huge, techno-logically advanced plants under construction in the first five-year plan. The emphasis on efficiency became more striking and disturbing to the regions following the center–region conflicts over the second five-year plan in 1932. In the aftermath of the conflicts, the planning of individual projects shifted from the regions to specialized planning insti-tutes under the central industrial ministry. These planning institutes promoted construction plans that projected costs at a fraction of what the regions anticipated.[6]

The introduction of huge new plants initiated in the second five-year plan promised to put significant new strains on the system,[7] which had still to overcome the problems that had plagued the first five-year plan. The transportation infrastructure continued to lag behind the develop-ment of the economy as a whole, deepening problems of supply in both industry and agriculture. Similarly, the shortages of qualified cadres which had been keenly felt in the first five-year plan threatened to become even more severe. The "giants" were built with advanced technologies that required training for even basic operations and specialized knowl-edge for repair work and for the organization of labor. The accidental destruction of expensive and complex equipment by poorly trained laborers straight from the village was a common occurrence in the 1930s. The potential for breakdowns, shortages, and accidents was greater in the second five-year plan than in the first.

Perhaps the most significant factor complicating fulfillment was the legacy of the region's first five-year plan. In their determination to develop certain sectors of the local economy, regional planners had attempted to convince central officials of the vastness of local reserves of given ores, or of the tremendous capacities of given plants, before local geologists or engineers were able to calculate their potential with certainty. In many cases, mine and plant capacities proved to be signif-icantly lower than the regions predicted. Deficiencies could be hidden in the course of construction, but certainly not after these enterprises were opened for production. By the mid-1930s, Moscow was demanding the prompt and full use of capacity projected in the first five-year plan. Regional officials, particularly those in the related enterprises, were profoundly worried, given the virtual certainty of plan underfulfillment.

The Urals coal industry was perhaps the clearest example of such a situation. The lack of local supplies of cokeable coal had been the single greatest hindrance to the development of the Urals as a metals and machine-building centre. Coking experiments on Urals coal had been conducted throughout the 1920s but had produced no clear results. In the late 1920s, Urals Party leaders, concerned that new investment in coal production would go to the Moscow or Don basins, exerted intense pressure on local geologists and metallurgists to produce favorable results. The result was a split between senior specialists trained before the revolution, who resisted the pressure and were subsequently prosecuted for "criminally delaying the development" of the regional coal industry, and the new cadre of Soviet-trained specialists, who took the opportunity to discredit their bosses by exaggerating the success of their experiments.[8] Moscow never saw fit to question their claims, and over the next five years hundreds of millions of rubles were spent developing mines in the Kizel basin and building coking plants – though in fact Kizel coal never was cokeable.[9]

Intensifying the pressures of the second five-year plan was the center's insistence on complete and prompt fulfillment of targets. In the first five-year plan period Moscow had reluctantly accepted the underfulfillment of the plan's wildly ambitious targets. With the second five-year plan and its reduced targets, this was no longer the case. At the January 1933 plenary meeting of the Central Committee, Sergo Ordzhonikidze made it clear to the delegates that the central leadership was prepared to deal with underfulfillment in industry in the same way as it was dealing with the current underfulfillment of grain collection targets:

> These days, the discipline of industry is not especially deserving of praise. It is not uncommon that directives of the Party and government are held up for discussion – "can they be fulfilled?". We decisively must put an end to this. I don't think that economic managers would like it if the Party instilled discipline in industry in the way we have been forced to do among the directors of sovkhozy (state farms). I don't think any factory director would envy the sovkhoz director who must be driven from the Party, fired from his position and thrown in jail ... [10]

Targets were not to be questioned, and excuses for underfulfillment would not be accepted. In his speech to the Seventeenth Congress, Stalin declared that "reference to so-called objective conditions cannot serve as a justification [of underfulfillment]," and that any attempt to use this excuse would cause "the removal [of the officials concerned] ... and the promotion of new people to their places."[11] Economic managers and other regional officials understood that their careers were on the line. As the chairman of the Urals Non-ferrous Metals Trust warned his subordinates in the fall of 1935, "If you do not turn things around, there will be casualties (budut zhertvy)."[12]

Despite the apparent moderation of the second five-year plan, its targets would have been extremely difficult to achieve under any circumstances because of the irregularity of financing, continuing problems of supply, shortages of trained cadres, and exorbitant demands for increased efficiency in construction and production. As new enterprises came on line and were expected to carry a growing burden of production, the danger of systematic underfulfillment increased. But it was the extravagant promises offered by the regions in the context of the free-spending first five-year plan that made failure to achieve second five-year plan targets virtually inevitable. When that failure became evident, regional leaders would be exposed to the wrath of central leaders unwilling to accept any excuses.

Regional coping strategies

Since the publication of Joseph Berliner's *Factory and Manager in the USSR* in the mid-1950s, it has been accepted that economic managers engaged in a range of practices intended to ease the pressures of plan fulfillment. These practices included hoarding inputs, underestimating production capacity, adjusting the assortment of output to simulate fulfillment and deliberately lowering quality in the interests of increasing output.[13] These practices were very widespread at the factory level and not especially well hidden. The local and central press reported on them frequently, but they usually provoked little more than formal reprimands (*vygovory*).

The coping strategies of the regional leadership, that is, of the members of the *obkom*, have received considerably less attention in the literature. They were intertwined with those of the managers and not fundamentally different from them. Both groups sought to mask their failures and advertise their successes. Both had a strong interest in protecting the perquisites of their respective positions. The strategies of regional leaders involved public condemnation of managerial practices in which they privately colluded. They tried to reduce plan targets while at the same time projecting an image of aggressive loyalty to the "Central Committee line." Often, they passively resisted central directives which they perceived to be counterproductive of regional – or their personal – interests, and sought to deflect blame if things went wrong or coping strategies were uncovered. From their positions in the *obkom*, it was somewhat easier for regional leaders than economic managers to control Moscow's access to information on their "successes" and "failures."

The second five-year plan marks the origins of a functional regional clique in the Urals. In this period, the top regional leaders strove to isolate or remove those in the *obkom* whose loyalties were not exclusive to them so as to prevent the dissemination of potentially damaging information. When they found out that members of the regional Control Commission were leaking information on fulfillment problems to the press, the offending parties were removed from their posts.[14] After Moscow created state and Party control commissions independent of regional authorities and invested them with the power to purge any officials who failed to implement central directives,[15] the issue of control took on a new urgency.

The clique employed a range of tactics to ensure its control, mostly in the nature of unsubtle positive and negative reinforcements. The positive reinforcements were largely financial. The members of the clique and "especially important members of the oblast Party aktiv" were ensured an excellent standard of living in exchange for their loyalty. They received large apartments, dachas, special access to consumer goods and food supplies and large supplements to their salaries. The central fund for this kind of graft ("podkup" or "podkarmlivanie") was run out of the economic administration of the oblast Executive Committee, but the leaders of the major city Party committees and trust directors had their own "slush funds."[16] Negative reinforcements were the flip side of the graft coin. Those who made trouble for the members of the clique were removed from their posts, thereby losing all the attendant privileges.[17] The Party chistki of the mid-1930s, including the verification and exchange of Party documents, were favoured means of removing untrusted colleagues.[18] It was generally not difficult to find some element from an enemy's past and use it to get him purged. Once the offending parties had been removed, those who replaced them were carefully chosen, known friends of the clique. They were coopted, rather than elected by an obkom plenum as had been the practice in the 1920s and early 1930s.[19] Leading Party and state workers who came to the oblast on orders from Moscow were greeted with great hospitality, established in luxurious surroundings and then carefully observed. If they then criticized local practices, they were "discredited in their practical work as a result of which they were usually sent to distant districts, or beyond the borders of the oblast."[20] If they were accepted into the inner circle of the clique, their professional reputations were systematically protected and advanced. According to Kabakov (testifying under interrogation after his arrest), all key positions in the oblast were under the control of the clique by 1935.[21] This even included the local representative of the NKVD, Reshetov, who was very much in the inner circle of the clique, and a close personal friend of Kabakov.[22]

> What resulted was a "wall" which not even the most determined and brave could break through ... It was impossible to expect that anyone would attempt to aggregate and draw conclusions from scattered evidence of wrong-doing and criminal activity ...

That would mean casting suspicion on all elements of the Party, state and economic leadership of the oblast.[23]

This "wall" of defensive mutual loyalty gave members of the clique confidence that they were "untouchable."[24] Those within the group counted on regional leaders to protect them privately from political campaigns or the fall-out from economic failures, whatever their rhetoric in public. At Party and state meetings whose minutes would be read in Moscow, regional leaders aggressively defended the "general line of the Party" and denounced any deviations from it; local industrial managers might be publicly chastised for enterprise failures at such fora and threatened with dismissal. Afterwards, however, Kabakov was known to take them aside and tell them that they were trusted and did not have to fear for their positions. In some cases, the heads of regional organizations were fired amidst scandal and then returned to their positions when things had calmed down.[25] Meanwhile, the oblast leadership colluded with trust directors in masking plant capacity and defending exaggerated spending plans before central organs.[26] When spending plans were rejected on the grounds of poor production results, good results were faked.[27] In many cases, the People's Commissariat was convinced of "continuous forward movement" with little more than creative manipulation of real production figures in monthly, quarterly and annual reports.[28] The clique was not merely aware of these various managerial practices: it coordinated them and protected those who engaged in them. If central officials uncovered clear evidence of these practices, a scapegoat was promptly found – usually from outside and well below the level of the clique – and he and "his" crimes were public condemned.[29]

In the mid-1930s, the Sverdlovsk oblast clique had good reason to believe that it was well protected by its network of "friends" in the Party and state apparatuses, major enterprises, the courts, the press, the NKVD and so on. Each member had much to gain from participating in the clique, and even more to lose from fighting it. As Kabakov put it under interrogation, "a large quantity of the *aktiv* were imperceptibly enveloped into the clique [by means of illegal gifts] such that within a year or so when they understood the criminal nature of what they were involved in, they were already beholden to us."[30] They were tied to the clique not only in terms of the lifestyle which they had come to enjoy, but also out of fear of being publicly implicated in its "illegal" coping strategies.

Fighting bureaucratism and the former oppositions

While central leaders had little knowledge of the regional coping strategies and of the depth of the systematic deception orchestrated by the regional clique, they carefully watched the fulfillment of their directives and were frustrated by what they called "bureaucratism": an apparent inertia or incompetence of the apparatus. As Moscow saw it, the grain collections campaign of 1931–2, the Stakhanovite movement and the Verification and Exchange of Party Documents, among other policy initiatives, were the objects of considerable "footdragging" until regional organizations were threatened with specific punishments for non-fulfillment.[31] On several occasions, such punishments were enacted to make an example to others,[32] but there is no clear evidence to suggest that the center ever contemplated combatting "bureaucratism" with the sort of onslaught of political violence that constituted the Terror. The Terror was a war declared against former oppositionists and other "enemies of the people." Ironically, it was regional officialdom that drew the connection between "bureaucratism" and "enemies of the people." The essential tactic of scapegoating was to blame purported enemies – "wreckers" and "saboteurs" – for the shortcomings of one's own organization. It worked well as long as the problems of fulfillment were relatively minor or could be hidden from the center. But when problems rapidly accumulated, as they did towards the end of the second five-year plan, the practice of scapegoating escaped the control of the clique and the center was given the impression that regional organizations were nests of "enemies." It was in the process of investigating the activities of these "enemies" that the regional leaders' systematic deception of the center was uncovered.

Central leaders had observed that "when we issue directives, we are uncertain whether they will be implemented."[33] In the speech announcing the creation of the Commissions for Party and Soviet Control, Stalin made it clear that these organs would be empowered to remove "officials ... who think that Party and Soviet laws were written not for them, but for idiots."[34] The threat to remove top officials followed in the aftermath of the disastrous grain collections campaigns of the previous two years, in which many local officials had shown a lack of enthusiasm for central targets in the face of widespread famine. But when the Commissions were created in 1934, the worst of the famine was over and industrial production was beginning to surge forward. Moscow was less certain about attacking high officials once things had started to improve.

The Commissions were immediately established in an ambiguous position. For example, the plenipotentiaries of the Commission for Party Control were given formal independence from the regional Party organizations that they were assigned to oversee. They were allowed to issue their own instructions and they could apply to the bureau of the Commission to have regional Party decisions repealed. But they were instructed to issue "all of the most important instructions with the participation of the regional Party committees."[35] They were encouraged to remove officials who violated or ignored central directives up to and including *obkom* secretaries, but they were criticized by the Commission leadership if their actions were perceived to be disruptive of the work of the *obkom*.[36] The plenipotentiaries never really understood how they were supposed to deal with the regional committees. As one plenipotentiary declared: "I don't know what to consider normal relations, and what abnormal."[37]

The Commissions did manage, however, to make themselves a thorn in the side of the regional clique. On several occasions, the Commission for Party Control investigations revealed information threatening to the clique. Within the first year of its work, the Sverdlovsk oblast Commission for Party Control uncovered evidence of financial irregularities in the economic administration of the oblast Executive Committee.[38] In essence, it had discovered the regional fund used by the clique to buy the loyalty of "especially important members of the aktiv." It proved to be a serious scare for the clique because disbursements had been directed by the top *obkom* leadership.[39] But the *obkom* immediately purged the head of the economic administration and several other Executive Committee members, accusing them of stealing the money for personal use.[40] No further investigation was held, and charges were limited to embezzlement.[41] A year and a half later, Party Control Commission investigations of the Stakhanovite movement and the Party *chistka* in Smolensk oblast uncovered evidence of "bureaucratic inertia" in the *obkom* which it passed on to Commission chairman N.I. Ezhov in Moscow, leading to a discussion of the problem in the Orgbureau of the Central Committee.[42] There are no minutes of the meeting, but it would have been a grave humiliation for Kabakov to be dressed down by the top central leaders. When Kabakov returned home, two *obkom* department heads were fired, and there was a wave of arrests of "saboteurs" of the two campaigns.[43]

Such incidents reinforced the tendency to believe that initiating local repression, finding specific targets on whom to lay the blame for problems, was the best way to convince Moscow that everything was under control. In testimony to his interrogators, Kabakov described the tactic as "being louder than anyone else in defense of the general line of the Party, and in certain circumstances not being afraid to sacrifice certain of our people to make it more convincing, and particularly when it seemed clear that they were sure to be purged anyway."[44] It seemed to work very well as long as the scandals were well separated in time and central investigations could be stopped short. But as we shall see, when Moscow refused to stop its investigations, as it did in 1936, the clique began to turn on itself.

Declining production and growing tensions in the oblast

According to statistics published in 1937 by the Commissariat of Heavy Industry for internal use, the 1936 plan was overfulfilled nationally by 5 percent.[45] Aside from the well-known necessity of approaching Soviet statistics with caution, there are good reasons for doubting the value of this figure. In a recent article, Roberta Manning demonstrated that a serious economic downturn had begun in 1936. She observed that downward pressure on growth rates had accumulated in the previous several years. The majority of unfinished projects from the first five-year plan had been brought on line, while new capital investment had declined. Other resources, such as the labor force, had already been stretched to their limits; and the state budget was under pressure from the rapidly increasing burden of military spending. Meanwhile, bad weather had made 1936 a terrible year for Soviet agriculture.[46] But for regional officials, these factors only further complicated the fulfillment of a plan they already knew to be impossible.

The 1936 economic year began in the Urals with the near-collapse of production at the Eastern Ore Trust. In the first five months of 1936, the Trust had produced 28 percent of its plan to date.[47] The whole production cycle of metal production and machine-building – the core of Urals industry – was affected. Smaller metallurgical plants were shut down and the larger ones were getting only a portion of their planned raw material, thus making it impossible for them to supply machine-building factories.[48] Only the existence of old reserves was preventing more widespread shut-downs, but the reserves were being rapidly depleted.[49] Production was also hampered by the gross inadequacy of the electricity supply, which led to frequent blackouts.[50]

The failure to complete first and second five-year plan construction projects constituted another impending crisis. The Central Urals Copper Trust was supposed to supply one-half of all-union copper production by 1937, but construction was nowhere near completion.[51] The reconstruction of Eastern Steel Trust factories for the production of high-quality steels, ongoing since 1930, required the investment of hundreds of millions of rubles in order to bring production to capacity, in addition to the huge investments already made in the project. This was a particularly sensitive case, because the Trust was expected to produce special alloys for the defense industry and the delays occurred as the military threat from both Japanese and German fascism became obvious.[52] Other projects nearing completion proved to be fundamentally defective. The Sinara Pipe factory lacked the iron ores for pipe production which the regional geological administration had claimed were present.[53] Regional officials were finding it increasingly difficult to hide the fact that coal from the Kizel region was unsuitable for metal production, after years of construction and investment based on the opposite assumption.[54]

As regional officials were reaching the limit of their ability to mask problems of production and construction, Moscow showed no tendency to lessen its demands on them. At its December 1935 plenary meeting, the Central Committee made it clear that the center expected substantial increases in the productivity of industry on the basis of Stakhanovite methods.[55] To make matters worse, the Council of People's Commissars increased the pressure on industry to meet targets for lowering the cost of construction and production. The 1936 investment plan for heavy industry was raised by 9.5 percent over 1935, and the target for cost reduction was 11 percent. At the same time, funding was concentrated on projects closer to completion, resulting in the freezing of financing to a wide range of on-going projects.[56]

The combined pressure of overstrained production capacity and increasing central demands created unprecedented tensions within the Party and economic apparatuses in Sverdlovsk oblast. Tensions between factory Party officials and factory directors, as well as between directors and shop (tsekh) managers, grew with the level of underfulfillment, accidents and breakdowns. Each was determined to show that the others should bear the burden of blame for the problems of the enterprise. Regional plenipotentiaries of the Commission for Soviet Control noted that in the summer of 1936 firings and "administrative penalties" (administrativnye vzyskanii) were being conducted on "on a massive scale."[57] As of October 1936, plan fulfillment in the Urals non-ferrous metals industry was (officially) hovering at about 80 percent and the rate of accidents had increased to 142 per 1,000 work hours (versus 88 in 1935).[58] Dismissing suggestions that educational measures for workers and engineers would reduce accidents, a Urals trust director insisted that show trials of "wreckers" were called for.[59]

Until 1936, the obkom clique had been able to prevent internal conflicts from getting out of hand. But the pressures of central demands for efficiency and budding regional economic crises were threatening the capacity of the clique for united action. Clique members continued to send to Moscow reports of regional "successes" into the fall of 1936, but the divergence of these reports from reality was becoming ever more visible. For example, the credibility of the claim made by the chairman of the Eastern Steel Trust to the Central Commissariat of Heavy Industry regarding "huge, remarkable successes ... new world records [of efficiency] ... systematic overfulfillment [of plan]"[60] was undermined by a Party Control Commission report to Moscow a few months earlier that noted the frequency of accidents and breakdowns, the failure of the Trust to report production of defective metal and the exaggeration of overall production figures.[61]

When uncovered, inflated claims reflected badly on those who made them. When they were accepted, they created problems for others. The chairman of the Eastern Ore Trust made enemies among many directors of metallurgy trusts by delivering an ever-declining quantity and quality of ores. The declining quantity of ores slowed the production of metals, while the high level of impurities in the ores resulted in the production of poor-quality metals and in damage to the smelting equipment.[62] Similarly, inaccurate claims made by the head of the Perm railroad that his organization had met its shipping targets created problems for trusts whose production plans were upset by delivery delays.[63] Because of the interconnectedness of the regional economy, the failures of any trust could not but affect others. Each of the trust directors – all members of the *obkom* clique – believed he was doing the best he could and resented others for complicating his work.

These mutual hostilities started to fracture the clique in 1936. The level of mutual reliance and trust declined as each feared he was the object of the intrigues of others.[64] The fear was intensified by the knowledge that each possessed potentially damaging information about the activities of the others.[65] When scandals and crises that drew the attention of Moscow had been infrequent, the clique had been able to work together to control them and deflect criticism. But as underfulfillment and other failures of the leadership became increasingly difficult to hide, clique members were in a bind. To defend other members was unpalatable and left one open to the accusation of participation in their "crimes." To denounce them was to risk a denunciation in response.

In the summer of 1936, when the first of the famous show trials of Trotskyite–Zinovievite "counter-revolutionaries" was held in Moscow, central party leaders had not yet imagined a giant nation-wide conspiracy.[66] But their calls for vigilance stimulated denunciations of "enemies" everywhere, and tensions in the regions within Party and state organs were so great that local leaders could not stem the flow of mutual recriminations and accusations. The more the center looked, the more it found – and the more it discerned the outlines of regional "conspiracies" which it was determined to uncover and root out.

The Terror

In a recent article based on newly available archival documents from the Moscow Party archives, David Hoffman has argued that the Terror in Moscow began quite suddenly in the summer of 1936, when, after receiving a top-secret letter of 29 July from the Central Committee calling for the rooting out of all Trotskyites, the Moscow city and oblast party committees sent a letter in the same spirit to all factory committees:

Upon receipt of this letter, the tone of party committee meetings changed overnight – accusations and counteraccusations proliferated, as party members suddenly began to blame preexisting problems of lagging production on the presence of Trotskyists in the factory.[67]

An examination of the Party and NKVD archives of Svedovsk oblast suggests that the July Central Committee secret letter was indeed decisive, but not because the central leadership intended it as a signal to initiate a terror. Rather, the letter inadvertently ignited existing tensions in the oblast.

The inability of the *obkom* to control the growth of denunciations first became obvious in the Urals non-ferrous metals industry. The enterprises of the industry were particularly vulnerable to mutual recriminations. Moscow was showing great impatience with "unsatisfactory" production figures. Production was at 80 percent of the plan and showing a tendency to decline.[68] Glavtsvetmet showered enterprises with demands for explanations of breakdowns, the decline in the quality of output and other production problems.[69] The rate of accidents was high and rising. Over half of all serious accidents (involving worker injury or death) in the Soviet non-ferrous metals industry occurred in the Urals.[70] Enterprises were also under fire from Moscow for the "completely insufficient development of the Stakhanovite movement."[71] Relations among factory and trust officials and local Party organizations shifted from tense to openly hostile. The potential for denunciations was clear, but they exploded with particular violence here because of the industry's preexisting reputation for being a focus of oppositional activity.

In the aftermath of the Kirov murder, a large group of oppositionists had been "discovered" in the administration of one of the largest construction projects of the non-ferrous metals industry – the Central Urals Chemical–Copper Combine. The head of construction, E.R. Shul'man, was accused of having hidden his participation in the "Workers' Truth" opposition in the early 1920s and of promoting oppositionists to prominent positions in the administration.[72] Though the issue was resolved rather quietly – the Commission for Party Control barred him from leading work for a year, without even excluding him from the Party – the project administration and the local Party organs were tainted by the incident, and, by association, the local non-ferrous metals industry acquired the reputation for harboring oppositionists. By the spring of 1936, under pressure of criticism from the Central Committee for the high accident rate and poor results in the Stakhanovite movement, a search for "wreckers" and oppositionists was under way.

Following the secret letter of 29 July 1936, the Party Control Commission launched an investigation encompassing most of the enterprises of the regional non-ferrous metals industry. Some of early purge targets were those who had made unfortunate remarks at meetings discussing the trial of the Trotsky–Zinoviev Bloc.[73] Others were removed for reputed links with the opposition. But a large number of documented expulsions in August and September clearly involved tensions at work. For example, the head of the labor department of the Kirovograd Copper Smelting Plant and his assistant were denounced for "anti-soviet actions" on the grounds that they had kept wages for engineering personnel at 450 rubles a month when less-qualified workers, probably Stakhanovites, were making up to 750 rubles.[74] At the same factory, Stakhanovites denounced engineering personnel as Trotskyists for failing to promote Stakhanovite methods and attacked the factory Party Committee for protecting the engineers.[75] At the Krasnoural Copper Smelting plant, tensions between district factory Party committees exploded into a war of denunciations. Each accused the other of protecting counterrevolutionaries as a result of which both organizations were purged and the district committee first secretary was arrested.[76] In the next few months, the circle of mutual denunciation spread wider and wider until the directors of the largest non-ferrous metal enterprises in the region – the Urals Non-ferrous Metallurgy Trust, the Urals Copper Mining Trust, and the Central Urals Copper–Chemical Combine and others – had been arrested.[77]

Because of continuing limitations on access to the archives of the Commission for Party Control and the NKVD, it is still impossible to trace the progress of denunciations on a case-by-case basis.[78] However, it is clear from Kabakov's testimony to his interrogators that any hopes he had had for restraining the progress of mutual denunciations vanished in September, when the regional NKVD representative, Reshetov, was replaced.[79] With the arrival of his successor, Dmitriev,

> the situation changed radically. The ground under our feet got so hot [sic], that I immediately understood that the unmasking of my colleagues and me was only a matter of time.[80]

Kabakov was probably trying to flatter his interrogators, but he did have reason to be worried in September. Reshetov had been his friend and ally. He and others had relied on Reshetov to share information and to protect the clique.[81] Dmitriev was not likely to do the same. According to K.G. Sedashev, the Eastern Steel Trust chairman, Kabakov was "horribly disturbed" by Reshetov's removal.[82] Fears about Dmitriev were quickly realized. It proved impossible to stop his investigations.

Parallel to events in the non-ferrous metals industry was a series of arrests in the oblast state apparatus. Investigations of individuals known to have been members of the Left Opposition in the 1920s led to F.I. Striganov, the head of the oblast administration of local industry.

Striganov was known to have been personal friends with two members of the Left opposition. At the end of August and in mid-October 1936, Striganov had been forced to do public penance for these contacts. The first time he avoided being purged,[83] but the second time he was not so lucky. He was arrested by the NKVD the same day. As in the case of the non-ferrous metals industry, the interplay of unsolicited denunciations and NKVD-inspired "naming of names" in the course of interrogation is difficult to establish,[84] but within three months many of the top leaders of the oblast state apparatus had been implicated, including the chairman of the regional Planning Commission, M.I. Fuks, and the chairman of the regional Executive Committee, V.F. Golovin, who was also second secretary of the *obkom*.

Striganov's position had not been helped by the consistent underfulfillment of the plan for local industry.[85] For the most part, the underfulfillment had been the result of underfunding. Budget cuts had generally hurt low-priority projects the hardest, as Moscow had set out to ensure the completion of the most economically significant construction projects and expand production at the largest existing plants. Local industry was low priority almost by definition. It often received less than a quarter of its requested budget.[86] It also received less attention and assistance from oblast organizations in planning, the organization of the Stakhanovite movement and so on. All this created considerable anger among officials in local industry toward oblast economic organs. Included in the materials of the NKVD investigation of Fuks is an unsolicited 27–page denunciation of the entire oblast administration written by V.A. Riabov, an assistant sector director in the administration of local industry. Riabov's denunciation was remarkably detailed and damaging. It contained copies of correspondence between Fuks and Golovin reinforcing his argument that the two knew about problems in local industry and took no action. And it showed how the oblast Planning Commission deliberately exaggerated plans for local industry as a way of increasing financing.[87]

Following Striganov's arrest, Fuks became the focus of criticism from the *obkom* and from within the oblast Planning Commission. At a closed Party meeting, he was criticized for not making changes in the Commission after the arrest of Striganov. Rather than following the typical *obkom* pattern in immediately identifying a few scapegoats as a way of cutting off further investigation, Fuks took no immediate action, but at the same time scared the Commission leadership into thinking he might do so by "hysterical shouting, swearing and table pounding. Hooligan, saboteur and wrecker were his favourite expressions."[88] When he finally took action in early 1937, he fired almost a third of the Commission staff – but not before he had been denounced by a host of sector heads and other Commission workers.[89]

How Golovin got caught up in this, aside from Riabov's denuncia-tion, is not clear from the documents currently open to researchers. But as soon as it was evident to Kabakov that Golovin – the second highest official in the region – would be arrested, he took action. According to the interrogation testimony of his personal secretary, A.I. Kostinaia, before the arrest of Golovin was publicly reported Kabakov composed an article for *Pravda* harshly criticizing Golovin in order to make it look as if he (Kabakov) had initiated Golovin's unmasking. Kostinaia quoted Kabakov as saying: "We have to write in the sharpest possible terms about Golovin in order to deflect criticism from ourselves."[90] She claims that Kabakov was "extremely upset" by this turn of events – and there was good reason. Even if Golovin did not denounce him (and he did not), Kabakov would have to explain how it was that key oblast offi-cials, including top trust directors, the heads of leading state organs, and an *obkom* second secretary (Golovin) had been members of a counter-revolutionary organization without his knowledge. His only hope was that the spread of arrests would be halted by the fall of a leader of the stature of Golovin.[91]

The February Central Committee plenum, which followed four weeks later, showed that this was not to be the case. It was clear from the speeches of central leaders that the flurry of mutual denunciations in the fall and winter and the investigations which they had provoked had already revealed too much about the tactics employed by regional lead-erships to hide the local state of affairs and resist central policy. In the opening speech, Politbureau member A.A. Zhdanov spoke of the decline of collective leadership in the regions, that is, the emergence of the sort of local decision-making which involved only a narrow group, permitted no discussion and no criticism. Zhdanov called this "cronyism" (*semeistvennost'*). Stalin called it "collusion,"[92] asserting that:

> instead of a leadership group of top workers, we had a small family of close friends, . . . the members of which were careful to live in peace . . . , not to air their dirty laundry, to sing each other's praises, and from time to time, send the center nause-ating and contentless reports of "successes."[93]

Neither Stalin nor other central leaders directly equated this "collu-sion" with oppositionist activity. Rather, as Zhdanov put it, it was the "scandalous lack of attention to Party work which aided the penetration of hostile elements into leadership posts."[94] But the distinction was exceedingly fine. Before 1937, it had not been difficult to distinguish between the "struggle against bureaucratism" and the "search for enemies." The former addressed the problem of bureaucratic "inertia," the latter focussed on the activities of "elements" hostile to the regime.

But as economic problems had split local officialdom against itself and provoked an avalanche of accusations, denunciations and incriminating information, it had become impossible to tell who was an "enemy" and who was a mere "bureaucrat." According to Zhdanov's formulation, "bureaucrats" had aided the penetration of enemies into leadership posts, but how was one to tell if their promotion was by oversight or by design? The central leadership could not, and did not, limit its response to an NKVD round-up of enemies. Rather, the solution promoted by the plenum was a campaign of "self-criticism." Officials from the factory floor to the Central Committee were encouraged to criticize their own "mistakes" – and those of others. In essence, the central leadership promoted the continuation and intensification of the flow of denunciations in the apparatus.

At the Central Committee plenum, regional leaders were compelled to rise to the podium and admit to their "errors." When they returned home, they were expected to organize similar meetings at all levels of the apparatus. The result of these meetings was a new wave of denunciations.[95] Purges and arrests affected every regional organization from the factory cell to the *obkom* – and especially the *obkom*.

By the end of May, the majority of members of the Sverdlovsk *obkom* had been denounced and were under arrest in the custody of the NKVD. Details of the regional coping strategies, including the faking of production reports, the *obkom* "slush fund," and the subversion of central policy initiatives, as well as information on disastrous construction projects – the fact that Urals coal could not be used for metallurgy, that ore reserves had been exaggerated, that billions of rubles had been invested on false pretenses – was communicated via the NKVD to the central leadership. Rather than clarify who were the enemies and who were mere "bureaucrats," the self-criticism campaign and the arrests it provoked created the impression of a colossal conspiracy against the regime.

The decimation of the regional leaderships in the summer of 1937 initiated a second, new phase of the Terror. The NKVD became more active, arrests more indiscriminate and summary execution commonplace. The central leadership was panicked that in the event of war with "the fascists," legions of internal enemies would join with them against the Soviet Union.[96] The sense of panic was reinforced by a consistent decline in industrial output. The decline followed not only from a further decrease in central investment, but also from massive arrests among economic managers and the unwillingness of those who replaced them to take initiative for fear that they too would be arrested. Moscow made no attempt to control the use of denunciation. Terror was pursued with a sense of urgency. As Molotov put it: "The danger of opposition was so great ... [and] there was not enough time ... "[97] Each arrest provoked others as NKVD officials followed the threads of "conspiracy." As the use of terror grew in ferocity and momentum, the idea of conspiracy was mythologized and detached from the original "crimes" of regional leaders, "crimes" which were provoked not by opposition to the regime, but by a need to cope with economic plans which could not be fulfilled.

Though there was no criminal plan of action or inter-regional collusion, regional leaders did resist central policy and did deliberately misrepresent the state of regional economies in their reports to Moscow. It was the only way they could cope with plans that made demands beyond the regions' economic capacity. Central leaders had told them that there could be no discussion, no excuses for anything other than complete fulfillment. Because they were not permitted to cite "objective reasons" for economic problems, they had to find local scapegoats when crises and scandals emerged. As plans became more demanding and regional economic capacities failed to keep pace, the tendency to shift blame increased, as did the issuing of misleading reports and resistance to central policy.

These coping mechanisms ultimately proved to be self-destructive. Misleading and self-congratulatory reports led to conflicts among mutually reliant industries. Scapegoating was successful on a small scale, but its widespread use created explosive resentments. In 1936, when underfulfillment could no longer be masked, tensions flared. As Moscow attacked what it thought was "bureaucratism," the seams of something more sinister – "conspiracy" – became visible. The call by the Central Committee to round up former oppositionists was the match to the powderkeg. The regional leadership could not control the explosion of tensions in the Party and state organs. The more the resulting accusations and denunciations revealed about economic problems, the more Moscow encouraged them. But the center did not stop even when the regional coping mechanisms had been exposed. Scapegoating had always involved labelling the victim as "saboteur," "wrecker," "alien element" or "oppositionist." Because Moscow had not accepted "objective reasons" for economic problems, denunciations were couched in these terms. The Terror raged on long after the "conspirators" had been arrested and shot, because Moscow was chasing labels. People can be arrested and shot. Labels are more durable.

NOTES

This article is a condensed and edited version of chapter 6 of James Harris's book, *The Great Urals: Regionalism and the Evolution of the Soviet System* (Ithaca, NY, 1999). It is published with permission of Cornell University Press.

1 James R. Harris, *The Great Urals: Regionalism and the Evolution of the Soviet System* (Ithaca, NY: Cornell University Press, 1999).

2 J. Arch Getty, *The Origins of the Great Purges: The Soviet Communist Party Reconsidered, 1933–1938* (Cambridge, 1985), 63; Graeme Gill, *The Origins of the Stalinist Political System* (New York, 1990), 262. Note that the formal reviews of Party membership known as *chistki* should be distinguished from the terror of 1936–8, known in English as "the Great Purges."

3 *Pravda*, 7 August 1936, 1; 13 August 1936, 1.

4 The statements of Urals leaders, given under NKVD interrogation, were the main source of the center's impression of conspiracy. The transcripts of these interrogations, currently held in the FSB archive in Ekaterinburg (Gosudarstvennyi arkhiv administrativnykh organov Sverdlovskoi oblasti, or GAAO SO) are one of the main sources used in this chapter. Such a source must be approached with extreme caution. Given the brutality of NKVD methods and its propensity to demand confessions to imaginary crimes, the initial impulse of the researcher is to assume that the transcripts represent the ideas of the interrogators, rather than of the interrogated. This, however, seems to be much more true of interrogations from the summer of 1937 than those from an earlier period (the fall of 1936 to the spring of 1937), which are the only ones employed in this chapter. Before the summer of 1937, NKVD questions were relatively broad and open-ended. The statements are plausible in commonsense terms and can often be verified against other credible sources; those interrogated were not under the same pressure as later to "confess" to fantastic charges such as spying for foreign governments or plotting the assassination of Soviet leaders. Of course, even the early interrogations featured forced confessions: the transcripts generally begin with an initial denial of "membership in an underground Trotskyist organization" and proceed days or weeks later to a confession of such. Once this "confession" had been made, though, "Trotskyism" became a vague label, a frame, for the description of concrete events and actions: hostilities with co-workers, the masking of poor results and so on; and revelations sometimes surprised NKVD interrogators (see, for example, GAAO SO, f. 1, op. 2, d. 22861, l. 113). It was not until some time in the late spring of 1937, as the number of arrests accelerated, that the NKVD appears to have ceased its investigations and simply demanded confessions that conformed to a sort of "master-text" that it had developed.

5 Eugene Zaleski, *Stalinist Planning for Economic Growth, 1933–1952* (Chapel Hill, N.C. 1980), 108.

6 For a selection of other regional criticisms of planning institute projections in 1933, see Rossiiskii gosudarstvennyi arkhiv ekonomiki (RGAE) f. 4086 Glavnoe upravlenie metallurgicheskoi promyshlennosti (GUMP), op. 2 Obshchaia dokumentatsiia, d. 684, General'nye smeta kapital'nogo stroitel'stva GUMP'a s prilozheniiami ekspertnykh zakliuchenii, ll. 412–51; for an example from the Urals, see Gosudarstvennyi arkhiv Sverdlovskoi oblasti, f. 241–r Oblplan, op. 1 Prezidium d. 879 Osnovnye problemy razvitiia promyshlennosti vo vtoroi piatiletke, l. 48.

7 Top central leaders made no secret of transportation problems in their speeches to the Seventeenth Congress. For comments by Stalin and Molotov, see *XVII s"ezd vsesoiuznoi kommunisticheskoi partii (b), stenograficheskii otchet* (Moscow, 1934), pp. 26, 362–3. For more detail on this issue, see E.A. Rees, *Stalinism and Soviet Rail Transport, 1928–1941* (New York, 1995).

8 GAAO SO, f. 1, op. 2, d. 43927 Delo Volkova, Mikhaila Semenovicha, ll. 62–4; d. 43935 Delo Anitova, Sergeia Ivanovicha.

9 A similar scenario was played out in the Urals copper industry, where geological surveying teams were compelled to fake results on reserves in order to

garner a potential billion rubles of investment that might otherwise have gone to Kazakhstan. GAAO SO f. 1, op. 2, d. 22861 Delo Sedasheva, l. 33.

10 Rossiiskii tsentr khraneniia i izucheniia dokumentov noveishei istorii (RTsKhIDNI), f. 17 Tsentral'nyi komitet, op. 2 Plenumy, d. 514 Stenogramma plenuma Tsentral'nogo komiteta VKP(b), ianvaria 1933 g., l. 111.

11 *XVII s"ezd*, 33.

12 The complaints of Stakhanovites had already resulted in the purging of the labor organization department of the Trust. RGAE, f. 8034 Glavtsvetmet, op. 1, d. 839 Stenogramma soveshchaniia aktiva tresta "Uraltsvetmeta" po voprosam organizatsii truda i Stakhanovskogo dvizheniia na predpriiatiiakh tresta, 20 oktiabria 1935, l. 214.

13 Joseph Berliner, *Factory and Manager in the USSR* (Cambridge, Mass., 1957), chs. 6–10.

14 Under interrogation after his arrest during the Great Purges, Kabakov suggested that they were trying to embarrass the regional leadership as part of a plan to take over the *obkom*. GAAO SO, f. 1, op. 2, d. 17368 Delo Kabakova, ll. 29–30.

15 The Commissions for Party and Soviet Control (KSK and KPK), created to replace the Workers and Peasants Inspectorate (Rabkrin), were given the power to remove "any responsible official up to and including members of the Central Committee" by the Seventeenth Party Congress in early 1934. *XVII s"ezd*, 35. Their work is described in greater detail below.

16 GAAO SO, f. 1, op. 2, d. 17368, t. 1, l. 68; ibid., d. 22861, ll. 63–4, 174.

17 Ibid., d. 17368, t. 1, l. 68.

18 Tsentral'noe khranenie sovremennoi dokumentatsii (TsKhSD), f. 6 KPK, op. 1 Protokoly, d. 62 Zasedanie biuro, 21 aprelia 1936, ll. 92–124. This will be described in greater detail below.

19 GAAO SO, f. 1, op. 2, d. 17368, l. 70.

20 Ia.P. Ivanchenko refers to the drink-soaked banquets used to greet incoming central workers ("primenia[li] pri etom metody pyshnykh vstrech, s obil'nymi popoikami"). GAAO SO, f. 1, op. 2, d. 22861, l. 174.

21 Ibid., d. 17368, t. 1, ll. 50–1.

22 The NKVD shared with members of the clique materials it received which could have proved dangerous to its members. Ibid., d. 22861, ll. 36–7; d. 17368, t. 1, l. 64.

23 Ibid., d. 17368, t. 1, l. 64.

24 Kabakov used the term. Ibid., l. 69.

25 Ibid., d. 22861, l. 46.

26 Ibid., d. 22947 Delo Zharikova, l. 80; d. 20017, l. 143; d. 22861, l. 29; d. 17368, t. 2, l. 254.

27 Kabakov claims that this tactic was used "more than once" with Uralvagonstroi, Sreduralmed'stroi and others. Ibid., d. 17368, t. 1, l. 62–3.

28 Ibid., d. 22861, l. 185 from the testimony of Ia.P. Ivanchenko.

29 For example, in 1934, after hundreds of millions of rubles had been spent to improve the production capacity of the plants of the Eastern Steel Trust, director Ia.P. Ivanchenko understood that the Trust was still years and millions of rubles from being able to increase production substantially. The clique conspired to promote a "reduced production plan" but the newspaper *Za industrializatsiiu* examined the Trust plan and made a scandal of it. Ivanchenko and Kabakov arranged to deflect blame onto the head of the production department, who was subsequently fired. Ibid., d. 17368, t. 2, ll. 268–9.

30 Ibid., d. 17368, l. 68.

31 Gill, *The Origins of the Stalinist Political System*, 214, 264–7; Getty, *Origins*, ch. 3; Gabor Rittersporn, *Stalinist Simplifications and Soviet Complications* (Chur, 1991), 42–4.

32 See, for example, Nobuo Shimotomai, "A Note on the Kuban Affair: the Crisis of Kolkhoz Agriculture in the North Caucasus," *Acta Slavica Iaponica* 1 (1983), 39–56.

33 The quotation is of Sergo Ordzhonikidze from early 1934. RGAE, f. 7297 NKTP, op. 38 Sekretariat, d. 104 Stenogramma vystupleniia t. S. Ordzhonikidze na zakrytom partiinom sobranii sotrudnikov NKTP SSSR ob itogakh raboty XVII s"ezda VKP(b), l. 1.

34 *XVII s"ezd*, 34–5.

35 TsKhSD, f. 6, op. 1, d. 7 Stenogramma vtorogo plenuma KPK pri TsK VKP(b), ll. 53–4.

36 Ibid., d. 62, ll. 92–124.

37 Ibid., d. 17, l. 121.

38 *Pravda*, 12 September 1934. ("Beri skol'ko khochesh', no tol'ko molchi.")

39 GAAO SO, f. 1, op. 2, d. 17368, t. 1, l. 102.

40 According to Sedashev, then the first assistant to the head of the Eastern Steel Trust, the key players in the cover-up were Kabakov, Chudnovskii (the chairman of the oblast Court) and Ivanchenko (head of the Eastern Steel Trust). Ibid., d. 22861 Delo Sedasheva, l. 38.

41 Ibid., d. 20017, ll. 15–16.

42 TsDOO SO, f. 4, op. 14 1936, d. 10 Stenogramma X plenuma obkoma VKP(b), t. 4, l. 13.

43 TsKhSD, f. 6, op. 1, d. 59 Zasedaniia biuro, 29 fevralia–3 marta 1936, l. 186.

44 GAAO SO, f. 1, op. 2, d. 17368, t. 1, l. 65.

45 *Tiazhelaia promyshlennost' SSSR za 1936* (Moscow, 1937), 12. Though the volume was bound, it was never publicly circulated. The front cover indicated in bold print that it was a secret document ("ne podlezhit oglasheniiu").

46 Roberta T. Manning, "The Soviet Economic Crisis of 1936–1940 and the Great Purges", in J. Arch Getty and Roberta T. Manning (eds), *Stalinist Terror: New Perspectives* (Cambridge, 1993) 129–33.

47 GAAO SO, f. 1, op. 2, d. 22329 Delo Davydova, l. 2.

48 Ibid., l. 2.

49 At the Urals Copper Ore Trust, reserves had declined from almost 10 million tons in January 1933 to barely over 2 million tons in January 1937. RGAE, f. 8034, op. 1, d. 1015 Prikaz NKTPa "O meropriiatiiakh po likvidatsii posledstvii vreditel'stva na rudnikakh Tresta Uralmed'ruda," l. 19.

50 GAAO SO, f. 1, op. 2, d. 17368, t. 3, ll. 272–3; d. 22861, l. 76.

51 Ibid., d. 22947 Delo Zharikova, l. 19.

52 Ibid., d. 17368, t. 3, l. 266.

53 Ibid., d. 22329, l. 15.

54 Ibid., d. 17368, t. 3, l. 282; d. 22861, l. 75.

55 *KPSS v rezoliutsiiakh*, vol. 6, (Moscow, 1984), 284–95.

56 Zaleski, *Stalinist Planning*, 243–6.

57 Gosudarstvennyi arkhiv Rossiiskoi federatsii (GARF), f. 7511 KSK, op. 1, d. 187 Protokoly, soveshchaniia dokladchikov i agitatorov, postanovleniia Prezidiuma Obl'IKov o khode obsuzhdeniia i realizatsii reshenii III plenuma KSK pri SNK, iiun'-iiul' 1936, l. 82.

58 RGAE, f. 8034, op. 1, d. 938 Stenogramma soveshchanii aktiva Trestov "Uraltsvetmet" i "Uralmed'ruda" po voprosam okhrany truda i tekhniki bezopasnosti na predpriiatiiakh trestov, 10 oktiabr' 1936, l. 7.

59 Ibid., ll. 28, 40.
60 Ibid., d. 149 Dokladnye zapiski, telegrammy, perepiska obkoma s Tsentral'nym Komitetom i Narkomatami o sostoianii i razvitii chernoi i tsvetnoi metallurgii l. 21–3.
61 Ibid., ll. 26–9.
62 Ibid., d. 22861, ll. 33–4, 68; d. 22329, ll. 24–5.
63 They did not criticize him openly because Shakhgil'dian and Kabakov were known to be the "closest of friends." GAAO SO, f. 1, op. 2, d. 22861, l. 42; d. 17368, t. 3, l. 75.
64 In his suicide note, *obkom* second secretary K.F. Pshenitsyn noted that Kabakov and *obkom* secretary M.V. Kuznetsov "were always conducting intrigues against me." TsDOO SO, f. 4 *obkom*, op. 24 Lichnye dela, d. 1888 Delo Pshenitsyna, Konstantina Fedorovicha, ll. 15–20.
65 K.G. Sedashev described how, in the spring of 1937, the NKVD had accumulated a substantial body of materials on him, but Kabakov was afraid to act. "Kabakov couldn't ignore the materials of the NKVD, but on the other hand, he was afraid of me." GAAO SO, f. 1, op. 2, d. 22861, ll. 44–5.
66 In its commentary on the trial, *Pravda* noted that the accused "have no social base in the country and cannot have any serious number of supporters." *Pravda*, August 13, 1936, August 15, 1936.
67 David L. Hoffman, "The Great Terror on the Local Level: Purges in Moscow Factories, 1936–1938" in *Stalinist Terror*, 163–5. The date of the Central Committee's letter was July 29, 1936.
68 RGAE, f. 8034, op. 1, d. 903 Perepiska s Trestom "Uraltsvetmet" o prichinakh neudovletvoritel'noi raboty obogatitel'nykh fabrik, l. 1.
69 Ibid., d. 899, ll. 9, 11–2, 14–24; d. 903, ll. 41, 42, 56, 108–15.
70 Ibid., d. 899, l. 1.
71 Ibid., d. 903, l. 115.
72 TsKhSD, f. 6, op. 1, d. 103 Zasedaniia partkollegii, 23 marta–15 maia 1935, ll. 28–-30.
73 Ibid., d. 138 Informatsii, dokladnye zapiski obkoma, gorkomov o khode obsuzhdeniia materialov protsessa nad Trotskistko-Zinov'evskoi gruppoi. Spiski iskliuchennykh v khode obsuzhdeniia, ll. 35–6.
74 Ibid., l. 38.
75 Ibid., l. 36.
76 Ibid., ll. 59–67. GAAO SO, f. 1, op. 2, d. 20017, l. 1.
77 Ibid., d. 22947, l. 52: d. 20017, l. 131.
78 Typically, judging by the NKVD archival materials from the fall of 1936 which I have studied, four or more independent denunciations on a given individual led to his arrest. The accused was confronted with this material at the beginning of his interrogation.
79 The removal of Reshetov immediately followed the replacement of Iagoda by Ezhov as commissar of the NKVD. Arch Getty has suggested that the September 1936 explosions at the Kemerovo mines provoked the change (Getty, *Origins*, p. 126), but given the frequency of industrial accidents, this seems rather unlikely. It is possible that Ezhov used information he was receiving as head of the Commission for Party Control to discredit Iagoda and take over the NKVD. The Commission for Party Control had been much more aggressive than the NKVD in investigating denunciations and problems of industrial production in August and September (see reports of regional plenipotentiaries to the Commission for Party Control, July–October

1936: TsKhSD, f. 6, op. 1, d. 66) and, given the cosy relationship between the Sverdlovsk oblast NKVD and the *obkom*, this is not surprising.

80 Ibid., d. 17368, t. 1, l. 59.
81 Ibid., d. 22861, ll. 36–7.
82 Ibid., l. 37.
83 Ibid., d. 22862 Delo Striganova, Fedora Ignat'evicha, l. 23.
84 The interrogation process produced denunciations because of the refusal of interrogators to accept protestations that the accused "acted alone."
85 Ibid., d. 34606 Delo Fuksa, Mikhaila Isaakovicha, t. 2, l. 14.
86 Ibid., l. 17.
87 Ibid., l. 16.
88 Ibid., l. 3.
89 Ibid., ll. 18, 19, 42.
90 Ibid., d. 17368, t. 2, l. 133.
91 Ibid., l. 59.
92 RTsKhIDNI, f. 17, op. 2, d. 612, vyp. 1, ll. 6, 8. The Russian word, *sgovor*, implies collusion against a target, here presumably the state.
93 Ibid., vyp. 3, l. 93.
94 Ibid., vyp. 1, l. 6. The formulation can also be found in Stalin's speech d. 612 vyp. 3, l. 3 and *Pravda* articles on vigilance March 6, 10, 17, 1937.
95 Arch Getty describes the same process in Smolensk oblast in *Origins*, 149–53.
96 *Sto sorok besed s Molotovym: iz dnevnika F. Chueva*, (Moscow, 1991), 390.
97 Ibid., 399.

10

"SOCIALLY HARMFUL ELEMENTS" AND THE GREAT TERROR

Paul M. Hagenloh[1]

The "Great Terror" of 1937–38 in the Soviet Union has solidified in popular and academic memory as Stalin's attack on political and social elites. Early studies of the Terror concentrated on show trials of high-level party functionaries, while memoirs written by victims immortalized the picture of the Russian intelligentsia disappearing into the "whirl-wind" of Stalinist repression. Academic explanations of the Terror have duplicated this bias towards political causes and elite victims. Whether scholars emphasize Stalin's destruction of the old party leadership as the first step towards terrorizing the entire population or point to internal political conflict erupting into central attack on local officials (two posi-tions which arguably represent extreme opposite tendencies in a previous generation's scholarly debates), they seek explanations in "political" events such as the Kirov murder, party purges across the 1930s, show trials of old Bolsheviks and real or imagined "oppositionists," and the purge of the armed forces in 1937.[2] Historians also generally agree on the trajectory of the Terror: from the repression of political dissidents in 1934, repression expanded to wider circles of elites and former elites, decimated the party and state apparatus, and eventually engulfed all layers of society. When we think of the "Great Terror," we think of polit-ical purges carried out by NKVD officers knocking on doors at night and arresting party members or intellectuals who had some stain on their past, who had been denounced by others (often for mercenary ends), or in many cases who had the misfortune of being a political or social elite in the wrong place and at the wrong time.

This picture of the Terror is incomplete. The Terror was also the culmi-nation of a decade-long radicalization of policing practice against "recidivist" criminals, social marginals, and all manner of lower-class individuals who did not or could not fit into the emerging Stalinist system.[3] In August 1937 the Politburo provided local NKVD branches with arrest and execution quotas for broad categories of "marginals," including dekulakized peasants, ex-convicts, national minorities, and recidivist criminals of all types. The "mass operations of repression of anti-soviet elements" (as they were termed by contemporary officials) that followed were not tightly controlled political purges, but are best understood as chaotic, poorly planned, brutal police campaigns intended to eliminate the social by-products of the upheavals associated with collectivization and forced industrialization. Local officials, driven by the center to arrest and eliminate more and more "anti-soviet elements," in turn scoured local society for individuals who could be singled out and targeted. The targets were not only former Trotskyists, former Mensheviks, old Bolsheviks, and other disgraced elites, but also individuals who had been identified as "marginal" through previous contact with the punitive system – former kulaks, recidivist criminals, and ex-convicts.[4] These mass operations, responsible for most of the executions and incarcerations in 1937–38, were fundamentally separate in trajectory and scope from party, industry, and military purges taking place at the same time.[5]

This chapter brings the question of "marginals" to the forefront of debates about the Terror by examining the radicalization of regime policy and local police action against recidivist criminals and ex-convicts during the 1930s. I will focus in particular on changing definitions of "regular" as opposed to "political" offenders, including speculators, hooligans, violators of the internal passport system, and especially an expanding category of individuals termed "socially harmful elements." Police carried out increasingly repressive extra-judicial campaigns against these categories of regular criminals in the mid-1930s. Eventually, the term "harmful elements" became an omnibus definition of a "recidivist criminal" that provided police with the ability to bypass the judicial system altogether and purge urban areas of unwanted marginals on their own authority.[6] By the mid-1930s, local police forces were conducting constant purges of their bailiwicks of marginals and criminals of all types, attempting to quarantine their areas from "harmfuls" they believed were the cause of crime and public disorder. This radicalization of policing practice created the practical background for the mass operations against "anti-soviet" elements in 1937–38.[7]

Policing practices against "harmful elements," I argue, are a much stronger bridge between the period of collectivization, dekulakization, and forced industrialization, on the one hand, and the Terror, on the other, than are trends related to "political" repression (which, several scholars have convincingly shown, experienced a short period of "moderation," at least in terms of central policies, in 1934–35).[8] The vocabularies, the procedures and the classifications of targets that were employed in

1937–38 against marginal strata were a product of policing strategies earlier in the decade rather than of concurrent party purges. The "mass operations" were police operations involving both the security police of the NKVD and the regular police (the *militsiia*). Although direction came from the center, local police officials carried out the campaigns in the manner to which they had become accustomed when removing suspect populations from urban areas in the years that proceeded the Terror.

"Socially dangerous elements" and extra-judicial authority in the 1920s

The key to the radicalization of regime policy against marginals and recidivist criminals was the emergence in the mid-1930s of a broad category of offenders termed "socially harmful elements." The vocabulary of "harmful" and "dangerous" elements initially entered Soviet criminal justice in the 1920s via theoretical debates about the nature of the emerging Soviet legal system. The idea of basing penal sanctions on the level of "social danger" presented by an offender was central to radical conceptions of Soviet law. People's Commissar of Justice Krylenko, for example, campaigned in 1929 for the promulgation of a new criminal code with only three sections: socially harmful (*vrednye*), socially dangerous (*opasnye*), and especially socially dangerous crimes. Krylenko envisioned specific punishments only for the first category of offenses; people guilty of "dangerous" or "especially dangerous" crimes would be isolated from society until rehabilitated or shot.[9] Although reference to "dangerous elements" was adopted in a muted way in the 1926 criminal code, a Soviet jurisprudence based solely on "social danger" rather than on codified criminal law never gained enough support among regime officials to override the perceived need for a list of crimes and corresponding punishments.[10] Soviet criminal codes after 1926 did contain provisions that gave courts the right to sentence people not only for individual criminal acts but for past activities and present "connections with the criminal world." In practice, however, the idea of punishing individuals for the level of social danger they represented, rather than for the act of committing a defined crime, never became the basis of Soviet criminal justice.

The police, however, made use of their own definitions of "social danger" in extra-judicial sentencing in the 1920s with little regard to theoretical distinctions. During the Civil War and the first years of NEP, the political police (the OGPU) exercised the right to expel political opponents of the new regime as "socially dangerous elements."[11] With the onset of NEP, however, the definition of "dangerousness" began to change. Both the regular and the political police increasingly sentenced non-political offenders under the rubric of "socially dangerous elements," applying the term to recidivists guilty of crimes such as speculation, hooliganism, and banditry. In 1924, the USSR Central Executive Committee (TsIK) established a definition of "dangerousness" that would serve as the basis of extra-judicial sentencing for the rest of the decade. OGPU "Special Boards" (*Osoboe Soveshchanie*) were given the right to try and banish, exile, send to a concentration camp or expel from the USSR several categories of offenders, including those guilty of state crimes (articles 57–73 of the criminal code), counterfeiters and international smugglers, bandits, drug dealers, malicious (*zlostnye*) speculators, and finally:

> individuals deemed socially dangerous due to their past activities, in particular: those having two or more past sentences (*obvinitel'nye prigovory*) or four arrests[12] for suspicion of crimes against property or crimes against the individual and his dignity (*protiv lichnosti i ee dostoinstv*) (hooliganism, solicitation of prostitution, pimping, and so on).[13]

This working definition of "socially dangerous elements" as multiple criminal offenders became the most durable aspect of the Soviet police's extra-judicial sentencing powers. No matter what the fortunes of the OGPU/NKVD regarding "political" crimes (Article 58), they never lost the right to sentence "dangerous elements" in the Stalin period.

The concept of "socially dangerous elements" emerged in the extra-judicial practice of the NKVD and OGPU rather than in the legal organizations of the theorists who championed it. The term referred not to a vague group of various "internal enemies" or "former people" but to what police officials believed was a specific category of urban recidivist petty criminals with a specific kind of criminal past. This definition was elastic, and could be applied, with central sanction, to groups who did not necessarily meet the criteria of "recidivism" – for example, in the expulsion of suspect individuals from gold-producing areas in 1927, or the additional banishment of some 9,200 "dangerous" prisoners after their sentences ended in 1928.[14] These uses of the definition of "socially dangerous" to target specific groups of undesirables, however, were not the rule in the late 1920s. The number of individuals sentenced as "dangerous elements," furthermore, remained relatively low before the mid-1930s. In 1931, for example, the OGPU sentenced 7,457 "dangerous" individuals, identifying them as "declassed elements, professional thieves, and professional criminals,"[15] while the total number sentenced by extra-judicial bodies in 1931 was 180,696 and the total number "arrested" under the auspices of the OGPU, was 479,065.[16] The idea of automatic punishment for "dangerous" elements with past infractions underwent minor definitional changes in the following years, but until the early 1930s the basic outline of what constituted a "dangerous" element in police practice remained unchanged: an urban recidivist with contacts in the criminal underworld and a history of multiple offenses.[17]

By the end of NEP, the police had carved out an area of extra-judicial sentencing authority regarding recidivist criminals that would become a permanent part of the Stalinist police system. Although "dangerous elements" were neither central to policing practice nor to police officials' understandings of crime and public order in the late 1920s, the concept is crucial to the evolution of Soviet policing under Stalin. "Socially dangerous elements" became a flexible definition of a group of recidivist criminals who fell under the administrative jurisdiction of the police itself and for whom the accepted punishment was isolation from society, either by exile or sentence to the camps. This category would assume increasing importance in police practice as the political and social situation changed drastically at the beginning of the 1930s in the aftermath of Stalin's revolution from above.

"Socially harmful elements," petty crime, and public order in the 1930s

Use of the category "socially harmful elements" began to expand in roughly 1932, and by the end of 1934 was the most important element of policing activity in urban areas.[18] The growing importance of "harmful elements" in policing practice after 1932–33, and the connection between policing practices and the mass operations, must be understood in the context of changing trends in policing strategy, especially the growing propensity of the police to use the newly created passport system to enforce a social quarantine of major urban areas from criminal and marginal groups. These changes in policing strategies were driven by growing contradictions in the regime's attempts to reduce the administrative chaos characteristic of the years of collectivization, cultural revolution, and forced industrialization, and by the state's increasing inability to impose the sort of order demanded by central party officials. Moreover, the best approach to instilling order in Soviet society, was contested at all levels of the police and party hierarchies. Throughout the 1930s, the "moderate" vision of Soviet administration lost out to more radical measures when public and state order was at stake. The party leadership and the police themselves increasingly resorted to exceptional, campaign methods of policing that contradicted the overall ethos of "relaxation" in regime policy during the Second Five-Year Plan. The result was a paradoxical situation in which, while certain groups in the central leadership struggled to reduce arbitrariness in the criminal justice system, at the same time the leadership as a whole supported a gradual shift of punitive duties away from the justice system into the chaotic administrative competence of the police itself.[19]

Fitfully in 1932, and then more steadily in mid-1933–34, the regime took steps to reduce the arbitrariness and expansiveness of the repression that had accompanied dekulakization, collectivization, and forced industrialization. Expediency and efficiency in administration were the central goals of this process. For example, the well-known Instruction of May 8, 1933, which curtailed the abilities of the police to sentence suspects and ordered the release of some 400,000 internees in the overcrowded labor colony system,[20] came after an attempt two months earlier to shift some 200,000 inmates from the prison system to colonies and OGPU camps without releasing them, a measure that failed due to logistic and provisioning troubles and resulted in mass starvation of inmates en route to the camps.[21]

Local and central police officials, however, understood the end of the First Five-Year Plan not only as a step back from administrative radicalism but also as a "return to order": order in public spaces, order in the functioning of state administrative organs, and order in state economic institutions. Beginning in 1932–33, the regime responded to what it saw as outrageous deficiencies in public order (which were in reality social reactions to the upheavals of forced industrialization and collectivization) with a series of campaigns against violent crimes. In July 1933 the Politburo authorized the OGPU to execute individuals engaged in banditry in Western Siberian krai, and in August gave the same rights to OGPU officials in Ukraine, Belorussia, the Urals and several other areas.[22] In December 1933 the Politburo instructed the OGPU to "apply the highest measure of punishment (*vysshuiu meru nakazaniia*) to all participants in armed robbery" in Moscow. The same Politburo order instructed the OGPU to expel from Moscow all individuals who had two past convictions for property crimes or two past arrests for hooliganism to areas outside of Moscow oblast', and to send "beggars and declassed elements" to exile or concentration camps.[23] In March 1935 the Politburo ordered judicial and law-enforcement agencies in Moscow, Leningrad, and other urban centers to review "all cases of armed robbery (*grabezh s nasiliem*) . . . in abbreviated order (3–5 days), to shoot all street robbers and to publish notice in the press that such and such a robber, having committed a violent act, was sentenced to the supreme measure of punishment, and that the sentence was put into effect."[24] The Politburo subsequently expanded the operation to include some dozen large urban centers across the Soviet Union.[25] Central party and police officials understood the propensity of local police forces to "overstep" the intended boundaries of these sorts of campaigns against specific categories of offenders but preferred the dangers of overzealous police to high levels of disorder in public places and economic institutions.

This sort of wide-scale repression of serious urban crime did produce the results that police and party officials desired. "Serious" crimes, such as banditry, armed robbery, arson, and murder, decreased dramatically after 1933. Police officials believed that they had solved the problem of violent crime by the end of 1935, and to some extent they were right. According to repeated statements by police and party officials, urban violent crime was eliminated by about 1934–35; in one report, NKVD chief Iagoda crowed that the city of Chicago alone had more armed assaults and robberies in July and August 1935 than did all of the cities in the USSR combined.[26] In a speech to a conference of regional police chiefs in April 1935, Iagoda added to the picture with characteristic bluntness:

> The picture of crime, as you can see in the statistics from 1934, has changed sharply. The role of the old incorrigible (*materyi*) criminal has moved to the background, and this is natural, because the majority of them have been executed, or are now in camps. Today's criminal (hooligan, thief, robber) exists under the guise of a worker, a kolkhoznik, a student, a member of the Komsomol, etc.[27]

By mid-decade, these campaign methods of policing and maintaining order by social purging were no longer "exceptional" but had become the predominant form of policing practice in major urban areas. As regime officials struggled to impose "order" on state institutions and on urban landscapes upended by chaotic in-migration, they found that attempts to reform and improve the daily functioning of the police system in the early 1930s had not been successful enough to produce the level of effective, daily policing and control deemed necessary by the leadership for the smooth functioning of the new economic and state systems. As a result, central and local officials turned increasingly after 1933–34 to policies of mass campaigns, purges, and quarantine of important urban areas, making use of their own extra-judicial sentencing capabilities (against both "harmful elements" and passport violators) to purge urban areas of marginals and recidivist criminals that they believed threatened the workings and even the existence of the Soviet system.

Police made full use of the powers provided to them in the mid-1930s to sentence petty offenders extra-judicially and to bypass the struggling court system altogether. The number of individuals charged as "harmful" jumped dramatically after 1932–33 as the category began to emerge as a central part of policing practice. When the OGPU was abolished in 1934 and the all-Union NKVD created in its place, "harmfuls" were the only category of individuals that the "Special Board" of the NKVD retained the right to sentence extra-judicially. Sentencing authority was expanded in May of 1935 by the creation of local "police (*militseiskie*) *troiki*," three-man boards set up specifically to sentence "harmful" elements to up to five years penal servitude in camps.[28] Police used this limited sentencing authority liberally. Between June 1934 and November 1935 some 265,000 "harmful elements" were removed from major urban areas across the USSR, 75,000 of them from the cities of Moscow and Leningrad and their surrounding regions.[29] A different source suggests that roughly 120,000 "harmfuls" were sentenced internally by the police in 1935, roughly 141,000 in 1936.[30] Gabor Rittersporn, furthermore, has shown that "harmfuls" were the only category of offenders whose relative and absolute weights increased in the hard-regime camps between 1934 and 1936; in the latter year, they equaled the number of individuals in camps for "counter-revolutionary" crimes (103,513 and 104,826 respectively). Their numbers continued to climb, reaching 285,831 by 1939 (or 21.7 per cent of individuals in the camps).[31]

There was little chance that such "campaign" measures could have eliminated broad, low-level manifestations of disorder that were intrinsic to the emerging Stalinist economic and social system. Regime officials, of course, did not understand matters this way. The "return to order" envisioned by party leaders was incompatible with the range of behaviors that people had developed to survive in the social system forcibly created during Stalin's "revolution from above." As a result, party and local police officials expanded the definition of "harmful elements" to include persons whose criminal behavior they found threatening, thus blurring the distinction between petty criminals and the "harmful" category. This mixing of petty crime, especially speculation and hooliganism, with the category of "harmful elements" expanded the abilities of police to sentence individuals themselves and cemented the importance of the category in policing practice in the years preceding the mass operations.

Speculation, or buying and reselling scarce consumer goods for profit, became one identifying characteristic of "harmful elements" in the mid-1930s. By 1932, the party leadership viewed speculation as enough of a threat to the economic system to promulgate the drastic August 22 law, but implementation of this law took a back seat to the campaign against theft (the Law of August 7). Both laws, furthermore, were directed largely at crimes against food supplies. Definitions of speculation and tactics against it changed, beginning in 1934, however, as the NKVD and the Ministry of Finance began pressing for increased sanctions against small-scale urban speculators. Each agency had its own reasons for demanding action. The Finance Commissariat was concerned about the threat that small-scale speculation of consumer goods presented to the tax collection system, while police officials saw speculation at markets as one of the most uncontrollable instances of low-level crime and disorder.[32] Disagreements emerged as well about the exact definition of "speculation" as well. Police officials charged that justice bodies tended to charge only large-scale, organized speculators with suspect social pasts under the August 1932 law, and argued that petty speculators flooding markets with small amounts of consumer goods should be charged under the law as well.[33]

By mid-decade, the NKVD had gained the right to sentence petty speculators extra-judicially. The Politburo launched a campaign against speculation in 1934 that encapsulated the logic of extra-judicial repression used for the rest of the decade. Police officials arrested and "brought to responsibility" some 60,000 individuals for speculation in 1934, and in addition expelled 53,000 people from major cities that "did not have any defined employment, that gathered in markets, that speculated, but that were impossible to sentence according to the law of August 8, 1932."[34] In July 1936, the leadership ordered another campaign against speculation, this time complete with "a series of show trials" and an arrest quota. The NKVD was ordered to expel five thousand speculators over the course of the month of August from Moscow, Leningrad, Kiev, and Minsk.[35] During the campaign, the police sent a limited number of individuals to the courts but processed the majority internally. In these four major urban targets of the operation, from July 26 to September 1 courts sentenced 1,635 individuals for speculation and related crimes (Articles 107 and 150 of the Criminal Code), while police *troiki* sentenced 4,003. In other words, by the mid-1930s police sentenced speculators as "socially harmful elements" through their own extra-judicial apparatus (*troiki*), expanding and mixing definitions of "harmfuls" and petty criminals and increasing punitive pressure on them.

Definitions of the crime of "hooliganism" also mixed with definitions of "harmful elements" in the mid-1930s, expanding the types of petty crime that the police sentenced extra-judicially. By late 1934 and early 1935, violent crime in urban areas had reached what regime officials perceived to be "threatening levels."[36] Iagoda insisted repeatedly in the mid-1930s that the NKVD be provided with some measure of sentencing authority to deal with hooliganism, requesting as early as April 1934 that "hooliganism and knife-fighting be punished by incarceration in a concentration camp for 10 years" (a suggestion that party officials declined).[37]

The Politburo responded to the perceived increase in street violence not only by promulgating the well-known 1935 law increasing judicial penalties for hooliganistic acts and for the possession of certain types of weapons[38] but also by instructing local police to sentence hooligans as "socially harmful elements" through local police *troiki*.[39] In Serpukhov, in Moscow oblast, for example, the city police chief reported that in April and May 1935 the local police station sent 60 cases of hooliganism to the Special Board, compared to 75 cases sent to the city People's Court.[40] Specific orders to sentence hooligans in 1935 as "harmful elements," furthermore, meant that hooliganism became another identifying factor of "harmful elements" in the widespread campaigns against them in 1935–36.[41]

The passport system and social quarantine

The internal passport system provided the final arena for expansion of extra-judicial sentencing of regular criminals and radicalization of policing practices against them. The passport system is generally understood as an attempt to halt peasant migration to cities and to fasten peasants to newly created collective farms. In practice, the passport system was also a policing technique in urban areas, and by 1935 it was central to police efforts to maintain order in major cities. The passport system allowed police to identify and expel the "harmful" elements and criminals who they believed threatened public order. Passports became an integral part of the law-enforcement system by mid-decade, closely connected to the work of newly created constables (*uchastkovye inspektory*) and the residence registration system (*propiska*). The passport system, a quick and convenient way for police to expel offenders from major cities without even the formality of a hearing by a *troika*, added substantially to the extra-judicial arsenal of the police between 1933 and 1937.[42]

The initial passportization effort was a massive operation. Police issued over 12 million passports in 1933–34 to all residents of so-called "regime" locations (an ever-widening list of major cities such as Moscow, Leningrad, Kharkov, along with border zones and internal areas of particular state importance), plus just under 15 million in other urban "non-regime" localities. Several categories of individuals were refused passports in "regime" cities, including residents "not connected with industry or education or not carrying out socially useful labor," kulaks fleeing from the countryside, individuals who had arrived in cities after January 1, 1931 without an invitation to work or who, although they were presently employed, were "obvious labor shirkers (*letuny*) or have been fired in the past for disorganization of production," and *lishentsy* (disenfranchised persons). The OGPU also refused passports to individuals who "have served sentences of deprivation of freedom, banishment, or exile by sentence of a court or the Collegium of the OGPU [in accordance with a list of crimes provided by the OGPU] and also other anti-social elements who are connected to criminal elements." The list included not only all individuals who had been convicted of counter-revolutionary crimes, but all serious regular crimes and a slew of lesser ones, including bootlegging, speculation, and violent hooliganism.[43] The passport system, then, was intended to purge cities of not just peasants or *lishentsy* but of all manner of marginal and criminal individuals.

The initial distribution of passports was as chaotic as any other large-scale police operation in the early 1930s. "Oversteppings" (*peregiby*) were a common occurrence. Central officials complained that local police often refused passports to temporarily unemployed individuals because they were "not engaged in socially useful labor." Local police officials, acting with little guidance or control from the center, tended to expand the list of crimes that made individuals eligible for passports and routinely refused to give passports to people who had been arrested and tried but acquitted.[44] The initial refusal rates for passports were, however, surprisingly low. By August 1934, some 384,900 people had been refused passports, compared to 27 million issued (though police reports did note that masses of individuals who expected to be expelled from regime cities had fled without even applying for a passport).[45]

Police were given wide latitude to arrest and sentence individuals who refused to comply with the new passport regulations. In Moscow, police were instructed to "purge (*otchistit'*) Moscow of counter-revolutionary, kulak, criminal and other anti-soviet elements.[46] Special panels (*troiki*) were created to sentence individuals who refused to exit major cities. These *troiki* were authorized to carry out the following punishments: "minus 30," or prohibition from living in the thirty regime cities, for the unemployed or "labor shirkers and disorganizers of production"; up to three years of banishment to a special labor settlement for the second offense of "labor shirker," for violations of passport regulations, and for *lishentsy*, dekulakized peasants, or individuals with previous criminal records; or three years in a camp for repeat criminal offenders and "criminal and other anti-social elements."[47] Local police, in other words, were given wide prerogatives to eject "undesirables" from their areas as they implemented the passport system.

Extra-judicial repression, however, was relatively limited in the initial months of passportization: 40,332 violators were apprehended in the city of Leningrad by April 1934, of whom 18,051 were expelled on order of the police and 16,055 were sent to the OGPU *troika* for sentencing.[48] Most individuals who were condemned by OGPU passport *troiki* were "unemployed, not engaged in useful labor" or "criminal elements." *Lishentsy* made up relatively few of the sentences (probably because they wisely fled of their own accord).[49] Police officials reported that the population growth of Moscow had been halted. By January 1934 the Moscow population was 3,613,000, compared to 3,663,000 in 1933 and 3,135,000 in 1932. Leningrad reported an overall reduction of 176,000 people in the course of 1934.[50] On the whole, the passportization process resulted in massive flight from major cities but involved less overt repression, in the form of sentences to labor camps or colonies, than other police operations of the early 1930s.

Once passports had been issued, the number of convictions for passport violations climbed steeply as police began to use the system as a policing tactic. An August 1934 report notes that in support of the passport regime the police had carried out 603,917 searches of apartment buildings and seized 630,613 violators of the passport system; 65,661 violators, the majority of whom were "declassed and criminal elements," were sentenced in extra-judicial proceedings, while 3,596 were sent to courts for trial, 175,627 were ejected from passportized areas by administrative order of the *militsiia* (without even the formality of a sentence by a *troika*), and 185,080 were fined.[51] In 1935 the police reported a total of 1,370,000 violators of the passport regime, of whom 944,000 were fined and 90,000 were sent to courts.[52] Procuracy reports from Leningrad and Moscow for 1935 state that the vast majority of people prosecuted for passport violations in that year were sentenced by the police *troiki* rather than by the court system, and that "the overwhelming majority of violators of the passport regime [were] subjected to internment in concentration camps as a measure of punishment." The majority of people so sentenced were identified as "kulaks, *lishentsy*, criminal elements and people not occupied with socially useful labor (beggars, prostitutes, etc.)."[53]

The passport system was also used to gather compromising information to help identify and expel repeat offenders in the future, a task that would assume greater importance during the Terror as local officials searched for ways to identify and arrest "anti-soviet elements."[54] Every individual who lived in a passportized location was required to register his or her passport with the police.[55] Each police station kept card catalogs of passports issued under its jurisdiction. In 1934, central officials ordered local police administrations to compile card catalogs of all people who had been refused a passport or ejected from a particular city.[56] Central police officials also created master lists of all individuals who had fled prosecution or incarceration. Policing urban areas thus would become – in theory at least – a simple and rational process of checking passports against lists and card catalogs to see if the individual in question was a criminal. The expectations of the police leadership for this passport and catalog system were enthusiastic to the point of irrationality. Central officials believed that if the system were implemented correctly, cities could be effectively purged of all "alien" and "harmful" criminal elements and crime would disappear completely.

The passport system, however, was no more effective at imposing broad social order and smooth functioning of the social system than other policing strategies. As early as November 1934, central police officials reported that the sharp decline of urban populations that accompanied passportization had ended and that populations were growing again due to an influx of "undesirable elements." Central officials specifically blamed disorder on poor implementation of the passport system by local police administrations, making use of the charge, characteristic by this time, that all difficulties of law enforcement were caused by the failure of local policemen to follow central policies.[57] Central officials responded to continued social disorder by expanding the list of "regime" cities and expelling more and more individuals from them. By 1935 the list of regime cities had widened to include 120 locations (plus border zones).[58] By 1938 there were some 130 regime cities in the RSFSR alone and over 500 in the USSR.[59] Individuals living in these cities with previous convictions, either by courts or by extra-judicial bodies, were expelled as each city gained "regime" status.[60]

Not surprisingly, this movement of suspect individuals created panic among police officials in non-regime cities. Police in these localities balked at the idea of accepting expellees from regime cities and often refused to issue passports to them.[61] Frantic requests by officials in cities "overrun by socially harmful elements"[62] for inclusion in the list of regime locations resulted late in the decade in a fundamentally untenable situation. The basic tactic of law enforcement was identification and expulsion of "dangerous" elements, but this system left these individuals nowhere to go. The result was a permanent class of mobile "expellees" who by definition could not be reintegrated into Soviet society and who were seen increasingly as the central cause of public disorder.

By mid-decade, police officials believed that most crimes were committed by recidivists and "harmful elements" and that constant sweeps and expulsions, supported by the passport system, were the best defense against these groups. Instructions to urban constables in 1936, for example, state: "The constable should proceed from the idea that every person without a passport, every non-registered person is already a suspicious individual, he has either committed a crime, or escaped from prison or a camp and is covering his tracks, or he is a person who is preparing to commit a crime."[63] Another circular from 1936 noted that "as a rule, in those places where [the police] do not struggle with socially dangerous elements and do not sentence them through *troiki* to camps, but limit themselves to various 'registration' measures and other driveling half-measures, robbery and theft exhibit constant growth." The same instruction tells all police bodies to sentence individuals who are charged with theft, and who have previous sentences, to camps through NKVD *troiki*.[64] By 1936 police instructions make explicit what had been largely implicit in police practice in the preceding years: recidivist criminals guilty of petty crimes with previous sentences were deemed "harmful" elements and should be sent by *troiki* to the camps.

Increasing administrative pressure on petty criminals was also accompanied by a redefinition of categories of "regular" versus "political" crime. The dividing line was hardly absolute during NEP, but began to collapse in earnest after the regular police (*militsiia*) was secretly subsumed under the political police in late 1930.[65] As the decade progressed, policing and sentencing strategies that differentiated between "political" and "regular" crime based on the class position of the offender gave way to a tendency to call all public-order or economic crime "counter-revolutionary." Iagoda, again, provides vivid illustration of this attitude, this time in a speech to regional police chiefs in 1935:

> For us the most honored matter is the battle with counter revo-
> lution – this is absolutely correct. But in today's situation, a
> hooligan, a bandit, a robber – isn't this the most genuine
> counter-revolutionary? ... In our nation – a nation, where the
> construction of socialism has been victorious, where there is no
> unemployment, where every citizen of the Soviet Union is
> presented with the complete possibility to work and live honor-
> ably, any criminal act by its nature can be nothing other than a
> manifestation of class struggle.[66]

By 1935–36, extra-judicial campaign strategies for dealing with petty crime had not only failed to halt low-level disorder in urban areas but had driven the Soviet system further and further from the sort of "order" desired by the leadership. Policing tactics based on social purging created and recreated larger categories of threatening "marginals" who, in the view of police officials, had to be removed from society.

The expanded abilities of the police to engaged in creative redefini-tion of criminal categories to their own advantage, combined with increasing fear among party leaders that crime and disorder were the result of inadequate protection of society from recidivists, tended to feed the cycle of increasing pressure on "marginals" and "harmfuls." This institutionalization of extraordinary measures was not the only option available to policy makers in the mid-1930s, nor was it the only policing strategy advocated by police officals. Early in the decade the police lead-ership attempted to create a functioning constabulary; voluntary "groups for assistance to the *militsiia*" and "night patrols" made up of demobi-lized army soldiers were available to aid policing; and some police officials proposed an increase in the covert, "operative" activity of the *militsiia* to prevent regular crime and disorder.[67] Local police officials complained throughout the 1930s that none of these other tactics was particularly effective, but they did tout the positive results of expulsions. Central officials, in turn, increasingly acceded to expulsion and quaran-tine after 1934. The inescapable contradiction inherent in this set of policies was that expelled individuals were defined as incompatible with Soviet society and yet had to go somewhere. Although this combination of developments did not lead inexorably to mass repression, the whole explosive mess certainly created and recreated the necessary conditions for more radical solutions to the problem of "dangerous elements" and "marginalized" populations in general. This volatile mix of categorization, extra-judicial repression, fear of low-level disorder, and purges of urban marginals forms the basis for the "mass operations" of 1937–38.

The mass operations

The pressure on "recidivists" continued right up to the launching of the mass operations. In April 1937 Ezhov, the head of the NKVD, sent an appeal to Molotov at the USSR Council of People's Commissars (*Sovnarkom*), arguing that the "fundamental contingent" of offenders committing "brazen crimes" (*derzkie ugolovnie prestupleniia*) consisted of repeat offenders who had recently been released from penal institutions. Ezhov requested that the trade unions set up work programs to streamline the transition to the workforce of the roughly 60,000 individuals who were being released per month because they had served out their sentences, and ominously asked that the NKVD be accorded the right to sentence individuals who had served their time but were "unrehabilitated" to an additional three years in the camps.[68] A *Sovnarkom* commission debated the measure for several months. Vyshinskii objected strenuously to Ezhov's suggestion regarding *troiki*, and on July 1, 1937 the commission agreed to create a work program but refused to give NKVD *troiki* in camps the right to sentence prisoners to an additional three-year sentence. The commission sent a draft recommendation and an explanatory note to Molotov on July 2, 1937, the very day Stalin issued the Politburo order that authorized the mass operations.[69]

The present state of knowledge about the practical implementation of the "mass operations" is exceedingly fragmented, due in most part to lack of access to documents in state, party, and security-service (FSB) archives. Based on what we do know, however, the mass operations resemble police sweeps of "harmfuls" in the mid-1930s, or of "former" people in Leningrad after the Kirov murder, rather than the party purges or purges of industry that were taking place at the same time. On July 2, 1937 the Politburo ordered local party leaders to present estimates of the numbers of "kulaks" and "criminals" that they wished to repress in their jurisdictions. Local officials responded by presenting separate estimates of numbers of "kulaks" and "criminals" to be exiled or shot.[70] The relative weight of each category depended on local circumstances. The Moscow Party Committee initially informed the Politburo that some 2,000 kulaks and 6,500 criminals (*ugolovniki*) should be shot, and 5,869 kulaks and 26,936 criminals should be exiled. The party leadership of Western Siberian krai sent in estimates of 6,600 kulaks and 4,200 criminals to be executed (with no initial estimate of exiles).[71] From there, the mass operations spiraled into continuous arrests of "anti-soviet elements" by

brigades of NKVD operatives who were assigned to work a specific operative area (*sektor*) and fill arrest quotas (quotas which were overfulfilled
many times over during the course of the campaigns). The notorious
"special *troiki*" created for the mass operations then processed the cases,
and the NKVD carried out punishments summarily.[72] Denunciation and
interrogation were generally not the bases of these operations; rather,
individuals were selected due to elements of their biography that had
been collected in some way during the previous years, both by the secret
police and by local passport authorities. Operations in rural areas may
have relied more on party meetings and denunciation due to the fact
that the NKVD operatives were outsiders coming into a particular area
to carry out a campaign, but in urban areas the operations were much
more self-contained.[73] Police (*militsiia*) *troiki*, furthermore, continued to
sentence "harmfuls" to five-years of exile or camp sentences throughout
the period of the mass operations, and were abolished only in November
1938 when the entire process was called off by the Politburo.[74]

Additional evidence regarding implementation of the mass operations
campaigns comes from the attempts of local police officials to justify
their actions after the change of leadership in late 1938. For example,
the assistant chief of the Saratov police administration, while explaining
his involvement in the arrest and execution of a particular individual
who was picked up for no specific crime but had three past sentences
for hooliganism, noted:

> among other work in 1937 we carried out a cleansing (*ochistka*)
> of the city and the oblast of criminal elements according to the
> NKVD Order No. 447 [the July 1937 order that launched the
> mass operations]. It is necessary to note that not only did neither
> I nor my subordinates read Order No. 447 itself, but we did not
> even see it, but we fulfilled the written and oral orders, with
> references to the Order, that the head of the oblast NKVD gave
> to us . . . The basic instruction was to produce as many cases as
> possible, to formulate them as quickly as possible, with
> maximum simplification of investigation. As regards the quota
> of cases, [the NKVD chief] demanded [the inclusion of] all those
> sentenced and all those that had been picked up, even if at the
> moment of their seizure they had not committed any sort of
> concrete crime.

The assistant *militsiia* chief continued by outlining the extra-judicial sentencing process during the mass operations. Cases regarding criminals
from all areas of the region were sent to the Criminal Investigations
Department of the *militsiia*, complete with their preliminary investigations, where they were prepared for review, approved in batches, and sent

to the *troiki* for adjudication. The cases in question here were "regular" criminals, although it is impossible to tell whether they were sentenced by the *troiki* as "politicals." The individual whose arrest led to the investigation of the Saratov police chief, for example, was a worker who had been sentenced three times in 1935–6 for hooliganism and had "failed to sever connections with the criminal world", by which his accusers meant that he was seen "cavorting drunk in public with unknown criminal elements." The criminal elements remained unknown, but this unfortunate individual was still shot as a "socially dangerous element."[75]

The radicalization of policing practice against recidivist "regular" criminals was obviously not the only aspect of state terror at the end of the 1930s. In particular, national minorities, were the targets of several campaigns late in the decade that intertwined with and expanded the scope of the mass operations.[76] Dekulakized peasants who had managed to flee resettlement camps and survive unnoticed or unprosecuted until 1937 were also targets in 1937–8. The party purge and "vigilance" campaign in industry were part of the process as well. But now that we know that the majority of those sentenced in the Stalin period were not sentenced for "political" crimes (Article 58),[77] it is important to begin dissecting the process that led to masses of people being sentenced for "regular" crimes. The stated goals of the "mass operations" was the removal of marginal strata of the population from society. The process of criminalization and marginalization of these individuals across the 1930s is as important to understanding the Terror as analysis of Stalin's motives and high-level political activity.

Conclusions

This chapter has two main goals, a modest one and a more challenging one. The modest goal is simply to bring investigation of "regular" crime into the discussion of extra-judicial repression and the Terror. Extra-judicial repression was not directed solely at "political" offenders in the 1930s, nor was it carried out solely by the political police. Our overall picture of the decade should be one, not of two outbursts of state violence (collectivization and the Terror) separated by a period of relative calm, but of a period of violence against the countryside in the decade that began to wane just as state violence in urban areas against marginals and criminal began to expand, eventually spreading back to the countryside in the mass operations. The paradox that has vexed historians of the Soviet police and judicial systems – that Terror unfolded at the same time as Vyshinskii was promoting the reimposition of order in the criminal justice system – does not seems so paradoxical in this light. Vyshinskii indeed promoted regularization in the legal sphere, but as the police gradually gained more and more practical control over the sentencing of "regular" criminals, his shrill campaign against the ambitions of Iagoda and Ezhov became more and more superfluous. The Soviet criminal justice system in the 1930s may have exhibited, in Harold Berman's classic phrase, a "surprising degree of compartmentalization of the legal and the extra-legal," but this did not translate to compartmentalization of "political" and "criminal" offenses, and as the 1930s progressed, Vyshinskii's efforts notwithstanding, the justice system had less and less to do with the policing and punishment of either one.

The second goal of this chapter has been to trace the ways that extra-judicial police campaigns against regular criminals and "socially harmful elements" in the mid-1930s formed part of the context for the mass operations of 1937–38. While the pictures historians have of the party purge, of purges of elite "enemies" of the regime, and of the purges in Soviet economic institutions are reasonably well developed, we know little about the implementation of the mass operations. What we do know, however, supports the idea that these operations were carried out through sweeps of urban areas, checks of social backgrounds, and utilization of information gathered during passportization rather than on the basis of elaborate processes of denunciation, interrogation, and further denunciation. A twisted but identifiable line of continuity in policing practices runs from the 1920s through the urban purges of "harmful" elements in the mid-1930s up to the mass operations of 1937–38. The targets of the mass operations were not only those individuals directly and purposefully marginalized in the process of Stalin's "revolution from above" (*lishentsy*, dekulakized peasants, and former elites), but also included those indirectly marginalized as the result of forced industrialization, urbanization, and socialization of the economic system (speculators, hooligans, passport violators, recidivist criminals, and "harmful elements.") The mass operations had an internal logic of their own which was distinct from that of the concurrent party or industry purges, a logic not of "surveillance," denunciation and show trials but of mass arrests of previously identified social outcasts. The radicalization of police campaigns against "marginals" across the decade drove the Stalinist system towards increasing social bifurcation, increasing politicization of all crime, and the final attempt in 1937–38 to remove all "anti-soviet" elements from society altogether.

NOTES

This chapter, previously unpublished, is a revised version of a paper presented at the conference "Police and Security Services under Communist Rule," held at the Zentrum Für Zeithistorische Forschung, Potsdam, Germany, in May 1997, and at the annual conference of the American Association for the Advancement of Slavic Studies (AAASS), Seattle, November 1997. It is drawn from chapter 7 of the PhD dissertation that Paul Hagenloh is currently completing at the University of Texas at Austin entitled "Police, Crime, and Public Order in Stalin's Russia, 1928–1941."

1 Research for this chapter was supported by grants from the International Research and Exchanges Board (IREX), with funds provided by the National Endowment for the Humanities and the US Department of State, the Social Science Research Council (SSRC), and the University of Texas at Austin. None of these organizations is responsible for the views expressed. The author wishes to thank Joan Neuberger, Charters Wynn, Judy Coffin, and David F. Crew for guidance and support; Gabor Rittersporn and Thomas Lindenberger for incisive criticism at key points; and David Randall Shearer who has influenced and improved this project from its inception.

2 See J. Arch Getty, *Origins of the Great Purges: The Soviet Communist Party Reconsidered, 1933–1938* (New York: Cambridge University Press, 1985), and Robert Conquest, *The Great Terror: A Reassessment* (New York, Oxford: Oxford University Press, 1990). Roberta Manning's two contributions to *Stalinist Terror: New Perspectives* begin to challenge the idea that the Soviet regime was responding to purely "political" motives in launching the Terror. Manning nonetheless reverts to explaining the mass operations as an outgrowth of the concurrent party purge. Roberta Manning, "The Soviet Economic Crisis of 1936–1940 and the Great Purges," and "The Great Purges in a Rural District: Belyi Raion Revisited," in J. Arch Getty and Roberta Manning, eds, *Stalinist Terror: New Perspectives* (New York: Cambridge University Press, 1993).

3 Parallel stories can be told about economic crimes such as embezzlement (*rasstrata*) and abuse of power by state employees, about internal "political" enemies of the sort expelled from Leningrad following the Kirov murder, and about dekulakized peasants. Although campaigns against these groups are important to the evolution of regime perceptions of social disorder and threats to the Soviet state, they are not as important to the background of the mass operations as were "public order" crimes.

4 The best explanations of the mechanisms of the mass operations are Oleg Khlevnyuk, "The Objectives of the Great Terror," in Julian Cooper, Maureen Perrie, and E.A. Rees, eds., *Soviet History, 1917–53. Essays in Honour of R.W. Davies* (New York: St Martin's Press, 1995); Gabor Rittersporn, "'Vrednye elementy,' 'opasnye men'shinstva' i bol'shevistskie trevogi: massovye operatsii 1937–1938 gg. i etnicheskii vopros v SSSR," in Timo Vihavainen-Irina Takala, ed., *V sem'e edinoi* (Petrozavodsk, 1998), 99–122; and David R. Shearer, "Policing the Soviet Frontier: Social Disorder and Repression in Western Siberia During the 1930s," unpublished paper delivered at the AAASS in Seattle, WA, 1997.

5 For the a recent assessment of the scope of the Great Terror, see J. Arch Getty, Gabor T. Rittersporn and Viktor Zemskov, "Victims of the Soviet Penal System in the Pre-War Years: a First Approach on the Basis of Archival Evidence," *American Historical Review*, 98: 4 (October 1993), 1017–1049. My research suggests that the figures provided by Getty *et al.* of roughly 700,000 executions in 1937–38 are of the correct order of magnitude.

6 Throughout this chapter I will use the term "police" to refer to both the political police (the OGPU and later the NKVD) and the regular police (*militsiia*) in the 1930s. The *militsiia*, though separate from the political police in the 1920s, was taken over by the OGPU in late 1930. After the takeover, the OGPU(NKVD) leadership set policy for both branches of the policing system, and local *militsiia* officials were, in theory at least, under the direct control of local OGPU/NKVD administrations.

7 This chapter is based almost exclusively on archival documents, most from the State Archive of the Russian Federation (GARF), the Russian Center for Preservation and Study of Documentation on Contemporary History (RTsKhIDNI), and the Central State Archive of Moscow Oblast' (TsGAMO). The author would like to thank the patient and helpful staffs at all these archives. Collections used most extensively are GARF, fondy 9401 (OGPU–NKVD–MVD SSSR, 1922–), 9415 (Glavnoe upravlenie Militsii MVD SSSR, 1930–), 8131 (Prokuratura SSSR, 1933–) and 5446 (Sovet Narodnykh Komissarov SSSR, 1922–58, especially the incredibly useful Upravlenie Delami sections). Other archival collections will be identified the first time they are cited. Notes are limited to citations of items used in the preparation of this chapter.

8 See Gabor Rittersporn, "Extra-judicial Repression and the Courts: Their Relationship in the 1930s," in Peter H. Solomon Jr, ed., *Reforming Justice in Russia, 1864–1996: Power, Culture, and the Limits of Legal Order* (Armonk, New York: M.E. Sharpe, 1997); Peter H. Solomon Jr, *Soviet Criminal Justice Under Stalin* (Cambridge: Cambridge University Press, 1996), ch. 5; and J. Arch Getty, "The Politics of Repression Revisited," in *Stalinist Terror: New Perspectives*.

9 See the well-researched and generally excellent doctoral dissertation by Aleksandr Iakovlevich Malygin, "Gosudarstvenno-pravovoi status militsii RSFSR v period provedeniia Novoi Ekonomicheskoi Politiki (20–e gody)," Doktorskaia dissertatsiia iuridicheskikh nauk (Moscow: Akademiia MVD RF, 1992), 95.

10 Malygin, "Gosudarstvenno-pravovoi status," 85–87.

11 The individuals targeted by the OGPU in the early 1920s as "socially dangerous elements" tended to be political oppositionists, intellectuals, and artists, the core of the first wave of "expellees" from the new Bolshevik state. The causes of the shift in usage of the term in the early years of NEP are unclear. See George Lin, "Fighting in Vain: NKVD RFSFR in the 1920s," PhD dissertation, Stanford University, 1997, esp. 21–53.

12 The instructions stated that punishment was to be applied to individuals with four "*privody*," which meant seizure by a policeman whether or not a formal arrest was made.

13 Gosudarstvennyi Arkhiv Rossiiskoi Federatsii (hereafter GARF), fond 3316 (Tsentral'nyi ispolnitel'nyi komitet (TsIK) SSSR, 1922–1938), opis' 12, delo 29, listy 5–6. Hereafter all archival citations will follow the abbreviated format: GARF, f. 3316, op. 12, d. 29, ll. 5–6.

14 Malygin, "Gosudarstvenno-pravovoi status," 62, 101–103.

15 GARF, f. 8131, op. 37, d. 20, l. 41. These "dangerous elements" were sentenced to three years in a camp (for recidivists with 5–10 previous convictions), or to exile or banishment.

16 GARF, f. 9401, op. 1, d. 4157, l. 203. I am deeply indebted to Gabor Rittersporn for making this document available to me.

17 GARF, f. 9415, op. 3, d. 3, l. 143.

18 A shift of vocabulary took place at this time as well. The term "dangerous" elements gave way to "harmful" elements (*vrednye*), a shift that was unplanned, that did not initially entail any change in the criteria identifying these people, and that shows how far the usage of these terms had come from their theoretical meanings in the legal debates of the 1920s. Police instructions continued to identify "harmful" elements as those with multiple offenses for property crimes, and police continued to sentence them to exile, banishment, or labor camps. "Harmfuls" were increasingly seen as a specific,

separate category of offenders, and the terms "socially harmful element" (*sotsvrednye elementy, sotsvredniki* , or *"SVE"* in Russian) became a police short-hand for recidivist, intractable petty criminals who by definition could not be reintegrated into Soviet society. I use the term "harmful elements" here-after because it is predominant in the sources beginning in roughly 1932.

19 Peter Solomon shows that the party leadership's attempt to reduce arbitrariness was motivated not by political liberalism or any wish to create a "law-based" society but by the desire to "enhanc[e] enforcement and compliance." Solomon, *Soviet Criminal Justice under Stalin*, ch. 5.

20 Rossiiskii tsentr khraneniia i izucheniia dokumentov noveishei istorii (hereafter RTsKhIDNI), f. 17 (Politburo), op. 162, d. 14, ll. 76, 89–92.

21 See GARF, f. 5446, op. 15a, d.1073 for a series of documents on the process. Note that the archival record is unclear on whether all of these individuals were released or sent to resettlement camps (*trudposelki*) in Siberia and Kazakhstan. I presently believe the latter is true. RTsKhIDNI, f. 17, op. 162, d. 15, ll. 2, 14.

22 RTsKhIDNI, f. 17, op. 162, d. 15, ll. 2, 27.

23 RTsKhIDNI, f. 17, op. 162, d. 15, l. 161.

24 RTsKhIDNI, f. 17, op. 3, d. 961, l. 21.

25 RTsKhIDNI, f. 17, op. 3, d. 961, l .59; f. 17, op. 3, d. 962, l. 17. In the RSFSR, this campaign produced some 641 sentences by February 1935, including 352 death sentences, 261 which were carried out after review by higher courts. Tsentral'nyi gosudarstvennyi arkhiv (TsGA) RSFSR, f. 428 (Verkhovnyi sud RSFSR), op. 3, d. 17, ll. 1–2.

26 GARF, f. 5446, f. 18a, d. 904, l. 2.

27 GARF, f. 9401, op. 12, d. 135, document 119, l. 4.

28 Prikaz NKVD SSSR #00192 from 1935, which is recounted in detail in recent secondary sources on the police and referenced in procuracy documents in the 1930s, but which as yet is not declassified in Russia. See V.F. Nekrasov, *et al.*, *Organy i voiska MVD Rossii. Kratkii istoricheskii ocherk* (Moscow: Ob"edinennaia redaktsiia MVD Rossii, 1996), 258, and the procuracy report in Gosudarstvennyi Arkhiv Novosibirskoi Oblast, f. 20, op. 1, d. 220, ll. 32–3 (many thanks to David Shearer for a copy of this document).

29 GARF, f. 9401, op. 12, d. 135, document 147.

30 These figures, as with all figures from this period that western historians have been allowed to see in Russian archives, must be treated with great care. The exact figures for 1935 and 1936 are 119,159 and 141,318 individuals respectively identified as being sentence by *"troiki"* in 1935 and 1936. The report from which these figures are drawn was created in 1953 by the *nachal'nik* of the First Special Section of the MVD USSR to summarize the extra-judicial activities of the organs of state security during the years of Stalin's rule. The only *troiki* in operation in 1935 and 1936, however, were the *"militseiskie troiki,"* which were created in 1935 specifically to process cases of "harmful" elements and passport violators (categories which were completely intertwined by 1935) and which did not have the authority to hear political cases (which were heard by the *Osoboe Soveshchanie* in these two years). GARF, f. 9401, op. 1, d. 4157, l. 203.

31 Getty, Rittersporn, and Zemskov, "Victims of the Soviet Penal System," 1032., and Gabor Rittersporn, "Extra-Judicial Repression and the Courts: Their Relationship in the 1930s."

32 GARF, f. 5446, op. 15a, d. 1071, ll. 14–14ob, 57.

33 GARF, f. 5446, op. 15a, d. 1071, ll.16–20.

34 GARF, f. 5446, op. 15a, d. 1071, l. 16.

35 GARF, f. 5446, op. 57, d. 42, ll. 124–131, 164–166.
36 See the Procuracy report in GARF, f. 3316, op. 64, d. 1619, l. 39 for a typical formulation.
37 GARF, f. 5446, op. 15a, d. 1130, l. 4. GARF, f. 5446, op. 16a, d. 1270 contains a series of communications on the topic of policing and hooliganism.
38 See Peter H. Solomon Jr, *Soviet Criminal Justice under Stalin*, 224–225, for an account of the role of the court system in the anti-hooliganism campaign.
39 The NKVD issued a directive entitled "Ob usilenii repressii za khuliganskie deistviia" at roughtly the same time as the March 1935 law was promulgated. Unfortunately, I have no global statistical evidence regarding numbers of individuals sentenced extra-judicially under this directive. See TsGAMO, f. 792 (Gruppa Partiinogo i Sovetskogo Kontrolia pri Moskovskom Komitete VKP[b]), op. 6, d. 968, l. 125.
40 TsGAMO, f. 792, op. 6, d. 968, ll. 105, 126.
41 I will not deal with juvenile delinquency nor with "welfare cases" such as adult beggars and prostitutes in this chapter simply for reasons of space, though both were crucial categories of "marginals" and both were subsumed under the category "harmful elements" by 1935. The judicial campaigns against juvenile crime in 1935 were paralleled by an extra-judicial campaign. Beginning in 1935, homeless children over the age of 14 and who committed any crime (not just those included in the list that accompanied the March law) were the responsibility of the police (*militsiia*) alone. Police were authorized to send homeless juvenile offenders to labor colonies with neither a trial at court nor even a hearing by a *troika*. My research suggests that the number of juveniles processed by the police exceeds the number sentenced by courts in 1935–36. For a full account, see Chapter 4 of my dissertation, "Police, Crime, and Public Order."
42 For recent examination of the social as well as administrative logic of the passport system, see Nathalie Moine, "Passportisation, Statistique des Migrations et Contrôle de l'Identité Sociale" *Cahiers du Monde Russe* 38:4 (1997).
43 GARF, f. 9401, op. 12, d. 137, ll. 59–60. This list expands across the 1930s, becoming more restrictive as the decade progressed. It is beyond the scope of this essay to trace those changes, but I devote a dissertation chapter to the passport system.
44 GARF, f. 1235, op. 141, d. 1517, ll. 16–20ob.
45 GARF, f. 1235, op. 141, d. 1650, ll. 30.
46 GARF, f. 9401, op. 12, d. 137, ll.1–2, 200.
47 GARF, f. 9401, op. 12, d. 137, ll. 202–204.
48 GARF, f. 1235, op. 141, d. 1517, l. 22.
49 GARF, f. 1235, op. 141, d. 1517, l. 19; f. 1235, op. 141, d. 1650, ll. 6–26.
50 GARF, f. 1235, op. 141, d. 1650, ll. 27–29. Unfortunately, the report gives no suggestion of how many people were coming into the city compared with how many were leaving.
51 GARF, f. 1235, op. 141, d. 1650, ll. 27, 30–35.
52 GARF, f. 5446, op. 18a, d. 904, l. 10.
53 GARF, f. 3316, op. 64, d. 1619, ll. 79–80.
54 GARF, f. 5446, op. 15a, d. 1130, ll. 1–10.
55 This well-known *propiska* system became one of the hallmarks of Soviet urban administration.
56 See GARF, f. 9415, op. 3, d. 9, l. 43.
57 GARF, f. 9415, op. 3, d. 8, ll. 56–7.
58 GARF, f. 9401, op. 12, d. 135, document 146.

59 GARF, f. 9401, op. 12, d. 233, ll. 497–501. The proliferation of regime cities prompted a redefinition of the category in 1938, after which only the capital cities (Moscow, Leningrad, Kiev, and a few other locations) were off-limits to all offenders, while second-tier regime cities retained relaxed restrictions.

60 GARF, f. 9401, op. 12, d. 137, ll. 58–60.

61 GARF, f. 9401, op. 12, d. 137, ll. 51.

62 GARF, f. 5446, op. 20a, d. 946, ll. 73–74.

63 GARF, f. 9401, op. 12, d. 135, document 133.

64 GARF, f. 9401, op. 12, d. 135, l. 31.

65 For details on the collapse of the NKVD RSFSR, see Lin, "Fighting in Vain," 122–174.

66 GARF, f. 9401, op. 12, d. 135, document 119, esp. pages 2, 5.

67 See Paul Hagenloh, "Constables, 'Assistance Brigades,' and the Stalinist Police State in the 1930s," paper presented at the 1998 Convention of the American Association for the Advancement of Slavic Studies, Boca Raton, Florida, September 24, 1998.

68 GARF, f. 5446, op. 22a, d. 69, ll. 44–47.

69 GARF, f. 5446, op. 22a, d. 69, ll. 31–33; *Trud,* June 4, 1991, 1–4.

70 In other words, local police officials provided four separate estimates, one for each category. Tsentr Khraneniia Sovremennoi Dokumentatsii (TsKhSD) f.89, perechen' 73, dela 47–150 are all Politburo entries regarding orders sent to localities during the mass operations.

71 TsKhSD f. 89, p. 73, d. 49. *Trud,* June 4, 1992, 1. The mechanics of the decision to implement the mass operations are not the subject of this chapter. See Oleg Khlevnyuk, "The Objectives of the Great Terror," for the best published discussion of central directives about the campaign.

72 *Moskovskie Novosti* #25 (June 21, 1992).

73 See David R. Shearer, "Policing the Soviet Frontier."

74 For activities of the *militseiskie troiki* in 1937–38, see the memoirs of Mikhail Shreider: *NKVD iznutri. Zapiski chekista* (Moscow: Vozvrashchenie, 1995). Unfortunately, we have no sources that would allow us to separate the activity of the police troiki from that of the special during the mass operations.

75 All from GARF, f. 8131, op. 37, d. 131, ll. 36–39.

76 Khlevniuk, "Objectives of the Great Terror"; Rittersporn, "'Vrednye elementy,' 'opasnye men'shinstva,' i bol'shevistskie trevogi."

77 Getty, Rittersporn, and Zemskov, "Victims of the Soviet Penal System," 1033–1036.

Part V

NATIONALITY AS A STATUS

Nationality and ethnicity became exciting areas of study as a result of the collapse of multi-national states, the Soviet Union and Yugoslavia, the emergence of nationality-based successor states, and the outbreak of fierce ethnic conflicts in the Balkans and some parts of the former Soviet Union. This seemed to be a remarkable demonstration of the strength of national feeling despite seventy years of Soviet rule – or was it? It was certainly difficult to put this event in the category of popular revolutions fuelled by nationalist sentiment, which in a number of separating republics – and, for that matter, in the Russian Republic itself – was conspicuous by its absence. Journalistic accounts of the break-up of the Soviet Union and comparable events in Eastern Europe and the Balkans tended to talk in terms of age-old, primordial national hatreds. The tide of scholarly thinking, however, influenced by the work of Benedict Anderson, Eric Hobsbawm, Ernest Gellner, Rogers Brubaker, and others, was running strongly against ideas of primordial nationality and towards the notion of nationality as something socially and culturally constructed. In the Russian field, Ronald Suny, a social historian turned political scientist and specialist on the Caucasus, was in the forefront of this trend.

In the article reprinted here, Yuri Slezkine tells the strange story of how the Soviet regime, grounded as it was in a Marxist ideology in which nationalism was false consciousness, nevertheless fostered and promoted ethnic and national particularism. Slezkine (b. 1956) is a Russian-born scholar who emigrated to the United States in the 1980s and received his PhD at the University of Texas at Austin; his dissertation on Russian interactions with the "small peoples of the North" focussed on the construction of a notion of backwardness. In his "Communal Apartment" article, he outlined a deeply paradoxical situation. The Bolsheviks, internationalists for whom class was the "real" identity marker, ended up privileging nationality and encouraging national identities – or at least, in the early years, every kind of national

309

identity but Russian, for they feared the oppressive legacy of Russian imperialism ("great Russian chauvinism") *vis-à-vis* smaller nationalities. Over time, the regime's attitude to Russianness became warmer and they encouraged the idea of the Russians as a "big brother" in the Soviet family of nations. But the policy of fostering national cultures (Uzbek, Buriat, Armenian, and so on) and national territorial administrations remained unchanged, making nationality a key component in a Soviet citizen's identity and turning the Soviet Union, in Slezkine's term, into a "communal apartment" where each national "family" (or at least all the larger ones) had its own room.

The question of categorization raised by Slezkine – how the Soviet national territorial boundaries were drawn and ethnic classifications systematized – has been further investigated by several younger scholars, notably Terry Martin and Francine Hirsch, who focusses on the ethnographers' role. While Slezkine's study was based on published sources, since 1991 a whole cohort of dissertation writers has plunged into the former Soviet archives to elucidate national and ethnic questions. Peter Blitstein has worked on Stalinist nationalities policy and David Brandenberger on the emergence of Russian national ideology, both taking 1938 as their starting point. Amir Weiner and Jeffrey Burds have studied Ukrainian national problems in the postwar years; Matthew Payne, Paula Michaels, and Michaela Pohl work on Kazakhstan, Douglas Northrup and Marianne Kamp on Uzbekistan.[1] These studies are based on local (republic and oblast-level) as well as central archives, as is the interesting work of the young German scholar, Jörg Baberowski, on Azerbaidzhan. Along with regional studies like James Harris's on the Urals or Jonathan Bone's on the Far East,[2] they give us a picture of an infinitely more complex and variegated "Stalinism" than was usually recognized in the Russo-centric Soviet scholarship of the past. Baberowski's work on Soviet Azerbaidzhan in the 1930s, for example, describes astonishing mutations of central policies such as collectivization and the Great Purges as they were filtered through local culture and practice by local executants; the center's commitment to a Soviet "civilizing mission" was constantly frustrated in these culturally "backward" (especially Islamic) regions; and, as so often in Soviet history, frustration generated violence, both against and within national leaderships.[3]

The most ambitious of the dissertation-based nationalities studies is the work of Terry Martin (b. 1963) on Soviet nationalities policy in the period 1923–38. Based on a huge volume of previously unknown archival data, this study encompasses a wide range of topics including indigenization (*korenizatsiia*), affirmative action, territorial delineation, ethnic conflicts, the special position of "diaspora" nationalities, and the deportations of national groups (a practice which, contrary to previous scholarship focussing on the 1940s, first appeared as a practice in the

1930s). Martin proceeds from the same observation as Slezkine that the Soviet state, despite its Marxist objections to nationalism, was a great promoter of nationality and national identities. But he sharpens the contrast between the original Marxist premise that nationalism is false consciousness and the high Stalinist conversion to notions of primordial nationalism; and, using Ernest Gellner's theories about the relationship of nationalism and industrialization, sets out to find an explanation for the shift. For Martin, Soviet nationalism is an "ascribed" category, analogous to class in Fitzpatrick's analysis: one was officially identified as an Uzbek in one's passport, just as one was officially identified there as a kolkhoznik. That both these attributes came to seem "primordial" characteristics was in part a product of affirmative action policies (which operated in favor of "national minorities" as well as workers). Another contributory factor was the emergence in the 1930s of a new notion of "enemy nations," primordially understood and obviously analogous to the "enemy classes" that preoccupied the Bolsheviks in the 1920s. It was the "extreme statism" characteristic of Stalinism, in Martin's view, that led the Soviet state to substitute itself for tradition (for example, in its energetic sponsorship of folklores) and to deviate from Gellner's modernization model. "Modernization is the theory of Soviet intentions; neo-traditionalism, the theory of their unintended consequences," Martin concludes.

FURTHER READING

Brubaker, Rogers, "Nationhood and the National Question in the Soviet Union and Post-Soviet Eurasia," *Theory and Society* 23: 1 (1994).

Gelb, Michael, "An Early Soviet Ethnic Deportation: the Far-Eastern Koreans," *Russian Review* 54: 3 (July 1995), 389–412.

Hirsch, Francine, "Empire of Nations: Colonial Technologies and the Making of the Soviet Union, 1917-1939," PhD dissertation, Princeton University, 1998.

—— "The Soviet Union as a Work-in-Progress: Ethnographers and the Category Nationality in the 1926, 1937, and 1939 Censuses," *Slavic Review* 56: 2 (1997).

Kamp, Marianne, "Unveiling Uzbek Women: Reform, Liberation, and Discourse in Central Asia, 1906–1929", PhD dissertation, University of Chicago, 1997.

Massell, Gregory, *The Surrogate Proletariat: Moslem Women and Revolutionary Strategy in Soviet Central Asia, 1919–1929* (Princeton, 1974).

Martin, Terry D., "An Affirmative Action Empire: Ethnicity and the Soviet State, 1923-1938," PhD dissertation, University of Chicago, 1996.

—— "The Origins of Soviet Ethnic Cleansing," *Journal of Modern History* 70: 4 (December 1998).

Michaels, Paula Anne, "Shamans and Surgeons: the Politics of Health-care in Soviet Kazakhstan, 1928–1941," PhD dissertation, University of North Carolina at Chapel Hill, 1997.

Miller, Frank J., *Folklore for Stalin: Russian Folklore and Pseudofolklore of the Stalin Era* (Armonk, NY, 1990).

Motyl, Alexander J., ed., *Thinking Theoretically about Soviet Nationalities: History and Comparison in the Study of the USSR* (New York, 1992).

Northrup, Douglas, "Uzbek Women and the Veil: Gender and Power in Stalinist Central Asia," PhD dissertation, Stanford University, 1998.

Slezkine, Yuri, *Arctic Mirrors: Russia and the Small Peoples of the North* (Ithaca, NY, 1994).

—— "N.Ia. Marr and the National Origins of Soviet Ethnogenesis," *Slavic Review* 55: 4 (Winter 1996).

—— "Naturalists versus the Nation: Eighteenth-century Russian Scholars Confront Ethnic Diversity," *Representations* 47 (Summer 1994).

Suny, Ronald G., "Rethinking Social Identities: Class and Nationality," in Suny, *The Revenge of the Past: Nationalism, Revolution, and the Collapse of the Soviet Union* (Stanford, 1993).

Tillett, Lowell, *The Great Friendship: Soviet Historians on the Non-Russian Nationalities* (Chapel Hill, NC, 1969).

NOTES

1   Many of these were presented at a conference called "Empire and Nations: the Soviet Union and the Non-Russian Peoples," held at the University of Chicago, October 24–26, 1997, and will be published in a volume tentatively entitled *A State of Nations: Empire and Nation-Making in the Age of Lenin and Stalin* edited by Ronald G. Suny and Terry Martin.

2   See James Harris, *Regionalism and the Evolution of the Soviet System* (Cornell University Press, forthcoming); Jonathan Bone, "A la recherche d'un Komsomol perdu: Who Really Built Komsomol'sk-na-Amure, and Why," *Revue des études slaves*, forthcoming.

3   See his "Stalinismus an der Peripherie: Das Beispiel Azerbajdzan 1920-1941," in *Stalinismus vor dem zweiten Weltkrieg. Neue Wege der Forschung* (Stalinism before the Second World War: New Avenues of Research), ed. Manfred Hildermeier with Elisabeth Müller-Luckner (Munich, 1998); also "Stalinismus als imperiales Phänomen: die islamischen Regionen der Sowjetunion, 1921–1941," in Stefan Plaggenborg, ed., *Stalinismus: neue Forschungen und Konzepte* (Berlin, 1998), and "Kolonialismus and zivilisatorische Mission im Zarenreich und in der Sowjetunion, 1800–1941," in *Jahrbücher für Geschichte Osteuropas*, forthcoming.

11

THE USSR AS A COMMUNAL APARTMENT, OR HOW A SOCIALIST STATE PROMOTED ETHNIC PARTICULARISM

Yuri Slezkine

Soviet nationality policy was devised and carried out by nationalists. Lenin's acceptance of the reality of nations and "national rights" was one of the most uncompromising positions he ever took, his theory of good ("oppressed-nation") nationalism formed the conceptual foundation of the Soviet Union and his NEP-time policy of compensatory "nation-building" (*natsional'noe stroitel'stvo*) was a spectacularly successful attempt at a state-sponsored conflation of language, "culture," territory and quota-fed bureaucracy. The Lenin Guard duly brought up the rear, but it was Stalin who became the true "father of nations" (albeit not all nations and not all the time). The "Great Transformation" of 1928–1932 turned into the most extravagant celebration of ethnic diversity that any state had ever financed; the "Great Retreat" of the mid-1930s reduced the field of "blossoming nationalities" but called for an ever more intensive cultivation of those that bore fruit; and the Great Patriotic War [World War II] was followed by an *ex cathedra* explanation that class was secondary to ethnicity and that support of nationalism in general (and not just Russian nationalism or "national liberation" abroad) was a sacred principle of Marxism-Leninism.

If this story sounds strange, it is because most historical accounts of Soviet nationality policy have been produced by scholars who shared Lenin's and Stalin's assumptions about ontological nationalities endowed with special rights, praised them for the vigorous promotion of national cultures and national cadres, chastized them for not living up to their own (let alone Wilsonian) promises of national self-determination, and presumed that the "bourgeois nationalism" against which the Bolsheviks were inveighing was indeed equal to the belief in linguistic/cultural – therefore – political autonomy that the "bourgeois scholars" themselves understood to be nationalism. Non-Russian nationalism of all kinds appeared so natural and the Russian version of Marxist universalism appeared so Russian or so universalist that most of these scholars failed to notice the chronic ethnophilia of the Soviet regime, took it for granted or explained it as a sign of deviousness, weakness or negligence. This essay is an attempt to recognize the earnestness of Bolshevik efforts on behalf of ethnic particularism.[1] Uncompromisingly hostile to individual rights, they eagerly, deliberately and quite consistently promoted group rights that did not always coincide with those of the proletariat. "The world's first state of workers and peasants" was the world's first state to institutionalize ethnoterritorial federalism, classify all citizens according to their biological nationalities and formally pre-scribe preferential treatment of certain ethnically defined populations.[2] As I. Vareikis wrote in 1924, the USSR was a large communal apartment in which "national state units, various republics and autonomous provinces" represented "separate rooms."[3] Remarkably enough, the communist landlords went on to reinforce many of the partitions and never stopped celebrating separateness along with communalism.[4]

"A nation," wrote Stalin in his very first scholarly effort, "is a histor-ically evolved, stable community based on a common language, territory, economic life and psychological make-up manifested in a community of culture."[5] On the eve of World War I this definition was not particularly controversial among socialists. There was disagreement about the origins of nations, the future fate of nationalism, the nature of pre-nation nationalities, the economic and political usefulness of nation states and the relative importance of nations' "characteristic features," but everyone seemed to assume that, for better or worse, humanity consisted of more or less stable *Sprachnationen* [nations united by a common language] cemented by a common past.[6] Language and history (or *Schick-salgemeinschaft*/"community of fate," both the precondition and conse-quence of linguistic unity), were generally taken for granted; but even the more debatable items on Stalin's list were usually – if not always explicitly – considered legitimate. The Austrian Marxist theorist Otto Bauer, who attempted to detach nationality from territory, clearly assumed that the "community of fate" was ultimately the fate of a phys-ical community. Rosa Luxemburg, who believed that the "principle of nationality" contradicted the logic of capitalism, saw large, "predatory" nation states as tools of economic expansion. And Lenin, who rejected the concept of "national culture," routinely spoke of "Georgians," "Ukrainians" and "Great Russians" as having national traits, interests and responsibilities. Nations might not be helpful and they might not last, but they were here and they were real.

As far as both Lenin and Stalin were concerned, this meant that nations had rights: "A nation can organize its life as it sees fit. It has the right to

organize its life on the basis of autonomy. It has the right to enter into federal relations with other nations. It has the right to complete secession.
Nations are sovereign and all nations are equal."[7] All nations were not
equal in size: there were small nations and there were large (and hence
"great-power") nations. All nations were not equal in their development:
there were "backward" nations (an obvious oxymoron in Stalin's terms)
and there were "civilized" nations. All nations were not equal in their economic (hence class hence moral) personae: some were "oppressor
nations" and some were "oppressed."[8] But all nations – indeed all nationalities no matter how "backward" – were equal because they were equally
sovereign, that is, because they all had the same rights . . . [The section
omitted underlines Lenin's and Stalin's commitment to "a strictly territorial definition of autonomy" and their assertion that modern territorial
divisions should be "based on popular sympathies" and result in "the
greatest homogeneity in the national composition of the population,"
though with a guarantee of equal status for national minorities.]

The "practice" of the revolution and civil war did nothing to change
this program. The earliest decrees of the new Bolshevik government
described the victorious masses as "peoples" and "nations" endowed
with "rights,"[9] proclaimed all peoples to be equal and sovereign, guaranteed their sovereignty through an ethnoterritorial federation and a
right to secession, endorsed "the free development of national minorities and ethnic groups," and pledged to respect national beliefs, customs
and institutions.[10] By the end of the war the need for local allies and the
recognition of existing (and sometimes ethnically defined) entities
combined with principle to produce an assortment of legally recognized
(and increasingly ethnically defined) Soviet republics, autonomous
republics, autonomous regions and toilers' communes. Some autonomies
appeared more autonomous than others but "nationality" reigned
supreme. "Many of these peoples have nothing in common except the
fact that before they were all parts of the Russian Empire and now they
have all been liberated by the revolution, but there are no internal connections among them."[11] According to Lenin's paradox, the surest way to
unity in content was diversity in form. By "fostering national cultures
[nasazhdat' natsional'nuiu kul'turu]" and creating national autonomies,
national schools, national languages and national cadres, the Bolsheviks
would overcome national distrust and reach national audiences. "We are
going to help you develop your Buriat, Votiak etc. language and culture,
because in this way you will join the universal culture [obshcheche-
lovecheskaia kul'tura], revolution and communism sooner."[12]

To many communists this sounded strange. Did nations not consist of
different classes? Should not proletarian interests prevail over those of
the national(ist) bourgeoisie? Were not the proletarians of all countries
supposed to unite? And were not the toilers of the besieged Soviet state

supposed to unite with all the more determination? In spring 1918 M.I. Latsis attacked the "absurdity of federalism" and warned that the endless "breeding of republics," particularly in the case of "undeveloped ethnic groups" such as the Tatars or the Belorussians, was as dangerous as it was ludicrous.[13] In winter 1919, A.A. Ioffe cautioned against growing nationalist appetites and appealed for the "end of separatism" on the part of the "buffer republics."[14] And in spring 1919, at the VIII Party Congress, N.I. Bukharin and G.L. Piatakov launched an all-out assault against the slogan of national self-determination and the resulting primacy of ethnicity over class in non-Russian areas.[15]

Lenin's response was as adamant as it was familiar. First, nations existed "objectively." "If we say that we do not recognize the Finnish nation but only the toiling masses, it would be a ridiculous thing to say. Not to recognize something that is out there is impossible: it will force us to recognize it."[16] Second, former oppressor nations needed to gain the trust of the former oppressed nations:

> The Bashkirs do not trust the Great Russians because the Great Russians are more cultured and used to take advantage of their culture to rob the Bashkirs. So in those remote places the name "Great Russian" stands for "oppressor" and "cheat." We should take this into account. We should fight against this. But it is a long-term thing. It cannot be abolished by decree. We should be very careful here. And a nation like the Great Russians should be particularly careful because they have provoked such bitter hatred in all the other nations.[17]

Finally, backward nations had not developed a "differentiation of the proletariat from bourgeois elements" and thus could not be expected to have revolutionary classes consistently hostile "to their mullahs."[18] Taken as a whole and compared to more "cultured" nations, however, they were legitimate proletarians by virtue of having been cheated and oppressed. Under imperialism ("as the highest and final stage of capitalism") colonial peoples had become the global equivalents of the western working class. Under the dictatorship of the (Russian) proletariat, they were entitled to special treatment until the economic and psychological wounds of colonialism had been cured. Meanwhile, nations equaled classes.

Lenin lost the argument but won the vote because, as [trade union leader M.P.] Tomskii put it, while "not a single person in this room would say that national self-determination or national movements were either normal or desirable," most people seemed to believe that they were a "necessary evil" that had to be tolerated.[19] Accordingly, the scramble for national status and ethnoterritorial recognition continued unimpeded. The Kriashen were different from the Tatars in customs, alphabet and vocabulary, and thus needed a special administrative unit.[20] The Chuvash were poor and did not speak Russian, and thus needed a special administrative unit.[21] The Iakut deserved their own government because they lived compactly and were ready to "organize their lives through their own efforts."[22] The "primitive tribes" who lived next to the Iakut deserved a special government because they lived in widely dispersed communities and were not ready to run their own affairs.[23] The Estonian settlers in Siberia had a literary tradition and needed a special bureaucracy to provide them with newspapers.[24] The Ugrian natives of Siberia had no literary tradition and needed "an independent government" to "direct at the dark masses a ray of enlightenment and to cultivate their way of life [kul'tivirovat' ikh byt zhizni]."[25] Local intellectuals, Commissariat of Nationalities officials, "native conferences" and Petrograd ethnographers all demanded institutional autonomy, offices and funding (for themselves or their protégés). Having received autonomy, they demanded more offices and more funding [. . .]

When the X Party congress [1920–21] legitimized the policy of institutionalized ethnicity no one called it a "necessary evil," let alone bourgeois nationalism. What the X Congress (and specifically Stalin) did was to conflate Lenin's themes of national oppression and colonial liberation, equate the "nationality question" with the question of backwardness and present the whole issue as a neat opposition between "Great Russians" and "non-Great Russians." The Great Russians belonged to an advanced, formerly dominant nation possessed of a secure tradition of national statehood and frequently guilty of ethnic arrogance and insensitivity known as "great-power chauvinism." All the other nationalities, defined negatively and collectively as "non-Great Russians," were victims of tsarist-imposed statelessness, backwardness and "culturelessness [nekul'-turnost']," which made it difficult for them to take advantage of new revolutionary opportunities and sometimes tempted them to engage in "local nationalism."[26] In Stalin's formulation, "the essence of the nationality question in the RSFSR consists of the need to eliminate the backwardness (economic, political and cultural) that the nationalities have inherited from the past, to allow the backward peoples to catch up with central Russia."[27] To accomplish this goal, the Party was to help them:

a) develop and strengthen their own Soviet statehood in a form that would correspond to the national physiognomy of these peoples; b) introduce their own courts and agencies of government that would function in native languages and consist of local people familiar with the life and mentality of the local population; c) develop their own press, schools, theaters, local clubs and other cultural and educational institutions and native languages.[28]

There were to be as many nation states with varying degrees of autonomy as there were nationalities (not nations!) in the RSFSR. Nomads would receive lands lost to the Cossacks and "national minorities" scattered among compact ethnic groups would be guaranteed "free national development" (which called for the creation of territorial units).[29] Perhaps most remarkably, this triumph of ethnicity was presented by Stalin as both the cause and the consequence of progress. On the one hand, "free national development" was the only way to defeat non-Russian backwardness. On the other:

> You cannot go against history. Even though the Russian element still predominates in Ukrainian cities, it is clear that as time goes on these cities will inevitably become Ukrainianized. About forty years ago Riga was a German city, but as cities grow at the expense of villages, and villages are the keepers of nationality, Riga is now a purely Latvian city. About fifty years ago all cities of Hungary were German in character, but now they have been Magyarized. The same will happen to Belorussia, in whose cities non-Belorussians currently predominate.[30]

Once this had happened, the Party would redouble its efforts at nation building because, "in order to conduct communist work in the cities, it will be necessary to reach the new proletarian-Belorussian in his native language."[31]

However "dialectical" the logic of the official policy, its practice was unequivocal and, by 1921, fairly well established. In a sense, the introduction of the New Economic Policy at the X Congress was tantamount to the "lowering" of all other pursuits to the level of the already "NEP-like" nationality policy. NEP constituted a temporary but deliberate reconciliation with "backwardness" – backwardness represented by peasants, traders, women, all non-Russian peoples in general and various "primitive tribes" in particular. There was a special women's department, a Jewish section and the Committee for Assistance to the People of the Northern Borderlands, among others. Backwardness endlessly multiplied itself and each remnant of the past required an individual approach based on "specific peculiarities" and characterized by sensitivity and paternal benevolence. The ultimate goal was the abolition of all backwardness and thus all difference, but the fulfillment of that goal was postponed indefinitely. Attempts to force it through would be "dangerous" and "utopian" – as was the impatience of those otherwise "mature and politically aware comrades" in central Asia who asked, " What on earth is going on? How much longer are we going to keep breeding separate autonomies?"[32] The Party's answer was the vague but emphatic: "For as long as it takes." For as long as it takes to overcome "economic and cultural backwardness . . ., economic differences, differences in customs (particularly important among nations that have not yet reached the capitalist stage) and linguistic differences."[33] Meanwhile, nation building appeared to be a praiseworthy goal in its own right. There was beauty in difference.

With one exception. One particular remnant of the past had few redeeming qualities and was to be tolerated but not celebrated, used but not welcomed. This was the Russian peasant. The NEP alliance (*smychka*) between the peasantry and the working class seemed to mirror similar arrangements with other "underdeveloped" groups but its official rationale was quite different. The "peasant element" was aggressive, contagious and menacing. No one assumed that its brand of savagery would dialectically dissolve itself through further development because the stubbornly "somnolent" Russian peasant was incapable of development *as a peasant* (his was a difference "in content"). By equating ethnicity with development and dividing the population of the country into Russians and non-Russians, the X Congress recognized and reinforced this distinction. The Russian nationality was developed, dominant and thus irrelevant. The Russian territory was "unmarked" and, in effect, consisted of those lands that had not been claimed by the non-Russians known as "nationals [*natsionaly*]." Mikoyan's objection that this was too neat, that Azerbaijan was culturally and economically "ahead of many Russian provinces" and that the Armenian bourgeoisie was as imperialistic as any was dismissed by Stalin and by the congress.[34] [. . .]

But what was "nationality"? At the time of the February revolution, the only characteristic ascribed to all imperial subjects was "religious confession," with both the Russian national identity and the tsar's dynastic legitimacy largely associated with Orthodoxy. Not all of the tsar's subjects and not all Orthodox believers were Russians, but all Russians were expected to be Orthodox subjects of their Orthodox tsar. The non-Orthodox could serve the tsar in his capacity as emperor, but they had no immunity from occasional conversion campaigns and were legally handicapped in cases of mixed marriages. Some non-Orthodox were legally designated as "aliens" (*inorodtsy*), a term whose etymology ("non-kin," "non-native") suggested genetic difference but which was usually interpreted to mean "non-Christian" or "backward." These two concepts reflected the Muscovite ("premodern") and petrine ("modern") notions of otherness and were now used interchangeably. Some baptized communities were too backward to be "real Christians" and all aliens were formally classified according to their religion ("Muslim," "Lamaist") or "way of life" understood as degree of development ("settled," "nomadic," "wandering"). With the spread of state-sponsored education and the attendant effort to reach the "eastern aliens"[35] and to control (and Russify) the autonomous educational institutions of western non-Russians, "native language" also became a politically meaningful category. The names of languages, however, did not always coincide with the collective names that variously defined communities used to refer to themselves and to others. On the eve of the revolution, Russia had census nationalities, nationalist parties and national "questions," but it had no official view of what constituted nationality.

On the eve of the February revolution (exactly one day before Nicholas II left for Mogilev and the locked-out Putilov workers poured into the streets of Petrograd), President of the Russian Academy of Sciences S.F. Ol'denburg wrote to Minister of Foreign Affairs N.N. Pokrovskii that, moved by a "sense of patriotic duty," he and his colleagues would like to propose the formation of a Commission for the Study of the Tribal Composition of the Russian Borderlands:

> The most thorough determination of the tribal composition of the areas lying on both sides of Russia's borders with hostile states is of extraordinary importance at the present moment because a world war is being waged to a considerable extent over the national question. The determination of the validity of various territorial claims by various nationalities will become particularly important at the time of peace negotiations because, even if new borders are drawn in accordance with certain strategic and political considerations, the national factor will still play an enormously important role.[36]

Under the Provisional Government the nationality question moved farther inland and the new commission was charged with the study of the whole population of Russia, not just the borderlands. Under the Bolsheviks "the essence of Soviet nationality policy" came to consist in the "coincidence of ethnographic and administrative borders,"[37] which meant that most of the imperial territory would have to be divided into borderlands and that professional ethnographers would have to play an important role in the endeavor.

There was no time to discuss terminology. Aliens and Christians were replaced by an undifferentiated collection of *narody* (peoples), *narodnosti* (peoples sometimes understood to be small or underdeveloped), *natsional'nosti* (nationalities), *natsii* (nations) and *plemena* (tribes). There was no agreement as to how durable (and hence territorially viable) these entities were. In what seems to have been a common attitude, the head of the commission's Caucasian section, N.Ia. Marr, considered nationality to be too "transitory" and too complex to be pinned down by "primitive territorial demarcation," but worked hard (a lot harder than most, in fact) to uncover "primeval ethnicity [*etnicheskaia pervobytnost'*]" and "true tribal composition."[38] The most commonly used "marker of tribal composition" was language. Party ideologues championed "native-language education" as the basis for their nationality policy; education officials proceeded from a "linguistic definition of national culture";[39] and ethnographers tended to fall back on language as the most dependable, albeit not universal, indicator of ethnicity. Thus, E.F. Karskii, the author of *Ethnographic Map of the Belorussian Tribe*, adopted mother tongue as "the exclusive criterion" of national difference and claimed, in a characteristic *non sequitur*, that Lithuanians who spoke Belorussian should be considered Belorussians.[40] More controversially, the central Asian Sart (usually defined as settled Muslims) were decreed out of existence, the various Pamir communities became "Tajiks" and the Uzbeks were radically redefined to include most of the Turkic speakers of Samarkand, Tashkent and Bukhara.[41] Yet language was still perceived to be insufficient and the 1926 census included two unequal categories of "language" and "nationality," revealing large numbers of people who did not speak "their own language." Such communities were considered "denationalized" by ethnographers[42] and not entirely legitimate by party officials and local elites: Russian-speaking Ukrainians or Ukrainian-speaking Moldavians were expected, and sometimes forced, to learn their mother tongue irrespective of whether their mothers knew how to speak it.

What made "denationalized" Ruritanians Ruritanians? More often than not, it was the various combinations of "material life", "customs" and "traditions" jointly known as "culture." Thus, when dealing with areas where "Russian" and "Belorussian" dialects blend into each other, Karskii distinguished between the two nationalities by referring to differences in clothing and architecture.[43] Similarly, Marr classified Iranian-speaking Ossetians and Talysh as north Caucasians (Japhetids) on the basis of their "ethnic culture," "genuine popular religion," "way of life [*byt*]" and "emotional attachment to the Caucasus."[44] Sometimes religion-as-culture outweighed language and became a crucial ethnic marker in its own right, as when the Kriashen (Tatar-speaking Christians) received their own "department" and the Adzhar (Georgian-speaking Muslims) received their own republic (a similar appeal by Marr on behalf of Muslim, Armenian-speaking Khemshil proved unsuccessful[45]). Cultures, religions and indeed languages could be reinforced by topography (highland versus valley Caucasians) and chronological primacy (in the Caucasians case, a native-versus-settler distinction did not necessarily coincide with a dichotomy based on progress, as it did in Siberia[46]). Physical ("racial", "somatic") type was never used independently but sometimes – particularly in Siberia – was used to support other distinguishing features.[47] Finally, none of these features could be decisive in the case of the steppe nomads, whose "national awareness" or "tribal self-identity" were considered so strong as to make any other criteria practically useless. Linguistic, cultural and religious differences among the Kazakh, Kirgiz and Turkmen might be negligible, but their clan genealogies were so clearly drawn and so vigorously upheld that most ethnographers had no choice but to follow.[48]

To be sure, the actual borders of new ethnic units did not always correspond to those suggested by scholars. Kazakh authorities demanded Tashkent, Uzbek authorities wanted autonomy for the Osh district and the Central Committee in Moscow formed special arbitration commissions:

> Subsequently the Kirgiz [i.e., Kazakh] abandoned their claims on Tashkent but became all the more insistent in their demand that three *volosts* ... of the Tashkent *uezd* be included in Kazakhstan. If this demand had been fully satisfied, the portions of the canals ... that feed Tashkent would have wound up on Kirgiz territory ... Besides, the adoption of the Kirgiz variant would have cut the central Asian railway line by a Kirgiz wedge 17 versts south of Tashkent.[49]

Such odd strategic or "national interest" considerations (as in Kazakh versus Uzbek), as well as more conventional political and economic priorities at various levels affected the final shape of ethnoterritorial units, but there is no doubt that the dominant criterion was indeed ethnic. "Nationality" meant different things in different areas but the borders of most areas were seen as truly "national" and were, indeed, remarkably similar to ethnographic maps drawn up by the Commission for the Study of Tribal Composition. Bolshevik officials in Moscow saw the legitimation of ethnicity as a concession to ethnic grievances and developmental constraints, not as a brilliant divide-and-rule stratagem, and confidently asserted, after Lenin and Stalin, that the more genuine the "national demarcation" the more successful the drive to internationalism.

In the short run, national demarcation resulted in a puzzling and apparently limitless collection of ethnic nesting dolls. All non-Russians were "nationals" entitled to their own territorial units and all nationally defined groups living in "somebody else's" units were national minorities entitled to their own units. By 1928, various republics contained national *okrugs*, national *raions*, national soviets, native executive committees (*tuzriki*), native soviets (*tuzemnye sovety*), *aul* (*aul'nye*) soviets, clan (*rodovye*) soviets, nomadic (*kochevye*) soviets and encampment committees (*lagerkomy*).[50] Secure within their borders, all Soviet nationalities were encouraged to develop and, if necessary, create their own autonomous cultures. The key to this effort was the widest possible use of native languages – "native language as a means of social discipline, as a social unifier of nations and as a necessary and most important condition of successful economic and cultural development."[51] Both the main reason for creating a national autonomy and the principal means of making that autonomy truly national, "native language" could refer to the official language of a given republic (almost always indicated by the republic's name[52]), to the official language of a given minority unit or to the mother tongue of particular individuals. The proliferation of territorial units seemed to suggest that eventually there would be an official language for most individuals, even if it resulted in state-sponsored trilingualism (in 1926 Abkhaz-speaking Abkhazia, itself a part of Georgian-speaking Georgia, had 43 Armenian, 41 Greek, 27 Russian, 2 Estonian and 2 German schools[53]). To put it differently, all 192 languages identified during the 1920s would sooner or later become official. [. . .]

Duly codified and apparently insulated from each other (not least by means of dictionaries[54]), the various official languages could be used to reach the "toiling nationals." By 1928, books were being published in 66 languages (as compared to 40 in 1913) and newspapers in 47 (205 non-Russian titles in all[55]). How many people were actually reading them was not of immediate importance: as in other Soviet campaigns, supply was supposed to generate demand (or suppliers would engineer it). Much more ambitious was the requirement that all official business including education be conducted in native languages (the languages of the eponymous republics as well as the languages of local communities).[56] This was necessary because Lenin and Stalin kept saying it was necessary, because it was the only way to overcome national mistrust, because "speech reactions in native languages occur more quickly,"[57] because socialist content was only accessible to nationals in national form, because "developed" nations consisted of individuals whose native language equaled the official language equaled the nation's name, and because the adoption of rigid literary standards had created large numbers of people who either spoke non-languages or spoke their native languages "incorrectly."[58] By 1927, 93.7 percent of Ukrainian and 90.2 percent of Belorussian elementary-school students were taught in their "native" languages (that is, the language implied by the name of their "nationality").[59] High schools, vocational schools and colleges lagged behind, but everyone seemed to agree that the ultimate goal was a total coincidence of national and linguistic identity. Theoretically at least, a Jew from a shtetl was to be educated in Yiddish even if parents preferred Ukrainian (Hebrew not being an option), while a Ukrainian from Kuban' was to be taught in Ukrainian if scholars and administrators decided that her parents' vernacular was a dialect of Ukrainian rather than a dialect of Russian (or a Kuban' language in its own right).[60] As one official put it, "We cannot take the desires of parents into account. We must teach the child in the language he speaks at home."[61] In many parts of the USSR such an approach could not be implemented or even seriously argued, but the validity of the final goal (total ethnolinguistic consistency under socialism rather than total ethnolinguistic transparency under communism) was usually taken for granted.

Finally and most dramatically, the promotion of native languages was accompanied by the promotion of the speakers of those languages. According to the official policy of *korenizatsiia* (literally, "taking root" or indigenization), the affairs of all ethnic groups at all levels – from union republics to clan soviets – were to be run by the representatives of those ethnic groups. This involved the preferential recruitment of "nationals" to party, government, judicial, trade union and educational institutions, as well as the preferential "proletarianization" of mostly rural non-Russian population.[62] The specific goals were not clear, however. On the one hand, an ethnic group's share of the total population on a given territory was to be equal to its share in all high-status occupations, which in effect meant all occupations with the exception of traditional rural ones (precisely those that, according to ethnographers, made most nationalities "national").[63] On the other hand, not all territories were equal or equally self-contained, with the "republican" identity frequently domiinating over all others. Indeed, most indigenization campaigns assumed republic-controlling (non-Russian) nationalities to be more indigenous than others, so that if the share of Armenian office-holders actually exceeded the share of Armenians in the total population of "their own" republic, no one seemed to allege a violation of the Soviet nationality policy (the Kurds were to control their own village soviets; their proportionate representation on the republican level was not a clearly stated priority).[64] No other union republic could equal Armenia's success but most of them tried (with Georgia making particularly great strides). Nationality was an asset and there were no nationally defined entities above the union republic.

Yet even though administrative hierarchy tended to interfere with the principle of national equality, the idea of a formal ranking of ethnic groups was absent from the NEP nationality policy. No one bothered with Stalin's distinction between nations and nationalities, least of all Stalin himself. The dictatorship of the proletariat consisted of countless national groups (languages, cultures, institutions) endowed with apparently limitless national – that is, "nonessential" – rights (to develop their languages, cultures, institutions). The key themes were "national diversity [*raznoobrazie*]" and "national uniqueness [*svoeobrazie*]," both useful as paradoxical prerequisites for ultimate unity but also as values in their own right. The symbolic representation of the USSR at the Agricultural Exhibit of 1923 included:

> The majestic ancient mosques of Samarkand . . . ; the white minarets of Azerbaijan; a colorful Armenian tower; a strikingly Oriental building from Kirghizia; a solid Tatar house covered with grillwork; some picturesque chinoiserie from the far east; and further on the yurts and *chums* [nomad's tents] from

Bashkiria, Mongol-Buriatia, Kalmykia, Oiratia, Iakutia, the Khakass, the Ostiak and the Samoed; all of it surrounded by the artificially created mountains and villages of Dagestan, Caucasian Highland [*Gorskaia*] Republic, and Chechnia ... They each have *their own* flag; signs in *their own* language; maps of *their own* expanses and borders; diagrams of *their own* riches. Nationality, individuality and uniqueness are forcefully emphasized everywhere.[65]

If the USSR was a communal apartment, then every family that inhabited it was entitled to a room of its own. "Only through free national self-determination could we arrive in this apartment," argued Vareikis, "for only because of this self-determination can any formerly oppressed nation shed its legitimate mistrust of larger nations."[66]

But what about the Russians? In the center of the Soviet apartment there was a large and amorphous space not clearly defined as a room, unmarked by national paraphernalia, unclaimed by "its own" nation and inhabited by a very large number of austere but increasingly sensitive proletarians. The Russians, indeed, remained in a special position. They could be *bona fide* national minorities in areas assigned to somebody else, but in Russia proper they had no national rights and no national opportunities (because they had possessed and misused them before). The war against Russian huts and Russian churches was the Party's *raison d'être*, and the heavy burden of that war was the reason it needed the support of the yurts, *chums* and minarets. In fact, ethnicity-based affirmative action in the national territories was an exact replica of class-based affirmative action in Russia. A Russian could benefit from being a proletarian; a non-Russian could benefit from being a non-Russian. "Udmurt" and "Uzbek" were meaningful concepts because they substituted for class; "Russian" was a politically empty category unless it referred to the source of great-power chauvinism (which meant arrogant bureaucratic statism, not excessive national self-assertion) or to the history of relentless imperialist oppression (which meant that the tsarist state was a prison for non-Russian peoples). In Trotsky's March 1923 formulation of Lenin's policy:

> The relationship between the Great Russian proletariat and the Great-Russian peasantry is one thing. Here the question is one of class, pure and simple, which makes the solution of the problem easier. The relationship between the Great Russian proletariat, which plays first fiddle in our federal state, and the Azerbaijani, Turkestani, Georgian and Ukrainian peasantry is something else entirely.[67]

The Russians were not the only non-nation in the Soviet Union. The Soviets were not a nation either (the apartment was not larger than the sum total of its rooms). This is all the more remarkable because after March 1925 the citizens of the USSR were building socialism "in one country" – a country with a central state, a centralized economy, a definite territory and a monolithic Party. Some people ("great-power chauvinists") associated that country with Russia[68] but as far as the party line was concerned, the USSR had no national identity, no official language and no national culture. The USSR was like Russia insofar as both represented pure "socialist content" completely devoid of "national form."

One could not criticize socialist content, of course, but the campaign to foster national forms had numerous, though mostly inarticulate, detractors. While almost none of the delegates to the XII Congress spoke out against the Lenin/Stalin indigenization (*korenizatsiia*) program, the greatest applause was reserved for the few attacks on "local nationalism," not for the Party's crusade against great-power chauvinism.[69] Meanwhile, in the Tatar Republic great-power chauvinism consisted in complaints "that 'all the power is in Tatar hands these days'; that 'Russians are badly off now'; that 'Russians are being oppressed'; that 'Russians are being fired from their jobs, not hired anywhere, and not admitted to colleges'; that 'all Russians should leave Tataria as soon as possible,' etc."[70] In Povolzh'e, Siberia and central Asia, "non-native" settlers, teachers and administrators resented official pressure to learn languages they considered useless, hire "nationals" they deemed incompetent, teach children they called "savage" and waste scarce resources on projects they regarded as unfair tokenism.[71] Ukrainian peasants were not enthusiastic about the arrival of Jewish agricultural colonists, while the "overrepresented" Jewish officials objected to wholesale Ukrainianization.[72] The presumed beneficiaries were not always grateful, either. "Politically immature" parents, students and teachers exhibited an "abnormal attitude" towards native-language education and had to be forced along the path of "Yiddishization" and "Belorussification" (for technical reasons, this path rarely stretched beyond middle school and thus appeared to be an educational dead end).[73] "Backward" Belorussian settlers in Siberia preferred instruction in Russian, while "particularly backward" indigenous peoples of Siberia argued that insofar as literacy was of any value in the tundra, it was to get to know the Russian ways and learn the skills that could not be mastered at home.[74]

While NEP lasted, these arguments fell on deaf ears because the correct way out of backwardness lay through exuberant and uncompromising nation building (*natsional'noe stroitel'stvo*) – that is, in official terminology, through more backwardness. But in 1928 NEP came to an end and so did the toleration of all "survivals." The "revolutionaries from above" restored the original Bolshevik equation of "otherness" with "backwardness" and vowed to destroy it within ten years. Collectivization would take care of rural barbarians, industrialization would bring about urban progress and the cultural revolution would "liquidate illiteracy" (and thus all deviance). According to the apostles of the Great Transformation, "socialism in one country" meant that the difference between self and other would soon coincide with the borders of that country: all internal boundaries would presently disappear, schools would merge with production, writers with readers, minds with bodies. But did any of this apply to nationalities? Did this mean that national territories were a concession to backwardness that had to be withdrawn? That nations were to be eliminated like NEPmen or collectivized like peasants? Some serious signs pointed in that direction. Just as legal scholars anticipated the withering away of law and teachers predicted the imminent obsolescence of formal education, linguists and ethnographers expected – and tried to bring about – the fusion and consequent disappearance of linguistic and ethnic communities.[75] According to N.Ia. Marr's allegedly Marxist and hence obligatory "Japhetic theory," language belonged to a social superstructure and thus reflected the cyclical changes of the economic base. Language families were remnants of evolutionary stages united by the inexorable process of global "glottogony" and were destined to become merged under communism.[76] Similarly, the speakers of those languages ("nationalities") constituted historically "unstable" communities that rose and fell with socioeconomic formations.[77] "By freeing itself from its bourgeois aspect, national culture will become fused into one human culture . . . The nation is a historic, transitional category that does not represent anything primeval or eternal. Indeed, the process of the evolution of the nation essentially repeats the history of the development of social forms."[78] In the meantime, the need to speed up the study of Marxism-Leninism and "master technology" seemed to require both the abandonment of the "preposterous" practice of linguistic indigenization among mostly "assimilated" groups and the encouragement of the widest possible use of the Russian language.[79]

This was not to be, however. Linguistic purism did come under attack from the Marrists and latter the Party,[80] but the issue was not officially resolved until 1933–1934 and the principle of ethnocultural autonomy was never put into question. As Stalin declared to the XVI Party Congress in July 1930:

> The theory of the fusion of all nations of . . . the USSR into one common *Great Russian* nation with one common *Great Russian* language is a nationalist-chauvinist and anti-Leninist theory that

contradicts the main thesis of Leninism, according to which national differences cannot disappear in the near future but will remain in existence for a long time, even after the victory of the proletarian revolution *on a world scale*.[81]

Accordingly, for as long (very long) as "national differences, language, culture, ways of life, etc." remained in existence, the ethnoterritorial entities would have to be preserved and reinforced.[82] The Great Transformation in nationality policy consisted in a dramatic escalation of the NEP nation-building drive. The champions of the Russian language were forced to recant,[83] and all of Soviet life was to become as "national" as possible as quickly as possible. If there were no fortresses that the Bolsheviks could not storm, no plan that they could not overfulfill and no fairy tale that they could not turn into reality, then surely it would not take more than a few months to master Uzbek, let alone the "mere 600 to 700 everyday words" that made up the Nenets language.[84] On 1 March 1928 the Central Asian Bureau of the Party, the Central Committee of the Communist Party of Uzbekistan and the Uzbek Executive Committee formally decided to become fully "Uzbekified" by 1 September 1930.[85] On 28 December 1929 the Uzbek government required that all officials of the Central Committee, Supreme Court and commissariats of labor, enlightenment, justice and social welfare learn the Uzbek language within two months (the other commissariats were given nine months and "everyone else" a year).[86] On 6 April 1931 the Central Executive Committee of the Crimean Autonomous Republic decreed that the share of indigenous government officials be raised from 29 to 50 percent by the end of the year.[87] And on 31 August 1929 the predominantly Russian-speaking residents of Odessa woke up to discover that their daily *Izvestiia* had been transformed into the Ukrainian-language *Chornomors'ka komuna*.[88]

Only cities, however, were expected to become fully Ukrainianized or Kazakhified. The most spectacular aspect of the Stalin revolution among nationalities was the vastly increased support for the cultural autonomy of all "national minorities" (non-titular nationalities), however small. "The essence of indigenization does not fully coincide with such concepts as Ukrainianization, Kazakhization, Tatarization, etc. . . . Indigenization cannot be limited to issues relating only to the indigenous nationality of a given republic or province."[89] By 1932 Ukraine could boast of Russian, German, Polish, Jewish, Moldavian, Chechen, Bulgarian, Greek, Belorussian and Albanian village soviets, while Kazakhstan hosted Russian, Ukrainian, "Russo-Cossack," Uzbek, Uigur, German, Tajik, Dungan, Tatar, Chuvash, Bulgarian, Moldavian and Mordvinian rural soviets, not counting 140 that were "mixed."[90] It was a feast of ethnic fertility, an exuberant national carnival sponsored by the Party and apparently reaffirmed by Stalin's attack on Rosa Luxemburg in his letter to *Proletarskaia revoliutsiia*.[91] It turned out that the Chechen and Ingush were different nationalities (and not all Vainakh speakers), that Mingrelians were different from Georgians, that Karels were different from Finns, that the "Pontus Greeks" were different from the "Ellas Greeks," that the Jews and Gypsies were different (but not *that* different) from everybody else and that therefore all of them urgently needed their own literary languages, presses and education systems.[92] Between 1928 and 1938 the number of non-Russian newspapers increased from 205 titles in 47 languages to 2,188 titles in 66 languages.[93] It was considered a scandal if north Caucasians of Ukrainian origin did not have their own theaters, libraries and literary organizations, if the people of Dagestan had a Turkic *lingua franca* (as opposed to several dozen separate standards), or if the cultural needs of the Donbass workers were being served "only in the Russian, Ukrainian and Tatar languages."[94] Most official positions and school admissions in the Soviet Union were subject to complex ethnic quotas that aimed at a precise correspondence between demography and promotion – an almost impossibly confusing task given the number of administrative levels at which demography and promotion could be measured.[95] The dictatorship of the proletariat was a Tower of Babel in which all tongues on all floors would have a proportionate share of all jobs. Even shock-worker detachments at individual factories and construction sites were to be organized along ethnic lines if at all possible (the famous female Stakhanovite, Pasha Angelina, was a proud member of the "Greek brigade").[96]

The Great Transformation was not just NEP gone berserk, however. In nationalities policies as much as any other, it represented the last war against backwardness-as-exploitation, a permanent escape from social (and hence all?) difference, and the final leap into timelessness conceived as classlessness. Great Transformation goals and identities were valid only if they were obstructed by villains. Starting in 1928, real or imaginary non-Russian elites could no longer claim nationwide backwardness or nationwide rights. Collectivization presupposed the existence of classes and that meant that all nationalities without exception had to produce their own exploiters, heretics, and anti-Soviet conspirators.[97] (If classes could not be found, gender and age sufficed.[98]) Life consisted of "fronts" and fronts – including the national one – separated warring classes. "If in the case of the Russian nationality the internal class struggle has been extremely acute from the very first days of October . . ., the various nationalities are only now beginning to engage in [it] . . ." [99] Indeed, sometimes the social corrective to the ethnic principle seemed to dissolve that principle altogether, as when a prominent party spokesman declared that "the intensification of class conflicts reveal[ed] the class essence of many national peculiarities,"[100] or when a young ethnographer/collectivizer concluded that the whole "system that impress[ed] the superficial and usually naïve observer as a national peculiarity ... turn[ed] out to be a system of ideological defense of private property."[101]

Not all national peculiarities could be dissolved by class analysis, however. The rhetoric of ethnic diversity and the practice of ethnic quotas remained obligatory, and most local officials purged during the first five-year plan were replaced by their social betters from the same nationality.[102] What did change was the amount of room allowed for "national form." The ethnic identity of the Great Transformation was the ethnic identity of NEP minus "backwardness" as represented and defended by the exploiting classes. The members of the so-called Union for the Liberation of Ukraine were accused of nationalism not because they insisted on Ukraine's separate identity, administrative autonomy or ethnolinguistic rights – that was the official Soviet policy. They were accused of nationalism because the Ukraine they allegedly defined and celebrated was a rural Utopia from the remote but recoverable past, not an urban Utopia from the near but ethnically fragmented future:

> They remained emotionally attached to the old Ukraine dotted with farmsteads and manor houses, a predominantly agrarian country with a solid base for the private ownership of land. ... They were hostile to the industrialization of Ukraine and to the Soviet five-year plan, which was transforming the republic and endowing it with an independent industrial base. They sneered [glumilis'] at the Dnieper Hydroelectric Dam and at Soviet Ukrainianization. They did not trust its sincerity and serious-ness. They were convinced that without them, without the old Ukrainian intelligentsia, no genuine Ukrainianization was possible. But more than anything else they were afraid that their monopoly on culture, literature, science, art and the theater would be wrested from them.[103]

The continued existence of nationally defined communities and the legit-imacy of their claims to particular cultural, territorial, economic and political identities (which Stalin regarded as the principle of national rights and which I call "nationalism") was never in doubt. The crime of "bourgeois nationalism" consisted in attempts by some "bourgeois intel-lectuals" to lead such communities away from the party line – in the same way as the crime of wrecking consisted in the attempts by some "bourgeois specialists" to derail Soviet industry. To engage in "bourgeois nationalism" was to sabotage a nation, not to "build" it.

In 1931 the "socialist offensive" began to wane and in 1934 it was effectively halted for lack of an adversary. Addressing the "Congress of Victors" [XVII Party Congress, 1934], Stalin declared that the USSR had finally "divested itself of everything backward and medieval" and become an industrialized society based on a solid socialist foundation.[104] For purposes of official representation, time had been conquered and the future had become present. All essential differences had been overcome, all scholarly pursuits had become Marxist and all non-Marxist pursuits had disappeared. In the absence of backwardness, there was no need for the institutions that had been created to deal with its various manifestations: the Women's Department, the Jewish Section, and the Committee for the Assistance to the Peoples of the Northern Borderlands had all been closed down. The science of pedology had been banned because it claimed that women, minorities and the socially disadvantaged might need special assistance along the path to modernity. The science of ethnology had been banned because it assumed that some contemporary cultures might still be primitive or traditional. And all non-socialist-realist art had been banned because all art reflected reality and all Soviet reality was socialist.

According to the X Congress's equation of nationality with backwardness, nationality would have had to be banned, too. Once again, however, it weathered the storm and re-emerged chastened but vigorous. "High Stalinism" did not reverse the policy of nation building, as most authors on the subject would have us believe.[105] It changed the shape of ethnicity, but it never abandoned the "Leninist principle" of unity through diversity. It drastically cut down on the numbers of national units but it never questioned the national essence of those units. The abolition of the Central Asian Bureau was no more a call for ethnic assimilation than the abolition of the Women's Department was a prelude to an attack on gender differences. In fact, just as the newly emancipated Soviet women were expected to become more "feminine," the fully modernized Soviet nationalities were supposed to become more national. Class was the only legitimate kind of "content" and by the late 1930s class-based quotas, polls and identity cards had been discontinued.[106] Differences "in form" remained acceptable, however, and nationality (the most venerable and certifiably hollow form of "form") was allowed to develop, regroup and perhaps even acquire a little content.

The most striking innovation of the early 1930s was the emergence of the Russians as an ethnic group in their own right. As class criteria became irrelevant, the former default nationality became almost as saturated with ethnicity as all others. The noun "national" was criticized and later killed because there were no "non-nationals" left.[107] First cautiously but then more and more forcefully as the decade progressed, the Party began to endow Russians with a national past, national language and an increasingly familiar national iconography, headed principally by Alexander Pushkin – progressive and "freedom-loving" to be sure, but clearly celebrated as a great Russian, not a great revolutionary. By 1934, "derussifying" Russian proletarians and deliberately pulling away from Moscow in the course of "cultural construction" had become a serious crime, not a "mistake" born of well intentioned impatience.[108] And yet, the Russians never became a nationality like any other. On the one hand, they did not have a clearly defined national territory (RSFSR remained an amorphous "everything else" republic and was never identified with an ethnic or historic "Russia"), they did not have their own Party and they never acquired a national Academy. On the other hand – and this, of course, explains the lacunae – the Russians were increasingly identified with the Soviet Union as a whole. Between 1937 and 1939 Cyrillic replaced Latin in all the literary standards created in the 1920s, and in 1938, after a three-year campaign, Russian became an obligatory second language in all non-Russian schools. The Soviet past was becoming progressively more Russian and so were the upper echelons of the Party and state.[109] "Internationalism," defined as close ties among Soviet nationalities, and later "friendship of the peoples," defined as even closer ties among Soviet nationalities, became official dogmas[110] and both could only be expressed in Russian, the Soviet lingua franca. Still, no one ever suggested that there existed a "Soviet nation" (*natsiia*, that is, as opposed to the ethnically non-specific *narod*) or that Russian should become the *first* language in all national areas or institutions. Even in Karelia, where in 1938 the local Finnish standard was discovered to be "fascist," the orphaned Finnic-speakers were forced to switch to the newly-codified "Karelian" rather than Russian, which had already become "the language of interethnic communication."[111] The Russians began to bully their neighbors and decorate their part of the communal apartment (which included the enormous hall, corridor and the kitchen where all the major decisions were made), but they did not claim that the whole apartment was theirs or that the other (large) families were not entitled to their own rooms. The tenants were increasingly unequal but reassuringly separate.

The culture of the Great Transformation had been, by definition, rootless, fluid and carnivalesque. Old people acted like adolescents, children acted up, women dressed like men (although not vice versa), classes changed places and words lost meaning. People, buildings, languages and nationalities endlessly multiplied, migrated and spread evenly and thinly over a leveled, decentered landscape. But this proletarian postmodernism proved premature. The Great Retreat of the 1930s was the revenge of the literal – the triumph of real *korenizatsiia*, as in "taking root" or "radicalization." The forces of gravity (in both senses) pinned buildings to the ground, peasants to the land, workers to factories, women to men and Soviets to the USSR.[112] At the same time and in the same basic way, each individual got stuck with a nationality and most nationalities got stuck with their borders. In the early 1930s, at the time of the reappearance of college admissions tests and shortly before the introduction of student files (*lichnye dela*), employee cards (*trudovye knizhki*) and the death penalty for attempted flight abroad, all Soviet citizens received internal passports that formally defined them in terms of name, time and place of birth, authorized domicile (*propiska*) and nationality. One's name and *propiska* could be changed, nationality could not. By the end of the decade every Soviet child inherited his [*sic*] nationality at birth: individual ethnicity had become a biological category impervious to cultural, linguistic or geographical change.[113] Meanwhile, collective ethnicity was becoming more and more territorial. The administrative units created just a few years before in order to accommodate pre-existing nationalities were now the most important defining feature of those nationalities. To cite a typical and perfectly circular argument, "The fact that an ethnic group has its own national territory – a republic, province, district or village soviet – is proof that the ethnic group in question is an officially recognized nationality. . . . For example, the existence, in Cheliabinsk province, of a Nagaibak national district makes it imperative that a special nationality, the Nagaibak, be distinguished from the Tatars."[114]

In the same way, the Jews became a true nation after the creation of the Jewish Autonomous district in Birobidzhan:

> By acquiring their own territory, their own statehood, the toiling Jews of the USSR received a crucial element that they had lacked before and that had made it impossible for them to be considered a nation in the scientific sense of the term. And so it happened that, like many other Soviet nationalities completing the process of national consolidation, the Jewish national minority became a nation as a result of receiving its own national administrative entity in the Soviet Union.[115]

This view refers to two important innovations. First, the formal ethnic hierarchy was back for the first time since 1913. Different ethnoterritorial units (republics, provinces, districts) had always had different statuses, but no serious attempt had been made to relate this bureaucratic arrangement to an objective and rigidly evolutionary hierarchy of ethnicity. After the mid-1930s students, writers, and shock-workers could be formally ranked – and so could nationalities. Second, if the legitimacy of an ethnic community depended on the government's grant of territory, then the withdrawal of that grant would automatically "denationalize" that community (though not necessarily its individual passport-carrying members!). This was crucial because by the second half of the decade the government had obviously decided that presiding over 192 languages and potentially 192 bureaucracies was not a very good idea after all. The production of textbooks, teachers and indeed students could not keep up with formal "nationalization," the fully bureaucratized command economy and the newly centralized education system required manageable and streamlined communication channels, and the self-consciously Russian "promotees" who filled the top jobs in Moscow after the Great Terror were probably sympathetic to complaints of anti-Russian discrimination (they themselves were beneficiaries of *class*-based quotas). By the end of the decade most ethnically defined soviets, villages, districts and other small units had been disbanded, some autonomous republics forgotten and most "national minority" schools and institutions closed down.[116]

However – and this is the most important "however" of this essay – the ethnic groups that already had their own republics and their own extensive bureaucracies were actually told to redouble their efforts at building distinct national cultures. Just as the "reconstruction of Moscow" was changing from grandiose visions of refashioning the whole cityscape to a focused attempt to create several perfect artifacts,[117] so the nationality policy had abandoned the pursuit of countless rootless nationalities in order to concentrate on a few full-fledged, fully equipped "nations." While the curtailment of ethnic quotas and the new emphasis on Soviet meritocracy ("quality of cadres") slowed down and sometimes reversed the indigenization process in party and managerial bureaucracies, the celebration of national cultures and the production of native intelligentsias intensified dramatically. Uzbek communities outside Uzbekistan were left to their own devices but Uzbekistan as a quasi-nation-state remained in place, got rid of most alien enclaves on its territory and concentrated on its history and literature. The Soviet apartment as a whole was to have fewer rooms but the ones that remained were to be lavishly decorated with hometown memorabilia, grandfather clocks and lovingly preserved family portraits.

Indeed, the 1934 Congress of Soviet Writers, which in many ways inaugurated high Stalinism as a cultural paradigm, was a curiously solemn parade of old-fashioned romantic nationalisms. Pushkin, Tolstoy and other officially restored Russian icons were not the only national giants of international stature – all Soviet peoples possessed, or would shortly acquire, their own classics, their own founding fathers and their own folkloric riches. The Ukrainian delegate said that Taras Shevchenko was a "genius" and a "colossus" "whose role in the creation of the Ukrainian literary language was no less important than Pushkin's role in the creation of the Russian literary language, and perhaps even greater."[118] The Armenian delegate pointed out that his nation's culture was "one of the most ancient cultures of the orient," that the Armenian national alphabet predated Christianity and that the Armenian national epic was "one of the best examples of world epic literature" because of "the life-like realism of its imagery, its elegance, the profundity and simplicity of its popular wisdom and the democratic nature of its plot."[119] The Azerbaijani delegate insisted that the Persian poet Nizami was actually a classic of Azerbaijani literature because he was a "Turk from Giandzha," and that Mirza Fath Ali Akhundov was not a gentry writer, as some proletarian critics had charged, but a "great philosopher-playwright" whose "characters [were] as colorful, diverse and realistic as the characters of Griboedov, Gogol' and Ostrovskii."[120] The Turkmen delegate told the Congress about the eighteenth-century "coryphaeus of Turkmen poetry," Makhtum-Kuli; the Tajik delegate explained that Tajik literature had descended from Rudaki, Firdousi, Omar Khayyam and "other brilliant craftsmen of the word"; while the Georgian delegate delivered an extraordinarily lengthy address in which he claimed that Shot'ha Rust'haveli's *The Man in the Panther's Skin* was "centuries ahead of west European intellectual movements," infinitely superior to Dante and generally "the greatest literary monument of the whole ... so-called medieval Christian world."[121]

According to the new party line, all officially recognized Soviet nationalities were supposed to have their own nationally defined "Great Traditions" that needed to be protected, perfected and, if need be, invented by specially trained professionals in specially designated institutions. A culture's "greatness" depended on its administrative status (from the Union republics at the top to the non-territorial nationalities who had but a tenuous hold on "culture"), but within a given category all national traditions except for the Russian were supposed to be of equal value. Rhetorically this was not always the case (Ukraine was sometimes mentioned as second-in-command while central Asia was often described as backward), but institutionally all national territories were supposed to be perfectly symmetrical – from the party apparatus to the school system. This was an old Soviet policy but the contribution of the 1930s consisted in the vigorous leveling of remaining uneven surfaces and the equally vigorous manufacturing of special – and also identical – culture-producing institutions. By the end of the decade all Union republics had their own writers' unions, theaters, opera companies and national academies that specialized primarily in national history, literature and language.[122] Republican plans approved by Moscow called for the production of ever larger numbers of textbooks, plays, novels, ballets and short stories, all of them national in form (which, in the case of dictionaries, folklore editions and the "classics", series came dangerously close to being in content as well).

If some republics had a hard time keeping up with others, Moscow tried to oblige. In 1935 and 1936, for example, the new State Institute of Theater Art was in the process of training or had already released eleven national theater companies with all actors and full repertoires.[123] If a national repertoire was still incomplete, translations from mostly nineteenth-century Russian and west European literatures were actively encouraged or provided (the first productions of the new Bashkir Opera in 1936 were *Prince Igor* and *The Marriage of Figaro*[124]). In fact, in the late 1930s translation became one of the major Soviet industries as well as the main source of sustenance for hundreds of professional writers. The "friendship of the peoples" thesis required that all Soviet nationalities be deeply moved by the art of other Soviet nationalities. As Gorky put it, "We need to share our knowledge of the past. It is important for all Union republics that a Belorussian know what a Georgian or a Turk is like, etc."[125] This resulted not only in frenzied translation activity but also in histories of the USSR that were supposed to include all the Soviet peoples, radio shows that introduced Soviet listeners to "Georgian polyphony and Belorussian folk songs," tours by hundreds of regulation "song and dance ensembles," decades of Azerbaijani art in Ukraine, evenings of Armenian poetry in Moscow, exhibits of Turkmen carpets in Kazan' and festivals of national choirs, athletes and Young Pioneers all over the country. From the mid-1930s through the 1980s, this activity was one of the most visible (and apparently least popular) aspects of Soviet official culture.

The pursuit and propagation of national cultures were far from uneventful, of course. Within ten years of the First Writers' Congress most of the founding fathers of the new cultural institutions had perished; large areas had been annexed, lost and reannexed; numerous small ethnic units had been abolished as "unpromising"; and several nations and former "national minorities" had been forcibly deported from their territories. At the same time, the Russians had been transformed from a revolutionary people recovering a national past into "the most outstanding of all nations comprising the Soviet Union"[126] and the focus of world history. Once again, however, the legitimacy of non-Russian "Great Traditions" was not questioned. The main enemies of Russia-as-progress were "bourgeois nationalism," which now referred to insufficient admiration for Russia, and "rootless cosmopolitanism," which represented the opposite of *korenizatsiia*-as-rootedness. Even in 1936–1939, when hundreds of alleged nationalists were being sentenced to death, "the whole Soviet country" was noisily celebrating the 1000th anniversary of Firdousi, claimed by the Tajiks as one of the founders of their (and not Persian) literature; the 500th anniversary of Mir Ali Shir Nawaiy (Alisher Navoi), appropriated by the Uzbeks as the great classic of their (and not Chaghatay) culture; and the 125th anniversary of Taras Shevchenko, described by *Pravda* as "a great son of the Ukrainian people" who "carried Ukrainian literature to a height worthy of a people with a rich historical past."[127] The few national icons that suffered during this period were attacked for being anti-Russian, not for being national icons.[128] Similarly, when the Ukrainian poet Volodymyr Sosiura was castigated by *Pravda* in 1951 for his poem "Love Ukraine," the alleged sin consisted not in loving Ukraine too much but in not thanking the elder brother enough.[129] A major reason for gratitude was the recent Soviet annexation of west Ukraine and the subsequent "reunification" of the Ukrainian nation state, a Soviet/Russian achievement widely advertised as a fulfillment of Ukrainian national aspirations.

In fact, it was in this period of Russian delusions of grandeur that the theoretical justification for non-Russian national aspirations was clearly formulated. On 7 April 1948 Stalin said something that closely resembled his 1913 statement on national rights:

> Every nation, whether large or small, has its own specific qualities and its own peculiarities, which are unique to it and which other nations do not have. These peculiarities form a contribution that each nation makes to the common treasury of world culture, adding to it and enriching it. In this sense all nations, both small and large, are in the same position and each nation is equal to any other nation.[130]

This seemed to suggest that ethnicity was universal, irreducible and inherently moral. But this was only an overture. In summer 1950 Stalin put his pen to paper in order to exorcize the spirit of [the linguist] N.Ia. Marr, one of last saints of the Great Transformation whose theories and students had somehow escaped the fate of the other "simplifiers and vulgarizers of Marxism."[131] According to Stalin, language was not part of the superstructure – or, indeed, of the base. It "belonged to the whole nation" and was "common to the whole society" across social classes and throughout history. "Societies" represented ethnic communities and ethnic communities had "essences" that existed "incomparably longer than any base or any superstructure."[132] In short, it was official: classes and their "ideologies" came and went, but nationalities remained. In a country free from social conflict, ethnicity was the only meaningful identity.

This was the legacy that Stalin bequeathed to *his* successors and that survived 1984 to haunt Gorbachev and *his* successors [...]

Civilized Stalinism ("developed socialism") was the credo of the "collective leadership" that presided over the twilight years of the Soviet Union. Deriving its legitimacy from the "really existing" ethnoterritorial welfare state rather than future communism and past revolution, the new official discourse retained the language of class as window dressing and relied on nationality to prop up the system.[133] Every Soviet citizen was born into a certain nationality, took it to day care and through high school, had it officially confirmed at the age of sixteen and then carried it to the grave through thousands of application forms, certificates, questionnaires and reception desks. It made a difference in school admissions and it could be crucial in employment, promotions and draft assignments.[134] Soviet anthropologists, brought back to life in the late 1930s and provided with a *raison d'être* after the banishment of Marrism, were not supposed to study "culture": their job was to define, dissect and delight in the primordial "ethnos." Even abroad, in a world dominated by capitalism, the most visible virtue was "national liberation."

All nationalities were ranked – theoretically along the evolutionary scale from tribe to nation, and practically by territorial or social status. The status of a given nationality could vary a great deal but the continuing use of ethnic quotas made sure that most practical advantages accrued to the members of titular nationalities residing in "their own" republics. Sixty years of remarkable consistency on this score had resulted in almost total "native" control over most Union republics: large ethnic elites owed their initial promotions and their current legitimacy (such as it was) to the fact of being ethnic.[135] Dependent on Moscow for funds, the political and cultural entrepreneurs owed their allegiance to "their own people" and their own national symbols. But if the politicians were structurally constrained within the apparatus, the intellectuals were specifically trained and employed to produce national cultures. Limits were set by the censor but the goal was seen as legitimate both by party sponsors and by national consumers. A very large proportion of national intellectuals were professional historians, philologists and novelists, and most of them wrote for and about their own ethnic group.[136] They produced multi-volume national histories, invented national genealogies, purified national languages, preserved national treasures and bemoaned the loss of a national past.[137] In other words, they acted like good patriots – when they were not acting like bad nationalists. As time went on, however, it became increasingly difficult to distinguish between the two because the national form seemed to have become the content and because nationalism did not seem to have any content other than the cult of form. More ominously, the country's leaders found it harder and harder to explain what their "socialist content" stood for and, when Gorbachev finally discarded the worn-out Marxist verbiage, the only language that remained was the well honed and long practiced language of nationalism.

The Soviet regime's contribution to the nationalist cause was not limited to "constructive measures," of course. It forced the high priests of national cultures to be part-time worshipers of other national cultures, it instituted an administrative hierarchy that privileged some ethnic groups over others, it interfered in the selection and maintenance of national pantheons, it isolated ethnic communities from their relatives and sympathizers abroad; and it encouraged massive migrations that resulted in competition for scarce resources, diluted the consumer base of the national elites and provoked friction over ethnic quotas. Finally and most fatefully, it deprived the various nations of the

338

right to political independence – a right that was the culmination of all nationalist doctrines, including the one that lay at the foundation of the Soviet Union.

This points to another great tension in Soviet nationality policy: the coexistence of republican statehood and passport nationality.[138] The former assumed that territorial states made nations, the latter suggested that primordial nations might be entitled to their own states. The former presupposed that all residents of Belorussia would (and should) some day become Belorussian, the latter provided the non-Belorussian residents with arguments against it. The Soviet government endorsed both definitions without ever attempting to construct an ethnically meaningful Soviet nation or turn the USSR into a Russian nation state, so that when the non-national Soviet state had lost its Soviet meaning, the national non-states were the only possible heirs. Except for the Russian Republic, that is. Its borders were blurred, its identity was not clearly ethnic and its "titular" residents had trouble distinguishing between the RSFSR and the USSR.[139] Seventy years after the X Party Congress the policy of indigenization reached its logical conclusion: the tenants of various rooms barricaded their doors and started using the windows, while the befuddled residents of the enormous hall and kitchen stood in the center scratching the backs of their heads. Should they try to recover their belongings? Should they knock down the walls? Should they cut off the gas? Should they convert their "living area" into a proper apartment?

NOTES

This article is reprinted from *Slavic Review*, 53(2) (Summer 1994), 415–452, and has been abridged by the editor of this volume.

The first draft of this chapter was written for a seminar organized by the Program for Comparative Studies in Ethnicity and Nationalism at the Henry M. Jackson School of International Studies, University of Washington. I am grateful to the Program's co-chairs, Charles Hirschman and Charles F. Keyes, for their hospitality and criticism, as well as for their permission to submit the piece to the *Slavic Review*. I also thank Peter Blitstein, Victoria Bonnell, George Breslauer, Daniel Brower, Michael Burawoy, Jane Burbank, Sheila Fitzpatrick, Bruce Grant, David Hollinger, Terry Martin, Nicholas V. Riasanovsky, Reggie Zelnik, the Berkeley Colloquium for the Study of Russia ad Eastern Europe and the University of Chicago Russian History Workshop, for stimulating discussions and helpful comments.

1 Not the first such attempt, of course, but sufficiently different from the previous ones to make it worth the effort, I hope. My greatest debt is to the work of Ronald Grigor Suny, most recently summarized in his *The Revenge of the Past: Nationalism, Revolution, and the Collapse of the Soviet Union* (Stanford: Stanford University Press, 1993). On the last three decades, see also Kenneth C. Farmer, *Ukrainian Nationalism in the Post-Stalin Era* (The Hague: Martinus Nijhoff, 1980); Gail Warshofsky Lapidus, "Ethnonationalism and

Political Stability: the Soviet Case," *World Politics* 36, no. 4 (July 1984): 355–80; Philip G. Roeder, "Soviet Federalism and Ethnic Mobilization," *World Politics* 23, no. 2 (January 1991): 196–233; Teresa Rakowska-Harmstone, "The Dialectics of Nationalism in the USSR," *Problems of Communism* XXIII (May–June 1974), 1–22; and Victor Zaslavsky, "Nationalism and Democratic Transition in Postcommunist Societies," *Daedalus* 121, no. 2 (Spring 1992): 97–121. On the promotion of "national languages" and bilingualism, see the work of Barbara A. Anderson and Brian D. Silver, especially "Equality, Efficiency, and Politics in Soviet Bilingual Education Policy, 1934–1980," *American Political Science Review* 78, No. 4 (October 1984): 1019–39; and "Some Factors in the Linguistic and Ethnic Russification of Soviet Nationalities: Is Everyone Becoming Russian?" in Lubomyr Hajda and Mark Beissinger, eds, *The Nationalities Factor in Soviet Politics and Society* (Boulder: Westview Press, 1990). For a fascinating analysis of state-sponsored nationalism in a non-federal communist state, see Katherine Verdery, *National Ideology under Socialism: Identity and Cultural Politics in Ceaușescu's Romania* (Berkeley: University of California Press, 1991).

2 For an excellent overview of recent debates on the ethnic boundaries of political communities, see David A. Hollinger, "How Wide the Circle of the 'We'? American Intellectuals and the Problem of Ethnos since World War Two," *American Historical Review* 98, no. 2 (April 1993): 317–37.

3 I. Vareikis and I. Zelenskii, *Natsional'no-gosudarstvennoe razmezhovanie Srednei Azii* (Tashkent: Sredne-Aziatskoe gosudarstvennoe izdatel'stvo, 1924), 59.

4 For a witty elaboration of the reverse metaphor (the communal apartment as the USSR), see Svetlana Boym, "The Archeology of Banality: the Soviet Home," *Public Culture* 6, no. 2 (1994): 263–92.

5 I.V. Stalin, *Marksizm i natsional'nyi vopros* (Moscow, Politizdat, 1950), 51.

6 For early Marxist debates on nationalism, see Walker Connor, *The National Question in Marxist–Leninist Theory and Strategy* (Princeton: Princeton University Press, 1984); Hélène Carrère d'Encausse, *The Great Challenge: Nationalities and the Bolshevik State, 1917–1930* (New York: Holmes and Meier, 1992); Helmut Konrad, "Between 'Little International' and Great Power Politics: Austro-Marxism and Stalinism on the National Question," in Richard L. Rudolph and David F. Good, eds, *Nationalism and Empire: The Habsburg Empire and the Soviet Union* (New York: St Martin's Press, 1992); Richard Pipes, *The Formation of the Soviet Union: Communism and Nationalism, 1917–1923* (Cambridge, Mass., Harvard University Press, 1964); Roman Szporluk, *Communism and Nationalism: Karl Marx versus Friedrich List* (New York: Oxford University Press, 1988).

7 Stalin, *Marksizm i natsional'nyi vopros*, 51. See also V.I. Lenin, *Voprosy natsional'noi politiki i proletarskogo internatsionalizma* (Moscow, Politizdat, 1965), passim.

8 The "oppressor" was not always "civilized," as in most Marxist analyses of Russia *vis à vis* Poland or Finland.

9 "Peoples" and "nations" were used interchangeably.

10 *Dekrety Sovetskoi vlasti* (Moscow: Gospolitizdat, 1957), 1: 39–41, 113–15, 168–70, 195–96, 340–44, 351, 367.

11 S. Dimanshtein, "Narodnyi komissariat po delam natsional'nostei," *Zhizn' natsional'nostei* 41 (49) (26 October 1919).

12 S. Dimanshtein, "Sovetskaia vlast' i melkie natsional'nosti," *Zhizn' natsional'nostei* 46 (54) (7 December 1919). See also S. Pestkovskii, "Natsional'naia kul'tura," *Zhizn' natsional'nostei* 21 (29) (8 June 1919).

13 A.P. Nenarokov, K edinstvu ravnykh: Kul'turnye faktory ob"edinitel'nogo dvizheniia sovetskikh narodov, 1917–1924 (Moscow: Nauka, 1991), 91–92.

14 Ibid., 92–93.

15 Vos'moi s"ezd RKP(b): Protokoly (Moscow: Gospolitizdat, 1959), 46–48, 77–81.

16 Ibid., 55.

17 Ibid., 106.

18 Ibid., 53. In the same speech, Lenin argued that even the most "advanced" western countries were hopelessly behind Soviet Russia in terms of social differentiation (which meant that they could – and sometimes should – be regarded as integral nations rather than as temporarily isolated class battlefields). By being Soviet, Russia was more advanced than the advanced west.

19 Ibid., 82.

20 Fedor Kriuchkov, "O Kriashenakh," Zhizn' natsional'nostei 27 (84) (2 September 1920).

21 R. El'mets, "K voprosu o vydelenii chuvash v osobuiu administrativnuiu edinitsu," Zhizn' natsional'nostei 2 (59) (11 January 1920).

22 V. Vilenskii (Sibiriakov), "Samoopredelenie iakutov," Zhizn' natsional'nostei 3 (101) (2 February 1921).

23 V.G. Bogoraz-Tan, "O pervobytnykh plemenakh," Zhizn' natsional'nostei 1 (130) (10 January 1922); idem, "Ob izuchenii i okhrane okrainnykh narodov," Zhizn' natsional'nostei 3–4 (1923): 168–177; Dan. Ianovich, "Zapovedniki dlia gibnushchikh tuzemnykh plemen," Zhizn' natsional'nostei 4 (133) (31 January 1922); Gosudarstvennyi arkhiv Rossiiskoi Federatsii (GARF), f. 1377, op. 1, d. 8, ll. 126–27, d. 45, ll. 53, 77, 81.

24 "Chetyre goda raboty sredi estontsev Sovetskoi Rossii," Zhizn' natsional'nostei 24 (122) (5 November 1921).

25 GARF, f. 1318, op. 1, d. 994, l. 100.

26 Desiatyi s"ezd Rossiiskoi Kommunisticheskoi partii: Stenograficheskii otchet (Moscow: Gosudarstvennoe izdatel'stvo, 1921), 101.

27 Ibid.

28 Ibid., 371

29 Ibid., 372.

30 Ibid., 115.

31 "Belorusskii natsional'nyi vopros i kommunisticheskaia partiia," Zhizn' natsional'nostei 2 (131) (17 January 1922).

32 Vareikis and Zelenskii, Natsional'no-gosudarstvennoe razmezhevanie, 57.

33 Ibid., 60. "Nations that have not yet reached the capitalist stage" were not nations according to Stalin's definition.

34 Desiatyi s"ezd, 112, 114.

35 See, for example, "S"ezd po narodnomu obrazovaniiu," Zhurnal Ministerstva narodnago prosvieshcheniia L (March–April 1914): 195, 242–44.

36 Ob uchrezhdenii Komissii po izucheniiu plemennogo sostava naseleniia Rossii. Izvestiia Komissii po izucheniiu plemennogo sostava naseleniia Rossii (Petrograd: Rossiiskaia Akademiia Nauk, 1917), 1: 8.

37 I. Gertsenberg, "Natsional'nyi printsip v novom administrativnom delenii RSFSR," Zhizn' natsional'nostei 37 (94) (25 November 1920).

38 N.Ia. Marr, Plemennoi sostav naseleniia Kavkaza: Trudy Komissii po izucheniiu plemennogo sostava naseleniia Rossii (Petrograd: Rossiiskaia Academiia nauk, 1920), 3: 9, 21–22. See also N.Ia. Marr. "Ob iafeticheskoi teorii," Novyi vostok 5 (1924): 303–9.

39 "The richest associations and the strongest perceptions are those acquired through the mother tongue" (Segal', "Vserossiiskoe soveshchanie").

40 E.F. Karskii, *Etnograficheskaia karta Bielorusskago plemeni: Trudy Komissii po izucheniiu plemennogo sostava naseleniia Rossii*, vol. 2 (Petrograd: Rossiiskaia Akademiia nauk 1917).

41 I.I. Zarubin, *Spisok narodnostei Turkestanskogo kraia: Trudy Komissii po izucheniiu plemennogo sostava naseleniia Rossii*, vol. 9 (Leningrad: Rossiiskaia Akademiia nauk, 1925); I.I. Zarubin, *Naselenie Samarkandskoi oblasti: Trudy Komissii po izucheniiu plemennogo sostava naseleniia Rossii*, vol. 10 (Leningrad: AN SSSR, 1926); Edward A. Allworth, *The Modern Uzbeks: From the Fourteenth Century to the Present* (Stanford: Hoover Institution Press, 1990), 181; Alexandre Bennigsen and Chantal Lemercier-Quelquejay, *Islam in the Soviet Union* (New York: Praeger, 1967), 131–33; Teresa Rakowska–Harmstone, *Russia and Nationalism in Central Asia: The Case of Tadzhikistan* (Baltimore: Johns Hopkins University Press, 1970), 78.

42 *Instruktsiia k sostavleniiu plemennykh kart, izdavaemykh Komissiei po izucheniiu plemennogo sostava naseleniia Rossii: Trudy Komissii po izucheniiu plemennogo sostava naseleniia Rossii* (Petrograd: Rossiiskaia Akademia nauk, 1917), 1: 11.

43 Karskii, *Etnograficheskaia karta*, 19.

44 N.Ia. Marr, *Plemennoi sostav naseleniia Kavkaza: Trudy Komissii po izucheniiu plemennogo sostava naseleniia Rossii* (Petrograd: Rossiiskaia Akademiia nauk, 1920), 9: 24–25; N.Ia. Marr, *Talyshi: Trudy Komissii po izucheniiu plemennogo sostava naseleniia Rossii* (Petrograd: Rossiiskaia Akademiia nauk, 1922), 4: 3–5, 22.

45 Marr, *Plemennoi sostav*, 9.

46 Ibid., 59–61. Cf. S.K. Patkanov, *Spisok narodnostei Sibiri: Trudy Komissii po izucheniiu plemennogo sostava naseleniia Rossii* (Petrograd: Rossiiskaia Akademiia nauk, 1923), 7: 3.

47 See, for example, Patkanov on "Paleoasiatics" in Patkanov, *Spisok*, 8.

48 Vl. Kun, "Izuchenie etnicheskogo sostava Turkestana," *Novyi vostok* 6 (1924): 351–53; Zarubin, *Spisok*, 10.

49 I. Khodorov, "Natsional'noe razmezhevanie Srednei Azii," *Novyi vostok* 8–9 (1926): 69.

50 See, for example, S. Dimanshtein, "Desiat' let natsional'noi politiki partii i sovvlasti," *Novyi vostok* 19 (1927): vi; "Vremennoe polozhenie ob upravlenii tuzemnykh narodnostei i plemen Severnykh okrain," *Severnaia Aziia* 2 (1927): 85–91; N.I. Leonov, "Tuzemnye sovety v taige i tundrakh," *Sovetskii Sever: Pervyi sbornik statei* (Moscow: Komitet Severa, 1929), 225–30; Zvi Y. Gitelman, *Jewish Nationality and Soviet Politics: The Jewish Sections of the CPSU, 1917–1930* (Princeton: Princeton University Press, 1972), 289; Gerhard Simon, *Nationalism and Policy toward the Nationalities in the Soviet Union: From Totalitarian Dictatorship to Post-Stalinist Society* (Boulder: Westview Press, 1991), 58.

51 I. Davydov, "O probleme iazykov v prosvetitel'noi rabote sredi natsional'nostei," *Prosveshchenie natsional'nostei* 1 (1929): 18.

52 After the abolition of the "Highland" (*Gorskaia*) republic, the only autonomous republic that had no ethnic "landlord" and hence no obvious official language was Dagestan, one of the most linguistically diverse places on earth (see A. Takho-Godi, "Problema iazyka v Dagestane," *Revoliutsiia i natsional'nosti* 2 [1930]: 68–75).

53 V.A. Gurko-Kriazhin, "Abkhaziia," *Novyi vostok* 13–14 (1926): 115.

54 M. Pavlovich, "Kul'turnye dostizheniia tiurko-tatarskikh narodnostei so vremeni Oktiabr'skoi revoliutsii," *Novyi vostok* 12 (1926): viii.

55 Simon, *Nationalism*, 46. The number of Yiddish books and brochures, for example, rose from 76 in 1924 to 531 in 1930 (see Gitelman, *Jewish Nationality*, 332–33).

56 See, for example, Fierman, *Language Planning*, 170–76; Gitelman, *Jewish Nationality*, 351–65; James E. Mace, *Communism and the Dilemmas of National Liberation: National Communism in Soviet Ukraine, 1918–1933* (Cambridge, Mass.: Harvard Ukrainian Research Institute, 1983), 96; Simon, *Nationalism*, 42.

57 Davydov, "O probleme iazykov," 23.

58 The Ukrainian Commissar of Education, Mykola Skrypnyk, defined the Donbass vernacular as a "neither Russian nor Ukrainian" patois in need of proper Ukrainianization (see Mace, *Communism and the Dilemmas*, 213).

59 Simon, *Nationalism*, 49.

60 I. Bulatnikov, "Ob ukrainizatsii na Severnom Kavkaze," *Prosveshchenie natsional'nostei* 1 (1929): 94–99; Gitelman, *Jewish Nationality*, 341–44.

61 Gitelman, *Jewish Nationality*, 342.

62 For a survey, see Simon, *Nationalism*, 20–70.

63 See, for instance, Borozdin, "Sovremennyi Tatarstan," 118–19; 122–23; Dimanshtein, "Desiat' let," v–vi, xvii.

64 Simon, *Nationalism*, 32–33, 37.

65 A. Skachko, "Vostochnye respubliki na S.-Kh. Vystavke SSSR v 1993 godu," *Novyi vostok* 4 (1923): 482–84. Emphasis in the original.

66 Vareikis and Zelenskii, *Natsional'no-gosudarstvennoe razmezhevanie*, 59.

67 Quoted in Nenarokov, *K edinstvu ravnykh*, 132.

68 See, in particular, M. Agurskii, *Ideologiia natsional-bol'shevizma* (Paris: YMCA Press, 1980).

69 *Dvenadtsatyi s"ezd*, 554, 556, 564.

70 N. Konoplev, "Shire front internatsional'nogo vospitaniia," *Prosveshchenie natsional'nostei* 2 (1931): 49. See also N. Konoplev, "Za vospitanie internatsional'nykh boitsov," *Prosveshchenie natsional'nostei* 4–5 (1930): 55–61.

71 GARF, f. 1377, op. 1, d. 224, ll. 8, 32; N. Amyl'skii, "Kogda zatsvetaiut zharkie tsvety," *Severnaia Aziia* 3 (1928): 57–58; Fierman, *Language Planning*, 177–85; N. I. Leonov, "Tuzemnye shkoly na Severe," *Sovetskii Sever: Pervyi sbornik statei* (Moscow: Komitet Severa, 1929), 200–4; Leonov, "Tuzemnye sovety," 242, 247–48; D.F. Medvedev, "Ukrepim sovety na Krainem Severe i ozhivim ikh rabotu," *Sovetskii Sever* 1 (1933): 6–8; P. Rysakov, "Praktika shovinizma i mestnogo natsionalizma," *Revoliutsiia i natsional'nosti* 8–9 (1930): 28; T. Semushkin, *Chukotka* (Moscow: Sovetskii pisatel', 1941), 48; I. Sergeev, "Usilit' provedenie natspolitiki v Kalmykii," *Revoliutsiia i natsional'nosti* 7 (1930): 66; Simon, *Nationalism*, 25, 41, 73–74.

72 Gitelman, *Jewish Nationality*, 386, 398, 402–3.

73 Davydov, "O probleme iazykov," 22; Konoplev, "Shire front," 50; A. Valitov, "Protiv opportunisticheskogo otnosheniia k stroitel'stvu natsshkoly," *Prosveshchenie natsional'nostei* 5–6 (1932): 68.

74 I. Skachkov, "Prosveshchenie sredi belorusov RSFSR," *Prosveshchenie natsional'nostei* 3 (1931): 76; P. Kovalevskii, "V shkole-iurte," *Sovetskii Sever* 2 (1934): 105–6; I. Nesterenok, "Smotr natsional'nykh shkol na Taimyre," *Sovetskii Sever* 6 (1932): 84; G.N. Prokof'ev, "Tri goda v samoedskoi shkole," *Sovetskii Sever* 7–8 (1931): 144; S. Stebnitskii, "Iz opyta raboty v shkole Severa," *Prosveshchenie natsional'nostei* 8–9 (1932): 49–51.

75 For professional abolitionism during the first five-year plan, see Sheila Fitzpatrick, ed., *Cultural Revolution in Russia, 1928–1931* (Bloomington: Indiana University Press, 1978). On linguistics and ethnography, see Yuri Slezkine, "The Fall of Soviet Ethnography, 1928–38," *Current Anthropology* 32, no. 4 (1991): 476–84.

76 Slezkine, "The Fall," 478.
77 N.Ia. Marr, "K zadacham nauki na sovetskom vostoke," *Prosveshchenie natsional'nostei* 2 (1930): 12; S. Asfendiarov, "Problema natsii i novoe uchenie o iazyke," *Novyi vostok* 22 (1928): 174.
78 Asfendiarov, "Problema natsii," 174.
79 I. Davydov, "Ocherednye zadachi prosveshcheniia natsional'nostei," *Prosveshchenie natsional'nostei* 4–5 (1930): 30–34; M. Vanne, "Russkii iazyk v stroitel'stve natsional'nykh kul'tur," *Prosveshchenie natsional'nostei* 2 (1930): 31–40.
80 I. Kusik'ian, "Ocherednye zadachi marksistov-iazykovedov v stroitel'stve iazykov narodov SSSR," *Prosveshchenie natsional'nostei* 11–12 (1931): 75; E. Krotevich, "Vypravit' nedochety v stroitel'stve Kazakhskoi terminologii," *Prosveshchenie natsional'nostei* 8–9 (1932): 94–96; Fierman *Language Planning*, 126–29; Mace, *Communism*, 277–79; Roman Smal-Stocki, *The Nationality Problem of the Soviet Union and Russian Communist Imperialism* (Milwaukee: The Bruce Publishing Company, 1952), 106–41.
81 I.V. Stalin, *Sochineniia* (Moscow: Politizdat, 1952), 13: 4. Emphasis in the original.
82 Ibid., 12: 365–66.
83 See, for example, *Prosveshchenie natsional'nostei* 11–12 (1931): 102–6.
84 Fierman, *Language Planning*, 177; Evgen'ev and Bergavinov, "Nachal'niku Obdorskogo politotdela Glavsevmorputi t. Mikhailovu," *Sovetskaia Arktika* 4 (1936): 65–67.
85 P. Rysakov, "Praktika shovinizma i mestnogo natsionalizma," *Revoliutsiia i natsional'nosti* 8–9 (1930): 29.
86 S. Akopov, "K voprosu ob uzbekizatsii apparata i sozdanii mestnykh rabochikh kadrov promyshlennosti Uzbekistana," *Revoliutsiia i natsional'nosti* 12 (1931): 22–23.
87 B. Rodnevich, "Korenizatsii apparata v avtonomiiakh i raionakh natsmen'shinstv RSFSR," *Revoliutsiia i natsional'nosti* 12 (1931): 19–20.
88 Mace, *Communism*, 212. See also Simon, *Nationalism*, 39–40.
89 A. Oshirov, "Korenizatsiia v sovetskoi strane," *Revoliutsiia i natsional'nosti* 4–5 (1930): 111.
90 A. Gitlianskii, "Leninskaia natsional'naia politika v deistvii (natsional'nye men'shinstva na Ukraine)," *Revoliutsiia i natsional'nosti* 9 (1931): 37; A. Zuev, "Natsmeny Kazakhstana," *Revoliutsiia i natsional'nosti* 4 (1932): 48.
91 Or so most people thought. Cf. Stalin, *Sochineniia* 13: 91–92 and *Revoliutsiia i natsional'nosti* 1 (1932); and Iiul'skii, "Pis'mo t. Stalina – orudie vospitaniia Bol'shevistskikh kadrov," *Prosveshchenie natsional'nostei* 2–3 (1932): 9.
92 See for example I.K., "Indoevropeistika v deistvii," *Prosveshchenie natsional'nostei* 11–12 (1931): 97–102; I. Kusik'ian, "Protiv burzhuaznogo kavkazovedeniia," *Prosveshchenie natsional'nostei* 1 (1932): 45–47; I. Zhvaniia, "Zadachi sovetskogo i natsional'nogo stroitel'stva v Mingrelii," *Revoliutsiia i natsional'nosti* 7 (1930): 66–72; D. Savvov, "Za podlinno rodnoi iazyk grekov Sovetskogo Soiuza," *Prosveshchenie natsional'nostei* 4 (1932): 64–74; M. Bril', "Trudiashchiesia tsygane v riady stroitelei sotsializma," *Revoliutsiia i natsional'nosti* 7 (1932): 60–66; S.D., "Evreiskaia avtonomnaia oblast, – detishche Oktiabr'skoi revoliutsii," *Revoliutsiia i natsional'nosti* 6 (1934): 13–25.
93 Simon, *Nationalism*, 46.
94 *Revoliutsiia i natsional'nosti* 1 (1930): 117; A. Takho-Godi, "Problema iazyka v Dagestane," *Revoliutsiia i natsional'nosti* 2 (1930): 68–75; Gitlianskii, "Leninskaia natsional'naia politika," 77.

95 See, for example, G. Akopov, "Podgotovka natsional'nykh kadrov," *Revoliutsiia i natsional'nosti* 4 (1934): 54–60; A. Polianskaia, "Natsional'nye kadry Belorussii," *Revoliutsiia i natsional'nosti* 8–9 (1930): 79–88; Rodnevich, "Korenizatsiia apparata"; Zuev, "Natsmeny"; E. Popova, "Korenizatsiia apparata – na vysshuiu stupen'," *Revoliutsiia i natsional'nosti* 7 (1932): 50–55; I. Iuabov, "Natsmeny Uzbekskoi SSR," *Revoliutsiia i natsional'nosti* 9 (1932): 74–78; P. S-ch, "Partorganizatsii natsional'nykh raionov," *Revoliutsiia i natsional'nosti* 10–11 (1932): 143–48; I. Karneev, "Nekotorye tsifry po podgotovke inzhenerno-tekhnicheskikh kadrov iz korennykh natsional'nostei," *Revoliutsiia i natsional'nosti* 3 (1933): 86–92.

96 Kh. Khazanskii, I. Gazeliridi, "Kul'tmassovaia rabota sredi natsional'nykh men'shinstv na novostroikakh," *Revoliutsiia i natsional'nosti* 9 (1931): 86–91; A. Kachanov, "Kul'turnoe obsluzhivanie rabochikh-natsmen Moskovskoi oblasti," *Revoliutsiia i natsional'nosti* 6 (1932): 54–58; I. Sabirzianov, "Natsmenrabota profsoiuzov Moskvy," *Revoliutsiia i natsional'nosti* 9 (1932): 69–74.

97 A. Mitrofanov, "K itogam partchistki v natsrespublikakh i oblastiakh," *Revoliutsiia i natsional'nosti* 1 (1930): 29–36; Martha Brill Olcott, *The Kazakhs* (Stanford: Hoover Institution Press, 1987), 216–20; Mace, *Communism*, 264–80; Rakowska-Harmstone, *Russia and Nationalism*, 39–41; Azade-Ayse Rorlich, *The Volga Tatars: A Profile in National Resilience* (Stanford: Hoover Institution Press, 1986), 155–56.

98 In other words, women and children could become default proletarians. See Gregory Massell, *The Surrogate Proletariat: Moslem Women and Revolutionary Strategies in Soviet Central Asia, 1919–1929* (Princeton: Princeton University Press, 1974); Yuri Slezkine, "From Savages to Citizens: The Cultural Revolution in the Soviet Far North, 1928–1938," *Slavic Review* 51, no. 1 (Spring 1992): 52–76.

99 "*Vskrytie klassovoi rozni*," See N. Krupskaia, "O zadachakh natsional'no-kul'turnogo stroitel'stva v sviazi s obostreniem klassovoi bor'by," *Prosveshchenie natsional'nostei* 4–5 (1930): 19.

100 S. Dimanshtein, "Za klassovuiu chetkost' v prosveshchenii natsional'nostei," *Prosveshchenie natsional'nostei* 1 (1929): 9.

101 N. Bilibin, "U zapadnykh koriakov," *Sovetskii Sever* 1–2, (1932): 207.

102 See, for example, Olcott, *The Kazakhs*, 219; Rakowska-Harmstone, *Russia and Nationalism*, 100–1.

103 D. Zaslavskii, "Na protsesse 'vyzvolentsev'," *Prosveshchenie natsional'nostei* 6 (1930): 13.

104 Stalin, *Sochineniia*, 13: 306, 309.

105 For two remarkable exceptions, see Barbara A. Anderson and Brian D. Silver, "Equality, Efficiency and Politics in Soviet Bilingual Education Policy, 1934–1980," *American Political Science Review* 78, no. 4 (October 1984): 1019–39; and Ronald Grigor Suny, "The Soviet South: Nationalism and the Outside World," in Michael Mandelbaum, ed., *The Rise of Nations in the Soviet Union* (New York: Council of Foreign Relations Press, 1991): 69.

106 Sheila Fitzpatrick, *Education and Social Mobility in the Soviet Union, 1921–1934* (Cambridge: Cambridge University Press, 1979), 235.

107 *Pervyi vsesoiuznyi s"ezd sovetskikh pisatelei. Stenograficheskii otchet* (Moscow: Khudozhestvennaia literatura, 1934), 625.

108 Compare, for example, Stalin, *Sochineniia*, 8: 149–54; and S. Dimanshtein, "Bol'shevistskii otpor natsionalizmu," *Revoliutsiia i natsional'nosti* 4 (1933):

1–13; S.D., "Bor'ba s natsionalizmom i uroki Ukrainy," *Revoliutsiia i natsional'nosti* 1 (1934): 15–22.

109 Simon, *Nationalism*, 148–55.

110 After Stalin's speeches at the XVII party Congress and at the Conference of the Leading Collective Farmers of Tajikistan and Turkmenistan (see Stalin, *Sochineniia*, 13: 361; 14 [1]: 114–115).

111 Paul M. Austin, "Soviet Karelian: The Language That Failed," *Slavic Review* 51, no. 1 (Spring 1992), esp. 22–23.

112 This is, in effect, a crude summary of Vladimir Papernyi's delightful *Kul'tura "Dva"* (Ann Arbor: Ardis, 1985).

113 On the "passport system," see Victor Zaslavsky, *The Neo-Stalinist State* (Armonk, N.Y.: M. E. Sharpe, 1982), 92ff.

114 L. Krasovskii, "Chem nado rukovodstvovat'sia pri sostavlenii spiska narodnostei SSSR," *Revoliutsiia i natsional'nosti* 4 (1936): 70–71.

115 S. Dimanshtein, "Otvet na vopros, sostavliaiut li soboi evrei v nauchnom smysle natsiiu," *Revoliutsiia i natsional'nosti* 10 (1935): 77.

116 Simon, *Nationalism*, 61.

117 Greg Castillo, "Gorki Street and the Design of the Stalin Revolution," in Zeynep Celik, Diane G. Favro and Richard Ingersoll, eds, *Streets: Critical Perspectives on Public Space* (Berkeley: University of California Press, 1994).

118 *Pervyi vsesoiuznyi s"ezd*, 43, 49.

119 Ibid., 104.

120 Ibid., 116–17.

121 Ibid., 136, 142, 77.

122 Zaslavsky, "Nationalism and Democratic Transition," 102.

123 North Ossetian, Iakut, Kazakh, Kirghiz, Kara-Kalpak, Kabarda, Balkar, Turkmen, Taijk, Adyge and Kalmyk (see A. Furmanova, "Podgotovka natsional'nykh kadrov dlia teatra," *Revoliutsiia i natsional'nosti* 5 [1936]: 29–30).

124 A. Chanyshev, "V bor'be za izuchenie i sozdanie natsional'noi kul'tury," *Revoliutsiia i natsional'nosti* 9 (1935): 61.

125 *Pervyi vsesoiuznyi s"ezd*, 43. "Turk" stands for "Azerbaijani."

126 Stalin, *Sochineniia* 2 (XV): 204.

127 "Khronika," *Revoliutsiia i natsional'nosti* 8 (1936): 80; Rakowska-Harmstone, *Russia and Nationalism*, 250–59; Allworth, *The Modern Uzbeks*, 229–30; Yaroslav Bilinsky, *The Second Soviet Republic: The Ukraine after World War II* (New Brunswick: Rutgers University Press, 1964), 191.

128 Lowell Tillett, *The Great Friendship: Soviet Historians on the Non-Russian Nationalities* (Chapel Hill: University of North Carolina Press, 1969), passim.

129 Bilinsky, *The Second Soviet Republic*, 15–16; Robert Conquest, *Soviet Nationalities Policy in Practice* (New York: Praeger, 1967), 65–66.

130 Stalin, *Sochineniia* 3 (XVI): 100.

131 Ibid., 46.

132 Ibid., 117, 119, 138.

133 See, in particular, Lapidus, "Ethnonationalism and Political Stability," 355–80; Zaslavsky, "Nationalism and Democratic Transition"; Farmer, *Ukrainian Nationalism*, 61–73.

134 Rasma Karklins, *Ethnic Relations in the USSR: The Perspective from Below* (Boston: Unwin Hyman, 1986).

135 See Roeder, "Soviet Federalism," 196–233.

136 Rakowska-Harmstone, "The Dialectics," 10–15. Cf. Miroslav Hroch, *Social Preconditions of National Revival in Europe* (New York: Cambridge University Press, 1985).

137 See, in particular, Farmer, *Ukrainian Nationalism*, 85–121. Also Allworth, *The Modern Uzbeks*, 258–59; Simon, *Nationalism*, 281–82.

138 For a remarkably elegant interpretation of this tension, see Rogers Brubaker, "Nationhood and the National Question in the Soviet Union and Post-Soviet Eurasia: An Institutionalist Account," *Theory and Society*, 23: 1 (1994).

139 Victor Zaslavsky. "The Evolution of Separatism in Soviet Society under Gorbachev," in Gail W. Lapidus and Victor Zaslavsky, with Philip Goldman, eds, *From Union to Commonwealth: Nationalism and Separatism in the Soviet Republics* (New York: Cambridge University Press, 1992), 83; Leokadiia Drobizheva, "Perestroika and the Ethnic Consciousness of the Russians," in ibid., 98–111.

12

MODERNIZATION OR NEO-TRADITIONALISM?

Ascribed nationality and Soviet primordialism[1]

Terry Martin

In his 1913 pamphlet, *Marxism and the Nationalities Question*, Stalin began his definition of a nation as follows:[2]

> What is a nation?
>
> A nation is, above all, a community, a definite community of people.
>
> *This community is not racial, nor is it tribal.* The modern Italian nation was formed from Romans, Teutons, Etruscans, Greeks, Arabs, and so forth. The French nation was formed from Gauls, Romans, Bretons, Teutons, and so on. The same can be said of the English, Germans and others, who consolidated into nations out of different races and tribes.
>
> *Thus, a nation is not racial or tribal, but a historically constituted community of people.* [Emphasis added]

This was an unexceptional, orthodox statement of contemporary Marxist thought. European Marxists were then contesting the growing racialist and primordial ethnic thinking that justified both imperialism and the growing nationalist movements of Eastern Europe. In opposition to the widespread contemporary belief in the historic depth of national identity, Marxists asserted that nations were fundamentally modern constructs.[3] In Stalin's words: "A nation is not merely a historical category, but a historical category belonging to a definite epoch, the epoch of rising capitalism."[4] After October 1917, Soviet nationalities policy would be premised on this belief that nations were not primordial entities, but rather inevitable by-products of modernization.[5]

In 1938, the Communist Party's official theoretical journal, *Bolshevik*, published an article, "The Magnificent Russian People," that epitomized a radically different understanding of nations:[6]

> The history of the Great Russian people is the history of its heroic battles for independence and freedom against innumerable enemies, conquerors and interventionists, including "German elements" . . . In this difficult battle, full of dangers, the magnificent Russian people multiplied and developed its remarkable qualities as the People-Fighter (*narod-borets*) and People-Freedom Lover (*narod-svobodoliubets*) . . .

The author then went on to recount the defeat of thirteenth century "German elements," the Teutonic Knights, by Alexander Nevsky, and concluded his description with a hymn to the primordial essence of Russianness:[7]

> The people is immortal. The military capabilities of the Slavic warriors (*druzhina*) and the courage, endurance, resourcefulness and resoluteness of the Russian fighters (*voinov*) – all these qualities have been cultivated in the Russian people.

That article exemplified a dramatic turn in the mid-1930s, away from the former Soviet view of nations as fundamentally modern constructs, and towards an emphasis on the deep primordial roots of modern nations.[8]

This dramatic reversal in the Party's official theoretical approach to nationality warrants further analysis. This is especially the case since such reversals were characteristic of the 1930s, and so understanding them might shed some light on the social and political nature of Stalinism. To that end, I will first present an explanation for the Soviet turn towards primordial nationality in the 1930s. I will then link this argument to an emerging controversy in current Soviet historiography: the relationship between the Soviet Union and modernity.[9]

This relationship is actually quite an old concern. The best American scholarship of the 1950s identified modernization as the fundamental sociological trend characterizing Stalinist society.[10] Scholars like Barrington Moore, Merle Fainsod, and Alex Inkeles pointed to the modernizing goals that the Soviet leadership consciously sought to achieve: industrialization, urbanization, secularization, universal education and literacy. More powerfully, they also pointed to a number of trends that contradicted the Bolsheviks' original goals, but that were characteristic of all modernizing societies: the emergence of a hereditary class system, lower birth rates, authoritarian industrial discipline, middle-class respectability. Quite understandably, they interpreted these trends as an unavoidable consequence of the Soviet Union's transition from traditional to modern industrial society.

In the early 1980s, however, several sociologists began to draw attention to the prominence and persistence of traditional pre-modern practices in Communist societies.[11] Modernization was supposed to involve the transition from ascribed status groups (*sosloviia*) to economic classes.[12] Nevertheless, many characteristics of status societies seemed to thrive under Communism: a hierarchical distribution of privileges and information according to political status; the importance of ranks, titles, uniforms, honors and other status symbols. Likewise, modernization theory predicted the replacement of personalistic ties with bureaucratic ones. Yet the role of informal and personal relationships also appeared to intensify in Communist societies: *blat* [exchange of favors], *tolkachi* [industrial procurements agents using informal methods of obtaining goods], patron–client networks, paternalistic "big men" (*vozhdi*) and their submissive petitioners.[13] These social scientists argued that the distinctive quality of Communist societies was the coexistence of modern and traditional elements. They coined a new term to describe such societies: neo-traditionalism.[14]

Nationality is an excellent test-case for evaluating the utility of the modernization and neo-traditional paradigms in understanding Stalinist society. Almost all contemporary students of nationalism agree with the original Bolshevik premise that the emergence of nations and nationalism is a consequence of the transition from traditional to modern society. They do not associate that transition exclusively, as Lenin and Stalin did, with the rise of capitalism. Most would prefer to give independent weight to such factors as the growth of centralized states, ideology and industrialization.[15] I will focus initially on the characteristic role of industrialization in the emergence of nations and nationalism, since industrialization was the central modernizing process of the Stalinist era.

Ernest Gellner's theory of nationality as an inevitable consequence of the social organization of industrial society provides a highly useful orientation for thinking about the Bolshevik turn towards primordial nationality in the 1930s.[16] Gellner argues that pre-industrial states lack the sociological prerequisites for the emergence of modern nations. Such states are divided vertically into a series of isolated village-based cultures. Villagers share a common culture that structures their daily life. All communication – gestures, actions, words – is readily understood within this mutually shared cultural context. These village-based cultures can be described as primordial, rooted, "thick." They are also pre-national. Peasants typically identify themselves either as locals or by their faith, not by nationality. Pre-modern states are likewise divided horizontally between the peasantry and the ruling estates. These estates do have a state-wide organization and share a common identity. However, this identity is not a national, but rather a corporate one. The clergy usually serve a universalist faith. Members of the nobility, which is often multi-ethnic in composition, emphasize their estate identity and deny any common national culture with the debased peasantry. Nationality, therefore, has no place in the pre-industrial state.[17]

In Gellner's model, industrialization destroys the primordial village-based folk cultures by uprooting the peasantry and transplanting them into an urban industrial environment where they lack a common cultural context. In order for these newly urbanized peasants to communicate with one another in a way that will allow an industrial society to function efficiently, a new common culture must be created. The state insures the emergence of a common, high culture (that is, a written, codified culture) by establishing a universal system of education. Gellner emphasizes that no industrial state has functioned without one. The new high culture is not nearly so deep and all-encompassing as the old folk cultures. It consists of no more than "certain shared qualifications: literacy, numeracy, basic work habits and social skills, familiarity with basic technical and social skills."[18] It is constructed, state-wide, "thin." Its dispersion throughout the territory of a given state creates a modern nation.

Gellner's key insight, then, is that modern national cultures are not extensions or distillations of pre-existing village cultures. Rather, their emergence presupposes the prior destruction of those primordial folk cultures. This is the essence of the modern sociological interpretation of nationality. It was shared by the Bolsheviks in the 1920s and articulated by Stalin in the passages quoted in the opening paragraph.

However, there is a second, much more widespread modern interpretation of nationality: the one subscribed to by nationalists themselves. Gellner notes that "generally speaking, nationalist ideology suffers from pervasive false consciousness. Its myths invert reality: it claims to defend folk culture while in fact it is forging a high culture; it claims to protect an old folk society while in fact helping to build up an anonymous mass society."[19] Nations are in reality the consequence of the social organization of industrial society, Gellner argues, but they are perceived by nationalists as the embodiment, awakening and essence of ancient village-based folk cultures. For this reason, nationalists place great emphasis on accidental and often invented elements of folk culture that survive to become part of the modern high culture. It is this primordial interpretation of nations, however, that by and large captured popular imaginations and made nationalism the strongest political force of the modern era.

To sum up, Gellner's analysis provides us with two useful insights. First, the policies that Stalin implemented to an unprecedented degree – rapid industrialization, the uprooting of the peasantry, high levels of social mobility, the establishment of a standardized universal system of education – typically lead to the formation of a shared high culture and a shared national identity, Gellner's definition of a nation-state. Gellner's theory also predicts that, due to uneven industrialization, isolated and culturally distinct regions often fail to assimilate with the new state-wide high culture. Such failures to assimilate result in a distinct regionally based high culture and separatist nationalism.[20] In both cases, however, exactly the same process occurs: industrialization destroys village-based folk cultures and necessitates the formation of a new high culture, which in turn serves as the basis for a shared national identity. In modern industrial society, high culture and national identity coincide.

Second, Gellner's analysis emphasizes that there are two modern interpretations of nationality: the sociological view of nations as modern constructs and the popular understanding of nations as primordial. The former view, as we have seen, informed the Soviet nationalities policy in the 1920s, while the latter view came to predominate in the 1930s. The Bolsheviks, it would seem, went from being students of nationalism to nationalists. This was ironic, since the original Soviet nationalities policy was a strategy designed to accomplish the exact opposite process: to move the Soviet population from the popular nationalist understanding of nations to the Bolsheviks' own sociological concept.

Such a policy was naturally a highly ambitious endeavor. I will briefly outline the logic of the original Soviet nationalities policy, since this intervention profoundly influenced the outcome of Stalinist modernization.[21] The strength of nationalism as a mobilizing force during the Revolution and Civil War had both surprised and disturbed the Bolshevik leadership. Party leaders differed on how best to address the nationalities question. One faction, led by Piatakov and Bukharin, argued that with the abolition of capitalism in Russia, nationalism and national identities would disappear. Therefore, the Party should give no support to the existence of separate national identities.[22] Lenin and Stalin both disagreed and argued instead that the Bolsheviks' own modernizing policies would result in a short-term strengthening of national identity.[23] In other words, they accepted Gellner's substitution of industrialism for capitalism as the primary force generating national identity.

However, it was impossible for any Bolshevik to accept Gellner's contention that national identity, as the shared idiom of a modern industrial society, would almost always be a stronger force than class identity. The Bolsheviks viewed nationalism much more instrumentally. Nationalism was a uniquely dangerous mobilizing ideology because it had the potential to forge an all-class alliance for national goals. It did this by presenting legitimate class grievances in an inappropriate national form. This was possible, of course, due to the popular primordial understanding of nationalism. Gellner would later parody this Marxist argument as the "Wrong-Address Theory" of nationalism:

> Just as extreme Shi'ite Muslims hold that Archangel Gabriel
> made a mistake, delivering the Message to Mohammed when it
> was intended for Ali, so Marxists basically like to think that the
> spirit of history or human consciousness made a terrible boob.
> The wakening message was intended for classes, but by some
> terrible postal error was delivered to nations.[24]

The Bolsheviks believed this danger could be averted by a strategy
that would depoliticize national identity. Paradoxically, this strategy
involved the systematic promotion of all "forms" of national identity
that did not conflict with the existence of a unitary, socialist state. In
practice, this meant support for the following national forms: national
languages, national elites, national territories and national cultures. The
logic behind this policy can be summarized as follows. Nationalism is
a masking ideology that leads legitimate class interests to be expressed,
not in an appropriate class-based socialist movement, but rather in the
form of an above-class national movement. National identity is not a
primordial quality, but rather an unavoidable by-product of the modern
capitalist *and* early socialist world, which must be passed through before
a mature international socialist world can come into being. Since national
identity *is* a real phenomenon in the modern world, it cannot be unequivocally condemned as reactionary. *Some* national claims – those confined
to the realm of national forms – are in fact legitimate and must be granted
in order to split the above-class national alliance. This policy will speed
the emergence of class cleavages, and so allow the Party to recruit non-
Russian proletarian and peasant support for its socialist agenda.
Nationalism will be disarmed by granting the forms of nationhood.

To restate this strategy in Gellnerian terms, Soviet policy sought to
decouple high culture and national identity. This is exactly what Stalin
meant by his famous phrase about cultures "national in form, socialist in
content."[25] Socialism would provide the basis for a new Soviet high culture, a state-wide cultural idiom inculcated through a universal, standardized, and yet multilingual, system of education and propaganda.
Socialism, not nationalism, would be the state's unifying principle.
National identity was accepted, and indeed propagated, by the Soviet state
in order to avoid the emergence of defensive nationalism. Any hint of
Russification was avoided. The idea of sponsoring a Soviet national identity was rejected, since such an attempt would be interpreted by non-
Russians as a front for Russification. Instead, national identity was
systematically promoted at the sub-state level in the form of national
republics, with their own national elites, languages and cultures. Of
course, these national cultures had to accommodate the new Soviet high
culture. They, therefore, could not contain any fundamentally distinctive
religious, legal, ideological or customary features.[26] Soviet citizens would

share a common high culture, but not a common national identity. According to Gellner's theory, in the modern world, such an outcome was impossible.[27]

This decoupling of national identity and high culture would serve the long-term Soviet goal of transcending national identity. National identity would be depoliticized by an ostentatious demonstration of respect for the national identities of all Soviet citizens. This would in turn allow the Soviet state to demonstrate the superiority of its newly emerging socialist high culture without provoking a nationalist backlash.[28] The eventual universal acceptance of this high culture would result, over the very long term, in the gradual disappearance of separate national identities (though how exactly this would occur always remained shrouded in mystery).[29] Of course, such a development was impossible given a popular understanding of nations as primordial. Thus, the Soviet nationalities policy also represented a pedagogical effort to move the Soviet population from the popular understanding of nations as primordial and immutable to the Bolsheviks' own sociological understanding of nations as historical and contingent. The Communist Party would act not only as the vanguard of the working class, but the vanguard of Soviet nations as well: guiding them through the phase of modernization and national identity to socialism and transcendence of national identity.

However, the exact opposite occurred. Soviet policy initially inadvertently inculcated and strengthened popular primordialism. Then, in the second half of the 1930s, the Soviet state suddenly abandoned its previous belief in contingent nationality and began to propagate an extreme and crude form of primordialism. Why did this occur? I will argue that it was an unintended consequence of the extreme statism exemplified by Bolshevik national vanguardism. Take, for instance, the issue of assimilation. Typically, wherever nationality is seen more as a modern construct, such as in the United States and France, ethnic outsiders and immigrants are encouraged to assimilate with the shared national culture. In nations where a primordial understanding of nationality prevails, such as Germany or Israel, ethnic outsiders are neither expected nor encouraged to assimilate.[30] One would have anticipated, then, that the Soviet Union would have encouraged voluntary assimilation. In fact, it did not.[31] The reason, again, was to avoid the emergence of defensive nationalism. If a minority of non-Russians voluntarily Russified, this would lead to a growth in reactive or defensive nationalism among the remaining non-Russian majority. Therefore, even voluntary assimilation was actively discouraged. For instance, Soviet educational policy stipulated that all children must attend native-language schools, regardless of the fact that many non-Russian parents very much wanted their children to attend Russian-language schools.[32]

354

Thus, although the policy of systematically supporting national forms was intended to disarm nationalism and so prepare the way for an eventual transcendence of national identity, in practice it actively hindered that process. It required a constant routine of ethnic labeling and so inadvertently indoctrinated the Soviet population in the belief that ethnicity was an inherent, fundamental and crucially important characteristic of all individuals. In order to implement affirmative action programs, monitor their success, delineate national territories, assign children to native-language schools and administer dozens of other nationalities programs, the Soviet state constantly asked its citizens for their nationality.[33] It also asked their employers, their Party cell chairmen, trade union representatives, and so forth. All personnel forms had a line marked nationality. Moreover, affirmative action turned nationality into a valuable form of social capital. The nationality line in a job application form was not a neutral piece of information but a crucial advantage or disadvantage. The message broadcast by the state was crystal clear: nationality is one of the most important attributes of any individual.

Rather than indoctrinating the belief that national form was an essentially superficial and politically unimportant additive to socialist content, as was the Party's stated intention, this policy instead reinforced a popular belief in primordial ethnicity. It became second nature to label people nationally. When internal passports were introduced in 1932, there was no debate about whether to record nationality on them. It was included without reflection, just as it was on all personnel forms, as a necessary and crucial datum about any Soviet citizen.[34] Yet the national line on Soviet passports became one of the single most important factors in not only reinforcing the belief, but also creating the social fact, that national identity was primordial and inherited.

The analogy between the Bolshevik approach to class and nationality is both striking and instructive. Despite the Bolsheviks' theoretical commitment to the mutable and temporary nature of both these identities, they in practice turned them into ascribed status categories.[35] Former workers retained their proletarian status even as they entered administration, while a one-time trader or well-to-do peasant could not easily shed his status as nepman or kulak by entering a different profession. As with nationality, class was transformed into an ascribed status due to "the legal and institutional structures that discriminated on the basis of class."[36] It was necessary to label individuals by class and nationality in order to determine who should receive preferences.[37] As with nationality, this encouraged a belief that class was an essential quality of an individual (with disastrous consequences for those labeled kulak), instead of a temporary and mutable attribute. In both cases, practice diverged strikingly from theory. It was never the Bolsheviks' articulated intention either to abandon orthodox Marxist class analysis or to promote a primordial understanding of national identity.

This outcome was instead an unintended consequence of the Bolsheviks' own extreme statism. Their attempts to organize, classify and reward their population according to sociological categories led them to reify categories they themselves viewed as constructed rather than essential. The behavior of the Soviet state differed drastically from the role assigned to the state in Gellner's model, where the state's main task was simply to organize a universal standardized system of education, while the impersonal social forces unleashed by industrialization drove identity formation.[38] In the Soviet case, however, the state intervened actively to manage identity categorization and so dramatically altered the typical consequences of modernization. This contrast suggests a major difference between market-driven and state-driven industrialization. In the latter case, there is a tendency to transform the impersonal modern categories of class and nationality into ascribed status categories, modern equivalents of traditional status (*soslovie/Stand*) divisions.

If it was statism that generated ascribed status identities, then this phenomenon should have increased dramatically in the 1930s with the completion of Stalin's radically statist "revolution from above." Although carried out under a slogan of class warfare, this campaign resulted in the creation of an almost completely state-managed economy and society. By the early 1930s, class militancy was being downplayed and class-based affirmative action programs phased out. The 1936 constitution abolished the category of class enemies. In principle, this should have meant the abolition of ascribed class categories and a movement towards a unified shared Soviet identity, the Gellnerian prerequisite for a Soviet nation.

Yet, again, the opposite occurred. What Fitzpatrick has called "Stalinist *soslovnost'*" instead intensified.[39] Various population categories were assigned different legal privileges and duties. Peasants were the clearest case of a Stalinist neo-*soslovie*: they were legally denied passports and freedom of movement, required to pay special taxes and labor services, but also allowed a few special privileges such as the right to own a private plot and sell its surplus at market prices.[40] Another emerging neo-*soslovie* category comprised the "leading cadres and specialists," who "enjoyed a range of special privileges, including access to closed stores, chauffeured cars, and government dachas."[41] Other population categories were Stakhanovites, *spetspereselentsy* ["special settlers," that is, administrative exiles], and *edinolichniki* [non-collectivized peasants]. Once again, this emerging system was generated by extreme Soviet statism. "Stalinist *soslovnost'*" was a system where individuals were categorized according to their relationship to the state, and granted status perquisites (or alternatively punishments), according to service rendered to the state.[42]

If the practice of ascribing class could survive the formal de-emphasis of class categories in 1936, it is no surprise that the practice of ascribing nationality should intensify greatly in the 1930s. Moreover, nationality was now ascribed as a primordial and essential attribute, not simply a historical and contingent one. With the de-emphasis of class in the 1930s, Soviet propaganda increasingly focused on the twin poles of a powerful, paternalistic state and an obedient, contented people (*narod*). Indeed, the 1936 constitution inaugurated a cult of the popular (*narodnost'*). As one commentator noted: "The constitution should remind us that the popular (*narodnost'*) is the highest criterion of all cultural work."[43] This new cult of *narodnost'* led to a massive increase in the amount of attention devoted to folklore and *völkisch* artistic expression in the 1930s.[44] Dozens of new Institutes of National Culture sprang up across the Soviet Union after 1933, dedicated to the celebration and promotion of ethnically distinct, folkloric, primordial national cultures.[45] Massively publicized *dekady* of national art (invariably attended by Stalin and the Politburo) took place regularly in Moscow and emphasized national dance, song and folklore.[46] A highly clichéd essentializing rhetoric of national culture likewise emerged. Georgia, for instance, was invariably called "sunny socialist Georgia," whose fine weather explained its "joyful" national art.[47]

Prior to the mid-1930s, such "exoticization" of national culture – we would call it orientalism – was regularly denounced as a manifestation of Great Power chauvinism.[48] By 1937–8 it had become official state policy. On the one hand, the intensive practice of ethnic labeling had reified and essentialized national identities. On the other hand, the official shift in emphasis from class to people that took place with the triumph of Stalinist statism in the 1930s led to an increase in attention given to national culture as the literal embodiment of *narodnost'*. These two factors were the major forces driving the Soviet turn towards a primordial understanding of nations and national culture in the 1930s.

The new Soviet primordialism of the 1930s allowed the emergence of a previously absent category: the enemy nation.[49] In the 1920s, class ascription was used both to identify class allies for preferential treatment and to expose class enemies for punishment. The latter practice culminated in the dekulakization campaign, a total state effort to eliminate a reified class category. In the 1920s, however, there were no enemy nations.[50] It is true that the "former Great Power nationality," the Russians, were ineligible for national-based affirmative action, and their traditional culture was often stigmatized as imperialist.[51] However, Russians were never singled out for punishment. The belief that nationality was historic and contingent, as well as compatible with a socialist high culture, implied that all negative national characteristics could be removed through re-education rather than through a policy of national persecution analogous to dekulakization.

The shift towards primordial nationality and the extreme statism of the 1930s, which generated a xenophobic attitude towards all influence from abroad, combined to create the category of enemy nations.[52] These enemy nations were primarily foreign nation-states, especially Germany, who were perceived as a threat to the present-day Soviet Union, but were now imagined as primordial enemies of the Russian state.[53] Many of these enemy states, however, had substantial diaspora communities living within the Soviet Union. Given the new primordialism, it was assumed that these nationalities owed their highest loyalty to their "homelands" abroad and so represented an internal enemy. Therefore, beginning in 1935, these Soviet diaspora nationalities – Germans, Poles, Finns, Latvians, Estonians, Lithuanians, Koreans, Chinese, Kurds – began to be deported away from the Soviet Union's border regions.[54] With the onset of the Great Terror, suspicions of disloyalty escalated dramatically and these same diaspora nationalities (as well as Bulgarians, Macedonians, Iranians, Greeks and Afghans) were labeled enemy nations and targeted for mass arrest throughout the Soviet Union.[55] On the one hand, the emergence of the category of enemy nation, which during and after World War II would be extended to numerous indigenous Soviet nationalities, marked the triumph of primordialist thinking.[56] On the other hand, since the concept of enemy nations was not compatible with a belief in modern constructed nations, it also represented a final factor fueling the Soviet turn towards primordial nationality.[57]

Soviet primordialism, then, can be explained by a number of convergent factors. The pervasive Soviet practice of labeling individuals by national identity in order to administer affirmative action programs helped turn nationality into an ascribed hereditary status. Passportization reflected and exacerbated this trend. In addition, Stalin's statist revolution from above produced a paternalistic cult of the popular, which in turn encouraged a celebration of primordial, *völkisch* national culture. Finally, the emergence of the category of enemy nations both exemplified and further reinforced the tendency to think of nations primordially rather than instrumentally. The Soviet turn towards primordial nationality, then, was not intentional. It was the result of unforeseen consequences of the original Soviet nationalities policy combined with the affinity of primordial nationality with broader Soviet social processes such as the statist cult of the popular.

I will now conclude with a comparison of the impact of the Stalinist and Gellnerian models of modernization on the formation of national identity. Gellner's model demands an outcome where high culture and national identity coincide. Soviet policy, on the other hand, sought to decouple high culture ("socialist in content") from national identity ("national in form"), first in order to enable the transcendence of national identity, then later as a consequence of the Soviet belief in primordial nationality. This was Soviet policy. What, however, was the impact of that policy on the actual process of identity formation? Soviet policy most certainly did impede the development of a common Soviet national identity, which might otherwise have emerged in a much stronger form as a result of the Soviet Union's modernization. (Likewise, ascribing class undoubtedly inhibited the emergence of modern class consciousness.) However, were separate national identities and a non-national state-wide high "Soviet" culture able to emerge simultaneously and coexist? Clearly national identities greatly intensified under Soviet rule and, although this is a question awaiting future research, some evidence suggests at least a trend towards a common Soviet high culture.[58] For instance, in their interviews with émigrés of the World War II era, Bauer and Inkeles found that their Ukrainian and Russian émigrés shared an almost identical sociological profile and identical social attitudes, with one major difference: they disagreed markedly on all questions relating to their perceptions of the nationalities question. The authors found this result significant and puzzling.[59] My analysis of these data would suggest that, for these admittedly culturally similar nationalities, the Soviet policy of decoupling high culture and national identity was working. Ukrainians and Russians shared a common Soviet high culture, as well as radically different ascribed national identities.[60]

The second distinctive feature of Soviet nationalities policy was its peculiar evolution towards a primordial understanding of nationality in the 1930s. Here there is considerable reason to believe that Soviet primordialism had a strong impact on identity formation. Western travelers to the post-Stalinist Soviet Union reported an insatiable Soviet curiosity about their visitors' nationality and a marked refusal to accept a non-primordial identity, frequently leading to the following vignette: " 'What's your nationality?' 'American.' 'No' (shaking head in exasperation), 'I'm not asking for your citizenship, what's your nationality?' " American, like Soviet, was not a nationality. Something more primordial, like German or Chechen, was required.[61] More scientific post-Soviet survey and ethnographic research has confirmed the remarkable strength of popular primordialism across the entire Soviet Union.[62]

As I have emphasized, primordialism *per se* is not at all incompatible with modernization theory. Indeed, Gellner argues it is the typical interpretation of nationality in the modern era.[63] Rather, Soviet practice was unusual, indeed bizarre, in its combination of primordialism and the decoupling of high culture and national identity. Primordialists are typically nationalists, who cannot imagine the separation of culture and identity. National identity is primordial because it is the expression of an ancient, continuous cultural tradition. Yet, in the late 1930s, the Soviet state combined their 1920s belief that national cultures could be bled of all religious, cultural, ideological and customary "content," reduced to a set of folkloric völkisch rituals, with their 1930s belief that these national cultures were nevertheless primordial and essential, of sufficient strength to warrant the deportation and persecution of stigmatized enemy nations. Soviet policy had evolved into an oxymoron: ascribed primordialism.

Stalinist modernization, then, produced a divergent sociological outcome where, in contrast to typical modern industrial societies, an emerging non-national high culture and separate primordially imagined national identities coexisted. Yet there is also a certain compelling resemblance between the Soviet Union and Gellner's ideal-type pre-industrial empire. Like his empire, the Soviet Union was divided vertically into separate cultures. Soviet industrialization destroyed the remnants of pre-industrial folk culture, but did not lead to a common Soviet national identity. Instead, the authentic primordial village-based folk cultures were replaced by ascribed national identities, which were nevertheless imagined primordially. Likewise, the Soviet Union also resembled Gellner's pre-industrial empire in its horizontal division between the people and a state-wide elite status group: Stalin's "leading cadres and specialists," the future *nomenklatura*. In Gellner's paradigm, industrialization eliminates the old status elite, who either assimilate with the new state-wide high culture or form the leadership of national separatist movements directed against that new high culture. In the Soviet system, the state annihilated the old status elite, but then replaced it with a new neo-*soslovie* elite.

Modernization or neo-traditionalism? I believe that my evidence about nationality strongly supports the neo-traditional paradigm for understanding Soviet social processes. Let me again re-emphasize here that the neo-traditional model does not assert that Communist societies represent a return to traditional society. They most certainly do not.[64] Neo-traditional societies, rather, represent an alternative form of modernization, one that includes the most characteristic processes of market-driven modernization (industrialization, urbanization, secularization, universal education and literacy), but one which likewise produces a variety of practices that bear a striking resemblance to characteristic features of traditional pre-modern societies. The primordially imagined nationalities of the Soviet Union are not Gellner's village-based folk cultures. "Stalinist *soslovnost'*" is not Tsarist *soslovnost'*.[65]

The primary cause of unintended neo-traditionalist outcomes was not the persistence of traditional values into the Soviet era but rather, as I have argued throughout this chapter, extreme Soviet statism.[66] In Communist neo-traditionalism, the state substitutes itself for tradition, takes over some of the roles played by tradition in pre-modern societies. Gellner's folk-based cultures were the authentic product of tradition, while Communism's folkloric national identities were the invention of the state (usually with the enthusiastic participation of national elites).

If Tsarist *soslovnost'* already marked a state-sponsored endorsement of traditional status categories, Stalinist *soslovnost'* represented a novel creation of status categories by the Soviet state.

The Soviet state substituted itself not only for the role of tradition in pre-modern states, but also, of course, for the role of the market in non-socialist industrial societies. I have already noted the key role of this substitution in the creation of the neo-traditional status categories of ascribed class and nationality. The state's assumption of market functions further links these two sociological outcomes to the other major social practices accounted for by the neo-traditional model: namely, the dominant role of personalistic and informal relations, of patron–client networks, *blat* and *tolkachi*, paternalistic "big men" and their submissive petitioners. I have not addressed this aspect of the neo-traditional model, since these practices are not directly connected to issues of nationality.[67]

However, these practices can also be explained as a product of the Soviet state's substitution of itself for the market. The Soviet state tried to establish a modern, impersonal system for distributing consumer goods, wages and promotions.[68] However, on the one hand, this system proved incapable of successfully distributing goods efficiently. On the other hand, at each level of the distribution, this system relied not on the impersonal forces of the market, but rather on an individual bureaucrat whose personal interest did not coincide with the interest of the state. The result was the emergence of an informal system of distribution, based on the pervasive use of personal connections. At the top of the system, the result was patron–client relations and deferential petitioning to paternalistic "big men." At the bottom, the result was the exchange of favors through the system of *blat*. As with ascribed status categories, extreme Soviet statism was the root cause of neo-traditional outcomes.

Modernization is the theory of Soviet intentions; neo-traditionalism, the theory of their unintended consequences.

NOTES

This is an edited version of an article written for a volume edited by David L. Hoffman and Yanni Kotsonis, *Russian Modernity: Politics, Practice, Knowledge*, London: Macmillan, forthcoming.
1 The research for this chapter was funded by the International Research and Exchange Board (IREX) and the Social Sciences and Humanities Research Council (SSHRC) of Canada. I would like to thank Julie Hessler, Roman Szporluk, Matt Lenoe, Sheila Fitzpatrick and the participants at Yanni Kotsonis's and David Hoffman's workshop on New Approaches to Russian History, Jörg Baberowski's conference on Nationalities Policy in the Non-Slavic Regions (Tübingen University) and Roman Szporluk's seminar on

Nationalism and Socialism at Harvard University for helpful comments. The ideas for this chapter emerged out of a series of planned conversations with my friend and colleague, Matt Lenoe. For Lenoe's more penetrating ideas on neo-traditionalism, see Matthew Lenoe, "Stalinist Mass Journalism and the Transformation of Soviet Newspapers, 1926–1932," PhD dissertation, University of Chicago, 1997, 930–64.

2 I. Stalin, "Marksizm i natsional'nyi vopros," (1913) in *Marksizm i natsional'no-kolonial'nyi vopros* (Moscow, 1934): 4, emphasis added.

3 Within this broad paradigm, Marxists differed considerably on a variety of specific issues. For an overview, see Walker Connor, *The National Question in Marxist-Leninist Theory and Strategy* (Princeton, 1984), 28–42.

4 Stalin, "Marksizm," 10.

5 I use the word "primordial" in this chapter to refer to a belief in both the antiquity of modern nations and the fundamental continuity in a nation's essence across time. The primordialist/modernist dispute in nationalities studies is already an old and increasingly unproductive one. For a summary with bibliography, see the introduction to John Hutchinson and Anthony B. Smith, eds, *Ethnicity* (Oxford, 1996), 3–16.

6 B. Volin, "Velikii russkii narod," *Bolshevik* no. 9 (1938): 28. I translate "*velikii*" here as "magnificent" to convey its honorific content and distinguish it from the more neutral ethnonym "*velikorusskii*" (Great Russian), which the author also uses.

7 Ibid., 29.

8 For a detailed analysis of this turn in the period from 1933 to 1938, see Terry Martin, "An Affirmative Action Empire: Ethnicity and the Soviet State", *1923–1938*, PhD dissertation, University of Chicago, 1996, 932–82. For its continuation after World War II, see Yuri Slezkine, "The USSR as a Communal Apartment," Chapter 11 in this volume; idem., *Arctic Mirrors* (Ithaca, NY, 1994), 303–36; and Lowell Tillett, *The Great Friendship: Soviet Historians on the Non-Russian Nationalities* (Chapel Hill, NC, 1969).

9 For a volume of essays dedicated to this theme, see David L. Hoffman and Yanni Kotsonis, eds, *Russian Modernity: Politics, Practice, Knowledge* (London: MacMillan, forthcoming). See also Peter Holquist, "'Information is the Alpha and Omega of Our Work': Bolshevik Surveillance in its Pan-European Context," *Journal of Modern History* 69 (September 1997): 415–50.

10 Barrington Moore Jr, *Soviet Politics: The Dilemma of Power. The Role of Ideas in Social Change* (Cambridge, MA, 1950); Merle Fainsod, *How Russia is Ruled* (Cambridge, MA, 1953); Alex Inkeles and Raymond A. Bauer, *The Soviet Citizen: Daily Life in a Totalitarian Society* (Cambridge, MA, 1959).

11 Ken Jowitt, "Neotraditionalism" (1983), reprinted in *New World Disorder: The Leninist Extinction* (Berkeley, CA, 1992), 121–58; Andrew G. Walder, *Communist Neo-traditionalism: Work and Authority in Chinese Industry* (Berkeley, CA, 1986); Victor Zaslavsky, *The Neo-Stalinist State: Class, Ethnicity, and Consensus in Soviet Society* (Armonk, NY, 1982).

12 These theorists all were working within a classical Weberian framework for the transition from traditional to modern society. I would emphasize that their theory, and especially my version of it, does not assume a single, universal path from the traditional to the modern (indeed, it explicitly contradicts this view), as the much-criticized modernization theory of the 1950s frequently did. My approach comes out of the tradition that posits different modernization outcomes depending upon the historical traditions of a given society, the historical epoch when it modernizes, and the strategy of modernization chosen by a society's elite. See Barrington Moore Jr, *Social Origins of*

Dictatorship and Democracy (Boston, MA, 1966); Alexander Gerschenkron, *Economic Backwardness in Historical Perspective* (Cambridge, MA, 1962); David D. Laitin, *Language Repertoires and State Construction in Africa* (Cambridge, 1992).

13 For an early appreciation of the personalistic nature of Stalinist society, see Joseph Berliner, *Factory and Manager in the USSR* (Cambridge, MA, 1957), 182–230. For recent studies of these issues which, to my mind, exemplify the neo-traditionalist approach, see Julie Hessler, "Culture of Shortages: A Social History of Soviet Trade, 1917–1953," PhD dissertation, University of Chicago, 1996; Charles H. Fairbanks Jr, "Clientelism and the Roots of Post-Soviet Disorder," in Ronald Grigor Suny, ed., *Transcaucasia, Nationalism, and Social Change* (Ann Arbor, 1994), 341–76; Sarah Davies, *Popular Opinion in Stalin's Russia* (Cambridge, 1997), 147–82; Merle Fainsod, *Smolensk under Soviet Rule* (Cambridge, MA, 1958), 396–405; Golfo Alexopoulos, "The Ritual Lament: a Narrative of Appeal in the 1920s and 1930s," *Russian History* 24 (1997): 117–29; Sheila Fitzpatrick, "Supplicants and Citizens: Public Letter-Writing in Soviet Russia in the 1930s," *Slavic Review* 55 (1996): 78–105. For a provocative theory on the role of the personalistic in Soviet society, see Jan T. Gross, *Revolution from Abroad* (Princeton, 1988): 114–24.

14 The term was coined by Ken Jowitt in his provocative essay, "Neotraditionalism" (1983) in *New World Disorder*, 121–58. I am, however, more indebted to the version of the theory presented in Walder, *Communist Neo-Traditionalism*.

15 For an excellent theory linking the emergence of nations and state centralization, see Charles Tilly, *Coercion, Capital, and European States, AD 990–1992* (Cambridge, MA, 1992). For a non-Marxist theory emphasizing ideology, see Liah Greenfeld, *Nationalism: Five Roads to Modernity* (Cambridge, MA, 1992). For a non-Marxist theory emphasizing industrialization, see Ernest Gellner, *Nations and Nationalism* (Ithaca, NY, 1983).

16 Gellner's theory is stated in three works: *Thought and Change* (Chicago, 1964); *Nations and Nationalism* (Ithaca, NY, 1983); *Nationalism* (New York, 1997). Although I find Gellner's theory brilliant and in many ways convincing, by using it I do not mean to endorse all aspects of his theory. It needs an account of the role of state centralization and popular contention (as in Tilly's *Coercion, Capital, and European States*) and the role of individual actors. For the latter, see David D. Laitin, "Turning Megalomanians into Ruritanians" in his *Identity in Formation: The Russian-speaking Populations in the Near Abroad* (Ithaca, NY, 1998), 243–60.

17 Gellner softens this somewhat in his conclusion: "It is not denied that the agrarian world occasionally threw up units which may have resembled a modern national state; only that the agrarian world could occasionally do so, whilst the modern world is bound to do so in most cases" (Gellner, *Nations and Nationalism*, 138).

18 Ibid., 28.

19 Ibid., 124.

20 Ibid., 63–87.

21 The following is an extremely condensed version of an argument made in Martin, "An Affirmative Action Empire", 15–62. For other accounts, see Slezkine, "The USSR as Communal Apartment"; Ronald Grigor Suny, *The Revenge of the Past* (Stanford, CA, 1993).

22 See, for example, Piatakov's speech in *Vos'moi s"ezd RKP/b/. 18–23 marta 1919 g. Protokoly* (Moscow, 1933), 79–83.

23 See Lenin's comments in *Vos'moi s"ezd*, 50–66, 101–9; Stalin, *Marksizm*, 65–139.

24 Gellner, *Nations and Nationalism*, 129.

25 Stalin's original formulation of this idea in 1925 was: "Proletarian in its content, national in its form – such is the universal culture to which socialism is heading" (Stalin, *Marksizm*, 158).

26 For an account of Soviet attacks on such customs, see Gregory J. Massell, *The Surrogate Proletariat: Moslem Women and Revolutionary Strategies in Soviet Central Asia, 1919–1929* (Princeton, NJ, 1974); Jörg Baberowski, "Stalinismus als imperiales Phänomen: die islamischen Regionen der Sowjetunion, 1920–1941," in Stefan Plaggenborg, ed., *Stalinismus: neue Forschungen und Konzepte* (Berlin, 1998), 113–50; and the forthcoming dissertation from Douglas Northrup at Stanford University on gender in Uzbekistan.

27 Gellner states that when such a discrepancy prevails, an individual will either pursue assimilation or separatist nationalism, which will then end the discrepancy. Gellner, *Nationalism*, 75.

28 It would also allow the socialist high culture to be propagated more efficiently through the use of national languages. Isabelle Kreindler, "A Neglected Source of Lenin's Nationality Policy," *Slavic Review* 36 (March 1977): 86–100.

29 For Stalin's comments on this issue, see Stalin, *Marksizm*, 158, 192–94. RTsKhIDNI 558/1/4490 (1929): 1–2. The Bolshevik goal appeared to be the transformation of nationality into a purely symbolic identity, which would in no way interfere with their sociological transformation. This goal is somewhat similar to Herbert J. Gans' interpretation of what has happened to ethnicity in America. Herbert J. Gans, "Symbolic ethnicity: the future of ethnic groups and cultures in America," *Ethnic and Racial Studies* 2 (1979): 9–17.

30 For an excellent case study, see Rogers Brubaker, *Citizenship and Nationhood in France and Germany* (Cambridge, MA, 1992).

31 For a more detailed account of Soviet hostility to voluntary assimilation, see Martin, "An Affirmative Action Empire," 463–562.

32 GARF 296/1/169 (1926): 4–5.

33 On nationality-based affirmative action programs, see Martin, "An Affirmative Action Empire," 63–310.

34 I was unable to find any discussion of nationality in the documentation surrounding passportization in 1932–33, nor did Nathalie Moine, "Passeportisation, statistique des migrations et contrôle de l'identité sociale," *Cahiers du monde russe* 38 (1997): 587–600.

35 For the analysis of class, I am relying on Sheila Fitzpatrick, "Ascribing Class," Chapter 1 in this volume. See also Alec Nove, "Is There a Ruling Class in the USSR?" (1975), reprinted in *Political Economy and Soviet Socialism* (Boston, MA, 1979): 195–218.

36 Fitzpatrick, "Ascribing Class," 38, above.

37 On affirmative action programs for workers, see Sheila Fitzpatrick, *Education and Social Mobility in the Soviet Union, 1921–1934* (Cambridge, 1979).

38 One should note here that Gellner does understate the typical interventions of the state in identity formation. The nationalizing state typically does more than simply form a unified educational system, but also uses various forms of discrimination to pressure minorities towards assimilation, as the Soviet Union's East European neighbors did during the inter-war period.

39 The term "Stalinist *soslovnost'*" and the examples in the rest of this paragraph are derived from Fitzpatrick, "Ascribing Class," 34–5 above.

40 Fitzpatrick, "Ascribing Class," 34, above.

41 Ibid., 37.

42 Ibid., 34–8; Nove, "Is there a Ruling Class in the USSR?" 214–16. Here one should note that the extreme social mobility produced by Stalinist industrialization (as well as periodic attacks on elites) meant that an even relatively static estate system could not and did not emerge. The status system that did emerge does, however, bear greater resemblance to the estate systems of bureaucratic absolutism (such as Petrine Russia and its table of ranks) than classic feudalism, as in the former system the state's primacy allowed it to rank even its elites and provide upward social mobility to a greater degree than the weaker feudal state. In such systems, honor depends more on one's service (*sluzhba*) than one's birth. For the difference between the two systems, see Max Weber, *Economy and Society* vol. 2 (Berkeley, CA, 1968), 1068–88.

43 D. Mirskii, "O velikoi khartii narodov. Konstitutsiia pobedy," *Literaturnaia gazeta* no. 41 (20 July 1936): 2.

44 For the massive attention devoted to folklore in the 1930s, see the new journal, *Sovetskii fol'klor.* vols 1–7 (1934–41).

45 See, for instance, GARF 3316/29/601 (1936): 3–16; GARF 3316/29/605 (1936–37): 1–54; GARF 3316/13/20 (1934): 32ob.

46 On the coverage of the *dekady*, see *Pravda* and *Literaturnaia gazeta* in March 1936 (Ukrainian) and January 1937 (Georgian).

47 "Solnechnyi prazdnik iskusstva," *Literaturnaia gazeta* no. 3 (15 January 1937): 5.

48 See, for instance, V. Kovalenko, "Proletarskaia literatura SSSR v bor'be za leninskoe natsional'no-kul'turnoe stroitel'stvo," *RAPP*, nos 1–2 (1932): 49; Peredovaia, "Usilim vzaimodeistvie kul'tur narodov SSSR," *Literaturnaia gazeta* no. 24 (16 June 1930): 1.

49 The following two paragraphs summarize an argument presented in Terry Martin, "The Origins of Soviet Ethnic Cleansing," *Journal of Modern History*, 70: 4 (1998).

50 The closest thing to an enemy nation was the quasi-ethnic Cossack *soslovie*, which was periodically singled out for group persecution. Peter Holquist, " 'Conduct merciless mass terror.' Decossackization on the Don, 1919," *Cahiers du monde russe* 38 (Jan. –July 1997): 127–62; N.F. Bugai, "20–40-e gody: deportatsiia naseleniia s territorii evropeiskoi Rossii," *Otechestvennaia istoriia* no. 4 (1992): 37–40; Nobuo Shimotomai, "A note on the Kuban Affair, 1932–1933," *Acta Slavica Iaponica* 1 (1983): 39–56; Martin, "An Affirmative Action Empire," 606–32.

51 For a good example of the latter phenomenon, see GARF 2307/14/81 (1929): 27–28. Also, N.F. Iakovlev, "Za latinizatsiiu russkogo alfavita," *Kul'tura i pis'-mennost' vostoka* no. 6 (1930): 27–43.

52 For a more nuanced presentation of this argument, see Martin, "An Affirmative Action Empire," 696–789.

53 See the quotation in the second paragraph on the primordial quarrel between "German elements" and Russia, dating back to the Teutonic Knights and Alexander Nevsky.

54 In addition to Martin, "The Origins of Soviet Ethnic Cleansing," see N.F. Bugai, L. Beriia – I. Stalinu: "Soglasno vashemu ukazaniiu . . ." (Moscow, 1995); Mikolaj Iwanov, *Pierwszy narod ukarany. Polacy v zviazku radzieckim 1921–1939* (Warsaw, 1991); Jean-Jacques Marie, *Les Peuples déportés d'Union Soviétique* (Paris, 1995), 21–33; Michael Gelb, "The Western Finnic Minorities and the Origins of the Stalinist Nationalities Deportations," *Nationalities Papers* 24 (June 1996): 237–68; and *Belaia kniga o deportatsii koreiskogo naseleniia Rossii v 30–40-kh godakh. Kniga pervaia* (Moscow, 1992).

55 Martin, "The Origins of Soviet Ethnic Cleansing"; N.V. Petrov and A.B. Roginskii, " 'Pol'skaia operatsiia' NKVD 1937–1938 gg." in *Repressiia protiv poliakov i pol'skikh grazhdan* (Moscow, 1997), 22–43.

56 Bugai, *L. Beriia – I. Stalinu*, 27–250.

57 As noted above, when passports were introduced in 1932, there was no special concern about nationality and individuals were allowed to choose their own nationality when acquiring a passport. At the height of the terror campaign against enemy nations in 1937–38, an NKVD decree of April 2, 1938 declared that henceforth nationality should be determined by the nationality of the parents and not by the free choice of the individual. As examples to be watched carefully, the NKVD cited "Germans, Poles and others" who were trying to present themselves as "Russians, Belorussians and others." Obviously the concern was over members of enemy nations trying to change their national identity in order to avoid persecution. Here is clear proof that the emergence of the category of enemy nation directly influenced the most important force for ascribed primordialism: inherited passport nationality. For a summary of the decree, see Petrov and Roginskii, 36. For context, see Martin, "The Origins of Soviet Ethnic Cleansing" and Moine, "Passeportisation," 596–7.

58 On the not uncommon phenomenon of individuals claiming Russian as a native language (and therefore presumably a high degree of assimilation) while having another inherited national identity, see Robert J. Kaiser, *The Geography of Nationalism in Russia and the USSR* (Princeton, 1994), 276–78. For an ethnographic account of this phenomenon, see Bhavna Dave, "Becoming Mankurty: Russification, Progress, and Social Mobility among Urban Kazakhs," paper presented at the Annual Meeting of the American Political Science Association, New York, 1994.

59 Inkeles and Bauer, *The Soviet Citizen*, 338–76.

60 Of course, this finding is only suggestive. Ukrainians and Russians shared very similar cultures. One would not expect such similar social attitudes between Russians and, say, Uzbeks. If this observation is correct, however, one should be witnessing a marked convergence of Russian and Uzbek social attitudes (indeed the social attitudes of all Soviet nationalities).

61 A good account of ethnic self-identification is Rasma Karklins, *Ethnic Relations in the USSR: The Perspective from Below* (Boston, MA, 1986), 22–44. The dialogue is based on my personal experience. Neither of my two logical answers to the question, "What is your nationality?" – Canadian or Mennonite – was ever satisfactory to my interlocutors. We usually ended up with "German" (since my grandparents spoke this as their high language though they all spoke different Germanic dialects and none had ancestors from Germany itself), an answer that mollified them but bore no relation to my own national self-identification.

62 Laitin, *Identity in Formation*. See, in particular, the section "Primordial Solidarities are Strong," 239–40.

63 Gellner, *Nationalism*, 92.

64 I should here distinguish my argument about Soviet neo-traditionalism from Timasheff's famous thesis of the Great Retreat. Timasheff interprets the concerted state-sponsored shift in the 1930s as a shift in the direction of what he considered to be authentically traditional Russian social and cultural practices (among them would be popular folklore) as part of a retreat from Bolshevik ideology. My neo-traditionalist paradigm does not address most of the social and cultural practices that Timasheff deals with in his book (nor am I at all certain that it can). Indeed, my primary concern – ascribed status

identities – is not part of Timasheff's Great Retreat thesis. However, our arguments do overlap in dealing with the pronounced shift towards the völkish and folkloric in the 1930s. Therefore, I would like to emphasize strongly that my neo-traditionalist argument does not at all assume a retreat from Bolshevik ideology or practice of the period 1918–32. Quite the contrary. Ascribed status identities emerged due to the Soviet state's policy of categorizing its population in order to punish enemies and reward friends. This practice began in 1918, perhaps peaked in the period 1928–32, but continued throughout the 1930s and beyond, although the categories to be rewarded and punished evolved considerably. I see the cult of *narodnost'*, with its celebration of the folkloric and the völkish, as emerging out of the extreme Soviet statism that underlay Soviet categorization policies, not as a repudiation of it. For Timasheff's thesis, see Nicholas S. Timasheff, *The Great Retreat: The Growth and Decline of Communism in Russia* (New York, 1946).

65 A point emphasized by Fitzpatrick, "Ascribing Class," 36–7, above.

66 My argument, therefore, does not support Moshe Lewin's emphasis on the peasantization of Soviet institutions as an explanation for traditionalist outcomes. Moshe Lewin, *The Making of the Soviet System: Essays in the Social History of Interwar Russia* (New York, 1985), 3–90.

67 Perhaps this is overstated. It seems likely that the neo-traditionalist norms of Soviet society had a strong affinity with traditional clan relations, which were still strong in many regions of the Caucasus and Central Asia in October 1917. The current strength of those relations and similar clan-like ties (*semeistvennost'* in Stalinist parlance) in many Russian regions, may represent not so much persistence of traditional patterns as a neo-traditional phenomenon. This is also a reminder that Soviet culture did not always center on Russian norms.

68 The definitive work on the informal social practices which evolved as market substitutions is Julie Hessler, "Culture of Shortages." For the economics lying behind these social practices, see Janos Kornai, *The Socialist System: The Political Economy of Communism* (Princeton, 1992).

FURTHER READING

See also the "Further reading" lists at the end of each section introduction.

Boym, Svetlana, *Common Places: Mythologies of Everyday Life in Russia* (Cambridge, Mass., 1994).

Brooks, Jeffrey, *Thank you, Comrade Stalin! Soviet Public Culture from Revolution to Cold War* (Princeton, NJ, 1999).

Clark, Katerina, *The Soviet Novel: History as Ritual* (Chicago, 1981).

—— *St Petersburg: Crucible of Cultural Revolution* (Cambridge, Mass., 1995).

Davies, Sarah, *Popular Opinion in Stalin's Russia: Terror, Propaganda, and Dissent, 1934–1941* (Cambridge, 1997).

Dunham, Vera S., *In Stalin's Time: Middle-class Values in Soviet Fiction* (Cambridge, Mass., 1976).

Engel, Barbara A. and Anastasia Posadskaya-Vanderbeck, eds, *A Revolution of Their Own: Voices of Women in Soviet History* (Boulder, Col., 1997).

Fitzpatrick, Sheila, *The Culture Front: Power and Culture in Revolutionary Russia* (Ithaca, NY, 1992).

—— *Everyday Stalinism: Ordinary Life in Extraordinary Times. Soviet Russia in the 1930s* (New York, 1999).

—— ed., *Cultural Revolution in Russia, 1928–1931* (Bloomington, 1978).

Garros, Véronique, Natalia Korenevskaya, and Thomas Lahusen, eds, *Intimacy and Terror: Soviet Diaries of the 1930s* (New York, 1995).

Groys, Boris, *The Total Art of Stalinism: Avant-garde, Aesthetic Dictatorship, and Beyond*, trans. Charles Rougle (Princeton, 1992).

Günther, Hans, ed., *The Culture of the Stalin Period* (New York, 1990).

Hildermeier, Manfred, ed., *Stalinismus vor dem Zweiten Weltkrieg. Neue Wege der Forschung / Stalinism before the Second World War: New Avenues of Research* (Munich, 1998).

Inkeles, Alex, and Raymond Bauer, *The Soviet Citizen: Daily Life in a Totalitarian Society* (New York, 1968).

Kelly, Catriona and David Shepherd, eds, *Russian Cultural Studies: An Introduction* (Oxford, 1998).

—— eds, *Constructing Russian Culture in the Age of Revolution, 1881–1940* (Oxford, 1998).

Kiaer, Christina and Eric Naiman, eds, *Everyday Subjects: Formations of Identity in Early Soviet Culture* (Ithaca, NY, forthcoming).

Kotkin, Stephen, *Magnetic Mountain: Stalinism as a Civilization* (Berkeley, CA, 1995).

Lahusen, Thomas, *Life Writes the Book: Real Socialism and Socialist Realism in Stalin's Russia* (Ithaca, NY, 1997).

Lewin, Moshe, *The Making of the Soviet System: Essays in the Social History of Interwar Russia* (New York, 1985).

Siegelbaum, Lewis H., *Stakhanovism and the Politics of Productivity in the USSR, 1935–1941* (Cambridge, 1988).

—— and Andrei Sokolov, eds, *Stalinism as a Way of Life: A Documentary Narrative* (forthcoming, Yale University Press).

Stites, Richard, *Revolutionary Dreams: Utopian Vision and Experimental Life in the Russian Revolution* (Oxford, 1989).

Timasheff, Nicholas S., *The Great Retreat: The Growth and Decline of Communism in Russia* (New York, 1946).

Trotsky, Leon, *The Revolution Betrayed* (London, 1937).

INDEX